COMPUTER AND DIGITAL SYSTEM ARCHITECTURE

William D. Murray

University of Colorado at Denver

PRENTICE HALL

Englewood Cliffs, New Jersey 07632

Library of Congress Cataloging-in-Publication Data

Murray, William D.
    Computer and digital system architecture / William D. Murray.
    p. cm.
    Includes index.
    ISBN 0-13-165721-6
    1. Computer architecture. 2. Digital electronics. I. Title.
QA76.9.A73M87 1990
004.2'2—dc20   88-8543
                                                        CIP

For Addie

Editorial/production supervision
and interior design: **Cheryl Adelmann**
Manufacturing buyer: **Mary Noonan**

The author and publisher of this book have used their best efforts in preparing this book.
These efforts include development, research, and testing of the theories and programs to
determine their effectiveness. The author and publisher make no warranty of any kind,
expressed or implied, with regard to these programs or the documentation contained in this
book. The author and publisher shall not be liable in any event for incidental or consequential
damages in connection with, or arising out of, the furnishing, performance, or use of these
programs.

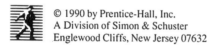 © 1990 by Prentice-Hall, Inc.
A Division of Simon & Schuster
Englewood Cliffs, New Jersey 07632

Printed in the United States of America

10 9 8 7 6 5 4 3 2 1

ISBN   0-13-165721-6

Prentice-Hall International (UK) Limited, *London*
Prentice-Hall of Australia Pty. Limited, *Sydney*
Prentice-Hall Canada Inc., *Toronto*
Prentice-Hall Hispanoamericana, S.A., *Mexico*
Prentice-Hall of India Private Limited, *New Delhi*
Prentice-Hall of Japan, Inc., *Tokyo*
Simon & Schuster Asia Pte. Ltd., *Singapore*
Editora Prentice-Hall do Brasil, Ltda., *Rio de Janeiro*

Contents

PREFACE   ix

1 INTRODUCTION   1

    1.1   Why Study Computer Architecture?   1

    1.2   Computers and Digital Systems   2

    1.3   A Brief Look at History   3

    1.4   A Baseline and Some Alternatives   6

    1.5   Descriptive Mechanisms   12

    1.6   Computer Performance Measures   14

    1.7   Summary   18

    1.8   Additional Reading   18

    1.9   Course Projects   20

2 DESIGN METHODOLOGY AND DESCRIPTIVE TOOLS   21

2.1   Outline of the Top-Down Approach   21

2.2   Requirements Analysis   23

2.3   Specifying the Design Objectives   27

2.4   Specific Architectural Decisions   30

2.5   Design Techniques and Tools   32

2.6   The Processor–Memory–Switch Descriptive System   33

2.7   Instruction-Set Processor Description   38

2.8   Description of Execution and Timing   44

2.9   Economics: Performance, Complexity and Cost   50

2.10   Summary   50

2.11   Additional Reading   51

2.12   Problems   53

2.13   Projects   53

3 SYSTEM STRUCTURE (THE PMS LEVEL)   54

3.1   The Computer as a Digital System   54

3.2   Model Range and Expansion Potential   55

3.3   Alternative System Organizations   61

3.4   Intermodule and Intercomputer Communication   67

3.5   Input/Output Subsystems   74

3.6   Reconfiguring, Upgrading, and Reliability   78

3.7   Levels of Memory   82

3.8   Processors and Software Issues   87

3.9   System Performance and System Cost   90

3.10   Summary   96

3.11   Additional Reading   97

3.12   Problems   98

3.13   Projects   100

4 THE MEMORY HIERARCHY   101

4.1   The Various Forms of Computer Memory   102

4.2   Characteristics of Memory Devices   103

4.3   Processor Storage   108

4.4   Primary-Memory Organization   110

4.5   The Cache   113

4.6   Secondary and Archival Memory   120

4.7   Intermediate Stores and Secondary-Memory Buffering   123

4.8   Virtual-Memory Methods   124

4.9   Memory-Design Rationale and Examples   128

4.10   Detection and Correction of Errors   131

4.11   Summary   134

4.12   Additional Reading   135

4.13   Problems   136

4.14   Projects   137

5 THE INSTRUCTION-SET PROCESSOR   139

5.1   A Variety of Processor Organizations   139

5.2   Languages and Processors   141

5.3   Processors and Operating Systems   152

5.4   Processor State   156

5.5   Environments, Context Switching, and Interrupts   166

5.6   Representation of Data   172

5.7   Instruction Representation and Instruction Sets   177

5.8   Summary   184

5.9   Additional Reading   187

5.10   Problems   187

5.11   Projects   192

6   PROCESSOR IMPLEMENTATION AND CONTROL   193

   6.1   Hardware and Software Techniques   193

   6.2   Virtual Machines and Actual Machines   196

   6.3   Control of the Hardware   200

   6.4   Fault Diagnosis and Maintenance   215

   6.5   Reduced-Instruction-Set Computers (RISC)   219

   6.6   Arithmetic and Other Function Units   226

   6.7   Processor Performance Issues   234

   6.8   Examples of Performance Evaluation   240

   6.9   Summary   245

   6.10   Additional Reading   247

   6.11   Problems   248

   6.12   Projects   251

7   INPUT/OUTPUT AND OTHER PROCESSORS   252

   7.1   Reducing Central-Processor Load   252

   7.2   External Devices and Their Control   254

   7.3   Peripheral-Device Controllers   258

   7.4   Memory and Central-Processor Interfaces   263

   7.5   Input/Output Processors   275

   7.6   Memory Processors   285

   7.7   "Hardware Engines"   289

   7.8   Summary   296

   7.9   Additional Reading   297

   7.10   Problems   298

   7.11   Projects   299

8   PARALLEL COMPUTER SYSTEMS   300

   8.1   Extreme Performance Goals   300

   8.2   Increasing Computer Performance   302

8.3   Vector and Array Processing   309

8.4   Pipeline and Array Processors   311

8.5   Interconnection Revisited   320

8.6   Multiprocessors and Multicomputers   326

8.7   Performance of Parallel Systems   334

8.8   Summary   341

8.9   Additional Reading   344

8.10   Problems   344

8.11   Projects   346

9   SPECIAL-PURPOSE COMPUTING SYSTEMS   347

9.1   Problem Analogs   347

9.2   Responding to Requirements   350

9.3   Designing the System   356

9.4   Processing and Arithmetic Units   360

9.5   Alternatives in Control of Computation   362

9.6   Examples   370

9.7   Summary   382

9.8   Additional Reading   383

9.9   Problems   383

9.10   Projects   384

10   SUMMARY AND PROGNOSIS   385

10.1   Methodologies for Design and for Research   385

10.2   Technology and Architecture   386

10.3   InstructionSet Processors and Controls   389

10.4   System and Language Issues   392

10.5   Performance Measures   395

10.6   Outlook   398

10.7   Additional Reading   399

10.8   Future Projects   400

APPENDIX A THE PMS AND ISP DESCRIPTIVE SYSTEMS   401

A.1   Introduction 401

A.2   Formal Definitions 402

A.3   PMS-Level Descriptions 408

A.4   ISP-Level Descriptions 411

**APPENDIX B SOME EXAMPLES OF INSTRUCTION-SET
PROCESSORS**   412

REFERENCES   434

INDEX   446

Preface

I designed this book as a text for graduate students or seniors in computer engineering, computer science, and electrical engineering. It is also intended for independent study by those interested in computer architecture and digital-system design. The book covers a need-based design methodology and reviews the alternatives available to the computer architect.

Your initial reaction might be, "How is this one different from all the others?" I wrote this book because I was not satisfied with texts available for the study of computer architecture in an advanced undergraduate or introductory graduate course.

Most computer-architecture textbooks follow one of three approaches: an introduction to computer design; a general review of computer architecture; or an investigation of a particular computer type. Those in the first category are aimed at the electrical engineer and devote a large percentage of their content to detailed computer subsystems. They are insufficient for a comprehensive study of computer architectures.

Books that review the organization of computers tend to cover the material in insufficient detail. Detail that is included generally pertains to one or two particular computers. These books generally have limited coverage of design alternatives and of methodologies for computer-architecture development. Subsequently, they must be supplemented with current computer literature.

In the third category are texts or monographs on a single type of computer or a single approach to computer design. While these books contain sufficient detail for serious study, they tend to have a narrow focus.

Closest to my needs were collections of papers on various alternatives to computer architecture, with discussions by the authors of groups of papers covering a specific topic. Although these excellent reference works are very useful, they are not organized as textbooks.

I have attempted to consider the issues faced by those who must design or select new hardware that meets economic as well as functional requirements. I address the composite of function, structure, organization, and performance of a computer or some other digital system. Throughout I focus on the effects of technology on the implementation of digital systems. Little attention is paid to design details of the logic or electronics of the system.

To some, "computer architecture" means the computer as seen by a user or programmer. My view of architecture is broader and is similar to that used by the architects of buildings, communities, and cities. I like the definition of architecture as "the science, art, or profession of designing and constructing . . ." (*Webster's New World Dictionary*, Second College Edition, published by Prentice Hall, 1986). Computer engineering is the profession and computer science is the science I refer to when addressing computer architecture.

The approach I have taken is to start with a discussion of the *methodology* to be used in developing a computer architecture, followed by examination of the *alternatives* that are available to the architect. I do not attempt to arrive at a definition of the optimum computer organization. (If it is possible to describe the "best" computer architecture it is reasonable to conclude that that should be the only computer architecture.)

Examples of architectures and subsystems are included to permit the reader to consider the results of prior undertakings and to evaluate these results. Examples are chosen from the mainstream of general-purpose computer design and from interesting deviations therefrom. These examples show that "good" or "successful" architectures are well matched to the functions for which they were intended, are characterized by a specific set of objectives, and usually feature the "elegance of simplicity" that we find in good solutions to all complex problems.

The material is presented with a top-down design-oriented approach. Computer architecture is a serious subject with many significant issues. A successful computer development does not result from merely assembling a group of electronic subsystems, but must start from a consideration of the requirements for the system with an orderly progression toward the detailed design, including an evaluation of the alternatives at each step of the process. The book is organized, each chapter is written, and examples and problems are selected to emphasize development of computers that are responsive to requirements, are balanced in their features, and are economically as well as technically sound.

The book is organized into 10 chapters, starting with an introduction and a review of computer organization in Chapter 1. In Chapter 2 I develop a design methodology and specify the descriptive tools available to help design a digital system. These tools include the processor-memory-switch (PMS) system for top-level description of the computer and the instruction-set processor (ISP) language for defining the programmer's view of the computer. Both of these tools were introduced by C. G. Bell and A. Newell [BellC71].

Alternatives available at the system and the major subsystem levels of computer architecture are covered in the next seven chapters. In Chapter 3 I examine alternative approaches to the top-level system structure and review the rationale to be used to select from among these alternatives. Then I look at methods for communication among subsystems at the top level and review the considerations that go into design of these subsystems: the memories, the processor(s), and the input/output subsystems.

The various types of computer memory are discussed in Chapter 4. The chapter begins with a review of the levels in the memory hierarchy and of the trade-offs relevant to designs at each level: primary, secondary, and archival memory. Questions related to organization and control of virtual memory and its mapping into physical memory are covered, followed by a discussion of errors in memory operations and their detection and correction.

The discussion of central-processor architectures in Chapter 5 shows that there are many alternatives available at this level of computer design. The requirements imposed on the processor design by the applications, programming languages to be used, and operating systems that control the computer set the framework for processor design. Internal registers for short-term information storage, the relationship of such registers to primary memory, and the alternatives available for organizing the internal registers (also called the processor state) are considered. The processor internal data structure and its instruction set, covered next, require a large part of the computer architect's attention.

Issues and alternatives in implementing processors and computer controls are covered in Chapter 6. Of particular importance are the uses of microprocessors and other highly integrated electronic circuits as well as possibilities and problems of microprogrammed controls. The effect on control structure of the languages, application programs, and operating systems are examined, as are the pragmatic questions of manufacturability and maintainability. The functional design of the arithmetic and logic units entails considerations of the trade-offs between speed and complexity.

If the central processor is not to be bogged down in the detailed control of input/output operations, a separate control for those functions must be provided. This might be a fixed-program controller or it can be a processor with its own instruction set. In many applications there are requirements for specialized processing that suggest that a special-purpose processor be attached to the system to relieve the central processor of some duties. Expansion of the control needs of the memory at various levels might lead to incorporation of an internally programmable memory processor. Processors of all three types are considered in Chapter 7.

When it is necessary to exceed the performance that can be achieved with conventional sequential architectures, parallel organizations can be used to permit concurrent processing activity. In Chapter 8 several different approaches to parallel computer design are introduced. Problems of connection, communication, and related performance issues are discussed.

The general-purpose digital computer does not match all requirements for data-processing systems. In many cases a special-purpose design is more cost effective. The determination of whether this is so and the approach to designing special-purpose digital systems is covered in Chapter 9. Chapter 10 includes a brief summary and a prognosis for the future for the methodologies and the alternatives covered earlier in the book.

Problems and/or projects for the reader follow each chapter. The problems are designed to reinforce understanding of topics covered. The solution of each problem emphasizes thinking about alternatives and minimizes routine calculation. The projects address design issues, most of which can be adapted to situations that might be faced by a reader currently involved in computer design.

I have covered the material in a graduate electrical engineering and computer-science course, "Advanced Computer Architecture". The material can be covered in a single semester if students enter with a solid background in computer-hardware organization. Students or independent readers should possess a good understanding of the organization of some representative computer, as would be obtained in a course on assembly language programming followed by either a course on computer organization or a course on use of microprocessors in electronic equipment. The reader should have a good understanding of at least one modern higher-level programming language, of boolean algebra and logic design, and a working knowledge of the role and functions of operating systems and compilers in digital computers. If significant time is needed to review computer organization fundamentals, Chapter 9 on special-purpose systems can be omitted.

I want to express my appreciation for the assistance and encouragement offered by my friends and associates: Harry Jordan, Rod Schmidt, and Hans Gethoeffer. Students in course EE 559 have been very helpful in developing the approach and the material used herein. The careful reviews and frank comments by the many external reviewers have permitted major improvements over the original draft manuscript. Tim Bozik and Cheryl Adelmann of Prentice Hall were especially helpful to this new author.

W. D. Murray

1

Introduction

As the title states, this is a book about the architecture of computers and other digital systems. By architecture we mean the design and implementation at the system level rather than at the component level. We are concerned with the function, structure, performance, and economics of the system being considered. We will examine each of these system aspects and will consider the interactions among them. As we will see, balance and consistency among features are characteristics of a successful computer architecture.

1.1 WHY STUDY COMPUTER ARCHITECTURE?

In examining computer architecture we will emphasize a design methodology (a rationale for architecture development) and the alternatives available at each level of system detail. We will learn how to construct a system from functional building blocks. Our objective is to meet the requirements with as economical a design as is possible. This is not an easy process that is accomplished by plucking items from shelves of components. The systems we are dealing with are complicated and there are other system architects who will be trying to achieve results better than our own. In our design we must achieve a result that meets the established requirements for performance, reliability, flexibility, and operability. The cost of development, construction, and operation, as well as the performance of our product, will be compared with those of our competitors.

Computer architecture is a scientific and engineering discipline. There is a logical approach to the discipline. There are tools available to assist us. There are needs for analysis, synthesis, and evaluation. There are means to measure whether we have been successful or not. There is a body of knowledge derived from theory and from past experience that must not be ignored. Perhaps most importantly, there are opportunities for creativity, professionalism, excitement, and satisfaction in undertaking the examination, evaluation, and development of an architecture for a computer or another digital system.

1.2 COMPUTERS AND DIGITAL SYSTEMS

It will be useful to define some terminology to establish a common framework for discussion. Starting with the fundamentals, the *computer* is assumed to be an internally programmed electronic digital machine with the associated software required for its operation, maintenance, and efficient use. It is a system of components or subsystems that broadly follows the definition given by von Neumann and his associates [BurkA46]: "Inasmuch as the completed device will be a general-purpose computing machine it should contain certain main organs relating to arithmetic, memory-storage, control and connection to the human operator. It is intended that the machine be fully automatic in character. . . ."

While its name is computer, its role may involve little computing in the usual sense. Its function might be that of data processing, file management, communication control, or some other tasks that require acquisition, storage, retrieval, manipulation, and dissemination of large quantities of information. In any event its major subsystems involve memory (storage and retrieval), input/output (acquisition and dissemination), and processing (data manipulation) functions, and the interconnection and controls to permit the assemblage of components to function as a working system.

To broaden the subject, a *digital system* is an assemblage of components or subsystems designed to perform a set of related tasks under control of one or more digital processors. The digital computer itself is then a digital system since it is an assemblage of subsystems controlled by a digital processor. In fact, the maturing of the discipline of computer engineering and the introduction of a wide variety of standard semiconductor building blocks for computer subsystems allow many computer designs to result from careful selection from inventories of standard subsystems. Thus computer design can be similar to digital system design.

In all of these systems the major subsystem functions are processing, storage, and control of system interfaces. Processors contain their own local storage (registers), an *arithmetic and logic unit* that performs operations on data, paths for transferring information among registers, individual flip-flops for holding temporary control information, and control logic to force the processor to execute instructions as called for by a program. In many cases a part of the control logic itself is a program (a *microprogram*) residing in a fixed or modifiable memory within the processor or in a separate store.

The memory of a computer usually is distributed over several physical modules. As noted, there is memory within the processors. Since the high unit cost of storage in the processors limits the amount of processor memory that is practical, a main working memory is assembled from lower-cost and lower-speed circuits. This *primary memory* holds active programs and their data. Primary memory is queried by the processor(s) to obtain instructions and data items and is the destination for the results of individual computations. The primary memory is supplemented by lower-unit-cost, but slower, secondary memory that in turn can be supplemented by even-lower-unit-cost archival memory. There might also be specialized memories that are used for buffers between processor registers and primary memory. There must be a mechanism to coordinate the operations of the various memories. For example, we might require a means to transfer "pages" or "segments" of information between primary and secondary memory.

Unless we can provide for communication with the external environment the activities of the computer or digital system will be of little use. This communication is accomplished by input/output controllers. These functional units control the flow of information between the primary memory and external devices, such as keyboards, printers, terminals, and the secondary and archival memory units previously described. Specialized forms of input/output processors might be useful for connection to long distance communications facilities or to real-time analog subsystems. Other specialized processors might be used to relieve the main (or central) processor of certain tasks such as memory management, mathematical operations, or control of special hardware.

This brief description of the major component subsystems of a computer outlines the scope of this book. As a frame of reference for study of the many alternatives available to the digital system architect, and for a consideration of the approach to designing a digital system, the reader should be familiar with some specific conventional digital computer (or even with a very unconventional computer system).

1.3 A BRIEF LOOK AT HISTORY

As seen in Fig. 1-1, machines for calculation go back at least to the seventeenth century (Blaise Pascal, Samuel Morland, and Gottfried Leibniz). Charles Babbage accomplished his monumental work on automatic computation during the 1800s, a century that also saw the mathematics of Boole and DeMorgan and the automatically controlled loom of Jacquard. Practical adding machines, bookkeeping machines, accumulating cash registers, and tabulating equipment were manufactured by the beginning of the twentieth century. In the 1930s digital computation (as opposed to analog computation where a machine directly reproduces the problem being solved, perhaps at a different speed) was accomplished with machines using electrical relays by Howard Aiken at Harvard University, George Stibitz at Bell Telephone Laboratories, and Konrad Zuse at the Technische Hochschule in Berlin. In the same time period John Atanasoff at Iowa State University developed a digital calculating machine using vacuum-tube circuits and Alan Turing presented his ideas on computing theory.

Following these origins of automatic computation, the ideas for the internally programmed digital computer generally are attributed to John von Neumann and his associates at Princeton University's Institute for Advanced Study, but must have been

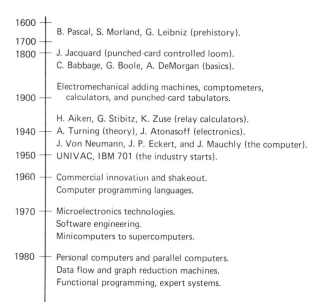

Figure 1-1   Looking back.

influenced considerably by the work of J. Presber Eckert and John Mauchly, who designed and built an electronic digital computer with externally wired programming, the ENIAC, at the University of Pennsylvania. These efforts were accomplished in the mid-1940s and were followed in the late 1940s and early 1950s by an explosion of activity toward development of a variety of digital computers at the institutions already mentioned, at MIT, at the Rand Corporation, at the National Bureau of Standards, at the University of Chicago and the University of Illinois, at the Los Alamos and Argonne National Laboratories, as well as at Cambridge, London, and Manchester universities and the National Physical Laboratory in Great Britain.

In the 1950s and early 1960s many corporations introduced electronic digital computers to follow the UNIVAC and the IBM 701 into the marketplace. In addition to Eckert-Mauchly Computer Corp. (later purchased by Remington Rand) and International Business Machines, these included Bendix (computer division bought by Control Data), Burroughs Adding Machines (later Burroughs Corp. and subsequently Unisys), Consolidated Engineering Corp. (Electrodata division sold to Burroughs), Control Computer Company (acquired by Honeywell), Control Data Corp., Digital Equipment Corp., Engineering Research Associates (with Eckert-Mauchly became Remington Rand UNIVAC, then Sperry Rand UNIVAC, then a part of Sperry Corp. [merged with Burroughs to form Unisys Corp.]), English Electric (merged with I.C.T. to form I.C.L.), Ferranti (merged with English Electric), General Electric (computer operation acquired by Honeywell), Honeywell (computer operations moved to a joint venture with Fujitsu and Cie. Bull), International Computers and Tabulators (became I.C.L.), Librascope (became a division of General Precision Equipment), Philco Corp., Radio Corporation of America (computer division acquired by UNIVAC, RCA later acquired by General Electric), Raytheon, and Scientific Data Systems (acquired by Xerox). The organizations have been as volatile as the products!

Competition among the various companies that were attempting to establish themselves in this new market led to a great deal of innovation and design variation in the electronics, the physical layouts, and the architectures of the computers of the 1950s and early 1960s. Many new ideas that were diversions from the "theme" established by the pioneers were introduced and tested by the marketplace and its users. Some of these ideas proved very useful and became a part of the mainstream of computer architecture; others were rejected and disappeared (at least for a time); a few were maintained in the architectural ethic of the companies that introduced them and characterized those companies' unique approaches.

Throughout the 1960s architectural innovation continued, but at a less explosive pace. New companies with new ideas entered the market, many older computer companies withdrew from (or sold their interest in) the market. This was a decade of settling and planning for broad applications for families of computers. All members of a family maintained the same architecture to facilitate customer migration from one level of machine to the next. (The migration usually was not without pain and difficulty. There were many small details in programs that had to be matched to the many small details in architecture for the move to be completed. Often those details were not obvious to the builder or to the user.) The concept of a "virtual machine" architecture that could be represented on a variety of physical computers was introduced by several companies.

The decade of the 1960s also was characterized by the introduction of "higher-level" computer languages, programming languages that were closer to the languages of the problems being solved and thus easier for problem solvers to understand. As with the computing equipment, some of the languages were readily accepted and continue to evolve, others were adopted only by small groups in narrow specialties, some became the base for orderly development of newer languages, and many simply faded from view. The acceptance and introduction of higher-level programming languages and of the operating systems that accompanied them to facilitate the automatic management of computer resources had a strong influence on the computer architectures that followed through the 1970s.

Another influence, that of rapidly advancing semiconductor technology, became very strong during the 1970s. The ability of the semiconductor manufacturers to offer individual components with hundreds, then thousands, then hundreds of thousands of devices on one chip of silicon less than 6 mm on a side permitted more and more computational capability to be placed in a given space for a given cost. This period might be characterized by the push of electronic technology on computer architecture, rather than the converse where architectures established the need for particular electronics capabilities. This led to the introduction of the microprocessor and with it the explosion of the microcomputer market with its subsequent settling and maturing.

In the same decade problems of developing and maintaining the large programs that were needed for many applications led to the start of software engineering, a discipline for orderly specification, design, validation, and maintenance of software systems. Computers were extended to higher performance levels with the supercomputers and to lower price levels with the minicomputers.

The 1980s were a period of further development at both ends of the performance spectrum, with the introduction of many personal computers at the low end and of a variety of parallel computing systems at the high performance end. New experimental architectures appeared, new languages more friendly to user needs were introduced, and artificial intelligence research spun off expert systems approaches to assisting computer end users.

The purpose of the last few paragraphs is not to present a comprehensive history of computers and computer architecture. That has been done so well by other authors. (See the Additional Reading section at the end of the chapter.) There is, however, an important purpose for having offered a brief overview of computer history. That is to emphasize that the architecture of electronic digital computers has been the subject of serious study and development for over forty years. Over that period many good ideas have been offered and rejected due to unavailability of the required technology or to insufficient strength of need. Some of those ideas subsequently have been recovered when the technology or the need was there. An excellent example is that of microprogramming, suggested by M. V. Wilkes [WilkM51], but which did not yield sufficient performance with the technology available. Most computers today use some degree of microprogramming in a form very much like that suggested by Wilkes.

How many other ideas of value still reside in the files of earlier computer architects, or are lost in our own individual files? What combinations of ideas, some of which have been rejected in the past, will be useful for future architectures? The serious computer architect is interested in learning those ideas and approaches that were considered and rejected as well as those that were accepted. Thus, in keeping with the emphasis on methodology and alternatives of this book, there are many references to computer architectures of the past. As specific topics are pursued, readings of material important to each topic are suggested.

1.4 A BASELINE AND SOME ALTERNATIVES

We should establish a *baseline* architecture against which we can describe and evaluate alternatives. Toward that end nothing is more appropriate than the original von Neumann computer architecture. The paper [BurkA46] in which the von Neumann architecture is laid out should be read by every student of computer architecture. The resulting product is interesting in itself, but even more useful are the establishment of a rationale for approaching the development of an architecture and the analyses that led to the selection from among alternatives available to those particular architects. The methodology is one that should be (but, unfortunately, too often is not) followed by any designer of a complex system.

The "Electronic Computing Instrument" (Fig. 1-2) described by von Neumann and his associates is comprised of four major parts (or "organs", in the terms of those authors): a "Memory Organ" in which information is stored, an "Input/Output Organ" for communication with the human operators, an "Arithmetic Organ" in which all calculations are performed, and a "Control Organ" that manages the operations of all the others. Thus, we have defined what we now call storage (or primary memory), the input/output subsystem, and the processor (or CPU, central processing unit). The separate control organ of the von Neumann computer design has been distributed among the other subsystems in modern computers.

Many specific quantitative data are provided on each of the major organs. The Arithmetic Organ handles fixed-point rather than floating-point arithmetic operations.

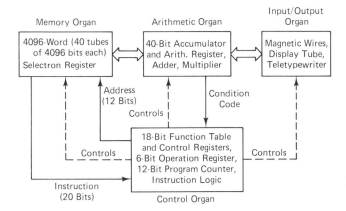

Figure 1-2 An "electronic computing instrument."

Data are represented in fractional binary form in a 40-bit word. Negative values use 2's complement notation. The "order code" consists of 21 instructions, including addition, subtraction, multiplication, and division (but a square root instruction is not included). Instructions and data take the same form to permit them to be held in similar registers and to permit instructions to be handled as data and modified. The instructions are executed in the sequence in which they are listed, but there are special instructions that permit transfer of control out of the sequence, such transfer to be either unconditional or as a result of some data condition. There also are instructions for communication with the external environment. There is a program counter (instruction pointer) that points to the instruction being executed and that is incremented to control the normal sequential execution. Instructions have the form of an operator and an address that indicates the location of the single argument. A special storage unit, the accumulator register, holds a second argument and is the target of the result of an arithmetic operation. A "selectron register" serves as the memory-buffer register. An arithmetic register holds the less significant half of the result of multiplication or the remainder from a division. All of this characterizes what we identify later as the instruction-set processor (ISP) level of description of the computer.

Equivalent detail is provided regarding design of the other organs. The applications expected require a memory of 4000 words with a factor of safety for growth. ("We believe that this memory capacity exceeds the capacities required for most problems that one deals with at present by a factor of about 10." From the very beginning computer architects have underestimated the appetite of computer users for memory!) An examination of those devices available to provide memory of the size required leads to selection of a storage cathode-ray tube (a "Williams tube") to store 4096 binary digits. Forty such tubes will allow for 4096 40-bit words, with individual words to be accessed in parallel with approximately uniform access time ("a quite small fraction of a millisecond"). As a result of the memory organization the computing machine can perform its 40-bit operations in bit-parallel manner and attain higher speeds than a bit-serial machine can. (The EDVAC under development at the University of Pennsylvania at the time is cited as an example of the serial approach.)

A second level in the storage hierarchy is needed. For this longer-term storage magnetic wire is selected for its low cost, compact size, and "since we have achieved reliable performance with them". Dead storage of very high capacity can be achieved with a library of wires used with the secondary store. Since it is necessary that humans place information on and review information on the wire, it is "now clear that the secondary storage medium is really nothing other than a part of our input/output system"[BurkA46]. The input/output will also include a means for viewing graphically the results of a given computation by means of a cathode-ray tube. Finally, the input/output subsystem includes a modified teletypewriter for keyboard input and printed output.

The Control Organ addresses memory to obtain pairs of instructions. Each instruction is decoded and executed according to its operation code field and is applied, where appropriate, to an argument to be found at a memory address specified by an address field. Instructions are to be executed in address-order sequence unless a specific transfer-of-control instruction (unconditional or dependent on some data condition) is executed. Error detection and error correction, where possible, are to be managed by the Control Organ.

With completion of the description at the system level, we have what now is called a processor–memory–switch (PMS) level definition of the von Neumann computer. We outline both the PMS and the ISP descriptive mechanisms in a later section of this chapter. The von Neumann design is specified at both the PMS (Fig. 2-5) and ISP (Fig. 2-7) levels in Chapter 2.

If that is the description of the von Neumann computer, and if so much of the design is still used, what are the alternatives that have been considered and are available to us? This is the specific topic of most of the book, but let us take a brief look at this time to gain some perspective on the alternatives. Some are mentioned in the summary given of the von Neumann design, but there are many others.

At the top, or system, level our von Neumann benchmark has only two subsystem modules of the computer itself: the processor and the primary memory. The Control Organ is really distributed between the two modules, residing mostly in the processor. In addition to the processor and memory, the system contains the input and output peripheral equipment, including the secondary memory. The system organization is very much like that of a small contemporary personal computer. Note that input/output (I/O) control is a responsibility of the processor module and that calculation of arithmetic results must be deferred while input or output transfers are being accomplished.

This suggests (it was considered by the von Neumann team and actually used by Eckert and Mauchly in their UNIVAC machine) that a separate subsystem module be incorporated to permit input/output operations to occur simultaneously with processor activity. The processor would then initiate input or output by signaling to an input/output controller and would then resume its computations until the controller signaled that the input or output had been completed. The presence of this separate controller was a feature that distinguished the earliest commercial business-oriented computer, the UNIVAC [EckeJ51], from the first commercial scientific machine, the

IBM 701 [BuchW53]. Other interesting differences between these two included decimal vs. binary arithmetic and storage, absence vs. presence of floating-point operations, exclusion vs. inclusion of multiply and divide operators, parallel-by-digit (digit-serial) vs. parallel-by-word arithmetic, and decimal vs. binary memory addressing.

For a separate input/output control to be fruitful it is necessary that transfers between the I/O control and memory be interleaved word by word with transfers between the processor and memory. If this can be accomplished with one I/O controller it should be easy to do it with more than one, and the use of multiple I/O controllers is seen in the evolution of computer architecture. As input and output devices become more powerful and their control more complex it might be desirable to make the I/O control an internally programmed processor with its instructions for each type of peripheral device held in main memory or in its own special memory (in which case we might call it an I/O computer).

Even with interleaving to permit word-by-word sharing among the processor and the I/O subsystem there might be a bottleneck at the memory interface. Perhaps it is desirable to break the large main memory into smaller parts, or modules, to permit the I/O controls and the processor to access different memory modules simultaneously. Now with modular memory and multiple accesses to memory, we introduce the need for a switching mechanism to permit the simultaneous information paths to be established. Once that is done if we need more processing power why not add additional processors, if we can solve the problems of coordination and synchronization that are introduced.

An example of a multiple-module system is the UNIVAC (now Unisys) 1100/20 with two processors, four memory modules, and 32 I/O channels, as shown in Fig. 1-3. This computer has four primary memory (main storage) modules, each with a controller (multi-module access unit), and two central processing units, each with an input/output subsystem of 16 channels. Each channel can interact with an input or output device concurrently with other channel-device communication.

We have introduced several variations from the initial von Neumann design at the system level alone. Even more striking variation is possible within the processor. Noting

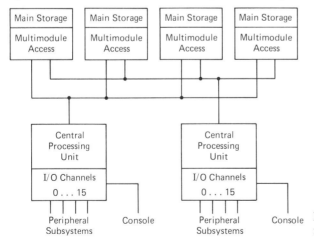

Figure 1-3 UNIVAC 1100/20 multiprocessor system.

that in matrix algebra we often make orderly sweeps through a matrix, repeating small groups of instructions with incremental steps in each dimension, we find that there is a lot of time consumed in the calculation of memory addresses as we "index" the matrix subscripts. Why not add a register in the processor to speed up memory indexing? The address of an argument then can be the sum of the content of the special "index" register and of the address field of the instruction. The instruction need not change while we repeat the loop of instructions since the value in the index register can be modified to address different arguments. If one index register is good, since there are three physical dimensions we deal with, wouldn't it be even better to have three index registers? Of course, the next step is to realize that even more than three index registers can be useful, particularly if we can use more than one for each argument reference (i.e., address = instruction's address field + [ixreg a] + [ixreg b] + [ixreg c], where [ixreg a] means "content of index register a"). When the computer includes index registers there must be a mechanism in instructions to select which registers are to be used.

Once electronic components have been supplied to add registers it is natural to consider using the registers for more than just indexing. We might want to use the added registers as additional accumulators so that information (data, addresses, instructions, pointers) can be held temporarily without taking the time needed to place it in primary memory, which consistently has been about an order of magnitude slower than processor registers. The resulting organization is called a *general register* processor. This idea can be extended to lead to "cache" memory as an extension of the general registers.

An alternative use for the components devoted to index registers is to implement a specially organized memory, a push-down stack or last-in first-out (LIFO) store. With this organization of the processor the accumulator is replaced by a top-of-stack register. A second data register, the next-to-top register, also is included in the processor. All arguments for operations reside at the top or in the next level of the stack. As information in the top register is consumed, that in the next to top moves to the top location and all information at a deeper level moves one location higher in the stack. (As you might expect, the information in memory does not move, but a pointer changes to indicate that "this" is now the top level.) Registers are used to point to the bounds of the stack and to the currently active top in primary memory. Management of the stack is accomplished automatically by the hardware.

Closely related to the question of quantity and use of registers in the processor is the number of arguments that can be referenced by a single instruction. Since arguments in memory are designated by their addresses, the issue is that of number of addresses per instruction. The von Neumann architecture called for an instruction to contain a single address field designating the address of an argument in memory. The accumulator can hold another argument. (The specifics of assignment of arguments depend on the individual instruction.)

Designers of some early computer architectures felt that there could be advantages to specifying the addresses of two or three arguments in each instruction. Then the location of two arguments and the destination for the result of a computation could be included in one instruction. Of course, the instruction word would have to be large enough to hold the codes for the operation and the multiple-address fields.

With the general register organization described earlier we might use a three-address format to specify the general registers to be accessed or the combination of general

```
        C
        A              CLRAC
      COPY               ADD    B
        B                MUL    A
      MUL                ADD    A
      ADD              STORE    C
    STORE
  x: push x on stack   op x: Accum <- Accum op x
  op: top <- top op next  CLRAC: clear accumulator
        (a)                    (b)


   MUL A B
   ADD A B            MUL A B B
   STORE B C          ADD A B C
  op x y: y <- x op y   op x y z: z <- x op y
      (c)                  (d)
```

Figure 1-4 Instruction variations for C = A + A * B. (a) Zero-address (stack). (b) One-address (accumulator). (c) Two-address. (d) Three-address.

registers and memory location(s) to be used. On the other hand, if we have a machine with a stack all arguments are assumed to reside at the upper levels of the stack and there is no explicit addressing in instructions. This would be a *zero-address* computer. Examples from the 1960s include *variable-address* machines. There are, indeed, quite a few variants on the addresses-per-instruction theme.

Examples of instructions and instruction formats for zero-, one-, two- and three-address computers are shown in Fig. 1-4. In each case, typical instructions and argument-identification sequences are shown above a definition of how the instructions are interpreted. In the stack machine the addresses of the arguments (C, A, B) are placed on the stack and operations that use those arguments cause the values to be called from memory. The COPY instruction copies whatever is at the top (in this example, address A) into the next stack register after pushing an opening into the stack. Arithmetic operations (MUL, ADD) use the top two stack values and place the result at the top. The STORE instruction transfers the top value to the memory addressed by the next value (C in the example). In the single-address machine the accumulator (initially cleared with CLRAC) is the temporary register to hold all intermediate values. Arithmetic operations use the accumulator value and the value in the designated memory location (A, B) as arguments and place the result in the accumulator. STORE copies the value from the accumulator to the designated memory location. In the two-address computer addresses of both arguments for arithmetic operations are specified and the result is placed at the memory location designated by the second argument. With STORE the value at the first argument location is copied into the address specified by the second argument. With the three-address machine addresses for both arguments and for the destination are specified and a specific store operator is not needed.

The simple example illustrates the trade-off between quantity of instructions and the size of instructions of the four addressing means. Readers are cautioned not to form any judgment on which is the best approach to number of addresses per instruction only from this simple example. Even though the three-address organization appears to be most economical in number of instructions (2) and the stack organization appears to use the least operators and arguments (7), the simple example is not sufficient to demonstrate the effects of execution of a real program in all four computer types.

Instructions are placed in successive locations in memory so that the normal instruction-execution sequence calls for execution of the instruction at location $n + 1$ following that of location n. Thus the designation of "next" instruction is implicit, unless it is necessary to break out of the normal sequence, in which case the target of the jump becomes the argument for the jump instruction. The format with the implicit next-instruction designation is fine when instructions are in a memory that has no time differences among accesses to different addresses. That was the case with the Williams tube memory of the von Neumann machine, as it is with most semiconductor memory.

When the magnetic drum was used for computer memory a new constraint was introduced. Now consecutive words on the drum are available to the magnetic recording heads at very tightly controlled time intervals. (If it is not tightly controlled addressing becomes very complex.) Then the placement of successive instructions must be selected carefully based on individual instruction-execution times. If this is not done the time from the end of one instruction to the finding of the next has great variation with much wasted time. For example, if instruction "n" is expected to take the time of 1/10 of a drum revolution we should place instruction "$n + 1$" at a location as close to, but not closer than, 1/10 of a revolution after that of "n". This was the case with many early drum computers that incorporated a "1 + next" form of addressing. Here an instruction contains two addresses, one for the argument for the instruction itself and one for the location of the next instruction. From this description it is seen that the timing is even more complicated than that of determining instruction-execution times. The location of the argument influences the timing and the optimum location of the next instruction.

In a few paragraphs we have seen possibilities for considerable variation among processor organizations as well as many alternatives for system organization. As these alternatives are pursued in more detail in later chapters we will search for means to arrive at combinations of features that are compatible and consistent with each other. We will find that there are good computer architectures using each of the variants to be examined. What makes them good (or successful, or both) is a design symmetry with features complementing each other. Usually we will see features combined in a manner to yield an "elegance of simplicity".

1.5 DESCRIPTIVE MECHANISMS

The discussion of computer architectural alternatives in the previous section uses the informal descriptive mechanism of plain English. The vocabulary includes terminology that might require at least a superficial knowledge of computers, but there are no special

Requirements:	Specification languages
System level:	Processor–memory–switch (PMS)
Program level:	Instruction–set processor (ISP)
Execution level:	Simulation languages
Logic level:	Register transfer languages
State machine level:	State diagram and Petri nets

Figure 1-5 Descriptive language hierarchy.

symbols or grammatical structures used to aid in the descriptions. As a result the short descriptions are not very quantitative. Of course, we could have used the English language to provide a more detailed and more quantitative description of the various alternatives, but that would require considerably more space, and even then would be subject to varying interpretations due to the ambiguities of the language used.

For a more concise and a more precise description of computer systems a more formal descriptive language is needed. Fortunately there are languages appropriate to each of the levels of detail needed. Figure 1-5 shows the descriptive languages available at each of the design levels. We are concerned with the system levels of computer architecture and do not wish to have the descriptions confused by details needed at the levels of circuit design and assembly.

Specification languages have been developed for definition of requirements for computer hardware and for computer software. When the requirements are specified in such a language the specifier (customer) and the receiver (supplier) have a common definition of needs for the item to be supplied. If any items are not specified they can be assumed not to be required. Wherever appropriate, quantitative values of any requirements can be identified.

For a description of computer architecture, two, or perhaps three, levels of detail are most useful. In order to describe the top-level systems, including the computer in its broadest form, a language that permits us to define the system in terms of its major subsystems and their interconnection is needed. Most manufacturers of computers use block diagrams for this purpose since they offer graphical illustrations of the systems. The block diagram, however, is not very concise and does not facilitate identifying the quantitative information needed, such as the full range of memory sizes that can be used or the limits on input/output equipment that can be attached. A superior descriptive language at this level is PMS, the "processor-memory-switch" language proposed by C. G. Bell and A. Newell [BellC71] and now accepted by many computer architects as the system-level hardware description language.

While PMS describes the total system it does not provide adequate description of the processors to allow for an understanding of the quantities of registers and their organization, of the instruction set, or of the execution sequences used by the processors. A level of detail usable to the assembly language programmer is needed to describe the processors at the instruction set level. Bell and Newell have introduced another language,

ISP, the "instruction-set processor" language and, like PMS, it has gained wide acceptance in computer architecture.

In order to develop a complete computer architecture it is necessary to go beyond the description of the computer to include information on its performance. A more complete definition than can be obtained with PMS or ISP allows a simulation of the architecture to test its operation, to predict its performance, and to allow programs for it to be developed. A number of hardware description languages and simulation languages have been developed for this level of detail. ISP itself has been extended to permit simulation as instruction-set processor specifications (ISPS) [BarbM81], allowing for simulation of processors and execution of programs written for them. For a little more detail on operation of the computer hardware, register transfer languages (RTL), as described by Barbacci [BarbM75], are useful to describe and to simulate the flow of information within the processor. The dynamics of execution are better represented in graphical form with Petri nets or with state diagrams to show conditions possible and transitions to succeeding conditions or states.

The fact that a computer is represented not only by its hardware, but also by software elements makes it difficult to use a hardware description language to specify computer performance. In particular, the operating system that manages computer resources has a strong influence on performance. If the processor control uses microprogramming in a control store the boundary between hardware and software is especially hazy. Abstract descriptions of computers must consider the hardware and the software that together describe a computer architecture as a "virtual machine".

1.6 COMPUTER PERFORMANCE MEASURES

From the start of the commercial computer industry (or at least as soon as there was more than one participant) there was a desire by potential computer users to have a means to compare alternative machines. Initially the comparisons were largely intuitive and based on the association of (desirable or undesirable) architectural features with problems to be solved. For example, early scientific problem solvers saw advantage in the large word size (36 bits) and the fast floating-point arithmetic of the IBM 701, whereas business users liked the large input/output capacity, the decimal arithmetic, and the character processing of the UNIVAC. Roughly in proportion to the number of entries in the race for commercial supremacy (or even commercial success) there grew a race to find claims of performance and economic superiority to support each entrant's architecture.

In an attempt to support or to discredit the vague claims there was a search for "objective" measures of computer performance. In absence of any metric that reflected the rate of solution of problems, simple and supportable indicators of performance were introduced. The two quoted most often were processor clock rate and, with the introduction of core memories, memory cycle time. While these two could indeed be measured and users could validate the speed claims there was little that a user could do to associate these "raw speed" rates with problem-solving capability. As our previous review of architectural alternatives demonstrated, there are many ways to organize a computer at the system-structure level and at the instruction-set level. Clock rate and memory cycle time are very low-level measures of hardware performance. While they can be useful in approximating the differences among models following a single architecture, they have little use in defining performances of different architectures.

Unfortunately, things that are easy to measure about complex systems usually do not yield data that are very meaningful. Figure 1-6 reflects the concept that as we move toward the systems level, where we could determine problem-solving performance if we had a measure, the measures that are available are not precise. The illustration shows where the performance measures that have been used at each level of computer description fit on scales of precision and of relevance to problems to be solved.

At the circuit level there are even more precise measures of performance than clock rate. Switching times of various saturating and nonsaturating transistor devices in different integrated circuits are very useful to the electrical engineer for selecting the best semiconductor devices for implementation of the computer logic. Even at this level switching time does not reflect circuit performance unless we also know the "breadth" of the device in terms of its ability to deliver its signals to other devices, known as its *fan-out* capability.

If we wish at least to reflect the time it takes to perform some useful operation we could list and compare some computer instruction execution times. For example, we might compare the times taken by different computers to add two numbers, to multiply or divide, to fetch or store, or to transfer a block of information to a magnetic tape. Again we find difficulty in correlating with problem solution times. What are the relative importances of addition and multiplication times? Will any one of these have the same significance for all the problems we want the computer to handle? These questions in 1959 stimulated J. C. Gibson [GibsJ70] to investigate the distribution of use of different instructions in solutions of typical scientific problems on early IBM computers. An approximation of the distribution in the form of selected quantities of each of several types of instructions was known as the *Gibson Mix*. Others soon made similar measures on their own favorite groups of problems on their own computers.

In an attempt to formalize this operational approach to performance measurement K. E. Knight [KnigK66] developed a set of equations that yielded a single measure of performance. In the equations parameters were given values to reflect typical instruction distributions for different classes of problems. An outgrowth of the effort was the

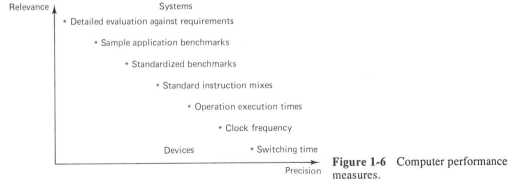

Figure 1-6 Computer performance measures.

presentation of *Knight's Scientific Mix* and *Knight's Commercial Mix*. The results are quantifiable and do reflect averages of typical problems converted to typical programs for specific computers, but are very sensitive to the programmer and the way the program was tuned to the computer architecture.

A brief look at some differences among computer instruction-set processor approaches shows the weakness of the instruction-mix approach to performance measurement. A three-address (three-argument) computer generally uses fewer instructions to obtain the result of an arithmetic expression than does a single-address machine. A computer with general registers uses fewer mem-ory references than does a machine without the registers. Reference to a register takes much less time than reference to primary memory. Furthermore, an instruction queue can mask the time it takes to fetch instructions in a linear sequence of commands. The standard-instruction-mix approach makes little allowance for these different processor organizations.

The next step in expanding the basis for comparison of architectures is to use standard small programs, each designed to represent a particular class of problem. These would be established by committees representing computer users in the specialties being approximated by the benchmark programs. Benchmark programs of this type have been developed to represent major problems in business and scientific specialties such as nuclear physics, dynamic meteorology, chemical processes, astrophysics, linear programming, economic analysis, and database management. The approach brings us a step closer to an evaluation based on a meaningful set of computer programs, but a step further from precision of evaluation. At this level the measures are strongly dependent on the software. If the programs are written in assembly language they can be optimized to take advantage of hardware features, but they do not reflect the capabilities of the translators. If they are written in a higher-level language, which language should be used? Higher-level language translators interact closely with operating systems and small samples of even realistic programs do not properly exercise the operating system. Finally, these benchmarks, if they are to use the compilers and the operating system, must assume that the system software is fully developed, making them barely useful for comparison of emerging products.

The most complete comparative evaluations have involved extensive effort:

- to quantify the class of problems to be solved,
- to identify the peripheral issues of importance like growth potential and reliability,
- to convert the problem-oriented statement into a broad set of required computer characteristics,
- to perform an initial screening based on the characteristics,
- to characterize different parts of the problem solutions as small programs expressed as algorithms in a standard form,
- to select a meaningful group of the small programs,
- to have the programs translated by hand or automatically under conditions

controlled to discourage a competitor from tuning the algorithms to favor its architecture,

- to run significant quantities of the programs on real or simulated versions of the architectures being compared, and
- to compile an evaluation of each competitor using all weighted factors previously determined to be significant.

Accomplishing a meaningful evaluation according to the procedure just outlined is a major task. Most organizations cannot devote the resources required to make this comprehensive an evaluation. Usually shortcuts are taken that reduce the validity of the results. Despite the amount of effort required, an evaluation of the type outlined should be worth undertaking by the developers of a new architecture before they make the much greater investment in detailed engineering design, manufacturing engineering, model building, software development, and field-support planning that are necessary before a new product can be taken to the market.

Although most computer users cannot afford the comprehensive analysis and evaluation outlined above we might expect that computer product developers can. Unfortunately, most developers of new systems, through impatience or unwillingness to face an objective evaluation, proceed with their development without a comprehensive evaluation of performance against competitive systems. The result is that there is little more than the simple measures of clock rate and memory cycle time available to the computer user for comparison of products. Most annoying (or amusing, depending on your perspective) is the fact that claims for the largest and most sophisticated computer systems are so often based on the unsophisticated measure of "millions of instructions per second" (MIPS) or the more advanced "millions of floating-point operations per second" (MFLOPS).

It would seem that a long-term objective should be to establish a means to identify an "ideal information engine" against which "actual computing engines" could be compared to find their information-processing efficiencies, just as actual thermal engines are compared with ideal-cycle thermal engines to determine their thermodynamic efficiencies. We are not close to achieving such measures, but continued efforts by those working in information theory, system theory, and computer science might arrive there at some future time. Meanwhile we should be doing the best we can, using all the tools that have been given to us to perform as good an appraisal as possible. We have developed much of the means and now need to exercise dedication to treat computer performance evaluation as an engineering discipline.

Even though performance measures are not precise it is necessary to consider performance when we compare alternative architectures. In the descriptions of alternative approaches in the succeeding chapters we use whatever means are available to describe and to compare relative performance levels. Much of the performance evaluation is qualitative, but even qualitative measures permit a numerator to be established in the performance/cost ratio.

1.7 SUMMARY

In this chapter we have established a base for the study of digital-system architectures. A brief review of the history of the digital computer suggests that at both the system and processor levels there should be a continuing review of architectural alternatives and a consideration of current technologies. Over the past four decades the architectural alternatives have seen little change, but the rapidly advancing electronics technologies have made different architectural approaches more feasible.

The main line of computer architecture starts from the computer architecture established in 1946 by the team led by John von Neumann at the Institute for Advanced Study of Princeton University. The "von Neumann" architecture is the baseline for further study and evolution. Many variations are possible at both the system and processor levels.

Serious comparison of the alternatives requires that we have standardized descriptive mechanisms or languages to specify the designs to the level of detail appropriate to our investigation. There are a number of such languages at each level of detail. For our purposes the processor-memory-switch (PMS) language at the system level and the instruction-set processor (ISP) language for processor definition of Bell and Newell are suited to our purpose and are accepted by many computer architects as quasi-standard descriptive mechanisms.

Almost since competition of designs was introduced in the computer field we have been attempting to derive meaningful and straightforward measures of computer performance. Simple measures have little meaning and meaningful measures are very difficult and expensive to develop. Despite all the effort, most currently used measures of performance revert to measurement of raw circuit speed.

1.8 ADDITIONAL READING

To obtain more detail on computer organization in preparation for investigating the advanced computer architectures covered in this book, the reader is referred to [ManoM82], [HamaV84], or [GorsG86], which cover computer organization in decreasing order of engineering emphasis. [KuckD78], [BaerJ80], and [TaneA84] look at alternatives to computer architecture with perspectives different from this text.

Material at the same level of detail as this text is offered in [BellC71] and [SiewD82], both of which contain collections of significant papers from the computer architecture literature with extensive commentary and explanations by the authors. Issues of *IEEE Computer* occasionally have been devoted to status reports on computer architecture or on specific aspects thereof. (For example, the June 1985 issue, Vol. 18, No. 6, is on multiprocessing technology.)

Special issues of IEEE [HuskH76] and ACM [BellC78a] publications contain useful papers from the history of computer development. [HuskH76] contains an interesting paper by H. D. and V. R. Huskey on early computer history. [RoseS69] is a useful summary of the field up to 1969 and [RandB73] offers a more comprehensive review.

[BurkA46] is only one of a number of excellent papers by von Neumann's group at the Institute for Advanced Study that are contained in a collection [TaubA63] that is recommended to any student of computer architecture or computer applications.

The early commercial machines, UNIVAC reflecting business-oriented architecture with emphasis on input/output flow and the IBM 701 for scientific computing with fast (for its day) internal operations, should be compared with the von Neumann design. These commercial ventures were described in [EckeJ51] and [AstrM52]. The Eckert paper is reproduced in [BellC71]. Additional detail on the IBM 701 can be found in [BuchW53].

The story of early programming language development was told in [SammJ69]. Its history was outlined in the special issue of *IEEE Transactions on Computers* [HuskH76]. More recent work on programming language development has focused on simplifying block-structured procedural languages [WirtN75], on introducing more powerful control and data-structuring features to procedural languages [WirtN77, WienR83], on languages for logic programming [ClarK82] and for functional programming [HendP80], and on formal means for specifying semantics [TennR81].

Evolution of the UNIVAC scientific computers, including the 1100/20 is covered in [BorgB78]. The index register was introduced as the *B-tubes* in the Manchester University computer in 1949 or 1950 [KilbT56], but was a part of Babbage's design of an "Analytic Engine" in 1830. The IBM 701 had three index registers and the IBM 7094 had seven.

The Burroughs B5000 [BartR61] and the English Electric KDF9 [DaviG60] were stack-based computers of the early 1960s. The Burroughs D825 [AndeJ62] contained four registers that could be used as an extension of a stack or as general registers. The D825 also had index registers and could be addressed as a zero-, one-, two-, or three-address machine with indexing of up to three levels for each address.

John W. Carr III described instruction sets of a two-address computer, the UNIVAC 1103, of 2 three-address machines, the University of Michigan MIDAC and the Soviet Strela, and of other early computers in [GrabE59]. Carr's papers on MIDAC and Strela are reproduced in [BellC71]. The Control Data 6600 and its successor Cyber 170 series used a three-address instruction format, employing general registers to hold arguments [ThorJ64]. The IBM 360 series [AmdaG64] and its successor large- and medium-sized IBM systems use multiple-argument addressing to specify combinations of general registers and memory locations.

Hardware description and simulation languages are of continuing interest to digital-system designers. *IEEE Computer*, Vol. 7, No. 12, of December 1974; Vol. 10, No. 6, of June 1977; and Vol. 18, No. 2, of February 1985 are special issues devoted to hardware description languages. IEEE, ACM, and AFIPS sponsor a biannual conference on the subject. PMS and ISP are described in [BellC71] and in [SiewD82]. [BarbM81] reviews the extension of ISP to ISPS and [BarbM75] compares various register transfer languages. [PeteJ83] reviews Petri nets and their applications to digital systems.

The concept of implementing a family of logically identical machines with different physical realizations for different performance levels was introduced with the IBM 360 [AmdaG64]. The distinction later was made between the "virtual" (logical) machine and the actual (hardware) machine. The term virtual machine also has been applied to the

logical machine seen by a user in a time-sharing environment [MeyeR70]. In developing
some principles of operating systems, Weiderman [Weidn71] introduced the idea that a
virtual machine is the combination of system programs and a virtual machine at the next
lower level.

Although developed in 1959, the Gibson Mix is first described in [GibsJ70]. The
performance equations of Knight were seen in [KnigK66]. A very good review of the
comprehensive evaluation of alternative architectures as conducted in the Department of
Defense Computer Family Architecture program was reported in [FullS77a,b].
[DennP87] outlines a comprehensive approach to evaluation of a new architecture for
NASA applications. A more complete description of the evaluation is contained in
[AdamG85]. [JordK87] summarizes application of the Exxon Research and Engineering
benchmarks for large-scale scientific computation. [FerrD78] reviews a number of means
to evaluate computer performance. The continued inadequacy of the MIPS/MFLOPS
performance measures is discussed in [ParkD83].

In this introductory chapter we have shown a few examples of real computers.
Throughout the book there are other examples.

1.9 COURSE PROJECTS

These projects are designed to demonstrate understanding of the material presented
throughout the book. In the Projects sections of succeeding chapters details of and
variations on Projects 1-A and 1-B will be assigned.

1-A. Investigate in detail some computer system. For that computer describe the characteristics
that are covered in the book. Your description should be sufficiently detailed to permit
comparisons with descriptions of other computers developed by others in the class. The
descriptive mechanisms introduced in this chapter should be used where possible.

1-B. Design a computer system (at the levels covered in this book) for your organization
(company, school, etc.). Start by identifying the needs of your organization and project
those needs five years into the future. As you proceed through the book add the design
detail needed to describe your computer.

1-C. Develop a table of significant characteristics of computers. This table should be useful for
comparing different computers whose characteristics are described by different people in
response to Project 1-A. (A starting point might be the table of Contents of this book.)

2

Design Methodology and Descriptive Tools

Before we consider the alternatives available to us in developing a computer architecture it is essential to establish a design methodology, a rationale for approaching computer design. We should learn *how* to design before we learn *what* to design. At the same time we should determine the tools that are available to permit us to specify our designs completely and concisely.

2.1 OUTLINE OF THE TOP–DOWN APPROACH

Unfortunately, the history of computer development contains too many examples of computers designed without a reasonable design methodology. In fact, too often computer design has proceeded without having even a broad architectural plan for guidance. As you would expect, the results have contained serious flaws. In the 1950s, there was some excuse for an ad hoc approach since computer architecture was little understood, many alternatives available to the designer were speculative and experimental, and almost any new computer design was worth evaluating.

In early commercial designs computer engineers paid little attention to the needs of those who had to program the machines. There was great devotion to "efficiency" of hardware to the extent that early higher-level languages were viewed with great suspicion and concern that the benefits of programming ease would be more than overcome by the resulting poor object programs. (Even today one occasionally hears comments of that type.) Programmers of many "advanced" early computers felt that the engineer was presenting the hardware design while saying, "There, I dare you to try to program that one!"

As the computer field matured users began to demand computer systems that aided programming. Higher-level languages and comprehensive operating systems became accepted parts of computer designs rather than curiosities. Computer architecture was seen as a starting point for design. Computer science and computer engineering developed as technical disciplines. The approach of initiating a design from the broadest aspect, rather than from the detail, evolved. In retrospect, it is difficult for the computer architect today to see how one could think that a complex system could be built from the bottom up. (In the 1950s aeronautical engineers felt that the approach most computer designers took was like designing an airplane from the rivets up.)

Undergraduate students and recent graduates might comment that the top–down approach is not used in our educational programs in engineering and computer science. A specific example is the usual sequence in computer education: introductory programming and logic design; assembly language programming and computer organization; operating systems, compilers, and architecture. It is true that this is a "bottom–up" approach, largely due to the overspecialization we find in academe. On the other hand, before one can understand the top level of design it is necessary to know a lot about the details that underlie that top level. To use the airplane design analogy, one must understand the principles of jet-engine thrust before attempting to design the airplane.

In this chapter we develop a rationale for approaching computer architecture. Our methodology is to approach the design from the top and work down toward the detail. We start with an understanding of the task to be accomplished and develop a statement of the requirements. Then we undertake satisfying those requirements with a system design. Using "stepwise refinement" we use the system design as the statement of requirements for the major subsystems. Subsystems design is then undertaken. The combination of the system and subsystem designs is our computer architecture that will be implemented by computer engineers.

Anyone interested in computer architecture should start by developing an understanding of this design methodology. A good "short course" for this is a reading of the early von Neumann design papers [TaubA63]. In those papers we see the top–down design approach taken by von Neumann and his associates. First they identify the problem areas in which the "computing instrument" will be used. Next they develop the general specifications for the machine, taking into account the limitations of the then-current technology. The general plan is carried to more specific levels by successive iterations of requirement analysis, examination of alternatives, and design specification. As we now know, the result was a computer architecture that has lasted for over forty years, despite continuing attempts to find the "non-von Neumann machine".

After we have developed our methodology we investigate the various descriptive mechanisms available for expressing our design concepts. We need descriptive notations for each of the levels of detail of our design. Thus, we review specification languages, system-design languages, hardware-function languages, hardware-design languages, and evaluation languages.

2.2 REQUIREMENTS ANALYSIS

Where do we start? Is the top-level specification "a brand new computer"? Perhaps "a new computer using the latest ultra-large-scale integration and super-speed memory" would do. If these do not sound sufficient, let us think of some of our alternatives at the system (processor–memory–switch) level: range of sizes of primary memory, input/output configurations, range of performance of central processing, secondary and archival storage, and interconnection of modules. Next we can look at some of the basic alternatives at the instruction-set processor level: numeric data word sizes and formats, other data forms and data structures, multiple-precision possibilities, types of operations to be in the instruction set, and quantity and organization of local registers. These are only a few of the design alternatives available, but it gives some indication of the information we need regarding the computer system requirements.

The starting point for requirements analysis should be an identification of the customer or groups of customers for the product. A listing of customer applications should include those currently being accomplished on the system that is to be replaced, those that the customer would like to add as part of the new system, and those that we can identify as useful to the new system.

It appears to be easy to identify customers and customer applications if there is only one customer, particularly if the customer currently is using a computer system. Even in this simplest case it is important that the system architect approach the subject with inquisitiveness and skepticism. There are applications being run on computers that need not be; there are applications that are separated and might perform better if combined; and there might be customer problems that are not being handled simply because the earlier architect did not allow for them.

The first step of requirements analysis becomes more difficult when there is not a specific single customer who can be queried to obtain information on needs. Rather there is a large customer community that is to be served with a product. In this case it is useful for the system architect to have interaction with those who understand the customer community and the types of applications that typically are handled by that community. In most large computer development organizations there will be a product planning or product management activity that will coordinate the needs of the customer, as stated by the sales organization that has the day-to-day contact, with the potentials for new system architectures, as can be outlined by the system architects. The specification of new computer architectures usually results from an iterative process involving communication between those who understand the applications and those who will develop the new systems.

In the typical company involved in digital-system product development the system architects perform a role that goes well beyond the functional design of a new system. As shown in Fig. 2-1, the architect is a key member of the product development organization.

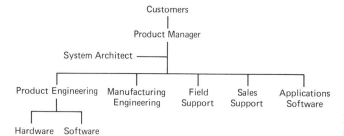

Figure 2-1   A typical product-development team.

Typically the architects serve as the technical arm (i.e., the "system engineers") for the product manager. In that broad role the architects are involved in coordination, evaluation, and support in addition to system analysis and system design. Successful product development takes all those who perform product engineering (hardware and systems software), manufacturing engineering, applications software development, sales support, and maintenance support and involves them early in the development process. Continued coordination is needed to assure success of the product. The digital-systems architect's role only starts with requirements analysis.

A review of a typical situation faced by the developers of a new computer system for a large customer community describes the requirements analysis process better. Let us take the role of the computer architect and attempt to clarify the applications to which our new system is to be directed. We see that most of the information we gather results in specification of the functions to be performed by our system, but we also obtain data that allow us to specify the performance required and to understand the economic constraints (or opportunities) that we face. Our example takes the form of an outline of questions to be asked as we generate the system specification.

A. *Function*: What are the major categories of applications for which the new system will be used? Do they involve bookkeeping, statistics, report and table generation? That is, are they what we might consider as primarily business uses? Are the applications mainly "scientific", that is, do they involve a high amount of numeric computation of high accuracy with relatively large data structures? Will the system be used for direct on-line control of processes and, if so, what are the natures and the dynamics of those processes? Will the system control the transmission and the routing of large amounts of information; is the application that of communications network control? Is the application a very unique and specialized one, such as the control of fuel mixtures and ignition in an automobile engine? Will the system be used interactively by humans; if so, how many, on what applications, and where? If the system will be used in several applications categories, what is the expected mix in terms of quantities and sizes of problems, time of the day or week for different applications, priorities of different applications, and nature of the control of the applications mix? Will the system be a subsystem of a larger system; if so, what particular constraints are imposed by that larger system, such as communications protocols? Now that the functional requirements are understood in complete detail, what is really not known and when will the functional requirements change; what contingencies should we allow for?

B. *Performance*: How much information must we be able to hold for short and long periods of time? How and at what rates will input be provided to the system and will results be transmitted? What is the total quantity of input and output expected over a larger period of time? How often will each of the major types of calculation and data-processing operations be performed? What are the requirements in each type of operation for precision and resolution of result, and what are the precision and resolution of the input information? How well are the algorithms for solution of the expected problems known, that is, what is the expected accuracy of our performance-requirements estimates? What are the priorities if the system nears saturation? Are there any special requirements related to performance monitoring, error detection, and recovery?

C. *Environment*: What is the physical environment in which the system will operate? Will it be in an office, a manufacturing plant, a mine, in space, in an internal combustion engine housing? How will it relate to any people who will be working with it and do they have any special characteristics, such as wearing space suits, visual limitations, unique operating equipment? In what language or languages will the system be presented problems and programs; what sort of translators will be running on the system? How will the system resources be managed and how will programs be assigned for execution; what are the expected characteristics of the operating systems? Will our system have to operate in a multiplicity of physical, interactive, or processing environments? Are there any variations of performance or functional requirements with any changes in environment?

D. *Time Frame*: When do we expect to announce the plans and the specifications for the system? When will we offer the system for evaluation and comparison? When will we deliver the first system and at what rate will we deliver additional systems? What are the plans for other models of a family of systems? What are the expected minimum and maximum useful lifetimes for the system and what allowances should be made for upgrading and renewing the systems once released?

E. *Competition*: What are the functional, performance, environmental, and economic characteristics of current successful systems in our target area? What are the characteristics of any that have failed? Do we know the characteristics of any systems that are to be introduced in the near future? What are the possible characteristics of competitive products, based on what we know about other organizations? For each of the competitive or possibly competitive products what can we identify about capabilities and limitations?

F. *Economic Constraints*: What are the present costs to our customers for a system of equivalent performance? What competitive cost will we expect at the time our product will be delivered? (We discuss technology trends in later chapters.) For our organization what are the relationships between implementation costs and competitive prices? (If we are designing a computer to be manufactured and sold in a competitive market the "whole manufacturing cost" [the cost including allocation of factory overhead] should be from one-quarter to one-half of the sales price to allow for sales and support costs, for amortization of research and development costs, for allocation of corporate support costs, and for profit.) In looking at the economic constraints and trade-offs it is essential that we be conservative in our estimates of costs. It is too easy for the system architects and engineers to be overly optimistic about what *other people* in the organization (sales, service, manufacturing, etc.) can or should do.

G. *Measures of Success*: How will we be able to establish that our architecture is successful? What performance-cost relationship will be satisfactory? What minimum level of performance is needed for success? What competitive advantages can we verify? How do we prove that our architecture satisfies the requirements?

One reaction to this discussion of requirements analysis might be that it appears to have many subjective elements and to require more estimation than analysis. There is a lot of truth in that reaction, but not much can be done about it. Characteristic of the requirements for almost any new large system is that the requirements initially are not fully understood by the customer or fully specified for the developer. Often with large systems we find that unimportant items are specified in excruciating detail, whereas important operations are ignored or glossed over. Computer architects must use their skills to fill the missing areas of the requirements specification.

Usually new computers and other new systems are developed in competition with other developers and success is measured on the basis of time and economics as well as on technical excellence. Often there is a unique technical innovation that might be advantageous to a new architecture, but the inventor does not know how it can be fit into the plan. A role of the system architect entails bridging the gaps (sometimes chasms) between the specific and the general, between the quantitative and the qualitative, between the known and the suspected, and between the achievable and the imaginable.

Most of us who consider ourselves engineering or scientific professionals find it distasteful to have to limit our creative abilities to satisfying any particular set of requirements. Why not let us be free to invent the "best possible" computer? Why inhibit the introduction of new ideas with constraints of the marketplace? There are two responses to these questions.

First, new invention and research in computer architecture should and can be conducted based on at least hypothetical needs. Often the existence of a feature helps to generate the need for that feature. When a computer architect can explain the benefits of some new approach customer requirements might be extended to take advantage of the new capability. Understanding the present domain of system requirements is needed to establish extensions to which new approaches can be aimed.

Second, and perhaps more important, is the fact that invention quite often is "pulled" by need. Many innovative new system designs result from the expression of "if only we could . . ." on the part of a user, followed by a realization that "if we can . . . , then indeed we can . . ." on the part of the system architect. Requirements analysis can encourage, rather than inhibit, creative development in digital-system architecture. The intent in starting with an analysis of requirements is to attempt to prevent a lot of energy being expended on a new architecture that is far removed from any possible application. We already have too many elegant solutions running around looking for problems to which they can be applied.

2.3 SPECIFYING THE DESIGN OBJECTIVES

Once the requirements for function, performance, time frame, and environment are identified development of the system specification starts with a statement of system objectives. This might be just a rephrasing of the requirements, but the requirements analysis usually uncovers incompatibilities, inconsistencies, or incomplete data sets for establishing a clear statement of objectives. The digital-system architect must resolve these problems, often by postulating a set of objectives and comparing these with the requirements as stated by representatives of the user community.

At the minimum, the statement of design objectives reflects a rewording of the requirements in terms that are understandable to the system architect and system designers. Most of us involved in design of a system would be happy to have our design objectives phrased as: "If a system to be first delivered by . . . , is able to accomplish these functions . . . , with this performance . . . , within these cost constraints . . . , with the following potential for future capabilities . . . it will be considered a success." Since the problem usually is not stated that clearly it is incumbent on us to develop a specification of design objectives in a form that permits us to be sure that the resulting design does indeed satisfy the objectives. Of course, our specification should be agreed to by those for whom we are designing the system.

You might see that there is something missing in the specification developed so far. There is no statement as to how we are to determine if the system design does meet the design objectives and thus satisfies the overall requirements. We must add to our specification of design objectives a specification of the methods that are to be used to verify that the objectives have been met. It is difficult to measure a paper design at this top level and the verification usually is performed as a "design review" by a team of evaluators. This team should consist of other system architects, implementers, and system users. Results of these early evaluations yield suggestions for modifying the architecture to correct shortcomings in satisfying requirements.

Since the total product development process consists of several nested levels of responsibility the approach outlined for system-level development can be repeated at each lower level. At each level there is a specification of objectives in terms appropriate to that level and a specification of the means that are to be used to verify the result. At any one level there might be segmentation into subsystems and components, usually reflecting the organization of people who are to accomplish the work.

With this approach of "stepwise refinement" the design at any level becomes the statement of requirements for the next level. Team leaders at each level perform the steps that have been outlined for the system-architecture level: analyze the requirements for activity at this level to arrive at a clear and mutually agreeable (with those at the next broader level) statement of need, specify (in terminology appropriate to this level) the design objectives, and specify the tests and the other verifications that will be used to measure our success. This process is represented in Fig. 2-2, which shows a specification tree with definition and verification at each level.

We have discussed the requirements analysis and the design objectives phases at the system-architecture level of a "methodology roadmap" (Fig. 2-3). Let us fill in some

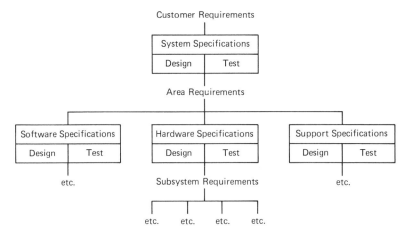

Figure 2-2   Nested levels of development and test.

of the detail of the design activity at this level. The design process requires a combination of *intellect*, *invention*, *intuition* and *iteration* (the "four I's"): *intellect* to apply the results of our education and training in our individual discipline, *invention* to exercise our creative abilities toward finding better approaches to problem solution, *intuition* to bring forth the results of experience with similar or analogous situations we have seen before, and *iteration* to evolve the product in ever-improving steps of design and evaluation. These are incorporated in the development of a digital-system architecture.

The creative aspect of design usually starts with the statement of a strategy for the design: what will our overall approach be and how will it result in something different from (and hopefully better than) existing designs? Within the overall framework we cause the design to take shape by comparing alternative ways to implement the functional parts of the design. In many cases we will experiment with an approach through a paper

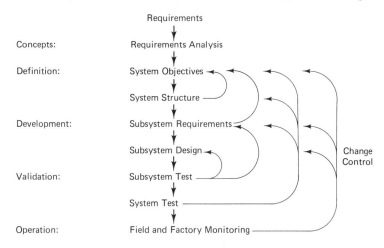

Figure 2-3   The product-development process.

evaluation, a computer simulation, or a physical breadboard. Often it will be necessary to ask designers at the next level of detail to work out an implementation of a concept to determine that it is feasible before we incorporate it in our architecture. Thus we see again that the top–down approach to system design does not have the levels of detail working independently and in isolation. There is much interaction among levels to ensure consistency and practicality of the result.

Application of the "four I's" to our design strategy yields an initial system architecture at the top (PMS) level. This is the "first cut" that will be subjected to reflection and evaluation to obtain an estimate of how well it satisfies the objectives. Comments from those who will use the system and from the designers who will implement the next level of detail will lead to ideas for improvement that can be incorporated as we continue the stepwise refinement of the architecture. This input from others might take place through informal review and communication or might be the result of a formal design-review process. It makes little difference which of the two approaches is taken as long as sound professional review is performed. The objective is to improve the architecture. The best people to accomplish the objective should be called on to perform the review. The approach must incorporate critical review to identify shortcomings and positive recommendations to overcome the shortcomings.

When the process of stepwise refinement of the top-level architecture has yielded a satisfactory product (which usually is refined further as we get into more detail), the subsystems that make up the system are designed. Again we follow the principles of design outlined before and there is a stepwise refinement of each of the major subsystems at this level. The result is the subsystem architecture (the ISP level). Sufficient information is available now to permit the specification of the requirements for the engineers who will perform the physical design and for the system programmers who will implement the operating systems and the language translators. Initial phases of the final operational software can be started at this point if desired, particularly if our own organization is to provide such operational software.

When the architecture has developed to this point it is possible to specify subsystem and system testing in more detail. It is necessary to identify tests that will verify each significant aspect of the architecture to ensure that the functional and performance requirements are being met. In most cases, engineers and programmers who specialize in test and evaluation can provide the detailed plans for the testing process using requirements data from the system architects. Manufacturing planning can be initiated when the architecture is developed to this point. Feedback from such manufacturing planning is important to the physical design.

The system architects are not free to wait for the result of their design to flow up from the implementers. As the "roadmap" in Fig. 2-3 indicates, the architects have a broad responsibility for success of the system. Throughout the period of physical design and construction of the prototypes the system architects must monitor results, be alert to possible problems, prepare alternatives to approaches that were specified, adapt the architecture to evolving requirements with orderly changes to specifications, and be available for consultation with any parts of the organization undertaking the development. As the architecture changes, a good record of each change and its impacts on the system must be maintained. The larger the organization doing the design and the more complex the system the more important it is that this record be maintained in a formal manner. With very large systems this process has been called *configuration control*, which has developed as a subdiscipline of system engineering.

Toward the final phases of the development cycle the system architects will be involved in review of plans for subsystem verification, for software development, and for system test and evaluation. If the system is to be manufactured in large quantities or it is a complex system requiring many operators and maintainers the system architects will be devoting significant time to transferring information for sales and training documents. Digital-system architecture is a profession that goes far beyond sketching great new ideas on the back of an envelope for others to worry about implementing. (This does not argue against the fact that many outstanding ideas have started with plans on the back of envelopes.)

You might question whether the formal approach indicated is appropriate to a small product, such as a personal computer. Much of the approach appears to be related to controlling complexity that is associated with very large systems. In the author's experience a formal approach to digital-system architecture is as important to development of a small system as it is to a large one. It is characteristic of most small systems that they will be produced in large quantities. Price competition is strong and product cost is important. With the rapid changes in electronics technology the "window of opportunity" for the product might be very short in duration and the introduction of new competing products might require a quick change in our approach. The relative need for strong design control is about proportional to the quantity of people involved. An orderly and professional approach to digital-system architecture is as appropriate to small systems as to large ones.

The disciplined approach outlined is recommended even when we are developing an architecture as a school exercise. As when one learns to program by starting with small examples, or when we learn to design electronic equipment by starting with small circuit examples, it is important that we develop a discipline applicable to a variety of digital-system requirements as we learn to undertake digital-system architecture.

2.4 SPECIFIC ARCHITECTURAL DECISIONS

After we understand the methodology and the approach to be followed we can consider the decisions to be made and the alternatives available at each design level. The balance of this book covers the design decisions and alternatives in developing a computer architecture. We must develop a skill in making decisions to select from among alternatives. Evaluation and comparison can be carried only so far. Sometimes we must base our decisions on the intuition gained from experience. A simplified tree showing the decision-making process at the top levels of design is shown in Fig. 2-4. This decision tree outlines the steps to be taken in formulating a system architecture.

The initial architectural decision probably has been made implicitly during the development of the requirements and objectives specifications. It is the determination of

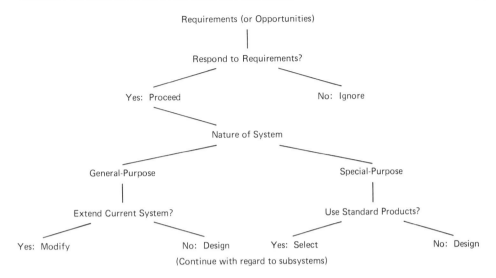

Figure 2-4   A digital-system-design decision tree.

whether the system we shall design (or select, if we are a user procuring a new system) will be a general-purpose digital computer or if it will be a digital system special to our needs. Perhaps we should say that we determine the extent to which we can use general-purpose digital-computer methodology in the system architecture, since degree rather than binary selection is characteristic of this decision (and of most of the design decisions we make).

Sometimes the architectural decisions for a large system result in selection of an existing digital computer as the system controller. In many cases the digital system is a single piece of equipment and the digital computer selected is a standard microcomputer, perhaps microprogrammed to perform effectively the tasks assigned to it. In some cases the system requirements call for a new specialized digital system that incorporates a new general-purpose digital computer. The design decisions that are so important in formulating the architecture must result from a careful consideration of alternatives.

Quite often in special-system design, and occasionally in the design of a general-purpose digital computer, we are faced with decisions on the balance between hardware and software. In Chapter 9 we see more detail on the trade-offs to be examined with regard to hardware vs. software solutions in special-purpose digital systems. In the case of digital computers themselves the issue more often is the balance between hardware control structures and microprogrammed control. This issue is covered at the instruction-set processor level of design in a later chapter.

Issues, alternatives, and trade-offs in architectures for system structure of general-purpose computers and of special-purpose systems at the PMS level, for organization of storage in the memory hierarchy, for the many different possibilities in organizing the central processor, and for design of other processors in the system are covered in later chapters.

2.5 DESIGN TECHNIQUES AND TOOLS

In the three previous sections we have developed the design methodology recommended for digital-system architecture. Lest the reader be left with the impression that from here on all that is available or needed to accomplish the architectural design is pencil, paper, and a creative bent, we should review some of the design techniques and the tools that are available to assist the digital system architect. Some of these are useful throughout the design process, whereas others fit into specific phases of the activity.

Several times earlier in this chapter we referred to "specification", a word that brings to mind visions of large volumes of detail presented in just barely readable form. While specifications of that description are found too often it is not necessary that they be overwhelming. Specifications of a system at any level can be clear, concise, readable, and even interesting. They must be so if they are going to be useful and used.

Just what should be in a specification and how should it be presented? First let us consider the information content. A specification should contain all the information needed to specify to the reader what is required—and only the information that is required. Detail that should be left to the discretion of the reader-designer must not be included.

This identification of what is necessary and what is sufficient often is not easy to accomplish; if it was, the specification would not be so important. It is relatively easy to write a detailed listing of how things *might* be done, particularly if the writer does not have to be accountable for the result. More difficult is the task of specifying what *must* be done. That is why we find too many specifications for requirements of large systems identifying insignificant (at that level) detail while omitting the fundamental requirements information needed by the receiver of the specification. Perhaps that type of specification should instead be called a "generalization"; it is not very specific to its objective.

As regards presentation of the information specific to the topic, there is no "best" format. Almost any form that is concise, precise, and readable is acceptable. On the other hand, within an organization it is a lot easier to convey information in specifications that are in a form well understood by the reader and the writer. Standardization is a desirable objective, but not overstandardization. Unfortunately, standards for specification writing usually violate the simple rule just proposed and burden the specification writer with unimportant detail, resulting in specifications that are difficult to write and to read.

Specifications usually are mechanisms to convey information between professionals in the same or related disciplines. Why should the specification not use the language of the discipline and a format appropriate to the discipline? The best specifications are those drawn up through interaction between the specifier and the receiver, making sure that both understand what is required and what is left to the discretion of the designer.

There are languages that are useful in conveying information about computer architectures concisely and precisely. The language itself can give guidance on what is necessary and what is sufficient at each level. At the requirements level there are languages that aid in development of concise and precise specifications. These *specification languages* have been developed mainly for very large systems involving extensive software development, but many are applicable to the specification of any digital system.

We need languages (or descriptive mechanisms) for representing our system and subsystem designs. The processor–memory–switch (PMS) and instruction-set processor (ISP) languages that were introduced in Chapter 1 can be used to describe systems at the top and at the instruction-set levels. Other hardware description languages are available at more detailed levels. These languages, important tools for conveying information, are covered in more detail in the next few sections.

When new concepts or new combinations of ideas are introduced sometimes it is difficult to determine whether the design will work as planned. In these cases test vehicles of some type prove useful. Simulation is quite powerful for evaluation of function-oriented ideas and there are a number of general and specialized simulation languages used in digital-system evaluation. When specifics of hardware are important the engineers usually construct breadboards to test general concepts before assembling more complete prototypes to measure design approaches. The attitude toward the evaluation, whether it be through simulation or hardware example, is that it is designed to demonstrate the feasibility of a well-thought-out idea, not that it is a part of an exhaustive trial-and-error design process.

Toward the conclusion of the design cycle more comprehensive evaluation is performed. A new architecture and its major components should be tested to verify that they satisfy the specification of requirements. Again, simulation can be quite useful for verification prior to construction and, again, the attitude should be one of testing to verify the validity of an architecture. When the engineering has been completed and prototypes built, tests are performed to verify that the physical representation of the architecture meets its requirements and that the resulting product is sound.

If new software is a part of the product development, initial software verification uses the simulator of the architecture. When the hardware is available, even in prototype form, more detailed verification of the hardware–software interfaces can be accomplished. The system architect has the responsibility for consistency of the total hardware–software system and wants to be sure that both parts work according to the specified requirements.

2.6 THE PROCESSOR–MEMORY–SWITCH DESCRIPTIVE SYSTEM

As implied by its title, the processor–memory–switch (PMS) language defines a digital system in terms of its major subsystems, the processors, the memories, the switches, the controls, and the special function units a system might contain, and of the interconnections among these major subsystems. PMS was introduced by C. G. Bell and A. Newell in 1970 [BellC70]. Their notations and terminology are used here and exceptions are identified. A more comprehensive and more formal description of the PMS language is included in Appendix A.

Each subsystem is defined by its type in capital letters: C for computer, P for processor, M for memory, S for switch, K for control, T for transducer, L for link, and D for function unit (or data operator). Lower-case characters specify the function of a particular unit or its characteristics, and the function is abbreviated after being defined. Subsystems also can be defined in PMS notation. For example, a memory might contain a special error-correction processor that might itself contain local memory. Processors contain their own memory cells, controls, and interconnections. Most modules contain control elements, links, and transducers. Where detail is not desired or necessary it is suppressed, particularly where the existence of a subsidiary module is obvious. (Definition of the memory local to the processor, the registers, will be included in the processor state, described at the instruction-set processor level.)

Characteristics of the subsystem types and the specific examples most used in the chapters that follow are:

Processor, P, a unit that executes a sequence of instructions held in a memory: a processor contains local memory in the form of registers and individual flip-flops and has data operators, links, transducers, switches, and controls (all to be described), but details on these are not included in the PMS description. An overview of the processor function might be included as a footnote. Specific processors used extensively in PMS descriptions in later chapters include: Pc (an abbreviation for Pcentral, the central processor, or CPU), Pio (for Pinput/output), Pcomm (a special processor for communications input and output), Pmath (for special mathematical operations), and Ppipeline (a processor that is organized as a "pipeline" of processors).

Memory, M, a module that stores information: a memory module is organized into addressable units that might be different from the word organization of the processors that access the memory. Memory modules might be subdivided into "frames" and a memory might contain several individual memory modules. A memory module contains a means to access the addressable units, with the specific mechanism dependent on the memory technology used. Some examples of memory modules used in the book are Mp (Mprimary, the main memory of the computer), Ms (Msecondary, which might be further specified as Ms.disk, Ms.tape, Ms.drum, or Ms.optical), Miop (for use only by an input/output processor). Sometimes the technology used is specified as .semi (semiconductor), .mos (metal-oxide semiconductor), .mtf (magnetic thin film), .mdl (mercury delay line), .adl (acoustic delay line).

Switch, S, a module that transfers information without changing its form from one of *m* modules of type *x* to one of *n* modules of type *y*: this would be defined as an "*m* by *n*" switch. Switches of characteristic 1 by 1 are Links, L, and are not ordinarily identified except as lines that connect two modules. The number of individual conductors of a link can be specified as a slash followed by a superior number (e.g., $/^8$). The organization of the switch might be identified: Stree, Scrossbar, Sduplex, or Sshuffle. (These are described in Chapter 3.)

Transducer, T, a unit that modifies the coding or the form of information: an example of the former is a decimal-to-binary converter; of the latter, the sense amplifiers of a magnetic memory; and of both, an analog-to-digital converter. A transducer often is included in a module of another type and is not identified when its existence is obvious.

Data-operator, D, or function unit, a module that changes the meaning of information or produces new information: an arithmetic function unit such as an adder or a multiplier is a D, as are smaller (e.g., shifter) and larger (e.g., fast Fourier transform unit) components that perform this type of activity. D units that are part of processors usually are not specified unless their operation is unique.

Control, K, the module that causes the operations of another system component to take place in the proper sequence: since most of our components are digital devices the K's usually establish the sequence of discrete state transitions that are the operations desired. The existence of many K's can be assumed from the nature of the modules being controlled and the K modules are not always specified.

Computer, C, a combination of the other subsystems containing at least one P and at least one M to operate as an internally programmed computing instrument: the use of the C in a PMS diagram is limited to the description of those systems that include standard or separately described computers as parts of the system.

The modules specify the contents of a system and the connections among modules specify the system topology. In many cases a system described is not fully populated with modules or will have variations in the possible interconnections or topologies. Footnotes to PMS diagrams identify the possibilities. Occasionally it is necessary to use multiple diagrams to record the complete PMS-level description, as with families of computers where different models have different topologies or different components.

Quantitative information can be provided for any module by appending to the module identifier as much detail as desired. These "attributes" are placed in parentheses and have the form: (attribute:value, attribute:value, . . .), with the identification of the attribute left out when it is obvious from the value used. Descriptive data usually is in lower-case to distinguish it from the module type. Abbreviations are used extensively to make the descriptions more concise. When not needed for clarity the detailed description in parentheses is replaced by descriptive data in the form of lower-case words or their abbreviations, with periods separating descriptive characteristics. An example of this form of description was used before in the description for Memory (function:secondary, technology:disk), abbreviated to Ms.disk. The descriptive information can be placed directly with the module identification on the PMS diagram or it can be footnoted if that is clearer. The name of a module or its model number is placed in quotations, as in "B-5500". An abbreviation is separated from a full name by a left slash: "Exchange\XC".

We can use as much quantitative descriptive information as is needed to form an adequate definition of a computer at the PMS level. Since the central processor is described in detail at the next lower level by its ISP, information on the Pc usually is limited to its specific name or model, the quantity of processors that can be attached and their numbering in the system, the technology used, and the date of introduction. Little more detail is provided for I/O and special-purpose processors, particularly if an ISP definition is included. Switches, data operators, controls, and transducers are defined by their function, capacity, performance, and name. Comments that are not part of the formal definition are placed in braces.

The various memory modules in a system require more detail at the PMS level, since computers and digital systems are characterized at this level by their memory capabilities. It is desirable to include in the definition of the primary memory the range of sizes and speeds of individual modules and the quantities of each size that can be included.

The organization of the memory in words, blocks, pages, and the size of each should be included. Access method, addressing modes, and technology are useful to our definition. Secondary memory and any special memories require almost the same level of detail.

The examples shown in Figs. 2-5 and 2-6 should suffice to provide an understanding of the simple and very descriptive PMS notation. Figure 2-5 is the PMS diagram of our benchmark, the computer described by Burks, Goldstine, and von Neumann [BurkA46] that initiated the von Neumann architecture. The reader should compare the PMS description with the English-language description used in Section 1.4.

We see in the diagram a primary memory of 4096 words of 40 bits each. The memory is constructed from 40 storage cathode-ray tubes called *selectrons*. The data path to the central processor is 40 bits wide. The central processor has a 40-bit 2's complement fractional binary word. It uses vacuum tubes with bistable logic. (In the 1940s there also were vacuum tubes with 10 stable states and some experimental computers used these tubes.) The central control for the computer was provided by the control section of the Pc. Information was transferred to and from the peripheral devices in serial (bit-at-a-time) form through the switch. The peripheral equipment consisted of a magnetic-wire secondary memory, a storage tube and a keyboard as a console, and a printer, each with a controller.

For comparison, Fig. 2-6 is a PMS definition of a much larger and more recent computer, the Denelcor HEP (heterogeneous element processor) [SmitB78]. The HEP computer was designed to exploit parallel organizations at the system and processor levels. As shown in the diagram, the system could contain up to 16 process execution modules (Cpem). Each Cpem contained its own program memory organized as 1 to 32 modules of 32 kwords of 64 bits and an instruction processing unit (Pipu). The Pipu was a parallel processor with a 64-bit data word. Concurrent execution of up to 16 independent tasks was handled by the 16 task queues, 16 function units, and 16 storage function queues. Further parallelism was introduced with a "pipeline" organization that had eight execution stages. Each Pipu contained 2048 data registers and 4096 constant registers.

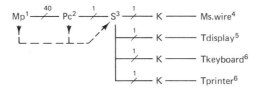

1. Mp\"Memory_Organ" (size: 4096 words, word-size: 40 bits, technology: 40 selectron_tubes) {each selectron displays 4096 bits}.
2. Pc (components: (D\"Arithmetic_Organ", K\"Control Organ") operation: (40-bit_word, fractional binary, 2's complement), technology: (vacuum tube, bistable logic)) {see ISP diagram for detailed description}.
3. S (operation: serial_by_bit) {data transfer between Pc and the selected (by instruction) device controllers}.
4. Ms.wire\Memory (function: secondary, technology: magnetic_wire) {store 4096 40-bit words in nonvolatile replaceable medium}.
5. Tdisplay (technology: cathode-ray_storage_tube) {same as Mp}.
6. {Tkeyboard, Tprinter: modified teletypewriter}.

Figure 2-5   PMS diagram of the von Neumann architecture.

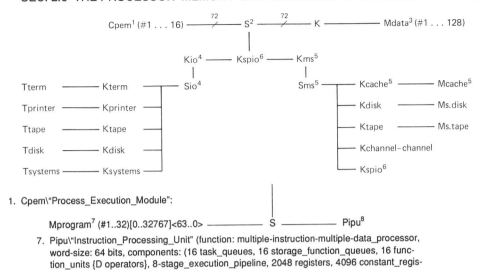

1. Cpem\"Process_Execution_Module":

    Mprogram[7] (#1..32)[0..32767]<63..0> ——————— S ——————— Pipu[8]

    7. Pipu\"Instruction_Processing_Unit" (function: multiple-instruction-multiple-data_processor, word-size: 64 bits, components: (16 task_queues, 16 storage_function_queues, 16 function_units {D operators}, 8-stage_execution_pipeline, 2048 registers, 4096 constant_registers)).

    8. Mprogram\"Program_Memory".

2. S\"Switch_Network" (function: (packet_switch, programmable routing) {a routing node contains 3 bidirectional ports with 2 word transfers}, propagation_time: 50 ns, message_throughput_time: 100ns).

3. Mdata\"Data_Memory_Module" (size: 128 kwords, word_size: (64-bit_data, 8-bit_error-correction code), access time: 50 ns).

4. "I/O_and_Control_Subsystem" (components: (Kio,Sio), function: programmed_control_of_peripheral_devices).

5. "Mass_Storage_Subsystem" (components: (Sms, Kms, Kcache, Mcache (8..128 mbyte), Kdisk, Ms.disk, Ktape, Ms.tape, Kchannel-channel, Kspio), function: simultaneous_operation_of_31_I/O_channels, transfer_rate: 2.5 mbyte/s_ea_channel).

6. Kspio\"Special-Purpose_I/O_Channel".

Figure 2-6   PMS diagram of the Denelcor HEP.

There were up to 128 data memory modules, each with 128 kwords of 64 data and 8 error-correction bits. Access time to a memory word was 50 nanoseconds. The process execution modules, data memory modules (with their controller), and the input/output subsystems were connected through a programmable packet switch, the switch network. Each routing node of the switch contained three bidirectional ports that transferred a double word (128 bits) every 100 nanoseconds. The time for a double word to flow through the routing node was 50 ns.

Three separate input/output subsystems were included in the HEP. The standard I/O subsystem with terminals, printers, magnetic tape drives, disk files, and external computer systems was connected to the switch network through the I/O and control system, a program-controlled switch. The mass storage subsystem, connected through a switch and controller, contained a "cache" memory of from 8 to 128 Mbytes, disk files, magnetic tape drives, and a channel–channel connection to another HEP. Thirty-one transfers could take place simultaneously at a transfer rate of up to 2.5 Mbytes/s each. Special–purpose input/output channels could be connected to the switch network directly or through the mass storage subsystem switch.

The reader cannot be expected to understand all of the operations of this very large system at this point, since we have not covered the details of alternative PMS and ISP organizations. These are topics of later chapters; the purpose of showing such a powerful system at this time is to contrast it with the simple von Neumann computer and to introduce the fact that there are many alternative system structures to be investigated. One whole chapter is devoted to parallel computer systems.

The processor–memory–switch language is a concise means to provide a top-level description of digital systems and computers. It is easy to read and its abbreviations can be followed and understood by anyone familiar with these systems. The growing acceptance of PMS in the community of computer architects makes it a reasonable standard for top-level system description.

2.7 INSTRUCTION-SET PROCESSOR DESCRIPTION

The processor–memory–switch level of description permits us to obtain an overview of the structure of a computer system, but it gives little detail on how processors in the system work. It certainly is insufficient to describe how to program the machine in assembly language. For these purposes we need a more detailed descriptive mechanism. We need more detail, but only enough to accomplish the objective of describing the operation of the computer so that programs can be written for it. We do not want to obscure the description with detail that is used for other purposes, such as for implementation of the computer, for manufacture, or for maintenance.

Another language originated by Bell and Newell [BellC71] meets our needs. Their instruction-set processor (ISP) language is concise, precise, complete, understandable, and easily learned. As stated in its title, ISP describes the instruction set of a processor and adds information on the primary memory (Mp) to the extent that it is needed for an understanding of processor operation. The information provided with this language is equivalent to that found in a computer assembly language programming manual. A detailed description of ISP is contained in Appendix A.

To write an assembly language program we need data on the internal "data structure" of the computer—its word organization, instruction formats, addressing, formats for numeric items (fixed point, floating point, multiprecision, whole word and part word) and characters, packing of small data items (characters, boolean values, short integers) into machine words. We require specification of the registers and the flip-flops (or switches) that are available to the user (the accumulator and/or the other data registers and the flags that can be set and tested) and those that are used but not made available (the instruction pointer, memory and I/O buffer registers, and the control flip-flops). The instruction set identifies the instructions available. We need to know how the instructions and the data are obtained from memory and details of the instruction execution sequence. All of this can be described with the ISP language.

In ISP we can describe data types, instructions, operations, and processors in a concise and precise manner. Conventions for naming and quantifying items are easy to remember because the meanings are obvious to anyone familiar with computer organization. The descriptions can be carried to sufficient detail to describe the processor operation completely or can be abbreviated to convey just the amount of information desired. Samples of special symbols that are used follow (several are different from the symbols used in [BellC71]):

<0..7>, specification of an 8-bit register with bits numbered from 0 to 7.

NR<15..0>, a register named NR of 16 bits, most significant numbered "15".

instruction\i<0..11>, instruction word, abbreviated "i", of 12 bits.

<0,1,2,3,4,5,6,7>, the same as <0..7> (i.e., commas separate items in a sequence).

[a..b], an assemblage of registers, as a memory.

[a..b][c..d], an assemblage of an assemblage of registers, as a paged memory.

[0..b]<7..0>, a memory of size (b + 1) bytes.

x:=y, an object identified as "x" is defined as "y".

@, concatenation = as A @ B.

L ← V, location "L" is assigned value "V".

C → A, condition "C" causes action "A".

A, B, C, actions "A","B","C" are concurrent.

D; E, action "E" follows action "D".

{this is a comment}, comment explaining an item defined in ISP.

"Name_of_item", the proper name of an item defined in ISP.

Logical, relational and arithmetic operators use normal symbols or abbreviations.

A description in ISP of a representative computer shows the utility of this language. The author's interpretation of the ISP of our benchmark von Neumann computer is shown in Fig. 2-7. The processor storage (Pc state) includes three 40-bit data registers, the accumulator (Ac), the arithmetic register (AR), and the selectron register (SR) (now usually called the memory buffer register). The last is included in the processor because it is used in arithmetic operations. We see also a control counter (CC) (now called a program counter) of 12 bits to permit addressing of all 4096 memory words. Two 18-bit registers, the function state register (FR) and the control register (CR), are used to hold instructions (each memory word of 40 bits is sufficiently large to hold two instructions with four extra bits). There are three flip-flops, condition (Cn), instruction control (Ic), and run. Cn has a value of 0 if Ac holds a negative value, or else it has a value of 1. Ic shows which of FR or CR holds the instruction to be executed next. If the instruction was in the left half of the memory word (In = 0) then the next instruction is in FR. Run is used to show that the computer is functioning correctly (Run = 1).

The memory (Mp state) is specified as 4096 40-bit words. In the data format description we see that the sign bit of the binary word is in Ac bit 1. Comments are used to specify that numeric values are represented in 2's complement fractional binary form. Next, we see the instruction format. The instruction is held in FR. The 6-bit operation

```
{Pc State}
   Ac<1..40>,                            {Accumulator}
   AR<1..40>,                            {Arithmetic Register}
   SR<1..40>,                            {Selectron Register}
   CC<1..12>,                            {Control (program) Counter}
   FR<1..18>,                            {Function state Register}
   CR<1..18>,                            {Control Register}
   Cn,                                   {Condition (Ac >= 0 -> Cn <- 1)}
   Ic,                                   {Instruction control (left = 0)}
   Run,                                  {Run flip-flop}
{Mp State}
   M[0..4095]<1..40>,                    {40 "selectron" tubes}
{Data Format}
   data<39..0> = Ac<1..40>,              {2's complement fractional binary}
   sign = data<39>,                      {sign bit}
{Instruction Format}
   i\instruction := FR,                  {18-bit instruction}
   op<1..6> := i<13..18>,                {6-bit operation code}
   addr<11..0> := i<1..12>,              {12-bit argument address}
{Instruction Interpretation Process}
   Run = 1 -> (Ic = 0 -> ((Ic <- 1, FR <- M[CC]<1..18>,
     CR <- M[CC]<21..38>); CC <- CC + 1; "Perform_Operation"),
     Ic = 1 -> ((Ic <- 0, FR <- CR); "Perform_Operation")),
   PROC "Perform_Operation" (op):
   (op = 0   ->,                                {continue}
    op = 1   -> Ac <- M[addr],                  {clear & add (CLA)}
    op = 2   -> Ac <- -M[addr],                 {clear & subtract(CLS)}
    op = 3   -> Ac <- abs(M[addr]),             {CLA absolute}
    op = 4   -> Ac <- -abs(M[addr]),            {CLS absolute}
    op = 5   -> Ac <- Ac + M[addr],             {add}
    op = 6   -> Ac <- Ac - M[addr],             {subtract}
    op = 7   -> Ac <- Ac + abs(M[addr]),        {add absolute}
    op = 8   -> Ac <- Ac - abs(M[addr]),        {subtract absolute}
    op = 9   -> AR <- M[addr],                  {load AR}
    op = 10  -> Ac <- AR,                       {register transfer}
    op = 11  -> Ac @ AR <- AR x M[addr],        {multiply}
    op = 12  -> (AR <- Ac / M[addr],            {division quotient}
                 Ac <- Ac MOD M[addr]),         {division remainder}
    op = 13  -> (Ic <- 0, CC <- addr),          {jump left instruction}
    op = 14  -> (CR <- M[addr]<21..38>,
                 Ic <- 1, CC <- addr + 1),      {jump right instruction}
    op = 15  -> Cn = 1 -> (Ic <- 0, CC <- addr),  {if Ac >= 0 jump left}
    op = 16  -> Cn = 1 -> (CR <- M[addr]<21..38>,
                 Ic <- 1, CC <- addr + 1),      {if Ac >= 0 jump right}
    op = 17  -> M[addr] <- Ac,                  {store accumulator}
    op = 18  -> M[addr]<1..12> <- Ac<1..12>,    {store field left}
    op = 19  -> M[addr]<21..32> <- Ac<1..12>,   {store field right}
    op = 20  -> Ac <- Ac x 2,                   {shift left}
    op = 21  -> Ac <- Ac / 2,                   {shift right}
    op = 63  -> Run <- 0),                      {halt}
{NOTE: Input/output operations not included (not fully defined).}
```

Figure 2-7   ISP description of the von Neumann computer.

code is held in instruction bits 13 through 18, while the 12-bit argument address field is in instruction bits 1 through 12. Instruction execution is specified to take place as follows:

> If Run is true (i.e., Run = 1):
>
>> If the next instruction will be in FR (Ic = 0):
>>
>>> Set Ic to 1 and transfer the next memory word to FR and CR. Then increment Cn to point to the next pair of instructions. Then perform the specified operation.

If the next instruction is in CR (In = 1):
    Set Ic to 0 and move the value in CR to FR.
    Then perform the specified operation.

Perform operation specifies how each instruction will work. There are 22 instructions, not including those required to copy I/O information between the accumulator and the console or the secondary memory. (Input/output operations are not detailed in the source paper. The specific codes for the other instructions were not identified and values are assumed.) Several operations can be described to demonstrate the ISP specification:

Clear and Add (op = 1): The value in the memory
    location specified by the instruction address
    is copied into Ac.

Multiply (op = 11): The result of multiplying the
    values in Ac and the designated memory location
    is placed in the concatenation of Ac and AR.

If Ac holds a nonnegative value jump to the
    instruction in the right half of the memory
    word designated by the address field (op = 16):
      If Cn = 1:
        Set IC to 1 and copy addr into CC and
        copy the instruction in the right half
        of the memory word designated by addr
        into CR.
    (Note that the sequence specified by the instruction
    interpretation process causes the value in CR to be
    transferred into FR as the next instruction to be executed.)

In order to obtain a good understanding of the ISP notation, and to see how this early computer operated, readers should carefully go over each of the 22 operations shown in Fig. 2-7.

A comparison with the ISP of a more modern computer also is useful. In Fig. 2-8 is shown an abbreviated ISP of the Intel 8086, a microprocessor introduced in 1978 and used in many personal computers in the 1980s. The processor has 8- and 16-bit arithmetic and communicates with memory in 16-bit words. The 8088 microprocessor of the original IBM PC and its clones is similar to the 8086, except that it has an 8-bit data bus. The 8086 can address 1 Mbyte of memory in 64-kbyte (possibly overlapping) segments. Input/output transfers of up to 64 kbytes are allowed.

The Pc state includes the following 16-bit registers: four data (AX, BX, CX, DX), two segment offset (SP, BP), four segment base (CS, SS, DS, ES), two index (SI, DI), and one program counter (IP). Register FL contains 16 flip-flops for status and control purposes. As indicated in the footnote, a queue of 6 bytes acts as an instruction stream buffer. This queue and two internal communication registers are transparent to the

```
{Pc State}
     GR[0..7]<15..0>,                  {16 General Registers}
     AX := GR[0],{Accumulator}         BX := GR[1],{Base Register}
     CX := GR[2],{Count Register}      DX := GR[3],{Data Register}
     SP := GR[4],{Stack Pointer}       BP := GR[5],{Base Pointer }
     SI := GR[6],{Source Index Reg.}   DI := GR[7],{Data Index Reg.}
{Register Aliases}
     AH<7..0> := AX<15..8>,            AL<7..0> := AX<7..0>,
     BH<7..0> := BX<15..8>,            BL<7..0> := BX<7..0>,
     CH<7..0> := CX<15..8>,            CL<7..0> := CX<7..0>,
     DH<7..0> := DX<15..8>,            DL<7..0> := DX<7..0>,
{Segment Registers}
     CS<15..0>,{Code Segment Reg.}     DS<15..0>,{Data Segment Reg.}
     SS<15..0>,{Stack Segment Reg.}    ES<15..0>,{Extra Segment Reg.}
{Control Registers}
     IP<15..0>,{Instruction Ptr.}      FL<15..0>,{Flag Register}
{Flag Assignments}
     CF := FL<0>,    {Carry Flag}      PF := FL<2>,    {Parity Flag}
     AF := FL<4>,    {Auxiliary Carry} ZF := FL<6>,    {Zero Flag}
     SF := FL<7>,    {Sign Flag}       TF := FL<8>,    {Trap Flag}
     IF := FL<9>,    {Interrupt Enable} DF := FL<10>,  {Direction Flag}
     OF := FL<11>,   {Overflow Flag}   {all others are unassigned}
     {NOTE: Pc also contains several registers not available to programmer.}
{Mp State}
     Mp[0..2⁴-1][0..2¹⁶-1]<7..0>,      {16 64-kbyte segments}
{Data Formats}
     uw<15..0>,   {unsigned binary word} ub<7..0>,      {unsigned byte}
     sw<S,14..0>,{signed binary word}  sb<S,6..0>,     {signed byte}
     pd<ld,rd>,   {packed decimal}      ud<0000,rd>,   {unpacked decimal}
     {NOTE: S := sign bit, ld, rd := binary-coded decimal format.}
{Instruction Formats}
     i\instruction[1..6]<7..0>,        {1- to 6-byte stream}
     op<0..7> := i[1]<7..0>,{operation} next := 2,
        d := op<6>,   {direction bit*}
        s := op<6>,   {sign extension*}  v := op<6>,      {variable bit*}
        w := op<7>,   {word/byte bit*}   z := op<7>,      {zero compare*}
        rega<2..0> := op<5..7>,                   {register select type a*}
        regb<1..0> := op<3..4>,                   {register select type b*}
     mr<7..0> := i[@], next := 3,               {mode/register byte*}
        mod<0..1> := mr<7..6>,                  {register/memory mode}
        rop<0..2> := mr<5..3>,                  {register/operator extension}
        rea<0..2> := mr<2..0>,                  {register/effective address}
     ldi<7..0> := i[3], next := 4,              {low-displacement byte*}
     hdi<7..0> := i[4], next := 5,              {high-displacement byte*}
     lda<7..0> := i[next],                      {low data byte (immediate)*}
     hda<7..0> := i[next + 1],                  {high data byte (immediate)*}
     {NOTE: Bits, bytes or fields with * are not in all instructions.}
{Memory Address Calculation}
     ea <- displ + GR[index] + GR[base],{Effective Address}
        mod = 00 -> displ <- 0,          mod = 01 -> displ <- ldi,
        mod = 10 -> displ <- <hdi,ldi>,  mod = 11 -> "Register_Mode"(),
     {NOTE: The rea value is used to select index and/or base registers.}
     aa <- offset + 16 * segment,       {absolute address 0 to 2²⁰ - 1}
     {NOTE: Offset is Effective Address for most variables, IP for
     instructions, SP for stack operations, SI & DI for string source and
     destination. Segment is CS, SS, DS, ES for instructions, stack,
     variables, string destinations.}
```

Figure 2-8   Partial ISP description of the Intel 8086.

programmer. Register aliases state that the 4 data registers can be viewed as eight 8-bit registers, each with "high" and "low" bytes. Under flag assignments, we see that only nine of the 16 flip-flops of the flag register are used.

The processor can address (in 64-kbyte segments) 2^{20} bytes of primary memory (Mp state). Data formats for word, byte, and decimal formats are shown. An instruction can take from 1 to 6 bytes. Special uses of certain bits in the operation byte are shown.

(The special-use bits are in locations not used by the operation itself.) The optional 5 bytes of an instruction include one to designate addressing mode or register usage, two for displacements from a base address, and two for (immediate) data.

Effective-address calculations for the four address modes specified in the second instruction byte are shown. Index and base registers are selected by the reg and r/m fields. The set of 133 instructions is not shown in this partial ISP description. Each of the instructions can be defined as the von Neumann machine operations are described in Fig. 2-7.

Since the other processors of a computer system (input/output, communications, special-function processors) operate in the same manner as the central processor(s) the ISP descriptive language is equally applicable for their description. To demonstrate this and to show another processor type we refer to Fig. 2-9, which is the ISP description of the Intel 8089, the input/output processor companion to the 8086 microprocessor.

The 8089 processor includes two I/O channels for concurrent communication with two I/O devices. Each channel contains three 20-bit general registers (GA, GB, GC), two 20-bit pointer registers (TP and PP, which is system-controlled), and four 16-bit user-accessible registers (IX, BC, MC, CC). The primary memory is shared with the central processor. There are 16 kbytes of input/output area accessible by way of the I/O bus. Both byte and word data formats are used.

Formats for the 2- to 6-byte instructions are shown. The first instruction byte is for field selection, with uses of the 8 bits specified. The second byte identifies the operation to be performed and the register (GA, GB, GC, PP) that holds the base address to which the displacement is added, as shown in the memory-address calculation. The operations are not included in this partial ISP description.

```
{Pio State}                                    {Input/Output Processor}
   CRS[#1,2][0..8], {2 Channel Register Sets (similar)}:
      GR[x]<19..0> & (x := A..C),              {3 General Purpose Registers}
      TP<19..0>, {Task Pointer}                PP<19..0>, {Parameter Block Ptr}
      IX<15..0>, {Index}                       BC<15..0>, {Byte Count}
      MC<15..0>, {Mask/Compare}                CC<15..0>, {Channel Control}
   {NOTE: Assembly/disassembly registers and 4 tag bits & a program status
    word in each channel are not available to the programmer.}
{Mp State (System Space)}
   Mp[0..2⁴-1][0..2¹⁶-1]<7..0>,                {shared with Pc via System Bus}
{Mio State (Input-Output Space)}
   Mio[0..2¹⁴-1]<7..0>,                         {accessed through I/O Bus}
{Data Formats}
   ub<7..0>, {unsigned byte}                   uw<15..0>, {unsigned word}
{Instruction Formats}
   i\instruction[1..6]<7..0>,                  {2 to 6 bytes per instruction}
   fs<7..0> := i[1],                           {field select byte}
      rbp<0..2> := fs<7..5>,                   {register, bit, pointer select}
      wb<0..1> := fs<4..3>,                    {displacement/data bytes}
      aa<0..1> := fs<2..1>,                    {memory addressing mode}
      w := fs<0>,                              {operand width (word or byte)}
   op := i[2],                                 {operand byte}
      opcode<0..5> := op<7..2>,                {operation code}
      mm<0..1> := op<1..0>,                    {memory base register}
   {NOTE: Additional bytes (up to 6) specify offsets, displacemenst, data.
{Memory-Address Calculation}
      tag = 0 -> as <- pointer + displ,        {address in Mp (1 mbyte)}
      tag = 1 -> ai <- pointer + displ,        {address in Mio (64 kbyte)}
   {NOTE: Tag and pointer are in TP for Instructions otherwise in GR[x].}
```

Figure 2-9 Intel 8089 I/O processor ISP (partial).

The fetch–execute cycle of the 8089 is similar to that of a simple central processor. Intel placed the functions of the 8086 processor and many peripheral interface devices on the same silicon chip in the 80186 integrated microprocessor system.

Just from these three examples we see possibilities for significant variation among instruction-set processors. In Chapter 5 we examine extensively such variations. We consider in detail the alternatives for processor state (internal registers and their use), for word size and organization, for instruction sets, for quantities of arguments per instruction, and for methods to control processor operations.

2.8 DESCRIPTION OF EXECUTION AND TIMING

In this book we seldom need descriptive mechanisms more detailed than that offered by the ISP language. On the other hand, the computer engineers who implement the architecture require a language for description at the next more detailed level. This allows formal definitions of the operation and of the performance of the computer designed, and is particularly useful for simulating execution. Simulation permits evaluation of alternative designs and allows programs to be tested before a physical model is built. It is also used for cost-performance studies of competitive real and hypothetical computers.

The ISP language of the previous section allows for a functional description of the way a processor works. What can be provided at the next level of detail is a description of the flow of signals within the processor, with information on timing and synchronization of this flow. This level of description is often called the *logic level*. At this level we should be able to describe the operation of the computer controls (the "microsequences").

In designing a processor the computer engineer is concerned with the elements used to hold information, the transfers of information among those elements, the transformations performed on the information during the transfers, and the timing involved in the transfer processes. Register transfer languages have been developed for the purpose of describing this performance of discrete systems (systems for which operation can be described as finite sequences of activities).

With a register transfer language we define the registers and the other storage elements of the processor, as we did in the ISP language, but our definitions are more hardware than function oriented. Machine operation is described in terms of the flow of information among storage elements during individual time periods, controlled by a "clock". Typical register transfer operations are shown in Fig. 2-10. Often information

```
REGISTER_A <- REGISTER_B
```

(a)

```
REGISTER_A  <- REGISTER_A + REGISTER_B
```

(b)

```
t0 : ADDRESSREG <- INSTREG.ADDR
t1 : MEMBUFREG <- MEM[ADDRESSREG], OVFF <- false
t2 : AACUMULATOR <- ACCUMULATOR + MEMBUFREG
t3 : if OVERFLOW then OVFF <- true
```

(c)

Figure 2-10   Register transfer language examples. (a) A simple transfer. (b) Register-to-register addition. (c) A microsequence.

transfers entail no change in information content, in which case we might reflect the transfer of information as shown in Fig. 2-10(a). When the transfer includes a change in the information the change (e.g., an addition) is included in the expression on the right side of the register transfer statement, Fig. 2-10(b). Specific clock cycles can be included in the description, as we see in Fig. 2-10(c), the execution phase of an addition operation in a single accumulator computer. In the last example t_0, t_1, t_2, and t_3 represent time cycles and a comma separates actions taken within a time cycle. Register names are capitalized. "INSTREG.ADDR" means "ADDR field of INSTREG". "MEM[ADDRESSREG]" means "the memory location designated by the value in AD-DRESSREG". OVFF is the overflow flip-flop.

Figure 2-11 shows a register transfer language (RTL) representation of a part of the instruction execution sequence of a simple computer, with the "add" and "jump to subroutine" instructions demonstrated. For reference, a PMS diagram of the computer (based on the DEC PDP-8) is shown in Fig. 2-11(a). The description at the RTL level repeats some information, Fig. 2-11(b), that would be in the instruction-set processor description if an ISP diagram did

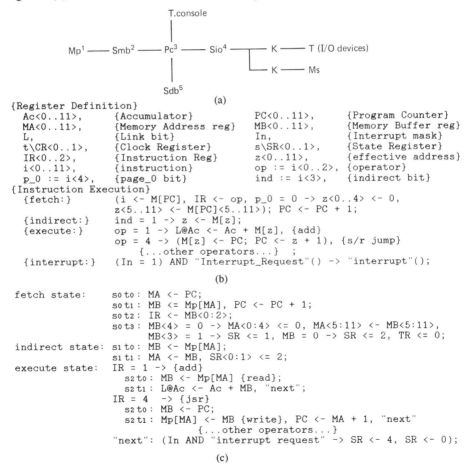

Figure 2-11   RTL representation of instruction execution. (a) PMS diagram. (b) Relevant ISP (extended). (c) Register transfer operations.

not accompany the RTL diagram. Registers are defined as in ISP. The simple computer shown has a 12-bit accumulator, memory address, memory buffer, and program counter registers, a 3-bit instruction register, a 2-bit state register, and a 2-bit clock (time cycle) register. A link bit and an interrupt mask bit are included in the hardware.

The instruction execution sequence at the ISP level is shown for comparison with the register transfer definitions. During the fetch cycle the memory location pointed to by the program counter contains the instruction. The first three bits represent the operation field of the instruction and the last seven bits represent the displacement of the effective address. Bit 4 is the "page-0" bit, specifying reference to the initial page. The program counter is incremented during this phase. Register transfer operations in the fetch phase (s0) are shown in Fig. 2-11(c). At time 0 the memory address register receives the value in the program counter. At the next clock pulse the memory value addressed is read to the memory buffer register and the program counter is incremented. During clock time 2 the operation code is transferred to the instruction register. In the final clock phase the memory-address register receives the address of the argument. If the page-0 bit is set, bits 0 through 4 receive a value 0; if not, the value remains as it was. At the same time bits 5 through 11 receive the value of the address field in the memory buffer register (the instruction that was fetched). Simultaneously, bit 3 of the instruction (MB) is tested to determine if the indirect (s1) or the execution (s2) stage is to be next and TR is reset to 0. All of these activities can take place during one clock time because they do not require use of the same transfer lines. The only true register transfer is "MA<5..11> <- MB<5..11>". Other activities reflect changes in flip-flop values (designated "<-").

If the instruction had an indirect designator (bit 3 = 1), then to go into memory again to find the effective address, "indirect" in Fig. 2-11(b). The register transfer operations for this case are shown as the indirect stage in Fig. 2-11(c). Two clock times are required, the first to obtain the value from memory and the second to move the resulting value to the memory address register and to set the state register to 2.

Two operations of the execute stage are demonstrated, "add" (opcode = 1) and "jump to subroutine\jsr" (opcode = 4). In the first case the values in the accumulator and the designated memory location are added and the result is placed in the accumulator, with any overflow going to the link bit. For the "jsr" case the value in the program counter is stored at the effective address and the program counter is set to the value of the next memory location. The execute stage register transfers, Fig. 2-11(c), show that for "add" at the first clock time the value of the argument is read from memory to the memory buffer register. At the next clock time the addition operation is performed. In the case of "jsr" the first clock time is used to move the value of the program counter to the memory buffer register. At time 1 the value is written to memory while the program counter receives the value in the memory-address register incremented by 1. No matter which instruction is being executed the interrupt request is tested to determine whether the next stage is interrupt ($s = 4$) or fetch ($s = 0$).

This simple example demonstrates how cycle timing and details of information flow can be shown in a register transfer description. It also shows how the resulting detail can obscure the higher-level description we want at the instruction-set processor level. The register transfer language description is the top-level description for implementation of the computer.

State-transition diagrams and state tables also can be used to demonstrate operation of discrete systems. In a state-transition diagram all states possible in the system are shown as nodes. A unique identifier is given to each node. Edges that emanate from a node indicate the possible transitions to other states. The conditions that cause each transition and any output resulting from the transition are specified at each edge. Thus, the state-transition diagram is a directed graph representing the relationships of the states and the control of changes of state. The state-transition diagram might be augmented with a state (or excitation) table showing the result of each control input in each state and an output table showing the value that will be generated from each input in each state.

State-transition diagrams are useful for representation of simple finite-state machines, such as lexical analyzers for programming languages, finite automata, and logical subsystems of a digital processor. An example is the binary counter shown in Fig. 2-12. The combined state and output table, Fig. 2-12(a), specifies that with the system in any state an input of 0 will cause the system to remain in that state and an input of 1 will advance the system to the next state. The output values are the same as the state transitions. For example, if the system is in state 01 an input of 0 keeps the system in state 01 and generates an output of "01". If starting at state 11, an input sequence of 1's generates a binary count modulo 4 ("00", "01", "10", "11"). The same information is conveyed by the state-transition diagram of Fig. 2-12(b). Here the system can be in any of four states (the nodes 00, 01, 10, 11). An input (x) of 0 keeps the system at the same state and generates an output specifying that state, while an input of 1 advances the system to the next state and transmits the value of that state. The state transitions are identified by the directed edges. Input and output values are specified as "x=input/output" at each edge.

It is not possible to represent the complete operation of even a very simple processor with state-transition diagrams of reasonable size. At the logic level there are too many states and too many transitions. However, the state-transition diagram can be used to represent major instruction cycles of a computer. The execution cycle of the computer defined in RTL in Fig. 2-11 is shown in Fig. 2-13. The overall fetch-execute cycle of four states is represented in Fig. 2-13(a) [to be compared with the cycle described in ISP in Fig. 2-11(b)]. The conditions that take us from the fetch instruction state (S_0) are: ind=1 (indirect bit set), which takes us to the indirect state (S_1), and ind=0, which takes us to the execute instruction state (S_2). S_2 unconditionally follows S_1. On exit from S_2 the

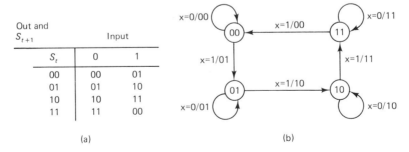

Out and S_{t+1}	Input	
S_t	0	1
00	00	01
01	01	10
10	10	11
11	11	00

(a)   (b)

Figure 2-12 State transitions for a modulo-4 binary counter. (a) State and output table. (b) State-transition diagram.

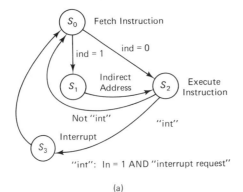

(a)

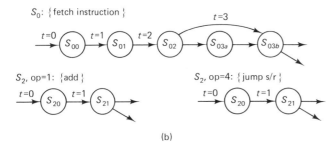

(b)

Figure 2-13 State-transition diagram for instruction execution of Fig. 2-11 (a) Fetch-execute cycle. (b) Examples of substates.

system can go to S_3, the interrupt state, or back to S_0, which also follows S_3. The path from S_2 is determined by whether the interrupt condition "int" obtains.

More detailed states are shown in Fig. 2-13(b), in which we see examples of the clock time steps that are represented in RTL in Fig. 2-11(c). Activity associated with each state is shown next to the symbol for that state. Readers should compare the two figures to see that the state diagram can represent actions of discrete systems expressed in ISP or in RTL. In either case the state diagram is less concise and shows no more detail.

Another form of directed graph, the Petri net, is useful to represent the control and the flow of data through a discrete system. In the Petri net the conditions that are possible in the system are represented by circles (*places*) and the transitions that are possible from each condition are represented by bars. Edges direct the flow between the transitions and the places. Availability of data (a *token*) in a place is represented by a dot in the circle. For a transition to "fire" it is required that data tokens be available at each of its inputs. When conditions for a transition are satisfied the transition will take place, causing the flow of data tokens to the places that are on edges from that transition.

Petri nets are very useful in representing the "data flow", as opposed to the "control flow" of a discrete system. As such, they have been useful in defining operation of Data Flow computers, which are covered in a later chapter. Petri nets also have been used to represent the flow of information and the "work" done in information-processing activities. This form of directed graph shows much promise for more formal descriptions of the flow of information in computers, but represents a level of detail too fine for most computer-architecture descriptions.

An example of a Petri net representing a process graph is shown in Fig. 2-14. When input data is available, a token is in P_0 in Fig. 2-14(a), the process represented by t_a is activated, producing tokens (results) at places P_1 and P_2, Fig. 2-14(b). At that time, either process t_b or t_c (but not both) can be executed, Figs. 2-14(c) and (d). After Figs. 2-14(a) and (b) have been repeated both t_b and t_c have been executed, providing the results needed for t_d, Fig. 2-14(d). Finally, t_d is executed, generating the system output as a token in P_5. Note that as soon as t_a has fired another input token can be placed in t_a, which can be fired as soon as t_a and t_d have cleared P_1 and P_2. This demonstrates that processes t_a and t_d can be executed concurrently.

There are other languages to assist us in simulating digital systems. These range from the high-level simulation languages SIMSCRIPT (derived from FORTRAN) and SIMULA (an ALGOL60 derivative) and variants of them to languages for simulating detailed operations of transistors on a semiconductor. In the latter case, following the simulation to verify correct operation, the languages can be used to place components on the semiconductor surface and to plan the interconnections. These "silicon compilers"

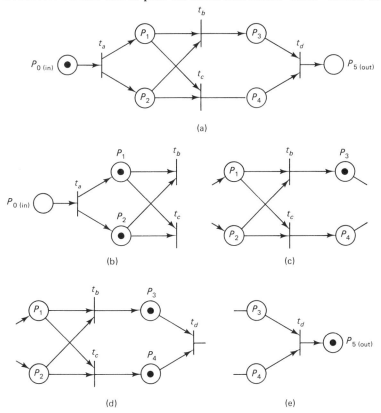

Figure 2-14 Token flow in a simple Petri net. (Processes are represented as "transitions," t_i. Value sets required by processes are represented by "places," P_j.) (a) A token has been placed in P_0, enabling t_a. (b) t_a fires, enabling t_b or t_c. (c) t_b fires, disabling t_c. Parts (a) and (b) are repeated, but now only t_c is enabled (the token in P_3 blocks t_b). (d) t_c fires, enabling t_d. (e) t_d fires, generating output.

permit computers to assist in designing integrated circuits with very large quantities of components. Languages at these extremes of system design are either too broad or too narrow for our evaluations of computer architectures.

2.9 ECONOMICS: PERFORMANCE, COMPLEXITY, AND COST

This chapter on design methodology should not close without some discussion about the importance of economics. Certainly the engineers who implement the architecture and design the hardware have great impact on the final cost of a system. However, insufficient attention to cost at the architectural level can assure that the resulting product will be expensive. Most problems of high cost (and of low reliability) are the result of complexity that is designed into products from the start.

Requirements for high performance do not translate into the need for complexity of hardware or of software. Well-conceived solutions to most problems are straightforward solutions. Complexity usually results from insufficient attention to developing a strategy for a design. The top-down methodology we have discussed is aimed at minimizing complexity by directing attention to the most important aspects of the design at each level. At the system level, what are the system requirements? At the processor design level, what is the combination of techniques that will best meet the requirements? At the implementation level, how do we implement the functional design specified with minimum components and minimum interconnection? In our systems software, what are the major functions and how are they related to each other?

Perhaps these questions of design philosophy have been addressed sufficiently in the past, but probably they have not. Hardware, software, and systems containing both remain more expensive than necessary and less reliable than possible due to excessive complexity. Usually the very performance objectives that caused the designer to formulate a complicated solution suffer because of the complexity. Beauty, elegance, and product success result from simplicity of design.

2.10 SUMMARY

An orderly approach to development of a computer architecture begins with an analysis of customer requirements. There might be a specific single customer or the customer might be hypothetical, defined by the market that the system is being designed to serve. The requirements for a computer system or for a family of computers is expressed in terms of the functions to be performed, the amount of information to be held and the rate of flow of the information, the physical and computational environments in which the system will operate, the date when the system will be introduced and its expected lifetime, status and expected actions of the competition, and economics of development, manufacture, and operation. It is important to establish specific measures to determine that we have succeeded in meeting the requirements.

The objectives of the architecture in response to the requirements must be specified. At each level of detail the objectives and the ways in which we can determine that the objectives have been met should be stated. The objectives for the design at any level of detail are translated to become the requirements for the next more detailed level. The system design process entails a high degree of iteration and feedback from the more detailed designs to the more general. System architects are involved throughout the product development process in evaluating designs, in correlating test results with system requirements, in providing guidance to those who develop support for the system, and in determining how any changes in requirements affect the system design.

In establishing the system architecture there are many decisions to be made, all of which entail selection from among possible approaches to satisfying particular objectives. In digital-system design the starting point is usually deciding the extent to which general purpose instead of specialized systems or subsystems should be used. At all levels of detail there might be standard modules available to obviate the need for unique new approaches to satisfying a function. Issues to be faced involve trade-offs between hardware and software approaches, including consideration of existing software techniques against new software development.

There are many tools available to assist the computer architect. Languages for expression of specifications for a design at the requirements, the system, the subsystem, and the components levels are essential to communication of design information. These language tools permit requirements, designs, and verification criteria to be specified with precision. It is important that the system designer not overspecify so that the freedom of the subsystem designers to perform their tasks is restricted.

The PMS language permits a definition of the system structure as an assemblage of communicating subsystems. The functional subsystems are the processor (P), the memory (M), the control (K), the switch (S), the transducer (T), and the data operator (D) components of the system. The PMS language permits a concise description of the characteristics of each component and of the interconnection among them.

Of most interest among the components is the structure and the functional organization of the processors. The ISP language allows a concise quantitative specification of processors at a functional level useful to the user and to the engineer who implements the processor. With many alternative approaches available at the ISP level, we must devote attention to balance and consistency in our selections.

If we wish to describe the digital-system components with more detail there are other languages available to us. Some of these languages permit the computer engineer to evaluate details of timing and performance of alternative implementations of an architecture. Other languages are useful in simulation of the digital systems for broader comparisons of performance.

At all levels of design, economics and reliability must be considered. Simplicity and not complexity should be emphasized in design.

2.11 ADDITIONAL READING

Since the beginning of their profession engineers have designed their products in response to needs and have used design tools appropriate to their specialties. However, very little was written on the methodology for engineering design prior to the advent of large systems in the 1950s. Teaching of method in design appears to have been passed on from experienced to new engineers through an oral tradition.

The author first learned about the then emerging discipline of *system engineering* and its methodologies for design of large systems in discussions with Harry H. Goode of the University of Michigan in the mid-50s. [GoodH57] remains an excellent guide to the tools and the methodology of system engineering. [BlanB81] covers the subject with a similar viewpoint.

[MillJ85] describes where the system architect fits in the development of large software systems. Its view of the role of the system architect is very similar to that described herein.

Difficulties with managing the development of large systems led the U. S. Air Force to publish a concise handbook for development of such systems, MIL-STD-499A(USAF), Engineering Management [USAF74]. While designed to provide guidance for development of very large systems, the standard is applicable to most digital-system development. [CandC85] assembled a step-by-step summary of the methodology for system development involving hardware and software. Methods for establishing and for responding to computer requirements are covered in [ThurK83].

Complexity of large software developments has led to efforts to specify a methodology for development of these systems. A special issue of *IEEE Transactions on Software Engineering* [BergG86] is devoted to the subject. [KingD84] and [JackM83] summarize two approaches. An issue of *IEEE Computer* [RzepW85] was devoted to specification of requirements for computer-based systems. [PresR87] offers a comprehensive view of software system development methods.

[TaubA63] provides excellent documentation of the approach taken by the von Neumann team. The first five papers cover the architecture and the use of the "electronic computing instrument" that we now call the von Neumann computer architecture. The first paper, "On the Principles of Large Scale Computing Machines", previously unpublished, and the second, "Preliminary Discussion of the Logical Design of an Electronic Computing Instrument" [BurkA46], cover the principles, the methodology, and the initial result. The third, fourth, and fifth papers cover "Planning and Coding of Problems for an Electronic Computing Instrument" and are interesting as descriptions of the origins of digital-computer programming.

Languages to specify requirements and designs have been used at all levels of digital system architecture. [DaviA82] gives a good review of an approach to developing a requirements language. An example of a language for formal specification of a large software system was shown in [BeicF84]. *IEEE Computer* Vol. 7, No. 12, of December 1974, Vol. 10, No. 6, of June 1977, and Vol. 18, No. 2 of February 1985 are special issues devoted to hardware description languages. IEEE, ACM, and AFIPS sponsor a biannual conference on the subject. PMS and ISP are described in [BellC71] and in [SiewD82]. [BarbM81] reviews the extension of ISP to ISPS and [BarbM75] compares various register transfer languages. [PeteJ83] reviews Petri nets and their applications to digital systems. [MillR73] compares Petri nets with other methods for modeling parallel computation.

The heterogeneous element processor (HEP) [SmitB78, KowaJ85] is an example of a parallel computer, the subject of Chapter 8. The Intel 8086 and 8089 [Intel83] were two members of a large and consistent family of microprocessor components and systems. The PDP-8 was an early (1965) minicomputer with a very simple organization. Much later its design was implemented as a microcomputer. The PDP-8 "design" shown in Figs. 2-11 and 2-13 is the author's version of an implementation. The "real PDP-8" implementation is described in [SiewD82].

2.12 PROBLEMS

2-1. Describe the advantages of a bottom–up approach to developing a system and compare them with the advantages of the top–down approach described in this chapter.

2-2. **a.** For a computer installation with which you are familiar, identify the customers and describe the needs of different customer groups.

   b. For the installation selected in Problem 2-2a, specify the requirements for the computer system(s) at that installation.

2-3. Draw a simple "flow diagram" showing activities that take place in input processing, internal computation, and output processing for each of the following classes of application:

   a. Numeric processing for the physical sciences.

   b. Transaction processing for an airline reservation system.

   c. Inventory management and automatic order generation for a retail store.

   d. Weekly status reporting for a geographically dispersed sales force.

2-4. Restate each flow diagram of Problem 2-3 as a set of design requirements for a computer system.

2-5. State advantages and disadvantages of using the English (or French, German, Russian, etc.) language to describe and specify a computer architecture.

2-6. Describe the von Neumann architecture of Fig. 2-5 in English-language phrases.

2-7. Describe the HEP architecture of Fig. 2-6 in English-language phrases.

2-8. Describe the operation of the von Neumann instruction set processor of Fig. 2-7 in English-language phrases.

2-9. Describe the memory-address calculations of the Intel 8086 (Fig. 2-8) in English-language phrases.

2-10. Draw a state-transition diagram for the instruction execution cycle described in Fig. 2-11(b) and 2-11(c).

2-11. Show how user requirements and design objectives are different for two computer installations with which you are familiar (or use hypothetical examples).

2.13 PROJECTS

2-A. For the computer that you are investigating for the course project (Project 1-A), outline the user requirements and specify the design objectives.

2-B. Outline the user requirements and specify the design objectives for the computer architecture you are developing as your course project (Project 1-B).

3

*System Structure
(the PMS Level)*

In this chapter we begin examining the alternatives available in computer architecture. Following the methodology covered in Chapter 2, the alternatives at the system level are considered first. Here we are looking at the processor–memory–switch (PMS) level description of the computer.

3.1 THE COMPUTER AS A DIGITAL SYSTEM

At the PMS level the computer can be viewed as a digital system consisting of several major units connected to permit the parts to interact as a single system. Whereas the major functional units of the general-purpose digital computer are fixed by their needs (storing, processing, communication with the environment), there are many possible arrangements for the allocation, distribution, and interconnection of the functions. The optimum arrangement for a particular computer is determined by the computational, physical, and market environments in which it will operate.

We must assume that those environments have been evaluated with sufficient attention so that we have a clear statement of the requirements and the design objectives toward which the computer is aimed. This was a key part of the methodology covered in Chapter 2. With this understanding of the needs, the computer architect can design the system.

With so much emphasis of the previous chapter devoted to a top–down approach to developing the architecture, it would be easy for the reader to assume that it is not necessary to pay any attention to the detail at this point. Lest we feel that we only need to "look up", a few remarks should be introduced regarding the need occasionally to "glance down" at the detail.

At the system level we are designing initially an abstract computer, or a virtual architecture. As the design proceeds and the architecture takes form it is necessary to take account of implementation issues that relate to more detailed capabilities of hardware and software. If we totally defer consideration of the implementation issues until a later stage of design we might find it necessary to redo some major aspects of our top-level design. It is much preferred that the architect proceed with the top–level design while having an understanding of the implications of the top-level decisions on the physical realization of the architecture.

It is necessary also to have an understanding of the potentials of the instruction-set processor (ISP) alternatives and of the technologies that might be applied to the realizations of our architecture in order that the PMS-level design can take advantage of techniques available at the lower levels. We are undertaking a top-down approach, but we must have some understanding of where our decisions are leading us.

In this chapter we cover PMS-level design and examine the alternatives available at this level. As these alternatives are considered we reference any implications on the ISP level of design and areas where the PMS design is particularly sensitive to ISP decisions and to advances in electronics technology.

3.2 MODEL RANGE AND EXPANSION POTENTIAL

Early in the development of the system architecture we must determine whether we are designing a system that will consist of just one realization or whether there will be a number of different models with different performance levels or different specializations. This question might be phrased in terms of the number and variety of physical computers that will reflect the architecture of the virtual computer we are designing. A brief look at the evolution of commercial computer offerings outlines the rationale that leads to today's system-level alternatives.

During the first decade of commercial computers many of the manufacturers had different models for different performance levels. For example, there were the UNIVAC 1101, 1102, 1103A, and 1105; the IBM 701, 704, and 709; the General Electric 210 and 225; and the Control Data 160, 1604, and 924. To some extent, the differences were due to a different application for each model, such as one model for business data processing and another for scientific computation. Examples from the early 1960s are the IBM 7080 (business) and 7090 (scientific) and the UNIVAC II (business) and 1103 (scientific).

Since it was difficult to transport programs from one machine to another, the cost of supporting software for different machines was approaching the cost of manufacturing the hardware, and the major manufacturers devoted attention to development of "families" of machines. Within a family there was sufficient compatibility that (in principle, at least) programs for one model could be transferred with minimum modification to other models (usually of higher performance and price). Examples of compatible families were the Burroughs B260, B160, and B300; the Digital Equipment PDP-4, PDP-7, and PDP-9;

the Honeywell 800 and 400; the IBM 7090, 7094, and 7094-II; and the Scientific Data Systems (later Xerox Data Systems) 910, 920, 930, and 940.

Computer family planning was carried a step further in 1964 when IBM introduced the System/360, a virtual-machine architecture that was realized in a range of actual machines called models 30, 40, 50, 65, and 75. (There were other models of the 360 series that did not implement the 360 architecture with complete fidelity and were not fully compatible with other machines of the series.) The benefits to both the users and the manufacturer were so striking that other manufacturers introduced virtual architectures with several physical realizations. Sperry Univac added the 1108 and 1106 to their 1107 architecture. RCA announced the Spectra 70 series, which closely followed the IBM 360 architecture. Digital Equipment offered the PDP-11 line with several different models. Burroughs had two virtual machines, each implemented as a family: the byte-structured B2500, B3500, and B4500 and the word-organized B5500 and B6500.

With a firmly established architecture a range of cost and performance levels can be introduced without the necessity for duplication of system software and all maintenance and user documentation. New larger and smaller models can be added to the family and evolution to a new family through realization of the architecture with newer technology can be introduced, as in the case of the IBM 370 series.

Most manufacturers had insufficient volume of manufacture to offer a wide variety in performance levels through different models, particularly at the high-performance end of their product lines. In this case architectural innovation at the PMS level led to "modular" computer organizations in which increased performance could be obtained by adding memory modules, input/output controllers, and/or processors, and we had multiprocessor and multicomputer architectures. Figure 3-1 is the PMS diagram for a successful multiprocessor system of the early 1960s, the Burroughs D825.

As the figure demonstrates, the D825 contained from 1 to 16 memory modules, each with 4096 49-bit (with a parity bit) words or 32k characters. (The 8-bit byte had not become a standard.) From one to four central processors and from one to 10 input/output controllers were the "active" modules that could gain access to memory independent of each other. Connection between the active modules and the memory was through the switching interlock, a distributed crosspoint switch that permitted each of the 14 active units to transfer a 49-bit word to or from one of the 16 memory modules at the same time. The two I/O exchanges also were crosspoint switches, each permitting connection of 64 peripheral devices to each of the 10 input/output controllers. These switches transferred information in 7-bit (including a parity bit) groups. System-level control was exercised by any central processor initiating a command that could cause memory, switch, or I/O controller action. These control paths are represented with dashed lines in Fig. 3-1.

Some information on the processors and I/O controllers is provided in the footnotes. This level of detail serves as a brief outline of the instruction-set processor description of the computer, a topic covered in Chapters 5 through 7. This PMS specification of the D825 demonstrates the organization of a computer system with many independent functional modules that communicate through high-performance electronic switches. Switching alternatives are reviewed in a later section of this chapter. Even in computers of the 1960s there was a wide range of alternative system organizations.

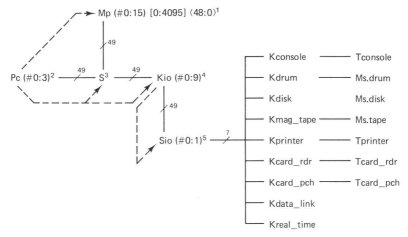

1. Mp (magentic_core, 4-micros_cycle, word_size: (1 parity, 48 data).
2. Pc (128 mag_thin_film_registers, 4 word_stack, 15 index_registers).
3. S\"Switching_Interlock" {14 by 16 distributed crosspoint switch}.
4. Kio {interrupt signaled to Pc}.
5. Sio\"I/O_Exchange" (10_by_64_crosspoint, speed: 2 million_char/s).

Figure 3-1   Burroughs D825 system configuration.

Similar issues face the architect of a new computer today. If it is known that the system is to have only one physical realization the PMS organization might be rather simple, leading to a structure with a single processor, a single memory, and a single input/output control without independent access to memory. That was the case with the simple 8-bit personal computers that brought computing to homes and small businesses early in the 1980s. The organization of those machines is very much like that of the von Neumann computer that we saw in Fig. 2-5. This straightforward structure, with all control in the central processor, is still used in "entry-level" personal computers and is found in special applications where a minimum computer size is needed.

Almost all computers today will allow input/output activity independent of the central processor. Typical of this organization is that of the original IBM Personal Computer, shown in Fig. 3-2. The central processor is an Intel 8088, similar to the 8086 that was shown in Fig. 2-8, except that data and address transfers are in 8-bit bytes, rather than by 16-bit words. Normal control paths from the central processor to other components are not shown in this figure nor in subsequent illustrations of this section or the next. A "numeric coprocessor" (Pnum), the Intel 8087, could be added as an option for higher-performance computation. Programs that made the 8088 act as the IBM PC are held in Mrom, a "read-only" memory not modifiable by users. User programs and data are stored in the primary memory (Mram), a dynamic random-access memory (DRAM). Both memories of the original PC had 250-ns access times.

The PC bus is a switch that connects the processor, the memories, and the input/output controller ("I/O channels"). As noted, the PC bus transfers 8-bit bytes at up to 4.77 Mbytes/s. Another switch, the Sio, connects any one of the peripheral-device controllers

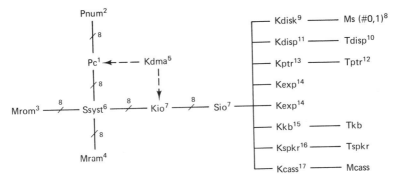

1. Pc\"Intel_8088" (HMOS, 4.77_MHz, 16-bit_ALU, 8-bit transfer).
2. Pnum\"Intel_8087" (fixed/floating-point_numeric_coprocessor, optional).
3. Mrom\read-only_memory (48..256 kbyte, 250-ns_access).
4. Mram\random_access_memory (64..640 kbyte, 250-ns_access).
5. Kdma\direct_access_memory_controller (byte-interlace_control).
6. Ssyst\"PC Bus" (8_bit_transfers_at_processor_clock_rate).
7. "I/O/ Channels" (Kio, Sio, 3 integrated, 5 expansion, byte_transfers).
8. Ms\floppy_disk (360 kbyte, 9 sect, 512 byte/sect, 250 kbyte/s_max).
9. Kdisk\5_1/4-in_disk_drive_adapter (optional).
10. Tdisp\monitor (16-color, monochrome).
11. Kdisp (controller, color/graphics, monochrome, monochrome/printer).
12. Tptr (7-dot_matrix_printer, 80 cps).
13. Kptr\"printer_adapter" {or monochrome display/printer adapter}.
14. Kexp\"expansion_slot" {for additional controllers, 8-bit duplex bus.}
15. Kkb\"integral_keyboard_controller" (15-stroke_buffer, self-test).
16. Kspkr\"integral_speaker_controller" {for 2-1/4 in dia. speaker}.
17. "Kcass\integral cassette controller" (optional).

Figure 3-2   A simple computer system, the IBM PC.

to the Kio, providing the communication with the external world. A "direct-memory-access memory controller" (Kdma) coordinates access to Mram by the Pc and the Kio to prevent interference between the two. The term *direct memory access* shows that the input/output subsystem can gain access to memory without interfering with operations of the Pc. The transfer of a block of information between a peripheral device and Mram is initiated by the Pc, which then can continue its processing while the transfer is taking place. At the completion of the transfer Kio signals the Pc that the information has been moved as directed and the Pc can then perform operations dependent on the transfer.

Several new terms have been introduced in the last two paragraphs. *Coprocessors* are reviewed later in this chapter and are a specific topic of Chapter 7. Various forms and uses of storage for computer memory are covered in Chapter 4. *Direct memory access* as a means to share memory among processors is included in several of the system organizations reviewed in later sections of this chapter.

Many features are available in different forms in both low-cost and high-performance computers. The same system organization can be used in different computers over a wide range of performance, just as it was with the "upward-compatible" models within an architectural family in the 1960s. We can develop very powerful computers with the relatively simple organization of Fig. 3-2. However, we do not need or want to restrict our system design to this simple PMS organization. Requirements for computers are not all the same. Often it is necessary to allow for change in the computer system to meet changing requirements. Almost any computer installation has to adapt to new input or output devices, such as larger or faster disk files or communications interfaces.

Computers with higher degrees of flexibility (and complexity) are the DEC VAX-11/780 with the system structure of Fig. 3-3 and the Model 3084 implementation of the IBM 370 architecture, shown in Fig. 3-4. The 11/780 was the first (1978) of the very successful VAX family of computers that included models with much higher and much lower levels of performance. Comparing the structures of Fig. 3-3 with that of Fig. 3-2, we see that the VAX, like the PC, had an optional numeric coprocessor, in this case the "floating-point accelerator" (Pfpa). A specialized program memory, the "writable user control store" (Mucs), in this system is available to user programmers. The "synchronous backplane interconnect" (Ssbi) is similar in function (but higher in speed and much larger in capacity) to the PC bus of the IBM PC. There are two forms of input/output connection, the "massbus" for connecting high-speed magnetic disk and magnetic tape storage devices, and the "unibus" for lower-performance peripheral equipment.

In the VAX we note three major additions over the PC structure: the "console subsystem" (Kcons, Sccons), the "multiport memory" (Mmp), and the "associative memory" (Mcache). The console subsystem includes a processor with its own memory

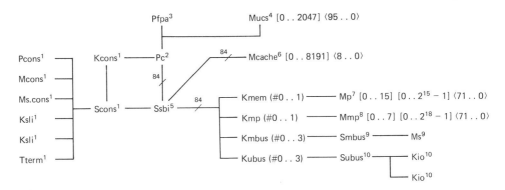

1. "Console_Subsystem" (operation, diagnostics, maintenance).
2. Pc\"VAX-11/780_CPU".
3. Pfpa\"Floating_Point_Accelerator" (optional).
4. Mucs\"Writable_User_Control_Store" (optional).
5. Ssbi\"Synchronous_Backplane_Interconnect" (13.3 Mbyte/s, wordsize:
   (46 information_bits {32 data}, 38 communic_control_bits)).
6. Mcache (associative_memory).
7. Mp\"Main_Memory_Subsystem" {8 bits for error correction}.
8. Mmp\"Multiport_Memory"; {8 bits for error correction}.
9. "Massbus_Subsystem" (1.3 Mbyte/s) {Ms: magnetic tape or disk (#0..7)}.
10. "Unibus_subsystem" {secondary memory and peripheral equipment}.

Figure 3-3 System structure of the VAX-11/780.

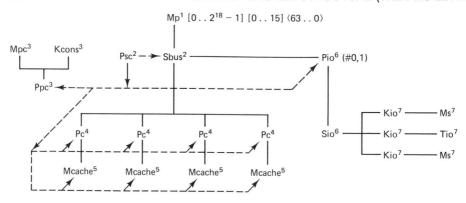

1. Mp (312-ns_cycle, 2-level_interleave).
2. Psc\"System_Controller" (64-bit_bus, 26-ns_cycle).
3. Ppc\"Processor_Controller" {with consoles and local control store}.
4. Pc (64 bit, 8 general_registers, 4 floating_point reg, 26-ns_cycle).
5. Mcache (size: 2^{12} words, 26-ns_cycle){synchronized by Psc}.
6. "External_Data_Controller" (24 channels, 3 Mbyte/s_each).
7. {Input/output devices with controllers connected to 24 channel Pio}.

Figure 3-4   IBM 3084 PMS diagram.

and peripheral equipment. The system facilitates maintenance of the (then) large VAX system. Multiport memory is a primary memory shared by two VAX-11/780 computers. It increases performance by connecting two computers together to operate as one. Mcache, the cache memory, is a high-speed local memory introduced in computers to hold recently used information. The function of the cache is to reduce the time consumed in references to the main memory by placing most-used information in a faster store. We discuss cache memory later in this chapter and in Chapter 4.

The 3084, largest of the IBM 370 series of computers before introduction of the 3090 models in 1986, demonstrates another step in system modularity. As is seen in Fig. 3-4, the 3084 has four central processors (Pc) connected to a single large memory through the Sbus. Each Pc has a cache memory (Mcache) to reduce the need for accesses to Mp. The Sbus also connects the "external data controllers" (Pio) and their peripheral devices to memory. As is the case in the VAX-11/780, there is a separate processor (Ppc) with its own memory (Mpc) for maintenance and operation control. Coordination among all of the modules, including the separate cache memories, and synchronizing access to memory is the function of the "System Controller" (Psc). The power of the 3084 is reflected by the transfer of a 64-bit "double word" every 26 ns over the Sbus, a rate of over 300 Mbytes/s.

The commercial success in the 1980s of the three systems of Figs. 3-2 through 3-4 might lead us to ask why we should not just pick one of these very flexible alternatives and start our detailed design? The reason that we cannot do that, of course, is that the flexibility attained as we make each step from the simplest serial approach toward the most "open" parallel approach does not come without cost. Every time we introduce a switch, a controller, or a transducer into our system we add cost. The costs are those of the particular items of hardware added, those of the software to coordinate operation of the new hardware, and those needed to protect other parts of the system from interference. No matter what system approach we start with, it is essential that we determine if there is not a less costly way to attain the desired result.

In addition, when we add hardware (or software) to a system we increase the "opportunities for failure". Any component has a probability that it will fail over the next hour of operation. The more components we place in the system the higher the probability that at least one will fail in the next hour. As we add to the system we want to be sure that the additions do minimum damage to system reliability. As will we see later, there are ways to add components to increase the redundancy of system functions to achieve increased *system* reliability even though we have increased the failure rate of the hardware by increasing its amount.

While useful as examples of what has been developed, a comparison of actual architectures, as in Figs. 3-1 to 3-4, does not expose clearly the alternatives available for consideration. It is preferable to develop the alternatives in an orderly progression of hypothetical (but certainly realizable) system structures. As we develop the progression we will see the need to consider some implementation issues, primarily related to the processing and the memory technologies available to us.

3.3 ALTERNATIVE SYSTEM ORGANIZATIONS

In examining the alternative PMS-level organizations of general-purpose computer systems we will introduce some specific data on subsystems. This should present a feeling for the reasonableness and for the realizability of each system.

Starting from the simple system of Fig. 2-5, let us consider what we might do to obtain incremental increases in system performance and flexibility. An obvious change to our computer organization is to add "direct memory access" (DMA) (described in the previous section) to permit the input/output system to share memory with the central processor. This entails the introduction of a switch and control between the memory (which we might call the "passive" component) and the "active" processor and input/output controller. The DMA controller assures that any attempt by the processor and the I/O controller to access memory simultaneously is resolved. The usual means to accomplish this is to simply prohibit interruption of the memory read/write cycle and to allow access immediately after a memory cycle to whichever active component is waiting for such access. Success of this simple control mechanism usually depends only on having a buffer in each active device to hold the request until the memory cycle is complete. If necessary we could add a buffer to the controller to allow it to hold a queue of requests for memory access.

Figure 3-5 shows the PMS-level organization of a typical modern computer with a single central processor (Pc), a single primary memory (Mp) of selectable size, and a single general-purpose input/output controller (Kio) that shares memory with the Pc. (In Section 3.4 we compare I/O controllers, or "channels", and I/O processors. For now we are not concerned with distinguishing between the two.)

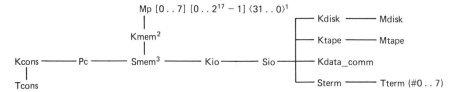

1. Mp (CMOS, 50 ns) {access from either Pc or Kio under control of Kmem}.
2. Kmem\"Direct_memory_access" (conflict_resolution, 1 request_queue).
3. Smem (1_word_interleave, data_rate: 20 MHz).

Figure 3-5   A representative uniprocessor system.

As shown in the PMS diagram, Mp is accessed by Pc or Kio through Smem, a switch that allows word-by-word (4-byte) interleaving between the two active devices (Pc and Kio). Kmem is a DMA controller that holds a request when the memory is busy. When an active device gains access (simultaneous tries are resolved arbitrarily by the electronics) any request by the other is deferred for a maximum of 50 ns, the memory cycle time. Mp is a CMOS semiconductor memory of 50 ns cycle time, available in 512-kilobyte increments to a maximum size of 4 megabytes (1,048,576 words).

The Pc is not defined in the diagram, but it has a console subsystem directly attached through a console controller (Kcons). Relatively little of the specification of the central-processor function can be presented in the PMS diagram. Further definition is provided in its instruction-set processor description.

Of most interest at the PMS level is the interface to the input/output subsystem. The diagram tells us that Kio (I/O controller), at the I/O device side, selects (under instructions transferred from the Pc) a specific I/O path to access the designated device and to initiate the designated transfer. Physical selection of the device is through Sio and the device controller appropriate to the device itself. Our example shows four different types of I/O devices, a disk memory (Mdisk), magnetic tape backup storage (Mtape), a group of terminals connected through Sterm, and a data-communication subsystem that is not given specifications.

From the PMS diagram with its footnotes we see a minicomputer system with a fair degree of flexibility in choice of memory size and I/O capability. A computer architect could have decided on this system following an analysis of customer requirements. Of course, to be sure there is a good balance in our design we must develop the further detail of the ISP description of the processor. On doing so, and on further consideration of future potential for the system, we might find that more flexibility is needed in the I/O subsystem. Once there is direct-memory-access capability that permits the I/O controller and the processor to communicate independently with memory it is easy to allow more than one input/output device to communicate at one time. It is quite reasonable to allow for three I/O subsystems of the type shown in Fig. 3-5 yielding the PMS diagram of Fig. 3-6. If processor performance is sufficient, the system shown can provide a good balance between central-processor and input/output activities. The structure shown is similar to that of the first commercially successful business computer, the UNIVAC II, and is characteristic of many small computers today.

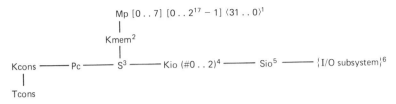

1. Mp (CMOS, 50 ns) {access from either Pc or Kio under control of Kmem}.
2. Kmem\"direct_memory_access" (conflict_resolution, 2-request_queue).
3. S (50-ns_cycle) {3 active modules can access Mp through Kmem}.
4. Kio {3 independent modules each connected to an Sio}.
5. Sio {connects Kio to up to 4 I/O subsystem controllers}.
6. "I/O_subsystem" (components: Mdisk, Mtape, Kdata_comm, Terminal_group).

Figure 3-6 Independent multiple input/output.

It is important to emphasize that here we are addressing the structure at the PMS level. With any of the organizations shown almost any individual component might be exchanged for an equivalent unit of higher performance, lower cost, larger capacity, or different physical configuration, as long as the interfaces to the other components remain compatible and the performance of each component is consistent with the system requirements. Variations in the capabilities of each major subsystem are discussed in later chapters.

As we add some capability to overcome some actual or perceived performance limitation we do not eliminate all constraints, but merely find the limitation at some other functional area. As we expand the input/output capability operating through the memory switch, we eventually provide sufficient I/O that the memory unit is saturated responding to I/O traffic, even when we have allowed for the fastest memory that is economically feasible. At that point we might "modularize" the memory so that different memory modules can be accessed simultaneously by Pc and Kio's, as shown in Fig. 3-7. The switch has become more complicated now, requiring that m memory modules be connectable to n active modules at the same time. The alternatives for organization of m x n switches are discussed in Section 3.4.

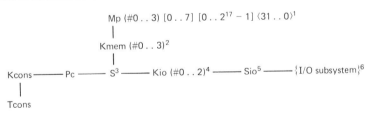

1. Mp (CMOS, 50 ns) {under control of Kmem}.
2. Kmem (conflict_resolution, 2 request_queue) {each controls an Mp}.
3. S (50-ns cycle) {3 active modules can access Mp through Kmem}.
4. Kio {3 independent modules each connected to an Sio}.
5. Sio {connects Kio to up to 4 I/O subsystem controllers}.
6. "I/O_subsystem" (components: Mdisk, Mtape, Kdata_comm, Terminal_group).

Figure 3-7 Computer with modular memory structure.

With a capability to connect *m* memory modules to *n* active devices, must we limit the *n* to 1 processor and *n* − 1 input/output controllers? Disregarding, for now, the operating-system software issues, we find no reason for such a limitation and we arrive at a structure in which multiple processors and I/O controllers can access memory modules simultaneously. (We find, of course, that operating-system issues *are* introduced even in the case of a single processor when there can be simultaneous I/O transfer.) The multiprocessor computer structure, shown in Fig. 3-8, is similar to that of Fig. 3-1 and is exemplified by both the Unisys A series (descending from the Burroughs B5500) and the Unisys (UNIVAC) 1100/2200 series. Both of these computer families employ multiple processors gaining access to multiple memory modules through a switch. Both have similar structures if specific switch configurations are ignored. The switch-configuration alternatives are covered in the next section. In systems of this type it is not necessary that all processors be the same and there are many examples of special-purpose processors in systems with this configuration, as is covered in Section 3.8.

Of course, this is not the limit of variation in system configurations. If we can use a switch to interconnect the active and the passive modules of a computer, we can just as easily connect combinations of the major modules or complete computers. Multiprocessors and multiple-computer systems represent major thrusts toward satisfying future needs for very large computers. At the top end of computer-capacity requirements we find the need for processing performance so large that efficiency of processor use is not of concern. One solution to these requirements aims at achieving a very high degree of processing concurrency with multiprocessor systems or multicomputer systems with a very large quantity (64 to 64,000) of processors or computers. A multiprocessor system implies sharing the main memory whereas in multicomputer systems each processor has its own memory.

Examples of multicomputer systems are shown in Figs. 3-9 and 3-10. The Carnegie Mellon University Cm* system shown in Fig. 3-9 contains multiple PDP-11 computers. While each PDP-11 "computer module" had its own memory, one Cm could communicate with the memory of another in the same cluster through the "map bus" (Smap). Intercluster

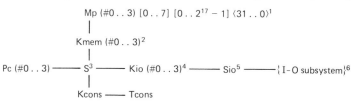

Mp (#0 . . 3) [0 . . 7] [0 . . 2^{17} − 1] ⟨31 . . 0⟩[1]

Kmem (#0 . . 3)[2]

Pc (#0 . . 3) ——— S[3] ——— Kio (#0 . . 3)[4] ——— Sio[5] ———{ I–O subsystem}[6]

Kcons ——— Tcons

1. Mp (CMOS, 50 ns) {under control of Kmem}.
2. Kmem (conflict_resolution, 2 request_queue) {each controls an Mp}.
3. S (50-ns_cycle) {8x4 switch, Pc and Kio access Mp through Kmem}.
4. Kio {4 independent modules each connected to an Sio}.
5. Sio {connects Kio to up to 4 I/O subsystem controllers}.
6. "I/O_subsystem" (components: Mdisk, Mtape, Kdata_com, Terminal_group).

Figure 3-8   Multiple processors (multiprocessor system).

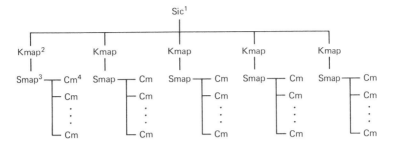

1. Sic\"Intercluster_bus" {packet switching among Kmap's}.
2. Kmap\"Mapping_processor" {microprogrammed communication controller}.
3. Smap\"Map bus" {communication within a cluster of Cm's}.
4. Cm\"Computer_module" {DEC LSI-11 modified as follows}:

5. Sloc\"Local_switch" {routes nonlocal memory references to Smap and accepts external references to this Cm}.

Figure 3-9 A multiple-computer system.

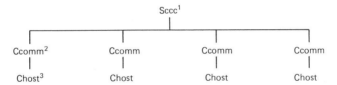

1. Sccc\"Common_carrier_communications_network".
2. Ccomm\"Communications_interface_processor" {standard protocols}.
3. Chost\"Host_computer" {various types at different locations}.

Figure 3-10 A network of computers.

communication was permitted using the "intercluster bus" (Sic). Communication among and within clusters was controlled by the "mapping processors" (Kmap). This experimental multicomputer system was a prototype for many similar commercial machines, as is covered in Chapter 8.

Multiple-computer systems can be distributed over a distance of many meters or of thousands of kilometers. In this case the communications network has very strong influence on performance of the system. Figure 3-10 demonstrates a typical distributed computer system communicating via a network. Here each different "host computer" (Chost) is connected to the communication network (Sccc) through a "communications interface processor" (Ccomm). Ccomm performs conversions from the data structures of the different hosts to the standard system message format. It also controls the transmission and reception of messages using standard communication protocols. A discussion of communication networks is included in the following section.

In developing the progression of system alternatives we have assumed that an increase in performance can be attained through system-level concurrency. This assumption and its limitations are covered in Section 3.9. Some more specialized techniques are available for further improvements in performance with any of the system configurations shown. An example is the "cache" or "lookaside" memory in which we hold copies of the latest information generated with an identification of the address in main memory at which the information resides. When an attempt is made to access the information the addressing of Mp is sidestepped and the information is obtained from the higher-speed (and higher-unit-cost) cache. Cache memories can be introduced as functional parts of a central processor or as specialized memory modules on a Pc–Mp switch. Cache memory organization is discussed later in this chapter and in Chapter 4.

With all of these possibilities it is easy to conclude that a computer can be configured in many ways and that we need not be too concerned about the particulars, especially if we provide for flexibility. That is far from the truth. The computer architect, like the architect of any complicated system, is not performing the proper role if the system is designed without concern for the trade-offs among immediate requirements, flexibility to meet future needs, and economics. Given that there are many ways to configure computer systems, how do we recognize a good design? Computer-system designs that have withstood the test of time and have remained successful are characterized by balance and flexibility. If the relationships among processor capability and performance, memory size and speed, and input/output traffic capacity are in balance, no single part of the system will be overloaded while some other part is operating well below its capacity. When the system design provides for change in the size and performance levels of the major subsystems we find a flexibility to adapt to different requirements.

The decisions about the system structure should be made by considering the range of performance levels required, the relative cost to the builder and to the user of having different modules of a type as opposed to different quantities of the same module of a type, and the need for flexibility to introduce specialized modules of any type. In considering the size/cost trade-offs we must keep in mind that in a particular type of equipment, cost does not increase in direct proportion to capability. In general, we obtain twice the performance for less than twice the cost. On the other hand, we must allow for the economics of quantity manufacture. It costs less per item to make two rather than one or to make 200 rather than 100 in a given period of time. This and other system-cost issues are expanded upon later.

Variation in performance is not the only reason for multiple-module system configurations like those shown in this section. Systems with a multiplicity of modules incorporate a redundancy that, if used and controlled properly, can lead to very significant increases in reliability as compared to single module computer systems of equivalent size. As is discussed in a later section, there are many circumstances in which computer failure or unavailability can have disastrous effect on broader systems. For now the reader is asked to think about the relative reliability of each of the system configurations shown in Figs. 3-5 through 3-10.

3.4 INTERMODULE AND INTERCOMPUTER COMMUNICATION

For any of the alternative system configurations that require connection among functional units with switches (other than the 1×1 links) we must pay attention to the specifics of switch design or selection. We are concerned with intermodule (or intercomputer) communication methods. The switch is required to communicate the desired digital signals between a source module and a destination module. Depending on the needs of our system structure we can select from among a variety of switch configurations and controls.

A comprehensive study of digital-signal switching would require a book of its own and there are communication-systems specialists to assist in the selection of approach and the detailed designs. An overview of communication-switching principles gives us sufficient background to perform our role as the digital-system architects.

Communication networks can be categorized as using either *circuit switching* or *message switching*. In the first case an electrical connection is made between the source and the destination for the time required to transmit the required information. In some cases the source module maintains the connection until it has received a response from the destination module, as when acknowledgment of receipt of a message is required in a communication network or when a processor is accessing information in a memory module in a computer system. The physical connection in a circuit-switched computer system can be maintained for a very short time (sufficient for a single word to be transferred), for a short finite interval (to transfer a page of memory data), or for a significant period of time (for a computer-terminal work session).

With message switching physical connections are established between two points only long enough to permit a message to be transferred from a buffer in a transmission node to a buffer in a receiver node. The two nodes need not be the source and the destination for the message, but could be intermediate "holding points" used as available to let the message pass generally in the correct direction from source to destination. The size of messages in this type of system can be single words or of much longer size. They can be of fixed size or of variable (to some specified limit) size. If of variable size they might be broken down into blocks of defined size. When the system is to support transmission over multiple routes from any source to any destination it is necessary that the message include identity of the destination (and perhaps of the source) and sufficient other information to permit separate messages or separate blocks of a single message to be reassembled in proper order.

Switches for computer systems that are installed at one physical location usually use circuit switching to communicate among processors and/or I/O controllers and the primary memory. For switches that are designed for direct transmission from a source to a destination there is little distinction between circuit and message switching for messages of small finite duration, such as a single computer word. It is where the physical routing of messages can vary from transmission to transmission that message switching is significant in computers. This is the case with systems that incorporate a large number of computers connected by a data-communication network.

In those situations where computers are accessed at relatively low data rates ($< 10,000$ bits/s.) by terminals that do not have data-processing capability, circuit switching commonly is used. In these applications we might have communication in only one direction (simplex); in either direction, but only one direction at one time (half duplex); or in both directions at once (full duplex). When the terminals have processing capability (i.e., "smart" terminals) or if the terminals contain buffer memory of significant size, message switching might be used. Architectural issues for systems of terminals connected to a data-communication processor (a specialized I/O processor) usually fall into the realm of the communications engineer. Detailed knowledge of capabilities and limitations of the physical communication devices are needed to evaluate alternative system configurations. Usually the computer architect specifies functional requirements and works with the communications engineer in evaluating technical and economic trade-offs to develop optimum communication interfaces.

Often the computer architect is involved with a system consisting of a large number of geographically distributed computers to be connected by a message-switching network. When such a system involves distances of from 0.1 to 10 km and relatively high transmission rates (> 1 Mbit/s) the network is defined as a local area network (LAN). For longer distances and/or lower transmission rates, common-carrier communications are used most often. In those cases involving long distances and very high transmission rates, communication networks dedicated solely to the computer systems might be required. In long-distance networks communication resources are relatively expensive and efficiency of link use is an important design criterion. Message-composition standards, header formats, and network protocols must be established by agreement between architects of the computer system and of the communication system. In those cases where we are working with an existing communication system a standard interface might already have been established and we merely adapt the new computer system to the standard interface.

Within the computer system we are more heavily involved with detailed specification or design of the intermodule communications. Let us examine switching approaches applicable to three interconnection categories: processor (including I/O processor or I/O controller) and primary memory, I/O processor or controller to or from peripheral devices, and computer to computer for closely spaced multicomputer systems. Each of the three categories is characterized by different connection times, message sizes, and transmission rates.

In the first category we generally view the processors and I/O controllers as "active" devices that initiate transfers to or from the "passive" memory modules. The active device specifies the memory address, the internal register location, and designates the direction of the transfer (memory read or write). Connection times are short, approximating the memory cycle time, since only one word of information is transferred during one connection. Any added time required for transferring the address and the read/write code can be masked by the time taken for the previous data transfer. Typical distinct activities of a read transfer are: (1) Move the memory-address code to the memory-address buffer. (2) Transfer a read signal to memory to cause information to be moved from the addressed memory location to the memory data buffer. (3) Transfer information from the memory data buffer to the designated register of the active device. The time involved here is a fraction of a microsecond, even if the modules are separated by several meters.

Connection between an I/O processor (or controller) and a peripheral device is maintained for the duration of time required to transfer a significant amount of information from the peripheral device to memory, or in the opposite direction, via a buffer in the I/O processor. The amount of information depends on the specific peripheral device, ranging from a single computer word to a block of bytes suitable to a magnetic tape drive. The connection might be maintained for several seconds. Note that this does not require that the memory be dedicated solely to this transfer for that time; the I/O processor can share the memory module with other processors on a word-by-word basis, using a direct-memory-access capability.

For those systems involving multiple computers at a single location, information might be transferred word by word or can involve small blocks of words. Control of the transfer is usually by an I/O control or an I/O processor, and information is moved from the memory of one computer to that of the other directly or via a secondary memory such as a disk file. Between the primary memory and the I/O control the switching is as described before for the processor–memory interface. Among I/O controls (for direct memory-to-memory transfer) or between an I/O control and secondary memory the interconnection is as for peripheral-device switching, also described before.

A variety of topologies is available for connecting modules. An orderly development in order of increasing complexity serves to demonstrate the possibilities. In every case we assume that an active device, such as a processor, initiates the connection, which is maintained until the transfer of information is complete (as might be signaled by the passive device). In looking at the interconnection schemes we are concerned with the number of active devices, m, the quantity of passive devices, n, and the extent of concurrency possible, p, designated by the triplet (m,n,p).

The simplest switch is the $(1,n,1)$ tree, where $m = 1$, n takes on any value, and $p = 1$. A typical tree structure is shown in Fig. 3-11. Control paths for the connection are shown as dashed lines. The desired control line is selected by a decoder in the active device. The active line controls the gates that "enable" the path to the selected passive device. It is possible to place the gates at either end of the wires connecting the modules. That is, they can be concentrated at the active module, as shown in the figure, or they can be distributed to the passive ones. In general, the first approach is less expensive since there are functions that can be shared and the control lines are shorter. The distributed approach has superior reliability since a failure of a switch requires shutdown of only one passive module for

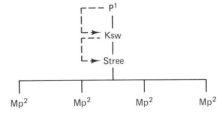

1. P: active module (Pc or Kio).   2. Mp: passive module (Mp).

Figure 3-11   A $(1,4,1)$ tree interconnection.

maintenance while the rest of the system continues in operation. This is more significant with the more complicated switches.

We should not let the single-line connection of this or the other interconnection illustrations mislead us into thinking that only a single wire is required for each link. Each connecting line represents the quantity of wires required for each parallel electrical signal. Usually the "width" of these paths is equal to the word size of the computer, unless bit-serial or byte transfers have been decided on, with the penalty of slower speed and added buffering at each end.

In some configurations we want to give a number of active devices access to a single passive device. An example is the computer of Fig. 3-6 with a single memory module, a central processor, and multiple input/output controllers. In this case an inverse tree of topology $(m,1,1)$, as shown in Fig. 3-12, is appropriate. Again, the control paths are shown as dashed lines. Here the control does not select the passive device, but makes a request for access that is granted if the passive device is not al.._:dy engaged. It is necessary to specify the action required in the case of a busy memory. Should the requesters queue up or should the denied requester just try again? (Perhaps all requesters are not to be treated equally. An I/O processor might be given priority over the central processor by being placed on the queue, whereas the central processor is not.) The comments made before about placing the gates at either end of the lines of the tree apply with the inverse tree as well. When access control and conflict resolution are handled at the memory, the switch is often called a *multiport memory*. It is used in the multiple computer and multiprocessor versions of the Digital Equipment VAX-11 series and in the model 308X multiprocessors of the IBM System/370.

A combination of a $1 \times n$ tree and an $m \times 1$ inverse tree, where each device might be a source, a destination, or both, is the $(m,n,1)$ bus. If $m = n$ we have the general $(m,m,1)$ switch (often called a *system bus*) for interconnecting m modules one at a time. In Fig. 3-13(a) a system bus for a computer with a single Pc, an Mp, and two Pio's is shown with its gates and control paths. As with the other switching arrangements, the control is established by the active device and if there is contention among the active devices a mechanism for conflict resolution is required. Usually the details of a bus connection are not shown, resulting in the system diagram of Fig. 3-13(b). The Tandem 16 multiple-computer system uses a dual bus to communicate among up to 16 computers. Within many computer processors a bus is used as the switch for register-to-register connection. Often a system includes several different buses, as we saw in the VAX-11/780 of Fig. 3-3.

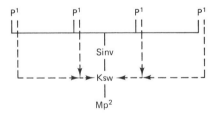

1.   P: active module (Pc or Kio).   2.   Mp: passive module (Mp).

Figure 3-12   A (4,1,1) inverse tree.

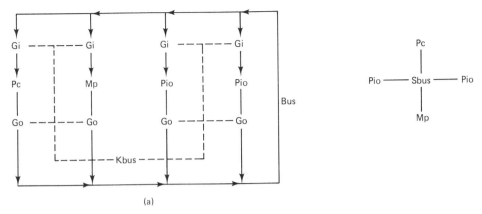

(a)

Figure 3-13 A (4,4,1) bus switch. (a) With gates and control lines. (b) Detail deleted.

Generalizing the connection schemes to permit $m > 1$, $n > 1$, $p = \min(m, n)$ leads to the crossbar switch, shown in Fig. 3-14. Here any five of the six active devices (Pc and Pio) can be connected to different passive devices (Mp) at any instant. In this diagram the gating elements are shown at the intersections of the vertical and horizontal lines representing the wiring between the memory and processing modules, an accurate representation of a crossbar built as a separate piece of equipment. Examination of the functioning of each of the switches shows that parts, except for the connection wires, can be associated with either the processing or the memory modules in a way that permits the rest of the crossbar to remain in operation when a module is deactivated for maintenance. This approach also permits electric power for the crossbar switches to be supplied by each associated module, rather than by a crossbar power supply. The result of the distribution of crossbar functions to other physical modules is an increase in reliability and maintainability. This representation of the crossbar switch, with control by the active modules, is shown in Fig. 3-15.

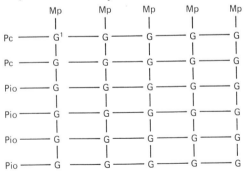

1. Control gating.

Figure 3-14 The (6,5,5) crossbar switch.

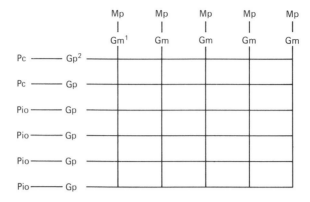

1. Memory gating includes conflict-resolution circuitry.
2. Processor gating with request-activation circuitry.

Figure 3-15   A distributed crossbar switch.

Addition of the switch to the processing and the memory modules usually results in a relatively small percentage increase in module circuitry and the reduction of reliability of any module is small. The Unisys A-series systems use the distributed crossbar, initially introduced in the Burroughs D825 that we saw in Fig. 3-1. The Unisys 1100 and 2200 multiprocessors use a multiple multiport memory equivalent with control at the memory modules, a technique employed more recently in Carnegie Mellon University's C.mmp.

In comparing the various switching and connection schemes discussed in the last few paragraphs we can use the number of individual connections to obtain an approximation of the cost of a switch. For example, each line of a (4,4,1) switch (a bus) requires the logic shown in Fig. 3-16 (a 4 x 1 multiplexer and a 1 x 4 decoder). For a 16-bit bus this logic is required for each of 16 connecting lines. Added logic, as is found in a microprocessor family's "bus controller" and "bus arbiter" (described in Chapter 6), would be required for control and for conflict resolution. Complexity or cost (measured in terms of component count or of area on a semiconductor surface) is approximately proportional to the number of inputs of a multiplexer or the number of outputs of a decoder. (We examined component counts of several multiplexers and decoders and found that the count increased approximately as the number of inputs (outputs) to the 1.07 power.) For a (4,4,1) switch, with which any of four modules can communicate with any other, this complexity measure yields a value of 8.

We can approximate the relative "cost" of different switches by using the count of inputs and outputs. A system that has a Pc, two Kio, and a single Mp and that uses a (3,1,1) inverse-tree connection, as shown in Fig. 3-12, requires a 3 x 1 multiplexer for transfers to memory and a 1 x 3 decoder for transfers from memory. For these the complexity by the measures just outlined is 6. This is three–quarters the complexity of the (4,4,1) bus that can be used to connect the same four modules. The reason for the difference is that the bus allows for some transfers that are not required, those among the Pc and the two Kio.

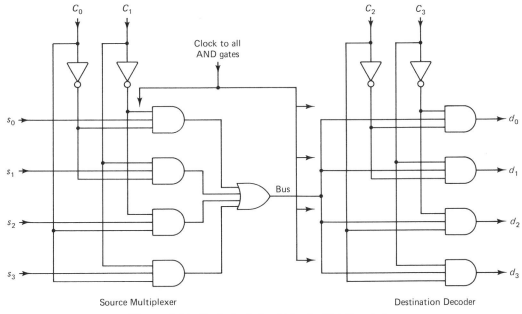

Figure 3-16 Basic logic for 1 bit of a (4,4,1) switch.

We can carry our analysis further to consider a system with more modules, say four Mp, two Pc, and two Kio. In this case an "asymmetrical" bus that permits transfers from Pc and Kio modules to any Mp appears efficient. A similar asymmetrical bus for transfers from Mp is needed. To allow sufficient memory access to the Pc and Kio we might find that two concurrent transfers are needed. The result is a set of four (4,4,1) buses, with a complexity of 32. A (4,4,4) crosspoint switch to permit simultaneous transfers to or from all four Mp is equivalent to eight of the asymmetric buses and has twice the complexity (64).

Finally, let us consider a system with eight Mp, four Pc, and four Kio, with switching implemented with a (bidirectional) (8,8,8) crosspoint switch. This entails an 8×1 multiplexer and a 1×8 decoder for each of the 16 individual connections (eight in each direction). The complexity of this configuration is 256. The large differences in "cost" (as reflected by the approximation of complexity) among the different configurations demonstrates that the performance increases that might result from concurrency of transfers increases system cost.

Differences in reliability among the switching approaches can be approximated by determining the number of different paths available for communication from any active module m to any passive module n. Then the relative performance of the various system organizations can be factored against both cost and reliability. When the length of the connecting wires between modules is large, reliability of the connection itself might be of concern. In these cases it is possible to increase the quantity of paths available in any of the connection topologies shown. An example is the duplex bus of Fig. 3-17. Reliability issues are covered after we have examined switches for the input/output subsystem.

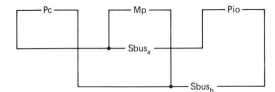

Figure 3-17   A duplex bus.

3.5 INPUT/OUTPUT SUBSYSTEMS

The input/output subsystem of the computer is the means for communication with secondary and archival memory, with other computers through data-communication facilities, and with the users at terminals, computer workstations, printers, video displays, or other devices. The input/output controller (Kio) or processor (Pio) is central to the I/O subsystem since it is the device that controls all I/O operations and synchronizes them with activities of the central processor(s).

The controllers (Kio or Pio) synchronize input or output data transfers, provide data buffering that allows for different transfer rates on the two sides of the controller, and perform any data transformations required to match the data structures of the I/O devices and the central processor. The determination of whether it is better to use an I/O controller that synchronizes I/O activities using internally wired sequences of operations or an I/O processor that is capable of executing sequences of instructions held in a memory is a decision to be made at the more detailed ISP level of design. Design of the input/output control mechanism at the ISP level is discussed in Chapter 7.

Issues to be faced when considering the input/output subsystem start with a determination of whether the subsystem is to be general-purpose (using standard peripheral equipment) or specialized (interfacing with system-unique equipment such as real-time process controllers). This determination is one of the first results of the requirements analysis covered in the previous chapter. That analysis also should have established the quantitative requirements for flow of input/output data, including the nature of the information, the required data structures, the rate of information transfer in each direction, and any special needs related to reliability or to the environment in which the system will operate.

From the specification of general I/O requirements an analysis of the input/output traffic expectations will enable us to establish the input/output subsystem architecture at the PMS level. It is not necessary to be concerned with the detailed characteristics of the I/O devices. (Detailed information is required at the ISP level and is covered in Chapter 7.) However, we do need to understand the characteristics of the devices and their individual controllers sufficiently to permit the traffic analysis to include information on the switching connection times and on the duration that connections are maintained. The wide variations in characteristics of peripheral devices and in the operations of any one device during different processing activities might cause our "traffic analysis" to be more of a "traffic estimate". That should not cause us concern. What is most important is that we specifically make decisions on input/output traffic based on the best information available to provide a start for the system design.

To obtain a feeling for the I/O design problem we might look at the range of data rates, the organization of data into batches, the data structures for transfer, and the response-time dependencies of typical peripheral equipment. Secondary and tertiary memories that use motion of a magnetic or optical medium impose particularly stringent requirements on the I/O subsystem. Such devices as disk files and magnetic tape drives can be characterized by high transfer rates of byte- or word-organized information (50 kbytes/s to 5 Mwords/s), by long times to gain access to a block of information (10 ms to 10 s) and by relatively large uninterruptible blocks to be transferred (256 bytes to 64 kwords). At the other extreme we have consoles with cathode-ray-tube displays with which we have small amounts of information to be transferred (several bytes to several display pages) in bit- or byte-serial form at relatively slow data rates (300 to 9600 bits/s). Between these two types we find printers, to which information is transferred bit-serially, byte-by-byte, or in single-line blocks; keyboard entry devices with speeds held down by human operators; and solid-state serial-access memories using magnetic bubble, charge-coupled device, or similar technologies with access times of several to several hundred milliseconds, transfer rates from 0.1 to 10 Mbit/s, and relatively small block sizes. Unique problems might be raised when there are specialized input/output devices such as digital-to-analog and analog-to-digital converters and other real-time control equipment.

The initial architectural issue to be settled is a determination of the maximum concurrency required in operation of the I/O subsystem. This allows us to specify the quantity of I/O controllers to be connectable at one time and the number of paths that should be incorporated in the input/output subsystem switches. Understanding the variation in data rates and in duty cycles of the different peripheral devices and knowing the amount of concurrency desired for each of the different types of devices allows us to determine how many different types of I/O controllers there should be and to allocate groups of peripherals to the different controllers.

An example of an I/O subsystem design to this point is shown in Fig. 3-18, in which the I/O subsystem peripheral equipment capacities and the general requirements for I/O controllers have been specified. This example system has a magnetic tape controller for four tape drives, a controller for two printers, a dual disk file controller for eight disk drives, and a display controller attached to 16 display terminals.

At this point we know the maximum complement of peripheral devices and the total data rate of all devices. However, more information is needed before we can develop specifics of the interconnection of controllers and peripheral equipment. It is necessary to establish the different input/output transfers that might be accomplished at the same time. This permits us to fix groups of peripheral devices that can share input/output controllers. The number of independent groupings then determines the number of Kio or Pio that is needed. The fact that two peripheral devices do not operate

Ktape[1] ———— Mtape (#0:3)   Kprint[2] ———— Tprint (#0:1)

Kdisk[3] ———— Mdisk (#0:7)   Kdispl[4] ———— Tdispl (#0:15)

1. Ktape {intermittent transfers, 1 to 16 4096-byte blocks, 1 Mbyte.s}.
2. Kprint {4096-byte block buffer, 2 printers operate independently}.
3. Kdisk {controls 1 to 8 disk files, 2 concurrently, 2 Mbyte/s each}.
4. Kdisplay {multiplexer, controls 1 to 16 displays, 2048-byte block transfers, 1 kbyte/s ea}.

Figure 3-18   A representative input/output subsystem.

concurrently is not the only factor used to determine the groupings. If there is a wide difference in transfer rates among devices it might be desirable to assign slow and fast devices to input/output controllers of two different speeds. We saw an arrangement of that type in Fig. 3-3, which showed that the VAX-11/780 included a "massbus" for high-speed transfers and a "unibus" for lower speeds. The groupings of devices, the specializations of the Kio, and the identification of the total quantity of concurrent transfers can lead to selection of a switching structure for the input/output subsystem.

While any of the switching approaches described in the previous section might be used in the input/output subsystem, the differences between the rates and the amounts of information transfer for I/O and for processor–memory interaction suggest that different switches are suited to the two applications. The I/O switch is characterized by relatively longer connection times, relatively lower transfer rates, relatively longer connection distances, and larger (sometimes much larger) quantities of items to be connected. Usually high-speed high-concurrency switches such as the crossbar are too costly for the input/output switch application. More common are the tree, the duplexed tree, and the I/O bus, all shown in Fig. 3-19. A simple tree is demonstrated

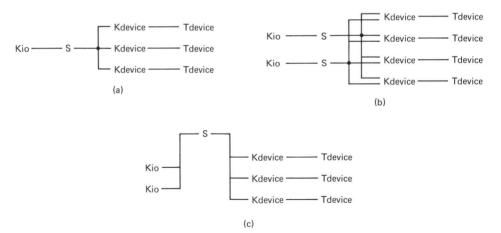

Figure 3-19   Input/output interconnections. (a) Input/output tree connection. (b) Dual trees. (c) Input/output bus.

in Fig. 3-19(a). Here any one of the transducers (Tdevice) can be connected through its controller to the input/output controller. The connection is maintained until the transfer of information has been completed. The switch typically transfers information in 8-bit bytes, possibly with a parity bit added.

If we have a number of devices that transfer information concurrently in pairs, but the specific pairings for simultaneous transfer are not known, we might use the dual-tree arrangement of Fig. 3-19(b). An alternative, if we can "interlace" transfers byte by byte between two device controllers and the two Kio, is to use an input/output bus, as shown in Fig. 3-19(c). This figure illustrates only a few of the switching schemes that might be used for attaching a group of I/O devices to a Pio or a Kio.

The variation in the rate or amount of data transfers of various devices might lead to use of different switches in different parts of the I/O subsystem, as demonstrated in Fig. 3-20. This is an example of how we might connect the input/output subsystem of Fig. 3-18. The configuration shown employs two I/O controllers with a duplex tree for connecting secondary memory (two disk controllers, each with four disk files attached, and a tape controller for the four tape drives). The printers and the displays are separated into two similar groups with a printer and its controller and a display controller with 16 terminals in each. A Kio is used for each of the printer-display groups. All of the Kio of the illustration are connected to a system switch of a type described in the previous section.

It is useful to compare the complexity of the input/output subsystem switches with that of the system switches. We noted in the previous section that these electronic switches are composed of a multiplexer to select from a number of sources and a decoder (or demultiplexer) to select the destination. The methods used to estimate the cost of system switches can be applied to the I/O switching design. A typical input/output switch might connect a Kio (or Pio) to eight bidirectional device controllers or to 16 unidirectional controllers. A bidirectional $(1,8,1)$ switch incorporates two 8×1 multiplexer and two 1×8 decoders and has a complexity of 16 by the measure used in the previous section. Since the complexity numbers presented before are for each connecting line, they must be multiplied by the number of bits transferred in parallel over each switch. The major difference in cost between the I/O switches and the system switches results from the byte- rather than word-size data transfers used in most I/O switches (although the slower input/output switch might be made with lower-performance and lower-cost transistors). It is suggested that the reader make similar estimates for other input/output switching configurations.

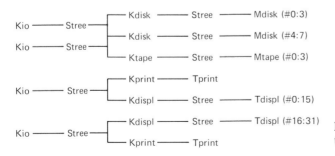

Figure 3-20 An implementation of the I/O subsystem of Fig. 3-18.

3.6 RECONFIGURING, UPGRADING, AND RELIABILITY

The different system configurations reviewed in the previous sections appear to yield different degrees of flexibility. The more "modular" the structure, the easier it is to modify system function and system performance by addition, deletion, or replacement of modules. However, the modularity that appears in the PMS diagram is not sufficient by itself to assure system flexibility. The modular system structure must be accompanied by facilities in hardware modules and in software to permit the system to operate effectively when individual modules are changed. Performance/economic trade-offs come into play here, as they do in almost all of our decisions on computer architecture.

We have seen that there are different ways to organize a computer system and to connect its functional parts. We must compare the different possibilities and measure their capabilities against our objectives. For example, if a major objective is to provide an architecture that yields a wide performance range with a single module of each major type a system configuration that emphasizes connection of many processors, input/output controllers and memory modules is appropriate. If our architecture is for a family of computers, and the quantity of systems to be built each year is significant, a system organization that permits us to attach one or two processors selected from one of several performance levels to a single memory module selected from a variety of sizes and speeds allows for a much simpler and less expensive switch.

Analysis of memory costs might show that there is a 10% increase in cost for a 20% faster memory that is suitable for the higher-performance version of two processors that we want in our series. It might be more economical to provide only the faster memory to permit our customers to upgrade their systems as their needs grow. These examples show that we must use iteration between system-level and module-level design to optimize our system configuration and that there must be interaction between the "wants" of the market and the "cans" of the architect and designer.

Modular computer organizations offer flexibility for selection of a configuration to meet specified size and performance levels. They permit systems to grow to meet new requirements by adding modules without replacing others. They facilitate gradual upgrading by replacement of selected modules. The price of the flexibility obtained is increased cost due to the additional hardware and software needed for switching and control. As we will see when we review performance and cost issues in a later section, the cost for a unit of performance of a single large module might be lower than that for multiple instances of a smaller module. The benefits of the modular organization must be weighed against the economics of total system cost.

In some situations very high degrees of reliability are required and multiple-module or multiple-computer organizations can provide redundancy to meet the requirements for increased reliability. A brief review of a few fundamentals regarding reliability of systems with redundant subsystems will give us an overview of the possibilities for design of high-reliability computers. Much more detail on the topic is included in the books and periodicals on system reliability referred to in Section 3.11.

The failure rate of an equipment is determined by accumulating the failure rates of the components. If failures of components are truly random the equipment failure rate is the sum of the failure rate multiplied by the quantity of each component. Rather than failure rate we usually use its reciprocal, the mean-time-between-failures (MTBF), to state the reliability of an item. When the equipment is used in a system, we are concerned with the probability p that it will not fail during a specified mission time, a period of time related to the functions being performed. With random failure mechanisms the probability of failure, $q = 1 - p$, is the mission time divided by the MTBF (or the failure rate multiplied by the mission time).

We will not attempt to establish any specific quantitative failure rates and reliabilities, but will compare different system configurations by assuming that the failure rate of processors increases roughly as the square root of performance and that the failure rate of memory modules increases roughly as the square root of capacity. Subsystem cost as a function of performance is assumed to increase by the same ratios. Both assumptions are based on component counts proportional to the square root of performance or capacity. We will identify the sensitivity of our result to these assumptions by also making the comparisons under linear increases of failure rates and costs with performance and capacity.

With these assumptions we can make comparisons of the reliability and the cost of the system configurations shown in Fig. 3-21. A system in which all equipment must be operating can be represented as a series of subsystems through which information must flow, as shown in Fig. 3-21(a). In this baseline the system-failure probability is the sum of the failure probabilities of the subsystems, since the system fails if any one subsystem fails. (Second-order effects of two or three subsystems failing simultaneously can be ignored if the subsystem-failure rates are low.) In the example of Fig. 3-21(a) the system-failure probability $Q_{simplex}$ is the sum of the subsystem-failure probabilities $q_p + q_m + q_{io}$. If, to simplify the analysis, we assume that the failure rates of all three subsystems are the same, q_0, the system failure rate is $3q_0$. In order to compare the various systems let us assume that the mission time and the subsystem MTBFs are such that the value of q_0 is 0.01 (i.e., the probability of success is 0.99). Then the system-failure probability is 3×10^{-2}. The baseline cost is established as unity.

Figure 3-21(b) shows how adding another computer in parallel provides redundancy for increased reliability. Of course, we also must add the hardware and software to control switching from the primary to the secondary system. All subsystems remain the same, so if we can ignore the cost and the increased failure rate due to the switching the subsystem-failure probabilities remain q_0. System failure now occurs only if both computers fail, and the system-failure probability is $Q_{simplex}^2$. The numeric value is about 9×10^{-4}, and the cost has been doubled. This duplex computer approach was included in the early von Neumann architecture and was implemented in the AN/FSQ-7, the computer built by IBM for the SAGE air defense system in the mid-1950s.

If the duplex system improves the reliability, perhaps "triplexing" will yield a further improvement. An example is the RW-400, an early 1960s multiple-computer system for military applications. The calculations for a triplex system with each computer

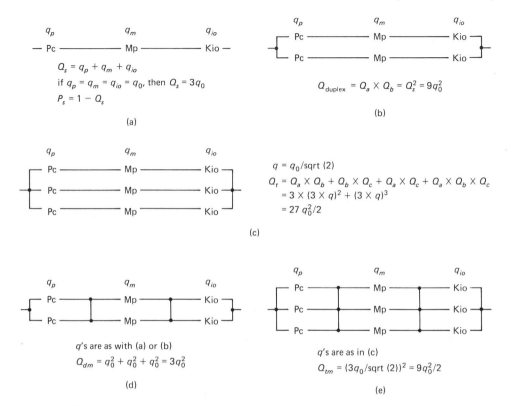

Figure 3-21 System reliability models. (a) A simplex computer. (b) A duplex system. (c) Triplexed computers. (d) A dual-module system. (e) Triplexed modules.

the same as that for the simplex yield a system reliability of $Q_{simplex}{}^3$ with a tripling of cost. An alternative is to introduce individual modules of one-half the performance of the simplex system and assume that two out of three computers must be operating for the system to meet its operating requirements. This system configuration is shown in Fig. 3-21(c). Now the module failure rates and costs have been reduced to $2^{1/2}$ of those for the simplex system, and the system-failure probability (if the Q's are small) is $Q_a Q_b + Q_b Q_c + Q_a Q_c$, or $3Q_a{}^2$. Each path has a failure probability $Q_a = 3q_0/2^{1/2}$, so the system-failure probability $Q_{triplex}$ is $27q_0{}^2/2$, or 14×10^{-4}. The cost is now $3/2^{1/2} = 2.1$, about the same as that for the duplex system.

With some increase in the switch complexity we might replicate independent modules, as shown in Fig. 3-21(d). Now the system operates if at least one processor, one memory module, and one I/O system are working. The q's are as for the simplex and duplex systems and the system-failure probability is the sum of the failure probabilities for the three stages, $Q_{dupmod} = 3q_0{}^2 = 3 \times 10^{-4}$. Again neglecting the switch, the cost is 2, the same as that for the duplex system. A final example is that of independent-module triplexing, shown in Fig. 3-21(e). Here at least two of the three modules of each type must be operational for system success. The system-failure rate $Q_{tripmod} = 9q_0^2/2 = 4.5 \times 10^{-4}$ and the cost is 2.1, as with the triplex system. The Burroughs D825, shown in Fig. 3-1, is a multiprocessor system that allows up to four Pc, 16 Mp, and two input/output exchanges. Its organization and its operating system were designed for very high reliability.

The results of the exercise are summarized in Fig. 3-22. Results of the same calculations under the assumption of a linear increase in failure rate and cost with performance and capacity also are shown. The results indicate that triplex computers, or triplexed modules, each of one-half the required capacity, are no more cost effective than duplex computers (modules). For about the same cost as the duplex (triplex) computers, modular systems with duplexing (triplexing) yield significantly lower failure rates.

The coarse approximations used in the development of these reliability estimates show how different configurations with different costs give different levels of reliability. When combined with other considerations this type of information helps us to decide on a system design. When we have more specific data on the subsystems and their components the reliability analysis can be refined and made more precise. Specification of required reliability should be a part of the requirements statement of any digital system. Often the requirement is specified in terms of *availability*, the measure of the percentage of time that the system is operational over a significant period of time (say, weeks). Calculation of availability takes into consideration the mean-time-to-repair (MTR) the system once there is a failure and requires knowledge of the maintenance response time as well as the MTBF. It is strongly influenced by the failure detection and diagnostic capabilities of the system.

3.7 LEVELS OF MEMORY

Information (instructions, data, status, and control signals) is stored at many levels of a computer system. Individual flip-flops and registers in the processors are the highest-cost (per bit) and the highest-speed memory elements of the system. Both are referenced at the

Failure probability and cost proportional to square root of performance:

System	Simplex	Duplex	Triplex	Duplex Module	Triplex Module
Failure probability	3×10^{-2}	9×10^{-4}	14×10^{-4}	3×10^{-4}	5×10^{-4}
System cost	1	2^+	2.1^+	2^{++}	2.1^{++}

Failure probability and cost proportional to performance:

System	Simplex	Duplex	Triplex	Duplex Module	Triplex Module
Failure probability	3×10^{-2}	9×10^{-4}	7×10^{-4}	3×10^{-4}	2×10^{-4}
System cost	1	2^+	1.5^+	2^{++}	1.5^{++}

Figure 3-22 Reliability and cost comparisons.

internal speed of the processor that houses them. At the other extreme are the archival memories that are four or five orders of magnitude less expensive and have nine or 10 orders greater access times than internal registers. Between the two, approximately following a straight line on a log–log plot of cost per bit against access time, are the cache memories, primary memory, and various forms of secondary memory. Detail on the technologies and the design of each of these forms of memory are covered in Chapter 4. At this point we are interested in where each fits in the PMS-level structure of the computer system and in the alternatives available for organizing systems using memory at the various levels.

If there were no difference in cost we would satisfy all of our memory requirements with registers internal to the processor. That obviously is not practical. If we use a manufacturing whole cost of 0.2 cents for a flip-flop assembled in a computer, the cost of a moderate-size memory (4 Mbytes) is about $64,000. That is well beyond what we can afford for the manufacturing cost of the whole processor in a small computer. Similarly, we cannot afford to use primary memory costs of about 0.005 cents per bit to implement a moderate-size secondary memory of 200 Mbytes. This manufacturing cost of over $80,000 is too great for a small system. We need a hierarchy of memory with units of different costs and speeds for a practical system.

The system-level issues focus on the architectures that can make effective use of the memory introduced at each level of the hierarchy. How do we take advantage of the speed of processor registers as well as the capacity of very large disk files? Can we design the system with facilities for automatic movement of information between levels in the hierarchy so that it appears to the user that the whole system has been implemented with the fastest memory? What can be done to permit indefinite growth of memory as far as the user is concerned, without the need for any change to programs or data?

Let us look first at the uses of processor registers, primary memory, and secondary memory. The registers in the processor can include general registers that hold instructions and data. (The organization of processors with general registers and with alternative uses of register hardware is reviewed in Chapter 5.) The amount of storage economically feasible for processor general registers is on the order of 1000 bytes. The registers operate at a speed consistent with the combinatorial logic that controls register-to-register transfers and performs arithmetic and other transformations. One view of the general registers is that they serve as multiple copies of the accumulator and the arithmetic register of the von Neumann computer model. These internal registers temporarily hold data and instructions being used currently by the processor. Due to the small quantity of registers only very active information can be held in them, and any information that is not used immediately might have to be stored in less valuable memory locations. Individual values reside in the processor registers for tens to thousands of processor instruction-execution cycles.

The primary memory, typically having a size of the order of several million bytes, holds active information not instantly needed by the processor(s). The information generally is organized into consistent groups of data items (data local to some procedure or program) or instructions (the code of the procedure or program), each group containing hundreds to thousands of bytes. The speed of operation on the primary memory is one or two orders slower than that of processor registers. Information tends to reside in the primary memory for thousands to millions of instruction execution cycles (for the lifetime of a procedure, for example). Connection between the primary memory and the processor(s) is provided by the links and the switches discussed in Section 3.3.

To mask the primary-memory access times from the user, the system can move small groups of bytes between the registers and the primary memory while the processor is using other registers. (The various methods for handling this are a topic of Chapter 5.) To a significant extent the system then can operate at register speeds. The processing speed attained through use of internal registers makes it desirable that there be a very large quantity of such registers, and we are faced again with the issue of relative cost of internal registers compared with primary memory. This leads to the introduction of *lookaside* or *cache* memory, with cost and performance fitting between those of processor registers and primary memory.

A cache memory is a relatively small high-speed high-cost memory (typically 2^{-10} to 2^{-5} the size, two to four times the speed, and over two times the unit cost of Mp). The cache holds the information from primary memory that was most recently used. Whenever access to primary memory is initiated the attempt is preceded or accompanied by a check to see if the information currently resides in the cache. If so, the access to primary memory is cancelled. The several methods of operation and several approaches to implementing cache memory are covered in Chapter 4.

The cache memory can be placed in several locations in a system, as shown in Fig. 3-23. It can be a part of a processor, part of a memory module, or a separate item connected to the processor–memory switch. In a uniprocessor system with a single memory module the cache is most effective when located with the processor, as shown in the left side of Fig. 3-23(a). There are two ways in which reading or writing to the cache can be faster than that to the primary memory. As noted before, the cache is made with faster memory circuits. Since the cache is small it can be placed close to, or made a part of, a processor to allow processor-cache communication with minimum time delay.

With a multiple-processor system it is possible that the same Mp location can provide information for two different processes operating in two different processors. If there is a cache with each processor, as shown in the right side of Fig. 3-23(a), one processor might have modified the information and there could be different values for a single variable in the different caches. With this arrangement information in different caches must be coordinated to be sure that the correct values are in all cache memories. This approach has been used in the large IBM systems (308X and 3090) with a separate processor, the system controller, used for cache management (see Fig. 3-4).

An alternative is to place the cache memory units with the primary memory modules, as shown in Fig. 3-23(b). Here a cache contains only information associated with its own Mp and there is no problem of different values for different caches. On the other hand, the cache is separated from the processors by the system switch and the speed advantage attained through elimination of switch transition time is lost.

A third organization, using the common cache memory shown in Fig. 3-23(c), provides economy of scale in that a single large cache would be less expensive than several smaller ones. However, the benefits of simultaneous access by different processors to different memory modules would be lost and the single cache could be a

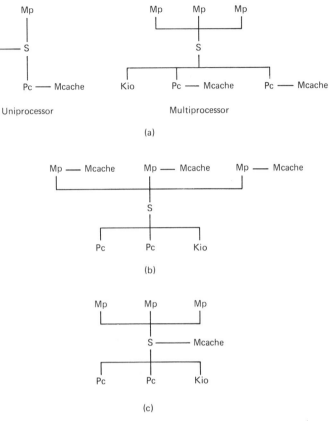

Figure 3-23   Cache memory in multiprocessor systems. (a) With the processor. (b) At primary-memory modules. (c) Independent cache.

performance bottleneck. The single cache might also be the weakest link in the reliability of the system. Finally, the processor–cache and cache–memory switches would be more expensive than a processor–memory switch of equivalent number of interconnection paths. Locating the cache memory in a multiprocessor system requires careful planning and analysis of expected performance and cost of the alternatives.

Just as primary memory acts as an extension of processor registers, secondary memory is a lower-cost extension of primary memory. A large-capacity disk file with a capacity of hundreds of megabytes and access time several orders longer than that of primary memory is typical of secondary memory. Usually the secondary memory is connected to the primary memory through the input/output network and a special processor or controller, as we saw in the previous discussion of input/output subsystems. Large blocks (thousands of bytes) of information, in the form of pages or of segments are transferred at one time. This works fine if relatively large blocks of information are transferred between primary and secondary memory at relatively long intervals (millions of execution cycles). Sometimes this organization causes significant delays when processing must stop while a block of information is transferred. Again, a memory with characteristics between those of the high-speed primary memory and the low-cost secondary memory is indicated.

The intermediate memory (Mint) might be a small high-speed disk or drum, a solid-state sequential-access memory using charge-coupled devices or magnetic-bubble technology, or a large low-speed semiconductor memory, all of which are outlined in Chapter 4. As with cache memory the system-level issue is one of location and connection. Several possibilities are shown in Fig. 3-24.

We can place the intermediate memory on the same switch as the input/output subsystem, just as we did with the secondary memory, Fig. 3-24(a). This approach is the most flexible and easiest to implement in the hardware, but it introduces software difficulties when we attempt to take full advantage of the speed of the intermediate memory. Here the intermediate memory takes the role of a special type of secondary memory and the operating system or the user software must determine when the higher-speed memory should be used. Little architectural support can be made available for this configuration since the use of the faster memory is so dependent on specifics of the programs being run.

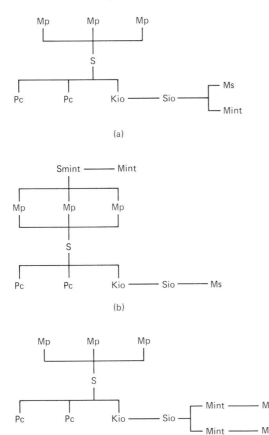

(a)

(b)

(c)

Figure 3-24 Intermediate-memory connections. (a) With the input/output subsystem. (b) A special interface with primary memory. (c) Part of the secondary-memory subsystem.

If the intermediate-memory controller is connected directly to the primary memory then block transfers of information between the two memory types can be made very rapidly. In this case the intermediate memory serves as a true "backup store" for the primary memory. Two complications arise here. With a modularized primary-memory organization like that of Fig. 3-24(b) there can be conflict for access to intermediate memory. The problem is similar to that of a multiple-processor system when two or more processors require access to a primary-memory module, except that the conflict lasts for the time required to complete the transfer of a block of information, and a process operating in the waiting memory module might be delayed for several milliseconds. A second problem shows up when we attempt to allow for transfers from the intermediate memory to secondary memory. We must either have the information first flow back into primary memory, using it as a buffer between secondary and intermediate memory, or we must provide another path from the intermediate memory to the secondary memory. In the latter case we also need a buffer to coordinate the data structures and transfer rates of the two different memory devices. Software difficulties regarding use of the intermediate memory can be substantial.

An approach that allows the architect to provide hardware support to the memory-management system is shown in Fig. 3-24(c). In this case, applicable to systems with very large amounts of secondary memory, an intermediate memory is assigned to each group of secondary-memory units. The intermediate memory resides between primary memory and secondary memory. Hardware buffers suitable to match the transfer rates of the intermediate-memory and the secondary-memory devices are provided between the two. In this case the secondary memory is the backup store for the intermediate memory, which is the backup store for the primary memory.

Concepts and problems described for intermediate memory are applicable to the situation we face when we want to introduce tertiary-memory devices like magnetic tape units or archival memories like optical recording devices. There are alternative ways to connect the devices; each alternative has advantages and difficulties in both hardware and software. We must examine the alternatives and select the approach that best meets the total system needs. In examining issues of this type at a subsystem level it is desirable that we localize any problems to that level as far as possible. In doing so we can minimize effects on other levels and we can make changes in the system with minimum side effect as new storage-device capabilities become available.

3.8 PROCESSORS AND SOFTWARE ISSUES

The processor is the most complicated of the major components in a computer system, and Chapters 5 and 6 are devoted totally to processor organization. Since processors are the "active" modules in the computer system, processor designs have significant influence on the system structure. Closely related to processor function and performance in a system are those system issues that affect the operating system and user software. Conversely, we see later that there are very important influences of software and programming language on processor organization.

The system organization examples shown earlier in this chapter included single and multiple central processors and single and multiple input/output processors (or controllers). Even though we discussed the possibility of different I/O processors for different groups of peripheral devices, we assumed that all central processors were similar to the extent that they could accomplish all needed calculations and processing. Whereas this general-purpose approach to processor function satisfies many computer-system requirements, there are cases in which the addition of one or more special-purpose processors can lead to improved system cost effectiveness.

An example of the effective use of special-purpose processors is seen in many microprocessor-based systems that have a general-purpose processor to handle system control, byte- or character-oriented processing, and boolean and integer arithmetic. Floating-point (to the user, real) arithmetic can be performed under program control. Even if the program control is a part of the hardware/software system provided to the user, real-arithmetic operations are much slower than are integer operations. A solution introduced by semiconductor manufacturers to permit use of their general-purpose microprocessors in a variety of systems was to include one or more specialized floating-point arithmetic processors in their catalogs.

As shown in Fig. 3-25, the Motorola MC68881 floating-point coprocessor could be added to a system with an MC68020 general-purpose processor to yield a very powerful 32-bit computer. The major microprocessor manufacturers provide many standard microprocessor components, several of which are included in the diagram, to permit design of a system with very few other components. The 68000 system shown in the figure contains a floating-point processor (Pfp) and a memory-management processor (Pmmu) as well as the M68020 Pc. The three processors communicate addresses over the processor interconnect bus (Kp), which controls processor interaction. The rest of the system is similar to those we have seen earlier in this chapter. A system switch, the system interconnect bus, connects the processors, the primary memory, and the peripheral controllers.

Specialized processors have been used in larger systems to handle unique requirements. A small degree of specialization was found in some early multiprocessor systems in that one of the physically identical processors was assigned as the "master", the executor of the operating system. With the other processors it might execute user programs and could communicate to assist in synchronizing tasks, but the other processors

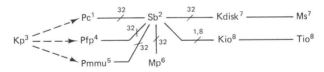

1. Pc\"MC68020" (32-bit_arith, 8 data_registers, 7 addr_reg, stack_ptr).
2. Sb\"system_interconnect_bus", ((n,1,1), 32 addr_lines, 32 data_lines).
3. Kp\"processor_interconnect_bus" (32 address_lines, processor_control).
4. Pfp\"MC68881" (eight 80-bit_floating-point_registers).
5. Pmmu\"MC68851_memory_management_unit" (Mp_control).
6. Mp {static or dynamic random-access memory and read-only memory}.
7. Kdisk, Ms {disk memory with direct-memory-access controller}.
8. Kio, Tio {bit or byte serial input/output devices with controller}.

Figure 3-25   Motorola M68000 system with coprocessor.

were prohibited from running the operating system. The first model in the Burroughs B5X00/6X00/7X00 series, the B5000, in 1963 allowed only one of its two processors to execute the master control program, its multiprocessing operating system.

The IBM System 370AP, attached-processor versions of the IBM 370 series, including the IBM 3033AP shown in Fig. 3-26, had one of the processors (the Pc) execute the operating system and control input/output operations. The other parts of a standard 3033 system include Pio, Sio, Mcache, Mp, and Kmsu. An attached processor, Pap, is similar to the Pc with its own Mcache, but it does not execute the operating system or control input/output transfers. The VAX-11/782 is another example of an attached-processor multiprocessor system. In all three of these examples all processors are almost identical and the specialization is software-directed.

A greater degree of specialization is seen when a scientific processor is added to a large system. When a user has problems involving floating-point variables with fast Fourier transforms or large quantities of simultaneous equations, but does not need a scientific "supercomputer", attaching a specialized floating-point arithmetic processor can be effective. IBM added the 2938 and 3838 scientific processors to their 360 and 370 systems to enhance their scientific processing capability.

Floating Point Systems has specialized in scientific processors to be added as "back-end processors" for more standard computer systems. As can be seen from Fig. 3-27, one might question whether the FPS scientific processor is a "back end" for a host computer or the host is really an input/output "front end" for the FPS scientific processor. The FPS 5000 can be connected to almost any host computer. The FPS 5000 contains Pio's, an Mp, and a system bus, appearing as a conventional computer. Its control processor is really a fairly conventional central processor, but its main role is to control the activities of the high-performance arithmetic processor (Pap).

With any of the approaches to attaching specialized processors we must be concerned with the processor-to-processor coordination required to make effective use of the specialized unit. In the example of Fig. 3-25 the two processors are very tightly coupled. The floating-point coprocessor is almost a special data operator for the main processor, which controls the coprocessor operations at an instruction-by-instruction level. With the almost-general-purpose attached processors, represented by Fig. 3-26, control still resides with the main processor, but is at a broader level. Control and synchronization signals

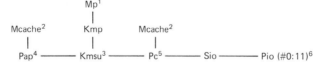

1. Mp\"Processor_storage_unit" (8 Mbyte, 8-way_interleave, 290 ns).
2. Mcache (64 kbytes, 58 ns, 64-bit_word).
3. Kmsu\"Memory_control_unit" {includes switch and cache coordination}.
4. Pap\"Attached_processor" (64-bit_word; 58-ns_major_cycle).
5. Pc (64-bit_word, 58-ns_major_cycle).
6. Pio {block multiplexer and selector channels}.

Figure 3-26   IBM 3033AP system configuration.

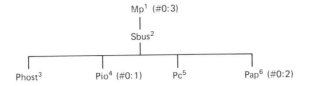

1. Mp (256 kwords, 38-bit_word {32-bit data & 6-bit tag}, 167 ns).
2. Sbus\"Address/data_bus".
3. Phost {various host computers from minicomputer to IBM 3090 in size}.
4. Pio {format, control and queuing input/output data}.
5. Pc\"Control_processor" (components: Mprogr, Dadd, Dmult, 64 reg).
6. Pap\"Arithmetic_coprocessor" (components: Mprog, Mdata, 2 Dadd, Dmult).

Figure 3-27 FPS 5000 series with a host computer.

flow between the two processors, but data and most instructions reside in the shared memory. Even looser control is provided by the host with the attached scientific processor shown in Fig. 3-27. There the host assigns a "job" by transferring programs and data from secondary memory. There is little communication thereafter until the job is completed.

Another systems issue closely related to the processor design is that of sharing memory for instructions and data as opposed to using specialized memory for the two. (Recall that the von Neumann team made quite an issue of the uniformity of data and instruction representations.) Sometimes the flexibility gained by using similar-sized words for data and instructions, which permits either to consume as much or as little of a shared memory as needed, is less important than the economic gains or the performance improvements one might obtain by having different word sizes and different memories for program and data.

Several computers designed for aircraft or space-vehicle control, where both the data and the program were of relatively stable and predictable size, used different memories for different functions. The stability allowed the architects to design the system with a read-only memory (ROM) for the program, a programmable read-only memory for constants (PROM), and a normal read/write random-access memory (RAM) for variable data. Computers of that type had a high reliability since the fixed information was much less likely to be altered by accident or by environmental hazards. When we discuss computers with microprogrammable control store in Chapter 6 we will see another example of different memory forms in different parts of the system.

The operating system, that piece of system software (possibly implemented partly in hardware) that controls management of computer resources, schedules processes, synchronizes possibly conflicting activities, and controls error-detection and error-recovery routines, is very important to the success of the computer system. Characteristics of the operating system affect the system architecture and features of the computer hardware can lead to a good or a poor operating system. Much of what has been covered under system configuration in this chapter influences, and is influenced by, the operating system. For example, a part of the price that is paid to obtain the flexibility and the reliability of the modular systems described is in the increased activities required of the operating system.

Other software that must be considered by the system architect includes the language translators, software to support maintenance of the system, programs and documentation for user and support personnel training, and the operational software that users employ to perform useful processing work. If the software is not considered at the time that the architecture is developed many problems that could be avoided and solved in the design will be deferred to be solved by the users.

Lest we assume that those are the only times when we must think of nonhardware items, let us remember that the computer architect is concerned with the *total computer system*. With any of the alternative system configurations, as well as with each of the alternatives available at more detailed architectural levels to be covered in later chapters, there are issues of operating-system software, of programming languages to support capabilities offered, of software for operation and maintenance of the systems, and of manufacturability and maintainability of the systems themselves. All of these are of concern to, and must be considered by, the computer-system architect.

3.9 SYSTEM PERFORMANCE AND SYSTEM COST

When we examined alternative computer system configurations in Section 3.3 we assumed that, for a given computer module, system performance would be proportional to the number of those modules. We did see that a modular organization imposes a requirement for a switch. The switch can introduce delays and reduce performance, but we assumed that the effects were not noticeable. In this section we examine these performance issues more carefully.

Let us consider first the effect of adding special input/output controllers (Kio) or processors (Pio). Input/output operations include a lot of detail related to packing or unpacking data, format modifications, and control related to the specific peripheral equipment involved in the transfer. While this processing can be performed by most central processors, doing so is not an effective use of that relatively expensive part of the machine. Most of the processing, aside from initiating the I/O operation and responding to its completion, can be performed just as well by a more specialized and less expensive processor or controller. A Pio or a Kio usually costs less than 10% of the cost of the Pc. If we can organize our programs (either manually or through the operating system) to have the Pc perform the overall command of I/O, while a Pio or Kio handles the details, we should be able to keep the Pc busy performing tasks that only it can handle.

It is reasonable to assume that, on the average, the addition of an independent input/output control module increases central processor performance by an amount almost equal to the total time taken for input/output transfers (to the limit of the central processor being fully busy with processing tasks). While it is possible that the system can be performing tasks that have very little I/O activity, with the result that a separate Pio or Kio has little effect on performance, this situation is rare today. Given that one Pio or Kio yields performance benefits, how about adding a second, or a third? We cannot prescribe the performance effect without having a detailed specification of the problems to be solved with the system. One can make pretty good estimates of relative percentage of I/O activity based on experience with applications in which the system will be used. History tells us that computers have more often been "I/O bound" than "processor bound".

If our central processor is designed for general-purpose applications we can provide for specialized operations, such as those performed by the floating-point processor of Fig. 3-25. We can estimate the increased performance in these cases by comparing the times required for the special operations on the central processor as opposed to performing them on the special processor. Even if the central processor cannot concurrently perform other tasks, there can be a significant performance improvement when we introduce a coprocessor.

Experience shows that large programs tend to run in "bursts" of processing and bursts of I/O activity. Similarly, an examination of large numeric problems shows that they tend to have bursts of setup and bursts of numeric processing. In each case the problems would have a central processor idle during I/O bursts or during numeric-processing bursts unless we can cause the central processor to turn to other tasks while the other processing is active. The multiprogramming operating systems that are a part of most of today's computers manage the task switching needed to keep a central processor as busy as possible, relieving the programmer of the difficult job of synchronizing processing and I/O. A multiprogramming operating system also manages other resources and schedules processes when all the resources each needs (memory, I/O devices, files, data structures, etc.) are available. When we have a comprehensive multiprogramming operating system of this type we can consider adding central processors and modifying the operating system to multiprocessing form.

Ever since multiprocessor systems were first introduced their performance has been a controversial subject. It was recognized early that two central processors do not perform twice as much processing as does one. There are penalties related to scheduling tasks on the processors, to conflict for memory, and to switching. The nature of these performance penalties is different in the case of distributing large single problems over a number of processors as opposed to assigning independent processes to different processors. In the former case there are significant intraprocess synchronizing problems that are being addressed as a part of studies of parallel processing and parallel computer systems, the topic of Chapter 8. Here we are concerned with the latter class of problems, where interprocess coupling is through the operating system or is a result of contention for resources.

When multiple-processor systems were first proposed, M. Minsky of MIT postulated that a system with n processors would see a performance increase proportional to $\log_2 n$. Recently expanded interest in such systems has led to evaluations of actual performance levels with results superior to those that would verify "Minsky's conjecture". Computer manufacturers claim a performance increase for each added central processor of about 90% the performance of the previously added central processor (performance proportional to the sum for i ranging from 0 to $n-1$ of 0.9^i). Hwang and Briggs in [HwanK84] use probability to develop the argument that performance is proportional to n divided by the sum for i ranging from 1 to n of $1/i$. In all of these cases performance for n processors is significantly less than n times that for one processor.

When developing the D825 computer shown in Fig. 3-1 in 1961 we postulated that, if we start with the need for multiprogramming and have a multiprogramming operating system, "useful processing work" for an n-processor system could approach n times that of an equivalent uniprocessor. The argument is developed in Fig. 3-28. Activity performed by a processor is separated to useful work, the fixed overhead of the operating system (including that for multiprogramming on a uniprocessor), operating-system overhead for handling multiple processors, and processing delays due to contention for other resources.

In Fig. 3-28(a) we see a typical distribution of activity for a uniprocessor with fixed operating-system overhead of about 10%. When a second processor is added the fixed overhead remains the same (arbitrarily associated with the first processor in the figure) and processor time is used for resource contention and for scheduling the second processor, as is shown in Fig. 3-28(b). The argument is extended to n processors in Fig. 3-28(c). From the figure we can see that the amount of useful processing work increases faster than the increase in processors as long as the overhead added with each added processor is less than the average overhead time for all existing processors. We postulated that for each processor added the variable overhead would be less than the fixed overhead until the quantity of processors was so large that there was a sharp increase in contention for memory or in input/output delays.

This argument was voiced more recently by J. Sanguinetti [SangJ86]. He reported on experimental results with a multiple-processor Elxsi 6400 system, showing performance gains greater than proportional to the number of processors. He suggests that the reason for performance gains at that rate is the reduced per-processor execution of operating-system kernel functions.

In Fig. 3-29 these various approximations to performance with increasing numbers of processors are plotted. The curves are shown for up to 16 processors. No matter which of the curves is most valid, current experience shows that there are users who find that systems with two to six processors are cost effective for their pool of problems. More experimental results are needed to permit the relationship of performance to number of processors to be specified more precisely. The issue is of great significance when we consider computer systems with much larger numbers of central processors for tightly coupled multiprocessing applications in Chapter 8.

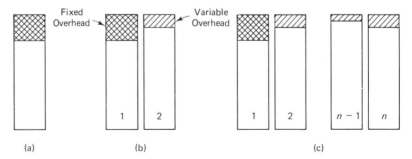

Figure 3-28   Output of multiprocessor systems. (a) One processor. (b) Two processors. (c) n processors.

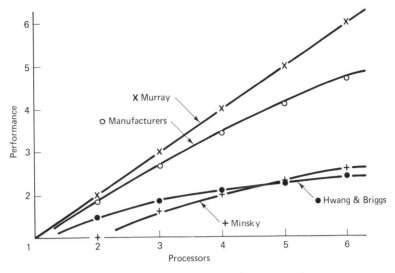

Figure 3-29   Multiprocessor performance estimates.

The general principles of system performance should be considered in the framework of performance/cost relationships. We saw that performance is not necessarily proportional to the quantity of functional modules. We also find that manufacturing cost is not proportional to performance of a module. It also is not directly proportional to the quantity of modules manufactured.

An approximate relationship between power p and cost c of machines of a given type, manufactured by similar means, is consistent among machines of many different types. That relationship, $p = k * c^m$, where m is about 2, has been used by engineers for many years. For example, a centrifugal pump of 10 horsepower costs about one-half that of a similar pump of 40 horsepower. This principle was applied to computers by H. R. J. Grosch in 1953 [GrosH53] and was soon named *Grosch's Law*. While some have argued that the exponent should have values ranging from 1.2 to 2, it is generally agreed that for a given machine (e.g., a processor) of some design (e.g., an IBM 370 CPU) manufactured at some time by some method (e.g., a 9370 processor) one gets almost four times the power for twice the price. This relationship is plotted in Fig. 3-30(a).

Another relationship, that between manufacturing cost and quantity, is significant to our decisions. Manufacturing planners apply an experience-based factor to develop a *learning curve* for projection of the cost of an item that is to be produced. Cost estimates are stated in terms of an *"L-percent learning curve"*, where L ranges from 70 to 90. This factor is used to represent the estimate that if the ith unit has a manufacturing cost of C, then the $2i$th unit will cost $L \times C$. Figure 3-30(b) shows 70, 80, and 90% learning curves starting from a unity cost. Whereas the learning curves do not directly reflect the ratio of average cost for production of $2n$ units against that for n units, as n becomes large (200) the ratio of average cost is within 2% of the factor (from 0.70 to 1.0) used in the learning curve. For example, with an 80% learning factor the average cost of producing 128 units is 0.810 the average cost for 64 units.

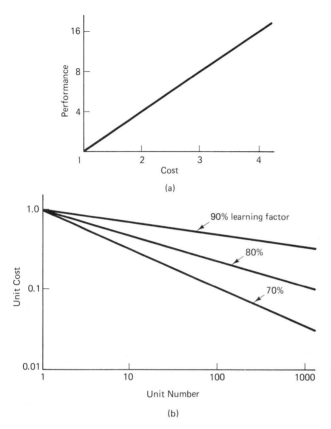

Figure 3-30   Performance/cost and cost/quantity relationships. (a) Performance/cost (Grosch's law). (b) Unit cost/unit number ("learning curve").

Let us attempt to combine the effects of these manufacturing-cost relationships by comparing the production cost of Q processors of performance level P with the cost of $2Q$ processors of performance $P/2$. In our example let us assume that Grosch's law holds and that our manufacturing learning-curve factor is 0.8. From Grosch's law, the cost (i.e., the component count or the complexity) of the smaller processor should be $(1/2)^{1/2} = 0.71$ the cost of the larger if we make the same quantity of each. However, if systems use the smaller processor they need twice as many and we must introduce the quantity factor. Manufacturing costs of the smaller, then, are $0.8 \times 0.71 = 0.57$ those of the larger. Therefore, the performance/cost ratio of the two is $2 \times 0.57 = 1.14$ in favor of the larger. (Note that if the quantity factor is 0.7, then the performance/cost ratio is about unity.) It appears that there is not a large difference between using a smaller quantity of larger processors and a larger quantity of smaller ones.

In our example so far we have assumed that two smaller processors working together can perform to the same level as the larger one. Our discussion of multiprocessor performance before raised questions on the performance of multiprocessor systems that must be answered before we can make a final evaluation of the better approach on a performance/cost basis. We also must factor in the increase of system cost for the multiprocessor system. This "textbook example" cannot be carried further without much more specific information, but it does show that a decision on our structure cannot be made only on the basis of a simple rule like Grosch's law (or Murray's postulate). Our plans must consider the total product line, the quantities to be produced, reliability, flexibility, operating-system issues, all of the items we have reviewed in this chapter.

The example does demonstrate that it is important that experts in manufacturing be a part of our top-level design team. System-cost projections for a product can be as complicated as are performance estimates. The two must be considered together when we compare a design with several small memory modules with one that incorporates one or two large modules. The same issues relate to selection of our approach to peripheral equipment for the system.

This leads to a final question to be answered on the topic of performance/cost relationships, the importance of any one of the major functional components to overall system performance and cost. We can perform simulations to determine the system-performance benefits of twice as much primary memory, of more input/output channel capacity, or of more processor power. We must also determine how each of these subsystems influences total system cost. Price lists from the major computer manufacturers indicate that peripheral equipment (including secondary memory) typically makes up about one-half of system cost. Of the other half, the distribution between central processors and primary memory ranges between 60%/40% and 40%/60%.

We hear hardware and operating-system designers say that "we can design for much larger memories because memory cost is becoming insignificant". If primary memory still is a large fraction of system cost, is that really true? Examination of cost trends of processor and memory electronics shows that electronic technology is making unit cost of memory much cheaper each year. However, that same technology is making the unit cost of logic in a processor much cheaper. In fact, the ratio of cost of a memory bit and a four-input gate or of a memory bit and a processor flip-flop has changed little over the years. It is still important to consider the effect on system cost and on system performance of each part of the computer system.

3.10 SUMMARY

A designer might be developing a single digital system that will be assembled using standard or specialized computers, or might be involved with a computer family that will have several models and will be manufactured in large quantities. The approach taken to the architecture will respond to these issues. If a product family is to be developed, the planned quantities of each member of the family influence the system organization.

There is a variety of computer system organizations, each with its own benefits and penalties. The "best" approach for a particular set of requirements is influenced by the need for flexibility of configuration and by the number of different performance levels to be implemented. Many different structures have been technically and commercially successful.

Within any particular system configuration the connection of the major functional units can be handled in different ways. Switches must fit the specific needs of the system topology and are influenced by the physical distances among modules of the systems. Even within computers to be installed at single locations a variety of interconnection schemes can be used. Each has specific characteristics related to the quantities of units that can be connected, the number of concurrent connections required, the duration of the connection, the quantity of information to be transferred during one connection, and the need for alternative connection paths. This connectivity can have a strong influence on system performance and on system cost.

Information flow among the major internal modules of the computer is different from that between the computer and its peripheral equipment. As a result the switching for the input/output system will be different from that between processors and memory. Here, again, the system designer must consider the amount of information to be transferred, the transmission rates required, the need for concurrent transfers, the format of information, and characteristics of the specific equipment to be connected.

Organization of the system and the switches used for connection affect system flexibility and reliability. Component redundancy and switching mechanisms that can be used to provide alternative system configurations increase system reliability. For some requirements reliability is as important as system capacity.

There are several technologies available for storage of information. While it is desirable that as much computer memory as possible operate at the fastest possible speeds, it is not economically feasible to use only high-speed stores. A hierarchy of memories, each with different speed and cost characteristics, is required. The system design must provide for interaction among the different memory levels. A major objective is to have it appear to the user that all of the storage has been implemented with high-speed components.

In addition to the central processors, computer systems might incorporate specialized processors that perform a limited number of functions effectively. In many systems special processors for numeric computation augment the general-purpose central processor(s). The computer operating systems that manage the computer-system resources and that schedule processing can cause a system to operate effectively if they are designed to take advantage of features of the system and its components. Conversely, the system can be designed to enhance performance of its operating system. The computer architect must consider hardware and software aspects of computer-system design.

Estimation of performance and manufacturing-cost relationships for a computer system is not a straightforward task. Variation of system performance with increases in individual module performance and with increases in the quantity of modules are influenced by how the functional modules are connected. The manufacturing quantities and rates of manufacture influence performance/cost relationships. There are several experience-based "rules of thumb" to assist in system design, but these rules must be applied with care and understanding.

3.11 ADDITIONAL READING

Multiprocessor computer organizations were first introduced in the early 1960s to meet the high-reliability requirements of military command and control systems. The Burroughs D825 [AndeJ62] was a large (for its time) computer used in several military programs. Surveys of multiprocessor systems were presented in [EnslP77] and [SatyM80]. [OrgaE73] offers a lucid description of the Burroughs B6700. The Univac 1110, described in [BorgB78], was the first of a sequence of multiprocessor systems from that company (now a part of Unisys). Digital Equipment's VAX-11 series is described in [Digi86a]. The IBM 308X, a newer multiprocessor, was presented in [CormR83] and [PadeA83]. The Carnegie Mellon University multiprocessors Cmmp and Cm* are discussed in [JoneA80] and [GehrE82]. A recent issue of *IEEE Computer* [WuChu85] is devoted to multiprocessing technologies.

Communications networks and associated issues are the topic of much activity of the IEEE Communications Society. Local area networks (LANs) were the subject of a special issue of *IEEE Communications* [TsaoC84]. [TaneA81] reviews computer networking methods and systems.

Those wishing to delve more deeply into reliability and probability can find many good textbooks on the subjects. [TrivK82] focuses on computer applications of the topics. *IEEE Transactions on Reliability* contain papers on equipment reliability. Issues of *IEEE Transactions on Computers* contain articles on reliability and fault tolerance in computers. The AN/FSQ-7 duplex computer is included in a paper on the SAGE system [EverR57]. [PortR60] summarized the RW-400 that was designed by Ramo-Wooldridge (a predecessor to TRW Corp.) and delivered as the AN/FSQ-27. Tandem Computers' computer product line designed for high reliability is described in [KatzJ77]. [ThomR63] presents AOSP, the operating system for the Burroughs D825 multiprocessor. [ShawA74] and its successor [BicLu87] on operating systems emphasize features needed for management of multiprocessor systems.

Performance of multiprocessor systems is reviewed in [HwanK84] and is the subject of much present research. The possibility of performance growth proportional to the number of processors is discussed in [SangJ86]. [StonH87] includes a discussion of effects of the relationship between processing and interprocess communication in a multiprocessing system. Principles of the capacity/cost relationships for machines can be found in most engineering handbooks and in books on design of specific types of machines. Application of those principles to computers was suggested in [GrosH53]. Further discussion of Grosch's law is still seen in the computer literature. A recent confirmation of the law was presented in [EinDP85]. The subject of manufacturing cost/quantity relationships deserves much more extensive coverage than can be provided in a book on computer architecture. This important topic is included in books on production operations and on management of manufacturing.

3.12 PROBLEMS

3-1. The VAX-11/780 system (Fig. 3-3) could be expanded to have multiple computers (up to four) connected through the multiport memory.

    a. Draw a PMS diagram of a dual VAX-11/780 (VAX-11/782) computer system.

    b. Describe problems you would have to address to have the system operate effectively.

3-2. A user wishes to use the VAX-11/780 (Fig. 3-3) as the central computer for a distributed system with up to 32 IBM PCs (Fig. 3-2) connected as "intelligent terminals". Draw a PMS diagram for such a system.

3-3. To the PMS diagram for a multiple-processor system (Fig. 3-8) add (by dashed lines) the control connections needed among modules. Describe the functions of each of these control connections.

3-4. Message switching is used to transmit data among a large number of computers that are distributed over a wide geographic area. In order to keep message buffers small, messages often are divided into "packets" of fixed size. Then a message consists of one or more packets. Different packets of a message might travel over different routes. Describe some problems and possible solutions regarding reassembly of packets into complete messages, including validating receipt of packets and complete messages.

3-5. Using the approach to measuring switching-system "complexity" described in Section 3.4, do the following:

a. Approximate the complexity of a single crossbar switch for a town that has 16,000 telephones.

b. Show how the cost (complexity) could be reduced by permitting only 512 pairs (any pairs) of subscribers to be connected at any one time.

c. Approximate the complexity and describe any control problems of your solution to part b.

3-6. Before the introduction of electronic switches, the cost of telephone switching was contained by placing groups of users on shared "party lines".

a. If all subscribers of Problem 3-5 are placed on eight-party lines, what is the complexity of a system with a single crossbar switch?

b. What type of switch is each party line?

c. How would you allow for communication between two subscribers on the same party line?

3-7. In a typical buffered "producer–consumer" process, data from two producers are transferred to a computer where they are stored in secondary memory. Each producer generates data at an average rate of 50,000 bytes/s. On demand from one of four consumers, data are taken from secondary memory, transformed, and transferred to that consumer. The average rate of data consumption for each consumer is 20,000 bytes/s. Central-processor time for data transformation is not significant.

a. Draw a PMS diagram for the system.

b. Describe the input/output switch(es) you have used, pointing to problems you anticipated and your solution to these problems.

3-8. Draw the PMS diagram for the RW-400, an early multiple-computer system, described as follows:

> An expandable central exchange is the switching center that permits communication among modules of various types in the RW-400 system. Up to 16 computer or buffer modules that provide system control and up to 64 passive auxiliary function modules can be attached to the central exchange. A computer or buffer module can initiate connection to an auxiliary function module for the period of time that such connection is needed.
>
> Each computer module (designated RW-40) consists of a processor and a word-addressed memory of 1024 26-bit words. A buffer module contains two logical buffer units, each with 1024 words of random-access memory, and the registers and control logic needed for it to operate as a system controller. Each logical buffer unit can be used as an extension of a computer module's memory or can be used as a buffer between a

computer module and an auxiliary function module. The buffer module can execute instructions held in its memory and can control input/output operations.

Auxiliary function units include magnetic tape drives, 8192-word magnetic drum storage units, punched-card readers, card punches, printers, plotters, and display consoles. A display console is used to monitor operation of the system and to manually control system configuration.

3-9. Write a PMS description, with a description of any switches, of a computer described as follows:

The machine has a memory of 16k 32-bit words organized into eight uniform modules. There is a single central processor and two I/O processors. I/O operations are initiated by the central processor through a message queue in memory. An interrupt system includes "I/O complete" signals. I/O processors access memory directly and memory references of the I/O processors and the central processor are interleaved. At any one time either I/O processor can be connected to any peripheral device through a peripheral controller. The peripheral equipment consists of two magnetic tape controllers, either of which can be connected to one of four magnetic tape drives; two 256-Mbyte disk files, each with a controller; two line printers (with controllers), one of which is at a remote location and is connected by a 2400-bit/s communication line. An operation-and-maintenance console with its own floppy disk drives is attached to the central processor.

3-10. A modular computer system contains two central processors, four memory modules, and three I/O processors. The probabilities of failure of individual modules over a "mission period" are $q_{cpu} = 0.02$, $q_{memory} = 0.005$, $q_{iop} = 0.01$. To be considered operational the system must have in operation either central processor, three of the four memory modules, and any two of the I/O processors. Failures of the switching system can be ignored.

a. Calculate the failure probability of the system.

b. What would be the failure probability if every module had to be operational?

3-11. The IBM 3084 (Fig. 3-4) has a cache memory associated with each processor following the cache placement model of the right side of Fig. 3-23(a). In a multiprocessor system of this type, more than one cache might contain copies of information in a single memory location. In the 3084, coordination of the cache memories is performed by the system controller (Psc). Describe the problem of read/write synchronization of cache data and show how the system controller might handle this problem.

3-12. Discuss the relative benefits and problems of an attached-processor system configuration, as in Fig. 3-26, as compared with a multiprocessor system (Fig. 3-8).

3-13. In a multiprocessor system, the processors have uniform access to a large shared memory that might be modular in form. With a multiple-computer system, each processor has its own primary memory. Both configurations permit sharing of secondary memory and peripheral equipment. Describe the characteristics of computational problems and problem mixes that would lead to superior performance of each of the two computer structures over the other.

3-14. Assume that multiprocessor performance follows the "manufacturers" curve of Fig. 3-29 (each added processor adds 90% of the performance of the previous one). Assume further that processor and memory performances increase in proportion to cost to the power 1.5. Describe (possibly with the use of a graph) the differences in system cost for the alternatives of adding processors and memory versus changing to more powerful computers as computational requirements grow through a factor of 4. In both cases assume that peripheral-equipment requirements increase by the same factor. Consider the situations where the initial processor cost is one-third and memory cost is two-thirds of system cost and where processor and memory costs are two-thirds and one-third, respectively. Discuss the conclusions you draw from the evaluation of cost and performance growth.

3.13 PROJECTS

3-A. For the computer system that you are investigating as a course project (Project 1-A), evaluate the range of quantities and the different models of major components (Pc, Mp, Pio, Kio) that can be attached, the quantity and the variety of peripheral devices that can be on the system, and the characteristics of the switches needed for connection. This information will permit you to draw the PMS diagram of the system you have selected.

3-B. After you have specified the design objectives (Project 2-B) for your course design project (Project 1-B), you are able to initiate your design at the PMS level. You should include in your design a complete definition of the switches needed for connecting components of the system. Your PMS-level design normally will not be finished at this stage; design of the components might lead to modification of the system-level design.

3-C. For a computer system that you are familiar with (possibly the one you are describing in course Project 1-A), lay out alternative PMS-level designs to satisfy the requirements.

4

The Memory Hierarchy

We begin our review of the major subsystems of the computer by examining the storage mechanisms available for the various computer memories. A feature that makes the internally programmed digital computer different from other calculating devices is the large amount of easily accessed storage for remembering instruction sequences as well as constants and data. Memory for storing instructions internally in the same form as data made the von Neumann architecture different from other computing machines. The relay calculators at Harvard University and at Bell Laboratories and the electronic calculating instruments of Antanosoff and of Eckert and Mauchly all held instructions in a separate mechanism, such as punched cards or a bank of wires.

It appears to be characteristic of computer users that no matter how much memory is provided they develop a thirst for more. As shown in Fig. 4-1, primary-memory capacity of large computer systems has grown by about a factor of 10 every 10 years. As we saw in Chapter 1, the von Neumann team felt that 4000 words would satisfy all needs with a factor of safety. The Burroughs B6500 was designed to have 16 times more memory than the B5500 that it replaced, and early customers ordered systems almost fully populated with memory. Maximum memory of IBM large computers follows the "factor of 10 every 10 years" slope of Fig. 4-1, and the "extended architecture" of the 308X and 3090 permits addressing of 2048 Mbytes (16 times that implemented with the 3090 Model 300E). As we will see, memory costs are falling rapidly. That is fortunate in light of the continuous growth in requirements for memory.

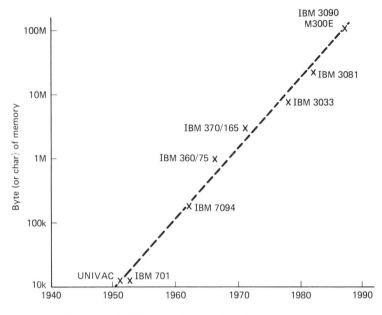

Figure 4-1   Memory-size trends in large computers.

It might be said that a modern computer does more remembering than computing. Specification of the memory must be accomplished early in the design and can be done after a careful analysis of system requirements.

4.1 THE VARIOUS FORMS OF COMPUTER MEMORY

General specification of memory capacity and performance is a part of the top-level (PMS) design. While the distribution of storage in a system is shown in the PMS design, the determination of how much storage is to be assigned to each memory level is dependent on the capabilities of the different types of memory devices. There are many technologies available for storing digital information. Very early computers used electrostatic storage assembled in banks of capacitors or in cathode-ray storage tubes. Acoustic and magnetostrictive delay lines have been used to store information in the form of waves propagating through the delay-line medium (glass, mercury, and solid metals were employed). Magnetic materials moving under a magnetic detector (head) were introduced early in computer history and remain with us today. For many years the magnetic core, a toroid of magnetic material threaded with electric wires, was the memory technique of choice for high-speed storage devices. Except for very special cases where the "nonvolatility" (its ability to remember even if power is lost) of the magnetic core is needed, core memories have yielded the stage to very-high-density semiconductor devices in very-large-scale integrated (VLSI) circuits. Optical techniques, made more useful with the advent of the laser, and methods where there are interactions between optical and magnetic effects have a place for very-high-capacity long-term storage.

At any point in time there is not a single memory technology that satisfies all requirements. Although it would be convenient if the memory technology that gave adequate speed were low enough in cost to satisfy all memory needs, this has never been true. Memories of sufficient speed to match the electronics of our processors never have been of sufficiently low cost to permit them to be used exclusively. The methods that are of low cost never have been fast enough to satisfy all needs. Now we have semiconductor devices that operate at the speeds of processor electronics. (They are the same as those used in the processor electronics.) We have somewhat slower, but somewhat less expensive, semiconductor memory devices that can be used in larger quantities. (In these circuits the memory elements are capacitors, as in some of the earliest computers.) Memory formed by placing magnetic material on the surface of a disk that rotates under a reading and writing magnetic head can be had in very large quantities at a cost much lower than that of equivalent size semiconductor memories. Magnetic tape still has the advantage (like that of flexible magnetic disks) that it can be separated from the equipment that uses it and stored, allowing for extremely large amounts of information to be stored in a few cubic meters.

This spectrum of memory devices, each having unique cost and performance characteristics, leads to incorporation of a hierarchy of memory devices in a typical computer system. There is a small amount (up to several thousand bytes) of relatively expensive very-high-speed semiconductor memory in the form of registers within the processors. Hundreds of thousands to millions of bytes of less expensive semiconductor elements serve as the primary memory (Mp). Between the two we might have a "cache", or hidden (to the user) store, with characteristics between those of the processor registers and primary memory. When we need more storage than can be provided by primary memory (and we almost always do) and when we need to store information even when the computer power is not on, there is a need for secondary memory (Ms) in the form of disk files with fixed or removable disks or of magnetic tape drives, both with capacities of thousands of millions of bytes. Sometimes we require a memory capability between those of primary and secondary memory and we might introduce an intermediate memory using a small disk file with fixed heads or memory made from one of the techniques that combine semiconductors and magnetic or electrostatic phenonema.

The distribution of storage of various types across the system levels is specified by the computer architect. This distribution is discussed in this chapter. In Chapter 3 we saw where the different memories might fit in the system structure. Here we look at the specifics of memory performance, cost, and size to permit the precise specification of storage for a computer system.

4.2 CHARACTERISTICS OF MEMORY DEVICES

The main characteristics that we are concerned with when examining devices for use in computer memory are the unit cost, the time to initially get at a unit (bit, byte, word, block) of information (the access time), the time between two successive read or write accesses (the cycle time), the sustained rate at which we can move a significant amount (thousands to millions of bits) of information (the transfer rate), and the size of memories that can economically be made (the capacity). We are also concerned with volatility in case of power loss, reliability, and susceptibility to the environment, but will assume that these concerns are being addressed by those doing the detailed design, and will not address these device-level issues.

In order to understand the important characteristics of different memory techniques, we should start with an understanding of how each technique operates. The semiconductor memories that we use in the processor registers and in the primary memory are assembled from transistors diffused into semiconductors (chips), each of which stores from tens of thousands to several million bits of information. Associated with the semiconductor memory are means for addressing the desired register or word and means to hold the information temporarily while it is being stored or after it is read. Access to information in the semiconductor memory devices can be made very quickly and access times range from several to several hundred nanoseconds (10^{-9} s). Successive reads or writes can be made in a time period (the cycle time) about the same as the access time. Since there is very little difference between the time it takes to get information from successive or from widely different locations, this type of memory is called random-access memory (RAM).

In some cases we might want to have memory that can be read from quickly, but do not want its information to be lost. Here we are willing to use special techniques to write into the memory. When writing is accomplished only once by physically changing connections, the memory is known as a read-only memory (ROM). If the interconnection pattern can be programmed to be set, the memory is called a programmable read-only memory (PROM). If rewriting can be accomplished when it is necessary, we have an erasable programmable read-only memory (EPROM). An electronically erasable PROM is abbreviated EEPROM. From the standpoint of access time and cycle time, all of the read-only memories are random-access devices.

Much more information can be held on a surface of magnetic material, such as iron oxide or chromium oxide or a film of magnetizable metal. Here the writing and reading of information requires that the surface (the magnetic medium) be moving across the "heads" that perform the writing and reading. In a write operation, these heads convert electric signals to magnetic codes in the medium. Reading has the opposite effect. The nature of the mechanism for storage and recovery of information requires that magnetic tape and magnetic disk storage devices incorporate physical motion of the media.

When access to a specific piece of information requires physical motion of a reading or writing head and/or of the memory medium, access to the information takes much longer than it does in electronically switched memories. Usually we cannot determine exactly how long it will take for the information desired to be placed under the reading or writing head, since we do not know the position of the information at the time the request is made. Thus, we must be satisfied to know the average time that is taken in getting to the information. For magnetic drums or small disk files, average access times are typically several thousandths of a second. For larger disk files, when there is significant time taken to move the read/write heads, average access is tens of thousandths of a second. In the case of magnetic tape, where it might be necessary to move a large amount of tape past the read/write head before we find the information desired, initial access might take seconds. With the memory devices that require physical motion we design our systems to transfer at one time large amounts of information that is in successive locations on the medium, attempting to make the time it takes to gain access to the first element of information less important.

Block-oriented random-access memories have been developed from time to time. With these devices initial access to information is made by electronic switching at speeds significantly longer than those for semiconductor memory, but still much shorter than that required for a disk file. Transfer rates are equivalent to those of disk files. Two techniques of approximately equal cost and performance are currently available for block-oriented random-access memory. These are the magnetic bubble memory that combines semiconducting and magnetic storage and the charge-coupled devices that transfer electric charge along a semiconductor surface. The lack of commercial success in previous attempts to introduce a form of memory technology between that of primary memory and rotating secondary storage makes most computer designers skeptical about the success of these latest candidates. However, we can expect that people will continue to search for memory technologies to fill the large gap between semiconductor memory and disk storage.

Speed and cost characteristics of memory devices are summarized in Fig. 4-2. In the illustration, access times and the reciprocal of transfer rates (i.e., the interbyte times) are plotted against cost per bit on logarithmic scales. The figure demonstrates the very large differences in unit cost and in speed for the various memory methods. The benefits of transferring large blocks of information to or from the magnetic storage devices can be seen from the fact that interbyte transfer times are very much shorter than the access times for those memory devices. The rapid decline in unit cost of all types of memory should cause us to treat the cost scale of Fig. 4-2 with care. The scale relates to 1987 costs (at the equipment manufacturing level) and should be expected to be reduced by a factor of 2 every 3+ years (a factor of 10 every 10 years), as we will see when we look at cost trends.

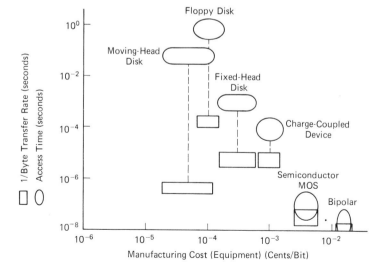

Figure 4-2 Memory technology: speed vs. 1987 unit cost.

Very low unit costs are obtained with disk files by making them with very large capacities. In that manner, the "overhead" cost of the motors, the head-moving mechanisms, the heads, and the magnetic surfaces are distributed over a very large number of bits. In Fig. 4-3 the ranges of capacities of four different memory devices are plotted against the unit manufacturing cost. Again, we note a very wide range in the capacity characteristic. As with the previous figure, the cost information must be adjusted with time to allow for the rapid fall in unit costs over relatively short time periods.

The performance, capacity, and cost data of Figs. 4-2 and 4-3 represent characteristics of the memory equipment. With those memory methods that make use of inexpensive storage media such as magnetic tape or removable disks, the unit cost can be several orders of magnitude smaller if one includes in the bit count all the information that is stored on media not presently mounted on the equipment. This is a suitable way to hold archival data that need not be readily available at all times. Of course, the "access time" for information so stored can be measured in minutes rather than fractions of a second.

There are many applications where large amounts of archival storage are required, but where access times of minutes cannot be tolerated. We continue to find specialized memory devices being developed to fill that need. Examples over the years have included very large (long or wide) magnetic tape systems, magnetic card systems in which the storage medium is a flexible plastic card coated with magnetic material, and banks of magnetic tape drives with automatic feeding and retrieval systems for the reels of tape. All of these storage devices have tended to be very complicated, rather specialized in characteristics, and not very reliable. As a result, acceptance has been limited to those users who have no reasonable alternatives. For archival storage where information does not have to be changed once it is recorded or where there is relatively little change, optical storage techniques are used. Optical disks using a photosensitive medium have capacities above those of the large magnetic disk files with comparable access times and significantly lower costs. The improvements in optical resolution attainable with laser writing and reading techniques have resulted in a new generation of optical storage equipments.

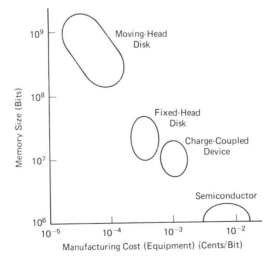

Figure 4-3 Memory technology: capacity vs. 1987 unit cost.

Combinations of lasers and magnetic thin-film technology offer promise for modifiable archival memory.

Evidence that one must consider system lifetimes in using memory cost data is shown in Fig. 4-4, a semilogarithmic plot of primary memory unit manufacturing cost against time for the past 20 years. Also shown is the history of cycle times of primary-memory techniques. We note that unit costs consistently have fallen by a factor of 10 each decade. That is roughly equivalent to halving every three years. At the same time, memories have become faster at a rate of around 10 times every 15 years. The combination of these effects results in a doubling of performance per unit cost every two years. As we will see when discussing technology trends for processor logic in a later chapter, equivalent performance–cost growth also has taken place there. Appreciation of these trends is of utmost importance when developing a new computer. We must realize that the computer we are starting to design now will compete with systems available from competitors several years from now. We cannot do our competitive cost and performance analyses by comparing with today's systems. We must forecast a continuation of the trends we have seen for over 20 years. Of course, we can expect the electronic technologies in our own organization to follow those trends, too. The mechanisms we find available for implementing our architecture will be more advanced, but we must be sure that our architecture takes advantage of the advancing technology.

The position in the computer system of the various types of storage were reviewed in Chapter 3. There we saw that the fastest and the highest-cost storage devices are the registers and the flip-flops used in the processor. Next in the hierarchy (in the direction of lower speed and lower unit cost) are the approaches used to implement the cache memory that serves as a buffer between the processors and the primary memory. Primary memory, or *main memory*, is the computer's working memory, where the active programs and data for those programs reside. The secondary memory is a lower-cost and larger-size extension of primary memory, in which programs and data are held in reserve and moved into primary memory as needed. Processor support for management of the interaction between the primary- and secondary-memory units is discussed in Chapters 5 and 6. Sometimes there will be a need for storage capability between the primary and the secondary memories. This can be provided by an

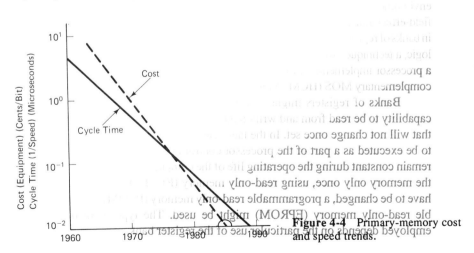

Figure 4-4 Primary-memory cost and speed trends.

intermediate store. Finally, the least expensive, the slowest, and the largest memory devices are those used for archival (or tertiary) storage.

Examples of system organizations with the various levels of memory are shown in the PMS diagrams of Chapter 3. There are no specific rules to allow us to establish how much storage should be provided at each level of the hierarchy. The allocation depends on the results of an evaluation of cost–performance trade-offs that consider alternative system configurations and memory technologies. It is influenced strongly by the specific memory equipment available to the system designer. A rationale for establishing the amount of storage at each level is developed and examples of memory distribution in several successful computers are shown in Section 4.9.

4.3 PROCESSOR STORAGE

Within central processors, input/output processors and controllers, and special-purpose processors, we find flip-flops, individual registers, and banks of registers for holding information that is in immediate use. The quantities of storage range from tens to several thousands of bits. This very-high-speed storage is implemented with the same electronics as used in the rest of the processor logic or with a slightly slower and less expensive form of electronics.

Individual flip-flops and small registers are made from semiconductor logic gate components. There are two generic forms of semiconductor device, the metal-oxide semiconductor (MOS) and the bipolar semiconductor. Metal-oxide semiconductors often are specified further as to whether the semiconductor material into which the device itself is diffused is negative (NMOS), positive (PMOS), or a combination of the two, in which case the device is said to be complementary (CMOS). When they are made with techniques that permit higher speed, they are identified as high-speed MOS (HMOS) devices. Most of today's bipolar semiconductors incorporate transistor–transistor logic (TTL) (possibly with Schottky-diode speedup) or emitter-coupled logic (ECL). For applications requiring very fast switching or operation under severe environmental conditions, we might find specialized semiconductors, such as gallium arsenide field-effect transistors (GaAsFET) used for the logic. When processor storage can be assembled in banks of registers that are on semiconductor components separate from the rest of the processor logic, a technique different from that of the logic might be used. As an example, we might find a processor implemented with high-speed TTL for the logic and controls and with high-speed complementary MOS (HCMOS) for the local memory banks.

Banks of registers might be organized as random-access memory (RAM) with the capability to be read from and written into or they might be designed to contain information that will not change once set. In the latter case, used for control stores that hold instructions to be executed as a part of the processor control or for constant stores that hold values that remain constant during the operating life of the computer, the information might be placed in the memory only once, using read-only memory (ROM). When values occasionally might have to be changed, a programmable read-only memory (PROM) or an erasable programmable read-only memory (EPROM) might be used. The type of memory implementation employed depends on the particular use of the register bank.

The uses of storage in the processors is a major topic covered in Chapters 5 and 6. There we see how processor memory is used for multiple accumulators, for holding base locations for primary-memory addressing (base registers), for memory-address indexing (index registers), for a combination of those uses (general registers), or for special buffers such as instruction lookahead queues. Many contemporary computers have controls that use microprogramming with a microprogram "control store" made from banks of RAM, ROM, or PROM registers.

Examples of processor memory banks are shown in Fig. 4-5, demonstrating the large general-register set of the Unisys 1100 computers, and in Fig. 4-6, showing the three specialized register banks of the Control Data Cyber series. The Unisys proces-

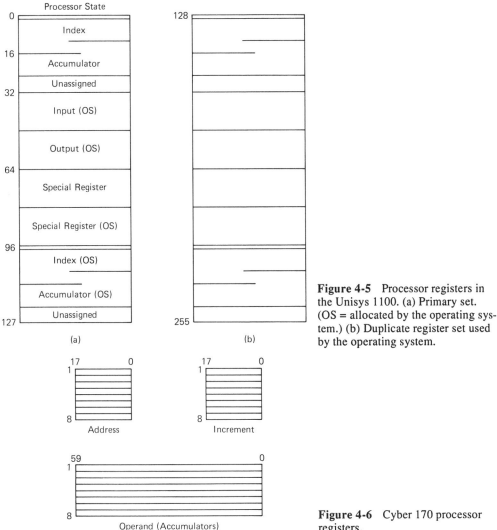

Figure 4-5 Processor registers in the Unisys 1100. (a) Primary set. (OS = allocated by the operating system.) (b) Duplicate register set used by the operating system.

Figure 4-6 Cyber 170 processor registers.

sors contain 256 registers. These 36-bit registers are truly general-purpose at the hardware level. The operating-system software introduces a specialization in assignment. Half of the registers are assigned exclusively for use by the operating system. The user-level registers are assigned special roles by the operating system, which also controls many of them during program execution. In the Cyber systems three different memory banks are used for memory base addressing, for memory-reference indexing, and for operands.

4.4 PRIMARY-MEMORY ORGANIZATION

Most primary memories of contemporary computers are constructed from semiconductor components. The exceptions are computers with specialized applications requiring "nonvolatile" memory that retains its information when there is no electrical power supplied and computers that must operate under extreme temperature conditions. In some of these cases magnetic-core techniques are still used. Whereas some of the very fast computers employ the faster and more expensive bipolar semiconductors in transistor–transistor logic (TTL) and emitter-coupled logic (ECL) devices, most primary memory uses metal-oxide semiconductor (MOS) devices implemented as dynamic random-access memory (DRAM). DRAM devices use capacitors for storage and require that information be rewritten ("refreshed") periodically, resulting in an increase of the effective cycle time. Semiconductor memory that is made from transistor flip-flops and does not require refreshing is known as static random-access memory (SRAM).

The organization of a typical semiconductor memory module is shown in Fig. 4-7. The module shown has n words of m bits each. The figure omits the details of the electronic interfacing devices that are required. The memory cells are contained in semiconductor components each containing from 64 kbits to several million bits configured in $64k \times 1$, $64k \times 4$, $256k \times 1$, $256k \times 4$, or similar organizations. (The main factor in lower semiconductor memory unit cost over time is the increase in the number of memory bits in an individual semiconductor component, the chip.) Each memory component contains an address decoder and a read/write buffer, as well as the circuitry (not shown) to control the read and the write operations. A memory module consists of the

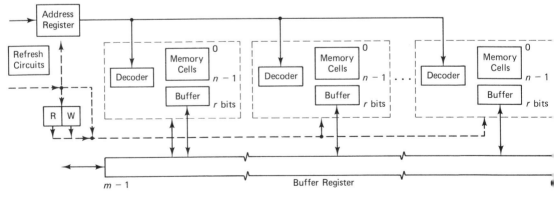

Figure 4-7   Components of semiconductor primary memory.

quantity of memory components (*m/r* in the figure) required to assemble the specified number of memory words. The module also contains the address register, a word-buffer register, the circuitry needed to "refresh" the cells (if DRAM is being used), and the read/write control circuits. The addressing and buffering circuits consume time during a read or a write instruction execution and result in cycle times longer than those for the semiconductor components themselves.

A typical memory printed-circuit board has from one-third to two-thirds of its surface devoted to the memory-cell circuits. The rest is for the addressing, buffering, interfacing, refreshing, and control circuits. This overhead of circuits on the printed-circuit board, of connectors and wiring to interconnect printed-circuit boards, of power supplies and cabinets is what makes the unit memory manufacturing cost higher than the cost of the memory components by a factor of about 2. The result is a range of economical sizes and "shapes" for memory modules, determined by the relative cost of all the individual functional parts. A 4-kword memory has a higher unit cost than a 64-kword memory. It might not be feasible economically to assemble a primary memory from a large quantity of small modules even if it is desirable from a performance standpoint. This is only one of the trade-offs that must be considered by the computer architect working with the memory designers.

In the opening section of this chapter we reviewed the trends in primary-memory size, performance, and cost. Despite the rapid and continuing drop in memory unit cost, the growth in memory capacity in typical systems results in primary memory consuming an increasing percentage of the cost of the central computer (i.e., the Pc, Mp, Kio, and associated switches). This is because processor and controller costs per unit of performance are dropping about as rapidly as are memory unit costs. Coupled with the increase in primary-memory sizes is the associated rapid growth of secondary-memory capacities. The combination is increasing the relative importance of storage to total system hardware costs.

Memory addressing is initiated in the processors, but the organization of the memory modules influences how the translation from logical addresses to physical addresses is accomplished. A physical location (address) is generally specified as the combination of a base address that identifies the beginning of an area of memory, an index that can change on each pass through a repeated sequence of instructions, and the offset specified by the computer instruction. This combination is illustrated in Fig. 4-8. The organization of the primary memory determines how the various fields are combined

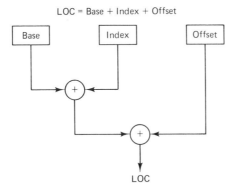

Figure 4-8 Typical primary-memory addressing.

relative to the physical structure of the memory. The addressing mechanism is important when we must provide means to coordinate addressing at the program level (logical address) with that at the hardware level (physical address). This subject is covered in a later section of this chapter.

Physical memory often is separated into functionally independent modules for the purposes of increased speed, for flexibility to change primary-memory size, and for increased reliability. There are two approaches to gaining performance increases through modular memory organization. With the first method, which we call *high-order inter-leaving*, successive memory addresses are contained in a single module, so that the higher-order bits of the physical address specify the module and the remaining bits specify the address offset within the module, as shown in Fig. 4-9(a). The performance increase over that of a single memory module results from the probability that instructions, reference tables, and data reside in different modules. (This separation can be forced by the operating system.) Thus, there is reduced opportunity for a memory reference for an instruction to have to wait for the completion of a reference to a table or to data. It is difficult to calculate the benefits of high-order interleaving without examining execution of sample programs in typical problem mixes since the effects are dependent on the distribution of programs and data among modules.

The other approach to modular memory organization, known as *low-order inter-leaving*, takes advantage of the "locality" of programs and data, the characteristic that a data item as well as an instruction tends to be in a memory location very close to that of the last item of data or instruction. In this case, successive memory locations are in different modules, as shown in Fig. 4-9(b). Here the higher-order bits specify the physical

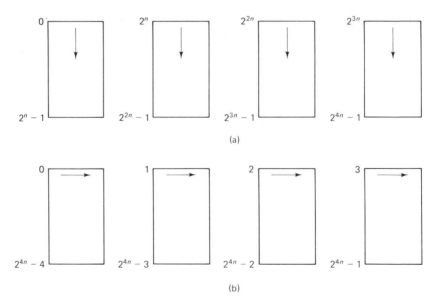

Figure 4-9   Memory-module interleaving. (a) High-order, address = module, offset. (b) Low-order, address = offset, module.

offset in a module and the low-order bits designate the memory module. We have true interleaving of successive instruction fetches. A stream of memory words can be transferred to a processor at a rate higher than that which would result with a memory module containing successive addresses. This approach is used in many high-performance computers with an effect very similar to that attained by using a physical memory word that is a multiple of the processor instruction (or data) words. It is possible with this approach to consider the interleaving when calculating the execution time of small program sequences.

It is difficult to make a general judgment about which of the two interleaving approaches is superior. The first certainly yields higher system reliability, since computation can continue when a module is not operating if its contents can be retrieved from secondary memory and placed in another module. The necessity to use statistical methods to forecast the memory-access overlap makes it difficult to argue for the performance of the high-order approach as compared with low-order interleaving. When considering the approaches, it is most important that we incorporate a memory organization that is compatible with the structure of the rest of the computer system and with the ISP-level organization of the processors. The memory must be organized to accommodate the features of the rest of the system.

Another issue relative to memory addressing is that of access to parts of memory words, such as bytes, individual bits, or instruction syllables. We must decide whether the part-word addressing is accomplished in the memory, imposing a requirement for more control logic there, or whether it is done in the processor after a whole word has been transferred. Small computers with 16-bit data words often use byte-level addressing of memory with bytes or pairs of bytes transferred to the processor in one access cycle. With higher-performance machines the time required to do the part-word addressing in the memory module usually is significant to performance and transfers of full words or multiple words are usually made.

Increasingly, designers are using a special-purpose processor, a memory-management unit (MMU), to handle memory addressing. The MMU is of particular use in coordinating byte, word, and multiword transfers. It also facilitates the design of different computers using standard microprocessor and memory components. Typical functions of an MMU include segment and page control (to be discussed in Section 4.8), separation of user(s) and operating-system space, and hardware support for memory protection. Memory-management processors are covered in Chapter 7.

4.5 THE CACHE

Earlier we stated that there might be a place for storage that is less expensive than the processor registers and faster than primary memory. The objective of such a store is to reduce the quantity of accesses to main memory by taking advantage of the "locality" of instructions in a sequence and of data items. If we can hold the most recently used information in a small fast memory that is easily accessible by the processor, we should be able to reduce the number of primary-memory references and make it appear that the system has a very fast primary memory. This local storage, the *cache*, becomes a buffer between the processor and primary memory.

The effect of the cache is similar to that of a large bank of general registers in the processor. With the registers, however, control of the interaction with primary memory is by instructions of the program. The cache memory usually is considerably larger than a general-register bank, and transfers between the cache and primary memory are automatic. The cache should operate as a lookaside store that can be queried to see if the desired information resides there before the longer time access to main memory is made. Of course, if it takes too long to make the query our objective is not satisfied. We might just as well have gone directly to primary memory and ignored the cache.

If we had an economical way to accomplish it, the best way to operate the cache is to use a content-addressable memory that would hold both the location in main memory to be accessed and the value stored at that location. The cache would be queried by sending it the address. If it held the designated address, it would respond by indicating "present" while it accepted the value on a write instruction or delivered the data on a read instruction. Almost from the origin of the digital computer, there has been a search for an economical content-addressable, or fully-associative, memory. So far, all such memories that work satisfactorily have had unit cost several times that of equivalent-speed random-access memories. The search continues.

In the absence of a means to attain content addressability in the memory itself, it is possible to approximate the effect by adding search logic to the cache-memory controls. One way to do this is shown in Fig. 4-10. With the "direct-mapped" cache organization, the main memory is divided into areas of uniform size, each having the same size as that of the cache (2^r lines of 2^m words in the figure). Addressing within each area is relative to the origin of the area and is the same as the address in the cache relative to its origin. A separate memory can hold a "tag" for each location of the cache that indicates in which of the 2^n areas of main memory is the data that is stored at that cache address.

The operation of the direct-mapped cache proceeds as follows: when a memory read instruction is executed the main memory and the cache are sent an address containing a tag field (the n higher-order bits), a line field (the physical memory word relative address of r bits), and a word field (m bits for selection within the line). The line field is transmitted to the decoder that causes the content of the tag memory and the cache data memory to be transferred to their respective buffers. If the tag so obtained matches the tag field of the memory address, the comparator signifies "hit" (the information is in the cache) and the reference to main memory is inhibited. The word field is then used by a decoder to select the specific word desired in the line that is in the cache data buffer. If there is no "hit" main memory must be accessed to obtain the information requested. At the same time, the cache is updated by placing the line of information received in the cache data memory and the tag field in the tag memory.

The problem with this very simple way to approximate content addressability is that there might be requests alternating between two locations that have the same line address (but different tags). When this happens, the first information must be overwritten to allow the next to get the position in the cache. Then a request for the first finds that the information no longer resides in the cache and must be obtained from main memory. We have a conflict for use of a cache location and do not get the benefits of the high-speed cache memory.

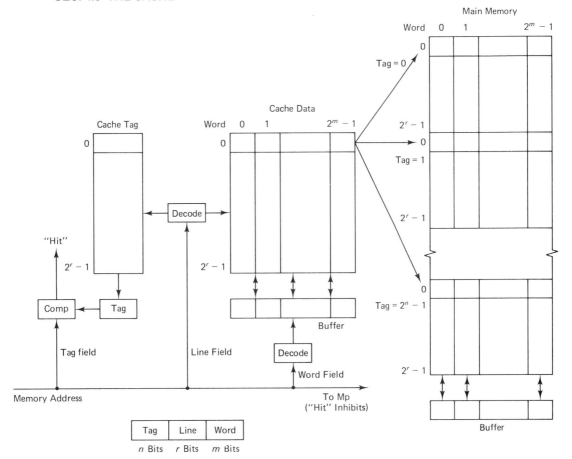

Figure 4-10   A direct-mapped cache.

A solution to the cache-conflict problem is to introduce search logic that allows us to implement a fully associative cache, as shown in Fig. 4-11. Here the tag is sufficiently large to hold the full address of a physical memory word (equal to the tag and line fields of Fig. 4-10). The tag memory is addressed separately from the cache data memory. When a memory read request is initiated the tag field is presented to the association logic, which searches the tag memory to see if that tag is present. If so, a "hit" is indicated and the location in tag memory where the tag was found is transmitted to the cache data memory as an address where the requested line is to be found. Since the information from any memory line can be held in any line location in the cache, there are no cache conflicts until the cache is full. The effect is the same as that obtained with a true content-addressable memory. Compared with the direct-mapped implementation, however, extensive logic is required to perform the associative search or significant time is needed to do a sequential search.

A compromise is shown in Fig. 4-12. In this "set-associative" approach the main memory is divided into 2^n smaller areas as with the direct-mapped cache. The cache is

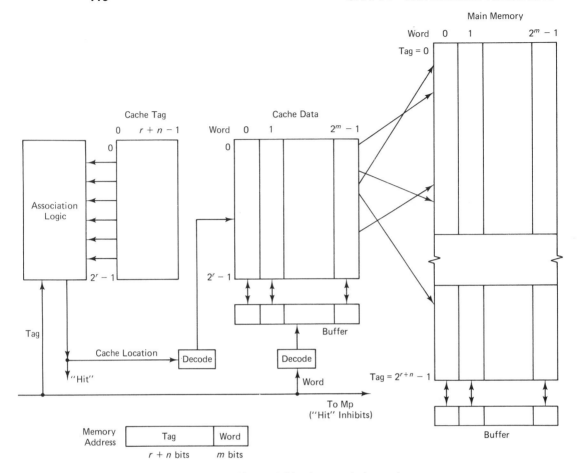

Figure 4-11   An associative cache.

organized into 2^s similar sections (sets) and operates as if it is 2^s direct-mapped cache memories. If there are 2^s sections it is possible for 2^s lines of information that have the same line address to reside in different sections of the cache. Operation is as with the direct-mapped cache, except that all 2^s comparators are queried simultaneously. If there is a "hit" the comparator that detected it is identified to show which of the cache data sections holds the information. It is seen that the limits of the set-associative cache as s goes from 0 to r are the direct-mapped cache ($s = 0$) and the fully associative cache ($s = r$). In the latter case there are no line addresses, as we saw in Fig. 4-11.

In the set-associative cache the larger the number of sections in the cache, the less likely that we will have a conflict for a location with a given line address. However, the smaller individual sections have the effect of making cache use less efficient since there are not as many different line addresses.

The designer must evaluate alternatives to cache design to find the optimum solution for the system being examined. An example of a study of this type, performed

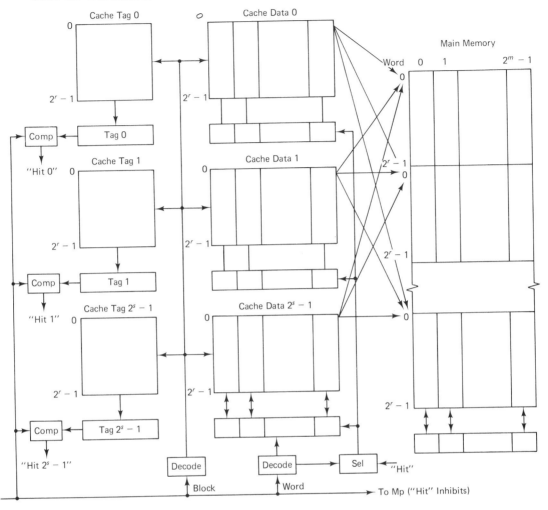

Figure 4-12 Set-associative cache organization.

by cache designers at Intel when the 80386 processor was developed, is shown in Fig. 4-13. The baseline for the study was a 16-Mbyte "pipelined" random-access main memory using 4 clock-time DRAMs. (The pipeline is a queue of memory requests. We discuss pipeline organizations in Chapter 6.) The other limit is attained by assembling main memory from high-speed (2 clock time) static devices (SRAMs), which shows a 47% improvement in performance over the baseline. This is consistent with other simulations that show that memory speed affects computer performance as the square root of the inverse of memory-access time. The optimal cache provides computer performance equivalent to that of a SRAM primary memory.

In all cases the cache memory itself is small enough to operate with a 1 clock cycle time. An added clock time is needed to check for a hit, and the effective speed of the cache

Cache Configuration			Cache Performance	
Size (kbytes)	Associativity	Line Size (bytes)	Hit Rate (%)	Improvement
1	Direct	4	41	0.91
8	Direct	4	73	1.25
16	Direct	4	81	1.35
32	Direct	4	86	1.38
32	2-way	4	87	1.39
32	Direct	8	91	1.41
64	Direct	4	88	1.39
64	2-way	4	89	1.40
64	4-way	4	89	1.40
64	Direct	8	92	1.42
64	2-way	8	93	1.42
128	Direct	4	89	1.39
128	2-way	4	89	1.40
128	Direct	8	93	1.42

No cache–2 clock SRAM access   100   1.47
No cache–4 clock pipelined DRAM   1.00

SRAM = Static random-access memory
DRAM = Dynamic random-access memory

Figure 4-13 Example performance data on cache memory. (Copyright 1985, Intel Corp., reprinted with permission.)

is the same as that of SRAM primary memory. Let us go through an example with the 16-kbyte direct-mapped cache to demonstrate the effect on performance. If a read reference finds the item in cache (a hit), the memory cycle time is 2 clock times (cache cycle). A hit occurs on about 81% of the read references. Otherwise (19% of the time), the primary-memory reference is completed, which takes 4 clock times. The effective memory speed is 2.36 clock times ($0.81 \times 2 + 0.19 \times 4$).

The figure shows the improvement attainable for various size caches with direct-mapped, two-way ($s = 1$) set-associative, and four-way ($s = 2$) set-associative caches, and with various line sizes (in bytes). The evaluation shows that a direct-mapping cache can be quite effective as long as the size is sufficiently large. The Intel simulations assumed a main memory of 16-Mbyte capacity. To attain at least a 70% hit rate (the minimum the designers felt was needed to be worth introducing cache) a cache of at least 8 kbytes is needed.

In the illustrations of cache memory in Figs. 4-10 to 4-12, lines of m words are transferred between the cache and primary memory. The size of the line (ranging from one word up) is determined by the primary-memory design; the cache design uses the same size lines. Where the lines do contain more than one word, we note that the characteristic of "locality" again is beneficial in reducing memory accesses since several successive words reside in a single line. We note that in the Intel simulations (Fig. 4-13) there is a measurable improvement in hit rate as the line size goes from 4 to 8 bytes with any given size cache with direct mapping.

Primary memory made from SRAM devices has a cost 6 to 8 times that of equal-size DRAM-based memory. (The devices themselves cost 10 to 12 times as much.) The smaller cache memories made with SRAM cost about twice as much as a large SRAM memory. This is due in part to the smaller size (a greater percent of the memory cost is due to the ancillary circuits) and in part to the added bits required for the tag field in each word.

The discussion of cache memory so far has focused on memory read operations. The cache can be used during write operations as well, but a new issue is introduced. When we use the cache for improving memory write performance we must determine whether we will write a copy of the cache content into primary memory each time we have a write (we do not inhibit the write on a "hit"). This is known as a "writethrough" operation. The alternative is to write to main memory only when it is necessary to overwrite into a cache data register that has been the subject of a write (called "writeback"). In the first case we impose a small delay on a memory operation that follows the write (unless it is inhibited by a cache hit) on each write operation. In the latter case a significant time is taken for writing, but only at the time that we need to reuse the cache register. A decision on using writethrough or writeback is influenced by many aspects of the memory and processor designs and can only be made intelligently after simulation of alternatives has been performed.

With the set-associative cache (or a fully associative cache), when we must overwrite into a cache location because that location is needed for information from a line having another tag, we face a question of which of the items now in cache should be overwritten. This replacement issue is similar to that faced in determining which block should be removed in a paged memory operating system. The three main alternatives are to remove the least recently used information (LRU strategy), to overwrite the oldest information no matter when (or if) it was used, or just to select randomly a line for overwriting. If we have decided on a writeback strategy for handling writes we might want a strategy that treats lines that have been subject to writes differently from those that have not in order to reduce the need for writing into memory. (This is similar to the treatment of "dirty," modified, vs. "clean," unchanged, pages in a paged memory system.) The simulations needed to decide between writeback and writethrough can include the parameters needed to decide on a replacement strategy.

Finally, we must determine whether our cache memory is to be used only for data objects or for both data and instructions. The cache is as useful for instructions as for data, but we might find a better way to perform the instruction buffering to cause the instruction stream to flow at the maximum speed. Some microprocessors incorporate multiple caches for different purposes, such as data, instructions, addresses, and/or a stack. Instruction lookahead is covered in Chapter 5.

The uses of the cache memory imply that it should be placed close to the processor in the system in order that delays in access can be minimized. It is easy to place the cache at the processor in a uniprocessor system, as long as we make sure that there is no interference between the central-processor cache and information transmitted to and from memory and the input/output controllers. In a large multiprocessor system, placing the cache with the processor can impose coordination difficulties, as we saw in Chapter 3. On the other hand, making the cache a part of the primary-memory system, while it eliminates the need for comparing the contents of several caches, introduces the processor–memory switch communication delays between the processor and the cache. The difficulty of optimizing the location of the cache in a multiprocessor system leads many parallel-computer designers to use multicomputer, rather than multiprocessor, organizations with small fast local primary memory in each computer and with a large shared memory for intercomputer coordination. These organizations are reviewed in the discussion of parallel computers in Chapter 8.

4.6 SECONDARY AND ARCHIVAL MEMORY

Despite the ever-increasing capacities of primary memories (see Fig. 4-1), there is a need for larger storage mechanisms than can be provided economically by primary memory. This need is growing about as rapidly as is the capacity of primary memories, as is reflected by the growth in capacity of disk files. For example, the IBM 2302 disk file used with the System/360 in the mid-1960s had a capacity of 112 Mbytes (access time: 107 ms, transfer rate: 156 kbytes/s). By the early 1970s the System/370 used the model 3330 disk file with a capacity of 200 Mbytes (access time: 38.4 ms, transfer rate: 806 kbytes/s). The 303X and 308X processing systems of the 1980s could use the model 3380 disk file with a capacity of 1260 Mbytes (access time: 24.3 ms, transfer rate: 3 Mbytes/s). In 1987 IBM extended the capacity of the 3380 to 7.5 gigabytes (7.5×2^{30}) for the 3090 system by tripling the bit density on the medium. The capacity of disk files has doubled every six years. Over the same 20-year period magnetic tape has retained the same basic size standards, but the drives have seen increased densities (from 1600 to 6400 bits/in) and faster tape speeds (120 to over 150 in/s). At the same time the computer systems are able to handle more disk and tape drives and system capacity for secondary memory has increased at a very rapid rate.

Interaction between the primary and the secondary memories is a major consideration of the system designer. The functional interaction is covered in Section 4.8. Here we are concerned with the physical interaction, the physical transfer of information between the two different levels of memory. The different characteristics of the memories at the two levels are centered on the very short access times and short interword-transfer times of primary memory and the long access times and the high block-transfer rates of the secondary memories. Figure 4-14 shows examples of the differences. We note that the random-access memory (primary memory) is characterized by access times about the same as the cycle times (one-half in the examples of Fig. 4-14). Transfer rates of random-access memories in words per second are the reciprocals of cycle times if there is no word interlacing or the reciprocals of access times with interlacing. The direct-access devices (disk files) have average access times (the time for head movement and for disk rotation) measured in tens of milliseconds and transfer rates of several million bytes per second. The serial-access mechanisms (magnetic tape drives) have access times of several

Type Memory	Average Access Time (s)	Block Transfer (s)	
		4 kbytes	1 Mbyte
Mp: 8-byte wd[1]	10^{-7}	10.2×10^{-5}	2.6×10^{-2}
Mp: 64-byte wd[2]	10^{-7}	6.4×10^{-6}	1.6×10^{-3}
Ms.disk[3]	2.5×10^{-2}	2.6×10^{-2}	3.8×10^{-1}
Ms.tape[4]	10^{1}	1×10^{1}	1.2×10^{1}

1. 64-bit/wd DRAM, 100-ns access, 200-ns cycle, no interleave.
2. 64-bit/wd DRAM, 100-ns access, 200-ns cycle, 8-wd interleave.
3. Disk, 15 surfaces, 3600 rpm, 45 kbyte/track, 2.8 Mbyte/s.
4. Magnetic tape drive, 3200 bit/in, 150 in/s, 450 kbyte/s.

Figure 4-14   Typical memory access times and transfer rates.

seconds (to move the tape to the start of a block) and transfer rates of almost a million bytes per second.

In Fig. 4-14 the average access times and the times it takes to make initial access and then to transfer two different-size blocks of information are shown. Of interest here are the differences in access times and in block-transfer times for the three different memory types. A "steady-state" flow of information can be attained when there is a reasonable balance in block-transfer times among the memories.

We are interested also in the percentage of available memory cycles used for transfers between secondary and primary memories when blocks are being transferred. For this we compare the transfer rates of the devices, ignoring the initial access times. When a block is transferred from the magnetic tape drive to the 8-byte/word primary memory, only about 1% of the memory cycles available are needed for the transfer (450 kbytes/s ÷ 40,000 kbytes/s [8 bytes in 200 ns] = 0.011). In the case of transfers between the disk file and primary memory, the transfers use about 7% of the memory cycles of the 8-byte/word memory (2.8 Mbytes/s ÷ 40 Mbytes/s), but less than 0.5% of the cycles with the larger memory (2.8 Mbytes/s ÷ 640 Mbytes/s [64 bytes in 100 ns]). When the amount of "cycle stealing" for secondary-memory transfers is low, there is little reduction in memory performance due to those transfers.

With the growth of secondary-memory capacities, allowing connection of several gigabytes on even medium-size systems, we must be concerned with means to address secondary memory effectively. Development of the physical address is accomplished in the processor and is a factor in our ISP design, to be covered in Chapter 5. At this point, as an introduction to the issues faced in coordinating memory transfers, we should look at the ways that might be used to address blocks of storage in primary and secondary memories. An example of physical-block addressing for primary and secondary memories is shown in Fig. 4-15. The example considers the addressing of a primary memory with 4k 4-kbyte blocks (16 Mbyte) and 16-Gbyte secondary memory implemented with sixteen 1-Gbyte disk file modules.

In primary memory we must be able to identify the block for transfers to and from secondary memory and to establish a location within the block for byte addressing. The memory itself might be addressed to the word (perhaps 4 bytes) with byte identity within a word handled in processor registers. We do not have to address secondary memory to the word or byte level, but merely must gain access to 4-kbyte (1-kword) blocks. The addressing format of the example shows the block address in primary memory as a 12-bit

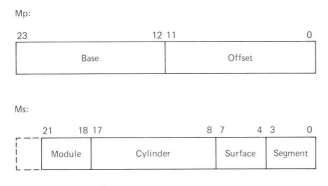

Figure 4-15 Memory block addressing.

base address with the 12-bit byte address concatenated with the base to form a 24-bit memory address. Secondary memory is addressed by specifying the module (4 bits), the cylinder (the same track on each of the surfaces within a disk file) (10 bits), the surface (4 bits), and the segment (an arc of a track holding the 4096-byte block)(4 bits). The combination of 22 bits allows us to address each of the 4096k 4-kbyte blocks and we have two additional bits in a 24-bit address field to allow for specifying this or some other assemblage of peripheral equipment. Beyond the module address, the cylinder and the surface addressing might not be separated in as orderly a way as is shown if the quantities of cylinders and surfaces are not integer powers of 2.

While the example shows that the same size address can be used to specify locations in primary and secondary memories, in most computers secondary-memory addressing is even more flexible, since the address of a segment is contained in a full memory word in a table held in special registers or in primary memory. The segment is accessed indirectly through the table.

Direct-access devices like disk files impose more constraints than random-access memory because of the physical motion of the heads and of the disk surfaces. The direct-access memory units are unidirectional; the disk cannot be stopped and reversed. The other major form of secondary memory, the magnetic tape drive, has its own set of constraints. Magnetic tape can be stopped and started. It can be read from (or written to) in either direction. However, the time required to stop and to restart the tape and the difficulty of maintaining the required bit-to-bit spacing if we allow writing in both directions limits what can be done in practice. Standard magnetic tape reels are 2400 ft long and can hold up to 0.18 Gbyte of information. The information cannot be packed continuously at the packing density specified. Interblock gaps of 9/16 in are provided so that there is space for the tape to be stopped and restarted between blocks. There is space at each end of the tape to allow for an end-of-tape indicator to prevent attempts to operate past the ends.

If we start from one end of the tape it can take almost 200 seconds to reach a block at the other end if the tape is operating at its read/write speed of 150 in/s. Even with the read/write heads retracted the time it takes to move from one end of the tape to the other is very long. It is difficult to speak of average access times with magnetic tape and information must be organized to allow for the particular characteristics of this memory medium. Most computer systems use magnetic tape as a backup to magnetic disk files. Magnetic tape drives have become a tertiary level store, with transfers of very large amounts of information between the disk files and the tape (using primary memory as a buffer) occurring very infrequently. In recognition of this use of magnetic tape storage a simpler form of magnetic tape drive, the "streaming" tape unit, has been developed. The streaming form of drive is unidirectional and is not designed to stop and restart often. As a result, streaming tape drives can be much less expensive than the bidirectional start–stop drives. For microcomputers the magnetic tape cassette becomes a simple single-channel streaming tape.

Beyond secondary memory in our hierarchy of computer storage we find a place for archival storage, memory that is seldom used but is needed to provide a library for long-term future reference. Characteristics required of memory at this level are long life without attention and very low unit cost. Since the information is not often referenced it is satisfactory if writing into memory takes a significant amount of time. The information is not changed often, if at all, so facility of writing is not important. Low cost and nonvolatility are the key criteria for measuring techniques for archival storage.

Optical storage methods have been used for several decades to implement long-term permanent storage. These archival storage devices record pulses of light on a photosensitive film that is on the surface of a reflective or transparent disk. The information is stored permanently once recorded, making the method suitable for archives of information to be kept for many years. By introducing the high optical resolution of lasers and/or holographic recording very large quantities of information can be stored.

Magnetic-tape drives that record on extra wide (>1 in) tape have been used for long-term storage of larger quantities of information than can be contained on standard tape. Archival stores also have been built with magnetic-tape drives and tape reel handling equipment to stow and to retrieve the tapes automatically. So far there are no standards for archival storage. The applications are specialized and no one technique has turned out to have the combination of performance, reliability, low unit cost, and ease of operation needed to have it stand out as a single candidate for archival storage. As with content-addressable memory, the search continues.

4.7 INTERMEDIATE STORES AND SECONDARY-MEMORY BUFFERING

In many systems there is a need for another type of store, analogous to the cache memory that resides between the processor registers and primary memory in cost and capability. This is the *intermediate store* that serves as a buffer between primary memory and secondary memory. There always has been a question whether there is a place for memory at this level. In some large systems where there is a wide gap between the capabilities of primary and secondary memories, system designers have seen an opportunity to provide an intermediate store with access time less than that of rotating files and higher than that of random-access memory, with reasonably fast block-transfer rates, and with costs between those of secondary- and primary-memory devices.

When core memories with 1- or 2-microsecond cycle times were used for primary memory, large ("bulk") core memories with 4- to 8-microsecond cycle times and with unit costs one-half or less than those of primary core memory were popular. High-speed (8-ms access time) drums also served a role between core and semiconductor memories and large disk files. Head-per-track disk files that do not require motion of the head assemblies have replaced drum memories as high-speed magnetic storage devices. The average access time of the head-per-track disk files is dependent on their rate of rotation, since head selection is controlled by electronic switching. On the other hand, it is not feasible to build very large secondary stores with head-per-track techniques since the head and electronics costs make the unit costs higher than those of large moving-head disk files. Fixed-head disk files have access times about one-third of those of the secondary-memory files and they have unit costs of 8 to 10 times those of the moving-head disk files.

Electronically switched block-oriented random-access memories have been investigated for many years. The bulk core memories were examples of this type of storage.

Other approaches used thin magnetic films and delay lines for storage to meet these requirements. More recently there have been two candidates vying to satisfy the requirements for intermediate memory. Magnetic bubble memory uses electromagnetic fields to concentrate a magnetic domain that holds a bit of information at a location in a magnetic film on a semiconductor substrate. An individual domain becomes a "cell" containing one bit of information that can be moved along the substrate by electrical pulses. Bubble memories were felt to have much promise during the late 1970s and early 1980s, but have been overtaken by improvements in semiconductor memory. Charge-coupled devices, on which a localized electrostatic charge is held on a semiconductor surface and can be moved under electrical signal control, offer promise to satisfy the requirements for a memory a little less expensive and a little less capable than bipolar or metal-oxide semiconductor memories. Whether the production difficulties of these devices can be solved before the inevitable reduction in unit cost of semiconductor memory has caught the new devices remains open to question. So often techniques that are outside the "main stream" of electronic technology have indicated much promise only to fall by the wayside as the mainstream of technology advances.

Alternatives to an intermediate store for disk file to primary-memory buffering can be provided by specialized random-access memory units. Disk-drive controllers of the VAX 8000 series of computers contain up to 256 kbytes of semiconductor memory to operate as a speed buffer between the disk files and primary memory. IBM also provides a cache in disk-drive controllers. In the case of the 8380 drive systems a cache of up to 256 Mbytes is available. With the 3090 system IBM introduced "expansion" storage, semiconductor memory that communicates with primary memory and with secondary memory in 4-kbyte blocks. The expansion storage of a 3090 system can be as large as 256 Mbytes. Expansion storage also is used for processor-to-processor communication in multiprocessor 3090 systems.

4.8 VIRTUAL-MEMORY METHODS

In Section 4.4 (see Fig. 4-8) a distinction was made between logical addressing (the address space of a program) and physical addressing (the address space of the machine). This distinction has been extended to allow different processes or users that are active in a computer to share the same physical memory space or for a single process or user to have a large logical address space implemented one or more parts at a time in a smaller physical memory. The logical address space in these instances is called "virtual" memory.

Virtual-memory management should not be the concern of the program writer. It is desirable that the user who programs in a higher-level language not need to have any concern about the physical levels of storage. As with other features of the computer hardware, memory management should be the concern of the operating system and language translators. The computer architect can provide capabilities that permit memory-allocation control to be totally transparent to the user. Modern virtual-memory capabilities attempt to provide such transparency.

The virtual memory seen by the user, even in assembly language programming, should be practically unbounded. The programmer should not have to worry about whether there is sufficient physical space for the programs or the data being generated. The hardware and the operating system, working in conjunction, should provide automatic management of physical memory. There are several basic methods for doing that in the computer design.

One way of accomplishing the task is to provide an almost limitless amount of virtual memory (logical address space) divided into a finite quantity of uniform-sized pages that correspond to blocks of physical primary memory. The computer hardware and its operating system perform the page-to-block matching and transfers so that the programmer does not have to know that the physical memory is significantly smaller than the virtual memory or that there are other users sharing the memory at any instant. With a paged memory the pages of information are transferred into blocks of physical memory as they are needed, totally under the control of the computer and operating system. Figure 4-16 shows the concept of paged virtual memory. At any time the physical memory can hold only a part of the virtual memory. There is no direct correlation between the pages of virtual memory and the blocks of physical memory, but the operating system knows which pages are "active" at any time and can decode the block assignments to unsort information in the blocks and construct the order of pages in virtual memory. In the example there are 16 blocks of 64 kbytes each in physical memory and up to 1024 pages of 64 kbytes each in virtual memory. As pages are needed they are transferred into physical memory and unneeded pages are removed. Page management can be undertaken totally by the software, but it is much easier and faster if hardware support is provided in the architecture.

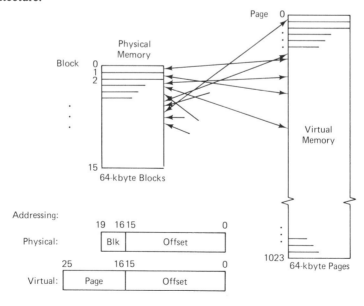

Figure 4-16 Physical and virtual memories.

Simple base addressing, as shown in Fig. 4-17, can perform the page/block correlation required to assist in page management. The figure shows a virtual address that
consists of a page identifier and an offset within the page. The page identifier is not used
directly as the base for physical addressing, but is used to access a page table in memory
or in registers. The page table shows if the desired page is presently in physical memory
and, if so, identifies the block (by giving the base address) in which the page resides. The
offset into the page is then the offset into the block. If the page is not present, as indicated
by the "presence bit", the page table identifies the address (perhaps indirectly through
another page table) of the location of the page in secondary memory.

For very large virtual memory it might be desirable to establish multiple-page
segments of virtual memory. Some segments might be shared by different user programs.
Then addressing is through a segment table to a page table to the physical block, as shown
in Fig. 4-18. In this case there is a segment table for each user program and a page table
for each segment. The offset to the virtual page remains the same as the offset into the
physical block. As with paged memory, a presence bit indicates whether the page resides
in physical memory.

An extension of segmented paged memory allows for segments of any size, as
shown in Fig. 4-19. Here the virtual-to-physical address mapping is straightforward, but
there must be a means to assure that separate physical segments do not overlap. Despite
the increased flexibility for allocation of segments of any desired size, the approach using
continuously variable segments has not been favored because of the additional burdens
of memory management that it imposes on the operating system.

In all approaches to mapping virtual-to-physical address space there are inefficien-
cies in memory use, called *holes*. As shown in Fig. 4-20(a), paged memory has unused

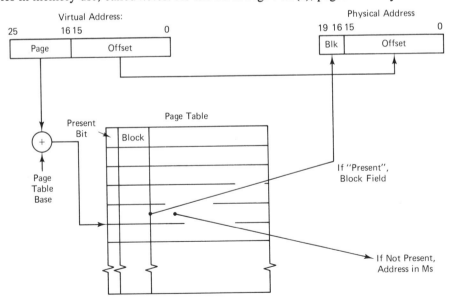

Figure 4-17   Paged-memory addressing.

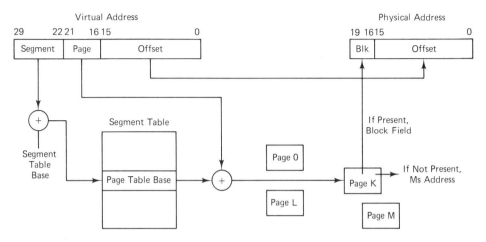

Figure 4-18 Segmented paged-memory addressing.

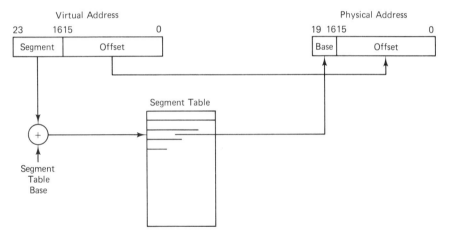

Figure 4-19 Addressing continuously-variable sized pages.

words in individual pages because it is unlikely that a segment will require memory exactly equal to an integer quantity of pages. With continuously variable segment sizes, Fig. 4-20(b), the holes result from the quasirandom sequence of assignment of segments to physical space. The figure illustrates a condition in which segments A, B, C, and D of different sizes were allocated physical space. Subsequently, segment A has been deallocated and segment X, of a smaller size, has been given the space formerly used by A. In the same manner, segment Y has replaced a large part of the space occupied by segment C. We note in Fig. 4-20(b) that there are unallocated spaces between segments X and B and between Y and D. These might be used by small segments that subsequently call for space, but it is likely that there will be a large quantity of small unused areas after the memory allocation has proceeded for a period of time. The holes experienced with paged memory are known as *internal fragmentation*, whereas those seen with segmented

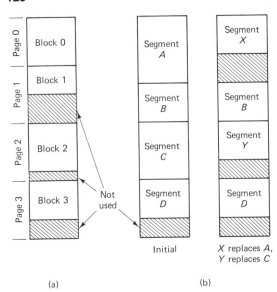

Initial

X replaces A,
Y replaces C

Figure 4-20   Holes in virtual-memory systems. (a) Paged. (b) Continuous segments.

(a)

(b)

memory are called *external fragmentation*. Both result in inefficient use of memory space, but that is a price that is paid for the flexibility of sharing memory among processes.

In all three approaches to virtual-memory, support for the page and the segment table management is provided by the architecture. Segment and page management could be done totally by the operating-system program, but at a higher cost in time. Most of today's computers provide some sort of page table management at the hardware level. The Burroughs B5500 and its successors through the Unisys A series have used continuously-variable-sized segments.

4.9 MEMORY-DESIGN RATIONALE AND EXAMPLES

There are a number of levels in the memory hierarchy and a variety of ways to implement the total memory system. In memory-system design we must decide how much memory of what type is to be assigned at each level. It would be desirable to have a simple methodology for quantifying memory-system design, but the wide variety of memory capabilities available to us precludes development of a simple design approach.

As computer systems have evolved, the approach to memory-system design has been influenced by the availability of particular memory forms (at the different levels) already in manufacture by the computer suppliers. Design decisions made many years earlier might determine how and how much physical address space can be specified for primary or secondary memory. Any change in the maximum address space can have severe effects on programs that were developed for prechange systems. (This is true particularly if users have found uses for previously unused or "reserved" bits in instruction or control words.) The necessity to retain "upward compatibility" when a new system is introduced has forced computer architects to approach changes in memory-system design very cautiously. As a result, the assignment of function and capacity to the various levels of the memory hierarchy appears to result more from past experience than from a prescribed rationale.

Despite this history, it is desirable that we have some principles and objectives even if we cannot write an algorithm for memory-system design. The overall objective is to attain maximum system performance at minimum cost. One way to approach the objective is to attempt to create the effect that at every memory level n, the system operates as though it has memory with performance of level n and with cost of level $n + 1$. For example, the caches evaluated in Fig. 4-13 aim at attaining a performance equivalent to the SRAM with total memory cost as close as possible to that of a DRAM memory. Our discussion of the methodology assumes that we are developing a general-purpose multi-user computer system for which we do not have tightly prescribed memory requirements.

The design approach might start by determining how large, and in what size increments, we should make the disk-drive secondary memory in a new system. Disk storage module sizes will have been determined by the state of the technology and by planned or de facto standards for disk sizes and rotational speeds (the latter established by the standard electrical power frequencies). For small computers, typical module sizes are 20, 40, 80, and 160 Mbytes. For medium-size computers, disk-drive modules range from 400 Mbytes to 1 Gbyte. Large systems use drives (based on the IBM 8380) of 2.4, 4.8, or 7.2 Gbytes. Then the computer architecture will be specified to accept as many drive modules as are necessary for the maximum-capacity versions of the system. For medium-size computers the maximum capacity typically is from 20 to 80 Gbytes and for large systems hundreds of gigabytes are used.

Primary-memory size then is established by evaluating various capacities in typical applications. The evaluations determine the memory size at which computer performance will be limited because too high a percentage of memory cycles are needed for transfer of information to or from secondary memory. These transfers occur as pages or segments are exchanged. Thus, the memory capacities are influenced by the approach selected for implementing virtual memory. There are no hard rules for the percentage of memory cycles that can be devoted to exchanges with secondary memory, but experience shows that processor performance is reduced significantly when more than about 5% of the memory cycles are used by the input/output system, including secondary memory. Whether we use simulations or make estimates based on simplified analyses, we must incorporate assumptions about typical process-code and data-segment sizes and the number of processes expected to be active (including the operating-system processes discussed in Chapter 5). Characterization of the processes allows for estimation of the amount of data and code exchanges with secondary memory for various memory sizes. From this, the minimum and maximum primary-memory capacities can be selected.

The amount of physical memory that can be addressed directly and by various indirect-addressing schemes is established by the central-processor organization, which is covered in Chapter 5. Thus, the memory capacities selected are influenced by and influence processor design. As described in Chapter 2, there must be interaction among the designs at the subsystem level.

Next the cost effectiveness of a cache should be considered. As shown in Fig. 4-13, the cache is introduced to attempt to attain the performance of a high-speed memory (in that example, SRAM) by adding only a little cost to that of the slower and less expensive primary memory (a DRAM). As was pointed out in Section 4.5, the unit cost of a SRAM cache is about 15 times that of an Mp made with VLSI DRAM. Its speed is about twice that of the DRAM. If DRAM primary memory is not fast enough to attain the performance required, then we could use SRAM for the primary memory, but the cost might be prohibitive (six or eight times that of DRAM memory). The issue then is whether a small amount of cache memory can increase performance to the desired level with only a small addition of cost. The example of Fig. 4-13 shows that a direct cache of 32 kbytes yields a computer performance increase of 38% (or 94% of the performance with an SRAM primary memory). If the cache size is about 0.2% that of primary memory (32 kbytes vs. 16 Mbytes) the increased memory cost due to the cache is about 3% (0.002×15). A 38% performance increase certainly is worth the 3% cost increase. However, a 35% performance increase is attainable at a 1.5% increase in cost with the 16K cache. The example is typical of the approach that must be taken.

A similar comparison should be used to determine the relative effectiveness of more internal processor registers as opposed to the introduction of the cache. The unit cost of processor registers is typically 10 times that of SRAMs and their speeds are about five times that of SRAMs. The comparison again involves the interaction of processor and memory-system designs. We note, however, that in many cases the processor architecture is fixed by requirements for compatibility with earlier models and this trade-off is not available to the architect.

Four examples of how computer architects have allocated storage in the memory hierarchy are demonstrated in Fig. 4-21. All examples are of computers that were available in 1987. In all cases the Pc state was established many years earlier when the architecture was introduced. These processor states are discussed in Chapter 5. Cache-memory sizes are related to processor performance, but the VAX 8700 has a particularly large cache. Maximum primary-memory size also is related to performance. In the case of the IBM 3090 the primary memory can include an expansion unit that transmits and

System	Pc State	Cache (kbytes)	Mp (Mbytes)	Max. Ms.disk (Gbytes)	Mdisk_buffer
VAX 8700	16w × 32b	64	32–128	214	To 256 kbytes /controller
Unisys 2200 (1 Pc)	128w × 36b	32	2–48	64	
IBM 9370 (model 90)	16w × 32b + 4w × 64b	16	8/16	40	
IBM 3090 (model 180E)	16w × 32b + 4w × 64b	64	32–64 (256*)	960	32–256 Mbytes /controller

*Expanded storage for block transfers.

Figure 4-21   Examples of the memory hierarchy.

receives information in 4-kbyte blocks. It acts as an "overflow" for the word-organized memory and as a buffer between Mp and Ms. Disk storage for all systems has a maximum capacity of 1000 to 3000 times that of Mp. Both the VAX 8700 and the IBM 3090 systems incorporate semiconductor memory buffers in their disk-file controllers.

4.10 DETECTION AND CORRECTION OF ERRORS

Errors can be introduced in any information when it is being transferred from one location to another. It is somewhat less likely, but still possible, that external electrical signals or transient power levels can introduce an error to information residing in a memory or processor register or in a secondary storage location. Circuits and software for detecting and correcting errors are a part of many primary- and secondary-memory systems. Methods for error detection and correction also have been added to processors to achieve very high reliability levels, as we will see when reviewing processor implementation in Chapter 6.

To detect a single bit error in a byte or a word of information a single bit of redundancy, a *parity bit* is added. The parity bit, a unit of information that is added to force the augmented word or byte to have an even (or odd, if that is our convention) quantity of ones, has been used in magnetic tape formats for many years. The parity bit also is standard in communication protocols, such as the 8-bit (including parity) ISO (International Standards Organization) and USASCII (USA Standard Code for Information Interchange) serial-transmission code.

More redundancy can be added to determine which bit is in error, allowing for single-bit error correction. The usual means for providing single-bit error correction with magnetic tape is represented in Fig. 4-22. With each 8-bit byte there is added a parity bit, resulting in a "9-channel tape format". Following each block of information on the tape there is added a redundant byte with its own parity bit. The extra byte, called the *longitudinal redundancy check* (LRC) byte, is formed by performing a count of the bits at each bit position for every

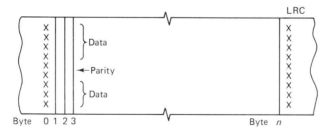

Parity bit (odd-parity example):
  bit 8 = (sum(bit i)+1)mod 2
Each bit in LRC byte i (even-parity example):
  LRC bit i = (sum(data bit i))mod 2

Figure 4-22   Parity bits and a check byte.

byte in the block and forcing the quantity of ones in the longitudinal direction to be even (or odd). Then a longitudinal redundancy check (also called a *cyclic redundancy check*) can be performed following the transfer of a block. Any single error in the block can be found at the coordinates of a byte parity error and a longitudinal parity error. Multiple errors can still be detected, but not necessarily identified for correction. Similar techniques are used for single-bit error detection/correction with communication codes.

More sophisticated coding techniques that permit multiple-bit error correction have been developed. *Hamming codes*, introduced by R. W. Hamming [HammR50] for digital communication applications in 1950, provide redundancy in single computer words to permit both error detection and correction. The principle of Hamming codes is the introduction of a set of parity bits each operating on a different independent group of data bits. These error-correction bits are placed at bit locations $2^0, 2^1, 2^2, 2^3, 2^4 \ldots$, and the data-bit positions are adjusted accordingly. For example, for an 8-bit data word, correction bits are added at positions 1, 2, 4, and 8, and the data bits are shifted to positions 3, 5, 6, 7, 9, 10, 11, and 12.

A pattern is formed from the binary representation of the position of bits in the augmented word (positions 1 through 12). The values assigned to the correction bits are established by the data bits for which there is a value of one in the related bit position. For example, in the least significant bit of the binary number representing bit position every other position has a 1 and every other bit of the augmented word is significant to calculating the value of the first correction bit. The data bits in the odd positions of the word are data bits 1, 2, 4, 5, and 7. For the next more significant bit of the position count, ones appear in locations 2, 3, 6, 7, 10, and 11 and data bits 1, 3, 4, 6, and 7 are used for generation of correction bit 2. The value to be associated with each correction bit is the exclusive-OR of associated data-bit values.

The syndrome to detect and locate an error is generated by multiplying the matrix that represents the pattern of the binary position count by the vector that is the actual augmented data word (with any errors). The value of the syndrome is the location of any single error in the augmented data word. If the value of the syndrome is zero there are no errors. The parity bit for the word that is added at bit location 0 shows that there is an odd or even number of errors, permitting the syndrome to be used for correction if we assume that there is only one error. If the syndrome indicates an error and the parity bit indicates an even number of errors, then we cannot make a correction; we have uncovered two or more errors.

An example of single-bit error correction and two-bit error detection is shown in Fig. 4-23. In the example we consider an 8-bit data word that should have the value 10011010. There is an error in the second bit and the memory location contains 11011010. A parity bit is included to provide even parity. For the 8-bit data word four redundant correction bits are required. The error-correction bits (c_i) are placed in positions 1, 2, 4, and 8. The parity bit is in bit position 0, so that the organization of the 13-bit augmented word is

$$p_0 \; c_1 \; c_2 \; d_1 \; c_3 \; d_2 \; d_3 \; d_4 \; c_4 \; d_5 \; d_6 \; d_7 \; d_8$$

The pattern for evaluating the word, obtained from an ascending binary count (reading each column from the top) from 1 to 12, is shown in the illustration. (The parity

Single-error correction: Given $x = 8$ data bits, d_i. $y = \log_2(x) + 1 = 4$ error-correction bits, c_j. Include parity bit p_0 for two-error detection. Total word of 13 bits, b_k, $k = 0..12$. Correction bits are at locations 1, 2, 4, 8, ... Parity bit at location 0:

> word: $p_0\ c_1\ c_2\ d_1\ c_3\ d_2\ d_3\ d_4\ c_4\ d_5\ d_6\ d_7\ d_8$.

Example: The code should be 10011010; but is 11011010 (error in second bit).

From the bit patterns applied to the correct code:
$c_1 = \text{excl\_OR}(d_1,d_2,d_4,d_5,d_7) = \text{excl\_OR}(1,0,1,1,1) = 0$,
$c_2 = \text{excl\_OR}(d_1,d_3,d_4,d_6,d_7) = \text{excl\_OR}(1,0,1,0,1) = 1$,
$c_3 = \text{excl\_OR}(d_2,d_3,d_4,d_8) = \text{excl\_OR}(0,0,1,0) = 1$,
$c_4 = \text{excl\_OR}(d_5,d_6,d_7,d_8) = \text{excl\_OR}(1,0,1,0) = 0$,

Generating the syndrome:

pattern matrix (binary representation of bit position):

```
position:    1 2 3 4 5 6 7 8 9 ...
(c4)     | 0 0 0 0 0 0 0 1 1 1 1 1 |
(c3)     | 0 0 0 1 1 1 1 0 0 0 0 1 |
(c2)     | 0 1 1 0 0 1 1 0 0 1 1 0 |
(c1)     | 1 0 1 0 1 0 1 0 1 0 1 0 |
```

c_1 = 0   data word vector
c_2 = 1   (neglecting parity bit)
d_1 = 1
c_3 = 1
d_2 = 1   result:
d_3 = 0   = 0 1 0 1
d_4 = 1   = 5
c_4 = 0   the error is in the
d_5 = 1   5th bit, d_2.
d_6 = 0
d_7 = 1
d_8 = 0

The parity error will show that there is an odd number of errors. We can rely on the error correction if we can be assured that the number of errors is less than 2.

Figure 4-23   Hamming-code error detection and correction.

bit is ignored.) The data and correction bits to be used are those that have a 1 in the row of the pattern. The sum of the values of all of these, modulo 2, should be 0, so that we can determine each value of c_i from the value of the data bits. For example, since the sum of the bits that are 1's in the bottom line of the syndrome matrix must be 0, we obtain: $c_1 = d_1 + d_2 + d_4 + d_5 + d_7$. For the (correct) data-word values in the example, $c_1 = 0$. Similarly, c_2, c_3, and c_4 are 1, 1, and 0, respectively. The parity bit p is 0 for even parity.

In the actual word there is a parity error, since data bit 2 is incorrect. (The parity error actually indicates that there is an odd number of incorrect bits.) The pattern matrix is multiplied by the actual augmented word (without the parity bit) to determine which bit is in error. The multiplication yields the value 0101 = 5, and the error is in bit 5, d_2, which can be changed to 0.

The central processor can be relieved of error-correction processing of the type shown by adding a fast special processor to each memory module, or error detection and correction processing can be handled by a memory-management unit (MMU) processor. Memory processors of this type are discussed in Chapter 7.

4.11 SUMMARY

Users appear to have a limitless hunger for computer memory at all levels. There is a variety of memory technologies that can be applied to formulate computer storage. The different characteristics of the resulting memory equipment cause us to establish a hierarchy of storage. Starting with storage in the processors and moving toward archival stores, the memory methods used result in slower, less expensive, and larger memories as we move up the hierarchy.

Semiconductor memory devices offer access and cycle times of from several to several hundred nanoseconds. Access time is almost independent of location and widely separated information can be read in succession as quickly as information that is in close address proximity. Storage that is based on the physical motion of a magnetic medium under a read/write head has much longer access times (to the start of the information desired), but transfer rates after the start has been found can be quite high. The unit cost of moving-medium memory is several orders of magnitude less than that of semiconductor memory when equipment is designed to contain very large quantities of information. Optical storage holds promise as a means to provide very large and very inexpensive means for storage for archival purposes. As with all technologies used in computer systems, the unit cost of memory has been falling at a rapid and continuous rate as performance has been growing.

Memory in the processors consists of flip-flops, individual registers, and banks of registers. The memory banks can use read/write memory, known as random-access memory, or might use read-only techniques. Access times for processor memory are of the order of several to tens of nanoseconds.

The main working memory of the computer is the primary memory. Most primary memory today is made from semiconductor storage elements assembled using integrated circuits that allow from 64 kbits to several megabits in a single electronic component. Much other circuitry is required in the assembly of a memory module. Primary memory can be organized in several ways, depending on the objectives. Modular memory can be structured to have the module designation in the higher-order bits or in the lower-order bits. In the first case successive words of storage are in the same module, leading to flexibility and reliability. Low-order interleaving allows for very-high-speed streaming of successive words since the next word to be accessed can be started before the previous word has been removed from its module. Part-word access can be accomplished in the primary memory or might be done in the processor after a full word has been retrieved.

A cache memory can be used to keep the most often used (usually the most recently used) information in storage that is faster than primary memory. To take advantage of the speed, management of the cache should be automatic. Fully associative cache management would be most desirable, but is expensive. Associative memory is approximated with direct-mapped or set-associative cache management techniques. The computer architect should perform an analysis to determine whether set-associative methods will provide sufficient performance improvement to warrant its added cost. Cache management is complicated with multiprocessor systems by the need to coordinate cache activities of the different processors.

Secondary memory is available to hold information not immediately needed by running programs. While the access times of secondary-memory devices are very long compared to those of primary memory, block-transfer rates of the two are compatible. Communication of information between primary and secondary memories is usually made in significant size blocks of words. Block transfers are suitable with both disk files and magnetic tape drives, although the special characteristics of the tape drives require that transfers be planned and managed well by the operating system. For long-term archival storage optical disk files and specialized magnetic tape systems currently are used. The applications for these devices remain specialized.

Other storage means are used for memories that might be needed between primary and secondary memory, as the cache resides between the processors and primary memories. There is some question whether there is sufficient demand for the electronic block-oriented random-access memories for intermediate storage to permit the candidate methods to become competitive.

Management of the transfer of information between primary and secondary memories usually is controlled by the operating system, but the computer architecture can include features to facilitate virtual-memory management. Virtual memory can be organized in pages, in segments of pages, or in continuously variable segments. Different forms of hardware support are available with each technique.

While the process of determining the sizes of each level of the memory hierarchy is not precise, there is a general methodology that can be applied. This entails working from the secondary-memory level toward processor storage and estimating the performance penalties that result from having too little memory at the next level down. The approach entails designing the hierarchy so that at each level n, performance is of memory at that level, whereas cost is close to that of memory at level $n + 1$.

The large amount of information contained in memory and transferred between memory levels creates opportunity for errors to be introduced in the information. Error-detection and error-correction techniques are available to prevent these random errors from interfering with the computer operation.

4.12 ADDITIONAL READING

The organization of primary and secondary memories, and techniques to implement such memories, are described only briefly herein. More complete descriptions are found in books for predecessor courses [GorsG86, HamaV84, ManoM82, and TaneA84]. Details of semiconductor techniques for memories can be found in texts on digital electronics (e.g., [AlleC86]) and in the issues of *IEEE Transactions on Electron Devices* and *IEEE Journal of Solid-State Circuits*.

The general registers of the Univac systems are described in [BorgB78] and can also be found in Unisys System 1100 and 2200 hardware description manuals. The use of registers in the Control Data Cyber series is the same as that in the CDC 6600, [ThorJ64].

Cache memory in various forms is included in most computers today. Cache organizations were described in [WindR73] and [BellJ74]. It is interesting to examine the different approaches to organizing cache memory of the computer manufacturers. Intel Corp.'s *Solutions* magazine of November–December 1985 [Intel85] includes an article on cache memory from which Fig. 4-13 was taken.

Virtual memory and methods for mapping virtual memory to physical memory are discussed in most current books on operating systems. [BicLu87], which updates [ShawA74] on the subject, has an excellent discussion of principles of virtual-memory management. Similar coverage is found in [MaekM87].

Error-correcting codes are discussed regularly in *IEEE Transactions on Information Theory*. [HammR50] is still considered the seminal reference on the topic and [HammR86] on coding theory and information theory includes many examples. [WakeJ78] reviews the subject from a designer's viewpoint.

4.13 PROBLEMS

4-1. Referring to Fig. 4-4, do the following:
  a. Develop the equation for unit cost of primary memory for future years and forecast the cost per bit in the year 2000.
  b. Develop the equation for speed of primary memory for future years and estimate the cycle time in the year 2000.

4-2. From the data available in the illustrations of this chapter, calculate the relative cost of the following two memories:
  a. 4-Mbyte DRAM Mp, 16-kbyte SRAM direct-mapped cache, with a hit ratio of 85%.
  b. 2-Mbyte SRAM Mp with no cache.
  Discuss the factors that would have to be considered in comparing the relative effect of the two on computer-system performance.

4-3. Consider two alternative approaches to a 4-Mword (16-Mbyte) primary memory for a 32-bit word computer:
  a. Four modules of 1-Mword × 32-bit memory with low-order interleaving (as shown in Fig. 4-9) and 32-bit transfers.
  b. A single module of 1-Mword × 128-bit memory with 4-word transfers.
  Describe the cost, performance, and reliability differences between the two approaches.

4-4. With technology available for a hypothetical simple computer, register-to-register operations take 20 ns and register-to-memory or memory-to-register operations take 100 ns. We are considering whether to design the computer with a single accumulator or to incorporate four general registers, permitting register-to-register operations. Write assembly language programs to run the following benchmark problem with each approach. (A to F are values of variables originally residing in memory or results that will be placed in memory):

```
real A, B, C, D, E, F;
begin
   E := (A + B) * (C - D);
   F := (A - B) * (C + D);
   A := E + F;
   B := E - F
end;
```

Identify the assumptions you are making about instructions and the notation you are using to identify registers.

What is the relative performance of the two approaches?

4-5. Consider a large modular multiprocessor computer system as shown in Fig. 3-23. Assume the following memory performance characteristics: cache read operation time (including check of tags), 2 clock times; primary-memory (DRAM) read cycle time, 4 clock times; and system bus (processor-to-memory and memory-to-processor) transfer time, 1 clock pulse. Describe how cache hits (or misses) can be signaled to inhibit (or initiate) primary-memory operations. Build a table showing effective memory read times with hit cache ratios of 80% and 90% for each of the three locations of the cache.

4-6. Memory-design engineers have estimated that both of the following approaches to secondary memory have the same cost:
   a. Two-Gbyte disk file with 8-ms average access time and 8-ms transfer time for a 32-kbyte block.
   b. Two-Gbyte disk file with 12-ms average access time and 12-ms transfer time for a 32-kbyte block and a 32-kbyte CMOS buffer with 8-ms block-transfer time (to or from Mp).

What is the relative performance of the two secondary-memory systems when a 32-kbyte block must be transferred every 50 ms? What if transfers are needed every 25 ms? What is the minimum interblock transfer time of each? What size blocks give the same minimum interblock time?

4-7. Consider an idealized memory hierarchy of an unlimited number of levels. Memories are all random-access, but each level is k times slower in access time than the previous level (closer to the processor). At each level the hit ratio has the same value (H).
   a. If level 0 is at the processor, what is the probability that a random reference will be satisfied by level i of the hierarchy ($i = 0, 1, 2, \ldots$)?
   b. Give a formula for the expected access time of a random reference.
   c. What would be the expected access time if the *miss* ratio was k times smaller at each higher level (i.e., inversely proportional to access time)?

4-8. Describe the memory-mapping operations needed to use paging to support multiprogramming on a machine with a *small* virtual address space and a *large* primary memory.

4-9. Consider the virtual-to-physical address mappings of Figs. 4-17 and 4-19. Describe the two mapping processes in ISP-like notation. Include a declaration of the registers needed for the mapping in each case.

4-10. Using the example of Fig. 4-23, show how Hamming coding would be used in error detection and error correction for the case where the desired data sequence of 11010110 is received as
   a. 11010010
   b. 11011010

4.14 PROJECTS

4-A. In describing the memory configuration for your evaluation Project 1-A, be sure to define the range of memory sizes available at each level. If there is a cache memory in the system identify its location (refer to Fig. 3-23) and describe its form (direct-mapped, etc.) and the mechanism used for writing to preserve cache coherence.

4-B. In designing the memories for your design Project 1-B, include specifications of memory speeds (access times, cycle times, transfer rates) and show the position of each memory in your PMS diagram.

4-C. Develop a PMS diagram for a memory subsystem that includes processor registers, cache, primary memory, and secondary memory. Include specifications for the memory at each level.

5

The Instruction-Set Processor

There are so many facets to processor organization that it takes two chapters to cover them. In this chapter we look at the instruction-set processor, deferring considerations of its implementation and of computer control until Chapter 6. Modern computers contain many combinations of the features that we will discuss. The features and alternative approaches are covered separately here in an attempt to describe each alternative clearly. We will see that some combinations work together naturally, whereas other combinations tend to complicate the processor design with little benefit.

5.1 A VARIETY OF PROCESSOR ORGANIZATIONS

The influence of user requirements on the organization of central processors is reflected in the characteristics of the different languages that are used for programming computers. The characteristics of the various languages influence the register organization and assignments, the instruction sets, the data structures, and the arithmetic and logic units. Equally significant are the effects of the operating system on processor organization. The operating system reflects the dynamics of the processing environment, and the computer and its operating system should be designed as a single virtual system.

Examples of ISP descriptions of typical computers in Chapters 2 and 4 showed that there can be a significant amount of storage in the processor. This memory local to the processor was identified as the Pc state in our review of the ISP level of computer description in Chapter 2. If we can build into the processor a reasonable amount of memory, how should it be used? We can allocate the registers as additional accumulators, as index registers, as specialized registers, or in different combinations at different times. When we provide the computer with a large amount of state we must pay attention to the need to store all of the state that is related to a process when that process is set aside for another to run. Some register organizations assist in the task of storing process state in primary memory.

With the understanding that we can provide sufficient components (or sufficient area on a semiconductor surface in the case of an integrated-circuit processor) for up to several thousand bits of storage in the processor, we must determine how we should allocate the storage. Specification of the function, quantity, and sizes of the storage establishes the processor state. The function of the processor storage to a large extent determines how the processor operates. Here we identify the storage that is seen by the assembly language programmer or by the language translator. In the next chapter when we review control of the processor we will see that additional storage that is transparent to the programmer might be required.

When a program consists of multiple procedures with different environments the computer must support switching of environments and procedure calls. If multiple-user processes are to be executed it is necessary to support changes in process context. When an interrupt system is implemented, environment or context switching can be initiated by an interrupt signal. In all of these cases we see that there are several different process states to be stored and managed.

After we have obtained a first approximation of the nature of the processor state we must specify the uses of each bit of the state under all conditions in which it will be used. The size of data words and the uses of the bits therein establish the range and the precision available for representing numeric values. In the detail of data representation we must include the identification of where the binary point is located, of the base for the exponent in floating-point representation, and of the code to represent negative values in all fields that can hold such values. We also must specify the codes for alphanumeric characters and decimal values and identify how they will be packed in a computer word. The specification of this detail for the processor registers influences and is influenced by the representation of similar information when stored in primary memory. We must specify registers that will be used for addressing memory or other registers and for buffers of information during transfers.

Once we have specified the processor storage we can identify the transfers and the transformations of information required to provide function to the processor. This leads to an identification of each instruction in the instruction set. The interaction between the functions desired and the way we have decided to represent information permit us to specify whether there will be independence between the instructions and the data types or if the former will depend on the latter. The organization and the quantity of processor registers is one input to the specification of the addressing modes and the forms of argument retrieval to be included in our instructions. In all of this we must be concerned with the influence of our decisions on the programmer and on the translators to be provided with our computer.

These items are covered in this chapter on the instruction-set processor. With them we will have identified the form and the function of our processor(s). The chapter includes several concrete examples to demonstrate how other architects have responded to the requirements for instruction-set processor design. Issues related to the control and the implementation of the instruction-set processor and to performance of alternate approaches are covered in Chapter 6.

5.2 LANGUAGES AND PROCESSORS

A specific view of the information-processing requirements can be shown in the characteristics of the languages used for programming the computer. Programming languages have a wide range of characteristics, some very close to the machine language of the usual computer and some very far from it. The difference has been called a *semantic gap*. Of course, we can narrow this gap by programming in a language close to that of the computer; much programming is still done in assembly language, but that just opens another more severe semantic gap between the problem language and the programming language. There are features that the computer architect can provide in designing a computer that is well matched to the programming languages that will be used.

If we know that only one language is to be used we can design the machine to speak a machine language very close to the programming language; we can use a *direct execution architecture*. We seldom have the luxury of being able to respond to such a narrow need and usually we will have to design our computer to be used with a variety of programming languages. Language and compiler developers can assist by designing translators that use as a target for translation an intermediate language that lies between the programming and machine languages. An intermediate language should have characteristics that take advantage of features of the computer hardware. The architect can assist the compiler designer by providing hardware features that allow the intermediate language to be a good target for the more popular programming languages.

There are two schools of thought about the "flexibility" needed in the machine to assist the assembly language programmer and the compiler writer. One argument is that a large instruction set, a rich variety of instructions, and a wide range of addressing modes give flexibility for the programmer and the compiler writer to optimize programs for efficiency of execution. The opposite view states that most programmers and compilers use only a small percentage of the features usually provided and that the language and the organization of the machine should be kept simple, permitting a few features to be used effectively. Our examples show that both views are held by designers and users and that commercially successful computers have resulted from each.

It is useful to start our look at computer support for language features by reviewing the characteristics of the types of languages with which people program. Then we can identify how the computer design can provide for those features. The evolution of programming languages has led to language characteristics that provide power to the programmer but that make the job of the computer architect more difficult in responding to those characteristics. This is not to be considered a poor outcome. It is desirable that intellectual effort be allocated to design of computers and of programming language translators so that our (virtual) computers are easier to use effectively.

The type of programming language that is closest to the language of the computer is symbolic assembly language. Programs for the earliest computers were written in symbolic assembly language and were converted to the raw machine codes by people called *coders*. The tasks performed by coders did entail little more than translating from the "symbolic" code with mnemonic instructions, like "ADD", to the machine bit pattern for each instruction. Each instruction in assembly language reflected a machine-code instruction. The location of the instruction in memory was represented by its position in the sequence of instructions. Locations for data were reserved by an identifier such as "DATA", usually following the instruction sequence. The programmer could designate a location, such as the target of a jump or a data location, by a label and the coder would change the label designation to the memory address so designated.

The amount of human effort required for the coding made it obvious that growth in the use of computers could be limited by the number of people who could perform these uninteresting tasks accurately. It also became obvious that the tasks performed by the coders could be done on the computer, using computer programs to specify the rules for translation. Thus, the *symbolic assembler* was created and the job of the coder was eliminated. (Most coders were employed immediately as programmers, since the limit on computer use was relieved and a much greater demand for programmers was created.)

A simplified model of the translation from an assembly language program is shown in Fig. 5-1. Statements (or lines) of code in assembly language bear a one-to-one correspondence to instructions of the computer, except that the program includes *pseudoinstructions*, or *assembler directives*, label names, and comments. These are added to aid the assembler or people who must read the program. The assembler of our example uses pseudoinstructions (START, END, ARRAY, MACRO) to identify starting and end points of instruction and data sequences. Labels (identified as character strings followed by a colon, such as SUB:) are translated to relative addresses by finding their locations in the instruction sequence.

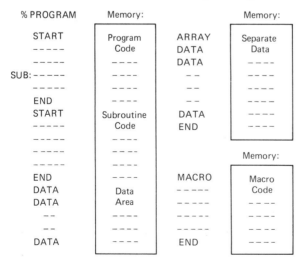

Figure 5-1 Assembly-language storage model.

Comments (separated by a special character such as %), which are used for person to person communication, are ignored by the assembler. Assemblages of instructions and data that constitute a program are placed in contiguous memory locations, although there might be separate areas assigned for *macro routines* that can be used by several different programs or for compound data structures like arrays.

Architectural support for assembly language programs consists of an understandable set of computer instructions that include a facility for assignment of processor registers as the individual programmer finds most useful. Memory-addressing modes should give the programmer the ability to use memory in ways that yield execution speed and efficiency of storage. The interaction between primary memory and processor registers should be easy to manage. Instruction mnemonics, addressing modes, and storage selection should be easy to remember after the programmer has gained experience with the system. If there are several models in a computer series, the different models should appear as the same virtual machine to the programmer. "Recipes" for using machine features optimally should be easy for an experienced programmer to comprehend and to remember. Introduction of radical new features or nomenclatures should be avoided unless there are significant benefits that result.

While relieving people of the detailed and routine tasks of coding to do more useful things, assemblers had a more significant benefit in reducing the amount of errors in machine language programs. Furthermore, it was found that the assemblers could include checks for many errors in the assembly language programs, such as misspelled or missing labels, addressing out of memory bounds, jumps to data, and use of instruction addresses when a data location was called for. Reliability and readability of programs have been as important as ease and speed in the evolution of languages for computer programming. Symbolic assemblers were of use in moving the vocabulary of programming from the machine toward the human, but they did not move the programming language any closer to the languages of the problems. "Higher-level languages" were needed and were introduced.

Before looking at specific types of high-level programming languages and their implications on computer architecture, it is useful to identify the characteristics of language with which we should be concerned. Each language has a specific structure that can be mapped to the computer storage model best suited to that language. The structure is reflected in the control mechanisms of the language: the nature of expression evaluation, command interpretation, instruction sequencing, and selection from among alternative evaluation paths. Subprogram capabilities, functions, procedures, subroutines, tasks, and coroutines are included in the control mechanisms. If the language includes subprograms, issues of *scope* and *extent* of named objects (variables, labels, subprograms themselves) are introduced. The scope indicates the program regions in which a named item is recognized and usable. Extent means the time duration over which an item is active (its lifetime). Some languages might permit an item's scope and extent to be divided into *blocks*, program substructures smaller than those of a subprogram. Included in the issues regarding subprograms are questions related to parameters (arguments) of the subprograms and how they are connected to the values of the calling program or subprograms. We will characterize different languages according to their control structures and will identify the computer control structures needed to handle the language effectively.

Variations also are possible in the nature of the data items a language can handle. There are different forms (types) of data items, such as integer or real numeric values, digits, characters, boolean (or logical) values. Whereas we usually think of variables and arguments as individual (scalar) items that have one value of a particular type at a time, most languages permit the definition of *compound data items*. These are collections of items, all of the same type (homogeneous data structures) or of different types (heterogeneous structures). The forms of compound data types (*vectors*, *arrays*, *records*, *structures* are names that are used), their construction from the scalars, and their relationship to the control structures are of interest.

"Autocoder" languages, such as FORTRAN, that permitted instructions to be formed using algebra-like expressions were a major advance over assembly languages. With autocoders a single statement in the program might lead to a sequence of machine-level instructions. Subroutines (functions and procedures) can be defined and called repeatedly from different parts of the program. In FORTRAN a data item is either *local* (within the main program or an individual subprogram) or *global* (known to the program and all subprograms). A subprogram can be invoked (called) only if it is not already active (i.e., subprograms are not *reentrant*). In Fig. 5-2 we see a model of a FORTRAN program and of its assignment to memory. We note that the memory assignment is similar to that of the assembly language model of Fig. 5-1. The machine code and the data for the main program and for each of the subprograms as well as the global data are packed into one sequence of machine words. Since only one invocation ("incarnation") of a subprogram can be active at any one time, only a single "execution environment" (set of locations for data and subprogram pointers) is needed. There also could be

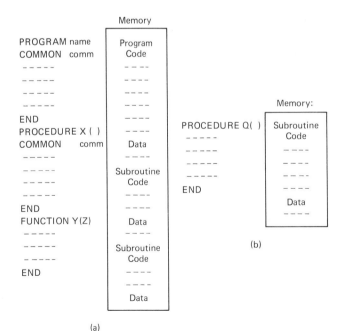

Figure 5-2 Static-language storage model. (a) Program with subroutines. (b) Separately compiled procedure.

independently compiled subprograms that would reside in separate memory locations like the independent macros of Fig. 5-1.

With FORTRAN programs overall memory management can be performed by the operating system, but movement of information within memory is seldom performed and the major parts of a program are considered to reside in contiguous locations. (Operating-system issues are covered in the next section.) Later implementations of FORTRAN compilers did not retain the requirement that programs, subprograms, and data be allocated a single continuous memory area, but data for any one program or subprogram did have to be kept in a single area. The programmer does have some control of memory use, as with the *equivalence* (defining two or more arrays as users of the same memory space) and *common* (global) data declarations. Of interest when we compare it with the block-structured language model is the allocation of contiguous memory locations to a data array. Arrays are an important data structure to this language for scientific problem solving and the mapping from an n-dimensioned array to the contiguous data area in "column-major" ordering is specified by the language.

A computer architecture adapted to the FORTRAN language model should have facilities for mapping a large contiguous virtual-memory space to the physical memory. Since only one execution environment is needed for each program or subprogram, the virtual-memory space can be viewed as a "static" item, known at the time the program is translated (compiled). The paged form of virtual-to-physical-memory mapping is suited to the FORTRAN model. Procedure invocation can be handled by a simple "subroutine jump" instruction that leaves the return address at a designated location. Parameter association is handled by placing the address of the argument in the location reserved for the parameter in the subroutine data area. (The normal parameter call mechanism is "call by reference".) The array data structure is important to most FORTRAN programs and hardware support for rapid addressing of arrays is needed. For this purpose "register relative" addressing of memory (the location of the argument is formed from the sum of the address designated in the instruction and a value found in a register) is useful. In total, the architectural-support requirements imposed by the FORTRAN language are only slightly different from those found to be useful for scientific programming in assembly language. This is reflected by the similarity of the storage models shown in Figs. 5-1 and 5-2.

The "static block-structured" languages that are derived from ALGOL-60 introduce an additional set of hardware-support requirements. In the model of Fig. 5-3, which represents languages like ALGOL-60 and PASCAL, we see the storage model, Fig. 5-3(b), for a typical program, Fig. 5-3(a). In these block-structured languages both individual instruction sequences (PROGRAM, PROCEDURE A, FUNCTION B) and their data can reside in different memory areas. A compound data item like a multidimensional array can be decomposed for memory-allocation purposes into groups of scalar values and groups of pointers to those values with pointers to those pointers to a depth that reflects the number of dimensions to the array. This is possible because memory allocation and use are completely transparent to the programmer. (We find no "equivalence" or "common" in ALGOL-60 or PASCAL.) The distribution of the program over a wide range of memory locations might appear to complicate things for the compiler and for the operating system, but they do not if the computer has included hardware support

```
PROGRAM example;
VAR q: ARRAY [1..m,1..n] OF INTEGER;
    r: RECORD
            s: INTEGER
            CASE b BOOLEAN OF
               TRUE: (c: INTEGER);
               FALSE: (d: ARRAY [1..4] OF REAL)
        END;
    x,y: REAL;
    z: INTEGER;
PROCEDURE A ();
    -----
END {A};
PROCEDURE B ();
    -----
END {B};
BEGIN {example}
    -----
END {example}.
```

(a)

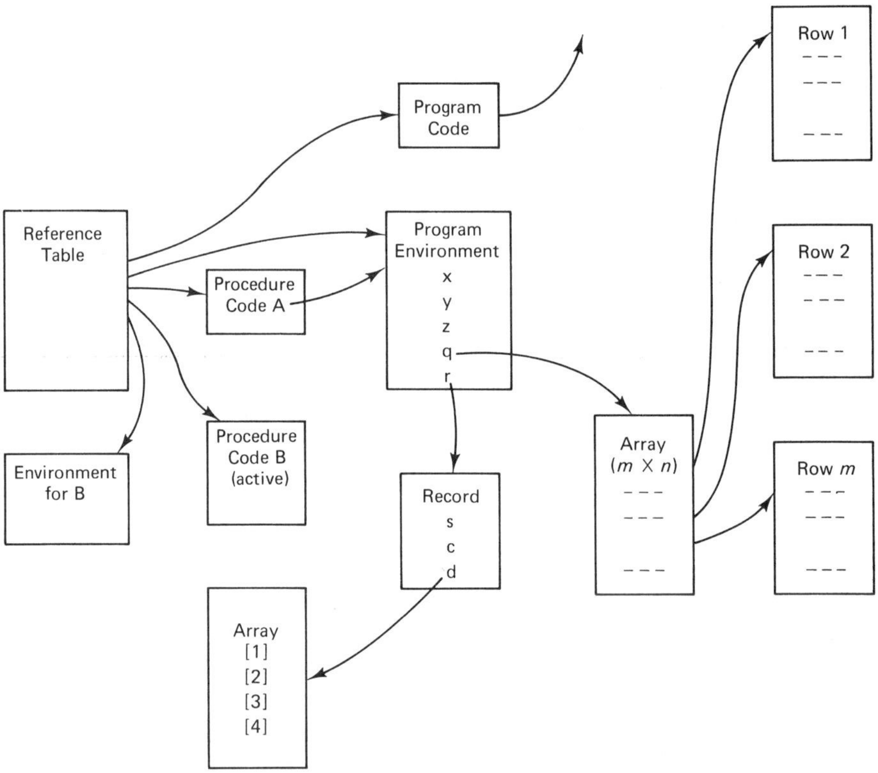

(b)

Figure 5-3 Block-structured language. (a) Program skeleton. (b) Storage
model.

for memory-segment linking. The benefits of reducing the requirements for large blocks of contiguous memory for each large program or compound data object can be substantial.

Although PASCAL and its offspring use the array, they also incorporate a heterogeneous compound data structure, the *record*. PL/1 and COBOL also use this form, calling it a "structure". The record, particularly with its "variant" field that permits a component to be of different types under different conditions, is particularly well adapted to the segmented approach to memory use shown in Fig. 5-3(b). The figure demonstrates that an effective indirect-addressing capability is important. This capability also is needed for implementation of the *pointer* data type in PASCAL and similar languages. A pointer variable is one that points to an item of some specified data type. Of course, the type pointed to can be a pointer and the data type can be used to build linked lists and tree structures.

With the static block-structured languages the scope of any identified item (variable, procedure, function, data type, constant) is established by the position in the program of the subprogram in which the item is defined. Thus, any variable is considered to be "local" or "nonlocal" with regard to the program or subprogram in which it is used. A means is required to connect the use of a nonlocal variable with the correct instance of that variable. Functions can be defined recursively (in terms of themselves); thus, subprograms must be "reentrant" (more than one incarnation active at one time). For each call of a procedure or a function there must be a complete execution environment, or data and parameter area, and a means to be sure that each is associated with the proper calling program or subprogram. To handle these sets of related execution environments, a flexible indirect-addressing mechanism is important. Indirection beyond that provided by the register relative addressing needed for FORTRAN arrays is very useful.

The procedure-definition facilities and the scope rules of block-structured languages encourage programming in small independent procedures connected only through parameter passing, a major aspect of modern structured programming technique. The effect of programming in small modules means that programs will execute a large number of subroutine calls. As we will see when we review performance issues related to instruction-set processors and their implementation, subprogram calls can average over 10% of all high-level language statements. Since the percentage of machine-level instructions required to initiate a procedure call and subsequent return usually is higher than that for other high-level control constructs, it is important that an architecture for these languages provide an efficient means for establishing new environments, for parameter passing, and for jumping to and from subroutine code areas.

Later developments in block-structured languages (PL/1, ALGOL-68, concurrent PASCAL, MODULA-2, EUCLID, ADA) added concurrent execution through parallel expressions and coroutines. This imposed a requirement for process synchronization if parallel computers were to exploit the concurrency. Data-type abstraction, the ability to define patterns for data types as well as the data types themselves, with languages like MODULA-2 adds to the generality of data definition and to the need for flexibility in assigning memory to data objects (name-location binding). The added features of concurrency and abstract data typing cause relatively minor extensions of the computer support already needed for the block-structured languages. A flexible indirect-referencing mechanism and an efficient means for invoking procedures are the key features required.

These block-structured languages are called "static" because the nature of the program structure (relationships among the program and all of the subprograms), the characteristics of all of the data items, and the scope of all variables and subprograms are completely defined when the program is written. Programs can be analyzed for syntax (parsed), translated to intermediate form, and optimized for execution on the target computer without regard for the specific data values to be used during execution. There are languages that are much more dynamic, where the translation can be affected severely by the input data. These languages, characterized by APL and LISP, were designed to have their programs translated by an "interpreter" and executed line by line, rather than being "compiled" in total before data is supplied.

These languages introduce a "dynamic" concept of data, wherein the structure or the type of a data item might change during execution. For example, an item named X can have an integer value at one instant and can be a multidimensional array a few instructions later. In APL, operator meanings might be dependent on the nature of the data being operated on. The languages are more algebra-like than the others we have discussed. Evaluation generally entails applying a function to a value to obtain a new value, to which a new function is applied. A more dynamic computational model is needed to represent programs in these languages.

As an example, the computational model for a simple program in LISP is shown in Fig. 5-4. The data structures include atoms and lists, where atoms are similar to scalar data items of the other languages, and a list (a rectangular box in the figure) contains two parts, each of which can be a list or an atom. The very simple syntax of LISP is shown by the representation of programs, Fig. 5-4(a), and compound data items, Fig. 5-4(b), as lists in the figure. The general computational model calls for a single imperative, "evaluate", that causes the innermost function to be applied to the value to yield a new value, with the evaluation repeated until there is a final value. The execution environments require dynamic association of names with values, as reflected by the *association list* shown in Fig. 5-4(c). This, or an equivalent mechanism, is used to associate an identifier with the most recently defined value for that identifier. When a value for an identifier is needed the association list is searched from the start (or from some intermediate marker if the scope of an identifier has been limited in a definition), examining the identifier of each identifier-value pair until the identifier is found. Then the value part of the pair is substituted for the identifier in the evaluation. The name-value binding is dynamic, as is shown by the association of X with "3" or with "*A N D*" in Fig. 5-4(c). The figure illustrates the need for an indefinite-level indirect-reference (pointer) scheme to support this dynamic language.

Languages based on predicate logic, such as PROLOG, are the subject of much interest for symbolic programming. Currently they are being used in artificial intelligence and for relational database management systems. In PROLOG the *Horn clause* forms the basic syntactic structure. The Horn clause takes the following form:

```
term0; term1 :- term2, term3,....termN.
```

which can be read as "the validity of term0 or of term1 is implied by the truth of term2

$(((f_1, f_2, x) (f_3, f_4, y) f_5, z) f_6, f_7 (f_8, x) f_9, f_{10}, z)$

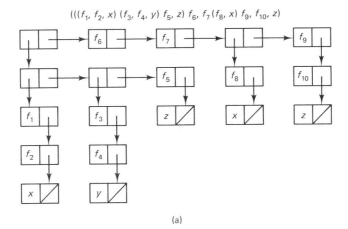

(a)

$((a_1, a_2, a_3) (a_4, a_5, a_6) (a_7, a_8, a_9))$

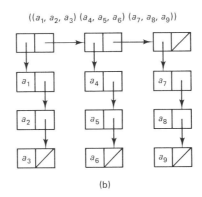

(b)

(x, y, z are variables, "3", "Q", "A", "D", "N" values)

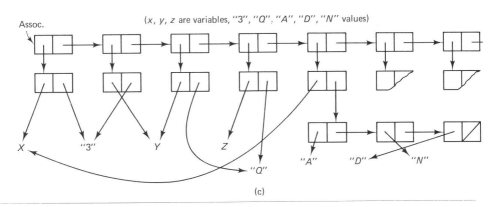

(c)

Figure 5-4 The computational model for LISP. (a) A program and its computation structure. (b) A data structure. (c) An association list.

and . . . termN". In PROLOG the separate alternatives on the left are expressed in separate clauses (implications). Terms are formed from atoms (constant strings beginning with a lowercase letter or an integer), variables (strings that begin with an uppercase letter), or functions of any number of arguments, where each argument is a term. More generally, the implication takes the form:

```
head :- body.
```

A clause without a body is an assertion or a rule, such as

```
larger (sun, earth).
```

(The sun is larger than the earth no matter what other conditions are true.) A clause without a head is a query, usually written:

```
?- larger (X, earth).
```
(Under what conditions is X larger than earth? Answer: X = sun.) General definitions can be formed with implications that use only variables as arguments for terms:

```
mother (X, Y) :- parent (X, Y), female (X).
father (X, Y) :- parent (X, Y), male (X).
grandmother (X, Y) :- mother (X, Y), parent (Y, Z).
grandfather (X, Y) :- father (X, Y), parent (Y, Z).
```

Following the definition of a set of implications and assertions, a query is evaluated by a scan of the implications and assertions with each evaluated from left to right, attempting to find matches of functions. When a match is found, tentative values of variables are assigned and the search is continued. If a matching of constants is found, the answer is produced (a value for a variable, or the value "yes"). If a match is not found, alternative possibilities are searched for. If none yield a complete match the answer "no" is returned. Matching against multiple variables (called *unification*) is a feature of the logic programming languages.

Architectures for these languages must have fast and flexible indirect referencing, simple and fast logical operators, methods to change the binding of values to variables rapidly, and the facility to hold nonnumeric strings of indeterminate size in memory and in processor registers. It is characteristic of PROLOG that individual operations are simple, but there are many of them, even in executing simple programs.

Object programming, represented by SMALLTALK, introduces other capabilities for the programmer and new requirements for hardware support if the computer is to reflect language requirements. In object programming, templates of similar data items and operations on the items (objects) are grouped into *classes*. Transfers and transformations to obtain values are initiated by message passing among objects, rather than by the procedure calls of the more common languages. Objects and classes are structured in a hierarchy of "inheritances" that identify the accesses (capabilities) allowed by other objects. For those who have become object programming-language users, the results in effective interactive computer use are striking.

Computer support for object programming languages include means for managing the inheritances and for implementing the message-passing mechanism of control. Figure 5-5 demonstrates how access to objects is managed in the IBM System/38, a computer designed to reflect object-oriented concepts. The definition of an object that has been "created" is held in a table that includes identification of the "owner" (the inheritance) and other attributes such as existence (rules about destruction). Operations allowable on all objects (generic) and those associated with a particular class (unique) are identified. Details of access to objects are removed from the programmer and all objects are "encapsulated" to make their definition, creation, and use high-level actions at the program level with the machine-level activities not seen by the user.

In the System/38 user-supplied symbolic names are converted to system pointers that identify the location of the object. If an access request (the operand) does not have associated with it an object location (the system pointer is "unresolved") the information is obtained through a context search in the name-location symbol table. Control of the inheritance rules is enforced by the user profiles that list the accesses allowed each user. Synchronizing multiple accesses to an object is handled by a "lock" similar to an operating-system semaphore. Tag fields in memory identify the nature of the information residing there and allow control of pointer accesses to object locations. Scaling and conversions of data to permit operation by "generic" type-independent operators is performed by the hardware. Resource management and process

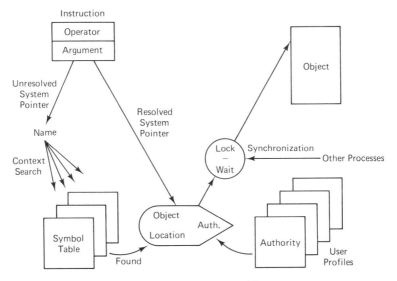

Figure 5-5 Access to objects.

scheduling are aided by queues and by the SEND and RECEIVE synchronizing operations supported by the hardware.

The System/38 was designed for business file-processing applications using programs written in high-level languages. Architectural features include implementation of the concept of objects in classes with inheritances. Capability-based addressing with a single-level storage system enforces the object discipline. The hardware and the software emphasize the data structures and the support processes needed to create, delete, address, and deliver "messages" (operations) to objects. The PMS structure of the System/38 is conventional, with a single processor, an I/O channel with the usual peripheral equipment, and a primary memory with a controller that controls access interleaving from the processor and the I/O channel. At the instruction-set-processor level the computer is microprogram controlled (see Chapter 6) with 32-bit microinstructions held in a control store. Virtual memory is implemented with a "virtual-address translation" unit, a translation lookaside buffer, and translation tables in memory. To a large extent, the System/38 appears as a direct implementation of a task-oriented operating system (covered in the next section).

The IBM System/38 is an excellent example of a computer designed to provide support for effective execution of programs written in a high-level language. Another example is the Burroughs B5500 (and its successors, now the Unisys A-series), which provided support for block-structured languages with its stack state, its indefinite-level indirect referencing, and its tagged memory. These characteristics are described in this and the next chapter.

These specific examples might be studied in detail to see how excellent language support was provided in two cases. Examples, however, do not give us guidance on principles to be applied more generally. W. A. Wulf [WulfW81] outlined the view of a compiler developer in specifying some general principles about hardware support for languages. The major characteristics desired are as follows:

Regularity: uniform treatment of features throughout the system, such as operations on different data types, use of registers, and source–destination description.

Orthogonality: ability to treat independently separate concerns like addressing, operations, and data types.

Composability: ability to compose the regular and orthogonal notions in arbitrary ways.

These three characteristics have been grouped under the term *orthogonality* by other investigators.

The difficulty of tailoring an architecture to any particular language is reinforced by the introduction of new languages with new characteristics. Recent examples are the extensions of LISP for artificial-intelligence applications, the rapidly growing interest in logic programming, and the purely functional languages such as HOPE and MIRANDA. As new languages are accepted, computer architects must understand their principle features to determine how new computers might provide maximum support.

5.3 PROCESSORS AND OPERATING SYSTEMS

The point has been made that the computer should be viewed by the system architect as a virtual machine consisting of the hardware and the operating system. When possible, the computer hardware and its operating system should be designed concurrently. There will be evolutionary modifications to the hardware and to the operating system, but if the two were designed as one virtual system the modifications required can maintain the compatibility initially established. When they are designed together it is easy for the hardware engineers and the operating-system designers to interact so that the hardware supports the software and the software takes advantage of hardware features.

Unfortunately, sometimes computers are not delivered with an operating system that meets the requirements of a particular user and an operating system must be designed well after the computer itself. The problems to be faced by developers of that operating-system software are not a subject of this book, but any communication that a computer architect might have with them can be useful in identifying hardware features that in the past made operating-system development more difficult. Alternatively, the computer architect is faced with situations in which a new computer must be designed to use an existing operating system. There have been several recent examples of computers (e.g., Sun and Unisys workstations, NCR "Tower") designed to use the Bell Laboratories UNIX operating system that almost has become a standard for university computer-science research. In this case, as well as when the total virtual system is being designed, the computer architect can provide features to support the operating system.

A review of the major functions of operating systems provides guidance on hardware support that might be useful. Operating systems provide for automatic resource management and process scheduling. The objective is to optimize, according to specified criteria, the application of the computer resources to execution of all the programs to be run. The first operating systems provided for sequencing of user jobs in order of their arrival after checking that the system had sufficient resources for each job to be run to completion. Jobs with similar resource needs were "batched" to be run in succession to maximize utilization of the expensive computers. These simple batch operating systems used a "job-control language" to permit users to specify resource requirements and any special characteristics of the programs to be run. The batch operating systems had little architectural influence and little support was required from the hardware. Register-based addressing and concurrent central processor and I/O activity permitted loading of a subsequent job while a job was active and allowed for execution of a job while the results of the previous job were being printed.

In 1961 much more sophisticated operating systems emerged. The Atlas computer at Manchester University was designed with a two-level store (virtual memory) and with flexible input/output capabilities, both managed by a program called the operating system. At about the same time Burroughs announced the B5000, a multiple-processor machine with virtual memory and with a "master control program" that performed resource management and process scheduling. At MIT an experimental time-sharing operating system, CTSS, was developed to be implemented on the IBM 7094. These were followed by the MIT Multics operating system and by the long line of operating systems provided with the IBM 360 series and its successors. In 1974 an elegantly simple time-sharing operating system named UNIX was described by Bell Laboratories. Principles of operating systems and of hardware support required to support them have evolved over this period.

The functions of an operating system can be separated into two main categories, resource management and process scheduling. The resources include all allocable parts of the computer hardware (registers apparent to the user, primary-memory areas, secondary memory, processors, input/output controllers, etc.) and software (shared data, virtual-memory segments, files, shared procedures, interfacing routines, diagnostic routines, software-derived buffers, etc.). Associated with each active resource is a "resource descriptor" that is data on the resource for the operating system. The descriptor defines the resource and includes information on the identity, lifetime, owners, quantity, users, and control procedures associated with the resource. When a process needs the resource the operating system references the descriptor to determine the resource status. If the resource cannot be allocated the process requesting the resource is placed in a queue to wait for release of the resource by another process. Figure 5-6 shows a data structure for maintaining a queue of processes waiting for availability of a sharable resource. Included at the head of the queue are pointers to the procedures for inserting and for removing processes from the waiting list. The resources might be reusable resources that are kept available even when not in use or can be consumable resources that are discarded after use. In either case the operating system must manage the creation, allocation and release, and destruction of the resources.

Process scheduling requires that there be information on each process in the system, represented as a "process descriptor". This descriptor contains information on the identification of, the resources required for execution by, the current status of, the owner of, the processes owned by, and the scheduling criteria for the process. Processes that have all of the required resources are placed on a "ready list" and are available for scheduling. Figure 5-7 shows a prioritized ready list with queues of processes waiting at each priority level. The scheduler is an operating-system process that takes ready processes in order and activates them as processors become available. During execution a process might require that a subsidiary process be activated, for example to request a resource. The

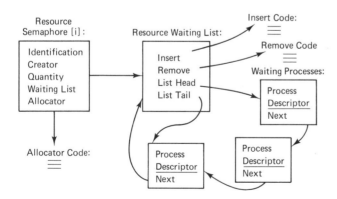

Figure 5-6 Operating-system re-source-management data structure.

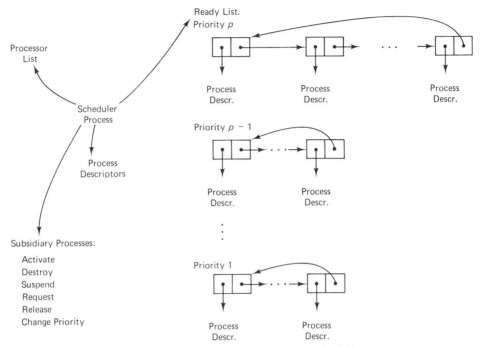

Figure 5-7   Operating-system process scheduling.

subsidiary process might lead to resumption of the original process, its return to the ready list, a change in its status, or its removal from the system.

The last two figures represent a general approach to resource management and process scheduling in a shared-resource multiprocessing environment. Many simplifications are possible in less-demanding environments, but the characteristics of operating systems are best seen in the general case. Hardware features that help the operating system can be deduced from the illustrations. Facilities for creating and for using linked lists are needed. To this end, indefinite-level indirect addressing can be very useful, as it is for handling higher-level programming languages.

Since the operating-system program consists of many individual concurrent processes, features that support process synchronizing are particularly useful. Hardware support for process activation and deactivation and for context switching is needed. Instructions like a combined "test–set–branch" assist in implementing synchronization primitives for process coordination. These are used to protect processes from damaging each other through uncontrolled modification of shared data resources. Almost every operating system is written in a high-level programming language, often a general language modified to add features to control hardware resources. The language-support features described in the last section are useful to the operating-system development. Some of the heavily used operating-system routines can be implemented at the hardware level as sequences of "microprogrammed" instructions, which are discussed in Chapter 6.

When multiple users simultaneously employ a computer they might interfere with each other's programs and data unless each is careful not to operate outside an assigned memory area. Rather than depending on users to observe the memory-use discipline required, most multiprocessing operating systems provide memory protection. Such protection can be provided if the operating system manages all memory allocation and relocation. All memory references are made through the operating system. To eliminate the need for operating-system intervention on each memory reference (an approach that would be a very heavy drain on computer performance), the checks that a reference is "in bounds" can be performed by the language translators or by the hardware. In either case the bounds and access parameters are set by the operating system. Most operating-system designers prefer that there be hardware support for memory protection as a part of virtual-memory implementation (Chapter 4). That is because the operating-system designer might not have control of the language translators and cannot be sure that the protection will be enforced during translation. Hardware support for memory bounds checking usually entails the use of upper and lower "bounds registers" that are set whenever a new code of data segment is entered. Each memory access is checked by the hardware to ensure that it is within the range specified by the bounds registers. Register-based addressing, described in Section 5.7, can facilitate bounds checking since the minimum bound is the value of the reference register.

With any real-time operating system and in most other operating systems there is a need to respond to external stimuli. Even with very simple systems, there are "I/O-complete" signals that a transfer has been accomplished. With a tightly coupled multiprocessing system, related processes might need means to interrupt each other for synchronization. A hardware-initiated interrupt system can relieve the operating system of much testing to determine if an interrupt-causing event has occurred. The interrupt system should be coupled with the operating system through easy-to-test flags, possibly accompanied by hardware-called control programs. The interrupt system then is a basic part of the virtual machine that is the hardware, its control structure, and the operating system. Computer interrupt systems are described in Section 5.5. Many of the features required by an operating system are similar to those required for object programming, which was described in the previous section (Fig. 5-5).

A dynamic operating system of the type described is called on many times while user programs are operating. The computer system must provide facilities for switching from user to operating-system tasks and back. These facilities are described in the next chapter when we address context switching.

5.4 PROCESSOR STATE

In the review of the instruction-set-processor descriptive language in Chapter 2 we were introduced to "processor state", the specification of the registers and the flip-flops in the processor that are apparent to the user. Examples in Chapters 2 and 4 showed how registers have been used in different processor architectures. In Chapter 4 the place of processor registers in the storage hierarchy was described and we saw the relationship between the processor registers and primary memory. Cache memory was introduced as a device to buffer primary memory. Now we examine some issues related to the processor state itself.

When we have a hierarchy of storage mechanisms we also have a need to control those mechanisms. The operating system manages virtual memory by controlling the interaction between primary and secondary memories. Movement of information between the cache and the primary memory is controlled by the computer hardware. Processor-register allocation, except for those registers used for operating-system controlled functions, is accomplished by the translators, assemblers, compilers, or interpreters that convert user programs to machine programs. The differences in control sources for the different levels of the memory hierarchy influence how much memory should be assigned at each level.

In Chapter 4 a comparison was made between the combination of a cache and a low-speed primary memory as opposed to a smaller but faster primary memory alone. A similar question might be raised with regard to processor storage and the cache. Would our system be more cost effective if we designed it to have a larger complement of registers instead of the cache? Even if processor registers have 10 times the unit cost of cache memory we could provide a large complement of fast processor registers for the same price as a typical cache. A specific trade-off analysis would be needed to answer this question for any individual computer design, but some general parameters can be considered. We must compare the cost of the support logic as well as that of the registers in the two cases. The comparison logic of the cache and the added switching must be compared with the increased busing for register-to-register transfers. Since much of the cache-memory operation can be overlapped with processor activities we have to examine whether the additional processor registers increase "in-line" performance more than the "off-line" performance increase due to the cache. Perhaps a small bank of fully associative registers acting as a local "lookaside" will prove better than a bank of registers and a cache. We should not be inhibited by prior history in examining how to use processor storage because much can be gained if we can find better ways to use this valuable resource.

In the last section we saw that hardware support can be provided to make the operating system more effective and easier to design. One feature that we might consider is the assignment of a specific bank of registers for exclusive use by the operating system, as was done by the UNIVAC 1107 designers (see Fig. 4-5). If we examine the question in light of today's electronic technology we might find better ways to use the registers given to the operating system. Establishing separate banks of registers makes it easier to establish independent operating modes for the operating system and user programs, leading to improved protection of operating-system resources. It also could eliminate most context switching when a user process and an operating-system process alternate. However, if it is more normal for several different operating-system processes to interact before control is returned to the user process the separate set of operating-system registers might not prove effective.

When considering a large quantity of registers we must appreciate that for the benefits gained with a large processor state there is the penalty that most of the state must be stored when we change context, as by responding to an interrupt or by initiating a call on a new procedure. It is true that if we allocate some of the registers to context switching we can save some state in the registers so assigned. However, that only helps if we are switching between two different contexts. The more general case of a procedure calling a procedure that calls a procedure . . . , or that of an interrupt interrupting an interrupt that interrupts an interrupt . . . , is not helped by a single level of storage devoted to context switching. It probably is more useful to use registers to facilitate moving to primary memory the state of those processes that are to be suspended rather than allocating them to hold such a state.

If we consider using registers for special operating-system related activities we might also consider other special uses. An example in Chapter 4 (Fig. 4-6) showed the use of three different register banks in the Control Data Cyber for addresses, for indexing, and for operators. The IBM architecture that started with the System/360 has two different sets of registers, the general registers and the floating-point registers. In the Intel 8086, we saw that the registers each have a designated function. A fourth example, that of the Digital Equipment VAX architecture is shown in Fig. 5-8. The VAX contains 16 general registers, certain of which (R12 through R15) are "reserved" for special use by the software. Although these registers have specified uses they can be used for any purpose. There is no hardware protection to ensure that the reserved registers are not loaded with undesired information by a user program.

If registers are assigned unique functions the control logic can use those registers directly and there is no need to address the registers in machine-level instructions. When we specialize we might be limiting the quantity of arguments that we can hold in the processor to less than the amount of storage available. If registers were truly general we might use all of them with more flexibility. Again, we see the conflict between the speed

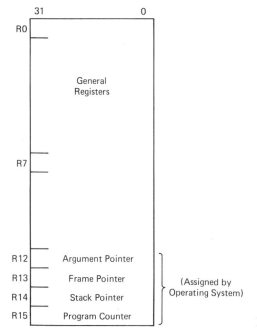

Figure 5-8 VAX register organization.

of specialization and the flexibility of generality. We have to decide in each specific case after analyzing alternatives and measuring the results against our objectives.

As will be seen when we discuss reduced instruction-set computers in Section 6.5, investigators at the University of California at Berkeley did perform a careful study of register use before specifying register uses in their RISC processors. They determined that a large (138) bank of registers organized to minimize data transfers on procedure call and return would be an effective use of hardware resources.

There are alternatives to treating registers as individual addressable entities. We might use some of the registers in special data structures such as a stack or a queue. In those instances the registers are connected in a designated way and are used as extensions of and as pointers to information structures in primary memory. The stack is a "last-in first-out" dynamic data structure that is accessed only by way of the most recent value entered. On the other hand, the queue is a "first-in first-out" dynamic data structure that has information entered at one end and removed from the other end. In both cases the data structures are of indefinite size, just enough to hold all the information contained. Hardware implementations should simulate the dynamic size variation as closely as possible.

It is unfortunate that the stack data structure usually is introduced by demonstrating its use in evaluating parenthesis-free postfix (inverse Polish) notation, for there are more important reasons for using this data structure. The stack used this way as a holder of operands certainly is useful, and is even more useful as a holder of operators to generate the postfix notation from an expression or a statement in infix notation that might contain parentheses. A simple set of rules permits the change in notation, allowing for the rules of precedence and associativity of the infix language. Figure 5-9 demonstrates this use of the stack in translation and in execution of arithmetic statements.

The statement with parentheses to be translated and executed is shown in Fig. 5-9(a). Generation of the parenthesis-free postfix equivalent using the stack to hold operators is shown in Fig. 5-9(b). At the point shown in the left side of Fig. 5-9(b) the statement has been scanned from left to right, operators and the left parenthesis have been stacked, and the output stream of operands has been generated. At the end of the statement the operators are "popped" from the stack to give the final output stream shown in the right side of Fig. 5-9(b). There are three simple rules about operators and parentheses:

    a. When an operator is found, if it has lower precedence than the one on the top of the stack (* is higher than +) place the one on the stack in the output stream before pushing the new operator on the stack.

    b. When a right parenthesis is encountered, clear the stack (by popping operators) until the first left parenthesis is encountered.

    c. When the end of statement symbol (;) is encountered, clear the rest of the stack by popping operators in sequence.

The reader should compare the result illustrated with the one that would come from

$$x := (a + b) * c + d;$$

x := a + b * (c + 3);

(a)

output stream: x a b c 3   output stream:

stack: +   x a b c 3 + * + :=

          (

          *

          +

          :=

Before Emptying Stack   Postfix Result

(b)

rest of sequence: + * + :=   postfix:

stack: 3   (x, (((3, c, +), b, *), a, +), :=)

         c

         b   infix:

         a   x := a + b * (c + 3)

         x

Between 3 and +   Result of Execution

Figure 5-9 A stack in arithmetic operations. (a) Statement in higher-level language. (b) An "operator" stack for translation. (c) An "operand" stack for execution.

(c)

(The result should be "x a b + c * d + :=".)

In Fig. 5-9(c) the evaluation of the expression is shown. Here the evaluation using a left-to-right scan of the postfix expression is straightforward:

> Push operands on the stack. When an operator is encountered, apply it to the appropriate number of operators from the top of the stack, pushing the result on the stack.

The result of the scan to the point that the first + has been encountered is shown in the left side of Fig. 5-9(c). The result of applying the rules to the whole expression is shown in the right side of Fig. 5-9(c), with parentheses added to create the triplets that show the order of evaluation. The result is that which would be found if we used the rules of algebra on the original statement. (Again, the reader should perform the evaluation of the altered statement shown before to obtain (x,(((a,b,+),c,*),d,+),:=).)

Notwithstanding these uses for arithmetic purposes, the main benefit of the stack data structure in a computer is for dynamic storage of execution environments. The example of Fig. 5-10 shows how the indefinite structure of the stack allows for storing the process state of several successive callers of other processes. The example includes recursive calls on a function that calls itself. The dynamic history of environments in call sequence is shown by identifying the process names in the stack of the illustration. At the point illustrated the operating system has initiated the main program, which called procedure A, which called function B, which called itself. Dynamic "calling-sequence" pointers placed in the stack word that separates environments trace the history of execution. The static "parent" pointers in the separator word identify the scope of

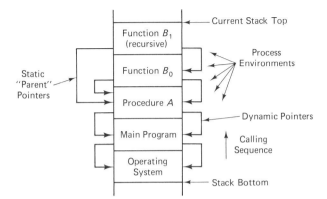

Figure 5-10 Process environments in a stack.

functions and procedures by pointing to the environment for the program segment in which the subprograms were defined. The stack data structure facilitates implementation of "reentrant" procedures that are called by different procedures, including themselves, with complete freedom (as far as the implementation is concerned).

When a stack is to be incorporated in the design we must decide the extent to which it should be supported by hardware. At one extreme, there need be no hardware support beyond allowing a general register to be used to designate the location in memory of the registers that address the stack. Many operating systems and compilers for general-register machines use several of the registers as stack pointers and stack bounds pointers when a stack data structure is needed. At the other extreme, we might design the whole processor around the stack data structure, as Burroughs did with their large machines starting with the B5000 in 1961. Most microprocessors take an intermediate stance, since they are designed to be used in a wide variety of user-designed virtual computers. The Intel 8086 instruction-set processor, as we saw in Chapter 2, has a register (SR) designated as the stack pointer and another (SS) as the pointer to the base of the current stack segment. The Motorola 68000 family of microprocessors contains two stack pointer registers, one for the current user program and one for the supervisor program.

The Hewlett-Packard 3000 computer series incorporated a hardware-controlled stack as its primary processor data structure. The HP 3000 stack, its pointers, and its extensions in the processor are shown in Fig. 5-11. The processor contained five stack control registers and four "top-of-stack" registers. The stack control registers were pointers to the stack in primary memory. Register DB pointed to the extent of the global data area in memory. The pointer identified the boundary between this set of processes and any others (including the operating system) that resided in memory. Registers SM and Q pointed to "stack markers" of environment boundaries, SM to the current marker and Q to its predecessor in the history of execution (the caller of the present process). The stack markers themselves (in memory) contained pointers to their dynamic predecessors and to the markers that identified their immediate ancestors in the static program structure, as was shown in the stack of Fig. 5-10. In memory the parameters for a procedure (values or pointers) were held immediately below the marker. Space for local variables and any temporary storage was built above the stack marker as the procedure

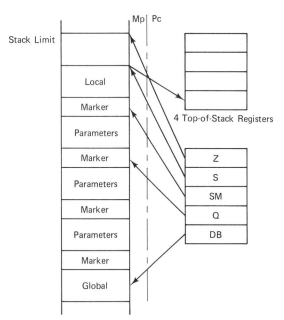

Figure 5-11 Hewlett-Packard 3000 stack.

was executed. For the current process, that whose marker was pointed to by register SM, the temporary storage was the active part of the stack. The four top locations of the stack extended into the processor and register S pointed to the topmost value that was in memory. The limit of the memory area allocated to the stack was contained in register Z. The HP 3000 stack organization was very straightforward and had many similarities to the stack of the Burroughs B5000. It is interesting to compare it with the "cactus stack" of the B6700 and its successors in the Unisys A series, shown in Fig. 5-12.

The B6700 Pc state was comprised of 4 top-of-stack registers, 32 display registers, and 4 stack pointer registers: S (top of stack in memory), F (control word for current process), SL (upper stack limit), and BOS (bottom of stack). As shown in Fig. 5-12, the stack, except for the extension to the four registers in the processor, was held in primary memory. Transfers between the registers and the rest of the stack as the stack was "pushed" or "popped" was in double word writes or reads masked as far as possible by instruction-fetch and operator-execution times. Larger versions of this system, such as the B7900, have more top-of-stack registers in the processor. Multiple-word transfers between the processor and memory are used to minimize stack operation delays. The inclusion of more of the stack speeds processing but means that more information has to be pushed when the environment is to be saved.

Boundaries between execution environments are identified in Fig. 5-12 by mark stack control words (MSCW) that are the bottom word in each execution environment. Each MSCW holds a displacement (dp) to point to the previous MSCW in the (dynamic) call sequence. It also holds a pointer (sp) to the parent environment, similar to that shown in Fig. 5-10. The display registers also point to the MSCWs showing the (static) relationship of scope of processes. These

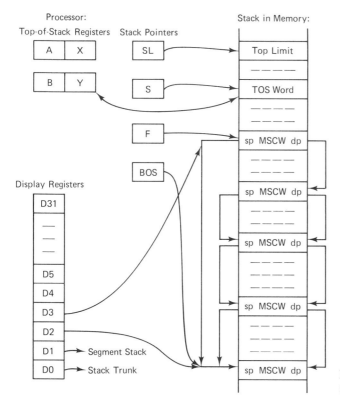

Figure 5-12 Burroughs B6700 stack and registers.

registers provide rapid automatic referencing of ancestor environments to support access to nonlocal variables and subprograms. Display registers D0 and D1 point to the MSCW of the *stack trunk* (the root of the cactus stack) and the MSCW of the *segment vector* (the stack branch that holds pointers to all program and subprogram code) for the program being executed. The cactus stack organization is, in effect, a data structure that contains all of the branches available to the operating system. There are separate sets of branches for each user active in the system.

If the stack is a natural data structure for connecting related processes the queue is a natural data structure for holding a waiting list of instructions that have been fetched from memory preparatory to their execution. The Intel 8086 contains a 6-byte instruction queue, the VAX-11/780 has one of 8-byte length, and the IBM 308X central processor contains a queue of four double words. Instruction queues usually have been kept relatively small in order not to require refilling when a conditional branch instruction is encountered. Many attempts have been made to form general guidelines about which of two branches is more likely to be taken in typical programs.

In the IBM 3090, when iteration sequences ("DO loops" in FORTRAN terminology) are being executed it is assumed that most of the time the sequence is repeated and the branch address to the start of the sequence is preexecuted and placed in the queue. For conditional branches two hardware support features are provided. The instruction queue is monitored for condition-code setting instructions (discussed in Chapter 6). If there are none the current condition-code setting can be assumed correct and the branch determined by that setting is followed. For the case where there is a condition-code setting instruction in the queue, a decision on most likely value is made by referring to a decode history table to determine what was the outcome of the previous test of the condition for the instruction. The approach is analogous to using history to predict the data that should be kept in a cache.

An interesting instruction queue is that of the Control Data Cyber series, inherited from the CDC 6600. As demonstrated in Fig. 5-13, this queue (it was called an *instruction stack*) of eight 60-bit words is fed by a buffer register that receives the instructions from memory. An instruction can contain 15 or 30 bits and the 30-bit instructions need not start at word boundaries. When an instruction word from the queue has been copied into the instruction registers, it is passed along the queue to make space for the next word. Thus, the instruction queue holds the last 16 to 32 instructions executed. Any time that a branch instruction is encountered in the instruction decoder, it is determined if the target of the branch already resides in the instruction queue. If so, the memory fetch is inhibited and the instruction words in the queue are cycled through from the beginning. As a result of this organization short loops of instructions (from 16 to 32) can be executed from the queue without requiring memory accesses. The attitude of the 6600 architects on conditional branches was that the outcome of tests for the conditional branch could not be forecast in general, but that in the loops encountered so often in dealing with arrays the exit from the loop will be the exception condition. Thus, it is better to have the queue, no matter how long, devoted to holding the sequence of instructions just executed. An interesting by-product of the design is the encouragement to programmers to write programs with many short loops in sequence rather than with fewer larger nested loops. (We are taught to use the latter approach when learning structured programming methods.)

In some of the very large computers the instruction queue was combined with effective-address calculations so that an argument queue could be filled as previous

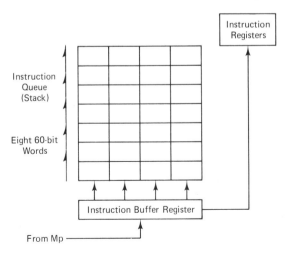

Figure 5-13   Instruction queue of the CDC Cyber computers.

instructions were being executed. Figure 5-14 is an example of such an organization, showing that instructions in the stream are decoded to determine how the physical address of the argument is to be obtained. The operator is passed to the instruction queue, whereas the address part is used to perform the effective address calculation and to fetch the operand. The effectiveness of this approach and the size of the queue required depend on the mix of indexed, direct, and indirect addresses. Whether this is an effective way to use registers, as opposed to using the hardware for longer independent instruction queues and larger general-register banks, is questionable. The approaches that might be used in very large computers are discussed in Chapter 8.

An interesting example of use of registers in a processor designed to support higher-level language is that of the MIT "Scheme-79" microprocessor (Fig. 5-15) that implements a dialect of the LISP language. Data in the computer memory (the *heap*) is represented as 64-bit (two physical word) list cells that have two parts (called CAR and CDR for historical reasons). Each 32-bit part contains a mark field, a type field, and a datum field. One role of a 7-bit type field is to identify whether the data field of 24 bits is a value or a pointer. Those familiar with LISP will see the uniform data structure of LISP data and programs in this computer word structure (see Fig. 5-4). The mark fields designate whether the cell is in use (CAR mark) or is being traced (CDR mark) during a garbage collection of discarded cells. The ADDRESS and MEMORY registers communicate with the processor registers (and with an INTER-RUPT register) over a 32-bit bus.

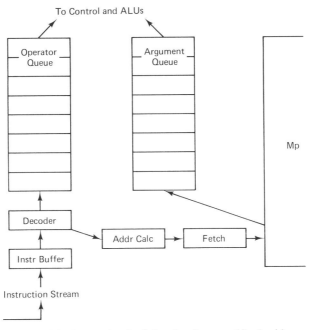

Figure 5-14   Instruction lookahead and operand lookaside.

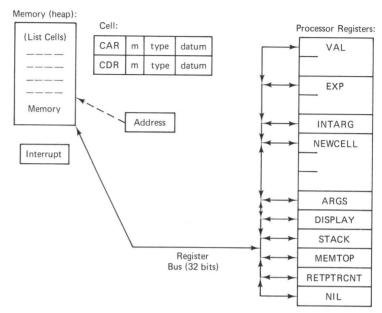

Figure 5-15   Scheme-79, a LISP microprocessor. (Adapted from [SussG81].)

The processor contains 10 functional registers, three of which require multiple physical registers. VAL (2 words) holds the value of the last expression evaluated. EXP (2 words) points to the expression currently being evaluated. ARGS points to the arguments for a procedure. STACK points to the stack of pending returns and their states. The stack itself is built from LISP cells in the heap. MEMTOP identifies the upper bound of the heap. DISPLAY specifies the current lexical environment. RETPTRCNT points to the return pointer count mark. NEWCELL (3 words) is used to build a new LISP cell. INTARG is a temporary holder of arguments during an evaluation. NIL is used as a target for a list terminator.

The heap memory holds data and program list structures, both of which have the same form (Fig. 5-4). Periodically, "garbage collection" must be performed to collect the discarded list cells. The same processor is used for evaluation and for garbage collection with different uses for the registers. Evaluation entails the traversal of a tree of cells. When a function is encountered, that function is applied to its arguments if they have been evaluated. Otherwise, the function is pushed onto the stack. The Scheme-79 organization is a direct implementation of LISP on a very simple processor.

The Symbolics 3600 computer is a LISP-based machine that has many of the features of the Scheme-79 microprocessor. The 3600 was developed for commercial applications of LISP-like language programming. It has sufficient generality to be useful with most other programming languages, but at less advantage compared with more conventional architectures.

5.5 ENVIRONMENTS, CONTEXT SWITCHING, AND INTERRUPTS

When characteristics of language were reviewed in Section 5.2, the "execution environment" of a process was defined as the information known to the process (more formally, the "bindings" that exist during execution). A process state change is required to activate a new environment whenever a procedure or function is called. When the subroutine is finished the former environment (that of the caller) must be resumed. We will see in the discussion of performance in Chapter 6 that a significant percentage of all instructions executed with compiled programs are procedure calls and returns. If execution environments cannot be created and released quickly a severe performance penalty can result. Memory that can be accessed very quickly is required to hold the environment so that instructions can obtain arguments with as little delay as possible. As much of the environment as is feasible should be available in processor registers when needed.

The different architectures treat the creation and the termination of execution environments in different ways. Stack-structured machines (e.g., Fig. 5-11 and 5-12) use stack operations to add to or delete from the top of the stack as information is produced or consumed in a process environment. When a new environment is called for, as in a procedure invocation, a marker is placed on the stack and initialization information (return address, environment of the caller, environment of the parent, parameter values) is entered. The new process (invoked procedure) then builds the rest of its environment by entering its local variables and temporary values during computation. When the process is completed and values have been returned to the caller (perhaps by leaving them at the top of the stack), the environment for the process is released by discarding information down to the stack marker and returning the calling-process state.

Many computers support the creation of execution environments by using a stack for the return information and register–memory exchanges to change environments. This involves transfers to memory locations of that part of the calling-process environment that is in registers, and transfers from memory of the part of the new environment that is needed to initiate the new process. In many cases a stack is used to hold pointers to memory blocks that hold the environments for processes that have called new processes (invoked procedures or functions). Most microprocessors have one or more stack pointers that are used in this manner. As we saw in Fig. 5-8, a stack pointer for the current process is included in the general registers of the VAX. When an architecture provides no hardware support for a stack, compiler and operating-system designers usually build one or more stacks with software, using general registers as stack pointers.

A user program usually contains many subprograms (procedures and functions). The execution environments that are associated with the sequences of invocation of the program and all its subprograms can be grouped together as a "context" for the program during its execution. The context of a program (or job) is the collection of hardware and software resources allocated by the operating system. The allocation can be static over the life of the job or can change dynamically as the processes of the program claim and release resources. The operating system must maintain a record of the context of each job that has been granted resources. This is a part of the resource-management activity of operating systems that we discussed in the last chapter. As an example, the VAX has pointers to five stacks for the set of operating-system and user processes (kernel, executive, supervisor, user, interrupt) that define a single "context".

Whenever the process scheduler of the operating system is called on to suspend a process and activate another, the record of the suspended process context must be saved and a record of the active one established. This activity is known as *context switching*. It is analogous to creation and suspension of execution environments, but it involves a larger amount of information and requires a larger amount of operating-system intervention. A computer architecture should support both execution environment management and context switching. Many of the features introduced for environment management can be used for context switching. However, since context switching should be performed much less often than subprogram call and return, it is important that those features needed only for context switching not impose a heavy burden on execution-environment control.

The operating system itself is a program containing subprograms. It requires resources and has its own context. During execution it becomes a set of processes, each of which has an execution environment. Operating-system processes interact with each other and with the user programs. If it is necessary to perform a complete context change every time the operating system is called (as on each subprogram call or each input/output initiation) a large percentage of the processor capacity will be consumed in context switching. If the call on the operating system only requires the temporary exchange of execution environments the performance reduction can be minimized. (The Unisys 1100 architecture is organized to handle this switching between operating-system and user contexts with its dual general register sets, shown in Fig. 4-5.) A significant part of control design (implementation of the instruction-set processor described in Chapter 6) must be concerned with execution-environment management and with context switching.

Much of the process switching that occurs in running programs on a computer is initiated by events external to the process being executed. Examples include completion of a block transfer of information from or to a file, completion of a spooled printing, arrival of a message from a communications line, initiation of a higher-priority job, a data-dependent software error (e.g., divide by zero), a hardware fault (e.g., printer not ready), or a data transfer (e.g., parity) error. All of these are characterized by the unpredictability of the event. Some of the events themselves are expected, but the time at which they will occur is not known. It is possible to use software to test for these events, executing a "polling" routine periodically during execution of a program. This approach has shortcomings if the external event must be responded to quickly and if the events can occur only sporadically. A large amount of processor activity might be devoted to searching for absent events.

Most systems designed to operate with a large quantity of external events incorporate an interrupt system. Any event that should be responded to generates a signal that is tested for by the hardware (usually after execution of each individual machine instruction). The existence of the signal causes an interruption of the process being run and the invocation of an interrupt-service routine, usually part of the operating system. There are many different interrupt-causing events, some requiring much quicker response than others, some having higher urgency than others. Different priority levels can be established for the different types of interrupt so that an interrupt-response process itself is not interrupted by another event unless it is of higher priority.

If we introduce a priority-based interrupt system it is useful to have a queue for each level to permit interrupt signals (events) to be held while the current interrupt response and those of all higher-priority events are completed. The priority queue might be implemented in hardware logic as a "daisy chain" of signals that are held in the logic queue until higher-priority signals have been cleared. Alternatively, the queue of events awaiting response can be placed in queues by the operating-system software. These would appear like the queues of ready processes waiting for scheduling in Fig. 5-7.

There are several ways that hardware features can support transfer of control to the specific procedure required in response to a given interrupt condition. There might be a single "interrupt flag" that causes a running process to be interrupted. A "program trap" then invokes the interrupt-response program that examines all interrupt lines to cause a branch to the specific service routine required. We also can have a number of interrupt flags, each invoking a different service routine after interrupting the running process. Often this is accomplished by having the operating system branch indirectly to the location specified at the memory address that is associated with the particular interrupt flag. Many combinations of these approaches have been used.

A complete example of a successful system will serve to describe context switching and interrupt processing. Figure 5-16 shows the registers used for environment, context, and interrupt control in the VAX. We will examine how the VAX handles environment switching when a procedure is called or context switching when

```
{General Registers:}
    GR[12]<31..0>,            {Argument Pointer}
    GR[13]<31..0>,            {Frame Pointer}
    GR[14]<31..0>,            {Stack Pointer}
    GR[15]<31..0>,            {Program Counter}

{Processor Registers (transparent to user):}
    KSP<31..0>,               {Kernel Stack Pointer}
    ESP<31..0>,               {Executive Stack Pointer}
    SSP<31..0>,               {System Stack Pointer}
    USP<31..0>,               {User Stack Pointer}
    ISP<31..0>,               {Interrupt Stack Pointer}
    PSL<31..0>,               {Processor Status Longword}
    PSW<15..0> := PSL<15..0>, {Processor Status Word}
    PCBB<31..0>,              {Process Control Block Base}
    P0BR<31..0>,              {Process 0 Base Register}
    P1BR<31..0>,              {Process 1 Base Register}
    P0LR<31..0>,              {Process 0 Length Register}
    P1LR<31..0>,              {Process 0 Length Register}

{Registers in Primary Memory:}
    PCB[0..23]<31..0>,        {Program Control Block}
        {Holds copies of KSP, ESP, SSP, USP,
         GR[0..13,15], PSL, P0BR, P0LR, P1BR, P1LR}
    PCEM<15..0>,              {Procedure Call Entry Mark}
        {First word of a procedure}
```

Figure 5-16 VAX registers for environment and context control.

a process is suspended by the operating system. The figure also will be used to present the extensive interrupt and exception-handling system of the VAX. Registers KSP, ESP, SSP, USP, and ISP are pointers to the location in memory of stacks for the four operating modes of the VAX system (kernel, executive, supervisor, and user) and of a special interrupt stack. (General register 14 points to the currently active stack.)

Subroutine invocation is handled in either of two ways. In the simpler of the two a jump to subroutine is executed (branch to subroutine is similar). This instruction causes the value of the program counter (general register 15) to be pushed on the active stack. (The value is stored in the location pointed to by the stack pointer and the stack pointer is incremented.) The program counter then is loaded with the target of the branch (determined by the effective address of the instruction argument). Return from subroutine entails popping the value on the active stack to the program counter (reading the value in memory pointed to by the stack pointer to the control-region base register, P1BR, and decrementing the stack pointer). Any movement of information related to the execution environments must be handled independently. This form of subroutine jump is similar to that included on most microprocessors. The stack is used only to hold program-counter values for correct return.

In the more extensive procedure call all of the general registers used by the procedure are saved, the parameters (arguments) are passed to the new procedure, and the stack, frame, and argument pointers (general registers 12, 13, and 14) are maintained. There are two procedure call instructions: CALLS with actual parameters on the stack, and CALLG with arguments in an arbitrary location. Both call instructions cause the program counter to be set to the value found from the effective address calculation. The first word of the procedure code is a procedure-call entry mask that specifies which registers the subprogram will use. Values (those of the caller) in these registers are saved as a new stack frame on the stack with the values of the frame and argument pointers, the program counter, the procedure-call register mask, and the processor-status word (the right half of the processor-status longword). The stack-pointer value is placed in the frame pointer to point to the new frame and a new stack-pointer value is formed by adding the size of the new frame to the old value. The argument pointer is set to the argument location specified in the CALLG instruction or to the former stack-pointer value in the case of a CALLS. In either case the argument pointer refers to the actual parameter list. With both instructions, the program counter is set to the address that results from the destination-argument effective-address calculation. The return-from-procedure instruction recovers the process state that was stored in the stack frame and returns the processor values to those that existed at the call, except for values returned by the procedure.

Context switching from any mode is effected by gathering the content of the general registers, the other mode stack pointers, the program-status longword, and the base and length registers for the program and control region page tables (P0BR, P0LR, P1BR, and P1LR). This current context is placed in a process-control block in memory, pointed to by the process-control block base (PCBB). Two instructions, "save process context" and "load process context", support context switching. The PCBB value is pushed on the currently active stack for recovery when the process is to be reactivated. The process that replaces the current process is activated by finding its process-control block in memory (its base address was placed on the stack when it was last deactivated) and loading it into the appropriate registers in the processor. The routines that control context switching are a part of the operating-system kernel.

We note that the processor-status longword (PSL) of the VAX includes a 5-bit interrupt priority-level field. This field reflects an extensive interrupt system with 31 priority levels, 16 (levels 16–31) for hardware-originated interrupts and 15 (1-15) for software. (Level 0 is for normal program execution.) When an interrupt request is made with priority higher than that stored in the PSL interrupt priority-level field the current process is interrupted and its state is stored by pushing the contents of the program counter (general register 15) and of the PSL on an interrupt stack in memory pointed to by the interrupt stack-pointer register. The interrupter provides a new program-counter value and the interrupt-service routine in the operating-system kernel generates a new PSL (including the new interrupt priority level). The interrupt-service routine initiates context switching (see above) as appropriate to the interrupt.

The VAX operating system considers interrupts as events (such as I/O device changes) that are unrelated to the currently executing program. It treats exceptions as events (like arithmetic overflow) that are related to the current process. Exceptions are handled in the same manner as interrupts except that the kernel-mode stack (pointed to by the kernel-stack pointer, KSP) is used to hold the program counter and the PSL.

The context-switching and interrupt-response systems of the VAX are quite powerful and are relatively straightforward. They typify capabilities required in a modern computer system. The specific features needed, which can be implemented as the VAX designers did or by alternative means, are automatic storage and recovery of process context, priority-sensitive interrupt response to hardware- and software-initiated interrupts, control of interrupt response with interrupt-enable flags and/or interrupt masks that control the interrupts to be responded to at any instant, and instructions available only to the operating system to control the context switching and the interrupt responses. Interrupt systems of the type described continually are active in providing communication between the central processor(s) and the input/output controllers.

The IBM System/370 does not provide hardware support for a stack since the architects of System/360 reasoned that a general-register state gave more flexibility. The System/370 general registers can hold pointers to execution environments and most of the call and return mechanisms are implemented with software. Several instructions are provided for subroutine linking. The BRANCH AND SAVE and BRANCH AND LINK instructions save the return information while changing the program-status word to specify a new instruction address. Linking to the monitor and the supervisor levels of the operating system is aided by MONITOR CALL and SUPERVISOR CALL instructions. The first of these uses monitor-mask information to determine if the transfer is to be acted on. The second provides for branching to the supervisor with access inhibits disabled to permit the supervisor to access all state information. PROGRAM CALL and PROGRAM TRANSFER link programs in different address space. None of the instructions provide any automatic passing of parameters or separation of execution environments. These functions are performed by explicit register save and restore operations in the calling and called routines or in the operating system. System/370 incorporates an extensive priority-sensitive interrupt system with results similar to those of the VAX, but context switching uses the facilities just described.

The stack-based Unisys A Series performs procedure calls and context switching using the operations on the cactus stack (see Fig. 5-12). Procedure invocation starts by pushing an inactive mark-stack control word (MSCW) on the active stack. The dynamic link to the caller environment (the current environment pointer in the F register) is written into the dynamic field of the MSCW and the F register is updated to point to the new MSCW. An "indirect-reference word" that is used to find a pointer to the procedure being called is pushed on the stack next. Now actual parameters are pushed on the stack, values for value parameters and pointers for reference parameters. The procedure-call instruction is executed, starting by using the indirect-reference word (just above the MSCW pointed to by the F register) to get from the program-segment stack (part of the current context) the pointer to the procedure code and the lexical level of the procedure environment (the procedure in which it was defined). The lexical level is used to determine the static-link field of the MSCW (the pointer to the environment in which the called procedure was defined). Return information (content of the three control registers that identify the next instruction, the 5-bit identifier of the current lexical level, and several flip-flops) is placed in a "return-control word" that is built in place of the indirect-reference word that has served its purpose. The new lexical level is set, the MSCW is marked "active", and its location is specified to the next display register. Execution of the new procedure starts. Responses to interrupts that do not require context switching are handled as procedure invocations.

Context switching following an interrupt with the A Series follows a similar process, except that a top-of-stack control word with values of the F and S registers and control flip-flops is placed on the stack for the procedure being suspended. That stack is pushed into memory and the operating-system stack is recovered using display register 1. Values of the display registers for the suspended environment need not be saved because they can be reconstructed from the static link information in the MSCWs of the process when it is reactivated.

We see that there are different approaches to changing execution environments and to context switching. Each takes advantage of features of a particular instruction-set processor. More of the required activity is automatic with a stack machine, but in all cases a large amount of information must be moved. The fundamental difference among approaches is the number of operating-system instructions that must be executed for changing environments or for context switching.

5.6 REPRESENTATION OF DATA

Once we have decided on the number of registers we will provide and how they will be used, we can address the issue of how information is to be represented. We must be concerned with representation of each of the types of information that are to be held in the processor registers and in memory. We also must be sure that the different formats are compatible in that they can be contained in common-sized words with little wasted space. Since the information will be stored in primary memory we cannot ignore the characteristics of the memory when we consider word sizes and information representation.

Let us look first at the way we will represent numeric data. Normally, we need to represent such data in both fixed-point and floating-point binary forms. There are several dimensions to the issue of numeric data representation. What precision is desired in fixed-point (in higher-level language, integer) and floating-point (real-value) computations? What range of floating-point numbers is needed? Should we place a "bias" in the range of floating-point values? Will the fixed-point values and the mantissa of the floating-point numbers be fractions or whole numbers, that is, where should we place the binary point? For a given word size, what is the best balance between precision (number of bits allocated to the mantissa) and range (number of bits and base of the exponent)? Should fixed-point values be organized as a special case of floating point or should the representations be independent? How will negative values be represented in each of the three fields?

While we address the issues of numeric-value representation we also must keep in mind that we must fit decimal, character, byte, and/or boolean information into the same words. We might want several different sizes for either fixed-point or floating-point data or for both. Beyond the representation of data, we must specify the format to be used for instructions, whether they be of fixed or variable size. The last issue is related to that of the addressing modes, the use of registers, and the quantities of arguments we will have for each instruction, and again we must consider the planned instruction set.

We start with an approximation of the size for the fixed-point word by determining the precision required for integer calculations. Then we select the form to be used for character and decimal representations, usually 8-bit bytes, and select an integer word size into which an integer quantity of 8-bit bytes fits exactly. (Occasionally we might have to consider compatibility with the older 6-bit character formats. This has affected several machines whose architectures are still active.) Next we formulate a floating-point word structure that is compatible with the fixed-point representation that we have selected. A comparison of the precision and the range that results might cause us to try alternative combinations. We then see if the word size is compatible with the instructions we have selected. Iteration through several trials might be required. This is the method, but what are the specific issues we need to consider?

Let us examine some differences among different fractional-mantissa floating-point representations. In Fig. 5-17 we see two 32-bit floating-point words. The exponent of one has an 11-bit field with a binary base and the other has a 9-bit field using a base of 16 (hexadecimal). (Whether we view the exponent itself as binary or hexadecimal makes little difference; in either case the exponent is represented as a binary code in the computer word.) In both cases the sign of the mantissa is placed in the most-significant-bit position. At first it might appear that we can represent a larger range of values of significantly more precision if we use the hexadecimal base of Fig. 5-17(b). The range seems to be expressible to 2^{2044} (16^{511}) and the precision to one part in 2^{23} (there are 23 mantissa bits including the sign), whereas the word of Fig. 5-17(a) with its binary base gives us a range of 2^{2047} and a precision of one part in 2^{21}. Let us consider what happens with a normalized floating-point value when we multiply it by 4 and attempt to add 1×2^{-7}, as shown in

31	30	20	19		0
	S	exp	mantissa		

range = 2^{2047}
resolution $\cong 1/2^{21}$

(a)

31	30	22	21		0
	S	exp	mantissa		

range = 16^{511} = 2^{2044}
resolution $\cong 1/2^{23} \cong 1/2^{20}$

(b)

Multiply and add:

initial value:	0.0110	1001 × 2^0	0.0110 1001 × 16^0
normalize:	0.1101	0010 × 2^{-1}	
multiply by 2:	0.1101	0010 × 2^0	0.1101 0010 × 16^0
multiply by 2:	0.1101	0010 × 2^1	~~1.1010 0100 × 16^0~~
			= 0.0001 1010 × 16^1
add 1 × 2^{-7}:	+ 0.0000	0001 × 2^1	+ 0.0000 0000 0010 × 16^1
result:	0.1101	0011 × 2^1	0.0001 1010 × 16^1

(c)   (d)

Figure 5-17   Normalized floating-point representations. (a) Binary exponent. (b) Hexadecimal exponent. (c) Binary exponent. (d) Hexadecimal exponent.

Figs. 5-17(c) and (d). Now we see that we have lost precision with the hexadecimal base since 1×2^{-7} cannot be represented by 8 binary digits × 16^1. The effective precision of the example in Fig. 5-17(b) is $1/2^{20}$ and not $1/2^{23}$. The hexadecimal representation has no greater range and no greater precision than the binary-based word. Further the "jumping" of the precision can lead to instability in some numerical problems.

Selection between fractional and whole-number representations of floating-point mantissas is determined by whether a bias toward the higher ranges is desired. As Fig. 5-18 shows, the whole-number representation, with the binary point to the right of the least significant bit, biases the range toward the high side by 2 to the number of bits in the mantissa. (It is claimed without substantiation that most physical problems lean toward very large values and that the positive range bias is desirable.) Before settling on the choice between whole-number and fractional representation we should examine our plans for the arithmetic and logic unit to determine if there are reasons there to make the decision one way or the other. If we have decided to make the fixed-point word a special case of the floating-point word (as will be discussed) we use the same format for the fixed-point value field. Otherwise, unless there is argument against it from the arithmetic and logic unit designers, we usually place the binary point to the right to let the fixed-point word directly represent an integer.

The argument for making the fixed-point word a special case (an exponent with value 0) of the floating point is for regularity in the arithmetic. If this approach is used fixed-point and floating-point operations are exactly the same. Operation on mixed types

Representation:

eeee.bbbb bbbb   eeee bbbb bbbb.

$2^{-8} \leqslant$ range $\leqslant 2^7$ $2^0 \leqslant$ range $\leqslant 2^{15}$

(a)   (b)

Figure 5-18   Fractional and whole-number mantissas. (a) Fraction. (b) Whole number.

is performed as if both are floating-point values. Conversion from floating point to fixed point entails adjusting to an exponent value of 0. The main disadvantage of the uniform representation is in the smaller fixed-point word that results.

We also must determine how negative values are to be represented. The 1's and 2's complement forms of negative binary numbers yield simpler arithmetic computations than does the sign-magnitude form. Of the two, the 2's complement has the advantage that there is only one representation of the value 0. While this might be an advantage, some designers have made use of the special - 0 for checking the arithmetic unit. Most designers prefer a uniform representation of negative numbers, and the arguments of W. A. Wulf referred to in the discussion of language issues before support this position. On the other hand, the architects of the IBM System/360 gave plausible reasons for having different representations of negative values with different numeric forms (and for using different arithmetic in fixed-point, floating-point, and decimal arithmetic operations).

A fourth possibility for representing a signed binary value is as an offset from some negative value, so that the binary representation is the true binary value with the bias subtracted. Figure 5-19 shows the four ways to represent 4-bit signed binary values. With sign and magnitude, 1's complement and 2's complement positive values all have the same representation, a 3-bit binary value with a sign bit of 0. Negative values (all with a sign bit of 1) have different representations. The figure shows the two values for 0000 with sign and magnitude (origin and 1000) and with 1's complement (origin and 1111). The bias 16 (or excess-16) representation covers the same range of values (-16 to +15) as does the 2's complement and there is only one representation of 0000 (1000). The biased format is used often to represent exponents since range checking is easy, but it is not well

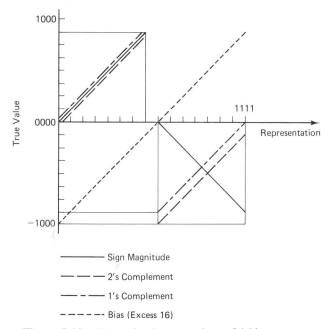

Figure 5-19 Alternative interpretations of 4-bit exponents.

suited to represent mantissa values due to the complexities it introduces in arithmetic operations.

In order to ease problems of moving programs from one machine to another the Computer Society of the IEEE developed a standard for floating-point operations for microprocessors. Computers that use the IEEE Floating-Point Standard [IEEE 85] must include single-precision arithmetic operations. Double-precision arithmetic is optional. The single-precision word has an 8-bit biased 127 exponent and a 24-bit signed fractional mantissa with an implied value of 1 added to the normalized fraction. In the double-precision case the exponent field contains 11 bits in biased 1023 form. The signed fractional mantissa has at least 53 bits, again with an implied 1 added to the left of the binary point. Exponent values of all 0's and all 1's have special interpretations, including "absolutely zero", infinity, and invalid condition, depending on the value of the mantissa.

The specification covers more than the representation of values. Arithmetic operators are specified to have results to an accuracy of better than one-half of the least significant bit value. Rounding is called for as are extensions for various intermediate calculations to be truncated at completion. A set of exception conditions and the actions to be taken in response to them is included. Several numeric coprocessors made by the semiconductor and system manufacturers follow the IEEE standard. These special-purpose processors are a subject of Chapter 7.

The final question on representation of data affects the controls more than the data structure. It is the issue of packing boolean values in a word as opposed to taking a full fixed-point word or a byte to represent boolean values. Packing can conserve a significant amount of space but introduces the requirement for taking time for packing and unpacking. The same issue faces us with regard to the representation of decimal values: Should we use full bytes or should we pack the decimal values two to the byte? No strong reasons appear to argue for or against either approach. We must evaluate each specific design to determine the proper trade-off between computation time and memory space.

That different groups of architects have arrived at different conclusions about data formats (and probably for different reasons) is demonstrated by Fig. 5-20. Here we see the fixed-point and the floating-point representations for numeric values in the Unisys A series, the IBM System/370 architecture, and the Unisys 1100 computers. Each approach was taken after significant evaluation of alternatives. In each case the data structures have shaped and been shaped by other aspects of the individual architectures. Numbering of the bit positions from the least-significant bit has been used in the illustration. In their literature many manufacturers use a left-to-right ordering of bit numbers.

The Unisys A series, Fig. 5-20(a), descendent of the Burroughs B6500, has a uniform representation of floating-point and fixed-point values. The mantissa is a whole number (the implied binary point is to the right of the least significant bit). In the case of double-precision values the mantissa consists of a whole-number part and a fraction part in the second word. A double-precision value with exponent 0 can be truncated to a fixed-point value by ignoring the second word. The octal-based exponent field for single-precision representations contains 7 bits in sign-magnitude format so that 0000000 is the exponent for the floating-point equivalent of a fixed-point value. The whole-number representation of the mantissa introduces a bias of 2^{39} (8^{13}) to the range of values that can be represented. A double-precision

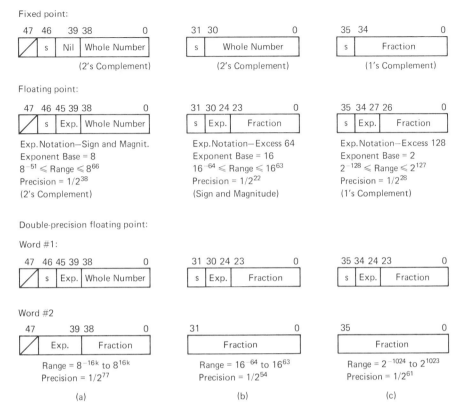

Figure 5-20 Fixed-point and floating-point word examples. (a) Unisys A series. (b) IBM System/370. (c) Unisys 1100.

exponent extends the range by 8^{256}. In double precision the second word contains the more significant part of the exponent and conversion from single to double precision entails adding a second word with values of 0 for the exponent and mantissa fields. The A series word actually holds 52 bits, the extra 4 as a "tag" to designate the nature of the word. Uses for this tagged memory are covered in Section 5.7.

The IBM 360/370 architecture includes a "halfword" integer in addition to the values shown in Fig. 5-20(b). The 32-bit word has different representations for fixed-point and floating-point values. Fixed-point values are in 32-bit whole-number signed 2's complement form. The single-precision floating-point representation uses a 7-bit base-16 (hexadecimal) number and the mantissa is a 25-bit sign and magnitude fractional value. For double precision the range (exponent) is not changed and the fraction is extended to add 32 bits. This architecture also includes an extended floating-point format with a 14-bit exponent and a 113-bit signed mantissa.

The 36-bit Unisys (formerly Sperry UNIVAC) 1100 fixed-point word uses 1's complement fractional representation, Fig. 5-20(c). Single-precision floating point has a base-2 8-bit exponent and a 28-bit 1's complement fraction. Double precision incorporates an 11-bit exponent and a 51-bit 1's complement fraction. The expanded exponent is held in the first (more significant) word. The double-precision fixed-point format of this computer is not shown.

As another example we might consider the floating-point representations in the VAX systems. There are five basic forms of fixed-point (integer) representation: byte, word, longword, quadword, and octaword. In each case the whole-number value is represented in 2's complement form or can represent an unsigned integer value. There are four forms of floating-point number, using from 32 to 128 bits. In addition to single precision (8-bit exponent and 24-bit signed mantissa) and double precision (8-bit exponent and 56-bit signed mantissa), there is a 64-bit format with an 11-bit exponent and a 128-bit format with a 15-bit exponent. All of the exponents are in biased form and are treated as base-2 values. Mantissas are 2's complement binary fractions.

5.7 INSTRUCTION REPRESENTATION AND INSTRUCTION SETS

Data is only one of the three types of information that must be represented in our registers. The other two types, instructions and control words, operate on the data. The control words, if they are used, fit into the computer word size after the data and the instruction formats have been established. The issues there are related to the types of special words that are needed rather than to their format. We will see examples of control words when we review the ISP descriptions of specific computers.

Several issues, only one of which is the instruction set itself, face us when we consider the instruction formats. The instruction set decided on establishes how many bits are required in the operator field and what special tags are needed to associate the arguments with the operators. The representation of the arguments reflects the addressing modes we have selected, the processor state of our design, and the number of arguments

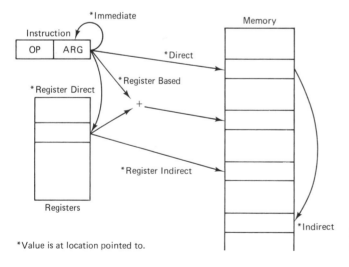

Figure 5-21   Various addressing modes.

we want to specify for each instruction. We consider addressing modes first since addressing-mode characteristics are related to the data structures discussed before.

Effective-address calculations establish the paths to arguments for instructions. Arguments can be accessed by immediate, direct, indirect, or register-based addressing, and by combinations of these. The different forms of addressing are illustrated in Fig. 5-21 and are described in what follows.

With the immediate form of addressing the argument value, sometimes called a *literal*, is specified in a field of the instruction itself. (With a stack-based architecture it might be a separate instruction.) Immediate addressing is used to specify small integer constants in a program. Larger integer or real constants must be designated using one of the other addressing modes to access the constant value held in a register or a memory location. Of course, immediate addressing cannot be used to specify the destination for a store instruction.

The location of the argument with direct addressing is specified by an address field of the instruction. The argument is found (or the result placed for a store operation) at the location so identified. With large addressable memory space the field required to specify an address is quite large and direct addressing often is limited to a small region, such as the current page or segment of the total address space. Zero-address (stack) machines might place a literal value on the stack followed by a load or store instruction, rather than using a field in the instruction itself. In this case the address is an integer constant just as with immediate addressing. A special form of direct addressing is register-direct address- ing, used with computers that have a set of addressable general registers. Here the address field is small since there is not a large number of registers. The field used for primary- memory direct addressing usually is large enough to hold the addresses of several registers.

With indirect addressing the location in memory specified by the address field is interpreted as an address. The latter address must be accessed to find the argument. Two memory references are required to obtain the argument, or to store a result. While this slows the execution of an individual instruction, the addressing flexibility gained might reduce the number of instructions required to solve a problem. Indirect addressing can be applied to a register so that the content of the register specifies the address of the argument. This is known as *register-indirect addressing*.

Register-based addressing entails adding the address specified in the instruction to the content of a register and using the result as the address of the argument. This also is called *displacement addressing* since the instruction-address field specifies a displacement from the starting location specified by the value in the register. Several different ways are used to designate the register. In the most general case (demon- strated in Fig. 5-21) a register and a displacement are specified in the argument field of the instruction. Special registers, called *index registers*, might be used to identify a base. Another alternative is to have a specific base register in the computer. This base register would be implied when the addressing mode calls for base addressing (or all addressing can be relative to this base). There could be separate base registers for data and for instructions. In this case arguments that refer to instruction would be addressed relative to the program base register. If the program counter is the implied register we have relative addressing. Relative addressing is very useful for instruction-sequence control within a program segment (a procedure, function, or program block, depending on the higher-level language).

We can make the register-based addressing more flexible by automatically incrementing or decrementing the value in a register with each address reference to it. This gives us an indexed (or autoindex) addressing mode. The modification of the address can be by the value 1, or can be specified in the instruction. For indexed addressing we can use general registers or special index registers as described previously.

It is possible to combine these fundamental addressing modes. For example, we might have register-based indirect addressing, where the displacement and the content of a register are used to designate a memory location in which is found the address of the argument. Another alternative is to obtain direct addressing from register-based addressing by using a register address to signify a base of 0, or to actually keep the value 0 in a register. There are many alternative combinations. The Motorola MC68000 microprocessors incorporate nine addressing modes. The National Semiconductor NS32000 microprocessors have 16 modes, including "indirect indexed" and an "external" mode that has two levels of indirection and two displacements. While a "rich" set of addressing modes might appear very attractive, we must be concerned with the complexity that is introduced when the programmer or the compiler writer must remember a variety of modes. This issue is discussed further in Chapter 6.

When we consider indirect addressing we must decide if a single level of indirection is sufficient or if we want indefinite levels of indirection. If the latter, will the indirect bit be placed at the source address or at the destination as a part of the information accessed? The three alternatives are represented in Fig. 5-22. Indefinite indirection is very useful for language and operating-system processes. If the indirect bit is placed at the destination

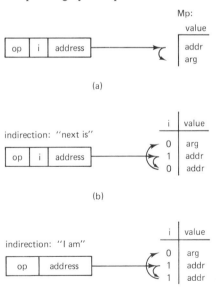

Figure 5-22   Indirect-addressing alternatives. (a) Single level. (b) Indefinite level–designation at the source. (c) Indefinite level–designation at the destination.

address we impose the requirement that every memory word contain such a "tag". On the other hand, placing it at the source means using a bit of every address field for this defined purpose. If the indirect bit is to be a part of each word we can consider expanding the tag field to several bits to designate how the word is to be interpreted. Tagged data and instruction words can be useful for memory protection, for maintaining access disciplines with operating systems, and for enforcement of inheritances with object-oriented systems. Uses of tagged memory are covered in Chapter 6 since they play a role in the control structure of computers.

For any of the addressing modes appropriate-sized fields must be established for each piece of addressing information and these must be compatible with the data structures we have selected. An instruction might be the same size as the computer word, we might place two instructions in a word, or the instruction might use a varying number of bytes (or "syllables", if the instruction is not broken into byte-size units). We will see examples of these different instruction formats.

We must determine the amount of memory to be addressed directly or as an offset to a based or an indexed address. If we are implementing a paged-memory system the direct-address field should be consistent with the physical block size selected for the memory mapping. The maximum size of the physical memory decided on determines how large the base-register fields and the index fields must be. The trend toward larger and larger physical and virtual address space has resulted in base and index addresses as large as the integer data fields.

Another of the "invariants" in computer history is the growth of the size of instruction sets, as can be seen in Fig. 5-23. Although at any one time there is a significant variation among the instruction sets of different computer architectures, the computers of each manufacturer experience a growth in instruction-set size over time. Whether the large instruction sets of today's computers are really useful has been questioned. The justification for growth in instruction-set size has been the addition of instructions to make programming easier and to allow compiled programs to run faster. It is almost never feasible to remove instructions because there are existing programs that use the instructions and compatibility must be maintained. A recent alternative to computer instruction-set processor design, the reduced-instruction-set computer (RISC), reverses this trend. The RISC approach is discussed in Chapter 6.

Do programmers and compilers really use all those instructions or have many been included only because it seemed to add little cost to the computer? Despite the claims of designers that the large instruction sets are of benefit to programmers and compiler

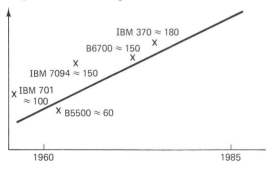

Figure 5-23 History of instruction-set size.

writers, much contradictory evidence is being accumulated. W. A. Wulf's argument for simpler features for the compiler writer was mentioned in an earlier section.

The instructions needed can be segregated into several groups: data transfer, arithmetic and logical transformations, shift, control flow, input/output, and special instructions. In the last category we find those instructions that are useful for process synchronization (e.g., test-set-branch) and other operating-system or translator activities. In some cases these instructions are reserved for use by the operating system and are called "privileged" instructions.

The issue of "regularity" or "orthogonality" of instruction sets has led to much debate. Orthogonal instruction sets are those in which an instruction operates on any data type appropriate to that operator. Nonorthogonal sets have different operators for different forms of data. For example, in Fig. 5-24 we see the difference between the DEC VAX (orthogonal) and the IBM 370 (nonorthogonal) approaches. The pros and the cons of orthogonal instruction sets were identified in our discussion of languages and translators before. The issue is specialization for flexibility and efficiency of execution, or generalization for simplicity and efficiency of translation. The success of both of the systems used in the example makes it difficult to decide the issue. Both approaches have vigorous proponents.

The way in which we represent instructions, the instruction format, is affected by the instruction set, the addressing modes, the processor state, and the quantity of arguments to be associated with each instruction. Whereas many earlier computers used a fixed number of arguments per instruction (we had one-address, two-address, and three-address machines), today we find two basic forms of instruction address, based on the processor state. Computers with hardware support for a stack are organized as zero-address (pure stack) machines and all others contain a variety of addressing formats, mixing register-direct, register-based, indexed, and immediate forms with no-, single-, dual-, and triple-argument selections.

(a)

Addressing modes (9): register, register deferred, autodecrement, autoincrement, autoincrement deferred, displacement, displacement deferred, literal, index (applies to other modes).

Numeric word sizes and types: integer (8, 16, 32, 64 bits), literal (6 bits, fixed or floating pt), floating point (32, 64 bits), bit field (0 – 32 bits), character string, decimal string.

Instruction association: Instructions can be associated with any combination of addressing mode and word size/type that is applicable to that instruction.

(b)

Instruction modes, word sizes and types, instruction association:

register-register: branching and status switching instructions, fixed point fullword and logical, floating point long and short.

register-index: fixed point halfword and fullword, logical and branching, floating point long and short.

register-storage and storage-immediate: branching, status switching, shifting, logical, fixed point, and input/output.

storage-storage: logical and decimal.

Figure 5-24   Orthogonal and nonorthogonal instruction sets. (a) DEC VAX.
(b) IBM 370.

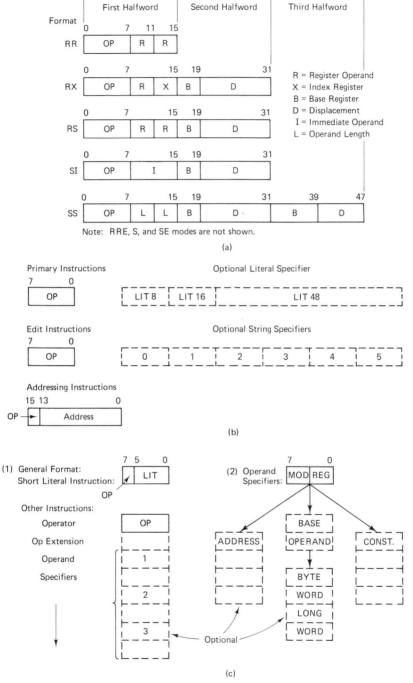

Figure 5-25 Examples of instruction formats. (a) IBM System/370. (b) Unisys A series. (c) DEC VAX.

Examples of three different approaches to instruction formatting are shown in Fig. 5-25. The IBM 370 architecture uses five distinct instruction formats, determined by the addressing modes. When memory references are included they can be base addressed or, in the case of the RX format, based and indexed. Two-address formats are used for register–register, register–memory, and memory–memory operations. Instruction sizes range from 2 to 6 bytes. VAX addressing uses variable-size syllable strings, but the strings can be from 1 to 54 bytes long, depending on the quantity of operands (0 to 6) and the addressing modes selected for each. The addressing modes for these two computers were described earlier and are shown in Fig. 5-24. With both of these general-register machines register-to-register operations use 2-byte instructions and total code space is most compact if a large percentage of the instructions can refer to data in registers.

The stack-based Unisys A series instructions are sequences of from one to seven 8-bit syllables. Addressing implicitly is to the stack and most operations require only one syllable. A second group of operators, including the input/output operations, use two syllables to extend the operator code to 16 bits. A final group, the edit operators, are used for string editing (included to provide for COBOL language translation) and take up to seven syllables, with the first specifying how many there are. Literal values are placed on the stack with the "literal" operator followed by the value that contains from 8 to 48 bits. Memory addressing for data is indirect through descriptors, using the tag fields of words to designate whether the content is a value or a reference.

A comparison of different approaches to the instruction-set processor should permit us to evaluate the performance of the alternatives. The discussion of performance in Chapter 2 showed that it is not easy to find objective means to measure performance, particularly in light of the different languages, programming styles, and processing environments. On the other hand, it is apparent from the review of the instruction-set processor in this chapter that there are different design philosophies that one can follow. We might be influenced by the "tidiness" of the RISC approach or of the stack-based architectures, or we might find that the breadth of environments for our design and the present investment in programs lead us toward a design that includes special-use registers and a wide variety of operations. In approaching a new design we should perform analysis and simulation to compare our alternatives. Above all, it is essential that the individual pieces of our architecture all complement each other; there must be balance (or symmetry) in the design. There is interaction among the issues of processor state, information representation, and instruction set. All of these interact with the system design at the processor–memory–switch level.

There are some general concepts related to performance to assist in establishing a strategy. Since performance is so heavily influenced by the alternative ways available to implement the instruction-set processor, we defer our discussion until Chapter 6.

5.8 SUMMARY

In this chapter we have covered instruction-set processors, the computer as seen by the programmer or the compiler. We discuss methods to implement the instruction-set processor in the next chapter. There are many ways to allocate the components (or the semiconductor surface) that we have decided we can afford for our processors. We examined these alternatives and developed a perspective on the trade-offs that must be considered in making selections.

User requirements can be expressed in terms of the languages that will be used for programming a computer. The different programming languages have different characteristics and impose different requirements on the architecture. Usually we need to have our architecture adapted to a variety of languages, rather than just a single one. The language of the machine itself forms the starting point for examination of languages. The human view of the machine language is built into an assembly language that requires that the programmer control the computer at the machine's level, but in a vocabulary that is adapted to the human.

Higher-level programming languages are designed to be closer to the languages of the problems we will solve using the computer. We are interested in characteristics of the different programming languages in order that our designs can be responsive to those languages. The characteristics of interest include the overall structure of programs written in each language and the data types and data structures that can be represented in the language. The way programs are executed is reflected in the control structure of the language. Here we need to know how a language treats expressions and their evaluation, the forms of commands available in the language, and the relationships of any subprograms to the main program and to each other. Data and control issues are combined when we consider the scope and the extent of items in the program structures that are obtained with the language.

We reviewed characteristics of several example languages, moving from FOR-TRAN, with its relatively static structure, through the block-structured language PAS-CAL, to the dynamic languages like LISP. Newer languages with different characteristics continue to be introduced. Currently there is great interest in logic programming languages such as PROLOG and in object programming with languages like SMALLTALK. Hardware features to support higher-level languages include flexible indirect addressing for implementing linked lists, means for establishing and deleting new execution environments for subprograms, rapid data and pointer movement in registers for parameter (argument) passing and return, and operators that resemble those most often used in the higher-level languages.

There is disagreement on how important it is to provide architectural features that match language characteristics. Some designers and compiler developers argue for features that permit the compiler to minimize the number of instructions needed to represent a user program. Others claim that "advanced" features will not be used if they lead to any complication and ask that the computer have a small and easy-to-remember set of features.

Just as the programming languages influence the architecture, so do the operating systems that control computer operations. Operating systems are a combination of hardware resources and programs. The two parts should be designed concurrently, but often cannot be. The computer designer might have to adapt to an existing operating system. Since the software part of the operating system is a program written in some programming language, the features that we found useful to programmers and compilers also are useful to the operating-system developer.

The major functions of the operating system entail management of computer-system hardware and software resources and scheduling of processes that are to be run on the computer. Architectural characteristics needed to support these include indirect addressing, means for context switching, and operations for synchronizing interacting processes.

In the architecture itself we addressed the questions of quantities and uses of registers in the processor, the Pc state. Processor registers provide for rapid access to information that otherwise has to be held in cache or primary memory. While a large number of processor registers can improve performance in executing any one process, the more registers there are, the more time it takes to store their values in memory when switching to another process, including an operating-system process. At any given cost level we have the ability to invest in more registers or in more cache memory. The performance improvements available with either investment must be evaluated.

Registers can be general-purpose, permitting any of the information that can be placed in primary memory to be placed in any register for fast access, or they can be specialized. The specializations can be to function, such as base registers, index registers, or address registers. Further specialization occurs if we organize the registers to support specialized data structures like queues or stacks. Using this approach leads to a different type of instruction set and a different control structure. Each computer control structure has its own advantages and shortcomings.

Registers also are used to provide fast access to instructions. An instruction queue of high-speed registers can mask the time it takes to fetch instructions from memory, especially in execution of short loops of instructions. In some cases the time it takes for effective-address calculation can be reduced by using additional registers to establish an argument queue as well as an instruction queue.

An important aspect of processor control is the dynamic mapping of execution environments in memory and processor registers. An execution environment is the virtual state needed by a process, the items required by a program or subprogram during execution. Groups of execution environments of the processes that make up a user program, or job, are the context of that user job. Usually the operating system controls the resources that make up a context. The processor controls must provide for context switching as jobs are changed. Many of the events that initiate changes of execution environments and of contexts are external to the process currently being executed. Mechanisms to signal these events and to respond to them are required. Different architects and engineers have used different solutions to this problem, but in most cases interrupt-generation and interrupt-response systems have been used.

Once the organization and the quantity of registers have been determined we must specify how information is to be held in the registers. There are several types of data that must be held and the format to be used for each might require compromise because of the necessity that the same register hold the different types at different times. Numeric data is in fixed-point (integer) and floating-point (real) forms. There might be several different-size formats for each numeric type. We also must arrange for storing decimal digits, alphanumeric characters, and boolean (logical) values.

When designing the fixed-point word structure we specify the location of the implied binary point and the code for representing negative values. With the floating-point data words we are concerned with two fields, the mantissa (magnitude) and the exponent. There is a trade-off between the size of each with regard to the resolution to which we can represent values and the range of values that we can represent. The alternatives for representing signed values are the sign and magnitude, the 1's complement, the 2's complement, and the biased forms. The mantissa and the exponent fields of floating-point words might represent negative values differently. The signed-value representation for fixed-point and floating-point numbers might be the same or can be different. We might use a unified format such that a fixed-point value is merely a special case (exponent of 0) of floating point. The base of the exponent can be 2, 4, 8, or 16; each has advantages and has been used in successful computers.

Instructions are held in the same memory words as are data. The formats of the instruction and data words must be compatible. A major part of the code for instructions is used to designate how to find arguments. Several argument-addressing modes are available, including immediate, direct, indirect, and register-based. There are many combinations of these four fundamental modes. Again there are questions of the best use of memory space. The addressing modes are associated with the way that data registers are used in the processor.

Related to the question of addressing modes is the design of the instruction set. Several issues are raised here. Should there be an independence (orthogonality) between instructions and addressing modes or should the mode be specified by the instruction? Do sophisticated or simple instructions give better support to programmers and compilers? Is it true that the larger the instruction set the better? These issues are the subject of controversy among computer designers and users.

5.9 ADDITIONAL READING

Design of computers to support higher-level programming languages has been the subject of study and research for many years. Early papers on the topic include [AndeJ61] and [WebeH67]. The topic has been covered in a series of workshops on high-level language computer architectures, led by Y. Chu. [Chuya75] is a good starting point for those who are interested in the principles, as is a special issue of *IEEE Computer* [ChuYa81]. [WulfW81], in that special issue, is an articulate statement of a compiler writer's viewpoint. [FlynM80] summarizes the issues relating languages and architectures. [TaneA78] discusses the relationship between modern programming technique and computer architecture. [MacLB82], a book on programming-language characteristics, identifies features that the computer architecture should support. More advanced coverage of the semantic aspects of programming languages is found in [TennR81]. An overview of logic programming is found in [KowaR79].

There are many books on operating systems, but few outline the principles as well as [ShawA74] (a second edition has been published as [BicLu87]) or cover the theory as well as [CoffE73]. Another view of operating-system function and design is presented in [PeteJ85]. [MaekM87] presents more advanced topics. The ATLAS operating system was described in [KilbT61] and [HowaD61]. The MIT work on CTSS and on MULTICS is discussed in

[CorbF62], [CorbF65], [DaleR68], and [OrgaE72]. [McKeR76], which compares operating systems, includes a good description of the Burroughs master control program (MCP). [RitcD78], a paper on UNIX, is suggested for any student of operating systems.

Comparing the processor state of different computers can yield a good understanding of differences in architectural approaches. Stack-based computers were described in [BullD77]. [OrgaE73] on the B5500/6500 architecture is an excellent review of the use of stacks. Principles of the IBM System/38 can be found in [DahlS78]. The instruction "stack" of the CDC Cyber computers is the same as that of the 6600 [ThorJ64], which was referred to in earlier chapters. The design of the Scheme-79 computer is found in [SussG81]. [MoonD87] describes the Symbolics 3600. The IEEE floating-point standard is specified in [IEEE 85].

5.10 PROBLEMS

5-1. The following are FORTRAN and PASCAL versions of the same algorithm ("place the values of X, Y, Z in descending order"):
   a. FORTRAN

```
program TEST ( )
read I, J, K
call ORDER (I, J)
call ORDER (I, K)
call ORDER (J, K)
write (I, J, K)
stop
subroutine ORDER (M, N)
L1 = M
L2 = N
M = MAXI (L1, L2)
if M = L2 then N = L1
stop
function MAXI (M, N)
if M > N then L = M else L = N
MAXI = L
stop
```

   b. PASCAL

```
program TEST( );
var I, J, K: integer;
procedure ORDER (var M,N :integer);
  var L1, L2: integer;
  function MAXI (M, N: integer);
    var L: integer;
    begin {MAXI}
      if M > N then L := M else L := N;
      MAXI := L
    end {MAXI};
  begin {ORDER}
```

```
        L1 := M;
        L2 := N;
        M := MAXI (L1, L2);
        if M = L2 then N := L1;
      end {ORDER};
    begin {TEST}
      readln (I, J, K);
      ORDER (I, J);
      ORDER (I, K);
      ORDER (J, K);
      writeln (I. J, K)
    end {TEST}.
```

Show how the program and subprogram codes and environments would be mapped to memory for each case (see Figs. 5-2 and 5-3). Include a location for each variable in each environment.

5-2. To provide architectural support for operating systems, describe the following:

    a. Use of indefinite-level indirect addressing to build a resource waiting list (Fig. 5-6).

    b. Use of register-based addressing (Fig. 5-21) to establish memory (upper and lower) bounds for a process.

5-3. Consider three simple processors of roughly equivalent capability but with different quantities of arguments for an instruction: 0 argument ("stack architecture"), 1 argument ("one-address architecture"), and 2 arguments ("two-address architecture"). All of the computers have 16-bit system buses and 16-bit arithmetic. Each machine can have in its instruction set as many of the following instructions as are needed for its architecture: LOAD, STORE, ADD, SUB, MUL, and DIV. Operators require 8 bits and addresses require 16 bits. Assume that memory addresses are represented by lowercase letters (a, b, . . .). For each of the three processors, do the following:

    a. Define the instruction formats and the instruction set.

    b. Use the instructions and addresses as appropriate to write a program segment that evaluates the following command:

```
    f := a * (b + c) / (a - d) + e;
```

    c. Identify how many bytes of memory are required to hold the program segment.

5-4. The following are characteristics of two computers, both of which have byte-addressable primary memory:

Computer A uses register-to-register operations (similar to the CDC Cyber). Arithmetic instructions have the following format: GR[A] <- GR[B] op GR[C], referring to registers for arguments and for results. The following instructions are available for memory references: LOAD GR[i] Mp[m] and STORE GR[j] Mp[n]. LOAD and STORE instructions require 4 bytes and register-to-register operations require 2 bytes.

Computer B is a stack machine and all arithmetic operations use the top elements of the stack for arguments and for results. The instructions PUSH Mp[m] and POP Mp[n] are used to load from memory to the stack and to store from the top of the stack to memory. PUSH and POP instructions require 4 bytes and arithmetic operations require only 1 byte.

    a. For each computer write the minimum program segment needed to evaluate the following expression (a, b, . . . refer to memory locations. The result ends in a register or at the top of the stack.):

```
(a + b)/c + a*(b - d) - e/(c - a)
```

   b. How many bytes of memory are required in each case?
   c. For computer A, how many registers did you need? How did you assign them to variables and to temporary results?
   d. For computer B, what was the maximum stack depth? Show the content of the stack when execution (first) required that depth.

5-5. Consider a general-register processor with register-to-register arithmetic and logical operations (op Rx Ry Rz) and register–memory operations only for LOAD and STORE (e.g., LOAD Rx My). Show how a stack can be implemented in such a machine. As an example, show the instructions for building a stack for a procedure with two parameters, three local variables, a return address, and a parent procedure pointer (see Fig. 5-10). Include a test to ensure that the stack upper limit is not exceeded.

5-6. Review the discussion of environment and context management for the VAX in Section 5.5. Consider a two-deep tree of contexts with a top-level system context and three user-level contexts. For each context there are several environments for each of the operating modes (kernel, executive, supervisor, user, and interrupt). Sketch the tree of contexts and environments, identifying the pointers and the memory areas that are used.

5-7. Add an interrupt facility to the ISP of the von Neumann computer of Fig. 2-7. Clearly identify your additions and describe how the facility works. Describe how the system resumes operation at the conclusion of interrupt processing. The interrupt action at the end of each instruction cycle (following perform operation) is as follows:
   "If interrupts are enabled and an interrupt is requested then the following sequence is accomplished: The accumulator value is stored in memory location 0; the value in the arithmetic register is stored in location 1; the condition value is stored in bit 1 of location 2; if $Ic = 1$ then the value in the control register is stored in bits 21 through 38 of location 2; Ic is copied to bit 1 and the value in the control counter is stored in bits 21 through 32 of location 3; other bits of locations 2 and 3 are cleared; the control counter is set to 4 and Ic is set to 0. Following that, instruction interpretation is resumed in normal sequence."

5-8. Consider two different processor organizations: The first has uniform data representation for fixed- and floating-point numbers and unified arithmetic operations, whereas the second has different formats for integer and real numbers and different real- and integer-arithmetic operations. Describe in detail how the two machines would handle the following sequence of operations: integer addition, convert result to real, real multiplication, convert result to integer, integer subtraction. Show an example that identifies data formats and demonstrates the sequence of operations for each processor.

5-9. We wish to compare three different data formats, all with base-2 exponents, that are candidates for our architecture:
   X. 32-bit word with single-word, double-word, and quadword floating-point formats. In each format each word has an 8-bit exponent and a 24-bit mantissa, so that the double-precision format has an exponent of 16 bits and a mantissa of 48 bits. Quadruple precision is double that size.
   Y. 48-bit word with single-, double-, and triple-word floating-point formats. The basic word has an exponent of 12 bits and a mantissa of 36 bits. Both fields are expanded by factors of 2 for double precision and 3 for triple precision.

Z. 64-bit word with single and double precision. The exponents are 16 and 32 bits and the mantissas are 48 and 96 bits for the two formats.

We have estimated that single-precision arithmetic operations take 2 clock times and each level of multiple precision adds another clock time (to make the additional register transfers). We are evaluating operations with two problem mixes:

Standard, 80% 24-bit, 15% 48-bit, 4% 72-bit, 1% 96-bit, and

Scientific, 50% 24-bit, 30% 48-bit, 15% 72-bit, 5% 96-bit.

To make the comparison, do the following:

   a. Prepare a table showing clock times for each candidate processor for 24-, 48-, 72-, and 96-bit operations.

   b. Calculate the average number of clock times for operations with each mix for each candidate processor.

   c. Calculate what percentage of data memory is used for each mix with each candidate processor. (For example, 24-bit precision only "uses" 2/3 (32/48) of the 48-bit processor word and 72-bit precision uses only 3/4 (96/128) of four 32-bit processor words.)

   d. Which basic word size do you choose? Why?

5-10. We have arrived at two possible instruction formats: a register-to-register or single-address format with either one, two, or three 12-bit syllables (12-bit operators, 12-bit register-to-register designators, 24-bit register designators and memory addresses); and a register-to-register or three-address format with a variable number of bytes (1-byte simple operators, 2-byte operators with register-to-register designators, and 1- to 9-byte memory-address designators). Discuss the advantages of each approach. Show examples to demonstrate the benefits of and problems with each.

5-11. Describe in words and give examples of memory-address calculations for each mode of addressing in the Intel 8086. The ISP of the 8086 is shown in Fig. 2-8. Each example should show the content of the instruction and the values in appropriate registers and memory locations.

5-12. For the von Neumann computer described in Fig. 2-7, do the following:

   a. Write an efficient symbolic assembly language program to sum a one-dimensional array of 50 integers. The result should be placed in memory. Use indirect addressing through a single memory location to facilitate indexing through the array.

   b. Add an index register facility, showing changes to the memory addressing, and write a program to sum the array described in part a.

   c. Identify the number of memory references (for instructions and for data) required in each of parts a and b.

5-13. The DEC PDP-10 was a 36-bit/word general-register computer with 2^{18} words of memory. Any of its 16 general registers could be used as an accumulator, and any except register 0 could be used as an index register. Indirect addressing could be accomplished to arbitrary depth with indexing allowed at each level. An instruction had a 9-bit operation code, a 4-bit accumulator designation, an indirect bit, a 4-bit index designator, and an 18-bit address field. The general registers occupied the first 16 locations in primary memory.

Write as much of a commented ISP description of the PDP-10 as is possible from the description given.

5-14. Trace the execution of a program to evaluate $Z = max(X,Y)$ on the von Neumann computer (Fig. 2-7). Identify the use of each memory word (instructions or data). For instructions, state the meaning of each field. For data, identify the value contained in the word at the beginning and at the end of the run. (You will have developed a symbolic assembly code.) Show the contents of Ac, AR, CC, CR, FR, Ic, Cn, and Run following each instruction. Initially, CC = 00000h, Ic = 0, Run = 1, and the following (hexadecimal) values are in primary memory:

Location	Hexadecimal Value	
0	00404	00518
1	00240	00404
2	00334	00504
3	00644	000FC
4	00400	00000
5	003A0	00000
6	00000	00000

(Hints on Fig. 2-7: Note the locations of instructions in words in the instruction interpretation process. Note the instruction format. Note the jump left and jump right instructions, unconditional and conditional.)

5.11 PROJECTS

5-A. Developing the data for a complete ISP description of a computer for the computer investigation project (Project 1-A) requires study. It is necessary to read carefully and to interpret the programming manual or the equivalent architectural description of the computer that you are investigating. The manuals should include data on Pc state, Mp state, instruction and data formats, argument addressing, instruction interpretation, and operation execution. It is not necessary to describe the complete instruction set, but representative instructions should be included. The examples of Appendix B show the level of detail desired.

5-B. In designing the ISP of the Project 1-B computer you should make decisions in the sequence of the descriptions of this chapter. It is necessary to make several iterations through the ISP design to arrive at the desired result. Trade-offs among data formats, instruction formats, addressing modes, and register uses are required. An examination of several of the examples of Appendix B demonstrates the level of detail required in the ISP description.

5-C. Compare the ISPs of two or three of the computers described in Appendix B. Describe the features of each and comment on the merits and the weaknesses (in your view) of the designs.

6

Processor Implementation and Control

The processor organizations described in the previous chapter are static in that a definition specifies the processor state, the instruction set, and the instruction-execution process, but it does not define how the processor is controlled to implement the fetch–execute cycle. This aspect of implementation might be considered a role of the designers at a lower level of detail, but the effects of the alternatives at this level must be considered at the architecture level. New technologies in hardware and software permit computer designs that give users greater control of the virtual machine that is programmed at the assembly-language level or by compilers.

6.1 HARDWARE AND SOFTWARE TECHNIQUES

Advances in semiconductor technology are felt strongly in computer-control design. Examination of the PMS- and the ISP-level descriptions of computers of earlier chapters reveals that there have been relatively few new architectures in the past two decades. We can see that computers are faster and smaller, but most system organizations and most processor states are quite similar to those of computers introduced in the 1960s. New semiconductor technologies allow us to implement the virtual machines differently, permitting increased ranges of performance and increased flexibility. The advance in flexibility results from our ability to exploit software control techniques that were identified but were not feasible with older technologies.

The factor that most affects the rapid reduction in unit cost and the growth in performance that were described earlier is the increase in component density, the quantity of transistors that can be diffused into one semiconductor. Improvements in semiconductor processing and in resolution of individual features that can be placed on a given area of semiconductor surface allow more and more devices to be placed in one physical component. As shown in Fig. 6-1 the quantity of individual devices (transistors, capacitors, resistors) on a single silicon chip has doubled about every 1.5 years since the planar transistor was introduced in 1959 and was followed by the integrated circuit in the mid-1960s.

The early small-scale integrated (SSI) circuits with up to 10 devices per component (chip) were followed by medium-scale integration (MSI), with hundreds of devices on a chip, in the late 1960s. The large-scale integrated (LSI) circuit examples of the figure include Intel microprocessors (4004, 8080, 80286, 80386) and dynamic random-access-memory (DRAM) components of sizes from 16 kbits to 4 Mbits. The component density is about four times as large for the simple and repetitive memory circuits as it is for the processor circuits that are more complicated and consume more power.

The effects of these advances go beyond more performance and increased capacity. They also permit a different approach to control structure and to arithmetic and logical function design. More complicated and more different functions can be provided in small and manageable arithmetic units. Features that used to be implemented by software can be built into the hardware control. Operations that directly support programming languages can be introduced. Computers that are *polymorphic* in that they take on different characteristics to perform different roles are feasible. Most computers today are controlled with some variation of the "microprogramming" that was suggested by M. V. Wilkes [WilkM51] in 1951, but that was not feasible for over a decade due to the low performance of the resulting machines. The continuing advances in semiconductors first

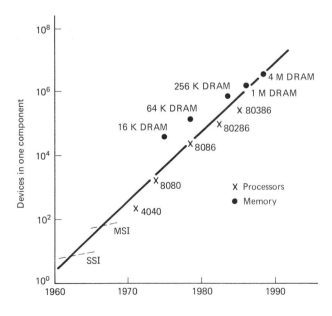

Figure 6-1 Semiconductor component density trends.

allowed control of the smaller machines within a family to be implemented with micro-programming. Then most computer controls took the same form. Further advances allowed even high-performance computers to be controlled with programmed logic arrays (PLAs). These semiconductor devices use a generalized interconnection matrix of logic gates. The array is specialized by breaking unwanted connections. The microprogramming approach can be extended to allow the system program developer and the user to have access to the control structure and permit tailoring of the computer to meet specific needs.

At the same time that hardware unit cost has been decreasing, there has been little change in software cost with the result that software development and maintenance has taken on a larger and larger percentage of the cost of owning and operating a computer system. This has had the secondary effect of making compatibility with existing systems an overriding factor in most computer acquisitions. The objective of compatibility is to permit retention of the software already installed. To some extent, architectural innovation has been stifled by these economic realities, but a new set of challenges appeared to the computer architects and engineers. They had to provide advances in performance and capacity without changing the instruction-set processors. To some, this has opened an opportunity for introduction of virtual machines that run the software of the major suppliers but that are implemented in different ways. This introduction of clones has been seen at both the low- and the high-performance ends of the performance spectrum. At the high-performance end there is the further challenge to provide innovative implementations that exceed the performance/cost capabilities of the virtual machines of the major manufacturers.

A large part of the support cost of a computer system is associated with fault diagnosis, fault recovery, and maintenance. In the control logic and in separate mainte-nance processors, we are able to address this aspect of support by using the flexibilities provided by the new technologies.

The electronics capabilities that permit advances in high-speed control structures also allow us to implement very powerful function units for arithmetic and logical operations. The very high component densities now available permit a large quantity of components to be assembled in parallel adders, multipliers, and shifters with such small dimensions that the designer can expect only very small propagation delays within the function units. Multiple function units are feasible when computation-speed requirements warrant.

At the upper end of the performance spectrum, there continues a need for computers that exceed the capabilities of the fastest conventional machines. Parallelism at the PMS level to address this set of requirements was discussed in Chapter 3. Facility for concurrent operation can be provided at the ISP level as well. Control structures for parallel operation of multiple arithmetic units are characteristic of all of the approaches to design of supercomputers.

While the software cost realities have had effect on stepwise improvements in comput-ers, they have not inhibited investigation of radically different approaches to computer organization. Instead, they have led to the development of new languages that will make easier the task of writing usable software and to the investigation of new architectures to support the new languages. One avenue of investigation has emphasized computers that are designed to facilitate both compiler development and computation of programs written in existing higher-level languages. On one branch of this road we find reduced-instruction-set computers (RISC) and on another we have the language-based computers.

Even more radical departures from current languages and architectures are found with the functional and logical programming languages and the architectures designed to support them.

No matter how interesting they are in their own right, alternative instruction-set processors and computer controls should be evaluated only in terms of their performance–cost ratios. Whereas absolute values of performance are hard to specify, relative capabilities of different approaches can be established.

In this chapter we examine various means to control the machine and many alternatives for control structure. Here we consider how to implement the instruction-set processor to make a computer of the assemblage of registers and flip-flops.

6.2 VIRTUAL MACHINES AND ACTUAL MACHINES

The idea of the "virtual machine", the computer with its system software as seen by the user was introduced in Chapter 1 and was discussed further in Chapter 5. When we examine the concept further we can see that there can be many levels of virtual machine, depending on who is the "user". At the highest level we find a virtual machine that consists of the computer, the operating system and other system software, and an *application package*, such as a spreadsheet, that permits a user to interact with the computer by entering data to obtain desired results. Here the user does not perform any programming in the usual sense, but merely describes data items and the relationship among those items to the computer. The virtual machine to that user is a *spreadsheet computer*.

The designer of spreadsheet programs and other operational software that provides information to nonspecialists sees another virtual machine. That is the computer with an operating system and programming-language translators. This virtual machine is more computerlike in that the programming languages usually require that instructions be provided in sequences that direct the order of evaluation of functions of the system. (Implementations based on nonsequential languages are covered in Chapter 9.)

System-software developers, those who design operating systems, translators for higher-level or assembly languages, and maintenance-support software, see the virtual machine that we have described by its instruction-set-processor description. There must be one or more levels of virtual machine below that level, for the instruction-set-processor description does not define how the various instruction-execution sequences are controlled. In fact, we are able to define virtual machines starting from the bare circuits and other hardware to any level desired by defining the controls that are implemented with combinations of hardware and software to yield a computer appropriate to the "user" at that level.

As an example of two different implementations of the same instruction-set processor virtual machine, we see in Fig. 6-2 how two models of the IBM System/370 were implemented. The processor differences are noted as follows: in Model 155 floating-point register data and storage control unit transfers are in 4-byte words, whereas in Model 165 they are in 8-byte double words; the arithmetic unit of Model 155 has two adders with 4-byte parallel data transfers, and the Model 165 arithmetic unit contains two adders and a shifter and uses 8-byte transfers; Model 165 has a separate effective address adder. Differences of this type were incorporated in the earlier System/360 models and were

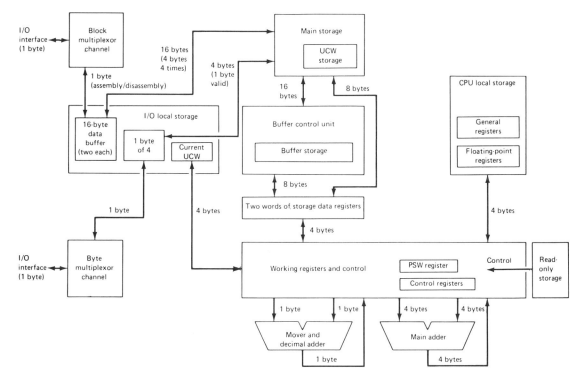

Figure 6-2 Implementations of the IBM System/370. (a) Model 155.

used later to distinguish among different 43XX, 937X, and 303X/308X/3090 models. In Chapter 3 we discussed differences among models at the PMS level.

The refinement of viewpoint on what is a virtual machine leads us to consider what it is that makes a computer operate as a computer. At the ISP level the description is static in that we see the processor and the memory states, the data and instruction formats, and the effects of the instruction-execution sequences. Descriptions of effective-address calculations and the fetch–execute cycle are somewhat dynamic, but even these emphasize the results that are found in user-visible registers. The sequences of register transfers, the operation of function units, and the processor state that is needed for control are not shown. This suggests that there are (at least) two levels of control structure, that which is seen by the user operating at the assembly language level and that which is used to implement that assembly language level machine.

In many examples we will find several assembly language control levels. Many computers are designed to have "privileged" operations and registers that are accessible only to the operating system. The UNIVAC 1100 system seen in an earlier chapter devoted half of the processor state to the operating system. The IBM System/370 architecture incorporates two states of operation, the *program state* and the *supervisor state*, with the latter having about 40 instructions that are not available to users operating in the program

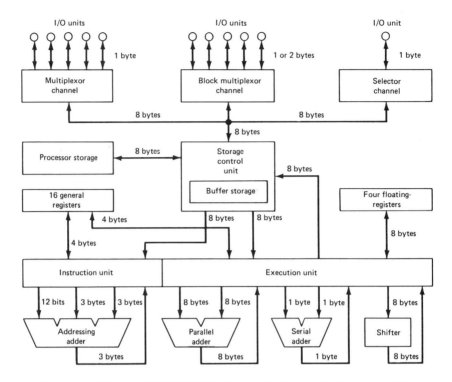

Figure 6-2 (Cont.) (b) Model 165. (Reprinted with permission from publications GA22-6942 and GA22-6935, copyright 1970 and 1972 by IBM Corp.)

state. The DEC VAX architecture includes four operating modes, the *kernel*, *executive*, and *supervisor* modes reserved for the operating system, and the *user* mode for normal programs. When designing the underlying controls of the computer we have to consider the differences among the operating states or modes.

Status flags and *condition codes* usually are incorporated in the computer to allow variation in control based on one or more sets of conditions. Many of the conditions should be visible to the user and the associated information will be testable by user programs. Other conditions will be hidden from the user, but will be available to the operating system. There might be conditions that are to be tested within the virtual machine presented to the operating system and will not even be visible to the operating system (except to those processes involved with error detection and failure diagnosis). The IBM System/370 provides a 64-bit (double word) *program-status-word* register for description of system status and sixteen 32-bit control registers to be used by the operating systems for control purposes. Certain locations in main memory are reserved for control and status recording.

The VAX systems include, in addition to the 16 general registers (see Fig. 5-8), banks of registers that are a part of the hidden processor state not seen by the users. The 64 internal data-bus registers (IDBRs) of the Model 780 are shown in Fig. 6-3(a). Twelve of these registers were used in the example of environment and context control described in Section

5.5 (Fig. 5-16). Other models have larger or smaller quantities of such registers that are controlled by the operating system. An asterisk after the name indicates that a register is an *architectural-processor register*, available to the system programmer in all but the smallest VAX systems. All models include the *processor-status longword* register shown in Fig. 6-3(b). That register includes, as the eight least-significant bits, four status flags for diagnostic uses and four condition code flags used for instruction-execution control purposes. The use of many of these registers in process switching was discussed in Section 5.5.

Most computers contain registers that are used for control and are not available to the programmer and the compilers. In Chapter 4 we were introduced to the general-register set (also called the control registers) of the Unisys 1100 and 2200 series (Fig. 4-5). One bank of 128 registers is available in the user program mode and another bank is reserved for use by the operating system. Each bank includes registers that are used for control purposes. A program-state register performs the same functions as the processor-

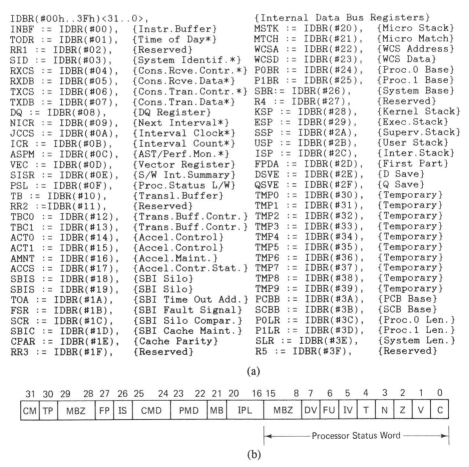

```
IDBR(#00h..3Fh)<31..0>,              {Internal Data Bus Registers}
INBF := IDBR(#00),  {Instr.Buffer}     MSTK := IDBR(#20),  {Micro Stack}
TODR := IDBR(#01),  {Time of Day*}     MTCH := IDBR(#21),  {Micro Match}
RR1  := IDBR(#02),  {Reserved}         WCSA := IDBR(#22),  {WCS Address}
SID  := IDBR(#03),  {System Identif.*} WCSD := IDBR(#23),  {WCS Data}
RXCS := IDBR(#04),  {Cons.Rcve.Contr.*} P0BR := IDBR(#24),  {Proc.0 Base}
RXDB := IDBR(#05),  {Cons.Rcve.Data*}  P1BR := IDBR(#25),  {Proc.1 Base}
TXCS := IDBR(#06),  {Cons.Tran.Contr.*} SBR:= IDBR(#26),   {System Base}
TXDB := IDBR(#07),  {Cons.Tran.Data*}  R4   := IDBR(#27),  {Reserved}
DQ   := IDBR(#08),  {DQ Register}      KSP  := IDBR(#28),  {Kernel Stack}
NICR := IDBR(#09),  {Next Interval*}   ESP  := IDBR(#29),  {Exec.Stack}
JCCS := IDBR(#0A),  {Interval Clock*}  SSP  := IDBR(#2A),  {Superv.Stack}
ICR  := IDBR(#0B),  {Interval Count*}  USP  := IDBR(#2B),  {User Stack}
ASPM := IDBR(#0C),  {AST/Perf.Mon.*}   ISP  := IDBR(#2C),  {Inter.Stack}
VEC  := IDBR(#0D),  {Vector Register}  FPDA := IDBR(#2D),  {First Part}
SISR := IDBR(#0E),  {S/W Int.Summary}  DSVE := IDBR(#2E),  {D Save}
PSL  := IDBR(#0F),  {Proc.Status L/W}  QSVE := IDBR(#2F),  {Q Save}
TB   := IDBR(#10),  {Transl.Buffer}    TMP0 := IDBR(#30),  {Temporary}
RR2  :=IDBR(#11),   {Reserved}         TMP1 := IDBR(#31),  {Temporary}
TBC0 := IDBR(#12),  {Trans.Buff.Contr.} TMP2 := IDBR(#32), {Temporary}
TBC1 := IDBR(#13),  {Trans.Buff.Contr.} TMP3 := IDBR(#33), {Temporary}
ACT0 := IDBR(#14),  {Accel.Control}    TMP4 := IDBR(#34),  {Temporary}
ACT1 := IDBR(#15),  {Accel.Control}    TMP5 := IDBR(#35),  {Temporary}
AMNT := IDBR(#16),  {Accel.Maint.}     TMP6 := IDBR(#36),  {Temporary}
ACCS := IDBR(#17),  {Accel.Contr.Stat.} TMP7 := IDBR(#37), {Temporary}
SBIS := IDBR(#18),  {SBI Silo}         TMP8 := IDBR(#38),  {Temporary}
SBIS := IDBR(#19),  {SBI Silo}         TMP9 := IDBR(#39),  {Temporary}
TOA  := IDBR(#1A),  {SBI Time Out Add.} PCBB := IDBR(#3A), {PCB Base}
FSR  := IDBR(#1B),  {SBI Fault Signal} SCBB := IDBR(#3B),  {SCB Base}
SCR  := IDBR(#1C),  {SBI Silo Compar.} P0LR := IDBR(#3C),  {Proc.0 Len.}
SBIC := IDBR(#1D),  {SBI Cache Maint.} P1LR := IDBR(#3D),  {Proc.1 Len.}
CPAR := IDBR(#1E),  {Cache Parity}     SLR  := IDBR(#3E),  {System Len.}
RR3  := IDBR(#1F),  {Reserved}         R5   := IDBR(#3F),  {Reserved}
```

(a)

31	30	29 28 27	26	25	24 23	22 21	20	16 15	8	7	6	5	4	3	2	1	0
CM	TP	MBZ	FP	IS	CMD	PMD	MB	IPL	MBZ	DV	FU	IV	T	N	Z	V	C

Processor Status Word

(b)

Figure 6-3 VAX-11/780 processor registers. (a) Internal data bus registers (IDBRs). (b) Processor-status longword.

status longword in the VAX systems. The unique characteristic of these Unisys computers is the use of the same register bank to contain data and control information.

The IBM System/370 has sixteen 32-bit control registers in addition to its sixteen general registers and four floating-point registers. As in the VAX, each bit of each control register performs a specific function. System/370 also has a 64-bit program-status word that contains masks and controls for interrupts (discussed in the next section), memory-access controls, condition codes resulting from instruction execution, exception (fault) codes, and the instruction address. Note that there is no separate program counter; its function is performed by the instruction-address field of the program-status word. The instruction address pointed to is the leftmost byte of the next instruction word to be fetched from memory.

The 32 display registers and the four stack-management registers (S, F, SL, and BOS) of the Unisys A series processors (Fig. 5-12) perform control functions related to data and control information that is held in the stack. Three addressing registers point to the next word to be fetched for instruction syllables, the base of the current program segment, and the base of the stack of descriptors (pointers to) of currently active program segments. All 39 of these registers contain 20 bits for access to 2^{20} words (6 Mbytes) of physical address. There also are three smaller registers to address syllables (bytes) of the instruction word, to identify which of 1024 stacks is currently in use, and to specify the lexical level (in the program structure) of the current program segment.

Thus, we have examples of four different commercially successful computer architectures, each representing a different virtual machine. We can approximate the relative cost of the different processor architectures by comparing the number of bits devoted to the combination of data and control state. The VAX-11/780 has 2560 bits, the Unisys 1100/2200 has 9252, the IBM System/370 uses 1344, and the Unisys A series devotes 1040 bits to these purposes. In both of the first two, most of the registers are organized as single register banks in order to minimize cost. The registers used for instruction queues are not included in this count.

The description of the internal data-bus registers of the VAX-11/780 and of the control registers of the other machines illustrates that the total amount of storage in a processor can be much larger than that described by the instruction-set processor that programmers and compilers see. Although these examples are representative of the larger computers, the inclusion of registers for control purposes is typical of all computers. The amount of this "hidden state" to a large degree is a measure of the complexity of the processor. Whenever it is necessary to store the current state of a process, as when a subprogram is called or when an operating-system process is invoked, some or all of the control-level state as well as most of that at the ISP level must be moved to memory, either with explicit instructions or automatically through pushing information on a stack.

6.3 CONTROL OF THE HARDWARE

A typical instruction-set processor consists of processor registers, function units, and buses for interconnection, as shown in Fig. 6-4. This simple example contains four general registers (R0, R1, R2, and R3), the program counter (PC), and the instruction

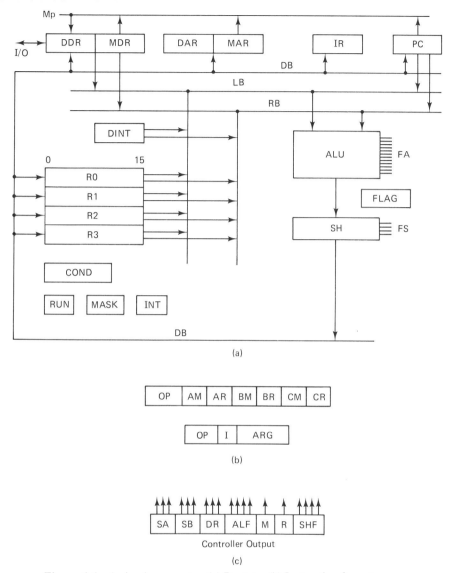

Figure 6-4 A simple computer. (a) Pc state. (b) Instruction formats. (c) Control signals.

register (IR), all of 16-bit size. An arithmetic and logic unit (ALU) and a shifter (SH) perform the information transformations. The processor has three 16-bit buses, two (Abus, Bbus) that receive information from registers for transfer to the ALU and a Dbus to deliver information to the registers. All register transfers go through ALU and SH.

The buses also are connected to the memory-address register (MAR) and the memory data register (MDR) of primary memory and to the input/output subsystem. The I/O subsystem interface includes a device data register (DDRi) and a device-address register (DARi) for each of 16 input/output devices. All of these "external" registers are 16 bits long. The device interrupt register (DINT) has a bit for each I/O device to indicate which device is signaling. The computer uses "memory-mapped" input/output addressing in which memory addresses are reserved for input/output devices (eight in the example). As the illustration shows, memory-mapped I/O permits the input/output subsystem to share bus addresses with the memory, reducing the requirement for separate input/output addressing. Since there is no separate connection between memory and input/output, information transfers between the two are prohibited while the buses are being used for internal processor transfers and direct memory-access (DMA) capability is limited.

The control structure of the computer also is shown in Fig. 6-4(a). The control state includes the status flag register (FLAG), a condition code register (COND), an interrupt register (DINT), and three control flip-flops (RUN, MSK, and INT). The condition codes in the COND register are used in controlling operations. Their values, indicating whether an operation has resulted in an overflow, a negative value, a zero value, or a carry out (for multiple precision), are set by logic in the ALU. The run flip-flop (RUN), is initialized to "on" and is set to "off" by a hardware fault or by a manually operated switch. Run permits the processor clock to be stopped for manual stepping for maintenance purposes. The mask interrupt flip-flop (MSK), is controlled by a control signal caused by set and mask instructions. The interrupt flip-flop (INT), is set by an interrupt signal from the interrupt register (DINT). DINT specifies which I/O device(s) is signaling or whether there is a hardware fault. Its value can be transferred to a general register as a part of an interrupt-response routine. In the event that there is more than one interrupt active, the response routine determines relative priorities. Inputs to the status flag register (FLAG), identify the status of the hardware modules other than the central processor.

As shown in Fig. 6-4(b), the instruction formats of this simple computer are either of three-argument or less than three-argument form. In the former case, the operation field of 4 bits is followed by three arguments, each with a 2-bit mode field and a 2-bit register designator. Addressing modes (see Fig. 5-21) include immediate, register, register indirect, and register-based (with possible indirection designated in the memory-address word). Each immediate or register-based mode indicates that the instruction is followed by a word that is to be interpreted as a 16-bit signed integer (for immediate) or an indirect bit and a 15-bit displacement. (Mp has 64k words.)

The fetch–execute cycle is similar to that which was described in Chapter 2 (see Figs. 2-11 and 2-13), except that indefinite-level indirect addressing is allowed. Instructions are taken from the memory address designated by the PC, brought to the MDR, and transferred to IR. There is an indirect bit in instructions that refer to memory and in the addresses held in memory to designate that indirection is called for. Instructions are decoded and effective address calculations are performed. After effective addressing and indirect referencing are completed, instruction execution takes place. At its completion the masked interrupt signal is used to determine if the interrupt phase is to be entered. The cycle is complete and the next fetch–execute cycle is initiated.

The controller uses data from the control state and from the instruction register (IR), and generates control signals, Fig. 6-4(c). Signals are required to select one or both source registers (SA, SB) and a destination register (DR). Three bits are sufficient to select the register connections to each bus (for sources, R0 to R3, PC, MDR/DDR, DINT, or none and for destination, R0 to R3, PC, MDR/DDR, IR, and MAR/DAR). Arithmetic or logical functions (ALF) and shift operations (SHF) are selected by controller outputs, 4 bits for selecting 1 of 16 ALU functions and 4 bits to select shift operations. Setting or clearing the mask interrupt flip-flop (M), requires a control signal, as does the run flip-flop (R). We require a total of 19 control signals.

A clock-pulse generator synchronizes the control logic. After an instruction is transferred from memory to the instruction register, signals from the instruction register are pulsed into the controller. The condition codes and status flags that signal the completion of asynchronous events like completion of a memory transfer are part of the control input. The controller can be implemented by either of two methods, "hard-wired logic" or "microprogrammed control".

In either case, at each clock pulse the controller generates a signal for each of the control lines of the computer. The signals cause register transfers and ALU/shifter operations as specified by the processor designer. A register-transfer language will have been used to specify operations on each clock-pulse time, as was shown in the example of Fig. 2-11. Since the simple computer of Fig. 6-4 has three buses that can be in operation concurrently, two source registers, a destination register, an ALU function, and a shift operation can take place during each clock period. (The processor registers are designed to permit information to be entered on the same clock pulse in which the current information is transferred from the registers.) Other activities that do not use the registers, such as memory read or write, also can take place during the same clock period.

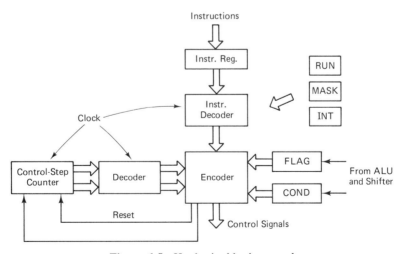

Figure 6-5 Hard-wired logic control.

   The hard-wired logic approach establishes control sequences with combinatorial (gate) and sequential (flip-flop) logic timed by the clock signals. Figure 6-5 shows a representative hard-wired control unit. At the beginning of a fetch–execute cycle the control step counter is initialized by the "reset" signal. The clock causes the binary count of the control step counter to be incremented at a fixed period. At each clock pulse the signals from the step decoder, the instruction decoder, the status flags (FLAG), and the condition codes (COND) are sent through the encoder to yield the required control signals. These signals control the gates of the buses and the inputs of the ALU and shifter of Fig. 6-4. In the control unit of Fig. 6-5 the control step counter, the instruction register, the status flags, and the condition codes are constructed from flip-flops and their contents are held until specifically changed. The step decoder, the instruction decoder, and the encoder are made with gates and contain no information storage capability. The two decoders are organized to use binary-coded information to select a control line for timing and for instruction selection and contain very regular logic structures. The encoder, on the other hand, has logic that is organized almost randomly to select the combinations of gate and function control signals needed to cause the proper microsequences to occur in the processor.

   Design tools analogous to those described in Chapter 2 are available to the logic and circuit designers for implementation of the control design. The operations of the encoder can be described with boolean logic equations as functions of the inputs from the decoders, the condition codes, and the status flags. The equations are reduced to minimum form, meeting established specifications for "fan-in" (number of inputs to a gate) and "fan-out" (number of gates that a gate output can drive). For minimum signal delay through the encoder a single "sum-of-products" or "product-of-sums" stage is desired. (Each signal traverses only one AND and one OR gate while it propagates through the encoder.) The two decoders also are designed with single logic stages to minimize propagation delays. Hard-wired controls usually are designed with gates of speed equal to those of the ALU and shifter.

   The cost of the random logic of the hard-wired controller can be reduced by using programmed logic arrays (PLAs) that contain groups of orthogonally directed conductors connected at their intersections by diodes or transistors. As shown in Fig. 6-6, two arrays are provided, an AND array that drives AND gate outputs and an OR array that has OR gate outputs. The connection to the arrays from the input signal lines and to the output control lines is determined by the interconnecting diodes. Where interconnection is not desired, the diode is "burned" open by electrical current that exceeds the diode's current-carrying capacity. The remaining diode connections implement the same combinatorial logic that is found in the decoders and the encoder of Fig. 6-5. The advantage of the PLA is that it can be made as a standard device that is customized to its function as a part of the manufacturing process. If it is necessary to change the control of a computer the PLA can be replaced with one that contains the newly desired connections. A PLA combines the decoding and encoding functions of Fig. 6-5 in a single set of sum-of-products equations. Usually a PLA implementation is somewhat slower than the random-logic design due to the large fan-in to the gates, requiring that slower components be used.

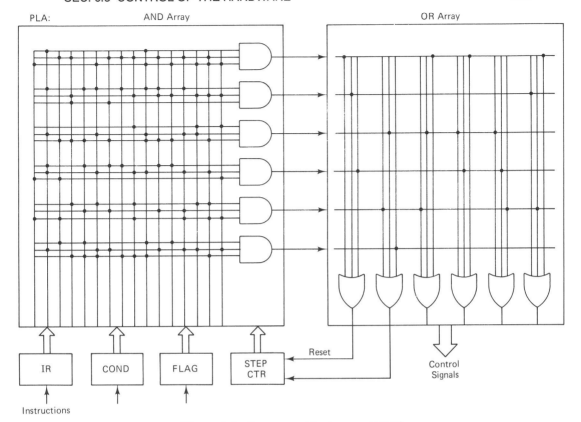

Figure 6-6 Programmed logic array control.

The second approach to computer-control organization, the microprogrammed controller, was invented with the realization that the control functions of the computer, as well as the computer itself, can be represented as a discrete-state machine. In both cases, at each state outputs are uniquely determined by the previous state and by current (data and instruction) information. The difference between the two state machines is that the control state machine outputs cause the closing of electrical control paths, whereas the computer state machine outputs can be interpreted as results of computations to be represented in human-understandable form.

A microprogrammed controller, as shown in Fig. 6-7, holds the possible control-signal combinations as words in a controller memory, the control store. The input information to the controller, including the operator held in the instruction register (IR), the status flags (FLAG), and the condition codes (COND), is decoded and used to select a word containing a microinstruction from the control store. That microinstruction is then decoded to yield control-input information for the next step, the designation of the next address (which might be combined with the input information), and the processor control signals. Operation of the controller is synchronized by a clock-pulse generator. The controller consists of the control store and a microsequencer (the decoding circuits, the address and instruction registers, and

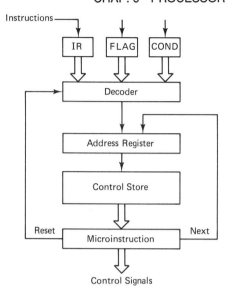

Figure 6-7   Microprogrammed controller.

the internal controls). A comparison of Figs. 6-5 through 6-7 shows that the three different controllers have similar inputs and outputs. In the microprogrammed case the encoding is done by specifying the output of each control word. Microprogram assemblers, design tools to assist the people who write microprograms, perform functions similar to the assemblers used by assembly language programmers.

The time taken between the availability of input signals and the generation of the output control signals in the microprogrammed controller usually is longer than that achieved with hard-wired logic. The total time is determined by summing the propagation delays through the decoding circuits, the time it takes to transfer the modified next address to the control-store address register (CSAR), the time to read the control-store value into the microinstruction register, and the decoding time. This is significantly longer than propagation times through a hard-wired logic controller, but the microprogrammed controller offers much more flexibility. Often the flexibility encourages computer architects to specify much larger and more complicated instruction sets than would be the case if they were restricted by the limitations of hard-wired controllers. We address this issue further in our discussion of performance in a later section.

The microprogrammed controller shown in Fig. 6-7 uses a control word that is only slightly encoded. All control-signal information in the word consists of signals to directly drive one or more gates for register or function selection. A control word for this microprogrammed controller that could be used to control the simple computer of Fig. 6-4 is shown in Fig. 6-8(a). The only field that is encoded is the next address field that selects the next microinstruction word. All other fields have a single output activated (designated as 1/8 for bus selection). This direct form of control-word output is identified as "horizontal" microprogramming since control lines are selected directly by reading a single control word from the control store. An alternative, the "vertical" form of microprogram word is shown in Fig. 6-8(b). In this case, all fields are encoded and the decoding to select one control line for each output field (other than the next address) is provided

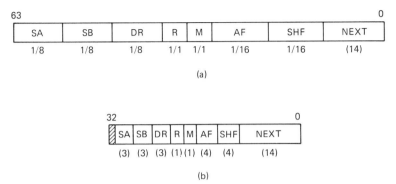

Figure 6-8 Horizontal and vertical microinstructions. (a) Horizontal. (b) Vertical (encoded).

as a part of the microinstruction decoder. The decoding circuits at the input and the output can be implemented with PLAs for increased flexibility.

The DEC LSI-11, a microprocessor version of the PDP-11, used an extreme form of vertical microprogramming, with the short microinstructions shown in Fig. 6-9. The four different formats limited the parallel operations that could be performed and the microcode was quite similar to assembly code. The LSI-11 contained microinstructions that were close to the instructions of the virtual machine, the PDP-11, and there was significant hard-wired control logic beneath the microcode. Since each of the microoperations was executed in a single clock period, the computer at the microprogram level has some characteristics of the RISC computers reviewed in Section 6.5.

It is possible to perform the control functions with two levels of microprogramming, introducing another discrete-state machine, the *nanocontroller*. Computer control implemented in this manner uses vertical (encoded) microinstructions that in turn act as input to the horizontal nanoinstructions. Since instructions at the two levels can be established

```
{Microcode Format}
    MW<23..0>,                  {Microword}
    FI<7..0> := MW<23..16>,     {Function Identifier}
    MI<15..0> := MW<15..0>,     {Microinstruction}
{Jump Instruction Format}
    JM<4..0> := MI<15..11>,     {Jump Operator}
    JA<10..0> := MI<10..0>,     {Jump Address}
{Conditional Jump Format}
    CJ<3..0> := MI<15..12>,     {Conditional Jump Operator}
    CN<3..0> := MI<11..8>,      {Condition}
    CA<7..0> := MI<7..0>,       {Condition True Jump Address}
{Literal-Register Format}
    LR<3..0> := MI<15..12>,     {Literal-Register Operator}
    LI<7..0> := MI<11..4>,      {Literal (Constant) Value}
    RG<3..0> := MI<3..0>,       {Register Identifier}
{Register-Register Format}
    RR<7..0> := MI<15..8>,      {Register-Register Operator}
    R1<3..0> := MI<7..4>,       {Register Identifier}
    R2<3..0> := MI<3..0>,       {Register Identifier}
```

Figure 6-9 A vertical microcode example, the LSI-11.

independently, there is increased flexibility in the control structure. The Motorola M68000 microprocessors use this approach. As we see in Fig. 6-10, the 10-bit-wide microinstruction selects an address in the nanostore or a branch back to the sequence of microinstructions. The 10-bit address field is large enough to select one of the 280 nanowords or one of the 640 microwords. The 70-bit nanoword is used to select control lines directly with no decoding and its next address field contains the address of the next microword. This two-level control structure reflects the complexity that has been criticized and is discussed under performance issues later in this chapter.

The control stores (micro- and nano-) usually are implemented with read-only memory (ROM) devices to take advantage of their high speed, low cost, and nonvolatility. A ROM is similar to the OR array part of the PLA shown in Fig. 6-6. During processor development random-access memory (RAM) might be used until the control sequences are validated, at which time the read-only memory is coded and installed. If the control sequences might be changed, programmable read-only memory (PROM) or erasable PROM (EPROM) can be employed, at least in prototype models of the computers. All of these alternative memories are slower than the ROM.

The controllers described are microprogramm*ed* so that the control sequences are fixed, at least for fairly long time periods. If random-access memory can be used in the control store, it is possible to change the control sequences by loading new micropro-

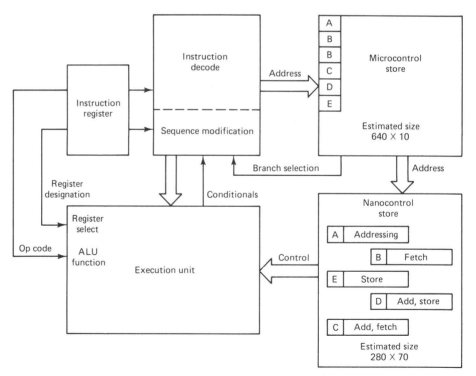

Figure 6-10   A two-level microcode example, the M68000. (Copyright 1979, IEEE. Reprinted with permission.)

grams, just as we load program code into the virtual machine. This yields a microprogram*able* computer with the microcode accessible to the system programmer or user. With this facility the computer can be adapted to particular applications or languages. The larger VAX computers include a writeable control store available to users as an option. In the VAX 8800 the control store of 16 kwords (of 144 bits) is all writeable. A part of the control store (1 kword in the 8800) is available to users.

In the mid 1970s a very flexible microprogrammable computer, the Nanodata QM-1 (see Fig. 6-11), appeared with two levels of control and six different storage units. The 18-bit vertical microcode that was held in the control store was accessible to the user and the control code could be moved from the main store (Mp) to the control store. The 360-bit horizontal nanocode, held in the nanostore was selected by the control code and directly drove the internal processor gates and controlled the arithmetic and logic unit (ALU). Two banks of thirty-two 18-bit registers each were used for control registers and general registers (local store) and for I/O buffering and index registers (external store). The 32-word 6-bit F Store was used for bus control registers. This interesting machine, characterized by the very wide nanoword, was intended as an "emulator" of other computers. It was used largely for research in microprogramming and emulation.

Another interesting microprogrammable computer of the 1970s, the Burroughs B1700, employed horizontal microcode. Different control structures were used to create various virtual machines (each defined by an *S language*) for translating or for executing programs written in different higher-level languages. Among the other interesting features of the B1700 and its successors, the B1800 and B1900, was the variable virtual-word sizes that could be realized with the 24-bit physical words. The memory was treated as a large string of bits that could be "sliced" into words of any desired length.

Microprogrammed control has become sufficiently popular that standard sequencers as well as the control stores are being provided by semiconductor manufacturers. An example is a computer control based on the Advanced Micro Devices AM 2910, as shown in Fig. 6-12. Here the operation code (OP code) of an instruction in the instruction register is mapped in a PROM to a control-store address that is generated by the next address multiplexer. The control-store address also can be a value in a register counter, an address obtained from the subroutine and loop stack, or a microprogram counter (similar to a

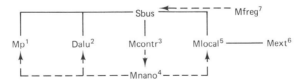

1. Mp\"Main_Store" (word_size: 18 bits).
2. Dalu\arithmetic_and_logic_unit.
3. Mcontr\"Control_Store" (word_size: 18 bits).
4. Mnano\"Nano_Store" (word_size: 360 bits).
5. Mlocal\"Local_Store" (size: 64 words, word_size: 18 bits).
6. Mext\"External_Store" (size: 64 words, word_size: 18 bits).
7. Mfreg\"F_Store" (size: 32 words, word_size: 6 bits).

Figure 6-11   A microprogram*able* computer, the QM-1.

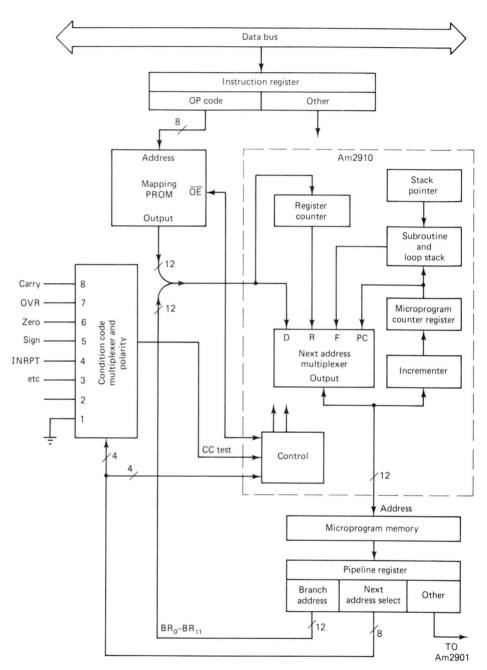

Figure 6-12 A standard microsequencer, the AM 2910. (Reprinted with permission of Advanced Micro Devices, Inc.)

program counter at the instruction-set-processor level). Microinstructions from the microprogram memory generate branch addresses of other microinstructions, signals (next address select) that are combined with condition-code information to control the microsequencer, and control signals for a microprocessor (the AM 2901 in the example). The microinstructions are buffered in a "pipeline" register. (Pipelines of instructions are described in Section 6.5.)

Standard sequencers of this type are used to assemble computers from a number of "bit-slice" microprocessors. Advanced Micro Devices has been a leader in high-performance bit-slice microprocessor technology and many different computers were assembled using their standard bit-slice components. An example is the 16-bit computer shown in Fig. 6-13 that employs the AM 2910 microprogram controller that was shown in Fig. 6-12. The 16-bit machine is assembled from four 4-bit AM 2901 microprocessors, the controller, four AM 7930 program control units, an AM 7914 priority interrupt module, and interfacing logic.

There continues to be much argument about the degree to which the computer architecture should support specific programming language features. As discussed in Chapter 5, some compiler developers argue for simple, regular, and orthogonal processor states and instruction sets, whereas others want to have available as many features as possible to support characteristics of languages and compilers. "Direct-execution" and "direct-interpretation" languages and architectures have been proposed for direct support of programming languages. Reduced-instruction-set computer (RISC) proponents argue for minimum features that are used extensively by compilers.

Figure 6-14 demonstrates the different approaches. In this representation of a "language space" the large variety of problem languages are dispersed. Programs to solve problems are written in one of the higher-level programming languages, more similar and tightly grouped than are the problem languages. The four different approaches to computer architecture to support translation are shown at different distances from the programming languages. The language of RISC machines is far from the higher-level programming languages, but the simple compilation-oriented hardware features are used directly by compilers for every programming language. Most conventional computers provide a variety of features to more directly match the characteristics of the programming languages, but they are designed to support a variety of languages and are close to none of them. Even closer to a selected few of the higher-level languages are the "language-based" computers like the Unisys A series that was designed to work with block-structured languages. A very close match to a single programming language is available with the direct-execution language computers that "speak" the higher-level programming language. The Nanodata QM-1 is an early representation of this last type of computer. Each of these approaches has different control requirements and each has a different control structure.

The real issue in selecting the method of control is one of performance for a given cost. Performance should be expressed in terms of the time it takes to solve problems of a user or a group of users. It should reflect the execution of programs written in the users' languages. It is here that the arguments made by proponents of "higher-level" machines with features to support compilers run counter to those of the reduced-instruction-set supporters. We discuss

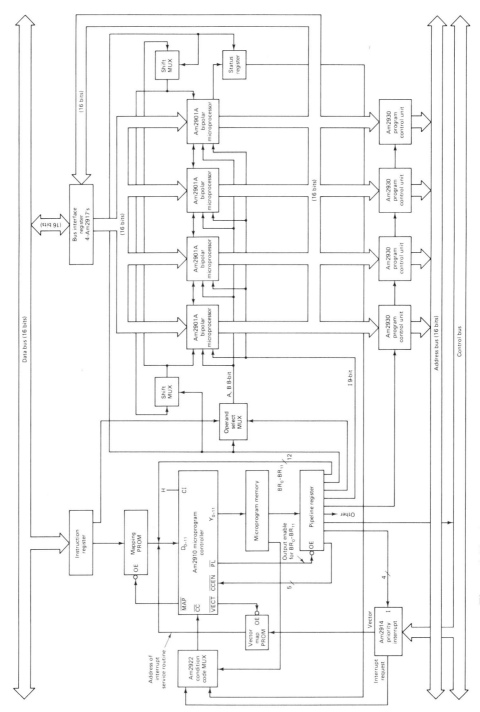

Figure 6-13 A processor made from bit slices. (Reprinted with permission of Advanced Micro Devices, Inc.)

212

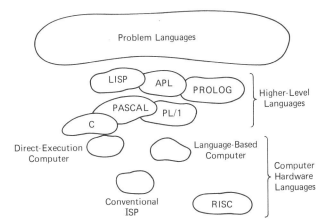

Figure 6-14 Architecture and language levels.

the issues in more detail in a later section, but at this point we should reflect on the benefits or hazards of microprogram flexibility. Is microprogramming flexibility a path to machines that match programming languages or is it an invitation to excess complexity?

The sequential control mechanism that we have described follows the von Neumann model of computation that has been used for computer design since 1946. When we examine special computer systems in Chapter 9, we consider alternatives to this "control flow" model. Three alternative models, "data-driven data flow computers", "demand-driven reduction machines", and "systolic arrays" are examined and compared with the more conventional control flow computers. All of these depend on information in the data or in the data structure to establish control of computation.

Somewhat related is the idea of placing control information in the words of data. This concept, called *tagged memory*, has been used in several experimental and commercial computers, most extensively by Burroughs in the stack-based B6500 and its successors (now the Unisys A series). As shown in Fig. 6-15, these computers had a 3-bit tag (and a parity bit) added to the 48-bit data fields. The tag was used by the operating system and the controls to determine how the word was to be interpreted. Scalar data had the tag 000 if it was single precision and 010 if double precision. (Recall that there is a uniform fixed-point and floating-point representation.) The operating system used the 0X0 tag to determine that an operand was scalar and the hardware examined the center bit to determine precision. Compiled programs did not have to specify the precision of the data before the programs were executed.

Other codes used by the operating system included the designation of data descriptors (pointers to data areas) as 101 and segment descriptors (pointers to instruction areas) as 011. In both cases the descriptors were used to point to memory segments outside the stack. The distinction between the two was used for memory protection and access control. The data descriptor permitted access to a total data area or to a particular scalar item within an area, using information in the information fields of the 48-bit word.

A program-control word (tag 111) controlled jumps to the code for other procedures and functions. The indirect-reference word (tag 001) was used for indirect addressing

```
{Memory Word Organization}
  Mp[n]<51..0>,                    {52-bit Word Size}
  P := Mp[n]<51>,                  {Parity Bit}
  TG<2..0> := Mp[n]<50..48>,       {3-bit Tag Field}
  IN<47..0> := Mp[n]<47..0>,       {48-bit Information}

{Data Words}
  TG = 000 ->                      {Single Precision}
    SP<47..0> := IN<47..0>,
    ES := SP<46>,                  {Exponent Sign}
    MS := SP<45>,                  {Mantissa Sign}
    ES := SP<44..39>,              {Exponent (Base 8)}
    MN := SP<38..0>,               {Mantissa (Integer)}
  TG = 010 ->
    DP<101..0> := Mp[n],Mp[n+1],
    ES := DP<97>,                  {Exponent Sign}
    MS := DP<96>,                  {Mantissa Sign}
    ED := DP<95..90,47..39>,       {Exponent (Base 8)}
    MI := DP<89..51,                {Integer Mantissa}
    MF := DP<38..0>,               {Mantissa Fraction}

{Descriptors}
  TG = 101 ->                      {Data Descriptor}
    DD<47..0> := Inf<47..0>,
    P := DD<47>,                   {Present-in-Mp Bit}
    C := DD<46>,                   {This-is-a-Copy Bit}
    I := DD<45>,                   {Indexed (Scalar) Bit}
    S := DD<44>,                   {Array is Segmented}
    R := DD<43>,                   {Read-Only Bit}
    D := DD<40>,                   {Double-Precision Bit}
    LN<19..0> := DD<39..20>,       {Length of Data Area}
    DA<19..0> := DD<19..0>,        {Data Area Address}
  TG = 011 ->                      {Segment Descriptor}
    P := DD<47>,                   {Present-in-Mp Bit}
    C := DD<46>,                   {This-is-a-Copy Bit}
    LN<19..0> := DD<39..20>,       {Length of Program Area}
    DA<19..0> := DD<19..0>,        {Program Area Address}

{Control Words}
  TG = 111 ->                      {Program Control Word}
    SN<9..0> := IN<45..36>,        {Stack Number}
    SI<15..0> := IN<35..20>,       {Syllable Index}
    LL<4..0> := IN<18..14>,        {Program Lexical Level}
    SD<13..0> := IN<13..0>,        {Index to Segment Desc.}
  TG = 001 ->                      {Indirect Reference Wd.}
    IN<46> := 0,
    AC<13..0> := IN<13..0>,        {Address Couple}
```

Figure 6-15   Tagged memory, the Burroughs descriptors.

within the stack. It was the means for pointing to nonlocal values in execution environments of ancestor procedures, using an address couple to designate an environment and offset as deep in the stack as was required. The stuffed indirect-reference word caused similar actions, but allowed for referencing other stacks in the cactus stack structure. Both forms of indirect reference were used for "target-designated" indefinite-level indirect referencing, permitting the computer to access a data location and find a data descriptor pointing to another location.

Several other special control words were tagged for operating-system interpretation. In the discussion of stack operations (see Fig. 5-12) and of context switching, we were introduced to the mark-stack control word that held pointers to the static and dynamic predecessor environments, the return control word that returned the previous environment, and the top-of-stack control word that held the processor state of contexts that had been saved.

The computer used all of the tags of Fig. 6-15 as a part of its control system. Interpreting for specific action, checking for validity of a word read from memory, and branching to specific error-recovery routines depended on values in the tags.

6.4 FAULT DIAGNOSIS AND MAINTENANCE

The control structure can be designed to include features that aid maintenance processes. Much of the automatic maintenance analysis is performed by diagnostic programs that are run periodically, at interrupt, on operator demand, or whenever the computer is turned on. The fault diagnosis can be made easier if there are facilities in the hardware that can identify faults or can initiate the diagnostic programs. A maintenance-support system requires means for detecting, isolating, and correcting hardware faults. The first step is the detection that a fault in the system exists. If the fault can be isolated, at least to the extent of locating a replaceable subsystem or printed-circuit card, then correction can be achieved by replacing the identified unit.

While the occurrence of some hardware failures is obvious in causing inoperability of part or all of the system, many failures are more subtle and more difficult to detect. This particularly is true in the case of intermittent faults that recur infrequently or of transient faults that are evident only if certain conditions exist. Fault detection usually entails comparing the results of an operation (a calculation or a transfer of information) with the correct result. The addition of parity bits or other error-detecting codes and checking for correct values on transfers, discussed in Chapter 4, is the primary means of detecting and, in some cases, of correcting transient errors in information. If a count is kept of errors made on transfers to or from a major unit such as a memory module or a register bank, that information can be used to determine that there is a fault that must be found and corrected. The error counts can be held in special registers and can stimulate an interrupt when a threshold is exceeded, or the registers can be polled periodically by the maintenance programs.

It is more difficult to identify errors that occur in units that transform information such as arithmetic or logical operators. Error detection again involves a comparison of results with the correct values. This might entail periodically performing a sequence of operations with known results as a part of the error-detection procedures in the diagnostic programs. When fault detection is needed continuously, the checking can be made a part of the function units. This can be accomplished by repeating operations with the same input conditions or through introducing redundant circuits to permit performance of the operation on two of the same circuits. In either case, a difference in the two results shows that an error has occurred.

Examples of error-detection logic are shown in Fig. 6-16. In Fig. 6-16(a) the outputs of two function units are compared. If a difference is detected an interrupt is initiated and the detector circuit that shows the error is identified. The diagnostic routine called by the interrupt processor finds the faulty unit to permit a replacement to be made or a count of

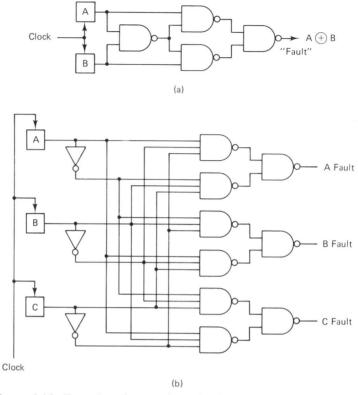

(a)

(b)

Figure 6-16 Examples of comparison circuits. (a) Two-way comparison
(each bit of A and B). (b) Three-way error detection (each bit of A, B, and C).

the fault to be recorded. Adding registers to hold the redundant results is costly and we
might exclude the redundant registers by designating a "primary" function unit that
delivers its results to the register and a "secondary" unit that is used for comparison. The
difficulty with this approach is that the specific difference in the results is not recorded
for fault analysis.

Figure 6-16(b) is an example of how "voting logic" can be used in a triplicated
function unit. A fault in any bit position can call an interrupt to initiate a diagnostic
procedure. In this case the faulty function unit can be identified immediately and the
correct value can be processed. When continuation of the processing is required (as
well might be the case when the cost of this level of redundancy is justified), the fact
that a unit fault has been detected and overruled is recorded in a register while normal
operation continues. If the fault was a transient error, such as might be caused by
electrical noise, it can be ignored and corrective action taken only if the offending
function unit records a history of errors.

Most diagnostic programs exercise the same virtual machine that is seen by the
users. Some have access to operators that are reserved for the operating system and
exercise its virtual machine. In either case it is difficult for the diagnostic procedures

to search inside the hardware to find and locate faults. With larger computer systems it might be desirable to perform some of the fault analysis using special control structures that can be introduced in a microprogram. Diagnostic programs run at this lower hardware level can evaluate the computer controls and the control registers that are not seen in the instruction-set processor. The larger VAX systems have a *writeable diagnostic store* for diagnostic procedures at this level. The *console processor* of these computers is used for maintenance support, as well as for operator access to the system.

As shown in Fig. 6-17, the IBM System/308X (and System/3090) contains a microprogrammed *processor controller* for system monitoring, diagnosis, and maintenance. The processor controller is a simple computer with a 128-kbyte microprogram memory that contains microprograms for the various monitoring and system-support manager processes. The functional controller is an I/O control for the specialized interface devices of the process controller. These interfaces include diagnostic-support systems (DSS) for the 3081 processor electronics and for the support units (3087, 3089), a logic-support system (LSS) for the processor logic, auxiliary storage for additional microprograms and data, fixed disk and diskette drive secondary storage, local system and customer engineering (CE) consoles, and data communication for automatic communication with a central maintenance station. Most large-scale computers now incorporate similar diagnostic processing capabilities.

A technique for stopping execution of a program for examination of conditions is to identify *breakpoints* at particular instructions. Hardware support can be provided for breakpointing by causing processing to stop when a breakpoint instruction is addressed. Flow tracing is used to track the progress of a program instruction by instruction. If a portion of a program where a fault is suspected can be traced, a breakpoint can be used to stop execution. The results of execution then can be examined to determine the reason for unexpected performance.

National Semiconductor NS32000 microprocessors provide good support for breakpoints and flow tracing. Breakpoint signals can be set on each access to a breakpoint address or after a specifiable number of accesses. Two breakpoint addresses can be effective at the same time, allowing for stops in either of two program branches. As shown in Fig. 6-18(a), three registers in the memory-management unit support breakpoint testing. Two of these (BPR0 and BPR1), hold the doubleword addresses of breakpoints for comparison with the address bus on every memory cycle. When a breakpoint appears on the address bus, other conditions specified in the associated breakpoint register are checked to determine if an interrupt should be initiated. The third register (BPCT), specifies the number of matches with the BPR0 register that are to be ignored before testing conditions for an interrupt.

The MMU also has four registers, Fig. 6-18(b), for flow tracing. When a bit in the memory-status register is set, two program-flow registers (PF0, PF1) hold the addresses of the last two instructions executed out of sequence (targets of branches). Two sequence-count registers (SC0, SC1) maintain a count of the number of instruction fetches between each program-flow change. Flow tracing is initiated by a program-setable bit in the

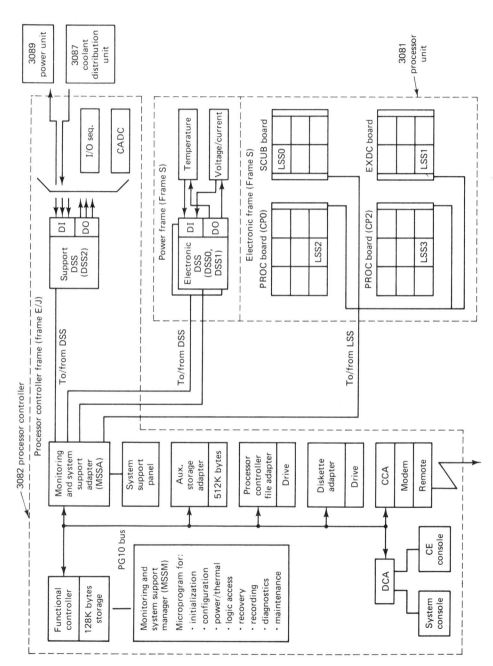

Figure 6-17 The IBM 308X processor controller. (Copyright IBM Corp., reprinted with permission.)

218

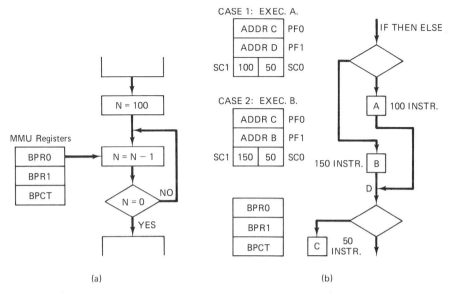

Figure 6-18   (a) Break points. (b) Flow tracing.

processor-status register. The trap is used to branch to a program-analysis routine. Flow tracing can be combined with use of breakpoints for more dynamic analysis.

6.5 REDUCED-INSTRUCTION-SET COMPUTERS (RISC)

The history of growth in instruction-set size and complexity was reviewed in Section 5.7. To a large degree this trend was driven by the desire of computer architects to provide instructions that were closer to the operations of higher-level languages, leading to variable-size instructions with a large number of argument-addressing options. The assumption that compiler writers desired (or even used) these features was questioned. In Section 5.2 W. A. Wulf's argument that simplicity and consistency are architectural features more desired by compiler writers was presented.

By the late 1970s many computer architects realized that much of the complexity that had grown into computer architecture was there because it was possible, not because it was necessary. As we saw in Section 6.3, microprogramming permitted and encouraged the use of complicated multiple-clock-cycle instructions with many effective addressing modes. The "hidden" processor that executed microcode required many registers that were invisible to the programmer (e.g., Fig. 6-3). In many computers the hidden processor state was larger than the visible state. At the same time the control memory to store microcode was four or more times the size of the cache memory. The complex control structure needed to implement many of the "higher-level" instructions had the effect of making even the simple instructions take longer, introducing a performance penalty on programs that were able to use only the simple instructions.

This situation caused a number of investigators to question whether computer architectures were really being optimized to performance of compiled programs. Several examined the history of execution of sample programs that were written in higher-level languages and translated to machine code by compilers. Other investigators questioned whether the valuable surface area of silicon semiconductors was being allocated in an optimum way with so much of it devoted to control memory and control logic.

At the IBM Research Laboratories John Cocke led a team investigating how compilers could use fast simple instructions. Their studies of instruction execution on a conventional computer showed that 80% of all computation used only 20% of the instructions in a typical instruction set. Furthermore, the simpler instructions tended to be in the 80%. The two-level control structure introduced with microprogramming (or three-level with nanocode, as in Fig. 6-10) for the complex instructions slowed down the simple instructions. All this suggested that a better computer architecture for higher-level-language programs would have a small set of simple instructions. It would incorporate few addressing modes and could be implemented with hard-wired (or PLA) control. An experimental machine, the 801, was developed following these principles and an operating model was running in 1979. The striking results of the project, confirming the conjectures of the investigators, were not published until 1982.

In 1980, a research team at the University of California at Berkeley led by D. A. Patterson also questioned the need for the complexity found in the more popular architectures. They felt that a simpler approach would lead to better use of silicon semiconductor surface area, easier VLSI design, and improved performance in execution of compiled programs. They studied execution records of higher-level-language programs and obtained results similar to those of the IBM group. The Berkeley investigators also found that a large percentage of instructions executed were for environment switching in procedure calls and returns. This suggested that compiled programs needed a computer with a small set of simple instructions and a large number of registers to facilitate environment switching (see Section 5.5). In principle, semiconductor surface area should be allocated to registers instead of to control logic. This principle was used in the Berkeley RISC I and RISC II computers.

At Stanford in 1981 J. Hennessy initiated similar studies of execution of compiled higher-level-language programs. The results showed that computers should incorporate one-clock-time instructions implemented by having a "pipeline" of instructions to overlap instruction fetch and execution. Optimizing compilers could be effective in using the pipeline and in register allocation. This led to the Stanford microprocessor without interlocking pipeline stages (MIPS) that has become a product of MIPS Computer Systems, Inc.

The objective of all these approaches to reduced-instruction-set computer (RISC) architecture is the facility in execution of code compiled from high-level-language programs. A key part of the Berkeley concept is the use of a large bank of registers for storing values that are local to a procedure and for those that are received from the calling procedure, with the argument that local data is required by procedures much more often than nonlocal data. Memory that is highly nonlocal ("global" in some programming languages) is held in primary memory, or is moved there as the depth of nesting of procedure calls fills the register bank.

The concept of the large register bank with overlapping windows for successively called procedures as used in the RISC II is outlined in Fig. 6-19. There are 138 registers, 10 at the low-address level for the global data area and 8 "windows" for representation of environments below the global level. Each 22-register window adds 16 physical registers since there is a 6-register overlap of adjacent windows. (The global window does not have the 6 low registers.) The overlap is used to pass parameters from the caller to the called procedure without actually moving the information. Parameters developed in the calling procedure are placed in the 6 upper registers of its window. The arguments of the called procedure (those parameters of the caller) are in the lower 6 registers of its window. Identification of the current group of 32 registers is by address mapping from the physical bank to a logical set, as shown in the illustration. The virtual register bank can be larger than the physical bank (can contain more than eight windows) and information not in the physical register bank is extended into in primary memory. Simulations showed that it is very seldom that more than eight windows are needed.

The IBM 801 and the Stanford MIPS emphasize use of optimizing compilers to take advantage of the simple instructions and the instruction pipeline. Both of these machines use a cache memory working with the general registers (32 in the 801 and 16 in MIPS) as alternatives to the register-window approach at Berkeley. Both use their compilers to optimize the use of general registers and to minimize the need for memory references.

Common to all three approaches are the use of register-to-register operations with only LOAD and STORE for memory references, hard-wired control to permit most operations to take place in one fixed time period, simple instruction formats with instructions not crossing word boundaries (in contrast to the examples of Fig. 5-25.), delayed branches that always allow fetch of the next instruction during execution of the current instruction, and pipelines to overlap instruction fetch, argument acquisition from registers, instruction execution, and result deposition in a register. The machines used different length pipelines: four stages for the 801, five in the MIPS, and three in RISC II.

```
PR[0..137]<31..0>,                      {138 31-bit Physical Registers}
LR(#0..7)[0..31]<31..0>,                {8 banks of Logical Registers}
GL[0..9] := PR[0..9],                   {Global Registers}
 (LR(#p)[0..9] := GL[0..9],             {Global Region for Process p}
  LR(#p)[10..31] := PR[m..m+21]
    & m := 10 + 16 * p,                 {Environment for Process p}
  LO(#p)[0..5] := LR(#p)[10..15],       {Low Registers for Process p}
  LC(#p)[0..9] := LR(#p)[15..25],       {Local Registers for Process p}
  HI(#p)[0..5] := LR(#p)[26..31],       {High Registers for Process p}
    HI(#p) := LO (#p + 1))              {Overlap of Process Registers}
  & (p := 0..7),                        {8 Process Environments}
```

Figure 6-19 Reduced-instruction-set-computer register windows.

Operation of a five-stage instruction pipeline (similar to that of MIPS) is demonstrated in Fig. 6-20. An instruction cycle, Fig. 6-20(a), is executed in five equal-length subcycles: instruction transfer (IT), instruction decode (ID), select argument registers (SR), operator execution (OE), transfer result to register (TR). If the instructions can be fetched from memory and placed in a queue (see Fig. 5-13) at the subcycle (rather than the cycle) rate, then it should be possible to overlap one or more of the subcycles to increase speed. With the simple register-to-register instructions of RISC architectures the subcycles can be overlapped, as shown in Fig. 6-20(b). Here the transfer (from the queue) of instruction $n + 4$ (IT) is taking place while instruction $n + 3$ is being decoded (ID). At the same time registers for the arguments of instruction $n + 2$ are being selected (SR), instruction $n + 1$ is actually being executed (OE), and the result of execution of instruction n is being transferred to a register (TR).

If the pipeline can be kept "full" of instructions, the execution rate is five times that of a purely sequential instruction-execution cycle. Attaining that goal requires careful design of the instruction set, a sufficient quantity of general registers to allow most instructions to use register-to-register transfers, fast load and store operations to permit memory references to be accomplished at the same rate, and instruction sequences that do not entail delays while an instruction must await the result of a previous instruction. In RISC each register-to-register instruction in the simple instruction set has the same format to allow the uniformly fast subcycles. A cache memory (see Section 4.5) permits

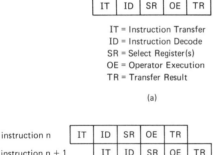

(a)

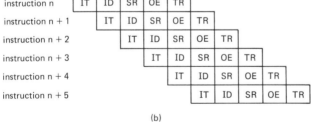

(b)

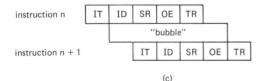

(c)

Figure 6-20 The RISC instruction pipeline. (a) Subcycles of an instruction execution. (b) A five-stage pipeline. (c) A bubble caused by dependency of instruction $n + 1$ on date from instruction n.

most LOAD from memory and STORE to memory operations to be accomplished in a cycle. (The time for a cache memory reference must be no more than four subcycles.)

The most difficult of the challenges described is the last: control of the instruction sequences to eliminate waiting. This problem has been called the appearance of "bubbles" in the pipeline. The problem has four components, the most straightforward of which is the delay of instruction $m + 1$ if one of its arguments is the result of instruction m. Here OE of instruction $m + 1$ cannot be accomplished until TR of instruction m has been accomplished and instruction $m + 1$ must be delayed until time $m + 2$ (one subcycle later), as shown in Fig. 6-20(c). A similar delay results when an argument for instruction $p + 1$ must be loaded from cache memory by instruction p. Here OE of instruction $p + 1$ cannot start until the completion of instruction p and instruction $p + 1$ should be delayed until the time slot for $p + 2$. If there is a cache fault (the value desired is not in cache memory and must be brought from primary memory), then the delay might be several cycles. Finally, a delay is introduced if instruction q calls for a branch out of the static instruction sequence. Here the next instruction cannot be fetched from memory until the branch instruction has been executed and the next instruction must be delayed until time $q + 5$. (This is a problem with all instruction lookahead methods, described in Fig. 5-14.)

In all of these situations execution-delay (bubble) difficulties are addressed through compiler design. In each case, the unused instruction slots (caused by delaying instructions one or more subcycles) initially are filled with NOOP (nil instructions). In all situations but the last the delays are data-dependent in that an instruction needs data from a prior instruction. A "data-flow analysis", well developed in compiler technology, is used to find instructions that are not dependent on the delayed or the delaying instructions. These are inserted into the sequence in the unused (NOOP) time slots to the extent possible, restoring execution speed to that determined by the subcycle time.

When an argument is not available in cache memory and must be obtained from primary memory, several time slots in sequence are empty and that number of instructions must be inserted. This situation cannot be predicted even by a very capable compiler (else it could ensure that the situation never would occur). The problem might be resolved by delaying for the time of primary memory fetch all instructions needing data from a LOAD. However, if this could solve the problem the cache would not be required for data at all. A better solution is to assume cache hits on all data memory references and to have the hardware detect cache faults, delaying the instruction-execution sequence until the data has been transferred.

The same technique can be used in the branch delay case, but selection of instructions for insertion is more difficult. If the branch is dependent on a condition these must be instructions that are executed no matter which instruction-sequence path is taken. Often this requires looking ahead so many instructions that it is not feasible to complete the search, and the technique works only when movable instructions can be found relatively near the branch. Sometimes the desired result can be obtained by moving the branch instruction (and the condition generator) back in the sequence, delaying some earlier instructions.

The operation of an optimizing compiler to find instructions that can be inserted out of their normal sequence is shown in Fig. 6-21. In Fig. 6-21(a) we see the higher-

```
C := A - B;
A := B + C;
if C > 0
    then B := C
    else B := B + 1;
```

(a)

```
  LOAD R[A] R[1]
  LOAD R[B] R[2]
  NOOP
  SUB  R[2] R[1] R[3]
  NOOP
* STO  R[3] R[C]
  ADD  R[2] R[3] R[1]
  NOOP
  STO  R[1] R[A]
* JGT  R[3]  #0    L1
  NOOP
  NOOP
  NOOP
  NOOP
  ADD  R[2]  #1    R[2]
  NOOP
  STO  R[2] R[B]
* JMP  L2
  NOOP
  NOOP
  NOOP
  NOOP
L1: STO  R[3] R[B]
L2: --
    --
    --
```

```
      LOAD R[A] R[1]
      LOAD R[B] R[2]
      NOOP
      SUB  R[2] R[1] R[3]
      NOOP
    * JGT  R[3]  #0    L1
      ADD  R[2] R[3] R[1]
    * STO  R[3] R[C]
      STO  R[1] R[A]
      NOOP
    * JMP  L2
      ADD  R[2]  #1    R[2]
      NOOP
      STO  R[2] R[B]
      NOOP
L1:   STO  R[3] R[B]
L2:   --
      --
      --
```

(b)   (c)

Figure 6-21   Moving instructions to fill pipeline bubles. (a) Higher-level-language statements. (b) Assembly-language program with bubbles. (c) Compacted assembly-language program.

level-language statements to be executed. A simple assembly language code for a typical instruction sequence, with NOOP (no operation) instructions inserted where a delay is needed, is shown in Fig. 6-21(b). The registers with letter (A, B, C) subscripts designate that the register contains the address of the letter variable of the higher-level-language program. Arithmetic operations call for three registers, two for source arguments and one for result destination.

The separate NOOPs are for delaying any instructions that require the data generated by the previous instruction. For example, the first NOOP is required because "SUB R[2], R[1], R[3]" uses as a source a value (R[2]) that is the destination of "LOAD R[B], R[2]". The sequences of NOOPs are caused by the branches (JGT, JMP). Instructions that the compiler can move are preceded by asterisks. In Fig. 6-21(c) these instructions have been moved out of sequence to replace most NOOPs and the sequence has been compacted. A program that had 23 subcycles has been reduced to one that takes 16 subcycles. The minimum program (without NOOPs) would take 11 subcycles. The pipeline has allowed 11 instructions to be executed in less than 4 instruction cycles.

Much of this process appears to be independent of RISC characteristics. However, it is the relative simplicity of the RISC architecture that makes it easier to implement this optimizing feature of the compilers. Compiler optimization techniques also are used to facilitate environment switching in the IBM and Stanford approaches. Instead of the register windows incorporated in the Berkeley designs, the others use the compiler to allocate general registers with minimum conflict.

The design philosophy used in RISC is similar to that prescribed by the von Neumann team: introduce complexity only if it can be justified by demonstrated improvement in performance. "If in doubt leave it out!" There are many similarities between RISC and the original von Neumann architecture (and with the simple computer described in Fig. 6-4).

Following the RISC machines just described, a number of organizations introduced computer architectures that were called "reduced instruction-set" computers. The variety among these designs led to argument as to what specific characteristics made a computer a RISC. (An internal publication of one manufacturer specified that their design was excellent because it contained "a large and rich instruction set"!) While there is still some disagreement, the characteristics of the first three RISCs are accepted as the features that are commonly seen in reduced-instruction-set computers:

1. relatively few instructions,
2. simple decoding with a fixed instruction format,
3. hard-wired, rather than microcoded, instructions,
4. fixed-clock-cycle execution of most instructions,
5. only a few addressing modes,
6. memory transfers only with LOAD/STORE instructions,
7. pipelined data path for concurrency,
8. large register set.

There is much debate on the merits of the RISC approach. Its emphasis on supporting high-level-language programs has similarities of objectives to the stack-based designs, but both run counter to the present "mainstream" of computer design. T. R. Gross and others at Stanford [GrosT88] report on experimental studies of the effects of the RISC features in the MIPS architecture. They separated their evaluation to examine architectural features and implementation characteristics. While their results are generally supportive of RISC, the degree to which such results can be extended to real programs must await further experience.

Some results of performance comparisons of different architectures stimulated by the RISC issue are reviewed in Sections 6.7 and 6.8. The results of the pioneer RISC efforts have led to many commercial RISC computers including those from IBM, Hewlett-Packard, and SUN. At least 20 purported RISC machines were available by mid-1987. As microprocessors for RISC, MIPS Computer Systems, Inc., offered its R2000 and R3000, both based on the Stanford design, Motorola released the 80010, and Sun agreed to sell or license its Sparc microprocessor, which is derived from the Berkeley RISC architectures. With this interest, RISC principles should have much influence on future computer designs.

6.6 ARITHMETIC AND OTHER FUNCTION UNITS

The virtual and the actual machines described before include registers and other processor state and the controls needed to establish the connections that transfer information from one location to another. No transformations on the information were described. That is, no arithmetic, logical, or shift operations were included in the control activities. Performing these operations requires that we introduce the D operators, the function units. It is interesting that our discussion of arithmetic and other functions, the computing part of the computer, comes so late in our description. We recall that the "arithmetic organ" was a major component of the von Neumann computer architecture. As the digital computer has evolved, the "memory organ", the "control organ", and the "input/output organ" (a subject of Chapter 7) have changed significantly, but the "arithmetic organ", the arithmetic and logic unit (ALU), has remained quite similar to that described by the von Neumann group.

A 2-bit section of a simple arithmetic and logic unit that might be incorporated in the computer of Fig. 6-4 is shown in Fig. 6-22(a). The control signals s_0, s_1, s_2, and C_{in}, outputs of the controllers of the previous section, determine the result F_i for input values A_i and B_i in each bit position i. As noted in Fig. 6-22(b), the three inputs s_0, s_1, and s_2 permit the selection of one of the eight basic arithmetic or logic operations or constants. The value of C_{in} determines whether 1 is to be added to the arithmetic operations or not. This ALU provides all arithmetic and logical microoperations required for all of the computer instructions.

The shifter needs four control lines. Lines s_3 and s_4 are used to select a left or right shift, a direct transfer without a shift, and no transfer (used for comparisons that produce no side effects). Another control, s_5, is needed to separate circular from noncircular shifts, and s_6 is used to control shifting the sign bit to distinguish between arithmetic and logical shifts. This shifter allows for shifting one bit position on a clock pulse so that multiple clock times are required for multiple-position shifts. With more powerful arithmetic units a "barrel shifter" that allows shifts of any number of bit positions in one clock time (see Chapter 3) might be incorporated. The shifter and the ALU together provide for all of the microoperations needed. Other computer instructions are implemented as sequences of these microoperations.

Readers who have designed a simple ALU might feel that there are approaches that use fewer components. (With VLSI, minimizing the sum of inputs to gates might be more meaningful than minimizing the gate count.) It is true that a design that builds an adder from a full adder circuit might require fewer gates, but the simplification comes at the expense of time since it will be necessary for the sum and carry signals to go through more gates. This examination of trade-offs between time and components is conducted by the circuit and logic designers, but we should be familiar with their methods.

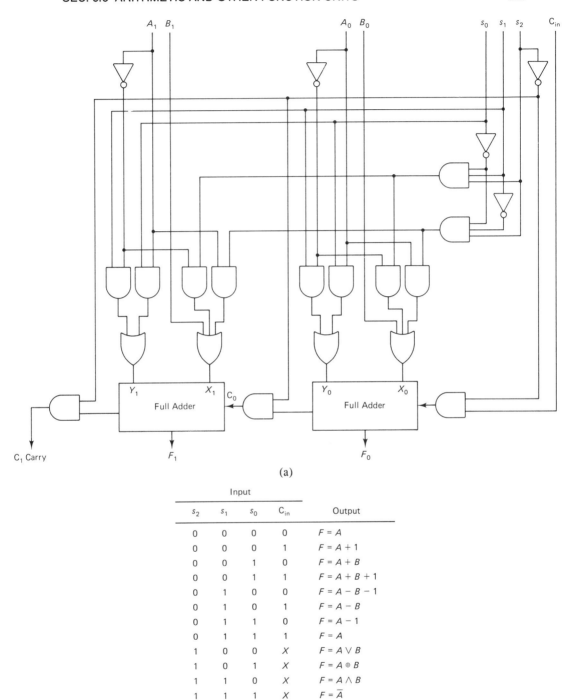

(a)

Input				Output
s_2	s_1	s_0	C_{in}	
0	0	0	0	$F = A$
0	0	0	1	$F = A + 1$
0	0	1	0	$F = A + B$
0	0	1	1	$F = A + B + 1$
0	1	0	0	$F = A - B - 1$
0	1	0	1	$F = A - B$
0	1	1	0	$F = A - 1$
0	1	1	1	$F = A$
1	0	0	X	$F = A \vee B$
1	0	1	X	$F = A \oplus B$
1	1	0	X	$F = A \wedge B$
1	1	1	X	$F = \overline{A}$

(b)

Figure 6-22 A simple arithmetic and logic unit (ALU) (a) and truth table (b).

Since this is a relatively simple arithmetic section, we might consider its performance and how it might be given more power. We get an idea of relative performance by counting the number of gates that signals must flow through for each operation. The sum (F_i) and carry (C_i) arithmetic operations of Fig. 6-22 each go through five gates at every bit position. However, before the output of the most significant bit has been produced, the carries must "propagate" from least to most significant position. For a 16-bit adder this is a path of $16 \times 3 + 2 = 50$ gates.

We can add logic to generate the carry output for each bit based on the initial carry input C_{in} and the values of A_i and B_i for all bits. With this "carry lookahead" technique the total number of gates traversed for the carry is about 5. The expense is a large number of components. The carry lookahead for a 16-bit ALU would cause an increase of almost 50% in the number of components required. Again, this evaluation is not in the role of the computer architect, but we must be aware of the possible impact when we ask for higher performance.

If floating-point arithmetic operations are to be included in the computer hardware, separate arithmetic is required for the exponent and the mantissa (magnitude) fields of the floating-point numbers. The exponent arithmetic is less extensive than that for the mantissa and an ALU like that of Fig. 6-22 and a simple shift unit can be used for exponent arithmetic. The mantissa ALU usually includes higher-speed multiplication and division and a variable-step shift unit. The fast shifter is useful for normalizing and aligning the mantissas in floating-point operations.

Whereas the add, compare, and shift operations are sufficient for constructing a multiplier-divider, the number of microoperation steps required for these long arithmetic operations is on the average one-half the number of bits in the magnitude field. In most computers used in numeric applications such calculations are too slow and "parallel" multipliers are employed. These multipliers examine groups of bits of the multiplier and add or subtract a value for each group, thus cutting down the number of steps in calculating the partial product to speed the multiply. The approach is demonstrated in Fig. 6-23 using 2×4 multiplier circuits to handle pairs of bits of the multiplier. In this example each multiplier circuit accepts 5 bits of multiplicand (one for overlap), 4 bits of partial product, 3 bits of the multiplier, and the carry from the previous multiplier in the same row to form a new partial product to be passed to the row below and an output carry to be passed to the multiplier on the left. The individual multipliers internally use carry lookahead techniques to obtain output values in a single clock period. The rows are offset by two 2 multiplier bit positions and ($n/2 \times n/4$) individual multipliers (in the example, 32) are needed for an $n \times n$-bit multiply.

Very-high-speed multiplication (in several clock pulses) can be achieved at the cost of a larger amount of hardware logic. High-performance-arithmetic processors use such multipliers to attain floating-point multiply times only slightly longer than those for addition and subtraction. This is achieved by using a large number of adders (perhaps one for each bit of the mantissa) to generate simultaneously the partial products for 1/4, 1/2, or all multiplier bits and one or more barrel shifters to generate carries from adder to adder. For vector processors (discussed in Chapter 8) that are used in scientific applications involving a large amount of matrix arithmetic, high-speed multiplication is essential to maintain flow of data through the arithmetic "pipelines".

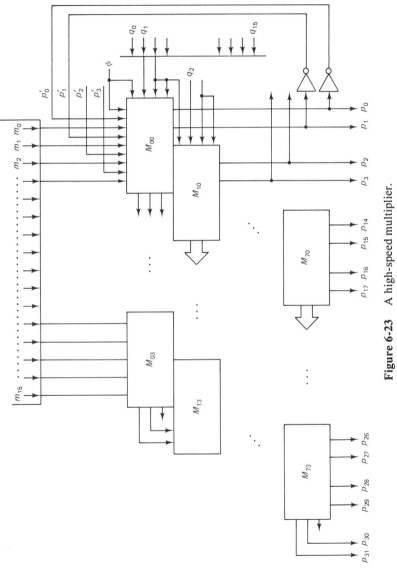

Figure 6-23 A high-speed multiplier.

Many high-performance computers employ several function units to permit concurrency and/or overlap in successive arithmetic instructions. The example of Fig. 6-24 demonstrates the nine different function units of the Control Data 7600, an approach that was introduced with the 6600 and has continued with the larger computers of the Cyber 170 series. In the 7600 an instruction can be initiated while another is being completed. (We saw the instruction queue for the Cyber computers in Fig. 5-13.) The multiple function units also permit two or more parts of a single instruction to be sent to different function units and allow a function unit to be freed for use by the next instruction while the current instruction's operations are being completed. As an example, while a floating-point addition is active in that function unit the normalization of the successive floating-point add can be initiated. The assignment of function units to instructions is controlled by a "scoreboard" that keeps the results in proper sequence as they are transferred to registers.

Another example of multiple arithmetic and logic units was seen in the IBM 370-165 of Fig. 6-2. In that case the function units are more general than are those of the CDC 7600. At the other extreme we find in the Burroughs B1700 low-level function units that continually yield, in a separate register for each, the result of nine different functions of two input arguments. This is equivalent to the simultaneous generation of all of the arithmetic unit operations of Fig. 6-22.

Multiple arithmetic and logic units can be organized as a "pipeline". Each unit can be specialized to perform only a limited number of functions ("D" operations in PMS notation), and data can be "streamed" through the pipeline with the required transformations applied by function units as called for by the instruction stream. An individual function unit can be organized as a pipeline of more elementary D operation units. As an

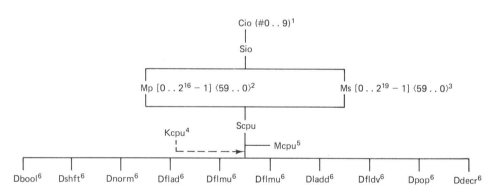

1. Cio\"Peripheral_and_Control_Processor" (processor, 4096-word_memory).
2. Mp (magnetic_core, cycle_time: 1 microsecond).
3. Ms\"Extended_Core_Storage" (magnetic_core, cycle_time: 3 microsecond).
4. Kcpu\"Scoreboard" {operation sequencing among Mcpu and D units}.
5. Mcpu (8 address_registers, 8 operand_registers, 8 index_registers).
6. {"Function_Units": boolean, shift, normalize, floating-point add,
   floating-point multiply, long add, floating-point divide, population
   count, decrement}.

Figure 6-24   Contol Data Cyber function units.

example, the pipelined floating-point adder of Fig. 6-25(a) has seven separate function units. A floating-point addition of two words, each with an exponent field (E) and a mantissa field (M) is performed stage by stage by comparing (subtracting) exponents to select one mantissa (from the word with the smaller exponent) for modification. The appropriate adjustment is made to the mantissa by shifting it left the correct number of bits. The mantissas are added and the result is normalized by counting leading zeros and shifting the exponent while the exponent is adjusted by subtracting the quantity of leading zeros found. While the arguments flow through the pipeline it is necessary to hold partial results in temporary registers, shown as shaded boxes in the figure.

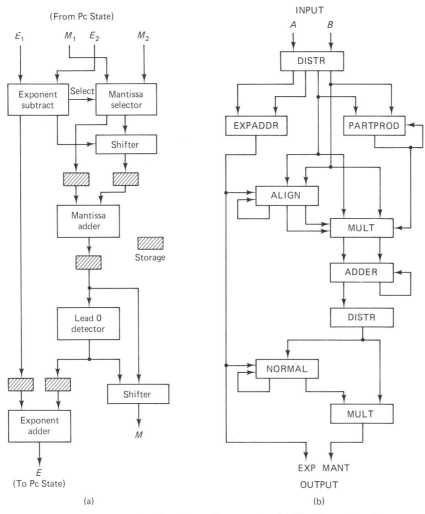

Figure 6-25 Pipeline function-unit examples. (a) Floating-point adder. (b) Dynamic multifunction pipeline.

Pipelined arithmetic and logic units also can be organized to perform multiple operations. In this case they can be static, connected to perform a single function at a time, or they can be dynamic, permitting different functions to be active in different stages of the pipeline. In the dynamic multifunction pipeline of Fig. 6-25(b), data flows through the pipeline and is directed to the stages required for each particular operation. At any time there can be an operation in execution at each stage of the pipeline. Data for any single instruction can take several clock times to pass through the pipeline, but data for an instruction can start in the pipe while that for the previous instruction is being processed in a later stage.

In the illustration input values (*A* and *B*) enter the pipeline from processor registers. A distributor sends exponent and mantissa fields or whole words to the exponent address (EXP_ADDR), partial product (PART_PROD), mantissa alignment (ALIGN) function units, or directly to a multiplexer (MULT). The multiplexer selects inputs for an add/subtract function unit (ADDER) that also serves as an accumulator for two-stage multiplication. A second distributor-multiplexer pair sends the result to a processor register directly or through the normalizer (NORMAL). The exponent-address function unit controls operation of the mantissa-alignment unit and the normalizer and also transmits the final exponent (if the data are floating-point) as part of the result. Several of the stages might require multiple clock pulses, as is shown by the feedback paths on the PART_PROD, ALIGN, ADDER, and NORMAL function units. Since it is desired that several operations be active simultaneously, registers must be provided in the function units for holding intermediate data.

Activity in the stages of a pipelined arithmetic and logic unit at successive clock times can be shown in "reservation tables", illustrated in Fig. 6-26. In Fig. 6-26(a) individual operations that can be performed in the multifunction pipeline of Fig. 6-25(b) are demonstrated. Fixed-point addition (or subtraction) can be performed in one clock time (as can boolean and relational operations, which are not shown). Fixed-point multiplication takes 3 clock times, 2 in PART_PROD overlapped with 2 in the ADDER. Floating-point multiplication starts in EXP_ADDR and PART_PROD, continues in PART_PROD and ADDER, ADDER, and NORMAL, taking 4 clock times. (Normalizing after multiplication requires only a single clock time.) Floating-point addition (subtraction) takes the most time to pass through the ALU, using 6 clock times with no overlapping operations. (With some added control complexity, the ALIGN and NORMAL units could be designed to take either 1 or 2 pulses, depending on how many shift operations are required to perform the function. At the cost of more components these units could accomplish any needed shift operation in a single clock time. As described earlier, the multiplier could be designed for single clock operation making multiple additions for accumulation unnecessary.)

Since the individual stages are active at different clock times with different operations, we might not be able to initiate an instruction on the clock pulse immediately following the start of the previous instruction. This is demonstrated by the superposition of reservation tables, delayed by one or more clock times, as shown in Fig. 6-26(b). Fixed-point multiplication (X's) can follow fixed-point addition (W) at the next clock time, since there are no conflicts at any times in any stages. (The reverse

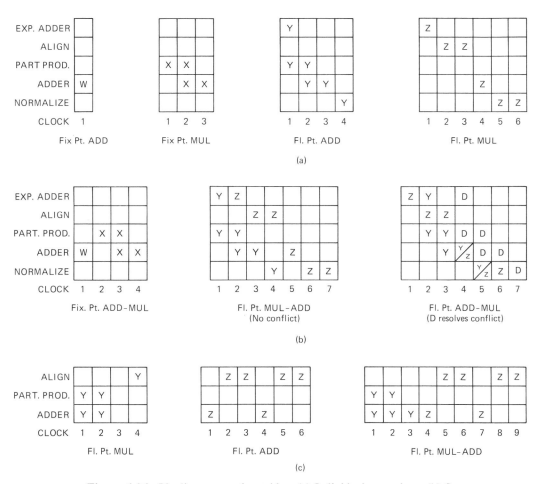

Figure 6-26 Pipeline reservation tables. (a) Individual operations. (b) Sequential operations. (c) Shared stages.

sequence does have conflict in the ADDER.) Floating-point multiplication (Y's) can be followed by floating-point addition (Z's) at the next clock time. However, when we attempt to start floating-point multiplication at the clock time immediately after floating-point addition we have conflict (called a pipeline "collision") in the ADDER at time 4 and in NORMAL at time 5, as indicated by the appearance of both Y and Z in those blocks. If the multiplication is delayed by 2 clock times (shown by D's) there is no conflict.

When examining individual reservation tables it appears that we can use ADDER for exponent as well as mantissa addition and can use the same unit (ALIGN) for mantissa alignment and for normalizing. We find no conflict within the individual floating-point multiplication and floating-point addition reservation tables for shared stages, Fig. 6-26(c). When the stages are shared it is necessary to delay floating-point addition until the fourth clock time after the start of floating-point multiplication, making the shared pipeline significantly slower than the ALU shown in Fig. 6-25(b). The reservation tables are useful for designing as well as in controlling pipeline operations.

There are many variations possible in organizing pipelined arithmetic units. Multiple-function pipeline units require more complicated control than do single-function units. Dynamic multiple-function units require more control than static multifunction arithmetic pipelines. The advantages of pipeline processing can be seen in the illustrations of sequences of instructions in Fig. 6-26(b). Whereas floating-point addition and floating-point multiplication individually take 4 and 6 clock times, respectively, the sequence of the two in either order takes only 7 clock times. Overlapped pipeline operations require that the instruction microsequences allow for the delays that are necessary when any instruction immediately follows any other. The information used for control of pairs of successive instructions is known as a *collision vector*. For each pairing (FLADD-FLMUL, FLMUL-FLADD, FLMUL-FLMUL, FXMUL-FXMUL, etc.) the collision-vector entry specifies the delay required before initiation of the second instruction.

Pipelined function units are only one approach to achieving parallel arithmetic operations in a processor. Another approach is to use an array of similar arithmetic and logic units, as was done in the ILLIAC IV, specified by the University of Illinois and implemented by Burroughs in the late 1960s. The structure of an ILLIAC IV array with its 64 processing elements (PEs), each with local data memory, is shown in Fig. 6-27(a). Four arrays could be configured independently or combined, as we see in Fig. 6-27(b). The single control unit of an array, shown in Fig. 6-27(c), caused execution of the same instruction in all PEs that were not masked out of the operation. Instructions were decoded in the advanced instruction station (ADVAST) and either executed in the control unit or passed to the PEs for execution. With those instructions that were passed to the PEs address or data operands were assembled in ADVAST and passed to the final queue (FINQ) to await transmission to the PEs. Control unit and PE instructions could be overlapped. The ILLIAC IV served as an experimental vehicle in parallel-processing studies for many years. Many of its features were incorporated in later parallel computer systems, the specific subject of Chapter 8.

6.7 PROCESSOR PERFORMANCE ISSUES

We should not leave the topics of processor organization (Chapter 5) and processor implementation (Chapter 6) without examining how they affect computer performance and computer cost. When we are faced with *claims* of better performance/cost by the proponents of each architecture, it is difficult to identify the *facts* of performance. The difficulties of measuring performance in solving real problems was discussed in Chapter 2. Most of the claims of performance today, particularly for solving scientific problems, are based on a measure of millions of instructions per second (MIPS) or of millions of floating-point operations per second (MegaFLOPS). Both of these measures identify the rate of execution of machine language instructions and have little relationship to how effective computers are for solving user problems.

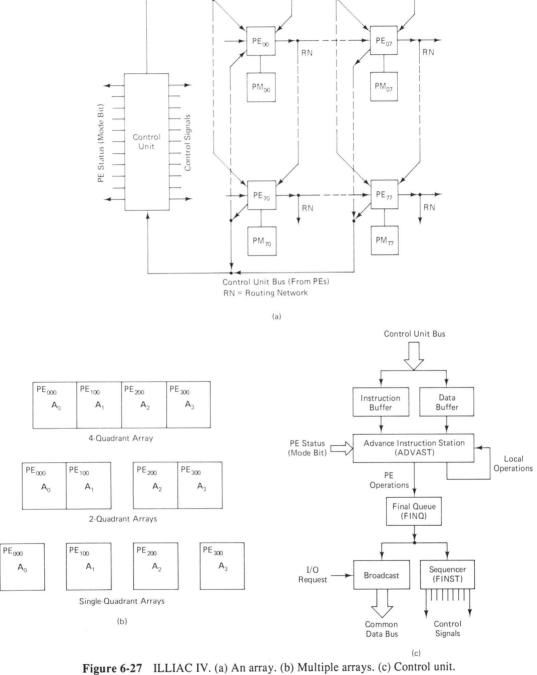

Figure 6-27 ILLIAC IV. (a) An array. (b) Multiple arrays. (c) Control unit.

Sets of simple representative problems (benchmarks) are a little more useful, since users and architects can compare the benchmark problems with their own objectives. A larger benchmark that has gained some popularity is the compiler written in a higher-level language then compiled and executed on the computer being evaluated. Compilers are used because they have a good mix of the characteristics of a variety of programs, because they are written in higher-level languages, and because they are more completely available to different evaluators than are most programs. Still these larger programs evaluate the total software and hardware system. It is difficult to isolate the effects of specific architectural features or even specific parts of the computer system.

In examining alternative instruction-set processors, it is useful to develop some principles of performance and cost. We can then attempt to interpret how different architectures match up against these principles. As we develop the principles it is useful to separate architectural (ISP) and implementation (control) issues.

Let us start by establishing the computer-related activities that can be influenced by different architectures. We assume that almost all programming will be carried out using higher-level programming languages. The activities that can be influenced by computer architectures are the human programming effort, automatic translation (by a compiler or an interpreter) of programs to machine code, preparation of data for the program, execution of the machine language program, and presentation of the results. How well a system accepts data and presents results is largely determined by system structure (concurrency of input/output and processing activity) and in the organization of the input/output processors or controllers. The central-processor organization can have influence in its interaction with the Pio or Kio and with the memory system. The facilities for I/O interrupt handling and for changing process environments are significant Pc characteristics for us to evaluate.

With regard to the question of higher-level-language programming, it is difficult to associate directly specifics of computer architecture and characteristics of problems people want to solve. The connection is through the programming languages to be used by people and to be supported by machines. The architectural aspect of the question is focused on how well the architecture supports the languages by providing features that lead to effective translators.

To separate the question of time it takes to run "typical" programs into activities that can be influenced by the processor architecture and those that cannot, let us consider the example of solving mathematics-related problems. If we use algebra as an example, we can view the solution at the problem level as a set of algebraic functions applied to arguments. We also must enter the arguments and write the results as part of the "useful work" in the problem solution. To a computer user all processing not related to these activities can be viewed as *overhead*. Included in this overhead are assignments of values to variables other than those used to report the final result, calls on and parameter passing to procedures, control constructs such as iteration statements and branches, declarations of data types and subprograms, and control of files. Much of the overhead is due to the characteristics of the programming language used to represent the problem, an issue for language designers rather than for computer architects.

Putting aside the high degree of processing overhead just due to the "semantic gap" between problem and programming languages, let us consider the activities that are required when programs are to be executed on computers. Then we can attempt to identify how well different architectures support each of these aspects of problem solving with computers. Our starting point is a program that has been written in some higher-level language to solve a specific problem.

The program must be translated to machine language, using features provided in the hardware and adjusting to limitations of the machine. We are concerned with how effective an architecture is in support of the translation process. How long does it take to perform the translation and what is the execution time for the machine language program that is the result of translation? Since the person who writes the compiler is a user of the computer, we must be concerned with the support the architecture has given that user. Have we provided the compiler writer architectural features that are understandable, consistent, easy to remember, and simple to employ? If we make the compiler writer's job too complicated we make the job more difficult and the result less reliable.

As was pointed out in the discussion of programming languages in Chapter 5, there are conflicting opinions on how the computer architecture should support compilers and compiler writers. One side holds that a rich set of architectural features offers more facility to generate efficient machine code, a greater ability to "optimize" the machine code to the machine. On the other side are those who say that the same features that might be used to generate efficient code complicate the machine so much that efficient code *cannot* be a result. This school argues that most advanced features are not used by the compiler writer or by the compiler. Although the conflict will continue, there is a distinct trend away from complicated-instruction-set processors. We see the results of some evaluations that support this trend in the next section.

It is easier to focus on effectiveness of alternative architectures in program execution. We are concerned with how well different processor organizations use time (execution speed) and space (memory size) in running programs. In both cases we should direct our attention to the programs as they are written in the higher-level language and attempt to make our measurements in those terms.

Starting with processor influence on space, we can determine how well a design handles the representation of all of the data structures that can be used in higher-level languages. How efficiently does an ISP permit storage of the different scalars (bits, digits, bytes, integers, and real values) to the precision needed? Can the design handle all of the compound data structures (arrays, records, files, lists, trees) called for in higher-level languages? What is the relative speed of access to each of the scalars and compound structures?

A specific issue here is the trade-off between the size of single-precision numeric values and the need for using multiple-precision values. If for numeric processing no multiple precision is used, then probably many single-precision values are being represented to a higher precision than is necessary for the problem. On the other hand, if we find it necessary to represent a significant percentage of numeric values in multiple-precision form, then the size of the data word probably is too small. The execution time penalty paid with multiple precision of numeric values must be compared with the space penalty if single-precision words are larger than really needed. For example, we might ask whether the problems our computer is designed to solve are handled more effectively with a 24-, 32-, 48-, or 64-bit numeric data word.

Another performance issue regarding data structures is the time it takes with different architectures to manipulate structures or substructures. The speed of machine instructions for moving items from memory to registers is significant, but probably is not as important as the total number of instructions required to find and move a compound data item. In many programs it is necessary to gain access to individual items in a compound data structure. Again, the sum of times of all of the instructions required is the significant metric, not the time it takes for any single instruction.

The same approach can be taken to evaluate how well a processor handles the expressions and the commands in a program. We can determine how many machine instructions there are to each higher-level operation and how much time each of the instructions takes. It particularly is interesting to measure the quantity of memory fetches and stores required to execute sequences of higher-level-language statements. Some of the memory references such as getting input parameters and passing results are reflections of specific actions in the program. Most memory activity, however, can be considered as overhead. It is caused by the lack of sufficient high-speed registers to hold in the processor every data item declared in the program and every temporary value calculated in all expression evaluations.

This leads us to the concept (taken from thermodynamics) of the "ideal computing engine". This is a hypothetical computer that, with a given quantity of components, would execute the higher-level-language program in minimum time. Its machine language would be reflected by execution of no overhead instructions. It would directly represent the program in the higher-level language. (This is not a proposal to build any of the "direct execution language" machines that have been proposed.) To specify such an ideal machine relative to any given electronic technology would require that we identify a "minimum reasonable" operation time for each operator in the higher-level language. (That task would carry us beyond the simple concept being developed here.) The ideal engine would execute a test program in time T_{ideal}.

Any example instruction-set processor architecture would represent an "actual computing engine". With the same electronic technology as the ideal engine it would execute the higher-level-language test program in time T_{actual}. The "execution efficiency" of the actual computer would be T_{ideal}/T_{actual}. We also might use the ratio of costs, comparing the component count for a processor that stored all variables and temporary values in high speed registers with that for an actual processor. While this concept of an ideal computer is sketchy, it is reasonable to think of characteristics of actual instruction-set processors that keep them from executing higher-level-language programs at "100% efficiency". A manageable approach to the problem entails taking several different simplified views of the issues.

One viewpoint is that we should minimize the number of machine-language instructions needed to execute a higher-level-language operation. There are four possible steps in this direction:

a. Eliminate all memory fetches and stores other than those related to program parameters.

b. Eliminate all data-manipulation instructions such as register-to-register moves.

c. Eliminate all "data-formatting" instructions, such as insertion and extraction of fields in words.

d. Combine the usual machine-level instructions to form higher-level instructions that match the higher-level-language operations.

Under the first approach the processor automatically would bring needed data to Pc registers and all instructions would involve register-to-register, or equivalent, addressing. This requires that we either introduce a large number of general registers or that we make register addressing implicit (the stack-based machine). The Berkeley RISC machine uses a large "register bank" organized as overlapping windows in an attempt to have instructions always operate on data that is in high-speed processor registers, as described in Chapter 5. Appraisals of performance of RISC approaches are included in the next section.

Stack-based machines have been introduced in attempts to meet the objective, but face some practical limitations. It is not feasible to place all of the stack in processor registers. (If it were, we might be close to our ideal machine.) In practice, a small number of high-speed registers form the high end of the stack. All operators use the stack for arguments and results, but behind the scenes information is being moved between these "high-stack" registers and the rest of the stack in primary memory. If the time for register–memory movement is overlapped with instruction fetches and execution, then the objective of masking memory data references is met. Even with a large number of high-stack registers and with multiple-word communication with memory it is not possible to achieve total time overlap.

We saw when reviewing the B6700 stack (Fig. 5-12) that in executing programs written in most programming languages it is necessary to make reference to values that are deep in the stack (referenced through the display registers). All such references require memory fetch time even though the fetch is implicit in the indirect reference. Compound data structures are stored in memory areas separate from the stack and are indirectly referenced from the stack, again leading to implicit fetching and storing to or from memory. (Issues of memory references for context switching using the "cactus stack" are separate from this discussion, which is centered on performance in execution of a single program.)

Current approaches to reducing the number of explicit register-to-register moves (approach b) have depended on the code-optimizing phase of compiling to plan register use. This can be reasonably successful if a sufficient quantity of general registers is available to the user program. Usually several of the limited number of registers are being used by the operating system and it is not possible to retain "register data locality" for more than a short sequence of instructions. The Stanford RISC (MIPS) and the IBM 801 have been more successful in use of registers by providing a larger quantity of registers than usual and by exploiting advanced compiler optimizing techniques for their assignment. Specific comparisons with conventional computers are described later.

With the restrictions of fixed register- and memory-word size imposed by hardware, it is difficult to find many ways to accomplish elimination of data packing (approach c). Of course, we can use full memory words to hold smaller units of information, but this can be a poor trade of space for time.

Approach d, higher-level operators, has been used in many computer designs. This is one of the "higher-level" features that architects have introduced to support compilers and compiler writers. The strategy here is that a few complex operations are better than many simple ones. This is the counter to the RISC argument. It is claimed that the major flaw in this strategy is that the introduction of complex instructions usually has the side effect of slowing down basic instructions. If, even with the higher-level operators, a high percentage of instructions actually executed is comprised of the simple ones, the addition of complex instructions might be detrimental to overall performance. If a very high percentage of instructions executed is comprised of short instructions, cutting the time or the quantity of long instructions has little payoff if short instruction times increase appreciably. Implementing complex operations also requires significant control logic. Whether that or an increased quantity of general registers is a better hardware investment remains an open question. Some specific data on this will be shown.

A review of processor activities during the fetch–execute cycle highlights some performance issues relative to implementations of instruction-set processors. A typical cycle is composed of

   i. instruction fetch,
  ii. effective address calculations,
 iii. argument fetch (if in memory),
 iv. repeat ii and iii for other arguments,
  v. execute instruction,
 vi. store result (if not to register),
vii. respond to interrupt (if signaled).

To increase performance many of the separate steps can be overlapped with others. Several approaches to accomplishing this were covered earlier in this chapter. In every case hardware must be added to achieve the concurrency. The computer architect and the computer engineer should examine carefully whether the added investment in hardware achieves sufficient improvement in performance. It also is important to evaluate whether that is the best way to use the added hardware. Are there better uses for the components or the semiconductor surface area?

6.8 EXAMPLES OF PERFORMANCE EVALUATION

An understanding of the distribution of instruction types and of addressing modes in compiled machine language programs is important as background for evaluating instruction-set processors. C. A. Wiecek reported measurements of instructions executed and addressing modes used in running several significant benchmarks on the VAX [WiecC82]. The benchmark programs were six compilers of simple programs, each consisting of over one million executed instructions. Several different compilers with different implementation languages were used to evaluate effects of specific languages. The differences were not significant.

Twenty instructions represented 65% of the instructions executed. The distribution of the instructions executed by general category is shown in Fig. 6-28. The paper reports that 74.2% of the standard VAX instructions were executed at least once. The sizes of the instructions and of the operand specifiers in instructions are shown in Fig. 6-29. If we can assume that the arithmetic operations and the conversions are the only instructions that directly represent operations in the higher-level-language programs, then the computer executes over 12 times as many instructions as there are operations in the program.

The average instruction length was 3.8 bytes, and on the average there were 1.8 operand specifiers per instruction. (See Fig. 5-24 for a description of the VAX instruction formats.) Interesting information is provided on register use and on the length of instruction sequences between branches. About 60% of all register reads and writes used 6 of the 14 general registers monitored. (The stack pointer and the program counter were excluded due to their special functions.) After a register was written into it was read by one of the next five instructions 75% of the time and was written into again after being read at most three times 93% of the time. On the average, sequences of 3.9 instructions were executed (including the branch) before a branch was taken.

Integer Arithmetic and Logical:		54.1%
(Approximate distribution:		
Moves:	31.9	
Compares:	14.1	
Arithmetic:	4.3	
Conversions:	3.8)	
Control:		30.9%
Addressing:		6.9%
Procedure Call:		4.9%
Variable Length Bit Field:		2.1%
All Other:		1.1%

Figure 6-28   Classification and frequency of instructions executed. (From [WiecC82].)

Bytes	Frequency	Specifiers	Frequency
1	3.3%	0	3.3%
2	25.0%	1	33.1%
3	23.5%	2	52.4%
4	18.6%	3	7.2%
5	12.2%	4	3.6%
6	7.7%	5	0.2%
7	8.3%	6	0.2%
8	2.5%		
9–16	1.7%		
17–32	0.2%		
(a)		(b)	

Figure 6-29   Distributions of instructions and operands. (From [WeicC82].)
(a) Instruction size. (b) Operands specified.

The experiment with the VAX instruction set serves as a background to evaluations of alternative architecture approaches. D. A. Patterson and C. H. Sequin, in developing requirements for the Berkeley RISC I architecture [PattD82], examined the distribution of higher-level statements in eight compiled programs written in Pascal and C. Then they multiplied each statement type by the average number of machine language instructions and memory references used to execute the statement. The number of instructions per higher-level statement was derived from C compilers for PDP-11, VAX, and MC68000 computers. The results are summarized in Fig. 6-30. The two illustrations of distribution of instructions cannot be compared directly, even though both are based on similar programs executed in similar ways. The data in Fig. 6-28 are presented from a viewpoint of machine instructions, whereas that in Fig. 6-30 comes from a higher-level-language orientation.

Patterson and Sequin used the information on instruction distributions to determine the relative importance of higher-level language constructs in compiled programs. The results were used in the RISC architecture. Since the RISC processor was to be made from a single VLSI chip, only a limited number of components (about 50k) could be allowed. The study of instructions led them to use the large bank of "windowed" registers (Fig. 6-19) and to eliminate the microprogram control store that is used in most microprocessors.

The results presented by Patterson and Sequin were striking. In 11 small benchmark programs RISC I exhibited average program sizes 1.1 times those of a Motorola MC68000 and 1.25 times those experienced on a VAX. Reduced instruction sets do lead to larger programs, but not much larger. On the other hand, the RISC I with a 7.5-MHz clock frequency executed the programs faster than a 10-MHz MC68000 and a 5-MHz VAX-11/780. The ratio of average execution times was 3.5 compared with the MC68000 and 2.1 relative to the VAX. The authors attribute the RISC performance to the fast simple instruction set that yields efficient compiled code and the register-window organization that substantially simplifies environment activation and parameter passing on procedure calls.

Statements	Occurence (High-Level Language)		Machine Instructions (Weighted)		Memory References (Weighted)	
H.L.L.[1]	P	C	P	C	P	C
CALL/RET[2]	15±1	12±5	31±3	33±4	44±4	45±19
LOOPS[3]	5±0	3±1	42±3	32±6	33±2	26±5
ASSIGN	45±5	38±15	13±2	13±5	14±2	15±6
IF[4]	29±8	43±7	11±3	21±8	7±2	13±5
WITH	5±5	—	1±0	—	1±0	—
CASE[4]	1±1	<1±1	1±1	1±1	1±1	1±1
GOTO	—	3±1	—	0±0	—	0±0

Notes: 1. P = PASCAL, C = C.
2. Includes parameter passing and register save/restore.
3. All machine instructions on each iteration.
4. Evaluation and jump.

Figure 6-30 Frequency of machine execution of HLL Statements. (From [PattD82].)

The IBM 801 RISC architecture described by G. Radin [RadiG82] exhibits similar performance benefits when compared with the System/370 architecture. In executing randomly selected modules of a PL.8 compiler, the 801 was superior to the 370 in code size (ratio of 0.9), number of instructions executed (0.8 those of the 370), and number of memory references (the 370 used twice as many). Radin tentatively concludes that "a general-purpose, register-oriented instruction set can be at least as good as any special vertical microcode set" and that "all the registers which the CPU can afford to build in hardware should be directly and simultaneously addressable". Stack machines and those that use registers for special purposes "all seem to make poorer use of the available registers".

M. E. Hopkins [HopkM84] described the features of the IBM 801 that contribute to its good performance. A major feature is that an optimizing compiler can plan register use to minimize memory references. Values in registers can be "reused" in subsequent instructions a larger percent of the time than they can in the more complex System/370. Hopkins called the 801 a RISC: "Reusable Information Storage Computer".

Another interesting comparison of architectures was presented by N. Wirth [WirtN86]. He compares three microprocessor architectures for "code density" (number of bits of code) and "simplicity of compilation" (size and speed of compilers). Wirth assumed that the same language (Modula 2) and equivalent compilers (scanner, parser, symbol table, symbol file generator, degree of code optimization) would be used on all microprocessors. The only difference was the code generator in order to focus on instruction-set-processor issues.

The architectures compared were the Lilith (a microprocessor developed at ETH Zurich), the Motorola MC68000, and the National Semiconductor NS32000. The first is a relatively simple stack-based architecture ("neither—extremely Spartan nor—lavishly baroque"). The others were selected because of their popularity for high performance work stations and for multiple processor systems. Lilith contains an expression stack ("a logical extension of the stack of procedure activation records") instead of "a set of explicitly numbered data registers" of the other two machines. This pure stack machine does not use addresses in instructions except for the explicit LOAD TO STACK and STORE FROM STACK operations.

The computers are outlined and their performance is compared in Fig. 6-31. Significant differences in the machine organizations in addition to the stack are noted in the addressing modes, and the use of a specific condition-code register (Lilith treats conditions as ordinary boolean operations on the stack). The results of compilation and execution also are shown. The Lilith permits a compiler to be written in fewer source code lines and generates a much smaller object code. The NS32000 and the MC68000 code generators are much smaller when generated in Lilith code than they are on themselves. The instruction ratios, Fig. 6-31(b), demonstrate that the number of machine instructions for almost all higher-level-language statements is larger on the Lilith. The average instruction length is smaller on the stack machine, permitting the larger number of compiler object-code instructions to take fewer bytes of code.

Microprocessor Characteristics:	Lilith	NS320000	MC68000
Instruction Length (bytes)	1, 2, 3, 5	1:11	2:10
Address Length (bits)	4, 8, 16, 32	8, 16, 32	16, 32
Mp Addresses/Instruction	0, 1	1, 2	1, 2
Addressing Modes	6	10	8
Max. Indirect Address Depth	2	3	1
Condition Codes?	No	Yes	Yes
Pc State- Data (words)	16 (stack)	8	8
Pc State-Address (words)	4 (stack mgt.)	4	9
Stack Use-Activation Records?	Yes	Yes	Yes
Stack Use-Expression Eval.?	Yes	No	No
Results:			
Compiler Source Lines	4,000	4,560	6,290
Compiler Object Code (bytes)	26,050	46,670	86,400
Object Code-Lilith Code Generator	10,190		
Object Code-NS Code Generator	15,340	22,960	
Object Code-MC Code Generator	21,650	48,630	
Average Instruction Length	1.5	3.6	5.8
Compiler Object Code (kbytes)	16.7	12.7	14.5

(a)

Microprocessors Compared	Lilith/NS32000	Lilith/MC68000
Instructions-Assignment	1.9	1.2
Instructions-Procedure Call	1.0	1.0
Instructions-Arithmetic Expr.	1.5	1.4
Instructions-Indexed Variables	2.4	1.6
Instructions-Compiler Object Code	1.3	1.2

(b)

Figure 6-31 Comparison of 32-bit microprocessors. (From [WirtN86].)
(a) Machine characteristics and results (b) Selected instruction ratios.

Wirth does not compare execution times, but it is reasonable to conclude that the Lilith can execute at least as many instructions per second as do the more complicated machines. He claims that the standard microprocessors, while being burdened by the need to satisfy many requirements, also are "products of an unbounded belief in the possibilities of VLSI". He also cautions designers against going from one extreme (complexity) to the other (RISC, with complicated code-generation strategies). Wirth argues for regularity of design (note the similarity to the argument of Wulf in Chapter 5) and claims that RISC should stand for "Regular Instruction Set Computer".

In this section we have not determined what is the best instruction-set processor. We have not even attempted to do so because the issues are very complex. There are so many different requirements for processors that it is doubtful that there is any one superior approach. It is more important that we develop a methodology and the tools to evaluate alternatives to permit us to make intelligent decisions on our designs. A few specific evaluations of performance give us some guidance in our selection from alternative approaches.

6.9 SUMMARY

In this chapter, a companion to Chapter 5, we have focused on the implementation of instruction-set processors. Advances in electronic technology and in software methodologies have caused large changes in the way instruction-set processors are created from a collection of electronic components. We have seen that there are alternative ways to implement a given instruction-set processor, just as there are alternative instruction-set processors.

The concept of a "virtual machine", a combination of a lower-level machine and its controlling software, can be brought to the level of an instruction-set processor. At this level the lower-level machine is the hardware itself, the processor state that we were introduced to early in the book. When we add the control hardware and software we create a virtual machine that is the processor described at the ISP level. Different combinations of basic hardware and controls can give different cost and performance versions of the same virtual machine. We can develop a family of processors all described by the same ISP.

We have examined what is needed to control a processor, to make an assemblage of electronic components a computer. There is much more state than we see at the ISP level. Many registers and individual flip-flops are needed for control purposes. In the four examples of popular computers we have seen four different approaches to implementation of four different instruction-set processors. Each has unique features and unique capabilities.

To direct our attention to the details of processor control we used the example of a specific simple computer. The processor state consists of four general registers and the registers needed for instruction interpretation. We included registers for communication with memory and "memory-mapped" input/output. A few flip-flops were added to hold condition codes and status flags. The processor has three internal buses and is similar to many contemporary microprocessors.

Our example processor was used to demonstrate hard-wired and microprogrammed control, the former offering higher speed and the latter lower cost and greater flexibility. Hard-wired control can be implemented with programmed logic arrays (PLA) for increased flexibility at slightly lower speed. In each case the controller generates the same set of control signals.

Microprogrammed control words can produce individual control signals directly (horizontal microprogramming) or the control-word information can be coded and the signals produced by a decoder (vertical microprogramming). It is possible to use two (or more) levels of control, often called "micro-" and the "nano-" levels. Within this one control technique there are alternatives. All microprogramming alternatives give the computer architect flexibility to specify sophisticated instruction sets.

In addition to the explicit control information found in instructions and that which is the result of instruction execution (condition codes and status flags), control fields can be a part of data words. This "tagged-memory" approach permits extensive validity checking to be performed during execution. It also can permit the instruction set itself to be simpler since the instructions do not have to contain the type of information that is placed in the tag fields.

During the 1980s there was movement toward simplifying computer organizations. Reduced-instruction-set computer (RISC) architectures appeared in several forms. The objective of this approach is to achieve maximum performance in execution of higher-level-language programs with minimum hardware. Whether RISC will achieve a major share of computer architectures remains to be seen, but many of the techniques employed in RISC are used in conventional computer designs.

A significant part of the computer control structure might be used for error detection, fault diagnosis, and maintenance. Some error detection can be in circuits as a part of the processor logic. For very high reliability, registers or arithmetic units can be triplicated and logic can be introduced to perform error detection and correction. The diagnostic logic can be quite extensive; a special console or processor is included in larger computer systems.

After reviewing controls we developed the requirements for the arithmetic and logic unit (ALU) and the shifter of our example processor. This established the logic that is controlled by the control signals produced. Starting with a very simple ALU and shifter, we saw that higher performance can be achieved at the expense of additional components. For very high performance multiple ALUs can be used or we can introduce independent function units. There are several different ways to organize the multiple arithmetic or function units, either to operate independently or as parts of a pipeline or array of concurrent processing elements.

We closed our discussion of processor organization and implementation with a discussion of processor performance. Of interest here is how computer performance is influenced by the instruction-set-processor design. Since most programs are written in a higher-level language and translated automatically to machine language, we are concerned with how the ISP and the control can give good performance in executing compiled programs. The compiler itself is one of the important programs that must be executed effectively. It is easy to talk about the need for performance, but it is difficult to specify and to measure. The principle of ideal and actual engines from thermodynamics is useful as a concept for identifying computer activities that are not contributing to production of useful "information work".

While we cannot carry the thermodynamic analogy to completion, we can use the concept to move toward more "efficient" processors. We can identify which operations represent actions specified in a program and which are "overhead". Overhead operations include most memory fetches and stores, most data moves, and data packing and unpacking. There are alternative means for reducing this overhead. Higher-level-language operators usually are converted to sequences of machine instructions. We can design machine instructions that better represent the operators in a program, but we must be sure that there is a net gain from the complexity that is introduced.

The results of several studies of processor performance were outlined. Statistics on which instructions are executed in running typical programs can be used in processor design. This information has been used by developers of RISC machines and by proponents of expression-stack architectures. Data on some of the studies were discussed. While we cannot identify the "best" approach to processor organization, there is a methodology for considering performance issues in our design.

6.10 ADDITIONAL READING

Soon after the integrated circuit was invented, G. E. Moore (then director of research at Fairchild Semiconductor and later a founder and chairman of Intel Corp.) predicted that the number of devices on a single silicon chip would double every two years. R. N. Noyce (another founder and former chairman of Intel) in 1977 [NoycR77] forecast a continuing decline in price per device at a rate of almost one-half each year for a decade. The curves plotted in Fig. 6-1 (and those showing the cost per bit of storage in earlier chapters) show that the projections of Moore and Noyce have been experienced closely. Details of the trends and the progress in electronics technology can be followed in *IEEE Transactions on Electron Devices* and *IEEE Transactions on Solid State Circuits*.

RISC principles were introduced by D. A. Patterson and others at the University of California at Berkeley. [PattD82] summarizes the principles and an implementation. Other implementations are described in [HennJ84], [HopkM84], [RadiG82], and [RadiG83]. [PattD85] gives an update on RISC approaches. [StalW86] and [StalW87] are surveys of the topic. [GimaC87] describes features of RISC machines and presents a large number of examples. [GrosT88] describes measurements on the MIPS RISC computer. A complete description of a RISC architecture is found in [KaneG87]. The issues continue to be argued in *Computer Architecture News* (ACM) and at the annual Symposia on Computer Architecture.

Descriptions of computer designs that show the control structure at the register transfer level can be found in [GorsG86], [HamaV84], [ManoM79], and [ManoM82]. These books also contain good descriptions of arithmetic and logic unit design. The argument for tagged memory is made in [FeusE73]. Use of tagged memory in the B5500 and B6500 is included in [OrgaE73]. The reasons for selecting a general-register organization rather than using a stack in the IBM System/360 architecture is described in [AmdaG64].

Before 1960, most computer controls used hard-wired logic. The paper by Wilkes [WilkM51] suggesting microprogramming was not followed until the 1960s when the technology for high-speed control memories became available. In 1964 IBM announced the System/360, in which the smaller models were microprogrammed. Microprogramming a computer to be a virtual representation of a higher-level language (Euler, derived from ALGOL-60) is outlined in [WebeH67]. The microprogrammable B1700 is described in [OrgaE78]. A good review of microprogramming in control is presented in [RausT80].

Direct-execution languages and direct-interpretation languages for computer architectures are discussed by M. J. Flynn [FlynM80] in a paper that refers to the detail contained in two Stanford University Technical Reports by him and L. W. Hoevel ([FlynM79], and [HoevL79]). These languages and architectures have been a topic of the Workshops on High-Level Architecture sponsored by the Computer Science Department at the University of Maryland.

Various approaches to pipeline processing are described in [HwanK84]. Much more detail on the design of pipelined arithmetic units and on pipelined instruction units is included in [KoggP81].

The argument for simplicity of instruction set processors is presented well in [WulfW81] and has been expanded on by the RISC developers. [PattD82], [RadiG82], and [HopkM84] cite comparisons of RISC and conventional instruction-set processors in support of the RISC concept. Comparisons with popular microprocessors are used in [WirtN86] to support the Lilith design at ETH Zurich. The commercially available microprocessors cited in the comparison are the Motorola M68000 [Motor84] and the National Semiconductor NS32000 ([HuntC87] and [Natio85]). The topic of architectural features for higher-level-language programming was covered in many papers in the ACM 1982 Symposium on Architectural Support for Programming Languages and Operating Systems; the proceedings contain the study of VAX instruction use [WiecC86] and the paper by G. Radin mentioned before.

More general references on computer performance are described in the Additional Readings section of Chapter 1.

For more on the other computers described in this chapter, the reader is referred to [ThorJ64] for a still-up-to-date description of the Control Data architectures, to [CaseR78] and [CormR83], as well as to IBM's Technical Publications Department, for descriptions of the IBM System/370, to [BarnG68] for the ILLIAC IV, to [WatsW72] for the Texas Instruments ASC, and to [StreW78] and Digital Equipment Corporation's VAX handbooks ([Digi86a] and [Digi86b]) for the VAX.

6.11 PROBLEMS

6-1. The VAX computer architecture and the implementation of the VAX-11/780 have been discussed in several chapters. The system structure (PMS) of the VAX-11/780 was shown in Fig. 3-3. Its user-accessible registers were shown in Fig. 5-8 and its user-transparent registers were outlined in Fig. 6-3. Its environment and context switching and its interrrupt operation were described in Section 5.5 and were illustrated in Fig. 5-16. The nine function units in the VAX-11/780 processor are connected to six buses (internal data, ID; visibility, V; physical address, PA; synchronous backplane interconnect, SBI; control store, CS; and memory data, MD), as shown in Fig. 6-32.

Function Units:	Buses:	ID	V	PA	SBII	CS	MD
Address Translation Buffer			B	S		D	B
Data Cache			B	D			
Synch. Backplane Interconn. Control			B	D	B		S
Memory Controller					B		
Floating-Point Accelerator		B	B			D	B
Data Path		B	B			D	D
Instruction Buffer and Decoder		B	B			D	
Control Store and Microsequencer						S	
Trap and Interrupt Arbiter		B	B			D	

Action of Function Unit: S = source, D = destination, B = both.

Figure 6-32 VAX-11/780 processor function units and buses.

Draw a PMS diagram of the VAX-11/780 *processor*. Describe and show a PMS diagram for a lower-cost and lower-performance model that retains the VAX architecture (i.e., remains a VAX virtual machine). The model you are defining should have significantly lower cost.

6-2. Identify the control signals needed for the simple computer shown in Fig. 6-4, assuming that it has a fetch–execute cycle like that shown in Figs. 2-11 and 2-13, and that it has an ALU like that of Fig. 6-22. Make some assumptions about part of the instruction set.

6-3. You are developing the controls for the simple computer of Fig. 6-4 and have decided on a microprogrammed controller like that of Fig. 6-7. Discuss the differences in cost and performance (if there are any) between a horizontal and a vertical approach to the microprogrammed control (Fig. 6-8). Draw the logic for the decoders required if vertical microprogramming is used.

6-4. Give examples to clearly show the use of breakpoints and of program flow tracing in fault diagnosis.

6-5. Show the operation overlaps in a three-stage RISC instruction pipeline (Fig. 6-20) with instruction transfer, instruction decode and source-register selection, operation execution and transfer to register each taking 1 clock time. In the example of Fig. 6-21 show how pipeline bubbles would be introduced and could be filled in the case of this three-stage pipeline.

6-6. Describe how you would implement multiplication in the simple computer of Fig. 6-4. Show the use of registers for multiplier, multiplicand, and result. Show the algorithm you would use with an example. Note that the result is double precision (at least during its generation).

6-7. Consider a computer with an instruction lookahead queue (Fig. 5-14). The addressing modes of this computer include register–register and register–memory operations. In both cases two arguments are specified and the destination of a result is the first argument (e.g., ADD R1 R2 means "add the contents of registers 1 and 2 and place the result in register 1"). The computer has 31-bit words and instructions can be either 16 bits (register–register) or 32 bits (register–memory). Instruction fetches, data fetches, and data stores all take 1 clock time. Instruction decoding also takes 1 clock time, as do arithmetic and logical operations and register transfers, except for division, which takes 2 clock times. Memory operations, instruction decoding, and other processor activity can be accomplished concurrently. For the following sequence of instructions (A, B, C, D, X, Y refer to memory addresses):

```
LOAD R0, A   {R0 <- M[A]}
LOAD R1, B   {R1 <- M[B]}
ADD  R0, C   {R0 <- R0 + M[C]}
COPY R2, R1  {R2 <- R1}
SUB  R2, D   {R2 <- R2 - M[D]}
MUL  R0, R2  {R0 <- R0 * R2}
SUB  R0, R1  {R0 <- R0 - R1}
STO  R0, X   {M[X] <- R0}
DIV  R2, R0  {R2 <- R2 / R0}
STO  R2, Y   {M[Y] <- R2}
```

show a timing diagram (Gantt chart) that demonstrates the independent operations of memory references, instruction decoding, and operation execution when:
a. instructions must start on word boundaries (NOOPs are introduced to fill words), and
b. instructions start on half-word boundaries.

6-8. A processor has a four-stage pipeline in which the pipeline reservation table is the same for all operations as follows:

Clock Time:	1	2	3	4	5
Stage 4				X	
Stage 3			X	X	
Stage 2		X			
Stage 1	X				X

Show how successive operations, W, X, Y, Z, etc., can be initiated to maximize execution speed.

6-9. The operations that follow evaluate the expression

$$A * B * C * (D + E) * F * (G + H)$$

as register–register operations in a computer with 16 general registers. Temporary values are held in registers designated T1, T2, etc.

Step 1: T1 <- A * B
Step 2: T1 <- T1 * C
Step 3: T2 <- D + E
Step 4: T1 <- T1 * T2
Step 5: T1 <- T1 * F
Step 6: T2 <- G + H
Step 7: T1 <- T1 * T2

Use the algebraic rules of commutativity and associativity to rearrange the computation for fastest possible execution if as many D units as are needed are available. How many steps are there to the program in this case? How many D units are required? How many more temporary registers are needed?

6-10. You are working with a single-address computer that incorporates immediate, direct, and indirect addressing. There is a single-instruction lookahead that masks the times for instruction fetch except on conditional or unconditional jump instructions. The computer uses 1 clock time for operations on literal (immediate) values, 2 clock times for operations on directly addressed values, 4 clock times for operations on indirectly addressed values, and 4 clock times on control conditional or unconditional jump instructions (since the instruction lookahead is ignored). You assume that an "ideal" computer would have an indefinite amount of local registers. It would execute all PASCAL operations (arithmetic, logical, relational, block exit, etc.) in 1 clock time.

You have written the PASCAL program shown in Fig. 6-33(a) to solve the problem of printing the largest value in a list of 10 integers.

The assembly language code for the program to be executed on the target computer is shown in Fig. 6-33(b).

a. Determine the number of clock times it takes to execute the PASCAL program on the "ideal" computer.

```
program BIGGEST();
const N = 10;
var TEMP, COUNT: integer;
    LIST: array[1..N] of integer;
begin
    TEMP := 0;
    for COUNT := 1 to N do
        if LIST[COUNT] > TEMP then TEMP := LIST[COUNT];
    write[TEMP]
end. {BIGGEST}
```

(a)

```
00          LOAD    #0          11 SKIP:  LOAD    OFFSET
01          STO     TEMP        12        ADD     #1
02          LOAD    #18         13        JMP     LOOP
03 LOOP:    STO     OFFSET      14 END:   PRNT    TEMP
04          SUB     #27         15        HALT
05          JGT     END         16        DATA    TEMP
06          LOAD    TEMP        17        DATA    OFFSET
07          SUB  i  OFFSET      18        DATA    LIST[1]
08          JGE     SKIP        19        DATA    LIST[2]
09          LOAD i  OFFSET      20            . . .
10          STO     TEMP        27        DATA    LIST[10]
```

(b)

Figure 6-33 Example program and code for Problem 6-10. (a) PASCAL program
(b) Assembly language code.

b. Determine the number of clock times it takes to execute the program on the target computer.

c. Repeat part b for the target computer without instruction lookahead with instruction fetches taking an additional 2 clock times.

d. Repeat part b for the target computer with a cache memory added. For this problem, assume that after a variable is first read there is a 100% cache hit ratio and operations on the value in cache take 1 clock time. Writing to memory takes an additional 2 clock times since a later instruction fetch is delayed.

6.12 PROJECTS

6-A. For your computer investigation project (Project 1-A) define the control mechanism and the hidden registers for the computer system. If your investigation is of a family describe the differences among models in the family.

6-B. Specify the control mechanism and the hidden registers for the computer you are designing for Project 1-B.

6-C. Design the controls for the von Neumann processor (Fig. 2-7). Specify the fetch–execute cycle using a register-transfer language (Fig. 2-11). Include execution of representative instructions. Specify the control-word format. If you choose microprogrammed control specify the size and organization of the control store.

7

Input/Output and Other Processors

In the original von Neumann design (and in some simple computers today) all processing was conducted in a single unit. The controller of the central processor (the "control organ") initiated the fetch-execute cycle by selecting the next instruction from memory and activated each of the register transfers and function operators at the time required to cause the instruction to be executed. Any effective-address calculations were performed in the central processor and the memory was a "passive" component of the system.

With that simple computer structure all input/output activity is performed under tight central-processor control. Transfers of any information between external devices and memory use processor registers as buffers. The computer architecture can be implemented with a single processor and storage and requires none of the switching discussed in Chapter 3. This structure is adequate in many cases, but processing performance suffers whenever there is input or output activity, since the processor resources must be devoted to the details of that activity.

7.1 REDUCING CENTRAL-PROCESSOR LOAD

If each external device is provided with a buffer register it might be possible to accomplish transfers between the memory buffer register and a device register without using a processor register. This would require that the processor perform the conversions between formats of the device registers and the memory and would still require that the processor be involved in the details of the register transfers. Different external devices have different formats and have many other different characteristics. A significant amount of processing is required.

When the central processor can be relieved of any input/output processing activities beyond initiating the I/O operation, then it can perform other tasks while input or output transfers are being made. The memory can be shared for both processor and input/output transfers as long as there are means for resolving any conflicts for access to memory. With this independent form of input/output control the processor periodically has to check to see if the input or output transfer has been completed or if it can be sent a signal from the controller of the input/output activity indicating that the transfer has been accomplished. The latter signal (or signals) can be made a part of the interrupt system of the central processor.

Design or specification of the input/output subsystem requires that we start with an examination of the characteristics of the many different types of peripheral equipment that might be attached to our computer. These input/output devices range from simple interfaces with human beings such as a keyboard to disk file memory drives with very large capacities and transfer rates. They include communications lines of various capacities with a variety of communications protocols and analog-signal interfaces for real-time processes. Details of all of the individual peripheral devices and of the quantities of each that might be connected are required before we can design the computer input/output system.

When we have identified the characteristics of the input/output traffic we can address issues related to the control of that traffic and of its coordination with the computer. We can specify any data buffering that might be required and can identify the signals that are needed to synchronize the flow of information. A mechanism for connecting the external devices with memory and for controlling transfers to and from memory can be designed. Most of the information needed for designing the input/output interface was generated when the requirements for the total system were developed, as discussed in Chapter 2. Details of the specific items of peripheral equipment to be used with the system completes the data needed for design to proceed.

The interface with common-carrier communications facilities or with special communications networks might require specialized input/output activities. As discussed in Chapter 3, there are protocols for initiating, conducting, and terminating messages and these depend on the nature of the communications switching and on the bandwidths of the transmission media. Input/output processing at the interface between the computer and a communications resource involves accomplishing the protocol in addition to synchronizing and monitoring other input/output operations. A specialized input/output processor for communications management might be more suitable than a standard input/output processor.

Systems with input/output facilities that can operate independently can share memory with the central processor. Any transfers of information between the I/O subsystem and the memory are conducted in the same manner as are Pc-Mp transfers. Means must be provided to resolve any conflicting requests for access to a memory module. Whereas the conflict resolution can be accomplished with simple logic at the memory module, there are cases in which more sophisticated processing at the memory interface is useful. Error detection and correction can be added to simple multiport memory control and priority-based access management can be added to the direct-memory-access memory interlacing. As the memory-control functions are expanded it might be worthwhile to introduce a special-purpose memory processor, or memory-management unit (MMU). Secondary-memory interfaces might also warrant special purpose processing.

There are other instances in which a processor might be used in a computer system to relieve the central processor of a particular set of functions. Special-purpose processors for these purposes might entail little more than adding independent control to a specialized arithmetic and logic unit or might involve the introduction of a processor more sophisticated than the central processor itself, with the Pc being used for management of the processes that are transferred to the special-purpose processor.

In this chapter we examine the specialized requirements that might lead to special-purpose processors. We characterize the special-purpose processors and examine the differences and the similarities between general-purpose and special-purpose processors.

7.2 EXTERNAL DEVICES AND THEIR CONTROL

The connection of the computer to its information-processing environments can involve a wide variety of transfer mechanisms. Before we can design the input/output interfaces we must understand the details of the devices and the systems that will be attached to the computer. In each case we must know the amount of information to be transferred, the formats in which the information will be found, the redundancy available for error detection and error correction, the rate at which the transfers will be made, and the controls that must be implemented to effect the transfers. A review of typical peripheral equipment demonstrates the nature of specifications that must be provided to define the input/output interfaces.

The minimum amount of information is transferred when a simple switch or flip-flop is used to identify that a particular condition has been reached or that a particular device such as a light or a bell should be activated. Even in this simple case there is a requirement for input/output control, since the central processor cannot be stopped to hold a single signal line at the level required to transmit the information. Instead, a boolean value is transmitted instantaneously across the input/output interface. Any storage of the boolean value inside the computer is accomplished in a processor register or in memory, whereas such storage outside the computer is effected in the peripheral device itself. In this case the amount of information and the format are the same, a single bit. Unless the information is to be transferred in the form of a pulse with a particular shape (this usually is accomplished in a pulse generator separate from the computer), the transmission rate is characterized by the time required to transfer the single bit of information. No format control or information transformation is involved, with the exception of an identification of the particular source or destination of the boolean value.

A slightly more complicated transfer involves a single byte of information from a keyboard that encodes keystrokes in the format needed by the computer or a byte of information to be transferred to a display or printer. Although a full byte of information is transmitted, there is no format transformation and the duration of the transmission is a single processor clock pulse. Here there is opportunity to include redundancy for error detection and correction and we might find that at least a single parity bit should be added to the data for error sensing.

It is easy to envision stepwise increases in complexity from these simple cases. The amount of information transferred might be the quantity of bytes that fill a line buffer for a printer or a display. Format conversion from or to a binary numeric value to or from a sequence of digits (possibly with a sign) might be required during the transfer. Multibit redundancy might be incorporated for longitudonal redundancy checking or for Hamming coding, as described in Chapter 4. Fixed- or varying-size blocks of information might be transferred between primary memory and some external device. Information buffering and transfer-rate coordination might be required. Several examples of secondary memory that require this type of control were described in Chapter 4.

The characteristics of some typical peripheral devices are summarized in Fig. 7-1. The ranges of block sizes shown for the keyboard and display are for unbuffered and display-page buffered terminals. Data are transferred as individual bytes (usually in USASCII/ISO format) in bit-serial or byte-parallel form. Transfer rates for terminals, which can be attached to a computer directly or over data-communication lines, are from 1200 to 19,200 bits per second. Block sizes range from 1 to 2000 bytes. This low-speed category of peripheral device imposes very little burden on the input/output subsystem and a small quantity of such terminals can be interfaced using central-processor control, as might be the case when the terminals are operator and maintenance consoles. Larger quantities of terminals for groups of users usually are connected to a separate I/O controller, as was shown in some of the PMS diagrams of Chapter 3.

A typical 80-column serial printer, such as is used with small computers, has characteristics very much like those of the display. The printer might be buffered or unbuffered and is connected either for bit-serial or for byte ("parallel printer port") transfers at rates similar to those for terminals. A high-speed (e.g., 1200 lines/min) printer usually will be connected for byte transfers into a buffer of at least 1-line (130-byte) capacity. Transfer rates are from 1200 to 50,000 bytes/s.

Magnetic-tape devices include the low-performance single- or dual-track cartridge

Device	Format	Parallelism	Transfer Rate (bytes/s)	Block Size (bytes)
Keyboard	Byte	Bit/byte	1200-19,200	1-2000
Display	Byte	Bit/byte	1200-19,200	1-2000
Serial Printer	Byte	Bit/byte	1200-19,200	1-2000
Line Printer	Byte	Byte	1200-50,000	130-6000
Cartridge Drive	Byte	Bit	1200-9600	2000-6000
Mag. Tape Drive	Byte	Byte	24k-1M	2k-16k
Floppy Drive	Byte/word	Byte	200k-1M	1000-6000
Disk Drive	Byte/word	Byte	1M-3M	2k-16k

Figure 7-1 Typical peripheral device characteristics.

drives that transfer bytes in bit-serial form at rates from 2000 to 6000 bits/s. Block sizes are those of page frames of a small computer (2000 to 6000 bytes). At the higher end of the magnetic tape unit performance range we find the standard-format nine-channel drives that use byte formats (EBCDIC or USASCII/ISO) with a parity bit in each byte. Here it is necessary to transfer blocks of up to tens of kilobytes at rates of 24 kbytes/s to 1 Mbyte/s. Special tape drives with 18 or more tracks have transfer rates several times faster.

As with the magnetic-tape drives, disk files have a broad range of performance and capacity characteristics. They include the low-performance floppy-disk drives for small computers and the large-capacity files for large computer systems shown in the figure. In both cases the format of the information can be in bytes or words, but transfers usually are made in bytes (which might be 8-bit internal slices, parts of binary words rather than independent bytes). Blocks of information similar to those of the magnetic tape units are transferred at rates of from 200 kbytes/s to 1 Mbyte/s in the case of the floppy-disk drives and from 1 to 3 Mbytes/s with the rigid-disk drives.

The peripheral equipment summarized in Fig. 7-1 covers a range of capabilities and is typical of devices that might be attached to a computer. There can be many other items that have characteristics overlapping those of the equipment shown in the figure and there might be special-purpose devices of greatly different character. Reflection on the requirements for control of the devices shown demonstrates that there are a number of coordination, control, and conversion functions that must be performed if these devices are to be used effectively in the computer system.

In our discussion of computer memories in Chapter 4 we saw that primary memory is designed to have "random-access" capabilities such that any word can be accessed in the same amount of time independent of its location. We saw that the information is stored in physical words of from 8 to 256 bits in size and that redundant bits might be added for detection or correction of errors made in transfers. Read or write times range from 25 to 500 ns for each physical word and we might use a low-order interlacing among modules to permit large blocks to be transferred at rates of up to 100 Mwords/s. The characteristics of transfers on the memory side of the input/output interface are quite different from those on the external side.

A comparison of information transfer on the two sides of the I/O interface allows us to identify some of the functions required for input/output control. When blocks rather than words are transferred and when the time to transfer each word is different from the time for access to the start of a block, a controller must synchronize the operations of the memory to those of the electromechanical external device. This is the case with both disk files and magnetic tape drives. Each memory access must be accomplished and the data-word transfer completed before the next byte can be transferred to or from the peripheral device. The input/output control must have priority over the central processor when there are simultaneous requests. This function of inhibiting central-processor access can be performed by logic at the memory or might be a part of the I/O control.

The difference in information-transfer characteristics at each side of the interface also leads to a need for buffers to hold information while the transfer synchronization takes place. For example, on output to a disk file a word of information is transferred from the memory to the I/O controller. The word will be held in the controller until the disk file can receive it. If there is a possibility that a central-processor access at this time could delay the next output from memory too long a 2-word buffer in the I/O controller might be required. With the slower external devices this second word of buffering seldom is required.

Often we find that while the transfer between the controller and the memory is in physical words, each of several or many bytes, the transfer between the controller and the external device is as a stream of bytes or bits. In these cases the buffer register(s) allows for both parallel and serial transfers. Usually this results in the need for a multiple-word buffer. If the controller is to be used with several different peripheral devices the buffering might permit any of words, bytes, or bits to be transferred on the external device side.

If the information on the two sides of the interface are in different formats we might have to perform format conversion at the interface. It is not desirable to burden a high-performance computer with decimal-binary conversion functions and these can be accomplished at the interface as a part of the I/O control function. Some external devices represent character information in codes that are different from the internal byte code of the computer, as in the case of internal 8-bit EBCDIC code and an external 7-bit USASCII/ISO code (see Fig. 7-2). This format conversion can be accomplished at the interface rather than involving the central processor. When the computer is connected to an analog external environment there certainly is format conversion at the interface.

A major source of error in information is electrical noise that can occur during transfers to or from an external device. It is desirable that error checking (and error correction, if there is sufficient redundancy in the information) be performed during such transfers. Facility to perform the error analysis, as was described in Chapter 4, can be included as a part of the input/output controller function. Since errors can be introduced on any memory transfer, similar error checking and correction can be performed at the memory side of the interface.

The input/output controller must be given instructions to direct which of many operations are to be performed by which of the many peripheral devices. The controller also must be able to provide information on the status of the external devices and on the controller itself in order that the operating system being executed by the central processor can perform its management functions. Thus, there must be methods for communication between the input/output subsystem and the central processor.

In any particular architecture we can identify all of the specific functions to be performed, can detail the characteristics of the external devices and of the computer interfaces, and can specify the control and the status information that is needed. When all of this information is organized it is possible to separate the information into those parts that are unique to single peripheral equipments or to groups of similar equipments, and those parts that are more general. This allows us to specify the function and the structure of the input/output controls and the function and structure of the specific device control-lers. In many cases, however, the device controllers have been designed as a part of the peripheral equipment and we do not have the freedom to allocate an increased role to those controllers.

	EBCDIC (8 bits)								USASCII (7 bits)			
	3 most significant bits								2 most significant bits			
	000	001	010	011	100	101	110	111	00	01	10	11
lsb												
00000	NUL	DS	sp	—					NUL	sp	@	'
00001	SOH	SOS		/	a		A		SOH	!	A	a
00010	STX	FS			b	s	B	S	STX	"	B	b
00011	ETX				c	t	C	T	ETX	#	C	c
00100	PF	BYP			d	u	D	U	EOT	$	D	d
00101	HT	LF			e	v	E	V	ENQ	%	E	e
00110	LC	ETB			f	w	F	W	ACK	&	F	f
00111	DEL	ESC			g	x	G	X	BEL	'	G	g
01000					h	y	H	Y	BS	(	H	h
01001					i	z	I	Z	HT	)	I	i
01010	SMM	SM	¢						LF	*	J	j
01011	VT	CU2	.	,					VT	+	K	k
01100	FF		<	%					FF	,	L	l
01101	CR	ENQ	(	_					CR	-	M	m
01110	SO	ACK	+	>					SO	.	N	n
01111	SI	BEL	|	?					SI	/	O	o
10000	DLE		&					0	DLE	0	P	p
10001	DC1				j		J	1	DC1	1	Q	q
10010	DC2	SYN			k		K	2	DC2	2	R	r
10011	TM				l		L	3	DC3	3	S	s
10100	RES	PN			m		M	4	DC4	4	T	t
10101	NL	RS			n		N	5	NAK	5	U	u
10110	BS	UC			o		O	6	SYN	6	V	v
10111	IL	EOT			p		P	7	ETB	7	W	w
11000	CAN				q		Q	8	CAN	8	X	x
11001	EM				r		R	9	EM	9	Y	y
11010	CC		!	:					SUB	:	Z	z
11011	CU1	CU3	$	#					ESC	;	[	{
11100	IFS	DC4	*	@					PS	<	\	|
11101	IGS	NAK	)	'					GS	=	]	}
11110	IRS		;	=					RS	>	^	~
11111	IUS	SUB	¬	"					US	?	—	DEL

NOTE: Capitalized strings are abbreviations for control characters.

Figure 7-2   Alphanumeric codes: EBCDIC and USASCII/ISO.

7.3 PERIPHERAL-DEVICE CONTROLLERS

For each class of data transfers we can specify requirements for input/output control. A simple input/output interface unit is shown in Fig. 7-3. As demonstrated by the illustration, a buffer register holds the data to be transferred until the peripheral device controller or the I/O bus can accept it. The source of or the destination for the data (the device address) is decoded to determine that this is the unit designated. An instruction on data to be transferred (the function code) and the status of the device being addressed (device status) are used for control. The transfer can be made over a single input/output switch or bus, or can involve separate data, control and address buses, as shown in the typical system of Fig. 7-4 . With the single link the different types of information

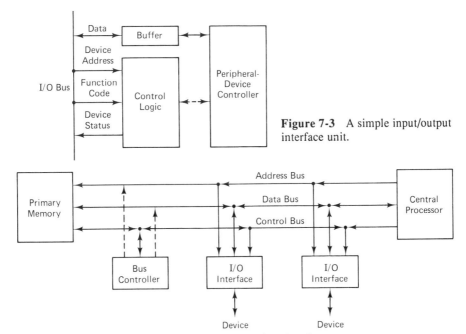

Figure 7-3 A simple input/output interface unit.

Figure 7-4 Input/output interface buses.

must be transmitted in sequence, whereas the independent buses allow the information to different locations in the interface to be transferred concurrently.

At the other side of the buses there is the interface with the primary memory and with the central processor. There are several ways to implement this interface. It might use the central processor itself to run the input/output programs, a direct-memory-access (DMA) unit might be added to allow the input/output operations to be removed from the central processor, or an independent input/output control or processor (sometimes called an I/O "channel") might be incorporated. The progression from program-controlled input/output through DMA control to input/output processor generally reflects a progression from low- to high-performance computer systems. We will examine all three approaches.

Figure 7-5 demonstrates how the interface of Fig. 7-3 would exchange information with a processor connected to the input/output bus using central-processor program-controlled input/output. The data are transferred to or from the accumulator (or any data register in the case of a multiregister computer). The function code and the device address are taken from those fields of the instruction register. The status of the external device and its interface unit are provided to the processor controls (Chapter 6). Communication with all interface units is through the I/O bus(es). Any interface unit (Fig. 7-3) will react to its own device address, will accept the function code, and will provide the device status. When an item of data is to be transferred it is sent from the data register after the central processor has determined (from the device status) that the peripheral interface unit is ready. If a block of information is to be transmitted the central processor repeats the operation after acquiring from memory the next word to be transferred.

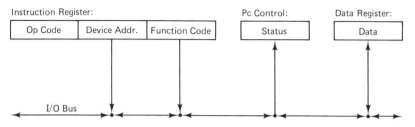

Figure 7-5 Input/output control at the central processor.

Each type of peripheral has a unique interface and requires unique control and buffering at the interface. For example, a serial-printer control needs a character buffer, controls of the paper feed, and paper-form sense inputs (paper out, top of form, paper moving) at the printer side. If it is a dot-matrix printer the controller also might contain the printed character generators. The character buffer might hold a single character, a line of characters, or more. Many serial dot-matrix printers for personal computers have buffering for a full display screen of 2000 (25 x 80) characters. On the side that connects to the computer input/output interface a controller requires a buffer register, an address decoder, a command decoder, and a status register. The control and the buffer register provide for bit-serial or for byte-parallel transfers. A parallel line-printer controller has similar requirements, but has at least a line of character buffers and the controls for print hammer timing if it is a full-character impact printer or for character generation if it is a dot-matrix character-forming device. Any of the printers might include more extensive forms handling and would require signal generators for forms control.

Typical of peripheral device controllers are the Intel 8295 dot-matrix printer controller shown in Fig. 7-6 and the Intel 8271 programmable floppy-disk controller of Fig. 7-7. At the interface to the processor or memory (connected through an I/O bus) each

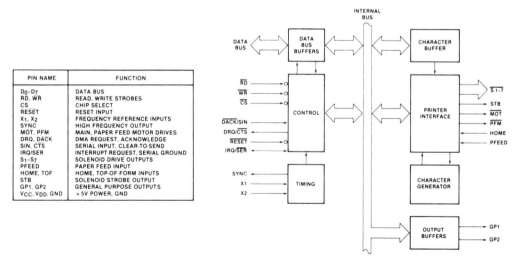

Figure 7-6 Dot-matrix printer controller (Intel 8295). (a) Pin names. (b) Block diagram. (Copyright 1979, Intel Corp., reprinted with permission.)

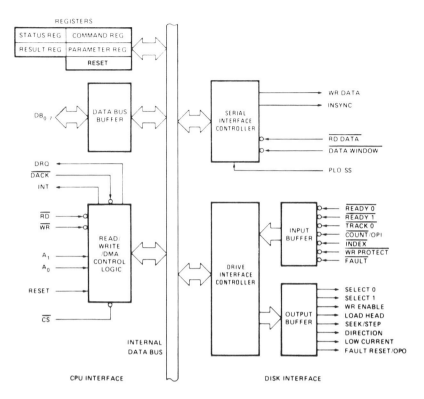

Figure 7-7 Programmable floppy-disk controller (Intel 8271). (Copyright 1979, Intel Corp., reprinted with permission.)

controller contains a data-bus buffer (a buffer register of 1 byte) and control logic. Logic unique to the type of peripheral device controlled is present at the device interface (to the right of the internal data bus in the figures). In both controllers the bus interface control logic includes detectors of read-select (RD), write-select (WR), chip-select (CS), DMA acknowledge (DACK), and RESET signals. The logic transmits DMA-request (DRQ) and interrupt-request (IRQ) signals.

Printers can be operated with parallel (by byte) or serial (by bit) transfers from the computer and the controller must adapt to either. The common control logic and the data-bus buffer are used in the parallel mode. In the serial mode the printer controller uses the DACK connector for the data input signals and the DRQ connection for a "clear-to-send" signal. The timing unit of the printer controller receives inputs to a crystal (XTAL1, XTAL2) for oscillator timing and transmits a signal for external synchronizing (SYN).

The printer controller contains a character buffer of 40 bytes, and the character generator that accepts character codes and sends signals to form the dot-matrix characters. These signals, called solenoid drivers (S_1 to S_7), are transmitted to the printer to control the print head and are accompanied by the solenoid strobe (timing) signal (STR). Motor-drive (MOT) and paper-feed (PFM) signal outputs, and paper-feed-switch (PFEED) and "print-head home" (HOME) inputs also appear at the interface to the printer. There are two general-purpose output signals (GP1, GP2) for use with printers that require additional controls.

The floppy disk controller receives a 2-bit input (A_0, A_1) from the computer to select its registers. The controller registers hold commands, command parameters, results of operations, status of the controller, and a reset command. Between the controller internal data bus and the dual disk drives there are a serial interface controller for the magnetic head electronics and a drive interface controller. The serial interface controller receives a signal specifying the nature of the data separator used in recording (PLO/SS) and signals for data input (RDDATA) and data-input timing (DATA WINDOW). To write on a diskette it sends write data (WR DATA) and timing (INSYNC) signals. The drive interface has an input buffer that receives "drive-ready" (READY 0, READY 1), "write-protected" (WR PROTECT), track-limit (TRACK 0), track-counter (COUNT), FAULT, and timing (INDEX) signals. The output buffer transmits drive select (SELECT 0, SELECT 1), head write (WR ENABLE), lower head (LOAD HEAD), track stepping (SEEK STEP), head DIRECTION, write-signal output compensation (LOW CURRENT), and FAULT RESET. These lines are connected to the drive electronics. The controller is designated as "programmable" since the computer can send specific commands and parameters to the controller registers and can receive status and results of queries.

More general peripheral controllers also are available from the semiconductor manufacturers. These give the computer designer flexibility to deal with a variety of peripheral equipments with the same basic interface unit. The Intel 8255 programmable interface unit shown in Fig. 7-8 contains controls for two different peripheral "groups" in addition to general control and data buffering similar to those of the device interface units of Figs. 7-6 and 7-7. Each peripheral group interface (A or B) has 12 connections that can be used as three sets of 4-bit input or output lines or as an 8-bit I/O set with four control lines. The "programming" of the programmable device interface units shown in Figs. 7-6 through 7-8 refers to the central processor or an input/output processor. The interface units themselves respond to program settings, but are not themselves programmable. Equivalent peripheral controllers for specific devices or for general use are available from other semiconductor manufacturers.

More flexibility is attainable with peripheral interface units that contain their own microprogram-controlled logic. The Motorola MC68120 intelligent peripheral controller shown in Fig. 7-9 contains an 8-bit CPU and a 2048-byte ROM for control of peripheral devices connected to any of three input/output ports. I/O ports 3 and 4 are for parallel 8-bit transfers and port 2 is for serial transfers with a programmable timer for the communications interface (serial I/O, port 1). A data buffer and an address buffer are included for connection to the computer system bus (like the I/O buses of Fig. 7-4). The 128-word dual-ported RAM holds data and control information. Six semaphore registers allow synchronizing of shared resources. We see here an example of a peripheral interface adapter that is truly an input/output processor. It can communicate directly with the central processor and the primary memory over the system bus or can be attached to an intermediate processor that exercises overall input/output control.

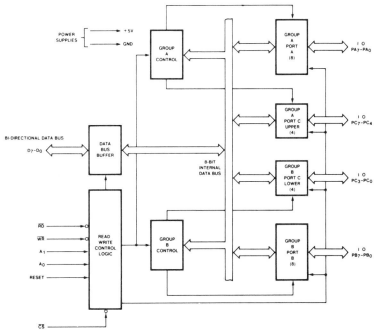

Figure 7-8 Programmable peripheral interface (Intel 8255A). (Copyright 1979, Intel Corp., reprinted with permission.)

7.4 MEMORY AND CENTRAL-PROCESSOR INTERFACES

Input-output control described so far has used the central processor for control of data transfers to or from memory. The control demonstrated by Fig. 7-5 used internal processor registers as buffers between the primary memory and the input/output bus. It is possible to have the central processor manage direct transfers between memory and peripheral devices without using its own data registers as buffers. Here the central processor specifies the device to send (receive) the data, the memory location from (to) which data is to be transferred, and the control information. Two approaches to moving data between memory and peripheral devices are demonstrated in Fig. 7-10.

Each peripheral device can be uniquely addressed, as shown in Fig. 7-10(a). Here a special input/output instruction contains the operation field (write to memory or read from memory), the identification of the peripheral device (address), and the memory address. Each device controller is organized as in Fig. 7-3. Data are transferred over the data bus to or from primary memory, which is instructed to read or write the data from or to the address specified.

With memory-mapped I/O, Fig. 7-10(b), a group of memory addresses is assigned to peripheral equipment rather than to the primary memory itself. Each peripheral device is given one or more addresses for data and for control information. Transfers to or from these "pseudomemory" addresses have the effect of transferring to or from the

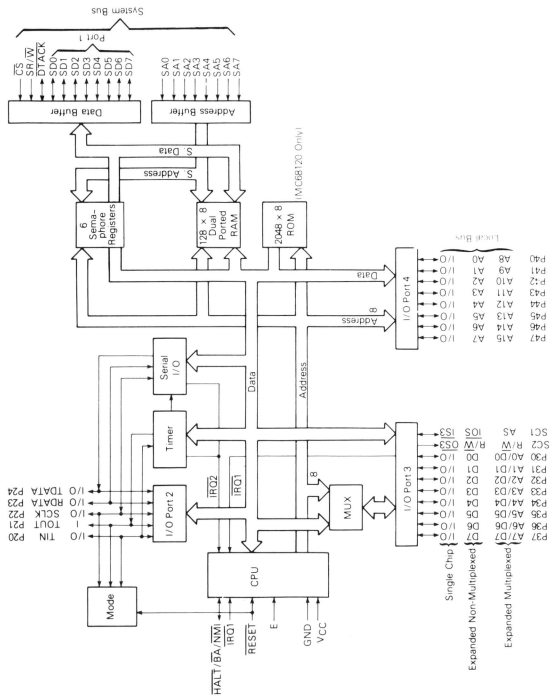

Figure 7-9 Motorola M68120 intelligent peripheral controller. (Courtesy of Motorola, Inc.)

264

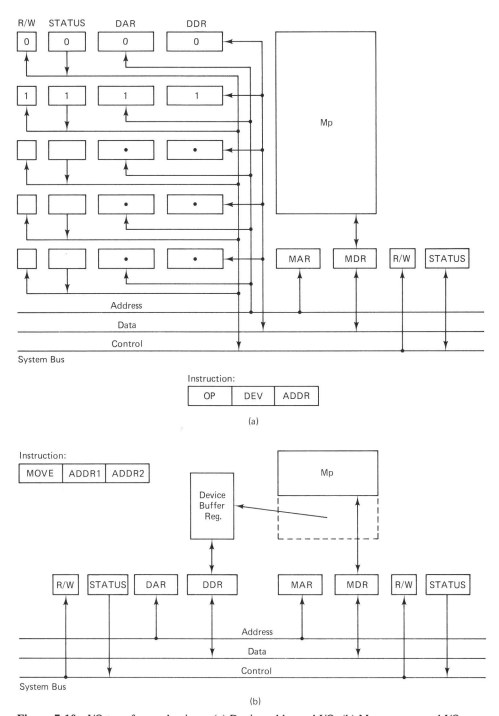

Figure 7-10 I/O transfer mechanisms. (a) Device-addressed I/O. (b) Memory-mapped I/O.

assigned peripheral device. The computer instruction set allows memory-to-memory transfers and the designation of an address that is allocated to a peripheral causes transfer to take place between memory and a device rather than between two memory locations. The device controllers are similar to those used for device-addressed I/O. The memory-mapped I/O technique is convenient even when communication between memory locations must be accomplished through processor registers.

Involvement of the central processor in the communication between memory and the external devices can be reduced by using a controller that handles details of word-by-word (or byte-by-byte) transfers after receiving a general command from the central processor. The central processor specifies the command, the device, the starting address in the device (if appropriate), the starting memory location, and the amount of information to be transferred. From this point until the transfer is completed the input/output controller manages the word-by-word or byte-by-byte data transfers. The input/output controller thus communicates with memory just as the central processor does, using the same switch or bus. To permit this sharing of memory and of the memory bus(es), coordination is needed to ensure that the processor and the I/O controller do not attempt to make transfers at the same instant. For this coordination direct-memory-access (DMA) capability is introduced. A DMA controller "steals" memory cycles from the central processor as the memory cycle times are needed for input or output activity, delaying processor access for the duration of the "stolen" memory cycle. DMA controllers typically control transfers for 4 to 64 peripheral device controllers.

Operation of a simple DMA controller is demonstrated in Fig. 7-11. To initiate input/output activity the central processor issues an input or an output command, speci-

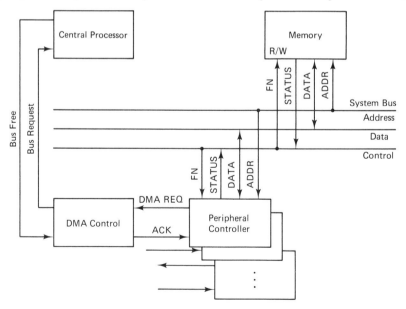

Figure 7-11   Direct-memory-access (DMA) control.

fying the device, the function, and the starting address in memory. The peripheral controller is selected by decoding an address and the function code is accepted as described before (see Figs.7-4 through 7-6). When the peripheral controller is ready to receive or to transmit a word (byte) of information, it requests access to the address and data buses by transmitting a request (DMA REQ) to the DMA control. If some other device has requested service the request is placed in a queue in the DMA control. The DMA control asks for use of the buses for a peripheral device by transmitting a "bus request" to the central processor. As soon as the processor has completed any memory transfer it inhibits its own access to the buses and returns a "bus-free" signal to the DMA control. The DMA control then sends the DMA ACK signal to the peripheral controller, permitting it to transfer the memory address and the read/write command to memory and to transmit or receive a word (byte) of data. The transfer is accomplished within a fixed amount of time, after which the DMA ACK signal is terminated and any further I/O operation is inhibited. The bus request signal is terminated and the processor is free to initiate its own memory (or input/output control) actions.

With this independent management of transfers the peripheral controller must have a counter and logic to keep track of the amount of information transferred and of the next memory address to be used. The central processor is not involved until the block transfer is completed or until an error occurs in a transfer. Since the processor is free to execute other instructions after initiating an input/output instruction, the processor must be advised when the whole block has been transferred. Methods to accomplish this communication are described later.

Due to the asynchronous operations, coordination is needed between the central processor and a DMA controller. After commanding an input or output operation the processor can resume processing not related to the input/output actions. (If there is no such processing the processor must wait for completion of the actions being undertaken by the DMA controller.) Figure 7-12 shows the synchronizing communication between a central processor, a DMA controller, and a peripheral controller. The DMA control can initiate a bus request at any time, but the bus-free response is only sent at the end of a

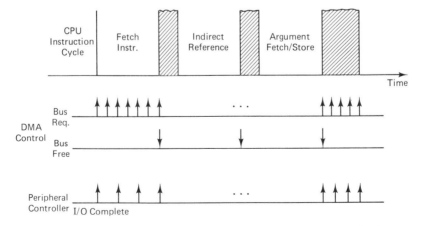

Figure 7-12　Peripheral controller, DMA, and CPU process coordination.

memory cycle. Then the processor delays its own memory accesses for a memory cycle time, allowing the peripheral device to gain access. Within a typical processor instruction cycle there are several memory accesses. The peripheral device can gain access at the end of any of these since the peripheral-memory transfers have no effect on the instruction cycle. An "I/O complete" signal can be transmitted by the peripheral-device controller at any time. The signal is responded to only at the end of a processor instruction cycle since the actions required themselves need processor instructions.

The simple DMA control shown in Fig. 7-11 requires that the management of detailed input/output transfers be accomplished by each peripheral controller. This I/O control management for many peripheral controllers can be combined with DMA control. In this case the DMA controller is an input/output controller of the type described in Chapter 3. DMA controllers of this type usually include registers to buffer transfers from several peripheral controllers. Then peripheral-device selections, commands from the central processor, memory addresses, and data transfers all flow through the DMA controller. The peripheral-device controllers return to the simple form shown in Fig. 7-3.

An example of a standard DMA controller is the Intel 8237 of Fig. 7-13. The connection of a DMA controller to the address bus, the control bus, and the system data bus is shown in Fig. 7-13(a). HRQ and HLDA are the "hold-request" and "hold-acknowledge" signals, respectively, for synchronizing memory activity with the processor. DREQ0-3 and DACK0-3 are the "DMA-request" and "DMA-acknowledge" lines, respectively, for up to four peripheral devices or for other 8237 controllers. The 8-bit latch register holds an added 8-bit address field if needed. Since the rate of data-transfer activity external to the computer usually is much lower than that between the central processor and primary memory, the "cycle stealing" by the DMA controller causes relatively little slowdown of processing when there is another task for the processor to accomplish concurrently.

The block diagram of the DMA controller is shown in Fig. 7-13(b). The 8237 contains four 16-bit base address and four 16-bit base word-count registers in the read buffer unit and four 16-bit current-address and four 16-bit current-word-count registers in the read/write buffer unit. Four read or write requests for the four independent DMA channels can be held in these registers, with the original requests in the read buffer and the current values (incremented or decremented on each transfer) in the read/write buffer. Temporary address and word-count registers in the decrementer and the incrementer/decrementer are used in actual control of a single block transfer. A mode register holds control information for each of the four channels. The command, request, and mask registers perform the actual control. The status register holds current status of each device being controlled. The five buffers (an I/O buffer for data, an I/O buffer and an output buffer for addresses, a read buffer and a write buffer) are receivers and drivers for connection to the internal and external buses. The temporary register holds data during memory-to-memory transfers.

Each of the four channels can be in a different mode. The modes are single (word) transfer, block transfer, demand (externally controlled) transfer, and cascade. In the last case controls are connected in cascade with other similar controllers to allow as much connectivity as desired.

Even if the central processor has been released from the task of detailed input/output control, it must be informed when an I/O task has been completed or when an externally

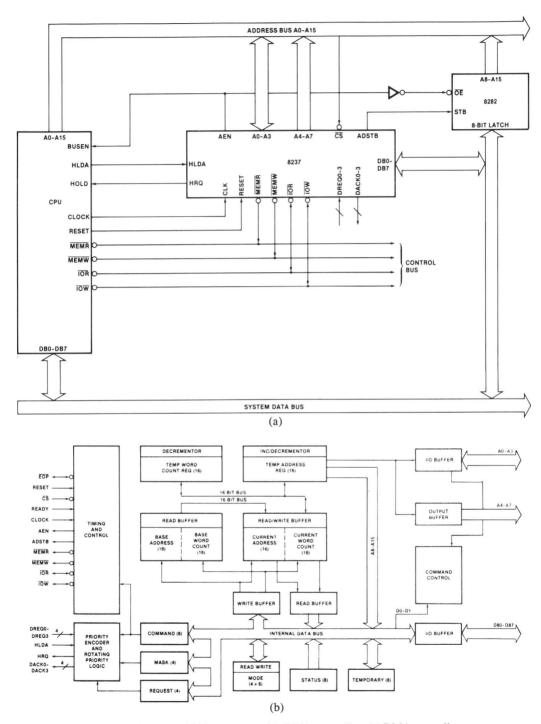

Figure 7-13 Intel 8237 programmable DMA controller. (a) DMA controller.
(b) Block diagram. (Copyright 1979, Intel Corp., reprinted with permission.)

stimulated I/O task is to be initiated. This can be accomplished by placing the "I/O complete" and the "I/O ready" information in status fields that can be tested by the central processor. In this form of process communication the central processor periodically "polls" the status registers of any input/output controllers or DMA controllers. The polling cycle must be short enough to respond to any I/O signals before information is lost. As an example, if data are available on an input communication line a command must be transmitted to the DMA controller to designate the memory location for the block of incoming data before the input buffer is filled and new information overrides old. Thus, polling by the central processor must take place very often and a significant amount of processor capacity might be devoted to it. (This is similar to the "busy waiting" activity in multiprocessing operating systems.)

An alternative mechanism that conserves processor time at the expense of additional hardware entails using interrupt signals to inform the central processor of input/output events. A priority-sensitive interrupt system of a central processor was described in Chapter 6. When an interrupt signal of priority higher than that of the process being executed is detected the processor branches to an interrupt-response routine that causes the processor state to be saved and initiates execution of an interrupt-service routine identified by the particular interrupt signal. The input/output subsystem must provide interrupt signals for each peripheral device to identify the nature and the priority level of any interrupts that can be initiated by that device. Usually the interrupt signal is generated in the device controllers. In large- and medium-size computers interrupt-signal detection and response mechanisms are included in the central-processor control logic.

For microprocessor-based systems standard interrupt controllers like the Intel 8259A shown in Fig. 7-14(a) are available. The interrupt controller is connected to the control, data, and address lines of a system bus. Control and status information is exchanged with the data bus through the data bus buffer. The read/write logic unit receives commands from the central processor and controls transfer of status information to the data bus. An interrupt-mask register allows for program control of the interrupt responses. Interrupt requests from the peripheral devices are accepted and, if not masked, passed to the priority-resolver circuits so that the interrupt-service register can hold the identity of interrupt requests that are being serviced. The INT output signals the central processor that an interrupt signal should be responded to and the central processor acknowledges receipt of the interrupt signal by transmitting INTA. The processor then services the highest-priority interrupt found in the interrupt-service register by executing an interrupt trap and a CALL of the service routine designated by the interrupt controller. Most standard interrupt controllers are expandable to allow for more requests. In this example up to eight additional 8259s can be connected in cascade, as shown in Fig. 7-14(b), to handle a total of 64 interrupts.

In Chapter 3 switches and links to connect modules of a computer system were discussed. Links were shown as single lines on the paper, but it was noted that a much larger quantity of physical wire interconnections are involved. In some cases the width of the link was identified by showing the number of lines. The control information and status information required to be transferred on the links were not specified.

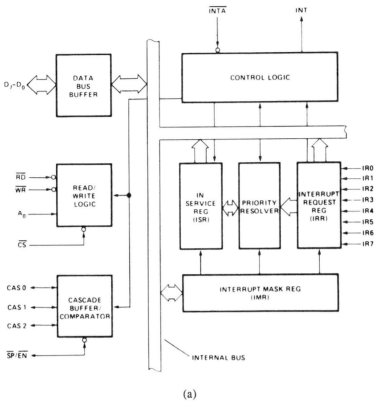

(a)

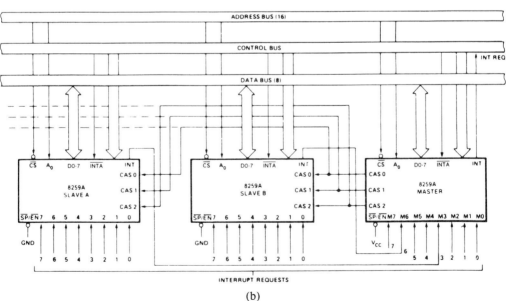

(b)

Figure 7-14 Intel 8259A programmable interrupt controller. (a) Block diagram. (b) Cascading the 8259A. (Copyright 1979, Intel Corp., reprinted with permission.)

Examination of a representative link reveals that usually there is a lot more than just the data to be transferred. The DEC VAX-11/780 synchronous backplane interconnect (SBI) bus of Fig. 7-15 will serve as an example.

The SBI is a bus to which the central processor, the primary memory, and two groups of input/output controllers (UNIBUS and MASSBUS) are connected. The SBI consists of 84 signal lines with the functions shown in the figure. In addition to the 32 information lines (B<31:0>) with the associated parity (P<1:0>), tag (TAG<2:0>), identifier (ID<4:0>), and mask (M<3:0>) lines, we see arbitration lines (TR<15:0>) to establish a fixed priority level for access to the information path, response lines (FAULT and confirmation, CNF<1:0>), control lines (UNJAM, FAIL, DEAD signal, INTERLOCK, and six CLOCK lines), interrupt-request lines (REQ<7:4>), giving a priority order for interrupt requests, and ALERT), multiport-memory control lines (MP<1:0>), and two spares. Any transmit/receive device (called a NEXUS) connected to the SBI can initiate a transfer by acquiring the bus (according to its arbitration priority) and transmitting the first transfer in a data exchange. Each transfer in an exchange takes place in a clock time and contains all the information needed to accomplish connection arbitration, information transfer, or transfer confirmation. The SBI allows transfers of up to 13.3 Mbytes/s. There is no separate bus controller.

The VAX 8600 and 8650 also use the synchronous backplane interconnect. Other members of the VAX 8000 family use one to four VAXbus interconnects (VAXBI). The VAXBI is a 32-bit synchronous bus that transfers address, data, and control information in successive 200-ns time periods.

In Fig. 7-16 the two input/output buses of VAX computers are shown. The UNIBUS connection between the UNIBUS controller (a DMA controller for word or byte transfers) and multiple low-speed peripheral devices has 56 lines: addresses (18 lines), data (16 lines), data control (6 lines), bus controls (13 lines), and initialization (3 lines). The MASSBUS

```
{Transmit/Receive NEXUS (Physical Connection)}
     SBI<83..0>,                    {Numbering only for Description}
{Bus Arbitration Group}
     TR<15..0> := SBI<83..68>,      {Transfer Request}
{Information Transfer Group}
     P<1,0> := SBI<67,66>,          {Parity}
     TAG<2..0> := SBI<65..63>,      {Information Tag}
     ID<4..0> := SBI<62..58>,       {Source/Destination Identity}
     M<3..0> := SBI<57..54>,        {Mask}
     B<31..0> := SBI<53..22>,       {Information}
{Response Group}
     FAULT := SBI<21>,              {Response Fault}
     CNF<1,0> := SBI<20,19>,        {Transfer Confirmation}
{Control Group}
     UNJAM := SBI<18>,              {Unjam (CPU console only)}
     FAIL := SBI<17>,               {AC Power Low}
     DEAD := SBI<16>,               {Power Failure}
     INTERLOCK := SBI<15>,          {Control Interlock}
     CLOCK<5..0> := SBI<14..9>,     {Universal Clock}
{Interrupt Request Group}
     REQ<7..4>:= SBI<8..5>,         {Interrupt Request}
     ALERT := SBI<4>,               {Alert (no interrupt request)}
{Miscellaneous}
     MP<1..0> := SBI<3,2>,          {Multiport Memory}
     SP<1..0> := SBI<1,0>,          {Spare}
```

Figure 7-15   VAX system backplane interconnect (SBI).

```
{Unibus Signal Lines}
     UB<55..0>,                        {Numbering only for Description}
{Address Lines}
     AD<17..0> := UB<55..38>,          {Device Address, <-}
{Data Lines}
     DA<15..0> := UB<37..22>,          {Data Signals, <-->}
{Data Control Group}
     CO<1,0> := UB<21,20>,             {Data Control, <-->}
     MSYN := UB<19>,                   {Master Synchronization, <-->}
     SSYN := UB<18>,                   {Slave Synchronization, <-->}
     PA,PB := UB<17,16>,               {Device Parity, <-->}
{Bus Control Group}
     BR<7..4> := UB<15..12>,           {Bus Requests, ->}
     BG<7..4> := UB<11..8>,            {Bus Grant, <-}
     NPR := UB<7>,                     {Nonprocessor Request, ->}
     NPG := UB<6>,                     {Nonprocessor Grant, <-}
     SACK := UB<5>,                    {Slave Acknowledge, ->}
     INTR := UB<4>,                    {Interrrupt, ->}
     BBSY := UB<3>,                    {Bus Busy, <-->}
{Initialization Group}
     INIT := UB<2>,                    {Initialize, <-}
     ACLO := UB<1>,                    {Line Voltage Low, <-->}
     DCLO := UB<0>,                    {DC Voltage Low, <-}

{Note- Signal direction: <- "to device", -> "from device", <--> "either".}
```

(a)

```
{Massbus Signal Lines}
     MB<53..0>,                        {Numbering only for Description}
     CB<30..0> := MB<53..23>,          {Control Bus}
     DB<22..0> := MB<22..0>,           {Data Bus}
{Control Bus Lines}
     CS<15..0> := CB<30..15>,          {Control/Status Signals, <-->}
     CPA := CB<14>,                    {Control-Bus Parity, <-->}
     DS<2..0> := CB<13..11>,           {Drive Select, <-}
     RS<4..0> := CB<10..6>,            {Register Select, <-}
     CTOD := CB<5>,                    {Transfer Direction, <-}
     DEM := CB<4>,                     {Demand, <-}
     TRA := CB<3>,                     {Transfer Data, ->}
     ATTN := CB<2>,                    {Attention (Status Change), ->}
     INIT := CB<1>,                    {Initialize Devices, <-}
     FAIL := CB<0>,                    {Power Not Available, <-}
{Data Bus Lines}
     DA<15..00> := DB<22..7>,          {Data Signals, <-->}
     DPA := DB<6>,                     {Data Parity, <-->}
     SCLK := DB<5>,                    {Synchronize Clock,->}
     WCLK := DB<4>,                    {Write Clock, <-}
     RUN := DB<3>,                     {Start, Continue, Stop, <-}
     EBL := DB<2>,                     {End of Block, ->}
     EXC := DB<1>,                     {Exception (Error), <-->}
     OCC := DB<0>,                     {Occupied (Command Accepted), ->}

{Note- Signal direction: <- "to device", -> "from device", <--> "either".}
```

(b)

Figure 7-16   VAX (a) UNIBUS and (b) MASSBUS lines.

controller (a DMA controller for block transfers) has 54 connections to high-speed secondary-memory-device controllers. The connections are for the control bus (31 lines) and the data bus (23 lines). A MASSBUS controller can transfer data at a rate of 1.3 Mbytes/s.

Whereas most large computer systems use switches and links uniquely designed for each individual architecture, there are standard bus designs that permit the semiconductor suppliers to offer standard bus controllers and bus arbiters and allow for standard interfaces for peripheral-device connections to computers. A simple standard interface is covered by the RS-232 specification for serial synchronous or asynchronous transmission of information. It is described in Section 7.5, which follows. Bus standards have been introduced for different computer-system applications.

A computer backplane bus is covered in IEEE Standard No. 796. It originated as the Intel Multibus for microcomputers. The standard includes specification of functional, electrical, and mechanical features of the high-speed bus. The assigned uses of the 86 signal lines are shown in Fig. 7-17. In addition to the 16 data lines (DATx) and the 20 address lines (ADRy), there are 16 control lines for data transfer and for bus scheduling and 9 interrupt controls (INTz and INTA). Power connection uses 22 lines and 3 are held in reserve. The functions are similar to those on the DEC SBI bus.

Another bus standard for computer systems is covered by IEEE Standard No. 696. This "S-100 bus" was designed initially for use with the Intel microprocessors. It has 100 signal lines and includes functions quite similar to those covered by the more recent IEEE Standard No. 796 of Fig. 7-17. A third IEEE standard, No. 488, covers buses for connecting electronic instruments to computers.

Standards for interconnection buses allow standard bus controls to be introduced. Since the two IEEE standards discussed evolved from Intel designs, it is to be

```
{Multibus Printed Board Connector}
    PC<1..86>,                                 {86-contact connector, 2-sided}
{Power Connections}
    GND  := PC<1,2,11,12,75,76,85,86>,         {Signal Ground, common connection}
    PLUS5  := PC<3..6,81..84>,                 {+ 5 volts dc, common connection}
    PLUS12  := PC<7,8>,                        {+12 volts dc, common connection}
    MINUS12  := PC<79,80>,                     {-12 volts dc, common connection}
{Address Bus}
    AD<23..0> := PC<9,10,77,78,28,30,
      32,34,44,43,46,45,48,47,50,49,
      52,51,54,53,56,55,58,57>,                {Address Lines}
{Data Bus}
    DA<15..0>  := PC<60,59,62,61,64,63,
      66,65,68,67,70,69,72,71,74,73>, {Data Lines}
{Data Transfer Commands}
    MDRC := PC<19>,                            {Memory Read Enable}
    MWTC := PC<20>,                            {Memory Write Enable}
    IORC := PC<21>,                            {I/O Read Enable}
    IOWC := PC<22>,                            {I/O Write Enable}
    XACK := PC<23>,                            {Acknowledge}
{Bus Control}
    BCLK := PC<13>,                            {Bus Clock}
    BPRN := PC<15>,                            {Bus Priority In}
    BPRO := PC<16>,                            {Bus Priority Out}
    BUSY := PC<17>,                            {Bus Busy}
    BREQ := PC<18>,                            {Bus Request}
    CBRQ := PC<29>,                            {Common Bus Request}
{Interrupt Control}
    INT<0..7> := PC<41,42,39,40,
                    37,38,35,36>,              {Interrupt Request}
    INTA := PC<33>,                            {Interrupt Acknowledge}
{Miscellaneous Control}
    INIT := PC<14>,                            {Initialize System}
    INH<1,2> := PC<24,26>,                     {Inhibit Memory}
    LOCK := PC<25>,                            {Lock Bus}
    BHEN := PC<27>,                            {Byte High Enable}
    CCLK := PC<31>,                            {System Clock}

        {Note- All signal lines are enabled in the zero state.}
```

Figure 7-17   IEEE Standard No. 796 (Intel Multibus).

expected that there are Intel controllers for those buses. The 8288 bus controller shown in Fig. 7-18 can be used to control transfers over a variety of buses like the Intel Multibus. It has two modes, one for an input/output bus and one for a system bus. If arbitration is desired of potential conflicts on a system bus like the Multibus, the 8289 bus arbiter of Fig. 7-19 can be introduced. The bus arbiter synchronizes use of a bus by multiple Intel 8086/8088 microprocessors and 8089 I/O processors. It is used with the bus controller of Fig. 7-18.

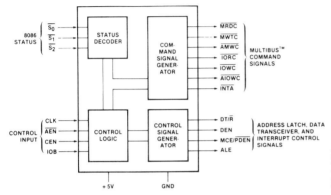

Figure 7-18 Intel 8288 bus controller. (Copyright 1979, Intel Corp., reprinted with permission.)

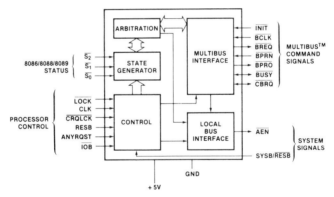

Figure 7-19 Intel 8289 bus arbiter. (Copyright 1979, Intel Corp., reprinted with permission.)

7.5 INPUT/OUTPUT PROCESSORS

We can provide another step in increased flexibility and in independence of input/output operation by introducing an input/output processor. This processor controls the different input/output activities by executing programs held in primary memory. Input/output programs can be written in assembly language or in higher-level languages. They can be developed by users or supplied with the operating system. An I/O processor has even more flexibility than the microprogrammable controller with programs written in microcode and executed as system-level routines selectable by the user. However, the differences between the microprogrammable controller and a full input/output processor in providing for input/output operation under operating system control are small.

The microprogrammable controller, as represented by the MC68120 intelligent peripheral controller of Fig. 7-9, can be compared with a microcomputer input/output processor, the Intel 8089 of Fig. 7-20. The I/O processor includes a small arithmetic and logic unit that executes add, logical, increment/decrement, move, and control instructions. Transformation and error detection/correction can be performed on transferred data. Bus control and bus arbitration are controlled by the I/O processor. The 8089 has its own fetch-execute cycle and is similar in operation to other microprocessors. (A partial ISP description of the 8089 was shown in Fig. 2-9.) There are two I/O channels, each with a channel control and a register file. Each register file contains four 20-bit address registers and four 16-bit control registers (index, byte count, mask/compare, channel control) available to the users. A 20-bit parameter pointer in each channel is not seen by users. A single channel-control pointer is shared by the channels.

A computer using the 8089 I/O processor and an Intel 8086 as its central processor (Fig. 7-21) includes a clock generator, a bus controller, and sufficient latches and transceivers to hold information to be placed on the address and data buses. Communication between the input/output processor and the central processor is through primary memory except for the I/O initiation signal that is placed on the 8089's channel-attention (CA) line by the 8086 and the local bus control line (RQ/GT). The latter operates in the same manner as the bus-request line of Fig. 7-11. The input/output processor, once I/O

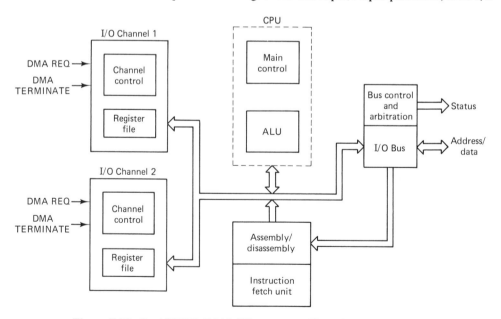

Figure 7-20 Intel 8089 8-/16-bit I/O processor. (Copyright 1979, Intel Corp., reprinted with permission.)

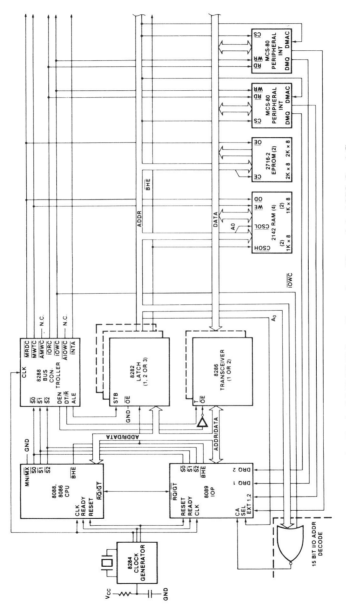

Figure 7-21 Typical 8086/8089 configuration. (Copyright 1979, Intel Corp., reprinted with permission.)

277

is initiated, reads 5 bytes that the central processor placed in a fixed shared memory location and branches to the program designated for the particular input/output operation. The input or output operation itself is performed by a peripheral controller. After completion of the I/O transfer, the 8089 signals I/O completion to the 8086. An interrupt controller can be added (see Fig. 7-14) for interrupt-based process synchronization.

The Intel 8089 is representative of input/output processors for large as well as small systems. Similar activities, albeit on a much larger scale, are performed by the input/output processors for the large systems. A major feature of the IBM System/360 over its predecessors was the use of a specialized processor for input/output. This processor, called a channel, in the System/370 is called the external data controller (EXDC). In the System/370 the central processor provides overall direction to the EXDC by executing one of 10 I/O instructions, such as START I/O and TEST CHANNEL. Control is passed to the EXDC by identifying a block of channel-command words in primary memory. These are executed in the EXDC to control individual transfers of data to and from memory. The channel-command word is a 64-bit double word with an 8-bit command code, a 24-bit data address in memory, 8 flag bits for condition codes, and a 16-bit data-length count.

The external data controller is implemented in different ways in the different System/370 models. In the 308X (Fig. 3-4) it is controlled by a channel-processing element, a microprogrammed input/output processor that executes the channel-command words held in primary memory. The channel-processing element controls up to 24 peripheral device controllers, 8 through each of 3 data-server elements (tree-structured switches with buffer registers). In the 3090 (Fig. 7-22) channel processing is distributed over the I/O processor, the primary data stager, the secondary data stager, and the channels (up to 48 for each EXDC). The I/O processor executes pageable vertical microcode to interact with the central processors by receiving instructions and posting interrupts.

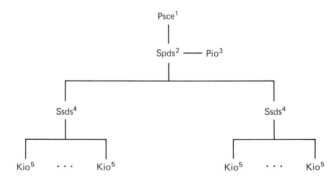

1. Psce\"System_Control_Element" {Not part of the Channel Subsystem}.
2. Spds\"Primary_Data_Stager" {Buffer for 2 Ssds}.
3. Pio\"I/O_Processor" (general_I/O_control, vertical_microcode).
4. Ssds\"Secondary_Data_Stager" {Buffer for up to 24 channels}.
5. Kio\"Channel" (peripheral_device_control, horizontal_microcode).

Figure 7-22 IBM 3090 channel subsystem.

Channel-control words are executed in the channels, which use horizontal microcode held in a writeable control store. The primary and secondary data stagers are speed-matching buffers and tree-structured switches, similar to those in the 308X. The system-control element is similar to the system controller of the 308X.

More comprehensive processing for input/output can be provided with standard components by using a standard microprocessor with switch control circuits to build an I/O-subsystem controller. For example, the Convex C-1 computer incorporates a Motorola MC 68000 microprocessor as its input/output processor. The Convex C-1 is shown in Fig. 7-23. The central system includes a powerful processor with separate instruction processing, address processing, and scalar and vector arithmetic units. A modular interleaved primary memory and a large cache memory provide storage. The input/output system is connected to primary memory through the P-Bus and the memory controller.

The input/output system itself is a Motorola MC68000-based computer with its own 512-kbyte primary memory, a 32-kbyte cache, a Multibus (IEEE Standard No. 796) switch, and a set of typical peripheral devices with individual controllers. The MC68000

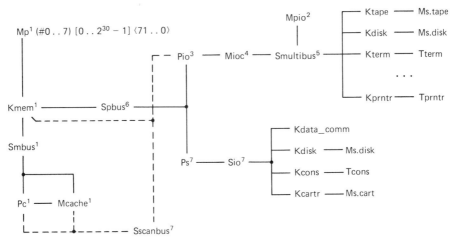

1. "Convex_C-1_Central System" (components: Mp (4-way_interleave, 100 ns_cycle), Kmem (DMA_control), Smbus (transfer_rate: 80 Mbytes/s, word_size: 72 bits {64 data, 8 parity}), Pc (components: "Instruction_Processing_Unit", "Address_and_Scalar_Unit", "Address_Translator Unit", 2 "Vector_Processing_Units", "Vector_Control_Unit"), Mcache\"Physical_Cache_Unit" (word_size: 36 bits, size: 2^{14} words, cycle_time: 50 ns)).
2. Mpio[0..2^{19}-1] <7..0>.
3. Pio {10-Mhz M68000 microprocessor}.
4. Mioc\"I/O_Cache" (function: bus-to-bus_buffer, size: 32 kbytes).
5. Smultibus\"Multibus" (capacity: 32 device_controllers).
6. Spbus\"P-Bus" (speed: 80 Mbytes/s).
7. "Diagnostic_and_Service_Subsystem" (components: Sio, Sscanbus {bypasses P-Bus for system diagnosis}, Ps\"Service_Processor_Unit").

Figure 7-23 Convex C-1 system.

is a standard microprocessor and its use as an input/output processor is determined only by the programs it executes. These programs, held in Mpio, consist of the executive (operating system) and device drivers. The central processor sends an interrupt signal to the Pio, causing it to read an I/O instruction from a message queue in primary memory. The device driver associated with the particular I/O activity required is called and executed by the Pio. Speed buffering for the peripheral devices is accomplished in Miocache. Another MC68000 processor is used for diagnosis and service, executing diagnostic programs held in Mp. It uses a separate switch (Sscanbus) to permit the Spbus to be included in the diagnoses.

When the input/output operations involve communication with remote devices or systems, another set of processing requirements is introduced. Each form of communication has a set of protocols that establishes the connection, identifies the sender and the receiver, synchronizes the transfers, checks for errors, and terminates the connection. A discussion of communication at the system level is included in Chapter 3. Here we are concerned with the processing needed at the interface between the computer and the communications network.

Standards for communication include rates of information transmission. These range from 300 to 9600 bits/s on standard lines with standard modems (modulator/demodulators) and to much higher rates on dedicated or local-area-network lines. Electrical connections and means for making and for breaking a connection are included in standards like the EIA (Electronics Industry Association) RS-232-C (internationally, CCITT v.24). Low-speed data communication that is conducted byte by byte with any amount of time greater than 1 or 2 bit times allowed between bytes is termed *asynchronous* communication. To conserve bandwidth (channel capacity), high-speed communication is performed in blocks of bits without spaces between and is termed *synchronous*. Blocks of information are preceded with headers for identification and for addressing and with synchronizing bit sequences for timing. They are terminated with standard bit groups that signal the end of a block. With asynchronous communication the standard code is the USASCII/ISO code that we saw in Fig. 7-2. This code has a 7-bit data field and a parity bit. A character (byte) is preceded by a "start" bit and succeeded by 1 or 2 "stop" bits. Synchronous communication (without breaks between characters or words) might use streams of ASCII/ISO code bytes or might just use streams of bits to be interpreted by the user(s).

Even with simple point-to-point (two-user) single-link (two-wire) communication under RS-232-C standards, a large number of signals might be required between the computer control (called *data communication equipment*) and the remote terminal (*data terminal equipment*). The RS-232-C standard is applicable to asynchronous and synchronous communication. Standard signals on the 24-pin connector are shown in Fig. 7-24. Not all signals are required with any one interface (for example, the connection always might be made rather than being dialed) and those not needed are ignored. The basic signals are: transmitted data (BA), received data (BB), request to send (CA), clear to send (CB), data set ready (CC), data terminal ready (CE), and received line signal detector (CF). Secondary signals (SBA, SBB, SCA, SCB, and SCF) are for a second link to a terminal device. A computer data-communications controller must provide for all of the signals that are required.

EIA ID	CCITT ID	Pin	Function
AA	101	1	Protective Ground
AB	102	7	Signal Ground (common)
BA	103	2	Transmitted Data
BB	104	3	Received Data
CA	105	4	Request to Send
CB	106	5	Clear to Send
CC	107	6	Data Set Ready
CD	108.2	20	Data Terminal Ready
CE	125	22	Ring Indicator
CF	109	8	Received Line Signal Detector
CG	110	21	Signal-Quality Detector
CH	111	23a	Computer Data-Signal Rate Detector
CI	112	23b	Terminal Data-Signal Rate Detector
DA	113	24	Terminal Transmitter-Signal Element Timing
DB	114	15	Computer Transmitter-Signal Element Timing
DD	115	17	Terminal Receiver-Signal Element Timing
SBA	118	14	Secondary Transmitted Data
SBB	119	16	Secondary Received Data
SCA	120	19	Secondary Request to Send
SCB	121	13	Secondary Clear to Send
SCF	122	12	Secondary Received Line-Signal Indicator
		9, 10	Test Pins
		11, 18, 25	Spare

Figure 7-24   RS-232-C connector assignments.

Standards for synchronous communication of groups of bytes are available. There are no start and stop bits between bytes and synchronization must be established at the beginning of a bit stream using special characters. The USASCII character stream standard for such communication entails sending a sequence of SYN characters (10010110 with even parity; see Fig. 7-2) before and between groups of message characters. This standard is used for both point-to-point and multipoint (where all users are attached all the time) communication systems.

Most multipoint data communication now uses the International Standards Organization (ISO) v.25 high-level data-link control (HDLC) protocol or variations of it. The more popular variations include synchronous data-link control (SDLC) and advanced data-communication control procedure (ADCCP). In all of these synchronous communication protocols continuous streams of bits are transmitted rather than streams of characters. Special groups of bits must be placed in the continuous bit stream to signal the beginning and the end of sequences of data and control bits. In HDLC the beginning and the end of a message "frame" are indicated by the unique flag code 01111110 repeated 0 or more times. The sequence of six 1's is unique because a transmitting controller inserts a dummy 0 after a sequence of five 1's and a receiving controller strips the first 0 that follows five successive 1's. The extra 0's and the flag code are not passed on to the computer receiving the message. Address and control codes of 8 bits each are followed by the text of packed bits. The text is followed by a 16-bit cyclic redundancy check field for error detection. With this protocol the groups of bits in a message can be of any size required by the computer(s) involved. The data-communication interface controller separates the long bit string into the appropriate groups.

Data-communications interface processing is more extensive than most input/output control, but the requirements for any protocol are well defined. Special-purpose controllers or processors of several degrees of flexibility (and cost) can be used. The processing might be performed by a hard-wired controller, by a microprogrammed communications controller, by a special-purpose communications processor, or by a data-communications computer having its own memory. In all cases the controller or processor is managed by the central processor or by an I/O processor. Interrupt signals are used to advise the central processor that a message has arrived or that transmission of a message has been completed.

A simple controller for asynchronous communication (a universal asynchronous receiver-transmitter, UART) is shown in Fig. 7-25. The UART is similar to a peripheral-device controller in its interface to the data, address, and control buses, and its data-buffer register. Controls include the selection of one of two registers (status or receiver) for reading (RD) or one of two others (transmitter or control) for writing (WR). Shift registers are used for serial input (receive data) or output (transmit data) at the modem (modulator-demodulator) interface. These registers transfer bytes in parallel to or from the data-buffer register. Transmitter and receiver pulses are synchronized with clocks in the transmitter and receiver controllers.

Standard UART, universal synchronous receiver-transmitter (USRT), and universal synchronous/asynchronous receiver-transmitter (USART) controllers are made by the semiconductor manufacturers. The Intel 8251A programmable communications interface shown in Fig. 7-26 accommodates a variety of asynchronous and synchronous protocols. (Like the Intel controllers of Figs. 7-6 through 7-8, it does not

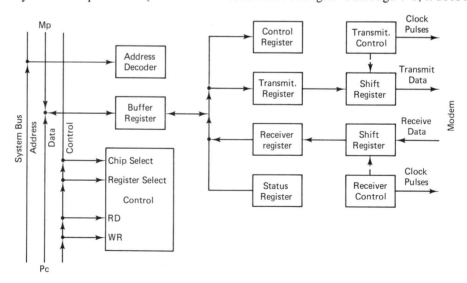

Figure 7-25 A simple universal asynchronous receiver-transmitter.

BLOCK DIAGRAM

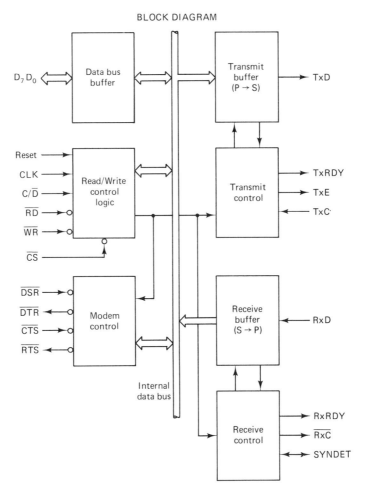

Figure 7-26 Intel 8251A programmable communication interface. (Copyright 1979, Intel. Corp., reprinted with permission.)

execute a program.) It is similar to the UART of Fig. 7-25, except that it handles both synchronous and asynchronous communication of 5- to 8-bit characters. Transmission rates can be up to 19.2 kbits/s in the asynchronous mode and to 64 kbits/s in the synchronous mode. This enhanced USART has error-checking and status-code transmission capability and operates under control of the central processor.

The National Semiconductor NS32490 network interface controller can be used to connect a computer to a high-bandwidth local area network (discussed in Chapter 3). It has dual DMA channels and an internal queue for transfer of packets of information meeting IEEE Standard No. 802.3. A block diagram of the controller is shown in Fig. 7-27. The receiver deserializer is activated when an input carrier signal (RXD, synchronized to the receiver carrier, RXC) is sensed. It takes the serial

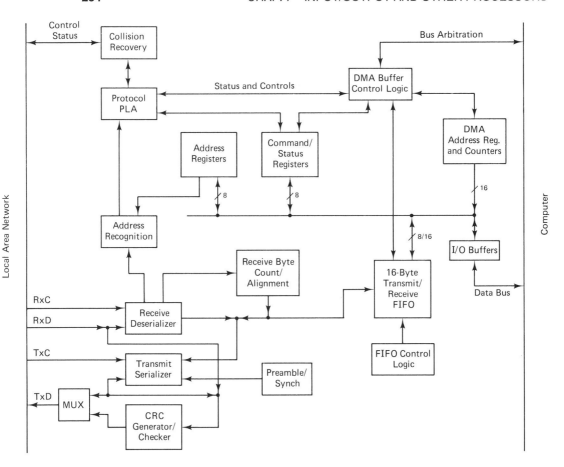

Figure 7-27   NS32490 network interface controller.

pulses and transmits them in 8-bit parallel bytes to the address-recognition logic or to the receive-byte logic. The transmit serializer operates in the reverse manner, taking bytes of data or preamble/synch information and transmitting them as a serial-bit stream (TXD) synchronized to the transmitter carrier (TXC). The cyclic redundancy count (CRC) generator/checker checks for errors in the incoming data (RXD) or generates the CRC byte for outgoing messages (TXD). The 16-byte receive/transmit FIFO (data queue) holds information while packets are formed (output) or decomposed (input). This queue acts as a speed buffer between the internal and external transfers. Memory addresses are held in the DMA-address registers, while the DMA counters maintain a count of bytes in a message (packet). The I/O buffer is a register to hold a word from or to the data bus. The controls include address-recognition logic, address and command-status registers, FIFO control logic, DMA-buffer control logic, and the PLA for communications protocol control. The NS32490 is a sophisticated processor with over 40 registers. It typifies current communications microprocessors.

7.6 MEMORY PROCESSORS

Input-output activities impose requirements for some processing at the connection between memory and the input/output or system bus to resolve conflicts for memory access and to permit "cycle stealing" by input/output devices. As the systems we consider are expanded to include multiple input/output processors, multiple central processors, and special-purpose processors, all having access to primary memory, the processing required at the memory interface becomes more extensive.

When cache memories are introduced there is a requirement for management of cache/primary-memory interaction. The existence of multiple processes, all addressing memory asynchronously, leads to the need for memory protection provided by a combination of operating-system software and of registers that can be associated with memory addressing. Virtual-memory capability is available to even small computer systems and the mapping of virtual to physical memory requires processing that can be performed in the central processors or can be assigned to logic at the memory interface. Relative addressing can be implemented with base registers at the memory. If the system uses tagged memory then interpretation of the tags and further memory action such as indirect referencing can be performed without central-processor action. Error detection and error correction on memory transfers can be provided at the memory interface. All of these requirements build to the point that we might consider the use of another special-purpose processor for memory management.

When the switching mechanism for memory with multiple users is a crossbar or an inverse tree (see Chapter 3), resolution of conflicts for access can be provided by relatively simple logic at the memory itself. Multiport memory control entails hardware for locking out a request for access while the memory is performing a read or a write operation. The lockout might involve queuing of requests or can merely defer the request and require that the requester try again. A signal acknowledging receipt of the request (a memory address) might be useful for synchronizing multiple access requests. If the requests are queued the queue can be priority-sensitive, granting access to input/output processors before central-processor requests are serviced. The processing for multiport memory control is similar to the bus control that was described in the earlier section on that topic. When there are multiple memory modules a multiport controller must be associated with each module.

Error-detection and error-correction methods were discussed in Chapter 4. These functions must be implemented in the module at each end of every link over which communication needing the detection and correction is to be carried out. Error detection using parity checking is used for transfers between primary memory and processors in almost all computer systems. With high-performance computers single-bit error correction, using techniques like Hamming coding, might be required. Although error detection and error correction can be accomplished by processors executing instructions or microinstructions, these approaches take a significant amount of time. The electronic logic to perform the functions during transfers is relatively simple.

While the mapping from virtual to physical address space that was covered in Chapter 4 usually is carried out in the central processor, it can be separated from the virtual effective-address computations and performed as a part of memory addressing. Checks that physical-memory references are valid (within designated bounds) can be made at the same time. This combination of memory mapping and memory protection can be performed by a special-purpose memory processor that incorporates flexibility to handle a variety of memory-mapping rules and of memory-access permissions. The processor required to perform these functions must be fast but will execute only a small group of functions.

As with many of the other applications for special-purpose processors, we find standard microprocessor memory-management units that can be used in computer architectures. For example, the National Semiconductor NS32082 paged memory-management unit (MMU) is a memory controller that is designed to work with NS32032 central processors. This MMU provides hardware support for demand paged virtual memory, including address translation, page-access protection, and software debugging support. The central processor, while operating in privileged state, passes an instruction (from a very small set) for execution by the MMU. Since the central processor designates instructions to be executed, there is no instruction-fetch subcycle. A description of NS32082 operation serves as an example of how memory-control functions can be performed by a separate special-purpose processor.

The 32-bit word NS32082 MMU has five major sections: a hardware-debug block, a register-file block, the translation-buffer block, the control block, and an input/output block. The hardware-debug block contains the seven registers used for program analysis and hardware debugging. In the register-file block are three addressable registers and a group of hidden working registers. This block contains the processor state for virtual-physical memory translation and protection. A 32-word associative cache memory makes up the translation-buffer block, used by the register-file block. The control block has the state machines and combinatorial logic for hard-wired control of instruction execution. Buffers in the input/output block provide the interface to the address and control lines of the system bus.

An ISP description of the NS32082 is shown as Fig. 7-28. The memory-management-status register (MSR) specifies the operational mode and current processing status. It contains all of the flags and control bits needed for user control of address translation, breakpoint management, and program tracing. Two program-control registers (PF0, PF1) record the addresses of the two most recent nonsequential instructions. The sequential-count registers (SC0, SC1) record the number of sequential instructions executed since PF0 and PF1 were last changed. Values in these four registers permit tracing of program flow for hardware and software debugging. Breakpoint registers (BPR0, BPR1) record breakpoint addresses and conditions for system breaks. Bits 24 through 31 of these registers control the various conditions for system breaks and identify the addresses (physical or virtual) to be used for breakpoint comparisons. The breakpoint count register controls the number of breakpoints that should be ignored before the system break is generated. System breaks are initiated by sending an interrupt signal to the central processor. Program-flow analysis and the use of breakpoints were discussed in Section 6.5.

Data to the MMU are computer-memory addresses that are limited to 24 bits. For each active process the MMU uses two tables in primary memory, a 256-word page table,

```
{Pmmu State}
    PTB0<31..0>,                          {Page Table Base 0}
    PTB1<31..0>,                          {Page Table Base 1}
    EIA<31..0>,                           {Error/Invalid Address}
    MSR<31..0>,                           {Memory-Status Register}
    BPR0<31..0>,                          {Breakpoint 0}
    BPR1<31..0>,                          {Breakpoint 1}
    BCNT<31..0>, BCNT<31..24> := 00h,     {Breakpoint Count}
    PF0<31..0>, PF0<31..24> := 00h,       {Program Flow 0}
    PF1<31..0>, Pf1<31..24> := 00h,       {Program Flow 1}
    SC0<15..0>,                           {Sequential Count 0}
    SC1<15..0>,                           {Sequential Count 1}

{Data Formats (an Address is the Data for the MMU)}
    addr<31..0>, addr<31..24> := 00h,     {logical address}
    offset<8..0> := addr<8..0>,           {offset within a page}
    ptr_off<6..0> := addr<15..9>,         {offset within a pointer table}
    pge_off<7..0> := addr<23..16>,        {offset within a page table}

{Format of Tables in Primary  Memory}
    pge_tbl[0..255][3..0]<7..0>,          {4-byte entry for 256 processes,
                                           addressed by PTB0, PTB1 in MMU}
    ptr_tbl[0..127][3..0]<7..0>,          {4-byte entry for 128 processes,
                                           addressed by a page table entry}

{Table Entry}
    index := (pge_tbl[p]) & (p =: 0..255),{selection from a page table}
    index := (ptr_tbl[q]) & (q =: 0..127),{selection from a pointer table}
    entry<31..0> := index[3..0]<7..0>,    {entry in a page or pointer table}
    v := entry<0>,                        {valid bit, 1 if page is present}
    pl := entry<2,1>,                     {protection level:
                                             mode-  supervisor   user
                                           value:
                                             00       read       none
                                             01       r/w        none
                                             10       r/w        read
                                             11       r/w        r/w }
    r := entry<3>,                        {referenced, set if accessed}
    m := entry<4>,                        {modified, set if written to}
    frame<14..0> := entry<23..9>,         {frame number}
    entry<30..24,8..5> := 0000000,        {reserved}
    bs := entry<31>,                      {memory-bank selector}

{Physical Address Calculation}
    (phys_addr := Mp[Mp[PTBn + pge_off] @ ptr_off] @ offset) & (n =: 0..1),
```

Figure 7-28   National Semiconductor NS32082 MMU.

and a 128-word pointer table that is pointed to by entries in the page table. Each table entry is a 32-bit word with bits assigned as shown in Fig. 7-28. Two page-table base registers (PTB0, PTB1) specify the base addresses of the page tables used in address translation. One register specifies the base for user mode and the other that for supervisor mode. The error/invalidate address (EIA) holds a virtual address that has generated an MMU exception, and when written into, removes page table entries from a translation buffer (not shown in Fig. 7-28).

The translation buffer is a fast content-addressable memory. The buffer holds the 15 higher-order bits of the virtual address and of the physical address, as well as two control bits. The cache permits physical locations for any virtual address to be read immediately if the physical frame number is already in the cache. If not, a reference to the page table is made to find the frame number. DMA capability is included to synchronize memory references with other processors.

Only six instructions are used in memory management. Two, for moving values between supervisor and user space, are executed by the central processor. The MMU can execute any of the other four after it is received from the central processor. These "slave" instructions are validate address for reading (RDVAL) or for writing (WRVAL), load MMU register (LMR), and store MMU register (SMU). The validation instructions are for providing memory protection and the register instructions are for reading or writing values in any of the 10 addressable registers. All other operations are built into the control hardware.

Just as we find a place for special-purpose processors at the primary memory, there are opportunities to incorporate processing at the interfaces with secondary memories. An example is a disk file queue processor for use with head-per-track disk drives. The queue processor maintains a queue of access requests and compares these with the current disk-segment addresses to permit accesses to be granted as the addressed segments arrive at the heads, rather than taking the requests in the order they were initiated. When there is a large amount of disk file activity, a queue processor of this type can mask much of the latency time of disk accesses. Of course, when there are relatively few requests very little is gained through use of the queued access methods.

Much more extensive processing is needed to implement a special-purpose processor for database management. Database machines have been proposed to relieve the central processor of some of the database-search functions. In the conventional approach using the central processor (host processor) the database-management system defines the database and the operations on it. An application request (query or modification of the database) is presented in the chosen query language and translated to the host machine language. The operating system running on the host processor controls access to the large database that is in disk files. A large amount of processor time is devoted to execution of details of database management and of data-file access.

In Fig. 7-29 a "back-end" database processor is introduced to perform the correlations required to map requests by name for information to the physical locations in the disk files. The database processor, which might be a general-purpose processor programmed for the purpose or might be specialized to the database-management functions, performs access validation, address translation, I/O request initiation, and maintenance of query and error statistics. The host processor has been relieved of all but the application-request (query language) activities. A disk-file controller with queuing to synchronize addressing of multiple disk accesses manages the physical data files.

An intelligent controller using associative processing can facilitate processing of disk-file requests. In this approach the database-management system is executed in the back-end processor and mapping from virtual to physical addressing for file access is handled in the intelligent controller. In some experimental systems very large associative processors such as the Goodyear STARAN (covered in Chapter 9) have been employed as intelligent controllers. This also appears to be a potential application area for data-controlled processing, also covered in Chapter 9.

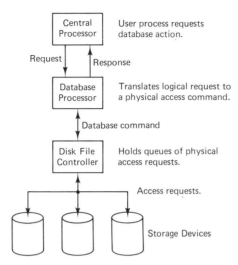

Figure 7-29 Database management processing.

7.7 "HARDWARE ENGINES"

There are many other opportunities for addition of special-purpose processors to a computer system. "Front-end" processing might entail special formatting and data-structure preparation prior to large-scale matrix processing. Special arithmetic processors might be provided as "back-end" processors to support general-purpose machines in specialized applications. Some applications might have very unique processing requirements and the need for general-purpose data manipulation might be relatively small.

One characteristic of the requirements that warrant consideration of a special-purpose processor is stability of the problem environment. If the requirements for computation can be established with little expectation of change and if the algorithms for solution of the computational problems are rigid, then there can be performance advantages in a special-purpose processor. Occasionally there is processing that requires such a high level of performance that it is not feasible to provide a general-purpose computer programmed to solve the problems. Sometimes a specialized processing requirement is needed only as an option for certain users of a family of computers. In any of these situations special-purpose approaches to processor design should be considered.

Special-purpose processors can incorporate specialization in the function units, in the registers for data structures to be processed, in the controls that implement register transfers, or in any combination of these three areas. A simple example of specialized function units is the provision of an optional floating-point arithmetic unit to be added to a computer as an alternative to programmed floating-point operations. As an alternative, we might provide microprogrammed floating-point operations as an option. In either case additional registers to hold the floating-point data can be included in the option.

In Fig. 7-30 we see an example of a large special-purpose scientific processor, the Floating Point Systems FPS 164. It is a scalar pipeline array processor that uses the IEEE floating-point arithmetic standard in the extended 64-bit format. The processor contains a local (main) memory for instructions and another, the table memory, for data. Four 256-word instruction caches and a 256-instruction subroutine stack allow short loops to be executed without further memory reference. There are three arithmetic units, an integer unit for effective address computation, a floating-point multiplier, and a floating-point adder. Three banks of registers, X and Y banks with 32 floating-point words each, and the 64-word address-register bank, feed the arithmetic units and receive results.

The FPS 164 is connected to a host computer and to secondary memory by its I/O bus. Main and local memories can be loaded from disk files and results can be transferred to the disk files over this fast bus. The FPS 164 can be viewed as an arithmetic coprocessor for a large host computer, or a small host can be treated as its input/output processor.

Applications for arithmetic processors of these kinds include calculations of fast Fourier transforms in signal processing, signal routing using Lee's algorithm for computer-aided circuit layout, and matrix inversion and multiplication in scientific processing. To attain the same levels of performance in these applications general-purpose processors would have to operate with much faster circuits than can be used in the special-purpose processors.

The Motorola MC68881 floating-point coprocessor (Fig. 7-31) is another example of a special-purpose arithmetic processor. This coprocessor operates in conjunction with the general-purpose MC68020 32-bit processor. The coprocessor communicates with the central processor, with memory, and with memory-mapped I/O over the system bus. A PMS diagram showing a typical system incorporating the coprocessor was shown in Fig. 3-25. As seen by the programmer, Fig. 7-31(a), the MC6881 has eight floating-point registers corresponding with the combined data and address registers of the MC68020. Instructions use the same register references as would be needed if the coprocessor was not present. The programming model also includes 32-bit control, status, and instruction-address registers.

Figure 7-31(b) is a block diagram of the MC68881. The bus-interface unit (BIU) contains eight coprocessor interface registers (CIRs) whose functions are described by their names, the register-selection and -control circuits, a status register, and a PLA for decoding conditions and status for the response register. Execution of floating-point instructions is initiated by a signal from the central processor received in the coprocessor interface register. The microinstruction control unit (MCU) uses vertical microcode and horizontal nanocode, similar to the MC68000 described in Chapter 6. The microprogram address is decoded by the microPC PLA and the instruction is decoded in an instruction decode PLA. The two are combined to select a microinstruction in the microROM. The microinstruction selects from the nanoROM a nanoinstruction that provides the control signals for the execution unit (ECU). The ECU is a conventional floating-point processor with data registers, a barrel shifter, a constant-value ROM, temporary registers, a shifter, and an ALU. The MC68881 implements the IEEE floating-point arithmetic standard. A queue (microPC stack) of microinstructions is kept in the MCU for execution of short loops without the need for PLA decoding.

Most microprocessor families include arithmetic coprocessors since many of the applications for the families do not require fast arithmetic processing. For those applications floating-point operations are programmed (or microprogrammed) in the central

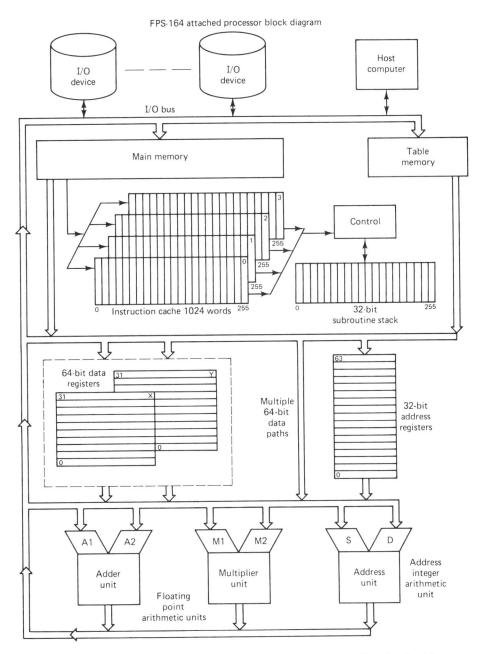

Figure 7-30 Floating Point Systems FPS 164 processor. (Reprinted with permission of Floating Point Systems, Inc.)

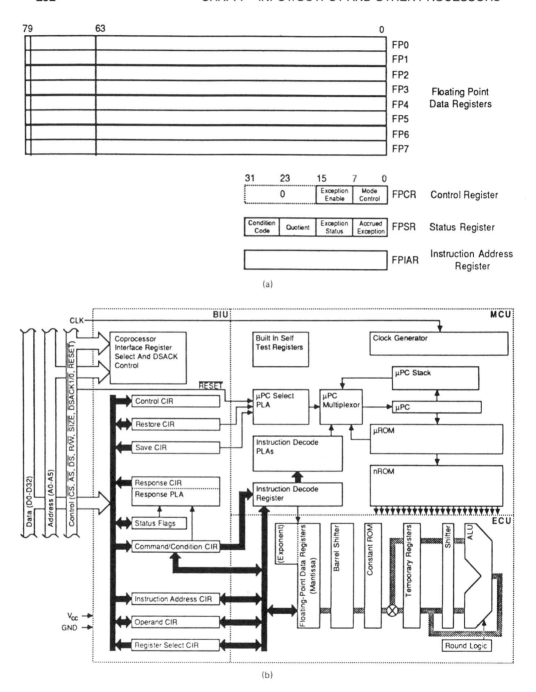

Figure 7-31   Motorola MC68881 floating-point coprocessor. (a) Programming model. (b) Simplified block diagram. (Courtesy of Motorola, Inc.)

processor. The arithmetic coprocessor can be designed into the applications that need high-speed floating-point operations or can be added to systems as an optional feature. The Intel 8087 arithmetic processor was an optional feature in many personal computers that used the Intel 8088 or 8086 as the central processor.

The Convex C-1 system was shown in Fig. 7-2, and we saw that the I/O processor of this system is a MC68000 microprocessor. It is interesting to see how the central processor of the system is organized and to specifically examine the features of its vector processor. In Fig. 7-23 five different processing elements were identified as parts of the central processor: instruction-processing unit, address and scalar unit, address-translation unit, vector-control unit, and two vector-processing units. Each of these might be called a special-purpose processor since each performs specific functions and communicates with the others over a bus. The instruction-processing unit fetches, decodes, and dispatches instructions to the address and scalar unit or the vector-control unit. Instructions are queued in an attempt to mask instruction-fetch times. The address and scalar unit is a 64-bit microprogram-controlled processor with eight 32-bit registers (a stack pointer and seven address registers, which also can hold single-precision data values), eight 64-bit accumulators to hold double-precision (longword) values, and a conventional ALU. Logical-to-physical address translation, including access control, is conducted in the address-translation unit, which contains eight 32-bit segment-description registers and an invisible cache.

Vector operations are executed in the vector processors. Each vector-processing unit contains four vector accumulators of 128 64-bit words and three D operators, one for simple vector operations (add, subtract, logical), one for complex (multiply, divide) operations, and one for memory operators. The vector-control unit has a vector-length register of 8 bits (7 significant) a 32-bit vector-stride (distance between elements) register and a vector-merge bit mask register of 128 bits, one for each element in a vector accumulator. An instruction involving vector operations is passed by the instruction processor to the vector-control unit. The instruction specifies the operation code and an entry address, the designation of the vector processor and the vector accumulator(s) to be used. When the D operator for the operation in the selected processor is free, the instruction is passed to that vector processor for execution. The vector processors can perform vector-vector or vector-scalar numeric, logical, compare, and move operations. The Convex C-1 appears to use a conventional processor as its Pio and a very specialized organization for its Pc.

A vector facility is offered as an optional addition to large IBM System/370 processors. The vector facility is attached to the instruction and execution elements of a central processor. It is an added instruction-execution processor with registers and a pipelined ALU for processing streams of data. As shown in the ISP diagram of Fig. 7-32, there are 16 vector registers, each of Z 32-bit words, where Z is an integer power of 2 dependent on the model. In the 3090 the value of Z is 128 and each 3090 processor can have a vector facility. Vector elements can be 32-bit integers for short floating-point values or two words can be used to hold 64-bit-long floating-point or product values. Vectors can be any length that can fit in memory. When vectors are longer than the size of a processor vector register the vector is processed in sections. The facility also contains

```
{Pvector State}
 ((VR[0..15][0..z]<31..0>,       {15 banks of z+1 Vector Registers}
  VMR<0..z>,                     {Vector Mask Register of z+1 bits}
  VSR<63..0>,                    {Vector Status Register}
  VAC<63..0>)                    {Vector Activity Count}
  & (z =: k2  - 1)) & (k =: 0,1,2..), {size varies with model}

{Vector Data Formats}
 int<31..0> := VR<31..0>,        {integer data (2's complement)}
 sfl<31..0> := VR<31..0>,        {short floating-point data}
 sgn := sfl<31>,                 {sign of fraction}
 exp<6..0> := sfl<30..24>,       {exponent, base 2}
 fra<23..0> := sfl<23..0>,       {binary fraction}
 lfl<63..0> := VR[m] @ VR [m+1], {long floating-point data}
 sgn := lfl<63>,                 {sign of fraction}
 exp<6..0> := lfl<62..56>,       {exponent, base 2}
 fra<55..0> := lfl<55..0>,       {binary fraction}
 prod<63..0> := VR[m] @ VR[m+1], {product}
```

{Note- Other vector registers are in the scalar processor.}

Figure 7-32 IBM System/370 vector facility.

a vector-mask (bit) register of length Z to identify which elements in a vector are to be processed. A vector-status register holds control information such as the section size, a count of the number of elements to be processed. A vector-activity-count register keeps track of the number of vector instructions executed.

The addressing modes of the System/370 are extended to include vector-storage/vector-register (VST), vector-register/vector-register (VV), vector-storage/scalar-register (QST), and scalar-register/vector-storage (QV) modes. Vectors can be operated on in memory with the vector result automatically placed in a vector register or they can be vector-register to vector-register operations. For vector-memory operations the hardware supports address calculations of the stride (distance between vector elements). New instructions include the basic arithmetic and logical operators, combined MULTIPLY and ADD/SUBTRACT/ACCUMULATE, ACCUMULATE, MAXIMUM, MAXIMUM SIGNED, and MINIMUM SIGNED. The vector facility is integrated into the 370 architecture and all scalar registers retain their function. The operating system is modified to manage the vector facility and to incorporate the few restrictions imposed on scalar operations.

A final example of uses for special-purpose processors is in digital signal processing. This application is characterized by the repetition of short loops of floating-point arithmetic operations, often requiring multiple words for high precision with dual datum values to represent complex numbers. In many applications the signals must be analyzed at such high rates that extremely high-performance general-purpose computers are required. When such a machine is used much of its processing capability is idle and only its ability to perform high-speed arithmetic is taxed. Often the same performance for the signal-processing analysis can be attained with a special-purpose microprocessor.

An example is the Texas Instruments TMS32020 digital signal processor shown in Fig. 7-33. It has the large set of specialized registers identified in the illustration. Most of these registers are devoted to masking transfers of instructions and data from and to memory. Half of the 64-kword (16-bit) primary memory is used for instructions and data can be held in the other half. In order to minimize memory access time two extensions of memory are implemented on the processor chip. A 288-word data extension holds a copy of a specific 32-word block and a 256-word block of data memory. A 256-word extension can be used for data or memory. The use of the latter is controlled by block-configuration instructions (CNFD, CNFP).

The signal processor includes single-instruction lookahead for its 16-bit instructions. There are immediate, direct, and indirect addressing modes. A high-speed arithmetic unit with two shifters performs the usual set of arithmetic operations on 16- or 32-bit fixed-point or 32-bit floating-point values. Addition or multiplication is accomplished in the 200-ns cycle time. This special-purpose microprocessor is representative of a variety

```
{Psp State}
  PRD<15..0>,                   {Period Register, for loading the timer}
  PC<15..0>,                    {Program Counter}
  RPTC<7..0>,                   {Repeat Counter, for a single instruction}
  TIM<15..0>,                   {Timer (counter)}
  ACC<31..0>,                   {Accumulator, for storage of ALU output}
  AR[0..4]<15..0>,              {Auxiliary Registers, for addressing data
                                 memory, temporary storage, integer data
                                 from Auxiliary Register Arithmetic Unit}
  ARP<2..0>,                    {Auxiliary Register Pointer, selects AR's}
  ARB<2..0>,                    {Auxiliary Register pointer Buffer}
  DP<8..0>,                     {Data memory Page pointer, current page}
  GR<7..0>,                     {Global memory size allocation Register}
  IR<15..0>,                    {Instruction Register}
  IFR<5..0,                     {Interrupt Flag Register}
  IMR<5..0>,                    {Interrupt Mask Register}
  PR<31..0>,                    {Product Register}
  ST[0..4]<15..0>,              {Stack for storing PC values}
  DRR<15..0>,                   {serial port Data Receive Register}
  DXR<15..0>,                   {serial port Data Transmit Register}
  SR[0,1]<15..0>,               {Status Registers}
  TR<15..0>,                    {Temporary Register}

{Register Aliases}
  ACCH<15..0> := ACC<31..16>,   {Accumulator High}
  ACCL<15..0> := ACC<15..0>,    {Accumulator Low}
  ARP<2..0> := ST[0]<15..13>,
  DP<8..0> := ST[0]<8..0>,
  ARB<2..0> := ST[1]<15..13>,

{On-chip Memory}
  Mcha[0..287]<15..0>,          {on-chip data Memory}
  Mchb[0..255]<15..0>,          {on-chip data or program Memory}
    {Note-Selection is by a block-configuration instruction.}

{Data Formats}
  uw<15..0>,                    {unsigned binary word}
  si<15..0>,                    {signed binary integer, 2's complement}
  s := si<15>,                  {sign}
  fr<14..0> := si<14..0>,       {binary fraction}
  sl<31..0>,                    {signed long integer, 2's complement}
  s := sl<31>,                  {sign}
  fr<30..0> := sl<30..0>,       {binary fraction}
  fp<31..0>,                    {floating-point value}
  sm := fp<31>,                 {sign of mantissa}
  mn<14..0> := fp<30..16>,      {fractional mantissa, 2's complement}
  ex<3..0> := fp<15..12>,       {exponent, base 2}
  fp<11..0> := 000h,            {not used}

{Mp State}
  Mp(#0,1)[0..2^16-1]<15..0>,   {Mp(#0) holds data, Mp(#1) holds program}
```

Figure 7-33   Texas Instruments TMS32032 digital signal processor ISP.

of devices being made to perform special signal-processing functions. A feature of all of these signal processors is a very-high-speed multiplier, often including multiplication of complex numbers.

7.8 SUMMARY

In this chapter we have considered when special-purpose processors might be more effective than general-purpose processors. We reviewed how the central-processor workload might be reduced by having some of it carried by processors designed to perform specific tasks. Input/output processing, memory management, and specialized arithmetic computations appeared as candidates for off-loading the central processor.

To start, we reviewed the external environments with which computers deal. Characteristics of the peripheral devices used in computer systems were examined. The controls needed for these devices establish specifications for input/output processing. The differences in speed of the peripheral devices and the primary memory impose a requirement for speed buffering and synchronization that are a part of the I/O control functions.

Different control functions are required at different points between the central processor and memory and the external environment. These functions usually are distributed among controllers. The peripheral devices themselves need controls for addressing, speed buffering, function selection, and status reporting. Many specialized peripheral controllers designed to perform with standard microprocessors are available from semiconductor manufacturers.

Input-output processing can be performed by the central processor with only hardware buffers required at the I/O interface. To permit the processor to continue to execute instructions for other processes while input/output information is being transferred to or from memory, a direct-memory-access (DMA) capability was introduced. In this case the processor instructs the DMA controller to perform a transfer that might involve a large block of data. On completion of the transfer the processor resumes the process related to the I/O transfer. The processor can communicate with the controller by polling sense lines or can be interrupted by the controller when processor attention is needed. When there are several system components using the same bus (or switch) there is a requirement for control of bus access. Several manufacturers supply standard controllers for DMA and for system bus management.

More general input output controllers can be introduced to relieve the central processor of all input/output control other than the call for transfer of a block of information. For flexibility in managing transfers we can use a microprogrammed controller, allowing a single controller to be used with a variety of peripheral devices. When a wide variety of input/output activities are required and when it is desirable to increase the separation of input/output processing and internal computation, an input/output processor that executes programs held in primary memory can be used.

Data communications and networks are of growing importance in computer systems. Unique input/output control requirements are introduced when data is transferred among different computers using standard communication protocols. Specialized communication processors often suit the need for this I/O control.

Modular computer organizations with several processors and controllers communicating with memory simultaneously call for management of the interface between the processors and the memory modules. Again special-purpose processing is indicated. This processing can involve error detection and correction, access control, virtual-memory management, and combinations of these. The memory-management unit (MMU) has become a key controller of high-performance computer systems.

Special-purpose arithmetic processors, or hardware engines, have found a place in high-performance scientific computers. These range from floating-point arithmetic coprocessors for microprocessor systems to free-standing array processors that attach to a large host computer. For applications like digital signal processing, special-purpose processors with very-high-speed multipliers have established themselves.

Special-purpose processors make more efficient use of their circuits than do equivalent general-purpose processors. Where generality is not required the specialized devices can prove themselves cost effective.

7.9 ADDITIONAL READING

Advances in peripheral equipment proceed at almost as rapid a pace as do those in semiconductors. Those who are interested in computer architecture and computer design should keep up to date on peripheral-equipment developments by following manufacturers' announcements, by surveying publications of the computer and electronics industry, and by attending meetings of the professional societies and reading associated publications. *IEEE Computer* is of special interest for the technical quality and the timeliness of its articles; issues often are devoted to a a single topic. *IEEE Spectrum* contains many articles giving an overview of topics on computers. For example, the June and July 1987 issues, respectively, had reviews of digital signal processors and of single-chip mathematics processors.

More detailed discussions of peripheral-device controllers are contained in the textbooks on computer organization referred to previously, [GorsG86], [HamaV84], [ManoM82], and [TaneA84]. Handbooks and user manuals of the microprocessor manufacturers (see, for example, [Intel83], [Motor84], and [Natio85]) are a rich source for detail on controllers of all types.

Input/output processors and other special-purpose processors also are described in detail in the handbooks and the user manuals of the semiconductor manufacturers. It is much more difficult to find detailed information on operation of the special controllers and processors used in systems made by the computer manufacturers, since most of the designs are proprietary. Digital Equipment Corporation publishes more detail on its computer hardware (e.g., [Digi86b]) than do most manufacturers. While handbooks and user manuals do not make for easy reading, the detail contained in them can be found in no other readily available source. Technical publications of the manufacturers that contain valuable information on topics covered include Intel's *Solutions*, *Digital Technical Journal*, *IBM Journal of Research and Development*, and *IBM Systems Journal*. The last contains an article on the IBM 3090 [TuckS86].

Standards on buses, interfaces, and communications are published by the Institute of Electrical and Electronics Engineers (see [IEEE 83]), the Computer and Business Equipment Manufacturers' Association, the American Standards Institute, the International Standards Organization and its constituent committees (e.g., Comité Consultatif International Télégraphique et Téléphonique, CCITT), and the Electronics Industry Association.

Publications of the IEEE Communications Society, such as *IEEE Communications* are sources for detail and for new developments in data communications.

[GorsG86] includes an interesting review of database processing and processors. [HsaiD83] is on database computer architectures. The *IEEE Computer* issue of September 1981 covered attached array processors. A bibliography on vector and array processors [LouiT81] was presented in that issue. The same publication contained a summary of the FPS 164 [CharA81]. The IBM System/370 vector facility is described in [BuchW86] and [PadeA88]. [PeleA76] is a comprehensive introduction to digital signal processing. Additional information on the Texas Instruments' digital signal processors is found in [Texas85] and [LinKS87]. Information on the C-1 can be obtained from the Convex Corp., Richardson, TX.

7.10 PROBLEMS

7-1. Identify the data rates and the data, status, and control signals, and specify the requirements for a controller for the following:
   a. A digital cassette tape drive that uses 4-channel audio tape.
   b. An x-y plotter that has a 4-color stylus.

7-2. Specify a device controller for a direct-access storage device (large disk drive) for a high-performance computer system (see Figs. 4-21 and 7-1).

7-3. You are asked to design a data concentrator for a system with a large number of special-purpose entry terminals. Each terminal can transmit a message of up to 40 words each second at an average rate of 900 messages per hour. A concentrator must take messages from up to 50 terminals and transmit them to a central computer after adding a 3-digit terminal identifier and a 10-digit message count to the head of each message. Parity and longitudonal redundancy checking are required.

7-4. Discuss the conditions under which there is advantage to the following:
   a. Memory-mapped I/O.
   b. Independent I/O addressing and control.

7-5. Expand the drawing of the DMA controller of Fig. 7-11 to cover DMA control at each of the memory modules of the modular system shown in Fig. 3-8. Discuss any particular problems that must be addressed with the multiple-memory DMA control design.

7-6. Describe the function of each signal line of the following:
   a. The Intel 8288 bus controller of Fig. 7-18.
   b. The Intel 8289 bus arbiter of Fig. 7-19.

7-7. Compare the communication interface controllers of Figs. 7-26 and 7-27. Identify which functional boxes of Fig. 7-27 match which boxes of Fig. 7-26. Describe the advantages of each controller.

7-8. Specify an instruction set for the NS32032 memory-management unit (Fig. 7-28).

7-9. Describe in detail the flow of information through the FPS 164 processor of Fig. 7-30. Identify the functions performed at each stage.

7-10. Discuss the features of the IBM System/370 vector facility (Fig. 7-32), identifying how the rate of vector processing is improved by each feature.

7.11 PROJECTS

7-A. In the computer (or computer family) that you are investigating as Project 1-A, determine how memory management and memory sharing are performed. Describe the nature of the input/output control subsystem.

7-B. Design the input/output control subsystem for the computer you are designing as Project 1-B. Identify any special-purpose processors that you find useful in your design.

7-C. Specify the ISP of a cache-memory controller, including an outline of the instruction set.

8

Parallel Computer Systems

Most processors that have been considered so far have been essentially sequential machines. Computation has involved serial flow from input data to final results. Concurrent operations on structured data, as in the addition of two arrays, is accomplished by repeating sequences of instructions on different combinations of data elements in the data structures. The power of the digital computer comes from its ability to perform repetitions of such sequences very rapidly. We did find cases where hardware was introduced to permit parallel operations to obtain higher performance than could be attained with the purely serial machines. Even in computers within a single family, we found that implementations could handle different-size information units to achieve different performance and cost levels. In general, the lower-performance members of a family use byte transfers, the intermediate members move words, and at the top end of the performance spectrum, multiple words are transferred.

8.1 EXTREME PERFORMANCE GOALS

In order to accomplish processing at higher speeds than is possible in a purely sequential fetch-execute cycle, some of the computers discussed in earlier chapters employ instruction lookahead queues to permit fetching an instruction from memory while the previous instruction is being executed. In some cases provision is made for effective-address calculations to be overlapped with the next instruction fetch, prior-instruction execution, or both. The hardware required to allow these concurrent activities adds some cost to the processors, but the performance increases are worth the added cost, particularly for those high-performance systems that tax the capabilities of the electronic components.

In high-performance processors multiple arithmetic and logic units or multiple special function units permit different computations to proceed simultaneously. Specialized processors can be added to relieve central processors of certain tasks that then are performed concurrently with central-processor activities. Cache memories introduce parallelism through a "lookaside" capability that allows a system to ignore memory references if the information is available in the higher-speed cache.

At a broader level, some of the system structures covered in Chapter 3 allow for concurrent processing in independent processors. Most computer systems at the higher end of the performance spectrum have at least two processors to permit simultaneous processing of several user jobs. In some cases the processes active in the different processors must be independent, interacting only through the sharing of computer-system resources. This mode of parallel processing is called *loosely coupled multiprocessing*. An alternative form, *tightly coupled multiprocessing*, requires synchronization of processes running in the different processors to permit passing of data among running processes. Multiprogramming operating systems control operations of the processors in these multiple-processor systems.

Parallelism at each system level is provided to increase computer performance beyond that which would be possible with a totally sequential computer made from equivalent electronic components. At the highest level of performance we find the *supercomputers* that require more computing power than is possible with the highest-speed electronics operating in a serial machine. Concurrent operations are essential to meet their performance goals.

The supercomputer was introduced at an early stage in the history of digital computers. In the late 1950s IBM introduced the 7030, "Stretch", a 64-bit computer for very-high-performance scientific applications. UNIVAC released the LARC, a 12-digit large-scale scientific computer at about the same time. Both of these computers incorporated local concurrency to achieve fetch-execute overlap. Neither machine was produced in large quantities and in both instances advances in electronics technology, largely influenced by the "pull" of need for performance in these powerful machines, made the supercomputers obsolete by allowing simpler computers to achieve almost equivalent performance. The Control Data 6600, introduced in 1964, was well organized to use local concurrency of arithmetic operations. It was commercially successful and established that company as a supplier of high-performance scientific computers.

The precursors of today's supercomputers, the ILLIAC IV, a University of Illinois architecture implemented by Burroughs, and the Control Data Star-100, were both installed in 1972 in the San Fransisco bay area. The Star introduced pipelined vector processing, an extension of the multiple specialized arithmetic units of the Control Data 6600 and 7600. Array processing was the key design feature of the ILLIAC IV, in which 64 processors executed the same instruction stream concurrently. Again the very large machines were not commercially successful but provided experience in vector and array processing that was incorporated in later supercomputers.

In this chapter we examine organizations of computers that incorporate a high degree of parallelism to attain high performance. Alternative approaches to achieving concurrency are considered, including pipelining and arrays of processors. Designs of vector processors that use multiple pipelines of arithmetic units are compared. Recent approaches to large-scale multiprocessing are reviewed.

If the objective of these powerful machines is a very high level of performance, it is necessary that we measure the performance increases attainable with each alternative design. Absolute measures are not available, but progress is being made toward identifying the significant parameters for increased performance of parallel systems. Some performance principles are outlined.

8.2 INCREASING COMPUTER PERFORMANCE

Independent of variations in computer architectures, advances in higher-performance electronic circuits and memory technologies have permitted computers to operate at higher sequential speeds. In Fig. 4-4 memory speed was demonstrated to increase by a factor of 10 every 10 years. Even more rapid gains are found with digital electronics used in processors. As shown in Fig. 8-1(a), the delay of a pulse traversing a single logic gate (AND-OR) stage has decreased by a factor of 10 every 7 years for over 40 years. The decrease in propagation delay is reflected by increases in computer clock frequencies, usually the reciprocal of propagation delay through 10 to 20 gate stages. We note that the trend has continued from vacuum-tube circuits of the 1940s and 1950s through germanium and silicon semiconductors into the newer gallium arsenide circuits.

At any given time there is a wide range of circuit performance levels and costs. For example, Fig.8-1(b) shows the differences in 1985 of propagation delay with three different silicon semiconductor technologies. Emitter-coupled logic (ECL) had the high-

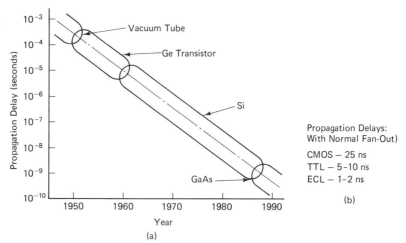

Figure 8-1   Digital-circuit propagation delays. (a) Average delays. (b) Mid-1980s examples.

est speed, with propagation delays of 1 or 2 ns (10^{-9} s). It was also the highest cost and the most power consuming technology shown. Another bipolar-transistor technology, transistor-transistor logic (TTL), was about five times slower, but was less expensive (a factor of about 2) and required less power. At the low-cost low-power low-performance end we found complementary metal-oxide semiconductors (CMOS) that were used in the large-scale integrated circuits of most microprocessors.

Through all of the history of the digital computer there has been a need for computers faster than those that could be built using serial architectures with the fastest existing components. To exceed the circuit-limiting speed always has involved doing things concurrently, using parallel circuits or subsystems. An early example of the serial–parallel trade-off is found in comparing the von Neumann design with that of other computers built at about the same time. The von Neumann IAS computer used 40-bit parallel arithmetic and accomplished memory transfers with 40-bit words. Another early machine, the EDVAC at the University of Pennsylvania, was designed with a serial acoustic delay-line memory and compatible serial registers. It used bit-serial transfers and arithmetic.

Registers were added to the early instruction-set processors to hold working copies of information that was in memory. This parallelism was expanded to the point where a large number of registers was included in the processor. The earliest supercomputer, the IBM 7030 (Stretch), incorporated instruction and operand buffers in its processor, as shown in Fig. 8-2. Queues of 2 instruction words (4 to 8 instructions) and 4 operands were filled from memory. Instruction decoding and index calculations were performed in the instruction and indexing unit, which was a processor with an arithmetic unit, 5 working registers, and 16 index registers. The updated (indexed) instruction entered the lookahead, where it was associated with the proper operand from an operand buffer. The operand buffers permitted arguments to be fetched before they were needed. Both instruction and operand words could be checked for errors and corrected by the error-corrector checker.

Instructions were transferred to the control and their arguments were transferred to the operand register. The 2-word (A, B) accumulator and (C, D) operand register held arguments for operations by the two arithmetic units. Wherever possible, both the serial and the parallel arithmetic unit were in use concurrently. Fixed-point numeric, logical, and decimal operations were carried out in the serial arithmetic unit and the parallel unit was used for floating-point arithmetic. All results were checked by the arithmetic check unit. System-level concurrency was achieved with an independent I/O exchange that communicated with the processor through the interrupt system. As with most supercomputers, only a few 7030s were delivered by IBM. The techniques and the components developed were used in the main line of IBM computers, the 7080, 7090, and 7094.

Similar approaches to in-processor concurrency were used in many other large computers. We saw in Fig. 5-13 the instruction queue of the CDC 6600 that has continued into current Cyber machines. A general instruction lookahead and operand lookaside were demonstrated in Fig. 5-14. Several of the processors of the earlier chapters included variations of these techniques.

In Chapter 3 system-level parallelism for concurrent operation was demonstrated by specific machines (the D825 of Fig. 3-1 and the IBM 3084 in Fig. 3-4), the general multiprocessor organization in Fig. 3-8, and the multiple computer system of Fig. 3-9. In

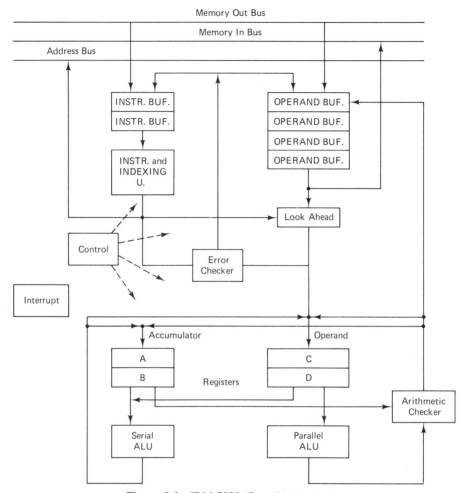

Figure 8-2   IBM 7030 (Stretch) computer.

all of those examples the concurrency was used to achieve a higher level of performance than that attainable with a single processor. Heterogeneous forms of processor parallelism were demonstrated by the systems with attached specialized processors in Figs. 3-25 through 3-27. Three examples of numeric coprocessors were shown in Figs. 7-30 through 7-32. These different approaches to parallel organization can be extended to yield very-high-performance computers.

Computer organizations have been characterized by M. J. Flynn [FlynM66] as single-instruction single-data stream (SISD), single-instruction multiple-data stream (SIMD), or multiple-instruction multiple-data stream (MIMD). The instruction and data flows in the three different classes of computers are demonstrated in Fig. 8-3. With the SISD organization a stream of instructions and associated arguments is processed in the ALU to produce results and data for successive instructions. The array-processor form of

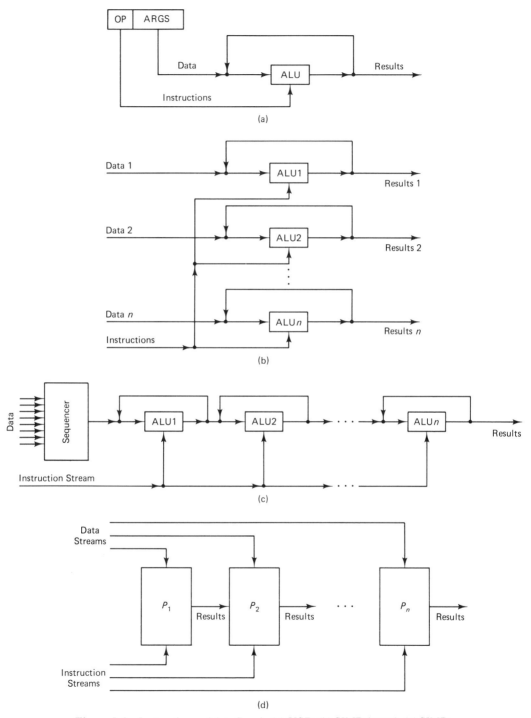

Figure 8-3 Instruction and data flow in (a) SISD, (b) SIMD (array), (c) SIMD (pipeline), and MIMD computers.

SIMD computation is an assembly of SISD processors using the same instruction stream to operate on separate (but possibly related) data streams. In the pipelined vector SIMD computer, elements of the multiple data streams are sent into the pipeline in sequence. Different operations are performed on the data in different stations of the pipeline (ALU1, ALU2, . . ., ALUn) and the data streams are reassembled at the end. MIMD computers are organized as separate SISD or SIMD machines with different (possibly synchronized) instruction streams operating on different (possibly coordinated) data streams.

Most computers are organized primarily as SISD machines. Pipelined processors (Fig. 6-25) and array processors like ILLIAC IV (Fig. 6-27) are both SIMD computers. The Texas Instruments Advanced Scientific Computer of Fig. 8-4 is an example of a vector processor with four independent pipelined ALUs. Each pipeline is fed by two stages of three 8-word memory buffer registers (X, Y, Z, X', Y', Z'). The common instruction-processing unit (IPU) has 16 instruction buffers, 16 base registers, 16 arithmetic registers, 8 index registers, and 8 vector-parameter registers. The instruction-processing unit is a pipeline processor that takes 8 word (16 instruction) groups from memory, decodes them, performs effective address computations, assigns instructions to an ALU pipeline unit, and obtains data from memory for the memory buffer for that pipeline.

The 8-stage ALU pipelines are similar to the pipeline that was shown in Fig. 6-25(b). Different sequences of function units are used in different operations. For example, the floating-point-add data flow is distributor $\rightarrow$ exponent adder $\rightarrow$ aligner $\rightarrow$ adder $\rightarrow$ normalizer $\rightarrow$ output. Once the values have been passed to the exponent subtract unit,

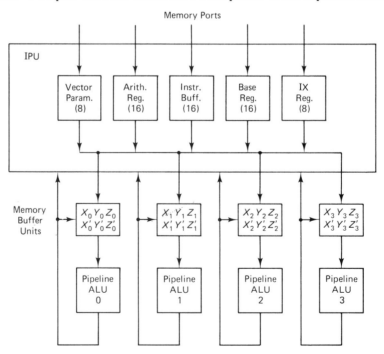

Figure 8-4 TI ASC processor organization.

another pair of values can move from the memory buffer to the receiver. The pipeline is static in that the connections are changed only when a different function is called, and data cannot leave the receiver until the connections are set. The memory buffers and the pipelined instruction-processing unit were designed to mask operand fetches from the 8-Mword (64 bits/word) memory. An independent peripheral processor executes the operating system. It and secondary-memory controllers communicate directly with memory.

Multiprocessors (Fig. 3-1) were predecessors of MIMD machines, but in most cases the multiple-processor organizations (discussed in Chapter 3) were "loosely coupled" in that there was little synchronization among processes being executed in different processors. More recent interest has been on "tightly coupled" MIMD machines (as well as in extension of the loosely coupled MIMD organization to very large quantities of processors).

The first commercially available MIMD computer was the Denelcor Heterogeneous Element Processor. The HEP system organization was shown in Fig. 2-6. This interesting computer architecture incorporates pipelined function units in each of up to 16 process execution modules (PEMs). Each PEM is a virtual MIMD multiprocessor implemented in a single physical processor. Up to 128 independent or related processes distributed over up to 32 tasks (half assigned to the operating system) can be handled concurrently. Each instruction with its arguments is transmitted as a packet for execution. An instruction can be transmitted every 100 ns. While that particular instruction takes from 800 to 3200 ns for execution, an instruction from another task can be initiated 100 ns later. The design objective was to maximize steady-state (rather than peak) instruction execution rates. When there are at least eight active tasks with independent processes the system can operate at 10 MFLOPS (million floating-point operations per second).

The major parts of a HEP process-execution module are shown in Fig. 8-5. Sixteen task queues each contain 16 task-status registers. A task is recorded in the registers of the task queue. Control and protection information is contained in a task-status word (TSW). For each of the 16 tasks up to 64 process-status words (PSW) follow the TSW in a queue. Each PSW contains a process identifier and the next instruction address. To service a task the next PSW is taken from the process queue for that task and placed in the snapshot queue. Information from the PSW and the TSW are combined and tests are made for memory-access rights to data and program memory and to general and constant registers. The PSW moves to the instruction-fetch unit where an instruction is copied from the program memory, and the PSW is updated before being returned to its queue or transmitted as a part of an instruction packet. An instruction packet with information on its arguments is transmitted from the instruction function unit to the operand fetch unit every 100 ns.

Arguments that are in the constant or general registers are copied into the instruction packet, which is then transferred to a function unit. If the arguments required are available in the registers, the packet is transmitted to one of the function units for execution. Each function unit except the divider is an 8-stage pipeline taking 100 ns/stage for instruction propagation. The eight divide-function units take up to 1700 ns for execution. The packet with its result is moved to the result store unit, which places the result value in a general register and returns the packet to the instruction-fetch unit to be returned to its process queue.

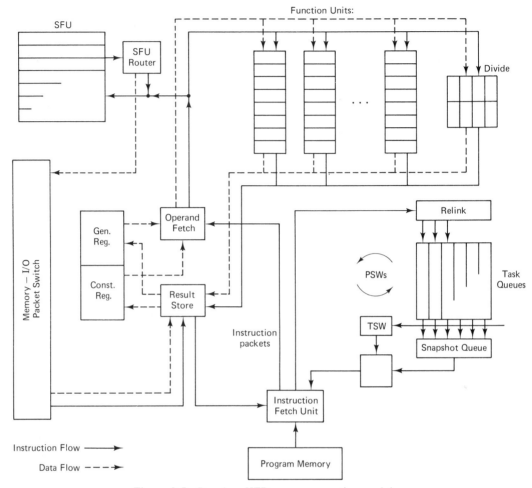

Figure 8-5 Denelcor HEP process-execution module.

If the instruction calls for transfer to or from data memory, the packet is placed in a storage function unit (SFU) queue. Instructions are removed from these queues at 100-ns intervals and transferred to the memory–I/O switch. Packets with data from memory are returned to the result-store section of the PEM to be placed in a register. (Writing to memory entails transmitting a packet with a value from a register to the memory–I/O switch. The "empty" packet is returned to the result store.) The result store transfers the modified packets to the instruction-fetch unit for return to the process queue and signals that the memory operation has been accomplished.

Maximum performance of the HEP is dependent on the availability of a new PSW every 100 ns so that an instruction packet can be built. The 10-MFLOPS rate can be sustained if at least eight process queues contain PSWs. Parallel versions of

FORTRAN compilers were developed to permit programs to be organized to exploit the parallel operations of the HEP. While not a commercial success, the HEP, like the ILLIAC IV and the TI ASC, is an example of an interesting experimental computer that has yielded a large amount of information on parallel computation and on parallel architectures. All three of these machines have helped to advance parallel processing and parallel computer architectures.

8.3 VECTOR AND ARRAY PROCESSING

Supercomputer architectures continue to fall into the categories of pipelined vector processors, array processors, tightly coupled MIMD multiprocessors, and loosely coupled multiprocessors or multicomputer systems. It is useful to outline the SIMD vector and array processors before we move to the newer MIMD computers.

As we saw in Fig. 8-3, both vector processors and array processors are classified as SIMD computers since a single instruction stream operates on different data streams. The example of inner-product calculations in matrix multiplication demonstrates parallel activity in both types of processors. Matrix multiplication (Fig. 8-6) entails building a matrix that has as a new element the sum of the products of elements of a row of the first matrix and elements of a column of the second matrix. In Fig. 8-6, if A is an $l \times m$ matrix and B is an $m \times n$ matrix, then $C = A * B$ is an $l \times n$ matrix, where each c_{ij} ($i = 1 \ldots l, j = 1 \ldots n$) is calculated from:

$$a_{i1} * b_{1j} + a_{i2} * b_{2j} + \ldots + a_{im} * b_{mj}$$

Each element c_{ij} requires m multiplications and (after initializing to 0) m additions. This can be treated as m multiply-add operations. If $l = m = n = 100$, reasonable for many problems in physical science, there are 10,000 elements to C, each of which requires an inner-product calculation of 100 multiply-add operations.

In the sequential pipeline processor (one without vector instructions) a short iteration loop of multiply instructions is executed. Address indexing through the arrays is used to select the stream of argument pairs (one from a row of one array and the second from a column of the other) to flow into processor registers. The sequence of multiplies is followed by a sequence of adds. This requires two separate SIMD operations. Alternatively, each individual multiply can be followed by an add (a "multiply and accumulate") in one step of a single SIMD operation. The computer instruction cycle proceeds as: fetch instruction, decode instruction, fetch argument 1, fetch argument 2, multiply, fetch old sum, add, and store into sum. With a floating-point add pipeline and a floating-point

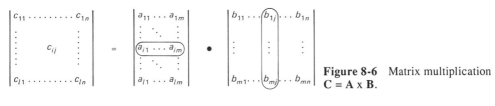

Figure 8-6 Matrix multiplication $C = A \times B$.

multiply pipeline there can be an overlap of microoperations in the instruction cycle, as was described in Chapter 6. If the pipelined computer incorporates vector operations the operations proceed in the same manner, except that the instruction(s) is fetched only once for the sequence of SUM($a_{ij} * b_{ij}$) shown before.

The inner-product calculation on a pipelined vector processor is shown in Fig. 8-7. Organization of the arrays that hold each of the argument matrices is demonstrated in Fig. 8-7(a). In the example the arrays are stored in "column-major" order and the successive elements to be read from matrix **B** are in successive memory locations. For matrix **A**, however, the successive elements are l locations apart. This separation of successive elements is known as the "stride" of the array. Matrix **A** could have been transposed before storing to place successive values in a row together, or matrix **B** could have been transposed to separate the elements by n locations. Performance of pipelined vector processors in applications such as matrix multiply is limited by the transfer capacity ("bandwidth") of the memory. The effective bandwidth can be increased by careful organization of the array in storage. A large memory word can be used to hold several successive matrix elements or successive elements can be

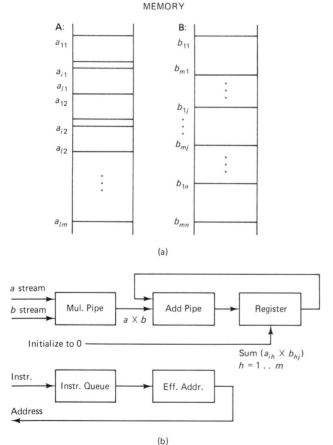

(a)

(b)

Figure 8-7 Matrix multiplication in a pipeline computer (a) Matrices in memory (column-major). (b) Pipeline process.

placed in different memory modules. Significant processing might be allocated to the "gathering" of elements of an array to store them in a way that maximizes overlap of computations.

The flow of elements from array **A** and array **B** into the multiply and add pipelines is shown in Fig. 8-7(b). A register that was initialized to 0 holds the intermediate results until an inner product has been calculated. If the add and multiply pipelines each have six stages, see Fig. 6-25(a), with a per-stage transition time of 50 ns, an individual multiply-add takes 600 ns, but another pair of inputs can be transmitted 50 ns after the first pair and the steady-state multiply-add rate is 20 MFLOPS.

Array processors handle the inner-product example in a different manner. Considering the multiplication of the same matrices as described before, we want to compute **C** = **A** * **B** on an array processor with k^2 processing elements (PEs) with l, m, and n all less than k. As shown in Fig. 8-8(a), the arrays are held in primary memory and there is a "memory manager" that organizes the streams of arguments from arrays **A** and **B** flowing into individual PEs. A pair of arguments, a_{gx} and b_{yh} $(x, y = 1 \ldots m)$ is transferred to each PE. All PEs concurrently execute multiply and each result is placed in a register. Then every PE adds its result to a value of c_{gh} that is in another register. The sequence is repeated until all values of a_{gx} and b_{yh} are consumed. At that point each of the k^2 PEs holds an inner product for one value of c_{gh}. These values are stored and the PEs are initialized for another set of k^2 inner products. The process is repeated until all l * m inner products have been computed.

If the arrays are large compared with the number of PEs, the computation can proceed in the different ways shown in Fig. 8-8(b). In Fig. 8-8(a) we assumed that a $k \times k$ segment of inner products would be calculated concurrently. It also is possible to calculate a $1 \times k^2$ row or a $k^2 \times 1$ column of inner products in one sequence. In these cases processing of the total matrix multiplication proceeds as a "wave" of individual parallel computation sequences. This row (or column) wave approach is useful if $k^2 < l$ (or $k^2 < n$) and if there is sufficient storage local to each PE to hold all m elements of a column of **B** (row of **A**). The columns of **B** (rows of **A**) can be loaded concurrently into all PEs by "broadcasting" their values. The columns of **B** (rows of **A**) do not have to be reloaded for computation of subsequent rows (columns) of the result matrix **C**.

Although the pipeline and array-processor approaches are different, the results are the same. In both cases processor hardware logic is added to permit operations to take place concurrently. Both forms of SIMD computer offer potential for very high performance if programs can be written to take advantage of the parallelism.

8.4 PIPELINE AND VECTOR PROCESSORS

Experience gained through development and use of the CDC Star-100 led to two commercially successful vector processors, one from Control Data and the other from Cray Research. Both machines contain multiple arithmetic pipelines and have independent scalar- and vector-processing units. Since the computers had a common parent, we will review the CDC Star-100 first to see the architecture that led to the more modern machines.

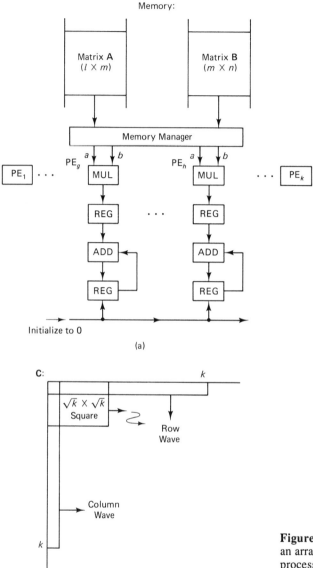

Figure 8-8   Matrix multiplication in an array computer. (a) Processing in processing elements. (b) Computation "waves."

Control Data started development of the Star in 1965 and delivered several machines in 1973. The architecture was built on a very large and fast (for its time) magnetic core memory. The 1.28-microsecond cycle time memory used 32-way interleaving of 512-bit "superwords" to attain block transfers at a rate of a processor word (64 bits) every 10 ns. A simplified diagram of the processor is shown in Fig. 8-9. The stream unit that separates the memory interface from three processor units holds read and write buffers

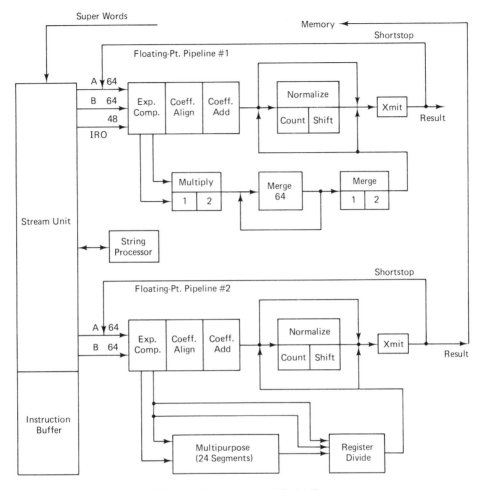

Figure 8-9 CDC Star-100 pipelines.

and a register file of 64 superwords. The microcoded system control and the control store are also in the stream unit. A superword can be moved to the 4-superword instruction buffer in 40 ns. The instruction buffer is like the instruction queue of the Cyber shown in Fig. 5-13.

A string processor that operates on strings of decimal or binary integers contains binary-coded-decimal and fixed-point adders. Two separate floating-point pipelines form the high-speed arithmetic section. Each pipeline has exponent-compare, coefficient-alignment, coefficient-add, normalize-count, normalize-shift, and transmit stages. Pipeline 1 also contains two 32-bit multiply units that can be combined for 64-bit arguments and three merge units for different-size multiplier results. In pipeline 2 we find a 24-segment multipurpose pipeline for a variety of arithmetic and logical operations and a nonpipelined register divide unit. Normalizing after multiply and divide is done in the same stage as it is after addition. For repeating operations on streams of data (i.e., vector operations) the "shortstop" paths permit results to be fed back into the pipelines without going to the register file.

The Star contained both scalar and vector instructions. Vector instructions identified the vector length, the starting location and the field size of each element of the two argument and the result vector, and the location of a control vector. The control vector had a bit to represent each entry of the result vector. The boolean value of each bit indicated whether or not the result should be stored. The computer had very powerful vector-processing capability. A peak execution rate of 100 MFLOPS was claimed for short (32-bit) arguments and it was 50 MFLOPS for long (64-bit) values. The sustained speed of the computer is much lower due to the requirement for scalar operations to perform vector startup. Scalar operation rates are about 1 MFLOPS with the result that average vector-processing speeds are from 5 to 10 MFLOPS. (The Texas Instruments ASC described earlier in this chapter has similar performance.)

The first commercially successful pipelined vector-processor supercomputer was the Cray-1. Design of the Cray-1 benefited from the experience of the architect, Seymour Cray, with the CDC 6600 and 7600 and the Star-100. The Cray-1 has 12 pipelined functional units that can be connected in many ways to form chains of operations. Control of this dynamically modifiable pipeline structure is more complicated than that of the multifunction pipelines of the Star-100, but it offers flexibility for vector processing. The million-word bipolar semiconductor memory uses 16-way interleaving of one to four 64-bit (plus parity) words and can transfer information at a rate of up to 320 million words/s. Twenty-four input/output channels can transfer information at up to 80 Mbytes/s each. These very high transfer rates are needed to keep the parallel pipelined processor busy.

The Cray-1 processor (Fig. 8-10) is organized into four major function units with three register banks and an instruction section. The instruction-execution section contains four instruction buffers, each holding sixty-four 16-bit "packets". An instruction uses one or two packets and the buffer can hold from 128 to 256 instructions. Branching within the buffer permits loops of those sizes to be repeated without further instruction transfers from memory. The 22-bit program counter (P) points to the parcel that is to be transferred to the next-instruction-parcel (NIP) buffer. The parcel is then moved to the current-instruction parcel (CIP) register for decoding and execution. If an instruction has a second parcel it is an address that is placed in the lower-instruction-parcel (LIP) register.

Effective-address calculations are performed in the integer-add and integer-multiply function units using addresses held in the eight 24-bit address registers (A0 through A7). A bank of 64 address-save registers (B00 through B77) buffers the address registers and the program counter from memory. Addresses can be transferred between the address registers and the 48 input/output control registers (CA, CL). Address values also can be transferred to the shift units, the input/output exchange address register (XA), and the vector-length register (used for vector control). Address registers can receive values from a scalar register or from the population count function unit.

The scalar function units, which perform fixed-point add, logical, shift, and population/leading-0 count operations, receive their data from the eight 64-bit scalar registers (S0 through S7). As with the address registers, there is a buffer between the scalar registers

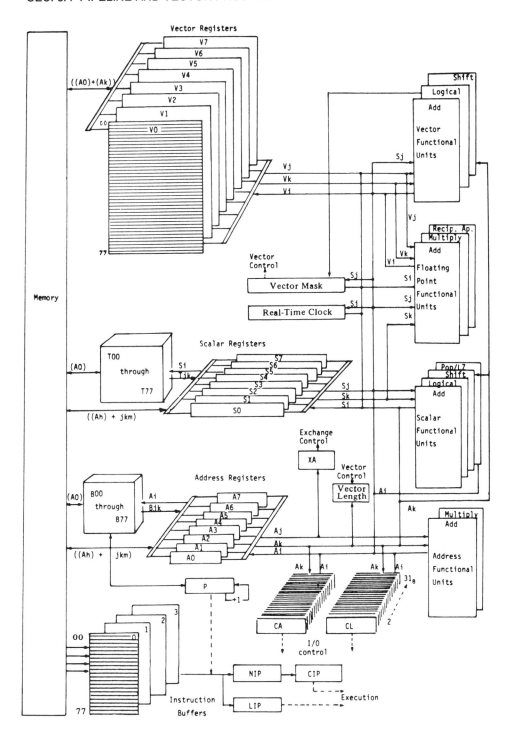

Figure 8-10 The Cray-1. (Reprinted with permission of Cray Research, Inc.)

and memory, the 64 scalar-save registers (T00 through T77). A scalar register can receive information from an address register or from the real-time clock. Fixed-point add, shift, and logical vector operations are performed in the vector function units. The eight vector registers (V0 through V7) each hold sixty-four 64-bit words. Data are streamed between the vector registers and the function units that handle vector instructions. The floating-point functions units (add, multiply, and "reciprocal approximation") can use data from either the scalar or the vector registers. A value from a scalar register can be added to a vector value in the vector adder. The vector mask holds a 64-bit boolean vector for control of vector operations.

In addition to the registers shown, there are base-address, limit-address, flag, and mode registers for addressing and control. Although the Cray-1 has a very large processor state (over 5000 bytes), its operation is straightforward. Its high performance is a result of an uncomplicated organization and very-high-speed circuits. The logic circuits have delays less than 1 ns, the registers have 6-ns cycle times, and the memory registers have a cycle time of 50 ns. The computer clock operates with a 12.5-ns period and all operations are expressed in multiples of this clock period. For example, the scalar add, population count, vector add, and scalar (double-word) shifts take three cycles (37.5 ns). Very flexible vector operations and powerful scalar operations are possible through chaining of function units. In many applications scalar operations can take place concurrently with vector operations, reducing the effects of vector initiation. All operations use register-to-register addressing and the buffering permits memory transfers to be masked almost completely. Peak performance of 250 MFLOPS and a sustained rate of 138 MFLOPS have been claimed [RussR78]. This is considered optimistic since the former would require over three instructions to be executed every 12.5-ns clock period. An Argonne National Laboratory report [DongJ85] gives the Cray-1 a maximum performance of 160 MFLOPS (presumably concurrent vector and pipelined scalar operations every 12.5 nsec) and a maximum sustained performance of 150 MFLOPS. ("It is easy to attain over 100 MFLOPS for certain problems, even using FORTRAN.")

A somewhat younger and even more direct descendant of the Star-100 is the CDC Cyber 205. The designation as a "Cyber" indicated that it was a standard Control Data product. An intermediate step, the Cyber 203, added a scalar processor to the Star architecture and used semiconductor memory with instruction-transfer rates of 50 MHz. The Cyber 205 takes another step by using large-scale integrated (LSI) circuits, a larger (one- to eight-Mword) 80-ns cycle bipolar semiconductor memory, a separate scalar processor, and up to four vector pipelines. As in the Star-100, memory transfers are of 8-word superwords that are four-way interleaved to allow a superword to be transferred each 20 ns, the processor minor cycle time. This gives an effective transfer rate of 400 million 64-bit (plus error-correction field) words per second. The system organization of the Cyber 205 is shown in Fig. 8-11.

The separate scalar unit also is the main controller of the system. It contains a 64-word instruction queue ("stack") similar to that of the other Cyber processors (Fig. 5-13). Virtual-memory management for both scalar and vector processing is accomplished at its memory-access interface. An instruction pipeline issues instructions to the vector-processing stream unit. A file of 256 64-bit general registers holds data for scalar and for vector processing. The scalar arithmetic unit has separate floating-point add, multiply, single cycle, and logical pipelines and a sequential divide/square root function

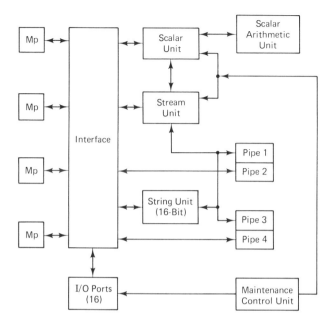

Figure 8-11 CDC Cyber 205 computer system.

unit. All but the last can accept a new instruction/data pair each 20 ns. The vector-arithmetic unit consists of the stream unit, similar to that of the Star-100, and up to four arithmetic pipelines. Each arithmetic pipeline unit has a data interchange (interface), a pipeline control, and five separate function units. The add, multiply, shift, and logical units are multifunction static pipelines like those in the scalar-arithmetic unit. Static pipelines must be emptied before being reconfigured, but are easier to control than the dynamic pipelines of the Cray-1. A fifth function unit contains a 16-word (128 bits/word) buffer to provide delays for controlled data streaming.

The separate scalar unit leads to much higher average performance than that of the Star-100. Peak 64-bit-word vector performance of 50 MFLOPS is claimed for each pipeline, but that reflects production of an add or multiply result every 20 ns. Any waiting for scalar unit operations, particularly to be expected with multiple vector-arithmetic pipes, slows the system. Peak performance can be approached only with very large vector lengths, where startup time and pipeline reconfiguration time are masked by the long vector-processing time. The Argonne report [DongJ85] states that "most tuned software employs long, contiguously held vectors". Pipeline startup is slower in the Cyber 205 than in the Cray-1 since there are many fewer processor registers. It is interesting that performance of the Cyber 205 is based on very-high-speed streams of information from memory through a rather small speed buffer (the general register bank), whereas the Cray-1 depends on its very large processor state.

The fourth SIMD processor to be outlined, the ILLIAC IV, was influential in design of today's tightly coupled multiprocessor systems. The ILLIAC IV was developed by Burroughs and the University of Illinois and was a contemporary of the Star-100. Both had long development cycles, were technically challenging, and yielded much information on parallel processing. A general outline of the ILLIAC IV was presented in Fig.

6-27. The system was designed to have four quadrants, each with 64 processing elements (PEs) arranged in an 8×8 array. The single-quadrant model that was built and used is represented in Fig. 6-27(a). Each processing element had its own data memory and could communicate with adjacent processors in the same row and in the same column (including end-around connections) through the routing network (discussed in the next section). A sixty-fifth processor executed instructions that were distributed among the PE memories and communicated function commands to all PEs. A single 64-bit control/status word was used as a mask to inhibit operation by individual PEs and as a means to transfer a vector of boolean values (such as $A_i > B_i$) from PEs. The control unit and a processing element are illustrated in Fig. 8-12.

The control unit instruction buffer, Fig. 8-12(a), received instructions in 8-word (16 instruction) blocks from PE memories. The 64-word buffer can hold 128 instructions to permit tight loops to be contained in the buffer. An associative memory is used to correlate program-counter references to locations in the instruction buffer. There is a 64-word local data buffer to hold control-unit data. Instructions flow into the instruction register, where they are decoded. Instructions related to control-unit operation are executed in the advanced station (ADVAST). Instructions for processing elements are passed with address or data operands to the final queue (FINQ) to be sent as controls to PEs by the sequencer (FINST) or to be broadcast over the data bus. There are four data registers (CAR0 ... CAR3) and a simple arithmetic unit (CULOG) in the control unit. It processes address calculations and program branch instructions. The boolean vector built from the value in the mode flip-flop of each PE provides a separate input to CULOG. Memory management for input/output operations (streams) is accomplished by the memory-access control unit.

One of the 64 processing elements is shown in Fig. 8-12(b). Commands are received from the control unit by the drivers and receivers block (D&R) and are interpreted using mode register (RGD) status and a mask bit to determine how the command is to be interpreted. Information on the status of the PE is transmitted to the control unit by the D&R. Command decoding is done by the operand select gates (OSG). Information broadcast from the control unit is received by OSG on the common data bus (CDB). Drivers and receivers (D&R) also are the interfaces to the adjacent PEs (N, E, S, W) using the routing network. The four data registers are an accumulator (RGA), an operand register (RGB), a multiplicand and routing register (RGR), and a temporary buffer (RGS). The floating-point function units execute add/multiply (MSG, PAT, CPA), logical (LOG), and shift (BSW) operators. The output of LOG is used to set the mode bit in RGD that can be transmitted to the control unit. Effective-address calculation and memory control are accomplished by the index register (RGX) and the address adder (ADA). The memory-address register (MAR) addresses the 2048-word processor-element memory. The data path to memory is through the memory-interface register (MIR) in the memory. MIR also is connected to the control-unit bus (CUB) for transmission of instructions or data to the control unit and to the I/O bus (IOB) for interaction with the front-end processor (a B6500 or a PDP-11).

Operation times of ILLIAC IV included 200 ns for a 64-bit floating point add, 400 ns for multiply, 80 ns for boolean or single-word shifts. Data transfers from memory could be

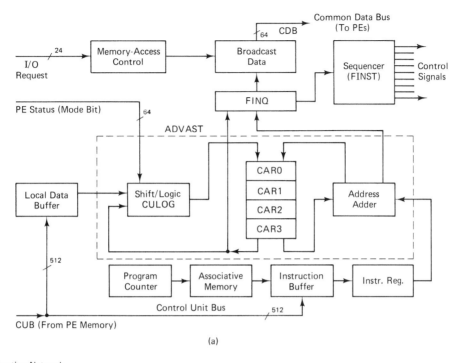

(a)

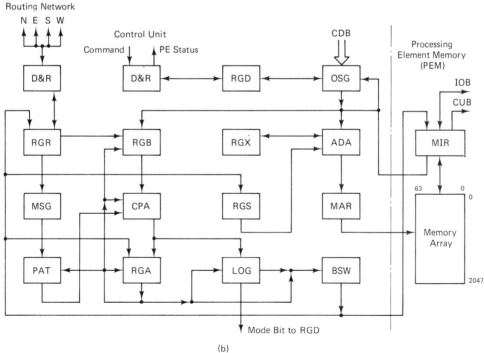

(b)

Figure 8-12 ILLIAC IV control and processors. (a) Control unit, (b) Processing element.

made at 240-ns intervals. Eight instructions (512 bits) were moved to the control unit in the same 240-ns period and most instruction fetches were masked by execution times, as were most address calculations. The peak instruction-execution rate of an ILLIAC IV PE was about 2 MFLOPS and the sustainable rate was over 1 MFLOPS. For problems suited to the array organization (e.g., dynamic meteorology and nuclear physics), a sustained rate of from 10 to 25 MFLOPS was achieved. The system was installed at NASA Ames and used in studies of parallel-processing hardware and software issues for almost 10 years. Several descendants of ILLIAC IV are discussed in a later section and in Chapter 9.

In describing the operation of each of these SIMD computers, we saw that the performance was dependent on the problem and the programs being run. The Star-100 was slowed down by vector startup time. ILLIAC IV ran with blinding speed on some problems and was excruciatingly slow on others. Even with a separate scalar processor, the Cyber 205 has reduced performance with small vectors. Experience with the Cray-1 has shown that problem and program tuning can have a large effect on performance. We defer discussion of these problem-algorithm and software issues until Section 8.7. At this point we should be aware that parallel processing must be addressed with both computer-architecture and computer-applications perspectives.

8.5 INTERCONNECTION REVISITED

In Chapter 3 system structures of computers with a relatively small number of modules were reviewed. Different possibilities for interconnection and for switching were discussed. In the computer switches described in Section 3.4 connection of up to 10 processors was shown. In Section 3.9 performance issues for loosely coupled multiprocessors with small quantities of processors were addressed. The interconnection scheme is crucial to performance of parallel computer systems involving very large quantities of processors and/or memory modules. Particularly in tightly coupled parallel systems it is important that operating modules be able to exchange information and to share resources.

For a first approximation to relative costs of different switching mechanisms we can assume that the cost at each node is determined by the number of connections for communication from and to that node. This assumption was used in the discussion of switching cost in Section 3.4. For densely packed computer systems, cost can be based on the amount of logic required for control. The cost of connecting cables and power amplifiers for transmission of signals over distances of more than a few centimeters is neglected. Systems that are distributed over meters or kilometers require a different set of assumptions based on specific communications technologies used, topics outlined in Chapter 3.

The logic required to take a signal, S_0, and to send it to one of n destinations, d_i $(i = 1 \ldots n)$, under control of $k = \log_2 n$ control lines, h_j $(j = 1..k)$, is shown in Fig. 8-13. This is a generalization of the specific design shown in Fig. 3-16. The generalization is useful here where we are looking at connecting a large number of processor

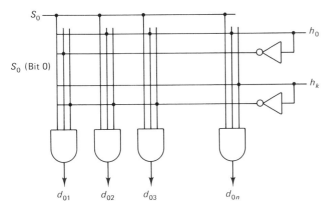

Figure 8-13 Switch control (one bit).

and memory modules. With a w-bit word there are w copies of the logic other than the control decoder. We can use the sum of inputs to all gates as a rough measure of the complexity (in number of transistors, number of input connectors, or area of semiconductor surface) of the switch. The cost is then

$$C_{\text{out}} = \log_2 n + w[n(1 + \log_2 n) + n]$$

Controlling input to a node from n sources requires the same amount of logic. An n-input OR gate replaces the drivers. Ignoring the first term, we require

$$C = w(2n + n \log_2 n)$$

for either the transmitter switch or the receiver switch.

If there are N nodes we must sum the cost for each node. For comparisons of different switches, we can assume that the number of nodes and the word size(w) is the same for all. Then N and w can be lumped into a single constant factor that can be ignored since we are considering relative cost of the different approaches. If the number of destinations (n) is the same for all nodes, then the cost of the different switches is the cost of switching at a node multiplied by the number of nodes (N):

$$C = N(2n + n \log_2 n)$$

We use this approximation to compare the cost of the connection schemes.

A simple approximation of performance, the connectivity, is the number of node pairs that can be connected by independent paths divided by the total number of nodes. Another performance measure that allows for the topology of the connection is the maximum number of edges (links) that must be traversed for any node to communicate with any other. (The average number of edges involved in node connection might be more valid but is more difficult to calculate.)

The crossbar switch of Figs. 3-14 and 3-15 is suited to the requirement for information sharing at high speeds. With p processor (active) modules and s storage modules the number of node-pair connections is $N = p \times s$. Each processor node must communicate with s storage units ($n = s$) and each storage module must communicate with p processor modules ($n = p$). For the crossbar connecting processors and memory modules the switch cost is

$$C_{pmcb} = p(2s + s \log_2 s) + s(2p + p \log_2 p)$$

If we are designing a system with a large number of nodes, all of which are transmitters and receivers, $p = s = N$, and

$$C_{cb} = 2(N-1)[2(N-1) + (N-1) \log_2 (N-1)]$$

or, for large values of N,

$$C_{cb} = 2N(2N + N \log_2 N) = 2N^2(2 + \log_2 N)$$

The connectivity of the crossbar is unity since any module can communicate with all N − 1 of the others. The maximum number of links traversed in any path also is 1 since there is a direct connection between all pairs of modules.

On the other hand, cost is of order $n^2 \log n$. It is easy to visualize a system of a very large quantity of relatively simple processors where the crossbar switch cost could overpower processor cost. (A 64-processor-module 64-bit computer like ILLIAC IV, if it used crossbar switching, would require over 8 million transistors for switch gating.) It is necessary for these applications that we introduce switch configurations that allow sufficiently high-speed communication at much lower costs (increasing on the order of $n \log n$, at most).

Early array computers such as the ILLIAC IV employed a two-dimensional inter-connection scheme in which each processing element could communicate with its nearest neighbors in either dimension ($n = 4$). A simplified 4×4 ($N = 16$) nearest neighbor mesh is shown in Fig. 8-14(a). Since the number of destinations is constant (4), the cost of the nearest neighbor mesh is

$$C_{nn} = N(2n + n \log_2 n) = N(2*4 + 4 \log_2 4) = 16N$$

and the connectivity is $4/N$. The maximum number of links to be traversed is 4 for the 4×4 mesh shown and, in general, is the square root of N for a square mesh. The Illiac IV model that was delivered had 64 nodes in an 8×8 configuration ($N = 64$). The cost for the switch gating is 1024, the connectivity is 1/16, and the maximum number of steps is 8.

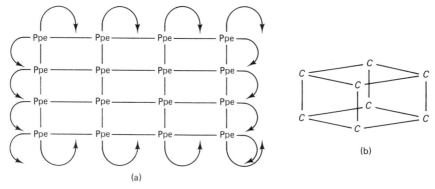

(a)

(b)

Figure 8-14   Two- and three-dimensional topologies. (a) Two-dimensional nearest neighbor. (b) 3-cube.

For higher-performance communication with large quantities of nodes, more-than-two-dimensional structures are promising. A popular arrangement is the indirect binary n-cube, or hypercube. With the binary n-cube there are n communication links from each node and a total of $N = 2^n$ nodes and the cost is

$$C_{bnc} = 2^n (2n + n \log_2 n)$$

The binary 3-cube ($N = 8$) is shown in Fig. 8-14(b). An interesting characteristic of this structure is that any node can transmit a message to any other in a maximum of n links. The connectivity (n/N) is $n/2^n$. For a 64-node computer ($n = 6$), the connectivity is 3/32 and messages can be passed in at most six steps. The cost of the switch is 1920.

A comparison of relative cost, connectivity as a ratio of nodes accessible versus total nodes, and the maximum number of steps required to communicate with another node for 64-node computers is summarized in Fig. 8-15. Starting with the nearest neighbor switch, an improvement in connectivity of about 50% can be achieved for twice the cost with the binary 6-cube. Maximum connectivity, a further factor of 11, can be achieved with the crossbar switch for an increase in cost by another factor of 34. Cost is inversely proportional to the square of the maximum number of steps to go from any node to any other.

Often it is useful to represent interconnection schemes by a ring of connected nodes that also are connected by chords, as demonstrated in Fig. 8-16. The reader might compare these with other ways to represent the same topologies to see that they are correct. With this form of illustration it is easy to obtain an estimate of complexity and of performance from the "density" of the net of connections. A comparison of Figs. 8-16(b) and 8-16(c) shows that the 2-dimensional mesh (nearest neighbor) with $N = 16$ is the same as the binary 4-cube. This is not the general case for other values of N. The barrel shifter, Fig. 8-16(d), connects a node to any node that is 2^k ($k = 0, 1, 2, 3, \ldots$) away. The barrel shifter was conceived for high-speed shifting in arithmetic operations.

Illustrations such as Figs. 8-14 and 8-16 show a topology conceptually (as long as it can be represented in three or fewer dimensions), but they do not demonstrate the methods needed to implement the switches. Most switching is built up from 2×2 switches ("routers"), as shown in Fig. 8-17. Two-function routers concurrently map a to x or y and b to the other, and four-function routers also map either input to both outputs. The control selects one of several possible connections between inputs and outputs. Larger switches can be assembled from these routers by combining multiple 2×2 switches.

The multiple-stage interconnections can use circuit switching, where the connection is established and the information is transferred, or message switching, where the message

Configuration	Cost	Connectivity	Maximum Steps
Nearest Neighbor (8 x 8)	1,024	1/16	8
Binary 6-Cube	1,920	3/32	6
Crossbar (64, 64, 64)	65,536	1	1

Figure 8-15 Comparison of 64-processor switches.

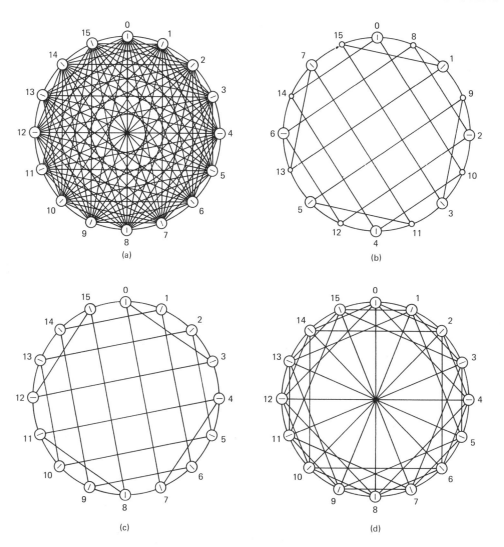

Figure 8-16 Chordal ring representations. (a) Fully connected (crossbar) ($N = 16$). (b) The binary 4-cube ($N = 16$). (c) The two-dimensional mesh ($N = 16$). (d) The barrel shifter ($N = 16$).

2-function: $(x = a, y = b)$ OR $(x = b, y = a)$

4-function: $(x = a, y = b)$ OR $(x = b, y = a)$
OR $(x = a, y = a)$ OR $(x = b, y = b)$

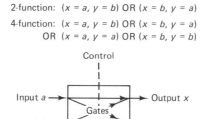

Figure 8-17 The basic 2×2 switch (router).

carries its destination and might stop at intermediate locations waiting for its path toward the destination to become available. These switching techniques were discussed in Chapter 3. Most of the connection topologies for large numbers of modules can be used with either control method. The general switch with t levels, each formed from switches with r outputs and s inputs, is known as an (r, s, t) *banyan network*. The shuffle-exchange network shown in Fig. 8-18 is an example of a banyan network with its inputs renamed. This network has also been termed a $2^3 \times 2^3$ delta network. Any input can be connected to any output by selection of control functions for each of the 2×2 switches. The routers permit any input to be "broadcast" to all outputs or to other combinations by selecting connections of an input to both outputs for some routers.

A switch like the shuffle exchange of Fig. 8-18 can be implemented with multiple stages as shown or can be built as a multistep single-stage switch. In the latter case only one stage of switches (in the dashed box in the illustration) is used. Registers must be added to the outputs (or the inputs) of the switch. Transfer of information from an input position to an output position can require several steps (as many as there are stages in the multistage network). Again we see a trade-off between time and logic circuits.

Figure 8-19 shows four more useful networks implemented with 2×2 switches (or as $(2, 2, t)$ banyan networks). All three of the three-stage networks of this illustration (a, b, d) and the shuffle exchange of Fig. 8-18 are "blocking" networks in that any one connection path can block other paths so that concurrent arbitrary interconnection of all inputs with all outputs is not possible. For example, in the baseline network, Fig. 8-19(a), if input 0 is connected to output 5, then input 1 can connect only to outputs 0 through 3 and input 4 or 5 can connect to any output other than 5. Nonblocking networks require more components. The Benes network, Fig. 8-19(c), is called a rearrangeable nonblocking network because, when in any state if a new connection is called for the existing connections can be rearranged to permit the addition. It has been the subject of network-capability studies. Of the three blocking networks, the baseline network allows arbitrary

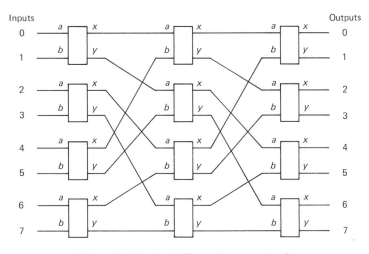

Figure 8-18   A shuffle-exchange network.

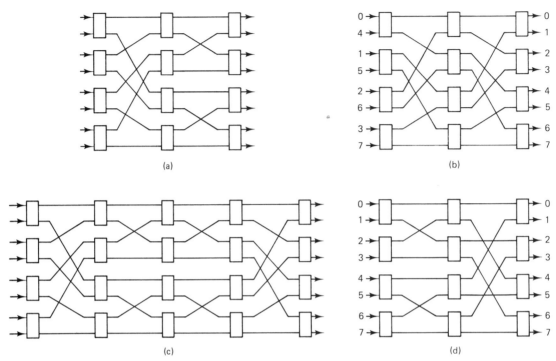

Figure 8-19   Implementation with 2 x 2 switches. (a) The 8 x 8 baseline network. (b) An omega network ($N = 8$). (c) The Benes network ($N = 8$). (d) The binary 3-cube ($N = 8$).

permutations to be established in two separate passes, whereas the others require at least three passes. The omega network differs from the 3-cube in that "broadcasting" is permitted in any switch and the input/output numbering is reversed.

The presentation of the binary 3-cube of Fig. 8-19(d) should be compared with Fig. 8-14(b). The 12 router switch settings can select any binary 3-cube connection or 4 routers can make any connection in three steps. Routers can be used to implement any hypercube (binary n-cube) switch by extension of the design shown in Fig. 8-19(d). The binary 4-cube, Fig. 8-16(b), can be built with an 8×4 array of routers (two binary 3-cubes plus an extra stage).

8.6 MULTIPROCESSORS AND MULTICOMPUTERS

In Section 8.3 vector processors and an array-processor SIMD computer were discussed. In both cases a single instruction stream was processed using multiple data streams. The computers are organized with a single control unit and with separate data units. To handle multiple instruction streams, MIMD computers require independent control and data units. The multiprocessor and multicomputer systems described in Chapter 3 were examples of MIMD-type architectures. The Burroughs D-825 (Fig. 3-1) was an ancestor of today's multiprocessor computers. Over 100 D-825 systems were delivered for U.S. government applications. Most of the systems delivered contained multiple processors, although an important objective was high reliability (see Section 3.6) rather than high performance. High-reliability duplexed computers, Fig.3-21(b), such as the AN/FSQ-7 built by IBM for the SAGE air defense system in the 1950s, were the predecessors of modern multiple-computer systems. The RW-400 (AN/FSQ-27) of Ramo Wooldridge (later TRW Corp) was an early multicomputer system that was designed for high reliability and for variable performance levels.

High-performance computer architectures are the subject of this chapter. We are concerned with how multiprocessor and multicomputer systems can be organized to attain very high performance levels. We also examine extensions of the ILLIAC IV SIMD design to achieve high performance. We want to focus on how to exploit high degrees of parallelism in computer designs.

Before looking at alternative parallel computer architectures we should review concurrent processing applications, the nature of computing tasks that can take advantage of processor parallelism. The early multiprocessors/multicomputers were designed with their operating systems to use their parallelism for independent computing jobs. These independent processes were coupled only through the sharing of hardware and software resources managed by the operating systems.

As experience was gained with these systems multiple tasks of a single job could be managed. Related processes shared resources and also were synchronized by common events that permitted information to be produced and consumed by different processes running on separate processors. An example of a single job with shared processes is the operating system itself. Coordination and synchronization of operating-system processes is required. Operating-system interaction with architectures was discussed in Section 5.3. Programming languages that incorporated resource sharing and process/task coordination were included in Section 5.2.

A high degree of interaction among activities assigned to separate processors is required for parallel processing of individual programs. Here a process is separated into subprocesses, some of which can be executed simultaneously by separate processors in a multiprocessor or multicomputer system. Parallel processing is the major objective of the concurrency introduced with high-performance parallel computers. ILLIAC IV and the pipeline vector processors of Section 8.4 were designed to exploit parallel processing in solution of problems involving matrix algebra.

A major difference among forms of concurrent processing is the degree to which they can make use of the independence of concurrent processes or to which they can exploit the coordination possible with parallel processing. Architectures for concurrent independent processes make use of statistics and distribute procedures and data almost randomly to yield a low probability of clashes for resources. Loosely coupled multiprocessors and multi-computers are well matched to these problems. For parallel processing, tightly coupled parallel computer designs can take advantage of the "locality" of instructions and data.

Parallel systems also have been classified as shared-memory or distributed-memory multiprocessors. An examination of representative systems will show that most use combinations of shared and distributed-memory organizations. Thus there is not a sharp distinction between multiprocessor (shared memory) and multicomputer (distributed memory) systems, as will be demonstrated in our examples.

The earlier examples incorporated combinations of parallel features. ILLIAC IV was an array processor that used pipeline features in its control. All three of the pipeline vector processors described previously had multiple (parallel) pipelined arithmetic sections. The combination is carried another step in the Cray X-MP, a multiprocessor version of the Cray-1. As shown in Fig. 8-20, the Cray X-MP is a shared-memory multiple-processor system that can have from one to four processors. The processors share a large 16-, 32-, or 64-way interleaved memory of from 1 to 8 Mwords. (The original Cray-1 had a 1-Mword memory and later models had 4 Mwords with 16-way interleaving.) As in the Cray-1, the 64-bit memory word is augmented by 8 bits for single-bit error correction double-bit error detection (SECDED). Synchronization among the four processors is accomplished by a common real-time clock and control signals flowing through the interprocessor communications unit.

The central processor is similar to that of the Cray-1, with eight 64-word vector (V) registers, 8 scalar (S) registers, 64 scalar buffer (T) registers, 8 address (A) registers, and 64 address-buffer (B) registers. The buffer of 512 16-bit instructions in each processor is twice as large as that in the Cray-1. The function units are like those of the Cray-1, except that a population pipeline and a second logical pipeline are included among the vector function units. There are three, rather than one, simultaneous interleaved paths to primary memory.

Faster circuits (9.5- rather than 12.5-ns clock period) alone yield a performance increase over the Cray-1 by a factor of 1.3. Increased memory block-transfer rates and the larger instruction buffer permit further speed increases of from 1.2 to 2 for vector operations running on a single-processor Cray X-MP. Multiprocessor configurations are claimed to provide performance increases of approximately 0.9 per added processor. Cray Research also has introduced the Cray-2, a four-processor vector machine with unchained pipelines and with a 4-ns clock period. The Cray-2 has a very large memory (256 Mwords in 128 banks). The Cray-3, a 16-processor computer with high-speed gallium arsenide circuits, has a performance objective 100 times that of the Cray-1. The parallel architecture of the Cray X-MP is extended in the Cray Y-MP.

In addition to the MIMD extensions of pipelined vector processors, there have been several advances in tightly coupled SIMD machines. The Burroughs Scientific Processor (BSP) architecture, Fig. 8-21(a), was based on experience gained with ILLIAC IV. The BSP incorporated several levels of parallelism, as shown in Fig. 8-21(b). At the system level, instructions are preprocessed in the control processor, while the parallel processor handles vector processing. The parallel processor contains 16 arithmetic elements (AE) and 17 processor memory modules, connected to the AEs by the alignment network. The 4- to 64-Mword secondary memory (file memory) is made from charge-coupled devices, described in Chapter 4. This file memory transfers blocks of information at a rate of 12.5 Mwords/s.

Within the control processor a 256-kword local memory holds scalar processor data and programs. The scalar processor operates at a clock rate of 12.5 MHz and performs at 1.5 MFLOPS. Array instructions are passed to the parallel-processor controller, which converts

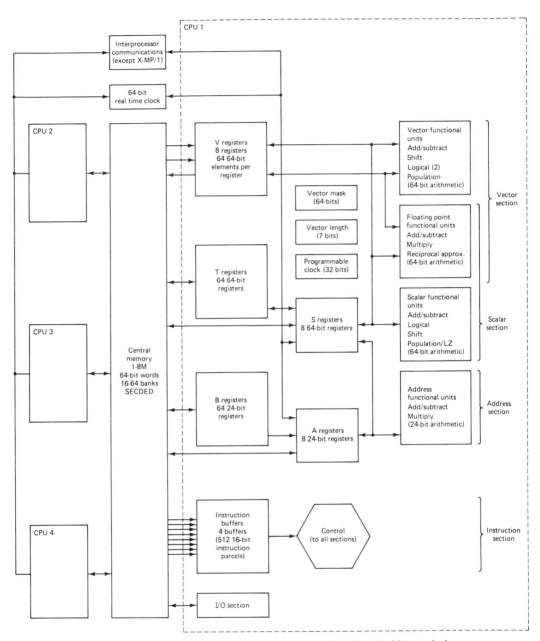

Figure 8-20   Cray X-MP-4 system organization. (Reprinted with permission of Cray Research, Inc.)

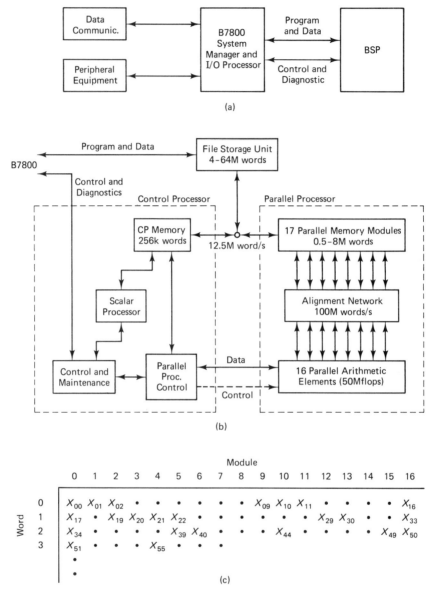

Figure 8-21 Burroughs Scientific Processor. (a) System configuration.
(b) Processor organization. (c) Memory organization.

each instruction to a microsequence for parallel-processor execution. The control and maintenance unit communicates with the B7800 host computer. The master control program (MCP) operating system of the B7800 controls the flow of data and programs to the BSP.

Each of the 16 parallel arithmetic elements of the parallel processor operates on the same microinstruction, unless masked out of operation. The 6.25-MHz clock gives each

AE 3 MFLOPS performance since most operations take 2 or less clock periods. The peak performance target for 16 AEs was 50 MFLOPS. Each AE has a five-stage pipeline that performs data-fetch, align, process, align, and store operations. The alignment network connects each of the 16 AEs with the proper one of the 17 parallel memory modules.

The use of a prime number of memory modules, larger than the number of processors, minimizes conflict for access to any memory module by different processors. The principle is demonstrated in Fig. 8-21(c). An array $X[0 \ldots m, 0 \ldots n]$, with $m = n = 9$, is shown. The 17 elements, X_{00} through X_{16}, occupy the first word of modules 0 through 16, respectively, while X_{17} through X_{33} are in the second words. Commonly used elements are a fixed distance apart. For a single row the element-to-element distance is 1, whereas for a column it is $m + 1$. Major-diagonal elements are $m + 2$ apart, and minor-diagonal elements are separated by m. Since there are a relatively large prime number (17) of modules, the probability of conflict for access by 16 processors is small.

The BSP was withdrawn by Burroughs (now Unisys) before it was completed. The decision reflected the company's concern about the economics of the supercomputer market. Several special-purpose systems also used the SIMD approach of ILLIAC IV. These are described in Chapter 9.

Most organizations for large quantities of processors (or computers) have been less tightly coupled than ILLIAC IV or BSP. Experimental loosely coupled multiprocessors have been studied at Carnegie-Mellon University. Sixteen PDP-11s, each with local memory, were connected to 16 modules of shared memory through a crossbar switch in the C.mmp. This computer was used for studies of hardware and software performance in large-scale multiprocessors in the 1970s. The results of those studies led to the Cm* (Fig. 3-9). The Cm* has five clusters of 10 computers connected through a distributed hierarchical switch. Computers within a cluster communicate through the Map bus, whereas intercluster communication takes place over the intercluster bus. The Cm*, like the C.mmp, has provided a large amount of information on large-scale loosely coupled microprocessor potentials and problems, both from hardware and software perspectives.

The Sequent Balance 8000 shown in Fig. 8-22 is an example of a loosely coupled multiprocessor produced as a standard commercial product. It uses standard microprocessor components in a highly parallel system organization. The shared primary memory of from 8 to 32 Mbytes is connected to the processors and the I/O control structure by two switches. The SB8000 bus is a time-multiplexed 32-bit bus for data transfers at 26.7 Mbytes/s. A 1-bit wide system link and interrupt controller (SLIC) bus transfers control signals among the system modules. System control is provided by the system control/ethernet/diagnostics control subsystem (Ksced). Standard peripheral equipment is managed by the multibus controllers (Kmultibus).

Two to 12 central processors (in pairs) each consist of a National Semiconductor NS32032 microprocessor (described in Appendix B), an NS32082 memory-management unit (seen previously in Fig. 7-28), and an NS32081 floating-point processor (similar to the MC68881 described with Fig. 7-31). A small local memory (Mlocal) holds the operating-system kernel code and data structures. The two-way set-associative

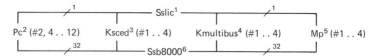

1. Sslic\"System_Link_and_Interrupt_Controller" (synchronous, 10MHz,
   fixed-length_packets, 8 interrupt_categories, 256 handlers/category,
   function: interrupt_and_control-signal_bus).
2. Pc\"Processor_Subsystem" (components: NS32032, NS32082, NS32081, Pslic,
   Ksb8000, Mlocal[0..2^{13}–1]<7..0> Mcache[0..2^{13}–1]<7..0>).
3. Ksced\"System-Control/Ethernet/Diagnostic_Subsystem":

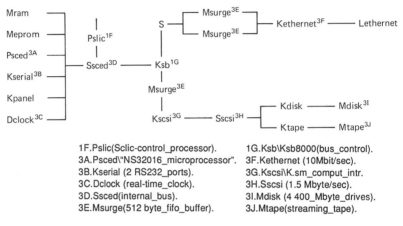

1F.Pslic(Sclic-control_processor).   1G.Ksb\Ksb8000(bus_control).
3A.Psced\"NS32016_microprocessor".   3F.Kethernet (10Mbit/sec).
3B.Kserial (2 RS232_ports).   3G.Kscsi\K.sm_comput_intr.
3C.Dclock (real-time_clock).   3H.Sscsi (1.5 Mbyte/sec).
3D.Ssced(internal_bus).   3I.Mdisk (4 400_Mbyte_drives).
3E.Msurge(512 byte_fifo_buffer).   3J.Mtape(streaming_tape).

4. Kmultibus\"Multibus_Controllers" (9 slots/controller).
5. Mp\"Memory_Subsystem"[0..3][0..2^{21}–1]<7..0> {Connects to Pslic & Ksb}.
6. Ssb8000\"SB8000-Bus" (10 MHz, 32-bit_data, 28-bit_addresses, 12 slots).

Figure 8-22   Sequent Balance 8000 system design.

writethrough cache (see Section 4.5) acts as a buffer to the shared primary memory. Two
controllers (Pslic and Ksb8000) provide interfaces to the two buses described before.

The system control/ethernet/diagnostics controller (Ksced) also uses a standard
National Semiconductor microprocessor for management of the local memory buffers
(Mram, Meprom) and the local controllers. The NS32016 is a 16-bit version of the
NS32032 that is used for the central processors. High-speed ethernet communications to
terminals and secondary memory are connected through 512-byte buffers (Msurge) to the
system bus controller (Ksb8000).

The hypercube (binary *n*-cube) connection mechanism described in the previous
section has been used for several multicomputer configurations. The starting point for most
of these was the California Institute of Technology Cosmic Cube, an experimental
multicomputer system based on message passing. As shown in Fig. 8-23, the 6-cube version
of the Cosmic Cube consists of 64 computers, each with an Intel 8086 microprocessor
processing element, an Intel 8087 numeric coprocessor, 128-kbyte local processing element memory, and a hypercube switch controller to communicate with five other computers. For input/output one of the 64 computers also is attached to the intermediate host
computer, also an Intel 8086-based microcomputer. Extensions can include more connec-

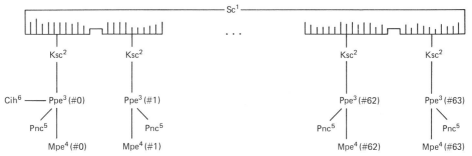

1. Sc\"Hypercube_Switch" (64 nodes, binary_6-cube).
2. Ksc\"Hypercube_Switch_Controller" {addressed by Ppe}.
3. Ppe\"Processing_Element" ("Intel_8086").
4. Mpe\"Processing_Element_Memory" (128 kbytes, DRAM).
5. Pnc\"Numeric_Coprocessor" ("Intel_8087").
6. Cih\"Intermediate_Host" {Intel 8086-based computer}.

Figure 8-23 The Caltech Cosmic Cube.

tions to intermediate host processors, to the limit of one at each hypercube node. The Cosmic Cube has been used in studies of applications of parallel processing.

A commercial extension of the Cosmic Cube, the Intel Hypercube iPSC (Intel Personal SuperComputers) was assembled from 2^k ($k = 2, 3, 4, \ldots$) microcomputers, each with an Intel 80286 integrated processor, an 80287 mathematical coprocessor, and 512 kbytes of dynamic random-access memory. A separate Intel 286/310 workstation is the host that handles input/output and the Xenix (Unix-based) operating system. Systems with 32, 64, and 128 nodes (5-cube, 6-cube, 7-cube) have been delivered and used experimentally in studies of parallel-computer organization and use. Similar computer organizations using other processors were the NCUBE (up to 1024 nodes) and the Ametek System 14 (16 to 256 nodes).

We have seen examples of computers with single processors that have a large word size for high-speed calculation of large floating-point values. This reflects the trend toward high-speed parallel arithmetic units. At the other extreme we find the Connection Machine from Thinking Machines, Inc., a computer with 2^{16} single-bit processors. A system diagram of the Connection Machine is shown in Fig. 8-24. Up to four host processors (VAX or Symbolics 3600) or special-purpose disk-file controllers and the parallel computer are attached to the (8, 8, 4) crossbar switch. Each link of the crossbar can transmit 64 Mbytes/s. The parallel computer has up to four quadrants, each with 2^{14} processors. Communication among the quadrants and with the host processors is controlled by the communication controllers (Kconn). The router switches (Srout) communicate among 1024 computing modules (Ccm) using a binary 10-cube interconnection.

Each computing module (Ccm) contains sixteen 1-bit processing elements (Ppe) and four processing element memory modules (Mpe) of 16 kbits. Processing elements can operate as single-bit processors or can be grouped as two 8-bit or one 16-bit processor. A memory module and eight processing elements are connected to each of two buses (Spe). The buses and the other two memory modules are connected to the router switch

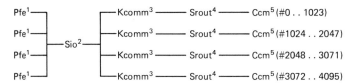

1. Pfe\"Front-End_Processor" {VAX, Symbolics 3600, or Kdisk}.
2. Sio\"Input/output_Switch" (crosspoint, 64 Mbytes/s/link).
3. Kcomm\"Connection_Machine_Controller".
4. Srout\"Router_Switch" (binary_10-cube).
5. Ccm\"Connection_Machine_Computer":

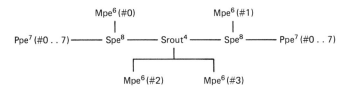

6. Mpe\"Processing_Element_Memory" (16 kbits).
7. Ppe\"Processing_Element" (1-bit_ALU, flag_register).
8. Spe {connects 1 Mpe to 8 Ppe}.

Figure 8-24   The Connection Machine.

(Srout) that can transfer information between the buses or can communicate with the other 1023 routers on a quadrant or with the communication controller. Communication among computing modules uses packet switching, where a packet contains a 16-bit destination address (2 quadrant, 10 router, 4 processing elements) and 32 bits of data. Message buffering takes place in a router switch if the output path is not free.

Raw computing power of 2^{16} MIPS is claimed for operations on single-bit data. This assumes all 2^{16} processors are operating concurrently at a rate of a million instructions per second (1 MIPS). Multiple-bit data operations are slowed down accordingly. For a document search problem, performance was determined to be equivalent to that of a single conventional computer operating at over 6650 MIPS. The Connection Machine approach is aimed particularly at the solution of large nonnumeric problems.

8.7 PERFORMANCE OF PARALLEL SYSTEMS

An example of calculation of the inner product of m elements in multiplying an $l \times m$ matrix by an $m \times n$ matrix was described briefly in Section 8.3. It demonstrated how pipelined processors and array processors act as SIMD machines. We will pursue this example in more detail to obtain estimates of performance of SIMD computers. In the sequential pipeline processor (one without vector instructions), a short iteration loop involving MULTIPLY and ADD operations is repeated many times. Address indexing through the arrays is used to select the stream of m argument pairs for the two vectors (a row of one array and a column of the other) to flow into processor registers. Let us identify the times for suboperations of an instruction as t_f, t_i, t_r, t_m, and t_s for instruction fetching, indexing, single-argument fetching, multiply instruction execution, and result storing, respectively. If the suboperations can be overlapped, the sequence of m multiplies takes m times the longest of the suboperation times plus the sum of the others, or the sum of all operation times and $m - 1$ times the longest:

$$T_{mp} = \text{SUM}(t_f, t_i, 2t_r, t_m, t_s) + [(m - 1) * \text{MAX}(t_f, t_i, t_r, t_m)]$$

The first term represents the pipeline filling time and the second reflects pipeline flow rate. Time for the addition sequence T_{ap} can be expressed similarly, except that t_a, addition execution time, replaces t_m.

If the pipelined computer includes vector operations, the operations proceed in the same manner, except that there is only a single instruction fetch for each of the two operations. The factor t_f does not appear as an argument for the MAX function. The time for m multiplies is expressed as

$$T_{mv} = \text{SUM}(t_f, t_i, 2t_r, t_m, t_s) + [(m - 1) * \text{MAX}(t_i, t_r, t_m)]$$

If t_f is not the largest of the times, the difference between the two approaches is that the introduction of the more complicated vector instruction results in less potential conflict for memory transfers.

A dual-pipeline vector computer permits "chaining" of the vector operations so that the result of multiplication in one pipeline flows immediately into the second pipeline for accumulation. The fill time of the second pipeline is masked and the total elapsed time for the m chained multiplies and adds is

$$T_{ch} = \text{SUM}(t_f, t_i, 2t_r, t_m, t_a, t_s) + [(m-1)*\text{MAX}(t_i, t_r, t_m, t_a)]$$

Unless $t_m = t_a$ it will be necessary that the two pipelines be synchronized. An equivalent result can be obtained with a multiple-function pipeline that has independent addition and multiplication stages. Here the elapsed time T_{ma} is the same as T_{mp} or T_{mv} for the single-instruction pipelines, except that t_m is replaced by t_{ma}, the time for execution of multiply and add in the pipeline function units.

Array processors handle the inner-product example in a different manner. The startup (scalar processing) time includes time needed to transfer the first pair of arguments for the multiply and an initial sum of 0 to each processor that is required (if m is not more than the number of processors, p). All active processors then execute a sequence of m multiply and add operations. If there are more elements m in each vector than there are processors p (the general case), then the sequence of operations must be repeated m DIV p times. If the fetching of arguments after the first pair is carried out concurrently with the arithmetic operations, then the time to perform the set of p inner-product calculations is

$$T_{ar} = \text{SUM}(t_f, t_i, 2t_r, t_m, t_a, t_s) + \{(m-1)*\text{MAX}[t_i, t_r, (t_m+t_a)]\}$$

similar to the time T_{ch} for the vector compute., but here the arithmetic operation times, t_m and t_a, are longer since the arithmetic units are not pipelined. When m is larger than p the total inner-product execution time is

$$T_{ip} = (m \text{ DIV } p) * T_{ar}$$

The relationships between scalar processing (pipeline filling or array loading) and vector processing are portrayed in Fig. 8-25. With an eight-stage pipeline processor, Fig. 8-25(a), the pipeline is initialized by the scalar operations (S.P.) and the vector operations are initiated, flowing from stage to stage as indicated by the diagonal arrow. If there is no separate scalar processor, the break between separate vector operations (vector processing *A* and vector processing *B* in the illustration) is much larger. The separate scalar processor assumed in the timing of Fig. 8-25(a) allows scalar and vector operations to be carried out concurrently. In optimum cases the gap between the two vector operations could be eliminated. A rough measure of the utilization of the processors is the area of actual (scalar and vector) processing divided by the area under the dashed line of the diagram.

A similar representation of timing for an array computer is shown in Fig. 8-25(b). In this diagram 16 array processors and a separate scalar processor (the host for ILLIAC IV or BSP) are shown. The array is initially loaded by the scalar processor and then array processing *A* takes place. The stepped reduction in processor use at the end of array processing *A* is due to the final calculation of the *m* REM *p* results when *m* is not an exact

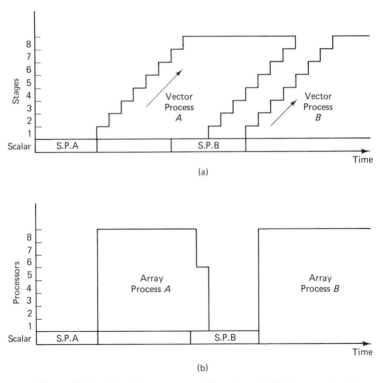

(a)

(b)

Figure 8-25 Parallel-processor utilization. (a) Eight-stage pipeline. (b) Eight-processor array.

multiple of p. Even with the separate scalar processor, there is a gap between array processing A and array processing B for initiation of B. Again processor utilization is measured by the area representing processor activity divided by the area under the dashed line.

While these diagrams are useful to obtain rough measures of processor use in the two types of SIMD machines, they cannot be used to compare pipeline and array processors. If the diagrams were drawn for the two different architectures implemented with the same amount of hardware, they could be used for that purpose.

Since pipeline and array forms of parallel computers were first introduced reports of both theoretical and experimental appraisals of performance have appeared. Even more than with straightforward computer architectures, realistic performance evaluation is very difficult to achieve. In a parallel architecture the utilization of the hardware provided is very sensitive to the particular problem being solved. For example, referring to Fig. 8-25, what is the actual relationship of scalar and vector processing in our particular problem mix? While accurate quantitative measures cannot be made, we can identify some principles of relative performance of different architectures for different problem characteristics.

Hwang and Briggs [HwanK84] develop a general expression for the speedup ratio S_k for a pipeline vector computer with uniform instruction times in terms of the number of stages in the pipeline, k, the number of instructions in a task, n, and the length of vector arguments in each instruction, N_i $(1 < i < n)$:

$$S_k = [k * \text{SUM} (N_i)]/[n * (k - 1) + \text{SUM} (N_i)]$$

This is better expressed in terms of the average length of vector arguments, $N_{avg} = \text{SUM} (N_i)/n$, as

$$S_k = (k * N_{avg})/(k - 1 + N_{avg})$$

The utilization factor, U, for the pipeline stages is S_k/k:

$$U = N_{avg}/(k - 1 + N_{avg})$$

Results of S_k and U for various values of N_{avg} with k ranging from 1 to 10 are shown in Fig. 8-26. The upper ($N_{avg} >> k$) and lower ($N_{avg} = 1$) limits for S_k are defined by the solid lines. As expected, S_k approaches k and U approaches unity as N_{avg} becomes larger. S_k levels off when N_{avg} is less than k. The equations and the curves of Fig. 8-26 reflect the ratio of processing area to total area under the dashed line in Fig. 8-25(a). Over a number of cycles of operation the N_i are the lengths of the individual processing times for activities of each pipeline stage and N_{avg} represents the average of all those times. The number of instructions, n, reflects the time for a cycle of scalar–vector computation. Similar results can be developed for the array computers. Here allowance must be made for times when not all of the processors are active, reflected in the "step down" of activity at the end of the vector-processing cycle in Fig. 8-25(b).

Bokhari [BokhS87] reported on an experiment running the sieve of Eratosthenes on a FLEX/32 MIMD multicomputer. The FLEX/32 had 20 computers connected in pairs over a global bus. Each computer contained a NS32032 microprocessor, a floating-point

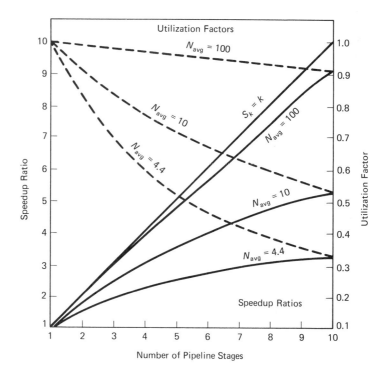

Figure 8-26   Vector pipeline performance.

coprocessor, a cache, and 1-Mbyte of memory. There were 2 Mbytes of shared memory accessible over the global bus. Bokhari ran a parallel solution to the problem of finding all the primes of P positive integers, where P ranged from 0.5 to 2 million. The problem was run several times for each value of P on 1 to 17 processors. (The other three were used for operating-system and monitoring functions.) A summary of his results for $P = 1$ million is shown in Fig. 8-27.

His basic algorithm took 35 s to run on a single processor. On three processors it took 13 s, a utilization factor of 90%. With five processors the time was 8 s, still a good utilization of 88%. After seven processors (time = 6 s, utilization 83%) the time leveled off, showing that a single processor was handling all the remaining work. He revised the algorithm to permit task splitting for "load balancing", also shown in the figure. The revision required more use of shared memory, so its single-processor time is longer (53s), but the distribution of tasks to processors results in a drop in elapsed time for any addition of a processor. Sample processors, times and utilizations are 3, 20, 88%; 7, 9, 84%; and 15, 5, 71%. The curve for the theoretical minimum time (reciprocal of the number of processors) for the basic algorithm is shown for comparison. These results show remarkably good utilization of a multicomputer system. The sieve problem is orderly and decomposable. It requires very little interprocess communication.

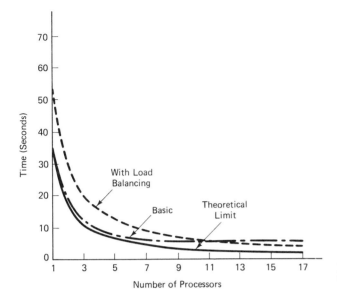

Figure 8-27   The sieve of 10^6 numbers on a multiprocessor [BokhS87].

Issues of decomposability of problems for multiple-processor systems were addressed by Cvetanovic [CvetZ87]. Computation was assumed to be decomposable and uniformly distributed to the N processors for the fraction of time, p, that the system spends on parallel sections of a problem. She considered three forms of decomposition of communication overhead: communication per processor inversely proportional to N, inversely proportional to the square root of N, and constant (independent of N). Problem solution speedup for the case of communication overhead proportional to N with various values of p are shown in Fig. 8-28. Values of N from 1 (2^0) to 2^{14} were considered. In all cases the speedup factor asymptotically approaches a value of $1/(1-p)$.

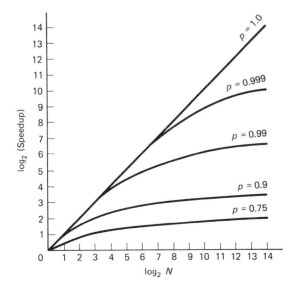

Figure 8-28   Speedup ratios for various parallel section fractions [CvetZ87].

H. S. Stone [StonH87] outlines a parametric evaluation of performance of multiprocessors considering the number of (uniform-sized) tasks, M, broken into task groups, k_i, each run on one of N processors, the units of time, R, for executing each task, and the units of time, C, for communications overhead for each communication between separate processors. Execution time T is

$$T = R * \text{MAX}(k_i) + (C/2) * [M^2 - \text{SUM}(k_i^2)]$$

The first term represents the longest running time on all the N processors, whereas the second reflects communications overhead. The latter results from multiplying half the communication time by the sum of the tasks performed by each processor multiplied by the external tasks that must be communicated with:

$$(C/2) * \{\text{SUM}[k_i * (M - k_i)]\} = (C/2) * [M^2 - \text{SUM}(k_i^2)]$$

If assignments are uniformly distributed so that $k_i = M/N$ for all i (assuming M is an exact multiple of N), then

$$T = (R * M/N) + (C * M^2/2) - (C * M^2/2N)$$

The time to perform all tasks on one processor (without communications overhead) is $R * M$. A comparison of the times shows that if $R/C > M/2$ then a performance increase results from the multiprocessor system with evenly distributed tasks.

The time for a single processor divided by that for multiple processors gives the speedup ratio:

$$S_N = R * M/[R * M/N + C * M^2 * (1 - 1/N)/2]$$
$$= N * (R/C)/\{(R/C) + (M/N) * [N^2 * (1 - 1/N)]\}$$

Utilization is S_N/N:

$$U_N = (R/C)/\{(R/C) + (M/N) * [N^2 * (1 - 1/N)]\}$$

Figure 8-29 shows utilization for various values of N (2, 8, 32), R/C (1, 8, 64), and M/N (2, 4, 8). It shows that communications overhead can impose a severe penalty on multiprocessor systems. Since the number of messages is related to the number of independent processes running on different processors, increasing the number of processors to handle larger quantities of processes is self-defeating unless communications times can be almost totally masked by processing times.

The illustration indicates that the masking must be large enough for R/C to be much greater than 64 for more than 32 processors. The case of $N = 32$ and $R/C = 64$ is particularly interesting. We can multiply the number of processors, N, by the utilization factor to determine if the added processors add anything to performance. We see that the speedup ($N * U$) is only 2 if there are twice as many tasks as processors ($M/N = 2$). When $M/N = 4$, 32 processors perform about as well as one. If $M/N = 8$ the 32 processors perform at half the speed of a single processor. This suggests severe problems for message-based large-scale multicomputer systems.

Holliday and Vernon [HollM87] studied the interaction between processors and memory in MIMD multiprocessor systems using general timed Petri nets to simplify discrete-time Markov chains. The model was applied to variable numbers of processors,

N =		2	8	32
U:				
R/C = 1	M/N = 2	0.33	0.018	0.001
	4	0.20	0.009	0.0005
	8	0.11	0.0044	0.0003
R/C = 8	M/N = 2	0.80	0.125	0.008
	4	0.67	0.067	0.004
	8	0.50	0.034	0.002
R/C = 64	M/N = 2	0.97	0.53	0.062
	4	0.94	0.36	0.032
	8	0.89	0.22	0.016

U = Speedup/N (Utilization)
N = Number of processors
M = Number of tasks
R = Task execution time
C = Communication overhead

Figure 8-29 Multiprocessor utilization [StonH87].

memory modules, and bus sizes. They considered various memory-request probabilities, assuming that processes on all processors are in any of three states: running, waiting for a memory module that is busy, or accessing a memory module. Fixed memory-access times are assumed. Their results are compared with several similar studies.

An interesting result is presented in Fig. 8-30. This shows the speedup ratio with a 10-processor/10-memory system and various numbers of buses, including the crossbar. Speedup ratio is plotted against memory-request probabilities. They note that when the number of buses is small there is a knee in the curves (at a speedup ratio of about 8.75) that represents a "critical memory-request probability". Request probabilities higher than that cause a rapid falloff in speedup ratio (and processor utilization). For the small number of buses the lower limit of speedup ratio is the number of buses. As the number of buses increases, approaching the crossbar, memory contention is more important than bus contention. The crossbar represents a system that is not constrained by the number of processor-memory paths.

This review of some evaluations of performance of parallel systems demonstrates the complexities involved in such evaluations. The results are not totally consistent because each is based on a different set of assumptions. Much more precise modeling is needed for realistic comparisons among architectural approaches. The studies do not resolve the issue of whether the better approach to high performance is a small number of very powerful processors or a very large quantity of simple processors (or computers).

8.8 SUMMARY

In this chapter we have reviewed how parallel organizations can lead to high-performance computers. Parallelism within individual processors and multiple-processor

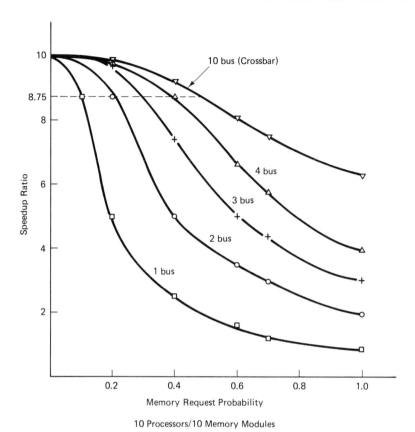

Figure 8-30 Processor–memory contention [HollM87].

approaches can yield performance beyond that possible with a straightforward sequential machine built with the fastest available components. History tells us that no matter how fast our circuits there always is a need for computer organizations that achieve higher levels of performance. Computer designs that respond to these pressures, while not always commercially successful, have spawned architectures and technologies that have been introduced into the main stream of computer design.

Our approach to the subject has used examples of high-performance computers that have been developed in the past, starting with a description of the IBM 7030 (Stretch). There we saw parallelism introduced in the central-processor organization. That description was followed by reviews of different approaches to parallel organization of the processors and of the systems. The examples concluded with an examination of alternative forms of computer control aimed at using parallelism and exploiting large-scale integrated circuits.

Computer organizations were categorized as single-instruction single-data stream (SISD), single-instruction multiple-data stream (SIMD), and multiple-instruction multiple-data stream (MIMD), reflecting the degree of parallelism and the independence of processes being executed concurrently. The Texas Instruments Advanced Scientific Computer (ASC) was an early SIMD machine and the Denelcor Heterogeneous Element Processor (HEP) was used to demonstrate MIMD principles.

Alternative approaches to SIMD design were examined. We compared pipelined processors with and without vector (multiple-indexed argument) instructions, starting with the CDC Star-100 and showing the evolution to the Cray-1 and the CDC Cyber 205. In the CDC computers statically reconfigurable pipelines are used and the design attempts to maximize the flow of arguments from memory. The Cray approach emphasizes flexible multifunction pipelines and a large number of processor registers to mask memory accesses. A very different SIMD approach was taken by Burroughs and the University of Illinois in the ILLIAC IV. This parallel computer used an array of 64 processors that had a single common control unit. All processors execute the same instructions on different arguments. Despite the differences in organization, the pipeline vector processors and the array processors have many similarities in results.

In preparation for considering large-scale parallelism, we reviewed various mechanisms for communicating among computer modules. The different switches exhibit different characteristics in the total number of nodes, the number that can be reached over a direct link (connectivity), and the number of steps required to reach any module from any other. Various switches that can be used to connect at least 16 nodes were compared for cost and performance. Basic logic building blocks can be used to implement the different switches.

Several examples of large-scale parallelism for supercomputers were reviewed, starting with parallel-processor versions of the pipeline vector machines. The Cray X-MP, with up to four processors connected directly to an interleaved primary memory with a crossbar, shows how parallelism at the system level is added to the parallelism in the vector processor itself to achieve extremely high performance. An alternative approach uses a large number of simpler standard processors in a loosely coupled multiprocessor to achieve system-level parallelism. The Sequent Balance 8000 uses National Semiconductor microprocessors and floating-point coprocessors in a unique system organization.

Tightly coupled multiprocessors (SIMD computers) have evolved from the ILLIAC IV. The Burroughs Scientific Processor (BSP) used 16 processors with common microcontrol sequences to perform the same operations concurrently. A feature of the BSP was the use of a relatively large number of memory modules dynamically connected to the processors to minimize memory-access conflicts. Other extensions of tightly coupled multiprocessors include the Caltech Cosmic Cube and the Connection Machine from Thinking Machines, Inc. Both use the hypercube (binary n-cube) interconnection scheme to permit distribution of processes among a large number of processors.

Our discussion of parallel architectures closed with a review of performance-evaluation principles applied to parallel systems. Some general principles of pipeline and array processors were reviewed and were followed by summaries of results of theoretical and experimental studies of parallel systems.

8.9 ADDITIONAL READING

[GorsG86] includes an overview of SIMD and MIMD computation. More detail on parallel computer architectures and related software issues are presented in [HwanK84], [KungS87], and [StonH87]. [KoggP81] covers pipeline computer architecture.

New material on parallel computers and parallel processing is presented at the annual parallel-processing conferences, sponsored in 1987 by Pennsylvania State University, and at the IEEE-ACM annual symposia on computer architecture. *IEEE Computer* magazine often devotes issues to the subjects. More detailed technical articles are found in many issues of *Communications of the ACM* and *IEEE Transactions on Computers*. [LiuMT82] was a special issue of the latter on parallel and distributed processing.

[FlynM66] categorized computers as SISD, SIMD, MISD, and MIMD. [RamaC77] is a good starting point for reviewing principles of pipeline computers. Parallel algorithms and architectures are covered in [KuckD77]. [JordH84] reviews pipelined-MIMD programming .

Many examples of parallel computers are covered in this chapter. For more information the reader is referred to Burroughs D825 [AndeJ62]; Ramo Wooldridge RW-400 [PortR60]; the SAGE AN/FSQ-7 [EverR57]; IBM 7030 (Stretch) [BlocE59]; Texas Instruments ASC [WatsW72]; Denelcor HEP [SmitB78] and [KowaJ85]; CDC Star-100 [HigbL73]; Cray-1 [RussR78]; Cyber 205 and Cray-1 [KozdE80]; ILLIAC IV [BarnG68] and [BoukW72] (and its predecessor, Solomon [SlotD62]); Burroughs Scientific Processor [StokR77] and [KuckD82] (prime memory [LawrD82]); C.mmp [JoneA80]; Cm* [GehrE82]; Cosmic Cube [SeitC86]; Connection Machine [HillW86]; and manuals of the manufacturers.

[DongJ85] summarizes data on many new supercomputers. Two specific computers are compared in [JordK87].

Several special issues of *IEEE Computer* ([WuChu81], [FreeH83], and [BhuyL87]) have been devoted to interconnection networks. Network topologies for large numbers of computer modules are covered by [FengT81], [HwanK84], and [SiegH84]. Specific examples are given by [BarnG68] (ILLIAC IV); [PeasM77] (the binary n-cube); [GokeR73] (banyan networks); [PateJ81] (delta networks); [StonH71] (shuffle); [WuC&F80] (multistage networks); [WuC&F81] (shuffle exchanges); and [LawrD75] (omega network).

Parallel-computer performance principles are reviewed in [HwanK84] and [StonH87]. [LiuMT82] contains papers on performance issues. [AgraA83] covers performance evaluation. [DennP87] outlines performance evaluations performed by NASA. Several papers on performance evaluation ([BokhS87], [CvetZ87], and [HollM87]) were cited in Section 8.7. [AgraD86], [HackJ86], and [SangJ86] contain much relevant information and references.

8.10 PROBLEMS

8-1. Consider a computer that has the following features of the CDC 6600: multiple concurrently operating D units (Fig. 6-2) and central-processor register-to-register operations (Fig. 4-6). The computer has two function units, D(#1..2) and four general registers, G[0..3]. D(#1) is a MOVE unit that executes instructions involving one source and one destination register, such as G[1] ← G[3], G[0] ← left shift G[2], etc. D(#2) is an ALU that performs operations with two source and (optionally) one destination register.

    a. Show how conflicts might arise as a result of concurrent operation of D(#1) and D(#2) if no assumptions can be made about the relative speeds of operation of the two.

    b. Describe in ISP a mechanism (like the CDC "scoreboard") to resolve or to prohibit the conflicts of part a.

8-2. If a program is to take advantage of the multiple processing units of an SIMD or an MIMD organization (Fig. 8-3), the problem must be converted to an algorithm with program sections or data items that are independent of each other. The independent program segments or multiple copies of the same segment can be run concurrently. For both independent program segments and independent data items, discuss the issues involved and describe how they would be handled by the program writer, by a compiler, and by an operating system.

8-3. In Section 8.4 both static and dynamic multifunction pipelines were described. Describe in detail the operation of each, using Fig. 6-25(b) as a model. Discuss the advantages and the difficulties with each pipeline organization.

8-4. **a.** Describe how the following data-dependent iteration statement that includes conditional control would be executed on a pipelined vector-processor version of an SIMD computer:

```
for I := 1 to N do
    if A[I] > 1 then A[I] := 1/A[I]
         else A[I] := -A[I];
```

    Describe the step-by-step execution at the machine code level defining any registers you need for the description.

    b. Repeat part a for the following statement:

```
for I := 1 to N do
    if A[I] > 1 then A[I] := A[N + 1 - I];
```

    Discuss any issues related to the meaning of a concurrent form of the statement.

8-5. In an array-processor version of an SIMD computer with four independent memory modules, show how to store a 4×4 array $A[I, J]$ so that all elements of any row or of any column can be accessed simultaneously.

8-6. Consider a multiple-computer organization with 64 independently operating computers. The computers communicate through a banyan network switch that uses two-function routers of Fig. 8-17. One mode of communication entails "broadcasting" a message from any one computer to all others. Extend the baseline and the n-cube switches shown in Figs. 8-19(a) and 8-19(d) to allow for 64 inputs and 64 outputs. For each switch, describe how broadcasting is achieved (show the router settings and the number of steps required). Show that for the $N = 64$ omega network, Fig. 8-19(b), with four-function routers, broadcasting is possible from every computer.

8-7. For the Burroughs Scientific Processor 17-module memory, Fig. 8-21(c) shows the distances between elements of a 10 by 10 array ($A[0 \ldots m, 0 \ldots n], m = n = 9$). For the general case of p memory modules and an array $A[0 \ldots m, 0 \ldots n]$, develop the expressions for the distances between adjacent elements of rows and of columns in terms of p, m, and n. Do the same for any value of m when $m = n$ for the distances between elements of major diagonals and of minor diagonals. From your results, show why p should be a relatively large prime number.

8-8. Consider a program dealing with operations on the array $\mathbf{A}[0 \ldots 63]$ to yield array $\mathbf{B}[0 \ldots 31]$. All results could be calculated concurrently if there were a sufficient quantity of arithmetic function units. The operations are repeated on $\mathbf{B}[0 \ldots 31]$ to yield $\mathbf{C}[0 \ldots 15]$, and on $\mathbf{C}[0 \ldots 15]$ to get $\mathbf{D}[0 \ldots 7]$, etc., until a final scalar value G is obtained. Show a diagram similar to Fig. 8-25 demonstrating the complete execution timing for generation of G from $\mathbf{A}[0 \ldots 63]$ and calculate the utilization of the processors for each of the following:

    a. A pipelined vector processor with two similar 10-stage pipelined arithmetic units and a scalar unit. The vector operations on each pair of arguments in $\mathbf{A}$ to yield a result in $\mathbf{B}$ take 16 clock times. Operations on successive argument pairs can be started every 3 clock times. Scalar processing to initiate the process on each cycle ($\mathbf{B} \leftarrow \mathbf{A}$, $\mathbf{C} \leftarrow \mathbf{B}$, etc.) takes 24 clock times and that to terminate the process after G has been generated takes 16 clock times.

    b. An array processor similar to the ILLIAC IV, but with 16 processing elements and a separate scalar processor. The arithmetic operations on each pair of arguments in $\mathbf{A}$ to yield a result in $\mathbf{B}$ take 16 clock times. Scalar processing to initiate the process in each cycle ($\mathbf{B} \leftarrow \mathbf{A}$, $\mathbf{C} \leftarrow \mathbf{B}$, etc.) takes 24 clock times and that to terminate the process after G has been generated takes 16 clock times.

8-9. State the starting assumptions and the steps needed to arrive at the expressions for speedup ratio S_k and utilization factor U developed by Hwang and Briggs. The expressions are discussed in Section 8.7 and are plotted for various values of k in Fig. 8-26.

8-10. H. S. Stone's parametric evaluation of multiprocessor performance to obtain execution time T as a function of execution time R and communications overhead C for each of M tasks being run on one of N processors is developed in Section 8.7. Examples of processor utilization for $N = 2$, 8, and 32; $R/C = 1$, 8, and 64; and $M/N = 2$, 4, and 8 are shown in Fig. 8-29. Using Stone's equations, calculate and plot the execution time T for $N = 1, 2, 4, 8$, and 16 processors with $M = 64$ uniform-size tasks, for $R = 128$ units, and with $C = 1$, 2, and 4 units.

8.11 PROJECTS

8-A. For the computer system you are evaluating in Project 1-A, describe which of its applications could be benefited by a parallel computer system. Discuss the relative merits of both pipelined vector processors and array processors, as compared with the computer you are describing, for the applications.

8-B. You have been designing a computer architecture in Project 1-B. Discuss how the requirements you started with would have to grow to warrant introduction of a parallel computer organization to your design. Describe how your design would be expanded to incorporate parallelism.

9

Special-Purpose Computing Systems

In Chapter 7 we reviewed situations in which special-purpose processors are better matched to a requirement than are general-purpose processors. Further investigation of computer-system requirements demonstrates that there also are cases where special-purpose systems are more suitable than general-purpose computers. In Chapter 2 a methodology for system development to meet a set of requirements was outlined. There we saw that one of the decisions to be made early in the development of a computing system is the selection between a general-purpose and a special-purpose approach.

9.1 PROBLEM ANALOGS

Special-purpose solutions should be considered if processing requirements are so specialized that a general-purpose computer is not economical. Sometimes this is the result of a need for a small number of operations to be performed at extremely high speeds as might be true for CAT (computer-aided tomography) processing in medical diagnosis systems. In this application the processing entails performing in real time correlations of signals from a large number of sensor scans taken from different angles. The correlation functions are all the same and are well-defined. Very few alternative control paths are involved in the processing. A special-purpose computer that contains a large number of correlation processors operating in parallel is more suited to the task than the very powerful general-purpose computer that would be needed to perform the same functions sequentially.

In these medical-imaging applications an irregular shaped object (part of the human body) is subjected to a stimulus (x-ray, ultrasound, magnetic) that is attenuated to different degrees by different constituents of the object. Since it is possible to measure only the composite effect of the object on any traversal of a signal, the interior of the object cannot be determined from individual traversals. However, signal-processing techniques, aided by knowledge of the shapes and the attenuating effects of abnormalities expected to be found in the object, permit an image of the object to be reconstructed from correlations of a large number of signal traversals from different angles. A simplified version of the process is depicted in Fig. 9-1. Scanning of the body part from different angles by the revolving transmitter and receivers is depicted in Fig. 9-1(a). An idealized model of the body part being scanned has a uniform outer layer and a homogeneous interior. Two possible abnormalities, both offering a reduction of attenuation by about the same amount, are present. The first (void a) forms a uniform layer on an arc of the interior of the surface layer and the second is a circular void (b) in the interior.

The instrumentation consists of a signal transmitter and an array of signal receivers. While the receivers can detect the amount of signal that is propagated through the object, only the total attenuation by the object can be measured on any scan by any one receiver. Resolution of each received signal is poor and processing is required to separate noise and to construct a smoothed signal over one rotation (scan) of the instrument. The processed signal produced over one scan is represented in Fig. 9-1(b). The scan indicates that there are abnormalities (areas of reduced attenuation) over 2 arcs. Further processing can form an image of the object with its abnormalities by comparing the actual smoothed signal with models that show the effects of each of many possible abnormalities. The required correlations can entail a large amount of processing at high speeds. All of the correlation processing for signal smoothing and for image construction is repeated many times. Very little control structure is required in the processing sequence. In many medical-imaging systems like this a special-purpose computer is more feasible than the very powerful general-purpose computer that would otherwise be required.

In another situation we might find that different functions are associated with different parts of a physical system. Examples of this are systems for chemical and biological process control, vehicle controls, and large system simulators. A solution to these requirements might entail using a number of specialized processors at different locations in the physical system being controlled rather than a centralized general-purpose computer. Here the cost of the special-purpose and the general-purpose computers might not be very different, but reliability and maintainability issues might lend weight to the special-purpose solution.

The special-purpose designs of these examples can be developed from analogs (models) of the physical systems. Computer requirements are established by determining the processing used in the analogs. This approach causes us to focus on the physics of the problem and leads us to processing solutions matched to those problem physics. In the radar data-processor example described in the next section the memory is organized to reflect the physics of radar returns. We will see other examples of the use of physical analogs in developing special-purpose computers.

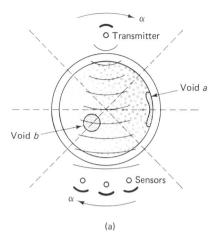

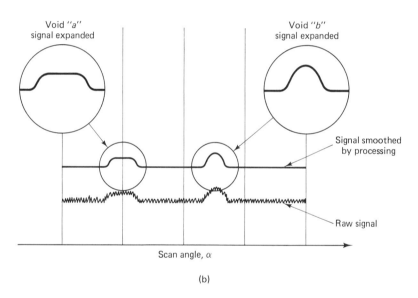

Figure 9-1 Medical-image processing. (a) Model of subject. (b) Signals sensed (picture "a" is reconstructed by the computer).

The selection of the design approach should follow a careful analysis of the requirements and an examination of the various alternatives that are available for solution. If several approaches appear to be feasible the selection is based on initial cost, hardware- and software-support costs, reliability, maintainability, and flexibility to adapt to anticipated system changes.

Special-purpose computers do not have to be designed starting from the basic circuits. Many building blocks ranging from controllers designed for large classes of problems to microprogammable processors, memories, I/O processors, and transducers are available to the custom-system designer. The decision on using standard components as opposed to a complete special design should be based on economics of design, manufacture, and system-lifetime support. A significant part of the cost of a special-purpose system can be in the custom test equipment that might be required for failure detection and diagnosis.

For some high-performance requirements conventional computer controls, even with the parallel architectures of Chapter 8, might not be satisfactory. Alternative control mechanisms based on data flow, string reduction, and graph reduction are possible. Where the computations are well-defined large numbers of simple processors can be organized on a single semiconductor chip as a systolic array.

In this chapter we consider the possibilities for special-purpose solutions to computer-system designs. Approaches to special-purpose design are reviewed and compared with general-purpose computer architectures. Several examples demonstrate how special-purpose systems can yield effective solutions to computational problems.

We saw in Chapter 8 that computer performance requirements beyond the capabilities of the fastest sequential computers led to parallel architectures. These architectures, represented by the CDC Star-100 and ILLIAC IV started as special-purpose approaches to specific problems. As experience was gained with these experimental machines, the designs evolved into standard products, in effect becoming general-purpose machines. The distinction between general-purpose and special-purpose computers might be in the extent to which the architectures have been accepted for standard products by the computer manufacturers.

9.2 RESPONDING TO REQUIREMENTS

The design methodology discussed in Chapter 2 identified requirements analysis as the first step toward developing a computer architecture. This analysis of requirements for a system should have determined the results that a computing system will produce (the output), the information available to generate those results (the input), the frequencies in which results must be generated, the precision and resolution required for the output, and the environmental, economic, time, and risk constraints under which we are operating.

When those requirements are understood by the developer and the customer it is possible to determine if a general-purpose computer or a special-purpose computer better solves the problem. A general-purpose computer (or a system based on it) and a programming system to adapt it to the problem offer advantages of flexibility to meet changes in the problem or to work on a variety of problems. On the other hand, a computer uniquely designed for the problem or class of problems might be more economical, or might be the only solution feasible with current technology. In many cases the decision is obvious, but in others detailed analysis of alternatives is required. To determine whether it is feasible to consider a special-purpose computer we should be convinced that the problem is clearly understood and that the parameters for problem solution are fixed. Before undertaking a special-purpose design we must be sure that the algorithms we have developed to attack the problem are realistic and will not be changed to make our design obsolete.

An example demonstrates the approach to be taken in deciding on and developing a special-purpose computer system. An analysis of the processing requirements for a radar data processor might show that a general-purpose computer would need processing speeds at the upper limit of current technology. At the same time the processing to be performed might not require many of the features and operations of the usual general-purpose computer. In this case a special-purpose radar data processor that is an analog of the physical situation might provide an economical solution. Figure 9-2 demonstrates a system of this kind and identifies the processing that is required.

The system consists of a search radar transmitter and receiver, a beacon interrogator transmitter, a beacon transponder receiver, beacon and radar antennas, and the data processor. The search radar covers a range of 250 miles and an accuracy of roughly 1/4 mile is required. The radar antenna gives an effective beam width of about 1.5 degrees. The radar transmitter generates a pulse signal at a rate of 360 Hz, allowing for return of a reflected signal at the longest range before the next pulse is transmitted. The compromise between the need to sample the target space as often as possible and to maximize the number of sequential pulses on a target in any scan (rotation of the antenna) leads to a rotation period of 10 s. The 1.5-degree beam illuminates a target for about 15 successive pulses. The radar receiver generates two outputs, an amplitude pulse indicating that an object has reflected energy, and a phase shift of the pulse indicating that the object is moving in a radial direction. The receiver sensitivity is set to permit a high percentage of noise pulses to be passed in order that low-level target signals not be lost. The time between transmission and reception of each pulse identifies distance.

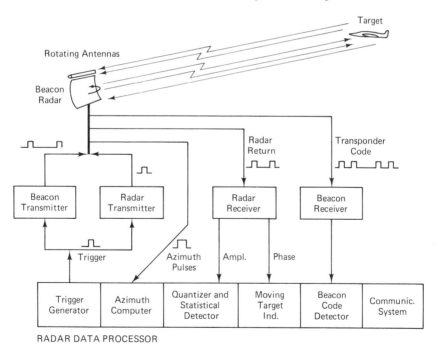

Figure 9-2 A pulse radar system.

The rotating radar antenna generates a signal every 1/10 of a degree of rotation to identify changes in azimuth. A special pulse is generated when the antenna faces north. The beacon transmitter whose antenna is attached to the radar antenna transmits a pair of pulses separated by a fixed time to query aircraft on their identity. Cooperating aircraft carry beacon transponders that transmit coded identifier-pulse sequences a fixed time after they receive the beacon inquiry. The beacon transmitter operates at the same pulse repetition rate as the radar. The beacon receiver reproduces the aircraft codes it receives.

The radar data processor must generate a reference signal to initiate the radar and beacon pulses (trigger generator). It must take the signals provided by the radar and analyze them to separate targets from noise at each range interval (quantizer and statistical detector). The azimuth (in pulse periods) of each target must be calculated (azimuth computer). It uses the radar phase data to separate moving targets from fixed objects (moving-target indicator). Signals from the beacon receiver must be processed to determine identities of cooperating targets (beacon code detector). Results from several radar sites are sent to a central location (communication system), where information on successive radar scans and from the separate sites are correlated for target tracking.

Analysis of the processing requirements establishes the functional design of the radar data processor. Rather than encoding the amplitude of the returned radar signal, the quantizer determines if the signal exceeds a threshold that is adjusted to allow for a fixed average number of returns (including noise) over each pulse period. To separate real targets from random noise a "sliding window" statistical detector records the output of the quantizer for the last 15 pulses at each range interval. If the number of returns exceeds a threshold, then the detector declares that it has found a target and the azimuth calculation is initiated. When the number of returns in the window falls below a lower threshold the azimuth calculation can be completed by averaging the azimuth at start and finish. This is accomplished by subtracting half the number of pulses that have occurred since the start threshold was exceeded (the "run length") from the current azimuth. Beacon identification information is added to the reports of targets.

In every 1/4-mile-range interval (2.688 microseconds) the data processor must determine if the radar receiver signal exceeds a threshold, must compare the amplitude and the phase signals, and must add the signal to a history of the last 15 signals. Then, if the detection threshold has been exceeded the processor must set a run bit and must add 1 to the run-length count, entering the beacon code if it is the same as the code now recorded at that range. When the lower threshold is reached the processor calculates the azimuth and resets the detector. Then it forms the output message of range, azimuth, and beacon code and places the message in a communications buffer for transmission. A fairly powerful general-purpose computer would be required to perform the calculations at the rate needed, but the observation that the radar beam space can be mapped onto a fairly small memory suggests a special-purpose processing approach.

A special-purpose radar data processor for the system of Fig. 9-2 is shown in Fig. 9-3. The detector memory is an analog of the space covered by 16 successive radar signals. The range of 256 miles is covered in 1/4-mile intervals by 1024 words. Each memory

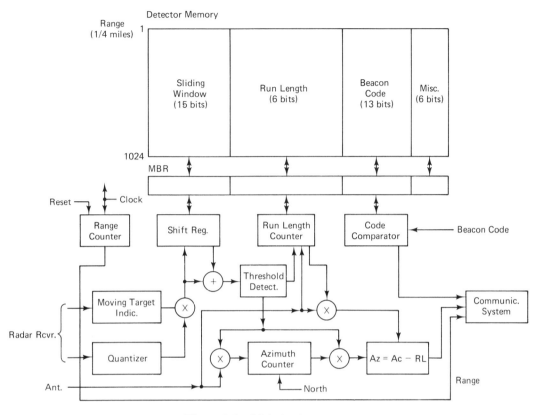

Figure 9-3   Digital radar processor.

word must hold the sliding-window detector record of the last 15 pulses (15 bits), the run-length count (6 bits to allow for extra noise pulses and very strong targets), a 13-bit beacon code, and 6 bits for status information. Memory addressing is coordinated with the radar pulses by the range counter that is stepped every 2.688 microseconds (1/4-mile target distance) by the processor clock. The range counter is reset to 0 at each radar pulse time. The azimuth counter is incremented at each pulse time and reset to 0 when the antenna faces north. Different functional parts of the detector operate on different memory-buffer fields during each 1/4-mile range period. The quantizer includes an analog integrator that is used to adjust the quantizer threshold so that an output pulse occurs a set percentage (typically 10%) of the time. The quantizer output also is adjusted for a moving-target indication when MTI is called for. A pulse from the quantizer and the number of pulses recorded in the sliding-window value are added and compared with the detection threshold. The new video input and the current window value are shifted to update the window. If the threshold has been exceeded the run-length counter is started and incremented on each pulse until the end-of-target threshold is reached. The beacon code input is updated with the current beacon code. (Beacon code processing can be much more extensive.) If the end of target is detected the azimuth calculation takes place and the range, azimuth, and beacon code are transferred to the communication buffer. This buffer is just a queue of messages that are transmitted with site identification and site status over standard telephone channels.

By making the computer memory an analog of the physics of the problem we are able to design a simple processor. The separate processes are carried out concurrently using slow and inexpensive circuits. It is feasible to duplicate the simple processor for high reliability. This approach to digital radar data processing first was used in the 1950s when high-speed digital circuits were very expensive. A drum memory could be rotated at a rate synchronized to the propagation time of the radar signals and the radar pulse timing could be generated by the drum. This form of radar data processor has been used in SAGE and other air defense systems and in air traffic control since that time. We will see extensions to other radar data processors in later sections.

A general-purpose computer program written in PASCAL to perform the radar data-processing tasks is shown in Fig. 9-4. The program accomplishes statistical detection using an exponential detector algorithm that is simpler (and less accurate) than the sliding-window detector implemented in the special-purpose processor. (The more accurate sliding-window detector is not easily represented in a higher-level programming language.) Beacon processing is not included. DETTYPE reflects the contents of each range interval in detector memory: TARG specifies that the detector threshold has been exceeded, DET is the exponentially decaying measure of hits identified by the quantizer, and RL is the run-length count of azimuth pulses since TARG was set to true. The record REPREC is the template for target information to be transferred to the communication system: RANGE and AZ are integer values representing range and azimuth counts, respectively, and NEXT is a pointer to the next record. REPTR identifies a pointer to a REPREC item. BOX is the detector memory containing a DETTYPE item at each range interval. REPORT and REPLIST are pointers to build and to point to the list of output REPREC records. PULSE is the amplitude output of the radar receiver. HIT and MSSGE are boolean values indicating a radar hit (PULSE exceeds the quantizer threshold, QUANT) and an output message. The constants MAXRANGE, QUANT, DETCONST, LOWER, and UPPER (not specified in the example) reflect the maximum range in 1/4 miles, the quantizer threshold, the exponential decay factor for the detector, the lower (end-of-target) detector limit, and the upper (start-of-target) detector limit.

After initializing the detector for each azimuth interval (AC), the processing at each range increment (BOX[I]) entails reading the radar receiver output (PULSE) and, if it exceeds the quantizer threshold, calling HIT and adding 1 to the detector value (DET). The detector value is reduced by multiplying it by the (less-than-unity) detector constant (DETCONST). If a target is already in process at this range (TARG = true) a test is made to see if we have reached the end of the target (DET <LOWER). If so, TARG is set to false, an output record (RANGE, AZ) is assembled and attached to the output list (NEXT points to the rest of the list and REPLIST points to a new entry), MSSGE is set to true, and the run-length count (RL) is reset. If it is not the end of the target RL is incremented. If a target was not in process then a new target count is started if the detector value exceeds the threshold (UPPER). After all range increments have been processed the azimuth count

```
program RADAR;
const MAXRANGE = {integervalue}; QUANT = {real value};
      DETCONST = {real value}; UPPER = {real value}; LOWER = {real value};
type DETTYPE = record
                        TARG: boolean;
                        DET: real;
                        RL: integer end;
     REPTR = ^REPREC;
     REPREC = record
                        RANGE, AZ: integer;
                        NEXT: REPTR end;
var BOX: array [0..MAXRANGE] of DETTYPE:
    REPLIST, REPORT: REPTR;
    I, AC: integer
    PULSE: real;
    HIT, MSSGE: boolean;
begin
    AC := 0; REPLIST := nil; MSSGE := false;
    for I := 0 to MAXRANGE do
                with BOX[I] do
                    begin TARG := false; DET := 0.0; RL := 0 end;
    repeat forever
        for I := 0 to MAXRANGE do
            with BOX[I] do
              begin
                  readln (PULSE);
                  if PULSE > QUANT then HIT := true else HIT := false;
                  if HIT then DET := DET + 1;
                  DET := DET * DETCONST;
                  if TARG then
                        if DET < LOWER then
                            begin
                              TARG := false;
                              new (REPORT);
                              with REPORT^ do
                                begin
                                    RANGE := I;
                                    AZ := AC - RL / 2;
                                    NEXT := REPLIST
                                 'end;
                              REPLIST := REPORT;
                              MSSGE := true;
                              RL := 0
                            end
                        else RL := RL + 1
                    else
                        if DET > UPPER then
                            begin
                              TARG := true;
                              RL := RL + 1
                            end
              end;
        AC := (AC + 1) mod(3600);
        while MSSGE do
            begin
              {transfer message to output queue};
              if REPLIST = nil then MSSGE := false
            end
end. {RADAR}
```

Figure 9-4   Radar-processing program.

is incremented, target messages are transferred to the message buffer, and MSSGE is set
to false. The process is repeated.

For each range interval (2.688 microseconds) about 25 PASCAL operations (approximately 50 machine instructions) must be performed. When beacon code detection

and message processing are added, over 100-machine level instructions are executed every 2.7 microseconds, requiring an operation time of about 27 ns. If we allow for a limited number of detection tests (say 100) each radar pulse period, instead of performing the test each 1/4-mile radar interval, we can reduce the operation rate by about 2. In either case it is feasible to use a general-purpose computer with today's technology, but the computer is more complex than the special-purpose processor. A microprocessor that is microprogrammed to perform the special-purpose processing yields an intermediate approach between the general-purpose and special-purpose computers.

We should consider the advantages of a general-purpose approach to determine if these outweigh the lower component count of the special-purpose computer. One might argue that one such advantage is the flexibility of a general-purpose computer to be programmed to perform many different tasks. We can change the role of the computer just by having it run different programs. The microprogrammed processor is somewhat less flexible since changing the microprogram probably involves a change in the ROM or the PROM that holds its microcode. The special-purpose hardware processor certainly does not have short-term flexibility, except for changing any parameters that are used.

For long-term flexibility to allow for adding new functions, for removing functions, and for changing other parts of the system, the special-purpose hardware processor can have equivalent or better flexibility than a general-purpose machine. Experience with major modifications to software systems has shown that these changes always are time consuming and expensive. Test and verification of software change usually is at least as large a job as hardware test and verification. The assumption that software is easy to change whereas hardware is inflexible has been disproved many times. In the actual radar data processor described before it was possible to add features (the beacon system), to adapt to changed external devices (multibeam radars), and to adapt to different processing needs (adding the air-traffic control functions to the air-defense radar sites). The question of hardware vs. software flexibility does not have simple answers.

The modularity of the special-purpose radar processor offered advantages for attaining high reliability levels. The radar processor, beacon processor, and communications buffer could all be duplicated so that a failure of one of each type of unit could be tolerated (see Section 3.6). Furthermore, the system could operate with limited capability even after loss of both radar processors or both beacon processors.

9.3 DESIGNING THE SYSTEM

Special-purpose system design starts with a complete specification of the problem solution stated in the terms of the appropriate basic science and its mathematics. Then we develop a data-processing analog of the solution, identifying each input, output, control-variable value, and computation. With the processing requirements so specified, it is possible to evaluate alternative processing architectures. At this point any special characteristics of the environment should be considered. These include the spacial configuration of the system; particular temperature, humidity, vibration, and/or electromagnetic levels; stringent reliability needs; and unique relationships to human operators. These factors influence how and by how much the processing capability should be distributed. Needs for any protection from the environment, such as electromagnetic shielding, can be identified and considered in system design. Parts of the system that should be replicated for failure protection can be specified. Human-machine interfaces can be designed.

An example of the relationship between the problem analog and a solution developed from the analog is shown in Fig. 9-5. This figure shows an outline of an aircraft control system. We see the objects to be controlled: the engines, the wing and tail stabilizers, and the wing flaps. The system inputs, in addition to the status of each item being controlled, are values from the instruments and the cockpit controls.

The range and the precision of all input and output variables of the flight-control system must be specified. The processing required at each interface to an input or output and where values are combined (Cs in the illustration) are identified. Any required redundancy can be added to the diagram at this point. Alternative distributions of the processing can be compared to determine if it is better to coalesce some processing functions. For example, all individual engine-control functions might be performed in the thrust-control computer. Many factors influence the design decisions. Performance, cost, reliability, maintainability, flexibility, and intangible factors that influence customer acceptance must all be considered. In a distributed system like the one shown the design might be affected by the capabilities of standard processors and by our ability to use the same processing and memory modules at many places in the system.

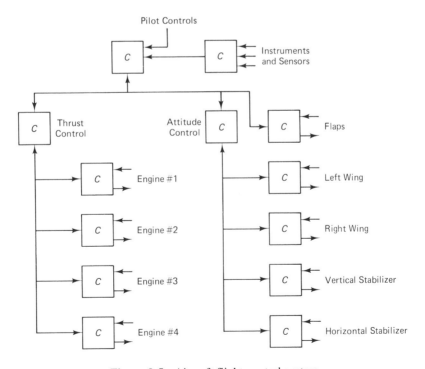

Figure 9-5 Aircraft flight-control system.

The examples of Figs. 9-3 and 9-5 show very different problem physics and very different processing solutions. In the radar-processing problem we are able to use a memory organization to model the problem, whereas the flight-control system is calculation-centered. In the latter example storage of information is needed, but it is not the key part of the problem analog.

With some physical problems it is useful to examine the data structures of the problem and to organize the processing memory around them. An example is the processing required for the receivers of a two-dimensional phased-array radar system (Fig. 9-6). The structure here is a two-dimensional antenna array, where signals that are returned from a radar pulse are detected at a large number of sensors, the outputs of which must be compared. Correlations are required among all receivers in each row and all receivers in each column. Finally, all rows and all columns are correlated and both results are combined. Processing and storage can be distributed as a direct analog of the problem data structure, as shown in the illustration, or all steps can be combined in one central correlator. In the distributed approach that is illustrated simple local correlators (Cl) are introduced at each sensor. The outputs of all local correlators of a column (vertical correlation) and of all correlators of a row (horizontal correlation) are combined in Cv and Ch correlators. The final combinations that yield output results and feedback controls to the sensors are performed in the central correlator, Cc. For each receiver the processing at each Cl is about as extensive as was that for the radar data processor of Fig. 9-3. Similar computation load is imposed on each Ch and Cv. If there are 100 receivers (a 10 × 10 receiver

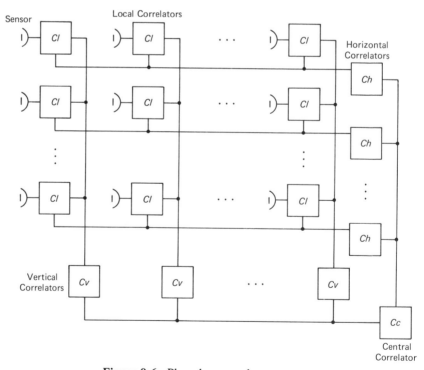

Figure 9-6 Phased-array radar processor.

array) the total processing is significant. If there are over 10,000 receivers, as is the case with a typical long-range phased-array radar, the total processing is sufficient to tax a general-purpose vector-processor supercomputer. An example of a special-purpose system to solve the problem (a "massively parallel processor") is described in Section 9.6.

With many geographically distributed systems communication among individual locations is significant. Communication as well as processing cost and performance must be considered in evaluating alternative designs. Often local processing can reduce the amount of information that must be transmitted, but the reduction of information might be detrimental to the processing that can be performed centrally. Our example of this is an extension of the radar data-processing system of Fig. 9-2 to incorporate multiple radar-site correlation for aircraft tracking, as shown in Fig. 9-7. In the system with centralized tracking sites, Fig. 9-7(a), processed information from all radar sites is communicated to the central tracking site, whereas in the distributed tracking example, Fig. 9-7(b), scan-to-scan correlation for tracking is performed at each site and track information is "handed off" to adjacent sites as needed. The first approach has higher communications costs because much more information is transmitted to the central location, but tracker computer cost is lower since a single larger machine is used. The centralized tracker also has more information with which it can make decisions regarding targets.

These simple examples outline some of the parameters that must be considered in designing a special-purpose computing system. In all these cases the special-purpose computer design was conducted as a part of the overall system design. Performance, cost, flexibility, and reliability of all hardware and software aspects of the system contribute to our design decisions.

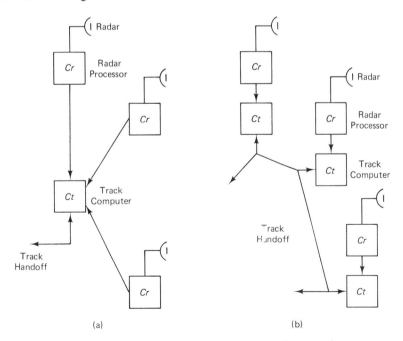

Figure 9-7   (a) Central and (b) local radar-track processing.

9.4 PROCESSING AND ARITHMETIC UNITS

In many systems, like the radar of Fig. 9-2, the processing requirements are unique. When the requirement calls for unique processing the system design usually entails designing custom function units or microcoding a general-purpose function unit to perform the tasks. Quite often, however, system processing can make use of standard functional units replicated as many times as needed. There are a number of calculation functions that appear in many applications.

For example, in closed-loop control systems (Fig. 9-8) a control function C drives a system S toward an objective. The control value is calculated from a combination of desired and actual conditions. In displacement control, Fig. 9-8(a), the desired output condition D_o, is compared with the actual condition D_a, and the control value C, a constant times the difference in conditions, is applied to "correct" the error. Displacement control can result in significant "overshoot" and an oscillating actual condition. Alternatively, we can control the rate of change of the difference between the actual and the desired situation. With rate control the rate of change of the error is used to generate the control value. Rate control, since it senses rate of error change, results in a steady-state fixed error. For control to a desired condition with minimum overshoot, displacement and rate control can be combined, as demonstrated in Fig. 9-8(b). Here the error and the rate of error change are combined to yield the control value C. Function units like those shown in Fig. 9-8 can be implemented with special-purpose digital logic. Since the control functions are used in many different applications, modular control function units or microprogrammed control units can be supplied as standard parts. Specialized processing units of this type are appropriate to the aircraft control system of Fig. 9-5.

The discrete fast Fourier transform (FFT) is used in many signal-processing applications like the medical image processing of Fig. 9-1. The discrete FFT of order n generates an output sequence y_i as functions f and g of an input sequence x_i, where i ranges from 0 to $n - 1$. Each output value is a function of functions of $1 + \log_2 n$ inputs. This transform can be implemented

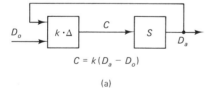

$$C = k(D_a - D_o)$$

(a)

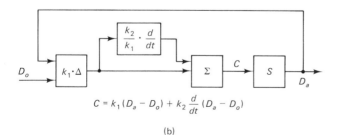

$$C = k_1(D_a - D_o) + k_2 \frac{d}{dt}(D_a - D_o)$$

(b)

Figure 9-8   Feedback-control functions. (a) Displacement control. (b) Displacement plus rate control.

with a special-purpose parallel processor (SIMD) that is assembled from a large number
of simple processing elements and router switches (Fig. 8-17). Organization of a one-dimensional FFT processor of order 8 is illustrated in Fig. 9-9. The eight output values, each a
function of four ($1 + \log_2 8$) inputs, are shown in Fig. 9-9(a) and the operations of the simple
processor-routers are demonstrated in Fig. 9-9(b). Usually functions f and g are combinations of
addition and multiplication. In many applications the input values x_i and the results y_i are complex
numbers. As in the previous example, the system requires a quantity of similar simple processing
units. A special-purpose computer assembled from building blocks of the special function units
that generate outputs f and g appears to be suitable for the task.

Convolution and correlation functions also are called for in many signal-processing
applications, such as the phased-array radar outlined in Fig. 9-6. Like FFT processing,
correlation and convolution can be implemented with arrays of special-purpose processors,
as shown in Fig. 9-10. In this one-dimensional example, for each output y_i ($i = 1 \ldots n$) a
set of weights w_j ($j = i \ldots m$) is applied to successive input values x_k ($k = 1 \ldots n$) according
to the equation shown in Fig. 9-10(a). Processing is accomplished by "streaming" the
inputs x_k through the weighting processors w_j, so that each multiplies the weight by the value
of x_k. The outputs of all active weighting processors (maximum of $m, n - i + 1$) are summed
to give the output sequence. For correlation the input values x_{i+j-1} are multiplied by w_j, and
for convolution the input values x_{i-j-1} are multiplied by w_j. Again a computer assembled
from special-purpose processor building blocks is called for.

In each of the examples of Figs. 9-8 through 9-10 simple standard function units are
used. The units are adapted to a particular problem by setting parameters of each unit: the
constant multiplier in the control case, functions f and g in FFT processing, and the weighting
factors in the correlator/convolver. By this means we obtain flexibility with standard components or circuits in special-purpose computer systems. At the other extreme we might find
that a large system is best constructed from a combination of special-purpose and general-
purpose computers. The radar tracking system of Fig. 9-7(a) is an example in which the radar

$y_0 = f(f(x_0, x_1), f(x_2, x_3))$
$y_1 = g(f(x_0, x_1), f(x_2, x_3))$
$y_2 = f(f(x_4, x_5), f(x_6, x_7))$
$y_3 = g(f(x_4, x_5), f(x_6, x_7))$
$y_4 = f(g(x_0, x_1), g(x_2, x_3))$
$y_5 = g(g(x_0, x_1), g(x_2, x_3))$
$y_6 = f(g(x_4, x_5), g(x_6, x_7))$
$y_7 = g(g(x_4, x_5), g(x_6, x_7))$

(a)

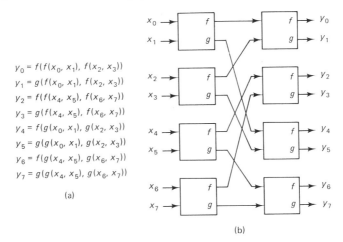

(b)

Figure 9-9   Fast-Fourier-transform processing. (a) Equations. (b) Computations.

For weights w_j $(j = 1 .. m)$

and inputs x_k $(k = 1 .. n)$

output $y_i = \sum_{j=1}^{m} w_j x_{i \pm j - 1}$ $(i = 1 .. n)$

(a)

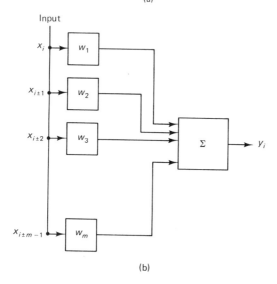

(b)

Figure 9-10 Correlation and convolution processing. (a) Equations (+ = correlation). (b) Processing.

processing functions are best handled by a special-purpose computer (Fig. 9-3) and track processing is more suitable to a general-purpose computer. When radar and track processing are accomplished at the same site, Fig.9-7(b), a special-purpose processor also might be more suitable for track processing. Both special-purpose and general-purpose track-processing computers have been used successfully in systems of this type.

It is interesting to consider whether several of the examples we saw in Chapter 8 are general-purpose or special-purpose computers. For example, ILLIAC IV and Star-100 were designed for solving mathematical problems involving matrix algebra. Many of the applications incorporated functions like those of the fast Fourier transform and the correlator/convolver examples. The class of problems addressed by these vector and array processors is sufficiently broad that the "standard" vector-processing computers, Cray-1 and Cyber 205, are now considered to be general-purpose computers and array processors have been introduced as standard products by several companies. This movement of concepts developed for specialized applications to general-purpose designs will continue. The distinction between general-purpose and special-purpose computers is not clearly defined.

9.5 ALTERNATIVES IN CONTROL OF COMPUTATION

The advances in the quantity of devices that can be placed on the surface of one semiconductor component has led to investigation of very-large-scale parallelism in computer architectures. In Chapter 8 we examined array processors and large-scale multiprocessors and multicomputers. Whereas the system organizations exhibited great variation, the individual processors in all the examples used the same sequential control structure that was proposed by von Neumann. There are also approaches that break away from the sequential instruction steps of the von Neumann architecture.

P. Treleaven and associates at the University of Newcastle upon Tyne [TrelP82] have characterized computer control as involving "control flow" or "data flow". In the former (conventional computer controls) the programmer (explicitly or through a programming-language translator) specifies the control sequence of the computations, whereas in the latter instruction control results from availability of data. The data-flow model of computation has similarities to the Petri net (see Section 2.8) in that operations are executed as the data required (like Petri net tokens) are available to them. The data-flow model has been identified as "data-driven" computation. Another new model of computation, the "demand-driven" model, uses a "reduction machine" that develops a computational graph and operates on it to reduce it to its final values.

These new models of computation are based on the use of functional or single-assignment languages in which all operations are functions that take values as arguments and produce values as results. One characteristic of such languages is "referential transparency", in that results of a function application are dependent only on the data values and are independent of other context and history. As a result the computational models using these languages possess an inherent parallelism and computation can proceed with a high degree of concurrency. The languages and the computational models have much similarity to the original version of LISP and its computational model, which were introduced by J. McCarthy [McCaJ60].

Two examples of data-flow computation are shown in Fig. 9-11. The distinction between "static" and "dynamic" data-flow computer architectures was first defined by

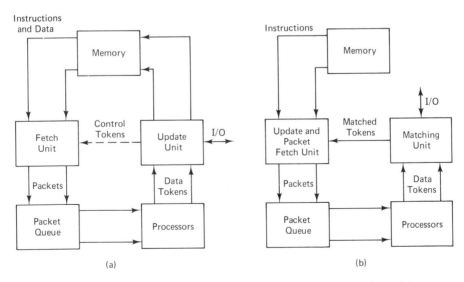

Figure 9-11 Data-flow computers. (a) Static model. (b) Dynamic model.

Arvind [Arvin81] and is shown in the figure. With both models data values (tokens) that are developed from computations or input to the system are associated with functions (instructions) that "fire" when all required data elements are available. The data tokens move on arcs of a process graph (like the Petri net) and the instructions are the nodes. Processors, each able to execute all functions or specialized to subsets of the functions available, are assigned to execute the ready data-instruction packets as the processors are available. When the instruction of a packet is executed the result is a new data token that is associated with instructions that are waiting for it. The memory holds instructions and data tokens that are waiting for additional data for a packet to be assembled.

In the static model, Fig. 9-11(a), data tokens are associated with instructions in the update unit and are passed to memory, where they are held until all data for the instruction are available. A control token is used to indicate that all data are available for an instruction. The control token commands the fetch unit to call the instruction and its data from memory, and the resulting packet is moved to the packet queue. The packet operator is "fired" when a processor is ready. In the static model only one data token can be on an arc at a time and the control tokens are needed for the association of an instruction and its data.

With the dynamic model token tags act as labels to associate data tokens with an operator and multiple tokens can exist on the arc of a graph. Token sets, the data required for an instruction to be executed, are assembled in the matching unit, which passes each matched token set to the fetch unit to obtain the instruction for assembly of the packet. The assembled packet is passed to the packet queue to wait for a processor.

In both approaches computation proceeds around a "ring", using those function units that are needed on any cycle through the processing unit. Introduction of the parallel computation that is required to achieve significant computational power requires a high-speed routing network (see Section 8.5) that permits data tokens to be passed from the multiple processors to the appropriate line of the update unit with the static model or of the matching unit in the dynamic model.

With reduction architectures for demand-driven computation, the computational graph is developed from a functional (or reduction) language representation of the program. Multiple-processor reduction-machine architectures can use "string reduction" or "graph reduction". Both approaches are described using a variant of J. Backus's FP language [BackJ78] to show the execution of a simple factorial program.

In string reduction (Fig. 9-12) the program is represented as a string of operators and arguments. The part of the program graph that can be executed by the multiple processors is moved to the processing unit. As that part of the graph is executed it is reduced to a smaller number of entries that requires less of the operations, and more of the total process is moved to the processing unit for evaluation. Eventually all of the remaining process can fit the processing unit and evaluation continues with unused portions of the processing unit made available for the next process program string. Figure 9-12 shows the evaluation of function factorial F applied to the value 3. The string F of 3 (where F is defined as *if* argument $A = 1$ *then* 1 *else* A *times* F of A *minus* 1) is shown in line a. In line b the string is reduced by substituting 3 for argument A. The definition of factorial has been shifted to the right (and out of the processor unit) to make room for the evaluable function. Line c shows that the equality has tested to FALSE and (concurrently) 1 has been

$p_0\ p_1\ p_2\ \ p_3\ p_4\ p_5\ p_6\ \ p_7\ \ p_8\ \ p_9\ \ p_{10}\ p_{11}\ p_{12}\ \ p_{13}\ \ p_{14}\ \ p_{15}$

$\wedge\ \wedge\ \wedge\ \ \wedge\ \ \wedge\wedge\ \ \wedge\ \ \wedge\ \ \wedge\ \ \wedge\ \ \wedge\wedge\ \wedge$

a. $F\overline{3}$; $F \equiv\, = [AI] \to \overline{1} * [AF - [A\overline{1}]]$; ...

b. $= [\,\overline{3}\,\overline{1}\,] \to \overline{1} * [\,\overline{3}F - [\,\overline{3}\,\overline{1}\,]\,]$; $F \equiv \{\text{definition of } F\}$

c. false $--\!\!\to * [\,\overline{3}F\,\overline{2}\,...\,]$; $F \equiv \{\text{definition of } F\}$

d. $*[\,\overline{3} = [\,\overline{2}\,\overline{1}\,] \to * [\,\overline{2}F - [\,\overline{2}\,\overline{1}\,]\,]\,]$; $F \equiv \{\text{definition of } F\}$

e. $*[\,\overline{3} = $ false $--\!\!\to \times [\,\overline{2}F\,\overline{1}\,...\,]\,]$; $F \equiv \{\text{definition of } F\}$

f. $*[\,\overline{3} * [\,\overline{2} = [\,\overline{1}\,\overline{1}\,] \to \overline{1} * [\,\overline{1}F - [\,\overline{1}\,\overline{1}\,]\,]\,]\,]$; $F \equiv \{\text{definition of } F\}$

g. $*[\,\overline{3} * [\,\overline{2}$ true $--\!\!\to \overline{1}\,...\,\emptyset\,...$; $F \equiv \{\text{definition of } F\}$

h. $*[\,\overline{3} * [\,\overline{2}\,\overline{1}\,]\,]$; $F \equiv \{\text{definition of } F\}$ ...

i. $*[\,\overline{3}\,\overline{2}\,]$; $F \equiv \{\text{definition of } F\}$

j. $\overline{6}$; $F \equiv \{\text{definition of } F\}$

Figure 9-12 String reduction.

subtracted from 3. At line d the second (FALSE) alternative to the conditional has been taken and the definition has been recopied with the new argument value, again shifting the definition itself to the right. In line e the equality test and the subtraction have been applied. The second alternative with a new argument value are shown in line f. The next evaluation (line g) finds the condition TRUE. (The subtraction has also been accomplished.) After this point the definition is not needed, and in line f we find a simple algebraic expression that is evaluated in two steps (lines h, i, j).

A string-reduction computer of this type has been developed at the University of North Carolina [MagoG80]. The computer is organized as a tree of processors with registers to hold string values at the leaves. The string that represents the unfolded program graph is shifted onto the leaves. A sequence of operations like that demonstrated in Fig. 9-12 is performed by processors that can execute the simple operations and can move the values at the leaves of the tree. Each processor is quite simple and the power comes from the many processors in the tree operating concurrently.

Graph reduction of the same program is shown in Fig. 9-13. With graph reduction the process is represented as a directed graph constructed from templates of the functions that are assembled to form the process. The process graph is traversed and operations are applied to the arguments to form new values for association with subsequent operations in the graph. As in the data-flow machines the arguments are represented as definite or indefinite sequences (streams) of values. As the program graph is unfolded it forms a tree with independent branches that can be evaluated concurrently.

The graph of factorial of 3 (EVALUATE F applied to 3, where F is *if* argument $A = 1$ *then* $\underline{1}$ *else* A *times* F of A *minus* $\underline{1}$) is shown in Fig. 9-13(a). In Fig. 9-13(b) the conditional has been evaluated and the second alternative (FALSE) has been constructed with $\underline{3}$ *minus* $\underline{1}$ as the argument for F. The process is repeated in Fig. 9-13(c). This evaluation of F yields the value 1 in Fig. 9-13(d). The multiplications are applied in Figs. 9-13(e) and 9-13(f) to yield the final result.

Most approaches to reduction machine architecture, like the data-flow models, assume that the program graph will be evaluated with an "applicative" order strategy in which argument values must be available before a function can be applied. It is possible to allow for treatment of "nonstrict" functions in a way that applies them to those

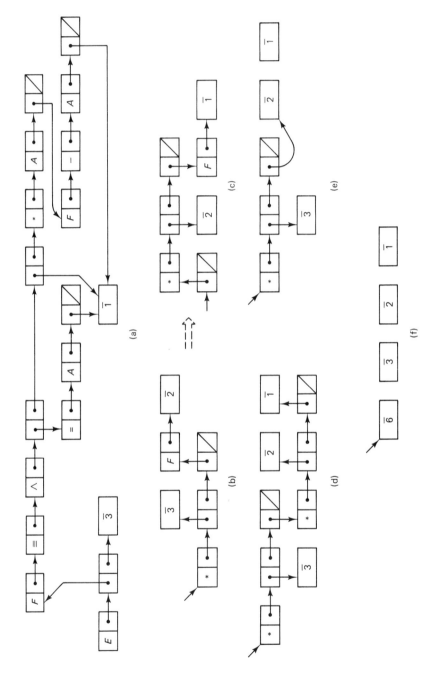

Figure 9-13 Graph reduction. (a) Evaluate F with argument 3. (b) $3 \neq 1$, multiply 3 by F(2). (c) $F(2)$ is $2 \times F(1)$. (d) Arithmetic expression. (e) Evaluate 2×1. (f) Result = 6.

arguments that are needed without waiting for the evaluation of arguments that might not be used by the function.

Another approach to graph reduction [TurnD79] uses principles of combinatory logic to form process graphs that contain no variables and that represent higher-order functions (functions that use functions as arguments and/or return functions as results). The basis for this approach is the reduction of a function of several arguments to a higher-order function of fewer arguments, called "currying" after the logician H. B. Curry. For example, given that the operator + is defined, we can define a function of two 2 variables, x and y, as

$$\text{plus } x \, y = x + y$$

Then we can define a function add$x$ of one variable y as

$$\text{add} x \, y = \text{plus } x \, y = x + y.$$

A particularly useful version of add$x$ is increment

$$\text{increment } y = \text{plus } 1 \, y$$

and the function increment can be defined (by currying) as

$$\text{increment} = \text{plus } 1$$

The concept is generalized to permit removal ("abstraction") of bound variables from any definition. "Combinators" are used to remove variables from the program and thus to form a process graph of higher-order functions.

An example, using the factorial function, is developed in Fig. 9-14. The function factorial, defined as

$$\text{fact } n => n = 0, 1, n * \text{fact } (n - 1)$$

has its bound variable n removed using the combinator rules of Fig. 9-14(a) to yield

$$\text{fact} = S(C(B \text{ cond(eq } 0))1)(S \text{ times}(B \text{ fact}(C \text{ minus } 1)))$$

with cond (conditional), eq (equal), times, and minus having their usual meanings. The variable n has been removed and the function is defined in terms of constants, combinators, and other functions. The application of the function to a value, fact 3, is represented by the graph shown in Fig. 9-14(b). The graph is traversed depth-first (left branch first). When an operator or a built-in function is encountered it is evaluated using as arguments the value in the right half of its cell and any needed arguments in the right halves of the previous cells. A defined function is replaced by its definition and evaluation continues. Any combinator is replaced by its equivalent reduction graph, which "pulls" any needed values back to the functions that will use them. For example, when the combinator S is encountered the graph is modified as shown in Fig. 9-14(c), reflecting the replacement of $Sfgx$ by $fx(gx)$.

Evaluation starts at the root node of the graph and proceeds toward the leaves with replacements made as soon as possible, following "normal-order" rules that permit replacement of parts of the graph even if all values are not yet available. In the illustration,

$$\overline{S}fgx = fx(gx)$$
$$\overline{K}xg = x$$
$$\overline{I}x = x$$
$$\overline{B}fgx = f(gx)$$
$$\overline{C}fgx = fxg$$

$$\overline{S}(\overline{K}E_1)(\overline{K}E_2) \Rightarrow \overline{K}(E_1 E_2)$$
$$\overline{S}(\overline{K}E_1)\overline{I} \Rightarrow E_1$$
$$\overline{S}(\overline{K}E_1)E_2 \Rightarrow \overline{B}E_1 E_2 \text{*}$$
$$\overline{S}E_1(\overline{K}E_2) \Rightarrow \overline{C}E_1 E_2 \text{*}$$

*If no earlier rule applies

(a)

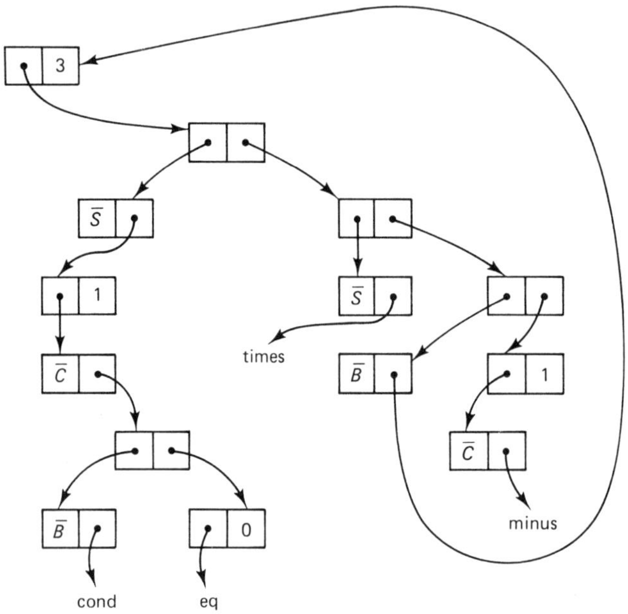

$$\text{fact} = \overline{S}(\overline{C}(\overline{B} \text{ cond(eq 0))1)}(\overline{S} \text{ times } (\overline{B} \text{ fact } (\overline{C} \text{ minus 1})))$$

(b)

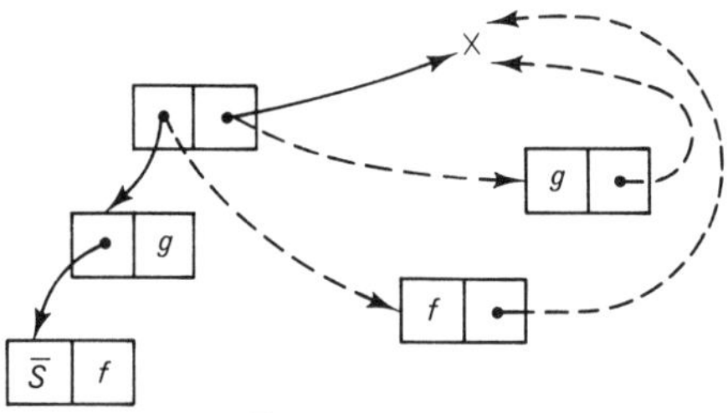

$$\overline{S}fgx \Rightarrow fx(gx)$$

(c)

Figure 9-14   The combinator model. (a) Combinator rules, E is any expression. (b) Graph of fact 3. (c) Example of reduction.

a box that calls for FACT of 3 would be the starting point for evaluation equivalent to those shown in string reduction and graph reduction. D. A. Turner suggests that the resulting evaluation will consist of more, but simpler, steps than does the usual evaluation of an equivalent function. Combinatory logic is the basis for experimental computers that have been built by the Unisys (Burroughs) Austin Research Center, Cambridge University, and the University of Kent at Canterbury.

The structure of very-large-scale integrated (VLSI) circuits encourages designs that repeat the same circuits many times to form a subsystem of over a million components on one semiconductor. The characteristic of repetition is one factor that permits memory components to be made with more devices than is possible in forming a processor (see Fig. 6-1). Attempts to find repetitive patterns for processor organization lead to the assembly of a large quantity of simple processors in an orderly structure. That is an objective of the data-flow and the reduction architectures described before. The "systolic-array" approach to exploiting VLSI in processor design takes advantage of the orderly nature of many numeric problems as are found, for example, in matrix arithmetic. A processor cell of a systolic array performs a simple set of operations, usually providing two outputs and a stored value as functions of two inputs and the previously stored value. Two typical cells and the functions produced are shown in Fig. 9-15(a). The operations shown are performed at each clock pulse on the streams of A and B input values.

The systolic array is formed by connecting the simple processors in an orderly manner so that the outputs of several cells form the inputs to others, as shown in Fig. 9-15(b). All cells perform the same operations simultaneously. Storage in each cell is

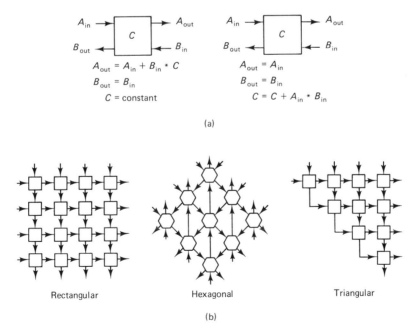

(a)

Rectangular   Hexagonal   Triangular

(b)

Figure 9-15 Systolic arrays. (a) Typical cell operations. (b) Two-dimensional topologies.

used as a one pulse delay for data synchronization. Cells at the boundaries receive system inputs, provide system outputs, or are connected to other systolic-array components to form larger arrays. Computation proceeds as a "wave" of operations flowing through the array at a rate set by the clock that steps data through cells at each pulse.

Systolic arrays can be formed with many different operations in cells and with many different topologies. The operations in the cells are usually simple arithmetic and logical operations appropriate to actions on small subsets of the data in an orderly data structure. The topologies are designed to match the data structures. A square array, the left side of Fig. 9-15(b), can be used to process adjacency matrices and similar graph algorithms. Linear vectors of cells (one-dimensional rectangular arrays) are useful for fast Fourier transform calculations, digital filters, arithmetic pipelines, and data queues. The hexagonal array of the center of Fig. 9-15(b) is the most popular systolic topology because it is useful for representation of matrix arithmetic (where the sum of products is used so often), pattern matching, and discrete Fourier transforms. Triangular patterns, the right side of Fig. 9-15(b), also are of use in matrix operations like orthogonal triangularization. Tree structures are more difficult to implement due to the larger number of interconnections, but the binary tree can be useful for parallel-function evaluation (as with the string-reduction architecture described before) or for operations on general tree structures.

The features of systolic arrays and of data-flow computation can be combined to yield "wavefront" computation. The difference between this and a systolic array is that the latter employs control flow and a clock controls the sequence of operations in all cells. Synchronizing the clock signal with the input data streams in a large array can be difficult. The wavefront array uses data-driven control, and a cell "fires" when data tokens are available at each enabled input. Both of these forms of highly parallel array-organized architectures are used principally in special-purpose computers.

All of these approaches to computer architecture that diverge from the sequential control-flow model require functional programming languages for representation of programs. They must show very significant benefits to influence people to forget their experience in using imperative (procedural) languages and to switch to a functional style. On the other hand, it can be argued that any program that has a deterministic result if presented with proper data can be unfolded and represented as a process tree that could be expressed with a purely functional program. If this is the case (it can be demonstrated using the techniques of denotational semantics introduced by Scott and Strachey [StoyJ77] and [TennR81]), then it should be possible to translate any deterministic program to a functional intermediate language for evaluation on a related architecture. It remains to be seen whether the claimed advantages of the noncontrol-flow approaches can be proved and if they can be made sufficiently general to have a lasting impact on computer architecture.

9.6 EXAMPLES

In this section we examine several special-purpose systems in some detail. The examples give a broad perspective on applications for and designs of special-purpose computers.

PIXAR Image Computer. Our first example, the PIXAR Image Computer, was introduced in 1986. PIXAR is a programmable system for generating and manipulating large digital images. It contains four parallel processors and can operate on high-resolution picture data at a rate of 40 MIPS. Although optimized for the special purpose of image processing, the computer is programmable to permit selection of specific image-processing applications. Typical applications include image synthesis, frame-buffered graphics, real-time video effects, and real-time simulation.

The PIXAR system is shown in Fig. 9-16. There are three central (channel) processors; six primary-memory (picture-memory) modules, each representing a picture of 4M pixels; two video controllers connected to the secondary memory and the host computer through a 2-Mbytes/s multibus and to primary memory through the video bus; a processor bus for high-speed communication (240 Mbytes/s) between the central processors and the memory modules; and the "Yapbus" (80 Mbytes/s) for image transfers to or from a high-speed disk file, a laser scanner, and another PIXAR system.

The central processors each contain four bit-slice microprocessors and four high-speed multipliers in an SIMD organization. A channel processor operates at 40 MIPS (10 MIPS/processor). The minimum image configuration is 2k by 2k pixels, with four channels (red, green, blue, transparency) per pixel. The image also can represent 4k by 4k monochrome pixels.The four microprocessors of a channel processor can be allocated to the channels for color-image processing or can be assigned to four adjacent pixels in monochrome applications. Each channel operates on 12 bits and a screen of image is mapped into a memory module. Three channel processors exceed the data-transfer capacity of memory for full-color processing, but one color processor and two monochrome processors can operate concurrently.

A full-color image (192 Mbits) can be transferred to an adjacent PIXAR in less than 1/2s. Picture-memory contents can be displayed on two video screens, each controlled by a video controller. Video formats are 525-line interlaced or 1024 by 768 interlaced for high resolution. The video displays can "focus" on parts of memory. Video controls are included.

1. Pch\"Channel_Processor" (#0, 2) {SIMD, 12-bit word, each contains
   4 bit-slice processors and a highspeed multiplier}.
2. Mp(#0..5)[0..2^{12}] <10..0>.
3. Kv\"Video_Controller" (#0, 1).
4. Smb\"Multibus" (2 Mbytes/s).
5. Spb\"P-bus" (240 Mbytes/s).
6. Syb\"Yapbus" (80 Mbytes/s, image_transfer).
7. Ms {disk drive}.
8. Ch {host computer}.
9. Cp {another PIXAR}.
10. Tl {laser scanner}.
11. Ms {high-speed disk drive}.
12. Svb {video bus}.

Figure 9-16   The PIXAR image-processing system.

PIXAR software operates under UNIX 4.2 BSD and includes libraries of software for special image-processing applications. It is claimed that PIXAR is 200 times faster than a VAX-11/780 programmed for image processing. Typical applications are satellite-image processing, seismic-image processing, medical-image processing, and automobile design.

In this special-purpose computer the memory became a direct analog of a 4M pixel video screen image. The SIMD processor is designed to operate on single pixels with different colors or on adjacent pixels. A general-purpose computer would have to operate at much more than 40 MIPS to be able to handle the processing of PIXAR since much data manipulation is implicit in the mapping between the PIXAR processor and its memory and the images it is producing.

GE Programmable Controller. In an earlier section process control was identified as an application in which special-purpose computers have been used. Often we find distributed process-control systems that are built using standard microprocessors programmed (or microprogrammed) to provide the specialized calculations required in different parts of the system. Several companies that specialize in industrial control offer standard controllers that can be programmed for specific control applications. Most such controllers contain simple processors, limited memory, and a large and flexible input/output system.

The General Electric Series 6 programmable controller is a special-purpose system of this type. Its modular organization gives it the flexibility for a variety of specific configurations and a capability for expansion as the systems in which it is used change and grow. Figure 9-17 is a PMS diagram of the system. The modular random-access memory (Mram) stores the controller programs. What is usually viewed as a central processor is distributed among three modules. All processor registers are in a separate register memory (Mreg). The arithmetic and logic functions are in an arithmetic control unit (Dac) that has four AM 2903 bit-slice processors (see Fig. 6-13). The logic controller Klc transmits microcode to Dac for execution. A separate programmable read-only memory Mprom is the control store for the microinstructions. The logic controller also controls operation of the input/output controller Kio, which really is the heart of the controller.

An expandable input/output switch Sio connects Kio to a wide variety of device controllers and transducers. These include electric power monitors, parallel and serial digital input and output devices, analog-to-digital and digital-to-analog converters, servo-motor controllers, and thermocouple sensors. The number of input/output devices is limited only because all devices must be serviced every 200 ms by the Dac. Programming is in the form of "relay ladder logic", where each rung of the ladder is for control of a specific device. While individual rungs might take different amounts of time, the total ladder must be executed in 200 ms or the system signals error and shuts itself down. The programmable controller is a flexible high-speed processor for control in real time of a wide variety of devices. Its flexibility comes from the modular organization that allows individual modules to be upgraded or replaced by similar modules of different function. The controller was designed to operate in the relatively hostile environment of manufacturing plants. Its operation can be learned easily by those who are not computer specialists.

PEPE. Our third example is a radar data processor that is quite different from those described in earlier sections. This special-purpose computer, the Parallel-Element Processing

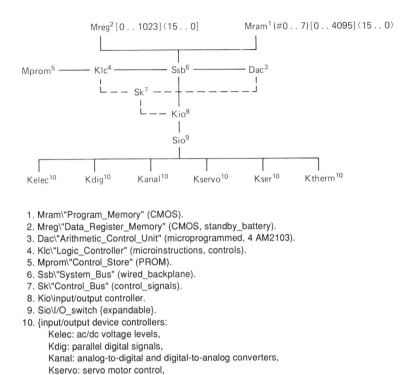

1. Mram\"Program_Memory" (CMOS).
2. Mreg\"Data_Register_Memory" (CMOS, standby_battery).
3. Dac\"Arithmetic_Control_Unit" (microprogrammed, 4 AM2103).
4. Klc\"Logic_Controller" (microinstructions, controls).
5. Mprom\"Control_Store" (PROM).
6. Ssb\"System_Bus" (wired_backplane).
7. Sk\"Control_Bus" (control_signals).
8. Kio\input/output controller.
9. Sio\I/O_switch {expandable}.
10. {input/output device controllers:
    Kelec: ac/dc voltage levels,
    Kdig: parallel digital signals,
    Kanal: analog-to-digital and digital-to-analog converters,
    Kservo: servo motor control,
    Kser: serial digital signals,
    Ktherm: temperature sensors}.

Figure 9-17   GE programmable controller.

Ensemble (PEPE) uses parallel-processing concepts initiated in ILLIAC IV. Its processing uses association and correlation functions and it is categorized as a parallel associative processor. PEPE was developed by Burroughs (now Unisys) for the U.S. Army Ballistic Missile Defense Agency. It exploited logic for radar-signal detection and analysis developed at Bell Laboratories.

PEPE was designed to handle a large amount of correlation processing for target filtering in a large radar system. It was connected to three other powerful computers: a specialized radar interface processor, the test and maintenance computer, and the host computer that passed programs and data values to initiate PEPE processing and to interact with standard peripheral equipment. The PEPE architecture allowed for an indefinite number of specialized processors, the quantity determined by the number of radar detectors to be serviced. A diagram of the system is shown in Fig. 9-18.

PEPE contains a global control section and the processing elements. The major functional parts of the global control section are input/output data-conversion units, parallel-element memory control (PMC), parallel-output data control (ODC), intercommunications control logic (ICL), and three processing-element control units (CCU, ACU, AOCU). The input/output data-conversion units connect PEPE to the three external processors, providing format conversion and buffering as required. All other parts of the

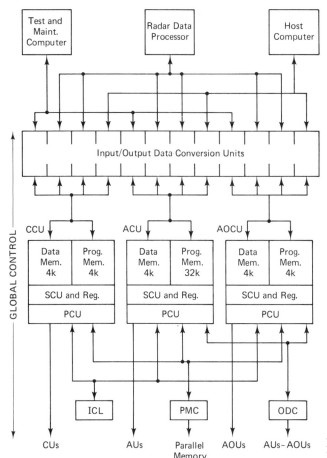

Figure 9-18 Parallel-Element Processing Ensemble (PEPE).

global control section control operation of the processing elements. Intercommunications control logic coordinates activities of the other controllers.

Each of the processing elements (Fig. 9-19) contains a correlation unit (CU), an associative output unit (AOU), an arithmetic unit (AU), and 2048 32-bit words of element memory (100-ns cycle time), shared through switch S by the three processing units. Each processor unit has its own registers. All units contain a 1-bit activity indicator, identifying if the unit should participate in parallel instruction execution, and a 21-bit activity history stack. The CU also has sixteen 32-bit correlation registers that contain radar data against which new radar returns are compared. The AU executes floating-point instructions using two data registers, a tag register to identify sets of elements, overflow and double-precision carry bits, and a fault-indicator bit. Output data is selected and organized in the AOU, which has an integer ALU, a single accumulator, and tag, overflow, and double-precision carry registers as in the arithmetic units. All accessing of the processing elements is associative, based on the content of processing-unit and element-memory registers.

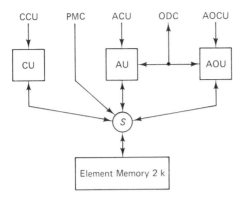

CCU   PMC   ACU   ODC   AOCU

CU   AU   ←→   AOU

S

Element Memory 2 k

Figure 9-19 PEPE processing element.

The three processing-element control units of the global control section (Fig. 9-18), correlation (CCU), arithmetic (ACU), and associative output (AOCU), control those functions concurrently in all processing elements. Each control unit has a 4-kword data memory and a program memory of size shown in Fig. 9-18. Each sequential control executes sequential instructions for address calculations and contains an accumulator, a second data register, a program counter, 16 index registers, a status register of 95 bits, and three stop flags. The parallel control transmits instructions to the processing elements. This part of the arithmetic control unit contains a queue of sixteen 41-bit parallel instruction words. (The other control units do not require the instruction queue since their processing units execute only short instructions.) Each of the control units is implemented with microprogram control and separate 2048 80-bit control stores for serial and parallel instructions.

Concurrent activities in PEPE include operations on different data in each processing element, simultaneous (overlapped) instruction execution in the three processing units of each processing element, and parallel operation of the three processing-element control units. The use of associative (content-addressed) logic in the processing elements permits instructions and data to be "broadcast" to all elements and minimizes requirements for synchronization of processing-element control. This feature can be exploited in PEPE since it is designed to handle a single type of signal-correlation problem. It is useful to compare this powerful special-purpose system with the Burroughs Scientific Processor (Fig. 8-21), which was designed for more general application, and with their common ancestor, ILLIAC IV (Figs. 6-24 and 8-12).

STARAN. Another special-purpose computer developed for signal processing uses associative-processing techniques. STARAN was developed by Goodyear Aerospace Corp. for applications that require that a large number of correlations be performed at high speeds. The STARAN system, shown in Fig. 9-20, consists of 1 to 32 associative-array modules, the array-processor controller, sequence-control and program pager logic units, the array-processor (microprogram) control memory with memory-port logic to control multiport access, and external-function logic for interfacing to a host computer and a large disk file memory. The host computer acts as the input/output processor for STARAN. Data and programs are stored in the disk file memory until needed by the STARAN associative-array modules.

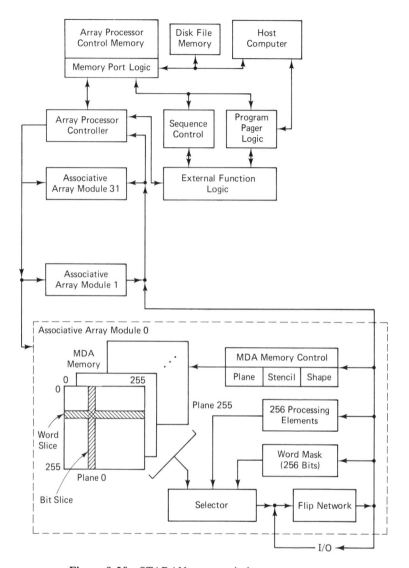

Figure 9-20   STARAN, an associative-array computer.

Each associative-array module holds from 1 to 256 memory planes. Each plane is organized as 256 256-bit words. Memories of all array modules are loaded under control of the array-processor controller, which then executes the microprogram to cause the array modules to operate as a SIMD computer, all executing the same instructions. The memory, called a multidimensional array (MDA), is addressed by plane, by "stencil" (position in a plane), and by stencil shape (word slice, bit slice, or some other of 256 combinations). The MDA memory control determines the 256-bit slice that is to be operated on next. That slice is transferred to the selector (a multiplexer) and to the FLIP network. The latter is a unique permutation network that moves 256-bit slices to the memory control, to the vector of 256 processing elements, to the word mask, or to the array input/output. The FLIP permutation network implements vector and array processing by moving strings of slices through the module.

FLIP uses the starting address (plane selection and stencil location) and the stencil shape to organize a flow of 256-bit streams to 256 processing elements of the association unit. The processing elements can perform serial arithmetic on each of the bit streams or can perform correlations on sequences of one or more bits of all streams. This latter mode is what categorizes STARAN as an associative processor. Flow of the data streams through the word mask allows different associative-array modules to mask different parts of slices.

Since 256 bits are processed in parallel in each of 32 associative-array modules, data correlations can be performed at a very high speed. This unique special-purpose computer has not been produced in large quantities, but has been successful in radar and communications processing, in map and terrain analysis, and in similar applications requiring correlation of large number of signals.

Massively Parallel Processor. Goodyear Aerospace developed another parallel computer for specialized signal processing for NASA. This Massively Parallel Processor (MPP) performs bit-serial operations concurrently on 128×128 arrays at a rate of 10 MHz. The MPP was designed to receive and to process digitized data from an array of 214 photosensors. The system (Fig. 9-21) consists of a large memory, a staging memory that holds 1024 128×128 memory planes, the 128×132 (four spare for reliability) array unit (ARU), an array control unit (ACU), the program and data management unit (PDMU), and a host computer. The PDMU acts as the system controller, managing transfers of information between the host computer with the peripheral equipment and the secondary memory and the MPP memory and moving programs to the ACU.

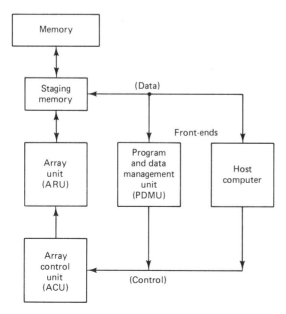

Figure 9-21 Massively Parallel Processor (MPP). (From [BatcK80]. Copyright 1980, IEEE.)

The MPP array unit has an organization similar to that of ILLIAC IV with a much larger quantity of simpler processing elements (PEs). As shown in Fig. 9-22, each PE can communicate with its nearest neighbor in two directions, including end-around transfers (not shown). To load the PE array, data are transferred in parallel to the leftmost column of PEs and are shifted to fill the whole array. Output from the array is performed by additional shifts out of the rightmost column.

Each processing element (Fig. 9-23) is a bit-serial processor with a 1024-bit RAM (a bit from each plane of the staging memory), and an N-bit shift register (N ranging from 2 to 30 bits, as shown). There are six 1-bit flags (flip-flops) that are the working state of the single-bit processor. A PE also contains a full adder and some logic at the interface to neighbor PEs (the P flag). A data bus (D) is connected to the flags and the RAM. The G flag holds a mask bit that, with data in the P flag, controls operation of the PE through the enable (E) unit. Boolean functions can be applied to values in the P flag and on the data bus (i.e., a value in any other flag). Input/output communication with horizontal neighbors (see Fig. 9-22) is through the S flag. The full adder uses values from the P, A (accumulator), and C (carry) flags. Multiplication and division are performed as sequences of serial add or subtract and shift operations, so that even at 10 MHz individual arithmetic operations can take a long time. The ARU has a separate tree of OR gates that is connected to the data bus for concurrent operations on all PEs.

MPP, like PEPE and STARAN, is a computer with a very large amount of parallel activity. It is a special-purpose SIMD computer uniquely designed for image-processing applications. Image-processing operations of MPP include feature extraction, pattern classification, pattern analysis, and scene analysis. Effective image processing requires that these operations be performed concurrently on a large number of image pixels.

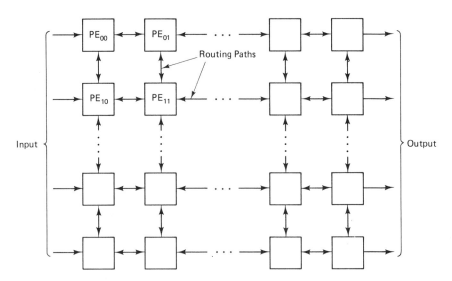

Figure 9-22   MPP array unit.

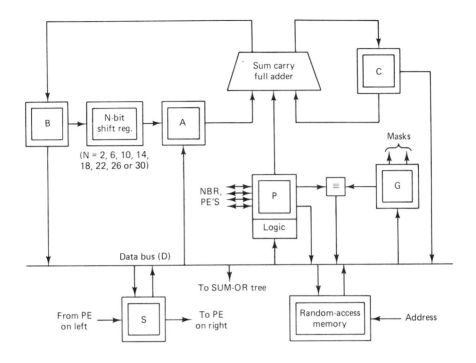

Figure 9-23   MPP processing element. (From [BatcK80]. Copyright 1980, IEEE.)

Antenna-Steering Processor. Systolic arrays and wavefront processors, discussed as one of the alternatives to sequential control flow in Section 9.5, have excellent potential for special-purpose computers. Processing along a "wave" of elements with input from adjacent elements in systolic arrays and wavefront processors is quite similar to the methods for interaction among processing elements in array processors like ILLIAC IV, STARAN, and MPP. Both the sequentially controlled systolic arrays and the data-driven wavefront processors are particularly well adapted to custom VLSI components. The alternative topologies for connecting processor elements in both forms of new architecture give flexibility to organize the arrays to suit individual problems.

Systolic- and wavefront-array designs have been used for signal processing using linear algebra algorithms, for beam forming in microwave- and sonar-signal processing, for bit-level correlators to be used in signal processing, and for implementing dynamic programming algorithms. Since the application is different from any we have discussed so far, a systolic-array processor developed at the Royal Signals and Radar Establishment in Great Britain is our next example.

The processor is used to form the beam of a phased-array receiver antenna. This requires simultaneous adjustment of the phase and the amplitude of the received signal in each of a large number (N) of channels. An optimum "weight vector" (found by a least squares algorithm) that minimizes a combined output signal is calculated and applied at each sample time. The calculations entail solving a set of linear equations that represent a triangular system:

$$\mathbf{R}(n) * \mathbf{w}(n) + \mathbf{u}(n) = 0$$

where $\mathbf{R}(n)$ denotes a triangular $(N-1) \times (N-1)$ matrix developed from operations on values arriving from the $N-1$ input channels, $\mathbf{w}(n)$ is the least squares vector of $N-1$ weighting factors, and $\mathbf{u}(n)$ is the vector produced from inputs from the reference (Nth) channel.

The systolic array for solving this set of equations is shown in Fig. 9-24. The diagonal of the matrix $\mathbf{R}(n)$ is held in the boundary cells and the nondiagonal elements are stored in the internal cells. The vector $\mathbf{u}(n)$ is represented in the rightmost internal cells. Calculations performed in each of the two cell types are shown in the figure. Boundary cells establish values of C, S to be passed to internal cells. If $x_{in} = 0$, then C and S are both 0 and the output control value k_{out} is set equal to k_{in}. For any nonzero value of x_{in}, new values of the cell weight d_i, the control variables C and S, and the next cell control, k_{out} are determined as

$$d_i' := d_i + k_{in} * x_{in}^2$$
$$S := k_{in} * x_{in} / d_i'$$
$$C := x_{in}$$
$$k_{out} := k_{in} * d_i / d_i'$$
$$d_i := d_i'$$

Similarly, the internal cells operate by passing the C and S values to their right, and, if x_{in} is nonzero, the cell weight and the output are

$$x_{out} := x_{in} - C * r_{ij}$$
$$r_{ij} := s_i * x_{out} + r_{ij}$$

The same set of unitary transformations applied to the data vector $\mathbf{y}(n)$ produces the vector $\mathbf{u}(n)$.

The result required for beam control is the residual of the least squares calculations rather than the full least squares weight vector. This residual is calculated by multiplying the outputs of the final boundary cell and the final internal cell, as represented in the figure by the boundary cell with the multiply symbol. Each systolic processing element (cell) performs addition and multiplication like the examples shown in Fig. 9-15. Delays are introduced to input sequences to synchronize the arrival of values at the two inputs of each cell. Each delay is the same as the time it takes for calculations to propagate through a cell. For a complete understanding of the systolic operations, readers should use pencil and paper to run sample problems through the array of Fig. 9-24.

In a high-performance signal-processing system the processing elements must handle two complex multiply and accumulate operations every 100 ns. For the precision required in the beam-forming application the complex operations represent about twenty 24-bit floating-point operations. Each element must be a powerful (200-MFLOPS) special-purpose processor in its own right. To perform the same task on a sequential

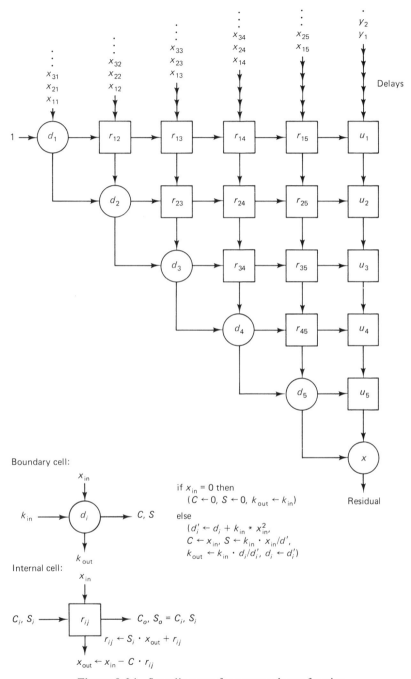

Figure 9-24 Systolic array for antenna-beam forming.

computer would require well over 200-MFLOPS performance for each channel. It is possible to build a systolic array of over 20 of the required cells in a single semiconductor chip. This would allow beam forming for $N = 6$ antennas. For more beams, multiple-chip systolic arrays are required.

9.7 SUMMARY

There are many instances where the computer architect is in the position of designing a specialized digital system. Use of a general-purpose computer should not be decided without a detailed examination of alternatives. Often a special-purpose design is more suitable for a combination of performance, cost, and reliability. Drawing a direct processing analog of any large system helps to determine if special-purpose alternatives should be considered. The analog also is the starting point for system design.

Several special-purpose computer architectures diverge from the usual control flow of computation. Data-flow techniques follow Petri-net principles in having operations execute when the data items needed are available. These data-driven computers use a large number of processors and large high-speed switches to permit the data to flow from the output of one processing stage to the input of the next. Reduction architectures use demand-driven methods to control processing. String-reduction and graph-reduction principles have been used to form new computational models. Combinatory logic can be used as a basis for a computing model that uses a normal-order evaluation of functional programs. Combinators are used to extract variables from function compositions to make the computer organization independent of the data to be used. Alternative approaches to exploiting very-large-scale integrated circuits (VLSI) include systolic arrays and wavefront processing. Whether these new techniques will be real competitors for control-flow approaches for general-purpose computers requires much more evaluation and comparison.

Several examples of special-purpose digital systems have been used to demonstrate the principles and the alternatives. In some cases a general-purpose computer to solve the same problem is much larger and more expensive than the special-purpose computer. Sometimes a general-purpose solution is not feasible at all. A detailed analysis of system requirements followed by careful specification and evaluation of processing approaches are needed to initiate the special-purpose computer design.

Many of the example computers are similar to or were derived from the parallel computers discussed in Chapter 8. Most of those parallel computers started as special-purpose systems directed at specific classes of mathematical problems. The distinction between general-purpose and special-purpose computers continues to be fuzzy and many of the concepts and technologies developed for special-purpose systems find their way into the mainstream of general-purpose design.

Most of the principles that have been stated throughout this book are applicable to special-purpose (or custom) system design. Architectures should be as simple as possible, flexible to adapt to change, manufacturable, and maintainable once installed.

9.8 ADDITIONAL READING

Much information on computing and data processing involving special-purpose computers is found in the literature on the particular application areas. For example, publications of the IEEE Communications Society include many articles on communications processing. *IEEE Transactions on Acoustics, Speech, and Signal Processing* and *IEEE ASSP* cover signal-processing techniques. Radar data processing often is covered in issues of *IEEE Transactions on Aerospace and Electronic Systems* and of the magazine of that IEEE Society. *IEEE Engineering in Medicine and Biology* and *IEEE Transactions on Medical Imaging* cover medical instrumentation and associated processing. Control systems data-processing requirements are found in *IEEE Transactions on Automatic Control, IEEE Control Systems*, and *IEEE Transactions on Industrial Electronics*.

The radar data-processing techniques described in Section 9.1 were developed for the SAGE air defense system and are outlined in [KranF60]. The SAGE system itself was described in [EverR57]. Although the techniques are old, the principles continue to be used in radar-based systems for air defense and air-traffic control.

Digital-signal-processing principles and functions are described in [PeleA76] and [WillC86]. The PIXAR image-processing system and principles of dynamic image processing are covered in [GlazD86]. The related computer, CHAP, is described in [LeviA84].

An excellent review of associative processors is found in [YauSS77]. The information on PEPE was taken from a hardware reference manual [TroyJ77]. Articles on STARAN and MPP are found in [BatcK77] and [BatcK80], respectively.

[TrelP82] reviews the distinction among different control styles. Data-flow architectures are described in [Arvin77], [DennJ80], [GurdJ86], and [WatsI82]. The February 1982 issue of *IEEE Computer* is devoted to data-flow architectures. Reduction architectures can be reviewed in [BerkK78], [MagoG80], [DarlJ81], and [TurnD79]. [TrelP83] compares these new architectures. An excellent treatment of a functional language is [BackJ78], supporting ideas presented in [McCaJ60]. [HendP80] covers functional programming in more detail. [Arvin81] includes many papers on functional languages and architectures. Denotational semantics, introduced by Scott and Strachey in 1971, are covered in [StoyJ77] and [TennR81].

Systolic-array architectures are reviewed in [KungH82] and [HwanK84]. A special issue of *IEEE Computer* [FortJ87] is devoted to systolic-array designs. Their applications and those of wavefront processors are also included. Systolic-processing principles are outlined in [KungH82]. An article on special-purpose systolic arrays for signal processing appears in [KungS87].

9.9 PROBLEMS

9-1. Convert the PASCAL program for search radar data processing of Fig. 9-4 to assembly language code for a real or a hypothetical computer. (If the latter, briefly outline the computer design.) From this program, estimate the memory cycle time and the times of arithmetic operations required to perform a cycle of the program in 2.0 microseconds (300-meter radar range interval).

9-2. Using a language like PASCAL or a flow chart, develop an algorithm for calculating the correlation function described in Section 9.4 and shown in Fig. 9-10(a). Convert the algorithm to assembly language code for a real or a hypothetical computer. Identify the speeds required of memory and of arithmetic operations for solving the correlation functions with $k = m = 100$ every millisecond.

9-3. Data-flow computation can be represented as a directed graph like a Petri net (Fig. 2-14), where the cells, rather than just "firing" when the required tokens are available, perform prescribed calculations when the required data are available. Draw a directed graph representing the data-flow computation for solution of four linear equations in four unknowns (reduction of a 4×5 matrix) by Gaussian elimination.

9-4. In ISP, show the design of processors to implement each of the two systolic cells of Fig. 9-15(a). Identify all registers and arithmetic-function units required in each case.

9-5. Convolution processing is described in Section 9.4 and is defined in Fig. 9-10(a). Since this processing involves "streaming" values of x_k through weighting processors w_j to obtain values of y_i, systolic arrays appear to be suited to convolution-processor design. Demonstrate the design of a systolic-array processor for one-dimensional convolution processing using one row of the rectangular array of the left side of Fig. 9-15(b) with the following:
a. Cells shown on the left of Fig. 9-15(a).
b. Cells shown on the right of Fig. 9-15(a).

In each case, define the inputs, any constants, and the outputs of the cells in terms of x_k, w_j, and y_i of Fig. 9-10(a).

9-6. Consider the description of ILLIAC IV in Section 8.4 and Fig. 8-12 and that of PEPE in Section 9.6 and Figs. 9-18 and 9-19. Discuss and contrast the mechanisms used in each to select a set of processing elements to participate in a vector operation. What aspects of the initial applications of the two computers might account for the difference in selection mechanisms?

9.10 PROJECT

9-A. Identify an information-processing problem that warrants consideration of a special-purpose computer. Develop the requirements in detail. Discuss factors that must be considered in comparing special-purpose and general-purpose computer approaches to the problem.

10

Summary and Prognosis

In the previous eight chapters we have outlined a methodology for digital-system design, have been introduced to several tools to help describe the architecture precisely and concisely, and have seen alternatives available to the computer architect for design of the system and its major components. In this chapter we consider where computer architecture is headed. What have we learned that will help us to design new architectures in the future?

Much of the material in the earlier chapters related the history of digital computers. Evolution of computer design and of the technological trends that influence the architectures have been presented. Now we should examine whether we can predict future architectures using the experience of the past. Projections of past trends should assist in identifying both opportunities and possible hazards for the architectures of tomorrow. If we look at the continuing rapid expansion of technological capabilities we learn to be cautious in predicting that anything "won't happen".

10.1 METHODOLOGIES FOR DESIGN AND FOR RESEARCH

A methodology for computer design was introduced in Chapter 2. The approach started with a careful specification of requirements for a digital system and worked from the top level of the architecture down toward the detail, with iterations of requirements analysis, evaluation of alternatives, system specification, implementation, and verification. This approach leads to a "need-driven" design, responding to user requirements. In the top-down approach we are cautioned to be aware of the varied possibilities for implementation at more detailed levels in order that the architecture can take advantage of expanding technologies.

An alternative methodology is used in computer research. It is "idea-driven", starting with a supposition that new concepts and new technologies will find applications if they provide sufficient advantage. The researcher should not be impeded by the necessity to demonstrate feasibility and economic advantage before pursuing new ideas. Most research results do find application, even if only in leading to further ideas. To be sure that the overall direction holds promise, the researcher might "wave a magic wand of success" over the idea to determine, if the results are as hoped for, whether the idea has possible application. This can serve to prevent an expensive foray into a project that has little chance for application.

This "suppose we could . . ." approach is useful over the whole range of computer design and implementation, from device-physics investigations to system-organization research. Progress in computer architecture requires that both the top–down design approach and the bottom–up research approach be followed. It is important that those involved in both areas exchange information and ideas with each other. A designer who neglects new ideas will find it difficult to keep up with competing designers. Research that pays no attention to possible applications may overlook branches where payoff can be very high. Often the need and the new idea can be offset in time because of mismatches of technologies. Microprogrammed computer control was cited as an example early in the book. Conversely, a technology may appear before there is an application need, as was the case when gallium arsenide (as well as some other III–V compounds) was used for electrooptical devices before it was recognized as a material for high-speed transistors.

10.2 TECHNOLOGY AND ARCHITECTURE

Need-driven advances in computer architecture were developed throughout this book. Advances in system structures, instruction-set processors, and processor implementations responded to demands for new functional capability, increased performance for lower cost, higher reliability, and combinations of these. The need-driven advances were evolutionary and architectures have changed slowly, as is evidenced by the age of many successful current architectures. IBM System/360–370, Unisys A series (Burroughs origin), Unisys 1100/2200 (Sperry origin), DEC PDP-11/VAX, and Control Data 6600/Cyber architectures all were introduced between 1960 and 1970. A new architecture sometimes was a response to reaching a technological limit that made it impossible to meet requirements with then-current designs. Several architectures started as special-purpose approaches to meeting a unique problem and found application to a variety of computing needs.

While computer architecture has evolved, computer technology has exploded. Device physics and processing methods have provided "much more for much less" at a consistent rate for the more than 40 years since the first electronic digital computer was introduced. Technology has influenced computer architecture by making new approaches feasible (e.g., personal computers) and by changing the balance among parts of computer systems (e.g., SRAM cache and DRAM primary memory), as well as in providing much more performance for much less cost.

It should be possible to project the technological capability expected in the future from the consistent trends of the past. Toward this end the data plotted in Fig. 4-1 (primary-memory size), Fig. 4-4 (memory cost and speed), Fig. 6-1 (semiconductor device density), and Fig. 8-1 (circuit speed) can be extended to the year 2000 with a high degree of confidence and to 2010 with reasonable assurance. From this projection of technology we can anticipate future computer architectures. Characteristics of computer technology expected in 2000 and 2010 are summarized in Fig. 10-1. The "change factors" (the quantity that is raised to the power of the number of elapsed years to determine future values) and calculated values for each of the characteristics are shown.

If present trends continue to 2000, large computers will have primary memories of up to 7 Gbytes, as large as today's "triple-density" disk files ("direct-access storage devices"). Primary memory will cost about the same as present computer memories since the cost per bit is falling at about the same annual rate (36%) that memory size is expanding (29%). By 2010 the large computers will have primary-memory capacities approaching 10^{11} bytes, using a full 36-bit word for addressing.

The number of devices (transistors) in a single component, the "device density", is growing at a rate of 58% per year, leading us to expect 10^9 devices on a dynamic memory chip or 2.5×10^8 devices on a processor chip by the year 2000. A computer using an Intel 80386 processor, 500-kbyte memory, an arithmetic processor, and input/output controllers will use about 10^7 devices. In 2000 we should be able to put 25 to 100 computers of this type in a single semiconductor component ("ILLIAC IV on a chip"). Since logic circuits will be 50 times faster and memory circuits 12 times faster than those used in 1988, it should be possible in 2000 for a very powerful computer, using extensive pipelining and parallel input/output to achieve 50 times the performance of an 80386-based machine, with 50 Mbytes of memory to be placed in a single semiconductor component ("Cray-1 on a chip"). The same capabilities, combined with advances expected in computer-aided design, should lead to very powerful single-chip special-purpose computers. These might be assembled using "application-specific instruction-set computers", like the special-purpose processors derived from Intel's 80386 or designed using advanced application-specific integrated circuits (ASICs).

Characteristic	Expected Values		Factor
	2000	2010	
Large Computer Memory Capacity, bytes (Fig. 4-1)	3×10^9	4×10^{10}	1.29
Primary Memory Cost, \$/bit (Fig. 4-4)	10^{-6}	5×10^{-8}	−1.36
Component Density, devices/chip (Fig. 6-1)			
Memory	10^9	10^{11}	1.58
Logic	2.5×10^8	2.5×10^{10}	1.58
Circuit Propagation Delay, seconds (Fig. 8-1)	2×10^{-11}	7.5×10^{-13}	−1.39
Memory Device Cycle Time, seconds (Fig. 4-4)	10^{-9}	10^{-10}	−1.23

Figure 10-1 Extension of technology trends.

When we extend our projection to the year 2010 we see, albeit less clearly, single-chip supercomputers with 100 times the capacity and 25 times the performance of the computer of 2000. It is difficult to visualize a "Cray Y-MP on a chip", but 2010 is only two decades away and the trends used in the forecast have been consistent for twice that long. We should consider the implications of these technological advances on computer architectures in more detail. First let us examine what might be the limits on the technologies to establish a degree of confidence in the projections.

Component density, the number of individual devices (e.g., transistors) that can be placed on (or in) a single semiconductor component, is limited by our ability to squeeze individual device "features" down to smaller and smaller sizes. The features of a metal-oxide transistor that are diffused into the semiconductor (Fig. 10-2) include source, drain, and isolation regions. At least two layers of conductors to connect the active source, gate, and drain features must be laid down over the semiconductor surface. A semiconductor "chip" with half a megabit of SRAM will have over 3 million such devices diffused onto a surface about 1 cm square. In each direction the linear density will be over 1500 devices per centimeter. In the semiconductor material and in materials deposited on the surface a transistor must have at least five specific distinguishable features, indicating that about 8000 features must be provided in the centimeter. The "feature resolution" must be at most 1.2 microns (1.2×10^{-4} cm) for the features to be separated. The ability to separate features clearly in the semiconductor production processes is dependent on precise electrooptical instrumentation. Higher component densities require more and more advanced methods for mask processing and mask alignment.

A 4-megabit DRAM with approximately 8×10^6 devices needs 0.7-micron process technology. In general, the wavelength used for optical lithography in semiconductor processing should be at most 1/10 the feature resolution size so a wavelength of 0.07 micron (700 Angstrom units) is required for 0.7 micron processes. This places the electrooptical processes at wavelengths of electrons, much shorter than those of ultraviolet light. The lithography processes at these wavelengths are called "electron-beam lithography". To place 10^9 devices on a 1 cm square semiconductor requires a feature resolution of 0.06 micron, requiring electrooptics working at 60 Angstrom units, in the X-ray spectrum. Moving to the component density shown for the year 2010 (10^{11} devices) requires that electron-beam

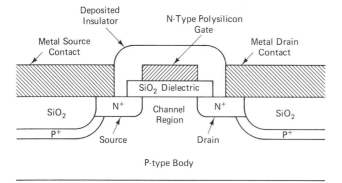

Figure 10-2   MOS transistor cross section.

lithography techniques be extended further into the X-ray spectrum near 6 Angstrom units. There is some question as to whether it will be possible to extend today's processing methods that far, or if other techniques will be needed, such as much larger chip sizes or three-dimensional semiconductor processing.

The more devices that are active on a semiconductor, the higher the power required and the heat generated, unless the individual devices use less power. Smaller devices use less power, but higher switching speeds require more power. There is a conflict among the requirements for more power to attain higher speeds, smaller devices to reduce power densities, and electrical current levels needed to separate signals from noise. At some point we might reach a practical limit of component density or component speed, although superconductor technology might come to the rescue here.

If it is possible to reduce circuit propagation delays as shown in Fig. 10-1, we find that in 2000 delay per stage will be about 20 ps (20×10^{-12} s). In that time light travels 6 mm and 25 gate stages will be traversed in the time it takes light to travel 15 cm. Will we be able to use today's designs at these speeds (or at 25 times these speeds, as projected for 2010)?

Straining the physical limits with advanced device technologies might be difficult. However, the trends of the past tell us that similar limits have been overcome for many years. Computer architects cannot afford to assume that "it will not happen". They must prepare to use the technologies that are projected to exist.

10.3 INSTRUCTION-SET PROCESSORS AND CONTROLS

How will advancing electronic technologies affect computer architectures? How can computer architects take advantage of advances in technology? These two questions cannot be answered before we have a clear picture of the technological capabilities, but we can anticipate several possibilities. Electrooptical devices offer the possibility of using light to transfer signals or to perform logic functions. Gallium-arsenide semiconductor devices offer high speed, but might require different physical configurations than silicon semiconductors. We know that we will have available circuits of much higher speeds than at present. We can be sure that there will be a major expansion of the number of gates and registers available to be incorporated into a processor. It is possible to consider how these advances can be incorporated into instruction-set processors and their controls.

If logic-circuit speeds expand more rapidly than memory circuits, as suggested by Fig. 10-1, we should design systems that allow more processing to be accomplished between accesses to memory. It might be desirable to use expanded instruction queues (Fig. 5-13) and multiple arithmetic pipelines (Fig. 6-25) in processors. Arguments would be prefetched from memory well before operator execution. Complex argument addressing might interfere with the smooth flow of operations through the pipeline and the *regular* instruction-set architectures of Wirth (Fig. 6-31) might be more suitable than either RISC or CISC approaches (Section 6.5). A more extreme possibility is that we move totally away from the fetch-execute cycle for individual instructions. Groups of instructions, perhaps representing functions or short procedures, and of data items might be brought to the processor for "batch" execution before another group is brought from memory. The present RISC/CISC argument might lose its significance because there would be no synchronization of individual instruction fetches and operator executions.

With so many more devices on a semiconductor we will find that a much larger quantity of processor registers can be introduced. If so, what is the best way to use these added registers? We can build a very large (1-Mbyte?) general-register state (Section 5.4). A large (256-kword?) stack implemented right in the processor (Section 5.4) could be feasible. On the other hand, we might prefer to devote as much of the semiconductor surface as possible to high speed primary memory (SRAM?) (Section 4.2) and return to the single-accumulator computer organization of von Neumann (Fig. 2-7). The best approach is not obvious and the reader might wish to consider how to design now for the anticipated level of circuit integration of 10 years from now (SuperLSI?).

New device technologies could lead to alternative instruction-set processor organizations, or even a return to very old approaches. Gallium-arsenide (GaAs) semiconductors have very low signal-propagation times compared with equivalent-size silicon (Si) transistors, allowing for very-high-speed logic. Initially it was felt that difficulties in attaining high yields of VLSI GaAs circuits would require different architectures for computers made with these devices. Determined application of semiconductor-processing techniques has solved most of the problems and GaAs computers can use the same architectures as silicon-device-based machines. The component densities of GaAs circuits may always lag that of Si circuits and architects might face a trade-off between circuit speed and number of components in a processor.

Gallium arsenide, gallium phosphide, lithium niobate, and other III–V compounds can be used as electrooptical semiconductors, opening possibilities for processors that take advantage of the propagation characteristics of visible or infrared light. There are questions about how "optical computing" can be accomplished. Optical buses for transmission of signals offer possibilities for very high communication bandwidths. Pattern-generation and pattern-interpretation techniques might be useful for function units. Possible use of electrooptics for logic and memory of computers is somewhat more speculative because it is difficult to find applications where electrooptics is superior to electronics for conventional computer architectures. If the electrooptical devices can attain pulse-transition times of the order of picoseconds (10^{-12} s) it might be attractive to reconsider a serial-by-bit computer organization similar to that used with vacuum-tube logic and electroacoustic delay lines in the 1950s.

The concept is illustrated in Fig. 10-3. In this instruction-set processor model a set of 1024 "optical delay lines" acts as processor registers for a simple serial ALU. An electrooptical switch selects source and destination registers. The optical delay lines are optical fibers with optical-pulse generators and optical-pulse receivers. When the value in a register is not being changed the receiver–generator pair merely regenerates the same sequence of bits. Information is read from a register by directing the optical signal through the optical switch to an input of the ALU. The ALU itself uses electrooptic logic to perform operations and to return the result as an optical train of pulses to the desired register by way of the optical switch. The delay in the ALU is designed to be precisely

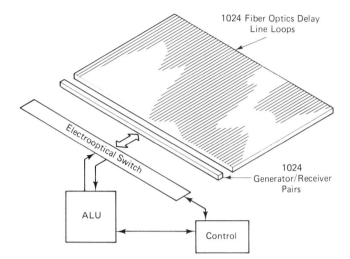

Figure 10-3 Serial computer with 20-GHz serial circuits.

the same as the delay time of the optical delay lines. Whether the concept is feasible or not depends on the electrooptical devices. If the pulse generators and the receivers can generate and detect 10-ps pulses at 20-ps intervals an optical-fiber delay line would need a path of 13 cm for a 32-bit word. This allows for a 640-ps propagation time through the optical switch and the ALU. This is a very sketchy idea of how we might deal with circuits with propagation delays projected for the 2000s in Fig. 10-1. Research on serial optical computers using similar concepts has been reported by Heuring, Jordan, and Pratt [HeurV88] at the University of Colorado at Boulder.

More speculative approaches to optical computers use other devices and physical principles for optical computation. These "integrated optical computers" are fabricated on the surface of an electrooptical semiconducting device. In one approach reported by L. C. West of AT&T Bell Telephone Laboratories [WestL87] a change in the transparency of optical transmitting devices is used instead of semiconductor "switching" to achieve logical gating functions.

There are other approaches to using the very large component densities and the device speeds shown in Fig. 10-1. If we cannot afford the time it takes go through the usual fetch-execute cycle with its multiple references to memory, we might consider the alternative control approaches described in Section 9.5. Systolic arrays (Fig. 9-15) that are dynamically reconfigurable might be feasible as a way to employ a very large number of high-speed semiconductor devices. Computation might proceed through the processor as a "wave" of values that converge to the desired set of results. Other possibilities include large-scale data-flow computation (Fig. 9-11) or the demand-driven execution of reduction machines (Fig. 9-13).

The requirement for compatibility with predecessor machines has inhibited radical changes in computer architectures. This is an "invariant" that we find when we examine trends in architectures. At some point, however, we might find that we cannot use the new technologies fully while retaining compatibility with current instruction-set-processor architectures. At that point we might be forced to examine at what level compatibility really is needed. Is it truly the compatibility of instruction-set processors as has been demanded in the past? Can we retain compatibility at the level of a standard higher-level language? Maybe an intermediate language with which a program can be represented by its parse tree would be a suitable "meeting ground" for retaining compatibility with old programs. The old programs might be translated to the inter-mediate- or higher-level language using a "reverse compiler". Again this is specula-tion, but it indicates the nature of ideas that should be included when considering architectures of the future.

10.4 SYSTEM AND LANGUAGE ISSUES

The projection of component densities of Section 10.2 suggests that a large amount of function will be available in a single component in the future. Computer organizations that incorporate a high degree of concurrent activity might be needed to take full advantage of the technology. History, status, potentials, and problems of parallel computers were covered in Chapter 8. Will it be possible to extend this parallelism to hundreds and thousands of processors? The pertinent issues here are identified by Gajski and Pier [GajsD85] as computer control, problem partitioning, process scheduling, processor synchronization, and memory access.

Experience with parallel computer systems so far has shown that hardware issues can be resolved and that it is possible to design, build, operate, and maintain large-scale multiprocessors and multicomputers. Hardware architectures probably will be available to take advantage of major advances in component densities and device speeds. More speculative is the question of operating systems, algorithms and programs, languages, and compilers that can exploit the hardware architecture capabilities. P. C. Patton, in a review of architecture and applications of multiprocessors [PattP85], concludes that effort is needed toward development of parallel algorithms and parallel programming languages, as well as parallel models of computation.

In Section 5.3 the operating system was described as software that takes the hardware computing machine and makes it a computer that is useful for problem solving. The operating system allocates computer hardware and software resources and schedules processes to use those resources. The more and the more varied those resources are, the more difficult is the design of an effective operating system. The more processes we have to schedule, the more important is an effective operating system. A. Shaw [ShawA88], in an editorial review of current issues in operating systems, points to problems of managing concurrency as the central issue we face in making highly parallel computing systems useful. Process communication is of particular concern. When large numbers of interact-ing processes are active concurrently in a parallel system, mechanisms must be available to communicate among the processes to synchronize their activities. Even when a parallel system is dealing with a large number of independent processes, these processes interact through demands for shared resources. In the latter case the process communication is among the independent user processes and the operating-system processes that manage the resources.

As we move to larger-scale multiprocessors and multicomputers, there will be a major expansion both in the number of resources (particularly processors) to be managed and in the number of user processes to be synchronized and scheduled. Unless methods are found to improve process synchronization and to reduce the overhead of process scheduling, we might find an increase in complexity of the operating system by order n^2 when processors increase by n. This can lead to the limit that the parallel processors will be saturated with operating-system tasks. To prevent this limit from occurring, multiprocessor and multicomputer operating systems must use processing that expands with the number of processors by less than order n. As was pointed out in Section 5.3, features of the computer architecture can be paramount to an effective operating system. Exploitation of technology toward highly parallel computers requires simultaneous and interactive development of architectural features and operating-system capabilities.

In a paper that compared approaches to high-performance computation, Gajski and associates [GajsD82] point out that "In all high-speed computer systems, it is important to achieve two goals: (1) the discovery of as much potential simultaneity as possible in the computations to be performed; and (2) the delivery at runtime of as much of the potential simultaneity as possible." The second point is addressed by computer architects, electrical engineers, and operating-system developers. However, no major advance in parallel computer systems can be successful unless problems can be analyzed to discover potential for concurrency and programs can be written to exploit that potential.

H. Stone [StonH87] coined the term "synchronizations per second" (SYPS) as a measure of interactions among processes in a parallel system. He points out that processing performancence can be limited by either a lack of hardware speed (too few MIPS) or an excess of synchronization (too many MSYPS). Attacking the latter problem requires that we look at the algorithms used to represent the solutions of problems and the programs that we write to reflect the algorithms. With conventional methods for algorithm development (flow charts, sequential pseudolanguages, procedural programming languages) we are encouraged to think in terms of serial solutions to problems, many of which are themselves parallel. The serial algorithms must be transformed to a parallel form, taking advantage of possibilities for concurrent execution.

Sequential programs can be analyzed to determine those "data dependencies" that establish operation successions that must be preserved. Often the dependencies are not inherent to the algorithm, but have been introduced by the particular selection of computational variables (particularly variables used to hold data temporarily). In such a case, modification of the sequential program can eliminate the data dependency. After excess data dependencies have been removed the remaining ones establish how the program can be decomposed for parallel execution. A compiler, Parafrase, that analyzes programs and converts them to parallel form for multiprocessing was developed at the University of Illinois [PaduD80]. It remains to be seen whether these techniques can be extended sufficiently to support the very-large-scale multiprocessing envisioned for the future.

H. F. Jordan [JordH86] focuses on algorithms that contain parallelism at a global level in an attempt to exploit "coarse-grained" concurrency on MIMD computers. He identified the concepts and constructs needed to write programs with global parallelism and used a FORTRAN implementation to demonstrate the approach. The characteristics of data dependencies in different classes of applications are described by S. F. Lundstrom [LundS87]. He relates these characteristics to requirements for memory organization in large-scale multiprocessors. There seems to be much potential in asking the programmer to specify certain parameters that will assist compilers and operating systems in taking advantage of parallel architecture features.

Parallel versions of procedural languages have been developed to permit programmers to represent parallelism in algorithms. Explicit direction of concurrent computation first was introduced for use in operating systems and appeared in systems programming extensions of general-purpose languages. In PL/1 the programmer specifically can dispatch tasks for concurrent execution. More general parallel constructs are used in Concurrent PASCAL, Modula, and ADA. The DOALL statement specifies parallel iterations in extensions of FORTRAN.

The work on parallel algorithms and languages outlined in the last few paragraphs demonstrates that it is possible to adapt sequential languages to parallel processing. There remains a question as to how far the approaches can be extended toward exploiting large-scale parallelism in architectures. Is there a limit on the amount of concurrent activity that can be identified and called for by programmers and compilers? As an alternative, proponents of functional and logic-based languages (Hope, Miranda, SISAL) argue that procedural languages take the natural parallelism of physical problems and force us to use sequential algorithms that are not naturally suited to parallelism. These arguments are closely associated with the issues of alternatives to control flow in computer architectures described in Section 9.5.

Even with a single central processor there will be very interesting alternatives for use of the expected circuit and device technologies. Probably the major hardware issue at the system level will be the question of optimum distribution of storage in the mem-ory hierarchy (see Chapter 3). When it becomes possible to place 10^8 to 10^{10} bytes of DRAM or 10^7 to 10^9 bytes of SRAM in a single component what will be the best way to allocate memory components among processor registers, cache, and primary memory? Will there be room for a memory level between primary and secondary memories?

For example, with the component densities projected for 2000 in Fig. 10-1 we can build a powerful processor with several thousand registers, a group of input/output processors, all the necessary interface logic, and 5 Mbytes of SRAM on a single semiconductor chip. Alternatively, the same technology will allow for the processor with a smaller number of registers, a 1-Mbyte SRAM and 50 Mbytes of DRAM on a chip. If both approaches have the same cost the optimum will be the one with superior performance. To project the performance levels of the two alternatives we must consider the relative speed improvements we can expect in logic circuits and in memory devices. The trends of the past indicate that processor (logic) speeds are increasing faster than memory speeds. This suggests (but certainly does not demonstrate) that the alternative with a large number of processor registers and the faster SRAM as a primary memory will prove to be superior.

Similar speed questions can be applied to the interaction between memories on the single-chip computer and magnetic secondary memories. Secondary-memory seek and latency times have been decreasing at a lower rate than primary-memory access times. Since any rotating-medium memory device will have to be located at least tens of centimeters from the processor-memory component, propagation delays will be much larger than "on-chip" memory-access times. A memory level between the primary and secondary memories might be more important in the future than it is today. With large SRAM primary memory on the processor chip it should be feasible to use another semiconductor chip for a 100-Mbyte DRAM intermediate memory. The intermediate memory would serve as a buffer for block transfers between the primary memory and the secondary memory.

Since 1959 a number of investigators have been intrigued with the possibility of modeling biological neural activities for computation. The approach uses a large quantity of simple and slow ALUs (possibly specialized function units) with a high amount of connectivity among the ALU cells. This approach has recently been identified as a "neural network" approach to computer organization. The architecture is an attempt to emulate the activities that have been postulated for the human brain. The highly parallel Connection Machine (Fig. 8-24) has been used for experiments on neural nets.

10.5 PERFORMANCE MEASURES

Computer-performance measures were described in Section 2.9. Performance was one of the issues discussed with each specific architectural subject in Chapters 3 through 9. Figure 10-1 shows that we can expect major improvements in electronic-device speeds in the future. This will certainly allow computer designers to claim major increases in the device, circuit, and arithmetic speeds of their machines. The rate of increase of memory and logic devices will lead to claimed MIPS and MFLOPS growth by factors of from 8 to 25 in a 10-year period. As stated in the earlier discussions, these simplified factors bear only a slight relationship to the rate at which computers solve problems.

Processor utilization is the percentage of time that a central processor is active. It is gaining favor as a measure of performance of the combination of computing machines and their system programs, particularly in multiprocessor systems. That a processor is "busy", however, is not an indicator that it is performing useful processing work. If processors (and other resources) are executing the operating-system processes required to coordinate multiprocessing they are performing overhead functions and not solving user problems. Processor utilization might create the illusion of high performance, but it is not a valid measure of actual performance.

Progress in development of useful performance metrics cannot be plotted in the simple form of Fig. 10-1, but progress is being made in this difficult subject. Reports of improvements in measures of performance of complex hardware and software systems appear regularly in scientific literature. The progress is slow because the subject is not responsive to simple solutions. The approaches include development of stochastic and deterministic models, and of experimental techniques to validate the models.

In the absence of deterministic means to describe accurately the performance of computer systems, models based on probabilities of various activities have been investigated. Queuing theory forms a basis for describing systems involving tasks that arrive and are held in a queue awaiting service. Queuing models have been used to evaluate computer performance since the mid-1970s.

In the queuing model a population (usually assumed to be infinite) of tasks arrives at a rate a, with a distribution of interarrival times t_a. Tasks that cannot be serviced immediately wait in a queue for a time t_q until the server (computer or processor) is free. When a task is taken from the head of the queue it is served in time t_s so that the total time T in the system is the sum of t_q and t_s. At any time there are N_q tasks in the queue and N_s tasks being served, where N_s can exceed 1 if there is more than a single server. There are $N = N_q + N_s$ tasks in the system at any time. Usually tasks are treated as arriving randomly, so that t_a has a Poisson distribution. The probability of a new arrival within some time t follows the (negative) exponential curve $(1 - e^{-at})$ and the probability of n new arrivals within time t is $e^{-at}(at)^n/n!$. The system capacity is usually assumed to be infinite (wait until served) and the queue discipline is first-in first-out (FIFO). The system is described in terms of the arrival-time distribution A, the service-time distribution B, and the number of servers c, as an $A/B/c$ queuing model.

Several queuing models of computer systems are shown in Fig. 10-4. The building block is an "open" queuing model with a single source of tasks that wait in a queue for service by one or more servers and then depart on completion. Figure 10-4(a) represents a single-server open model with exponential (Markov) arrival and service distributions. It is described as the $M/M/1$ queuing model. Several servers are shown in the $M/M/c$ model of Fig. 10-4(b) with $c = 3$. The open queues can be combined to form more complicated open models, and feedback can be introduced to yield queuing-network models. Figure 10-4(c) illustrates the "central service" queuing model of a simple single-Pc multiple-Kio system with a separate queue for each Kio (see Fig. 3-6). In Fig. 10-4(d) we see the model of operation of a four-Pc multiprocessor system with six Pio modules. Here the Pio share a single queue. There is a queue for tasks waiting to be assigned memory so they can enter the system and a queue of tasks waiting for Pc allocation. This last example is representative of queuing in a multiprocessor operating system (Section 5.3).

Calculations related to the open queuing models are straightforward. The more significant measures are average arrival rate a, average service rate s, traffic intensity r ($= a/s$), and server utilization u ($= r/c$). Performance is measured in terms of mean time in the queue (waiting time) W_q, mean time in the system W, expected number of tasks in the queue (queue length) L_q, and expected number of tasks in the system L. The expected numbers of tasks are related to the mean times by "Little's rule", $L = a/W$ or $L_q = a/W_q$. For the open-queue models of Figs. 10-4(a) and 10-4(b) we can calculate the ratio of mean waiting times to mean service times for various arrival rates. This is accomplished by calculating the probabilities of there being 1, 2, 3 . . . tasks in the system and dividing the result by the sum of the number of servers and the traffic intensity. The specific calculations are beyond the scope of this discussion and can be found in texts on queuing theory. Queuing-network calculations are more complex and require application of computational methods for any significant network.

Alternative stochastic models that are used in performance evaluation include stochastic Petri nets and Markov chains. When Petri nets (Section 2.8) are modified to add timing and probability factors or probability density distributions to the edges of the

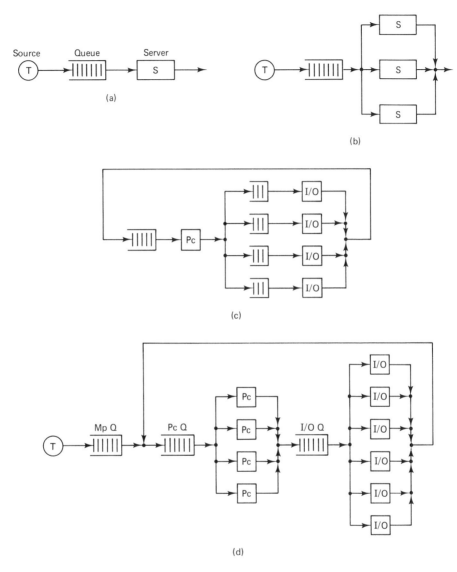

Figure 10-4   Queuing-model examples. (a) *M/M/*1 model. (b) *M/M/*3 model.
(c) Simple network. (d) Multiprocessor system.

graphs, they can be used to estimate performance of a system. The approach allows for
graphical demonstration of activities in the system, but is limited to relatively simple
systems because of the complexity of the calculations at this level of detail. Markov chains
are extensions of the technique to provide for analysis of activities in sequences of queues.
Although somewhat more general than the stochastic Petri nets, Markov chain analysis
requires insight about actions of the models and is limited to relatively small networks.

Probabilistic methods have been applied to specific hardware-configuration issues such as bus-controller and memory-interference studies. The methods particularly are useful for evaluating how well alternative configurations of individual computer architectures meet classes of problem requirements. For example, queuing theory can be applied to evaluate how many terminals or how many communication links are needed in a particular problem environment. Queuing theory also has been used to develop and to evaluate multiprocessing operating systems. Specific operating systems and their relationships to computer system structures can be evaluated using the techniques. So far the methods have not been very useful in development of computer architectures, except in modeling to answer specific questions, such as the size of buffers needed to handle conflict resolution in a modular system or the optimum size of a cache memory in an architecture. The many reports that appear on applications of stochastic analyses and stochastic modeling are contributing to an improved understanding of computer-system performance.

Benchmarking, simulation, and other models that require extensive computation to obtain comparisons of alternatives are very useful in the development of a computer. However, the cost of these techniques and the time it takes to obtain information limit their usefulness in developing insight on the relative merits of different architectures. They are useful in measuring details, but not in reasoning about architectures. For that purpose more deterministic methods are needed. The difficulty of the problem is reflected by the lack of realistic deterministic models at design levels beyond individual arithmetic units and controls.

Reasoning about performance of alternative architectures requires that we start with the problems we wish to solve on the computer. The desired "performance-measuring tool" would then identify the "information energy" that an "ideal computing machine" (hardware and systems software) would consume in solving the problems. Then actual virtual-computer architectures could be compared with the ideal machine to determine their relative performances and "information-processing efficiencies". This is the objective, but we are a long way from it. Progress will come slowly and will result from the accumulation of many individual investigations of computer performance and the factors that contribute to it.

10.6 OUTLOOK

In the descriptions of highly parallel computers and special-purpose systems in Chapters 8 and 9 we have seen approaches that move away from the von Neumann theme of computer architecture. There are designs that do not have "homogeneous" primary memory in which data and instructions are treated the same way. In one example (array processors) there are separate memories for holding data with each processor and a shared memory that contains instructions. Some approaches (data-flow architectures, reduction machines, and systolic arrays) introduce alternatives to the conventional control by sequences of instructions held in memory. Some architectures use a variety of specialized processors instead of the centralized "arithmetic organ" and "control organ" of the von Neumann design.

The search for a viable alternative to the von Neumann architecture is stimulating and can lead to innovative features. However, the history of computer architecture has seen many alternatives examined and rejected. A major invariant of the past four decades is the result that each attractive "non-von Neumann" approach has yielded interesting features that were added to the basic von Neumann architecture. The search should continue because the results have been useful and will continue to be useful to the evolution of computer architecture.

Whereas computer architecture has evolved, the technology used to implement the computer has exploded. We have traced some of the changes in the technology and have seen that increases in speed and capacity and the reduction of cost of computing devices have proceeded at exponential rates since the first electronic digital computer was introduced. Each time a physical limit was predicted to slow the trend, an alternative approach was found to continue the trend.

We still have questions on whether we have reached the physical limits of electronic technology. More significant to the topic of this book is the question of whether we have reached application limits. Can we continue to exploit advances in device technology through the evolutionary approach to advances in computer architecture? How will we best use the products of the device developers? Will we need to introduce a completely new approach to be able to take advantage of new semiconductor materials, electrooptics, magnetooptics, and other advanced techniques? The answers are not obvious, but the search will continue to be exciting!

10.7 ADDITIONAL READING

The field of computer architecture is broad and is influenced by many other disciplines. The breadth and diversity of the field make it difficult for an individual to keep abreast of significant new developments just as they make it important to do so. Despite the difficulty, it is essential that anyone who is engaged in computer design and use follow the technologies, devices, organizations, programming languages, operating systems, and applications of computers. There are many publications that offer overviews of advances in the field and direct readers to more detailed offerings. *Communications of the ACM*, *ACM Computer Architecture News*, and *IEEE Computer* should be on the reading list, or at least the browsing list, of anyone who is interested in computer architecture. More details on original work are reported in *IEEE Transactions on Computers*, *ACM Transactions on Computer Systems*, and reports of the conferences sponsored by the IEEE Computer Society and the Association for Computing Machinery.

Methodology for system development currently is addressed primarily within the specialty of software engineering. *IEEE Software*, *IEEE Transactions on Software Engineering*, and the newsletter of the ACM Special Interest Group on Software Engineering report on development methodologies and tools.

Advances in computing devices are reported in *IEEE Circuits and Devices*, *IEEE Electron Device Letters*, *IEEE Transactions on Electron Devices*, *IEEE Micro*, and *IEEE Journal of Solid State Circuits*. Several commercial publications cover new developments in electronics and computers from industry and the universities. Applications of gallium-arsenide devices to computers are reviewed in an issue of *IEEE Computer* [MiluV86].

Some specific references to more detail on other topics discussed in this chapter are included here. An overview of optical computing is found in [HwanA84]. [HeurV88] shows a possible design for a bit-serial optical computer that uses 1988 technology. Integrated optical computing is described in an issue of *IEEE Computer* [BatcT87]. The approach to integrated optical computing being pursued at AT&T Bell Laboratories is described in [WestL87].

Comparisons of data-flow and demand-driven control with conventional sequential control structures are covered in [GajsD82] and [TrelP83].

Parallel computer systems have been receiving a great deal of attention in recent years. [GajsD85], [PattP85], and [WuChu85] summarize the potentials and the problems in multiprocessing. Applications and compilation issues are discussed in [KuckD72], [PaduD80], and [LundS87]. [AlleF76], [KuckD76], [AllaS80], and [JordH86] discuss organization of algorithms and programs for execution on parallel machines. [HwanK84] and [StonH87], which were cited in Chapter 8, provide broad coverage of the issues. An update on operating-system issues is covered in [ShawA88].

There have been many reports on attempts to emulate biological systems for computation since the work of C. Rosenblatt in the late 1950s. Much of the effort has been devoted to investigating how biological neural systems operate. There is a resurgence of interest in using that knowledge to organize neural networks for computation with the idea that they might provide the optimum computation scheme for artificial intelligence. [LippR87] provides an overview of neural nets, which are the subject of [ShriB88].

The application of queuing models and other stochastic approaches to measurement of computer performance continues to receive attention. Foundations of queuing theory are covered comprehensively in [KleiL75] and [KleiL76]. Basics and applications to computers are discussed in [TrivK82]. [SaueC81] and [LaveS83] cover applications of queuing models to computer performance evaluation. Good outlines of the issues and the methods are described in [SpraJ80] and [AlleA80].

10.8 FUTURE PROJECTS

Reading this or any other book on computer architecture and completion of the problems and projects suggested in the book should not be the end of the "homework assignments" for anyone engaged in computer development. We should all "keep in shape" by retaining our ability to describe, analyze, and evaluate new computer architectures as they are introduced. The following is a continuing assignment for readers:

> For each new computer architecture that is introduced, investigate its characteristics. Describe its PMS organization, its instruction-set processor, and its control structure. Identify features that are improvements over previously described computers. Identify how those features will contribute to an increase in performance, a reduction in cost, an advance in the interface with humans, and/or an improvement in reliability.

A

PMS and ISP Descriptive Systems

A.1 INTRODUCTION

The PMS (processor–memory–switch) and ISP (instruction-set processor) descriptive systems used in this book were introduced by C. Gordon Bell and Allen Newell [BellC70]. The descriptive systems were formulated to describe computer architectures at the system level (PMS) and at the level useful for machine language or assembly language programming (ISP). A full definition of the descriptive systems as originally introduced is contained in [BellC71]. ISP was formalized as the processor simulation language ISPS (instruction-set processor specifications) by M. R. Barbacci [BarbM81].

PMS and ISP can be defined as formal languages, similar to higher-level languages used for computer programming. They are defined that way in the appendix of [BellC71]. The syntax of the combined descriptive system is rather simple. The allowable syntactic items (called "entities" by Bell and Newell) are combined in different ways to form "indefinite expressions" (general definitions of computers and their components) and "definite expressions" (specific representations of indefinite expressions). Computer components can be named and specified. Names can be abbreviated and combined to become definitions of other named items. Execution sequences can be defined to describe operation of processors and controllers. The descriptive systems can be understood by reading a few informal definitions and some examples, as were shown in Chapter 2.

This appendix contains a complete definition of the PMS and ISP descriptive systems as used in this book. The descriptive system is described in the form of a formal language. Some notations are different from those of Bell and Newell. The character set of the language is restricted to the printable characters found on most personal computers, word processors, and computer terminals. This permits a user to define a computer on these machines and facilitates communication of descriptions among individuals. The descriptive systems are modified to make a clear distinction between declarations, which are static definitions of the hardware, and commands, definitions of dynamic actions of the hardware during execution.

A complete formal definition of the syntax of the language is augmented by informal descriptions of the adaptations of the syntax to PMS- and ISP-level specifications. The formal description uses Backus–Naur form (BNF) definitions of all items used for specification. BNF is used extensively for definition of computer programming languages (e.g., [TennR81]). The concise and precise definitions permitted with BNF allow a computer specification to undergo automatic analysis by lexical analyzers and parsers as used in compilers. As a result, any computer description can be converted to a form for simulation on a computer. Those same characteristics lead to unambiguous descriptions for human interpretation.

A.2 FORMAL DEFINITIONS

The formal definitions that are applicable to both the PMS and the ISP descriptive systems are presented in Fig. A-1. The metalanguage (language used to define a language) of the formal definitions uses only 3 symbols: "|" (alternatively), "^" (superscript), and "::=" (is defined as). In the metalanguage, identifiers are underlined, spaces separate items, and multiple-word names are hyphenated. Any comments, including headings, are in italics. Each definition contains the name of the item being defined followed by the definition symbol and the definition itself. A definition may use more than one line. Definitions are separated by a blank line.

The semantics of the descriptive systems are not defined formally. Rather, they are incorporated as notes defining the meaning of symbols and as English-language comments following lexical or syntactical definitions where appropriate. Comments specifically related to semantic definition are preceded by "Sem-".

The vocabulary of the descriptive systems includes the upper- and lowercase English alphabets, the digits, a number of special symbols, and names of operations and system functions.

The following commentary describing the meaning of many of the definitions explains the Backus-Naur descriptive form for anyone not familiar with BNF.

Lexical Definitions. Lexical definitions describe the manner in which syntactic tokens are formed from strings of characters and connectors. Spaces are not permitted within the strings that form the lexical definitions. One or more spaces and other punctuation separate syntactic tokens that are identified through the lexical definitions.

This description of the languages used for both PMS and ISP consists of the lexical definitions, the syntactic definitions, and notes on semantics.

Lexical Definitions:

primitive-name ::= character ¦ character primitive-name

character ::= capital-alpha ¦ lower-alpha ¦ digit

capital-alpha ::= A ¦ B ¦ C ¦ D ¦ E ¦ F ¦ G ¦ H ¦ I ¦ J ¦ K ¦ L ¦ M ¦ N ¦ O ¦ P ¦ Q ¦ R ¦ S ¦ T ¦ U ¦ V ¦ W ¦ X ¦ Y ¦ Z

lower-alpha ::= a ¦ b ¦ c ¦ d ¦ e ¦ f ¦ g ¦ h ¦ i ¦ j ¦ k ¦ l ¦ m ¦ n ¦ o ¦ p ¦ q ¦ r ¦ s ¦ t ¦ u ¦ v ¦ w ¦ x ¦ y ¦ z

digit ::= 0 ¦ 1 ¦ 2 ¦ 3 ¦ 4 ¦ 5 ¦ 6 ¦ 7 ¦ 8 ¦ 9

phrase-name ::= primitive-name connector primitive-name

connector ::= _ ¦ - ¦ / ¦ .

proper-name ::= " primitive-name " ¦ " phrase-name "

number ::= simple-number ¦ simple-number base ¦ number ^ simple-number
  Sem- Numbers represent values from the domain of nonnegative integers.

simple-number ::= digit ¦ digit simple-number

base ::= b ¦ c ¦ d ¦ h
  Sem- b means "binary" (base 2), c means "octal" (base 8), d means "decimal", h means "hexadecimal" (base 16).

boolean-list ::= list-value ¦ list-value boolean-list

list-value ::= 0 ¦ 1 ¦ x

Syntactic Definitions:

description ::= specification-set

specification-set ::= specification ¦ specification , specification-set

specification ::= declaration ¦ command-list ¦ (specification-set)

declaration ::= name ¦ abbreviation ¦ definition ¦ set-declaration

name ::= simple-name ¦ proper-name ¦ specified-name

simple-name ::= primitive-name ¦ phrase-name ¦ selected-name

selected-name ::= memory-name ¦ register-desig ¦ primitive-name (simple-name)
  Sem- the last definition describes function composition.

memory-name ::= primitive-name ¦ memory-name [arithmetic-expr]

register-desig ::= memory-name < number-set > ¦ register-desig @ register-desig

number-set ::= number ¦ number-sequence ¦ number-set , number-set

number-sequence ::= arithmetic-expr .. arithmetic-expr

specified-name ::= simple-name (attribute-set) ¦ unit-spec ¦ memory-spec ¦ register-spec

attribute-set ::= valued-attribute ¦ valued-attribute , attribute-set

valued-attribute ::= attribute : attribute-value ¦ attribute-value

Figure A-1 Formal definitions of PMS and ISP.

```
attribute ::= simple-name

attribute-value ::= specification | number name | ( range ) name

range ::= character .. character | digit-set .. | number-set

digit-set ::= digit | digit , digit-set

unit-spec ::= primitive-name | primitive-name ( # number-sequence )

memory-spec ::= unit-spec | memory-spec [ number-set ]

register-spec ::= memory-spec < number-sequence >

abbreviation ::= simple-name \ declaration

definition ::= simple-def | conditional-def | select-def | procedure-def

simple-def ::= name-set := expression

name-set ::= name | name , name-set

conditional-def ::= boolean-expr ( specification-set )

select-def ::= SELECT register-desig ( select-list )

select-list ::= selection | selection , select-list

selection ::= ( test-set ) ( specification-set )

test-set ::= test-expr | test-expr , test-set

test-expr ::= number | boolean-list | OTHERWISE

set-declaration ::= specification & ( lower-alpha =: range )

procedure-def ::= PROC proper-name ( name-set ) : ( command-list )

name-set ::= primitive-name | primitive-name , name-set

command-list ::= command | command ; command-list
```

Commands:

```
command ::= evaluate | ( specification-set )

evaluate ::= assignment | conditional-action | repeat-action | decode-action |
  proper-name ( name-set )

assignment ::= register-desig <- expression

conditional-action ::= boolean-expr -> command

repeat-action ::= WHILE boolean-expr -> ( command-list )

decode-action ::= DECODE register-desig ( action-list )

action-list ::= action | action , action-list

action ::= ( test-set ) -> command
```

Figure A-1 Formal definitions of PMS and ISP. (Continued).

```
Expressions:

expression ::= arithmetic-expr | boolean-expr

arithmetic-expr ::= term | arithmetic-expr addop term

term ::= factor | term mulop factor

factor ::= simple-name | number | ( arithmetic-expr )

mulop ::= * | DIV | MOD

addop ::= + | -

boolean-expr ::= boolean-term | boolean-expr bool-addop boolean-term

boolean-term ::= boolean-factor | boolean-term AND boolean-factor

boolean-factor ::= boolean-value | NOT boolean-factor

boolean-value ::= simple-name | true | false | boolean-list | ( boolean-expr )
    | relational-expr

true ::= T | 1

false ::= F | 0

relational-expr ::= arithmetic-expr relop arithmetic-expr | boolean-value relop
   boolean-value

relop ::= EQ | NE | GT | GE | LT | LE

bool-addop ::= OR | XOR

comment ::= { text }

text ::= capital-alpha | lower-alpha | digit | punctuation

punctuation ::= ! | @ | # | $ | % | ^ | & | * | ( | ) | _ | - | + |
   [ | ] | : | ; | " | ' | ~ | ` | \ | space | < | > | , | . | ? | /
```

Symbols and words used in the syntactic definitions have the following meanings:

relational operators: "=" equal, "/=" not equal, "<" less than, ">" greater than, "<=" less than or equal to, ">=" greater than or equal to, arithmetic operators: "+" add, "-" subtract, "*" multiply, "DIV" integer divide, "MOD" modulo, boolean operators: "NOT" 1's complement, "AND" logical and, "OR" inclusive-OR, "XOR" exclusive-OR, miscellaneous: ":" is as follows, "\" is an abbreviation for, "@" concatenated with, "&" set values, ":=" has the value of, "=:" is taken from, "," concurrent evaluation, ";" sequential evaluation, "PROC" procedure definition, "SELECT" ..from the following values, "DECODE" ..the register and select an action, "OTHERWISE" ..take this action.

Figure A-1   Formal definitions of PMS and ISP. (Continued).

Any sequence of one or more characters forms a *primitive name*. *Characters* are letters or digits, as shown by the next three definitions. Examples of *phrase names* include Cray-1, System/370, 1100-40 and Ms.disk. "Unisys" and "English-Electric" are *proper names*. The dash connector is distinguished from the subtraction symbol by the context.

A *number* can be shown with or without its base designator. Numbers can be expressed with exponential notation. Numbers are formed from the digits. When it can be implied from the value the *base* usually is not shown. For example, A5F0 = A5F0h and 11011101 = 11011101b.

A *boolean list* is a sequence of 0s, 1s and x's, where x can represent either 0 or 1.

Syntactic Definitions. Syntactic tokens are separated by one or more spaces or by the specific punctuation shown in the definitions. The top-level definition is that of the description.

The *description* of a computer or any of its components is built from a set of specifications. A *specification set* has individual specifications separated by commas. Specifications can be evaluated concurrently and their order of sequential evaluation is not significant.

Each *specification* is either a declaration, a list of commands, or a set of specifications in parentheses. The parentheses can be used to establish the scope of any specification. For example, when a register designation (see description that follows) is declared within parentheses, that designation is the valid reference from any other specification within those parentheses. A *declaration* is a name, an abbreviation, a definition, or a set declaration.

The second alternative of *name* was included in the lexical definitions. A *simple name* is any of a primitive name, a phrase name, or a selected name. The specific strings that are allowed as simple names in attributes and attribute values are defined under PMS and ISP definitions that follow. *Selected names* are selected from items described by specified names, which are defined later. The names of items used in the examples to follow are selected from the PMS and ISP definitions described in the Appendix.

Examples of *memory names* are IR (the instruction register), Mp[127] (memory location 127), Mp[Mp[127]] (the memory location specified by the content of memory location 127), Mp[PC] (the memory address designated by the program counter), Mp[IR<6..15>] (the memory location designated by the sixth through fifteenth bit of the instruction register), and Mp[page][offset] (the memory location selected by the page and the offset fields).

Examples of *register designators* are R2<6..16> (register 2 bits 6 through 15), op-reg<3,5..7> (bits 3, 5, 6, and 7 of the operator register), and Mp[127]<7..0> (the first byte of the word at primary memory location 127).

A *number set* is assembled from numbers, sequences of numbers, and number sets separated by commas. A *number sequence* is formed from two arithmetic expressions (defined later) separated by two periods.

The first definition of a *specified name* is the general form. Examples include Processor(function: central, word-size: 32 bits, technology: CMOS), or Ms.disk(manufacturer: "Burroughs", head-per-track, access_time: 8 ms), or Computer(Pc.8088, Mp(size:(1..8) Mbyte, DRAM), Pio.#1, Pio.#2)

The last three forms of *specified name* permit abbreviation of attributes for concise specification of the quantity of units, the range of memory sizes, and the word size. Examples are Pc(#0..7) (eight central processors numbered 0 through 7, Mp(#1..4)[0..255] $[0..2^{10}-1]<15..0>$ (a primary memory of 4 modules each organized into 256 frames of 1024 16-bit words), Mcache[0..8191] (a cache memory of 8082 words), and Accum<15..0> (a 16-bit accumulator).

Examples of *ranges* include C..K (from C through K), 0,2,4.. (even nonnegative integers), 0,1,2.. (all nonnegative integers). Here the semantics can be inferred from the particular digits. A *digit set* is one or more (different) digits separated by commas.

There are two more alternatives for a *declaration*: abbreviation and definition. A name can be *abbreviated*, as CM\Control_Memory\M(function: control, size: 256 kbytes, technology: EPROM), IR\instruction_register, or Mp[0..2^{16}-1]\Memory(function: primary, size: 0..2^{16}-1).

A *definition* is a simple definition, a conditional definition, a selection from a list of definitions, or a procedure definition. In a *simple definition* a set of names is defined to be the same as an expression. The *conditional definition* tests a named item against a test expression and implements the set of specifications only if the two values are equal (e.g., op<0> = 0 (addr := instr<9..23>)). With the *select definition* a set of selections is tested to find the appropriate set of specifications. The *set declaration* uses a set notation to delineate values that subscripts may take in memory names. With a *procedure definition* we can define a set of commands that can be invoked by calling the procedure name. Note that the definitions are similar to the commands, defined later, but the former are used to select from static specifications and the latter initiate a selected command during execution.

A *command list* is a sequence of commands separated by semicolons. Note that a command list with more than one command is a single specification that will be evaluated concurrently with other specifications (declarations or command lists, including single commands). The command list defines actions to be taken by a processor or a controller while running.

Commands. A *command* is either to be evaluated or is a set of specifications enclosed in parentheses. *Evaluate* is used to represent operations in a computer module. The last form of *evaluate* is the procedure call.

In *assignment* the designated register receives the value that results from evaluating the expression. Assignment is distinguished from definition, defined earlier, in that here the numeric, boolean, or boolean-list value of the expression is assigned to the designated register during execution.

In *conditional action* if the boolean expression evaluates to true (T or 1) then the command is executed. If it does not evaluate to true the command is skipped. With *repeat action* a command list is evaluated repeatedly until a condition is not met.

With *decode action* the value of the designated register is used to select an action from the action list. If test-expression = register-desig then this command is executed. If no test-expression value equals the named-register value all of the decode-action commands are skipped and evaluation of the command list is continued. The value associated with the named register can be arithmetic or a boolean list. This determines whether an arithmetic expression or a list expression is to be evaluated.

Expressions An *expression* can be an arithmetic expression or a boolean expression.

Arithmetic expressions involve integer operations on integers or on integer-valued names. Multiplying operators take precedence over adding operators. Association is left to right. Parentheses force evaluation of inner expressions.

Boolean expressions and terms with operators at the same precedence level are evaluated from left to right. NOT takes precedence over AND, which takes precedence over OR and XOR. Boolean expressions operate on boolean values, boolean-valued terms, or boolean-valued names and return boolean values.

The *boolean value* true can be represented as T or 1 and the value false is represented as F or 0. As a boolean value, a *relational expression* is evaluated before a boolean expression in which it appears. Arithmetic expressions are evaluated before relational expressions in which they appear.

A *comment* is text enclosed by left and right braces. *Text* consists of spaces and any printable characters except the comment braces and the vertical bar. Any information within the first left and matching right braces is treated as commentary not a part of the formal description.

Further (informal) definitions specific to PMS and to ISP descriptive systems follow in the next two sections. Both of these use the formal definitions of Fig. A-1.

A.3 PMS-LEVEL DESCRIPTIONS

The major components of a digital system are defined here. In each PMS-level description the set of semantic definitions and abbreviations that follows is assumed to have preceded the computer description. For clarity in this section the character strings in a specification are enclosed in single quotations. (They will not be in the usual specification.) Included in these definitions are designations of attributes that are usually associated with each of the components:

'P\Processor' is a unit that executes sequences of instructions that are held in a memory. Unless there is only one processor type in the PMS description, the parameter of function must be included. Values of this attribute include central processor, typically described as 'Pc\ Processor.central\ Processor (function: central)', input/output processors: 'Pio\ Processor.input/output\ Processor (function: input/output)'; and other special-purpose processors whose function can be inferred from the attribute value, such as: 'Pdata_comm'. Usually only a very brief description of a processor is included at the PMS level since the ISP level of description defines the processor architecture in detail. Other attributes often described include quantity of processors that can be included in a system, model numbers within a family, hardware technology, means of control, clock speed, manufacturer, year of introduction.

'M\Memory' is a component that contains a bank of addressable registers to hold instructions or data. The attribute "function" usually is needed to distinguish among different memories. The usual functions are primary memory, 'Mp\ Memory.primary\ Memory (function: primary)'; secondary storage, 'Ms\Memory.secondary\Memory (function: secondary)'; and other memories whose function can be inferred from the attribute value, such as 'Mcache' and 'Mtertiary'. The attributes quantity of units, number of frames, number of words, and word size usually are included in a description of memory. Often technology, speed (access time, cycle time, latency time), manufacturer, and/or special characteristics are included in the declaration of attributes.

'S\Switch' is the unit that permits other units to communicate with each other. The switch can be merely a means to connect or disconnect a single path (usually not shown in a definition) or can be applied to the selection of one or more connections among multiple components. A complete definition of a switch will include the specification of the sources, the destinations, the number of connections allowed concurrently. In many cases communication is bidirectional and 'source' designates which component will initiate a conversation. An English language word describing the switch often is included in the definition. An example is: 'S\ Switch.duplex(4,8,2)\ Switch(sources: Pc(#0..3), destinations: Mp(#0..7), concurrency: 2, direction: bidirectional)'. As with other components the technology, the manufacturer, and other attributes might be defined.

'K\Control' is the component that controls connections and operations of other components. A control is distinguished from a processor in that its operations are dependent on its physical wiring instead of a sequence of instructions held in a memory. The main attributes that must be specified are the function and the components controlled (often implied by the function). Speed of operation and technology are among other attributes that might be significant. An example of a control component is 'Kio\ Control.input/output\ Control (function: input/output, number: 0..7, items_controlled: up to 8 peripheral equipment components)'. The last attribute might be defined by the switch between the control and the peripheral equipment.

'T \Transducer' is a component that changes the form or the coding of information without changing its meaning. The attribute that shows the original and the resulting form or code should be specified, although these often can be deduced from the components connected to the transducer or by its function identification. The transducers most often defined are those that are parts of peripheral equipment, such as 'Tkb\ Transducer.keyboard', or 'Tpr\ Transducer (function: printer, width: 80 columns, print_method: character serial, speed: 125 char/s, interface: byte parallel)'.

'D\ Data-operator' is a component that modifies information to produce different information, for example, an adder or an arithmetic and logic unit of a computer. The function attribute of a data operator usually is sufficient to define it, although speed of operation might be significant to a description.

'L\Link' is the connection between two components. The specification of a link must include identification of the components connected and the directionality of the connection. For example, links might be specified as 'Link (data, Pc-Sbus, bidirectional)' and 'Link (data, Sbus-Mp, bidirectional)'.

'C \ Computer' is an assemblage of components defined in terms of those components. A computer usually is defined in a PMS description only when it is the top-level definition, as 'Computer (manufacturer: "Burroughs", model: B5500, components: (Pc(#0..1), Mp(#0..4)[0..8191]<51..0>, Kio(#0..4)), technology: discrete transistors, introduction: 1961)', or when it is a component of a system, such as 'Cdata-comm\ Computer (function: data communication, manufacturer: "Perkin-Elmer", model: 2200)'.

As shown in the description of the Burroughs B5500 computer just given, a PMS definition can include other PMS-level components. Most computer components contain components of similar or different types: most processors contain memory registers, data operators, controls, switches, links, and transducers. A PMS-level description can carry the definition of components to any level desired.

A PMS description that follows the syntax defined herein appears as a specification set, in accord to the formal definitions of Fig. A-1. Although such a description is precise, it is not easy to visualize the physical or the functional configurations and interconnections from this formal a specification. The PMS diagram, a more graphic representation of the PMS definition, does offer a visual representation of the configuration and usually is employed. For the PMS diagram several special notations replace parts of the formal PMS descriptive system:

The links L are shown merely as lines connecting the other components. The function of a link can be defined by whether the line is solid (data and addresses) or is dashed (control). If some other function is to be assigned a link, that function is noted as an English-language phrase attached to the line. Direction of transfers can be designated with arrows at the ends of the lines.

When useful, the number of individual connection lines of a link is defined by a number over a slash through the link line. For example, '$/^8$' specifies a link that transfers 8-bit bytes in parallel.

In the PMS diagram the components are shown with minimum definition of attributes. A superscript number identifies a footnote that contains a more detailed description of the named item. For example, the 3 of 'Pc^3' specifies that footnote 3 contains a more detailed description of the central processor.

The footnote itself consists of the reference number followed by a period, the name, and the definition of the component. For example, '3. Pc("Intel_80286", CMOS, 20 MHz)'. A component definition can itself be a subsidiary PMS diagram.

Figure 2-5 in the text is a PMS diagram of the von Neumann architecture. The more formal PMS definition of that architecture is shown in Fig. A-2.

```
Mp\"Memory_Organ"\M(function: primary, size: 4096 words, word_size: 40
   bits, technology: selectron_tubes, organization: 4096 bits_per_tube),

Pc\Processor(function: central, components: (D\"Arithmetic_Organ",
   K\"Control_Organ"), word_size: 40 bits, data_format: (fractional_binary,
   2's_complement), technology: (vacuum_tube, bistable_logic)),

Lp\Link(function: parallel_processor-memory_connection, connectivity:
   half-duplex, concurrency: 40 bits_per_clock_pulse),

Ms.wire\Memory(function: secondary_storage, technology: magnetic_wire),

K(Ms.wire)\Controller(function: wire_memory_control),

Tdisplay\Transducer(function: data_output, technology: selectron_tubes),

K(Tdisplay)\Controller(function: display_control),

Tkeyboard\Transducer(function: keyboard_input, technology:
   electromechanical),

K(Tkeyboard)\Controller(function: keyboard_control),

Tprinter\Transducer(function: print_output, technology:
   electromechanical),

K(Tprinter)\Controller(function: printer_control),

S\Switch(function: Pc_input/output_connection, source: Pc, destinations:
   (K(Ms.wire), K(Tdisplay), K(Tkeyboard), K(Tprinter)), connectivity:
   half-duplex, concurrency: bit_serial),

Ls\Link(function: serial_I/O_connection, connectivity: half-duplex,
   concurrency: bit-serial, quantity: 5 links, connections: (Pc-S,
   S-K(Ms.wire), S-K(Tdisplay), S-K(Tkeyboard), S-K(Tprinter))),
```

Figure A-2 PMS definition of the von Neumann architecture.

A.4 ISP-LEVEL DESCRIPTIONS

The description of a computer at the instruction-set processor level uses the major component names used in the definition of PMS level of the last section. All registers that are visible to the programmer, and many that are not visible but are useful in understanding the computer operation, are defined. Names of physical registers are capitalized and logical register (part of other registers) names are in lowercase. Register names usually are abbreviated. A bank of registers with the same name is a memory from which a specific register can be selected using the set definition (e.g., R[0..15], R[n] & (n =: 0..15)).

An ISP description can include sections (with section titles as comments) on Pc state, Mp state, data formats, instruction formats, effective-address calculation, fetch-execute cycle, and instruction interpretation. The sections and their titles can vary according to the specific organization and function of the computer. In many cases it is not necessary to define each instruction of the instruction set and only representative examples are specified completely.

As prescribed by the formal definitions of Fig. A-1, a computer description in ISP consists of a set of declarations that define the computer and commands that define how it operates. The examples shown throughout this book serve to demonstrate ISP descriptions.

B

Some Examples of Instruction-Set Processors

This appendix contains ISP descriptions of some of the more popular computer central processors. The examples are sufficiently complete to allow the reader to understand and compare the architectures. The processors described fit into three categories:

Major computer families:
  IBM System/370
  Digital Equipment VAX
Popular 32-bit microprocessors:
  Motorola M68000
  National Semiconductor NS32000
  Intel 80386
Commercial RISC architectures:
  MIPS, Inc. 2000/3000
  Sun SPARC

The reader should compare Pc states, Mp states, data and instruction formats, addressing modes and translation, instruction interpretation, and instruction execution of the computers to obtain a good understanding of the differences in organization and in design philosophy.

{IBM System/370 ISP}

```
{Pc State:}
  GR[0..15]<0..31>,                     {General Registers}
  dr[n]<0..63> := GR[n] @ GR[n + 1]
    &(n =: 0, 2..14),                   {double-register pairs}
  FR[0,2,4,6]<0..63>,                   {Floating-point Registers}
  df[n]<0..127> := FR[n] @ FR[n + 2]
    &(n =: 0, 4),                       {double-length floating point}
  CR[0..15]<0..31>,                     {Control Registers}
  PSW<0..63>,                           {Program Status Word}
  PR<0..31>,                            {Prefix Register (transparent)}
  TR<0..63>,                            {Time-of-day clock Register}
  tod<51..0> := TR<0..51>,              {time of day (microseconds)}
  PT<0..63>,                            {Pc-Timer register}
  cpt<51..0> := PT<0..51>,              {central-processor time}
  CC<51..0>,                            {clock comparator}
  IR<0..47>,                            {Instruction Register}
  machine_state<0,1>,                   {Pc operating state}
    {stopped = 00, operating = 01, load = 10, check-stop = 11}
{PSW Assignments:}
  iomsk := PSW<6>,                      {input/output interrupt mask}
  exmsk := PSW<7>,                      {external mask}
  key<0..3> := PSW<8..11>,              {storage access key}
  em := PSW<12>,                        {extended-memory bit}
  mc := PSW<13>,                        {machine-check mask}
  ws := PSW<14>,                        {wait-state bit}
  ps := PSW<15>,                        {problem-state bit}
  insad<23..0> := PSW<40..63>,          {instruction address}
  {The following bits in the PSW are dependent on the value of em:}
  em EQ 0                               {basic control mode}
   (chmsk<0..5> := PSW<0..5>,           {channel masks}
    int_code<0..15> := PSW<16..31>,     {interrupt code (held in old PSW)}
    ilc<0,1> := PSW<32,33>,             {instruction length (in old PSW)}
    cc<0,1> := PSW<34,35>,              {condition code}
    prmsk<0..3> := PSW<36..39>),        {program-exception mask}
  {Note-In basic control mode, channel masks 6 through 31 are in CR[2].}
  em EQ 1                               {extended control mode}
   (PSW<0,2..4,17,24..39> := 0000000c,  {reserved bits, all = 0}
    rm := PSW<1>,                       {program-event recording mask}
    dt := PSW<5>,                       {dynamic address-translation bit}
    da := PSW<16>,                      {dual address-space mode bit}
    cc<0,1> := PSW<18,19>,              {condition code}
    prmsk<0..3> := PSW<20..23>),        {program-exception mask}
  {Note-In extended control mode, channel masks are in CR[2]. The
  interruption code is placed in real memory locations 134 and 135. See
  dynamic address translation under Logical-to-Real Address Translation to
  see the effects of t and s.}
  fm := prmsk<0>,                       {fixed-point overflow mask}
  dm := prmsk<1>,                       {decimal-overflow mask}
  eu := prmsk<2>,                       {exponent-underflow mask}
  sm := prmsk<3>,                       {significance mask}
{Mp State:}
  Mp[0..maxmem - 1]<0..7>,              {physical memory}
  maxmem := m * (2^20-1) &(m =: 1..2048),{implementation-dependent}
  Mv[0..2^24-1]<0..7>,                  {byte-addressed virtual memory}
  Mvx[0..2^31-1]<0..7>,                 {extended-storage option}
  by[n]<0..7> := Mp[n]
    &(n =: 0..maxmem - 1),              {byte, minimum addressable unit}
```

Figure B-1   IBM System/370 ISP.

```
hw[n]<0..15> := by[n] @ by[n + 1]
   &(n =: 0, 2..maxmem - 2),           {halfword = 2 bytes}
wr[n]<0..31> := hw[n] @ hw[n + 2]
   &(n =: 0, 4, 8..maxmem - 4),        {word = 4 bytes}
dw[n]<0..63> := wr[n] @ wr[n + 4]
   &(n =: 0, 8, 16..maxmem - 8),       {doubleword = 8 bytes}
qw[n]<0..127> := dw[n] @ dw[n + 8]
   &(n =: 0, 16, 32..maxmem - 16),     {quadword = 16 bytes}
sb[0..2^13-1][0..2^11-1] := Mv,        {standard 2-kbyte blocks}
lb[0..2^12-1][0..2^12-1] := Mv,        {4-kbyte block option}

{Logical-to-Real Address Translation (segmented memory):}
  {sx = segment, px = page address, bx = byte index:}
  logad := sx @ px @ bx,               {logical address}
  insad := sx @ px @ bx,               {instruction address}
  tf<0..4> := CR[0]<8..12>,            {translation format}
  ss := tf<3,4>,                       {segment selector}
  pg := tf<0,1>,                       {page selector}
  ss EQ 00                             {64-kbyte segments:}
  (sx<7..0> := addr<8..15>,
    pg EQ 10                           {4-kbyte pages}
    (px<3..0> := addr<16..19>,
     bx<11..0> := addr<20..31>),
    pg EQ 01                           {2-kbyte pages}
    (px<4..0> := addr<16..20>,
     bx<10..0> := addr<21..31>)),
  ss EQ 10                             {1-Mbyte segments}
  (sx<3..0> := addr<8..11>,
    pg EQ 10                           {4-kbyte pages}
    (px<7..0> := addr<12..19>,
     bx<11..0> := addr<20..31>),
    pg EQ 01                           {2-kbyte pages}
    (px<8..0> := addr<12..20>,
     bx<10..0> := addr<21..31>)),
  {segment table entries:}
  ptl<0..3> := dw<0..3>,               {page-table length}
  wr<4..7> := 0000b,
  pto<0..23> := wr<8..28> @ 000b,      {page-table origin}
  sp := wr<29>,                        {segment protection bit}
  cs := wr<30>,                        {common-segment bit}
  si := wr<31>,                        {segment-invalid bit}
  {page table entries, pfra = most significant bits of real address:}
  pg EQ 10                             {4-kbyte pages}
  (pfra<11..0> := hw<0..11>,           {page-frame real address}
   pi := hw<12>,                       {page-invalid bit}
   pfra<13,12> := hw<13,14>,           {extended-storage bits}
   hw<15> := undef),
  pg EQ 01                             {2-kbyte pages}
  (pfra<12..0> := hw<0..12>,           {page-frame real address}
   pi := hw<13>,                       {page-invalid bit}
   hw<14> := 0,
   hw<15> := undef),
  {Each block has a storage key accessed by the block number (not in
  addressable memory).}
  sk<0..6>,                            {storage key}
  acc<0..3> := sk<0..3>,               {access-control field}
  fp := sk<4>,                         {fetch-protection bit}
  rb := sk<5>,                         {reference bit}
  cb := sk<6>,                         {change bit}
  {segment-table locator, in Control Registers:}
  {With dual address space there are 2 possible virtual addresses.}
  pstl<7..0> := CR[1]<0..7>,           {primary segment-table length}
```

Figure B-1   IBM System/370 ISP (Continued).

```
    psto<17..0> := CR[1]<8..25>,        {primary segment-table origin}
    ssec := CR[1]<31>,                  {space-switch control bit}
    ssc := CR[0]<5>,                    {secondary space control (option)}
     ssc EQ 1 (secondary_space_control),{not defined}
    sstl<7..0> := CR[7]<0..7>,          {secondary segment-table length}
    ssto<17..0> := CR[7]<8..25>,        {secondary segment-table origin}
    {dynamic address translation (basic, extended, dual address space):}
    SELECT PSW<5,12,16>                 {see PSW Assignments above}
      ((x0x, 01x) (rlad := logad),
       (110) (sx LE pstl (rlad := pfra(Mp[pto(Mp[psto+sx]) + px]) @ bx)),
       (111) (sx LE sstl (rlad := pfra(Mp[pto(Mp[ssto+sx]) + px]) @ bx))),
    {Notes-If dual address space (DAS) is not installed (11x) has the same
    effect as (110) with DAS. Exception actions for invalid CR[0]<8..12> or
    PSW<5,12,16> values, invalid bit settings of segment or page table
    entries, and segment size greater than pstl are not shown. Protection
    mechanisms (key protection, segment protection, low-address protection)
    are not shown.}


    {Note-A segment- and page-table cache, the Translation Lookaside Buffer
    (TLB), is available with most models to enhance performance. The TLB
    holds 64-bit segment-table entries and 48-bit page-table entries. The
    most recent entries in the segment and page tables are held in TLB, and
    when a reference to a segment or page table is found in TLB it is not
    necessary to obtain the information from primary memory.}

{Real-to-Physical Aaddress Translation:}
  {Real address is adjusted by the "prefix" to assign different physical
  locations for the first block of real addresses for different Pc's.}
  em EQ 0                               {basic control mode}
   (absad<23..0>,                       {absolute (physical) address}
    rlad<23..0>,                        {real address}
    prfx<11..0> := PR<8..19>,           {address prefix}
    DECODE rlad<23..12>
    ((000h) -> absad <- prfx @ rlad<11..0>,
     (prfx) -> absad <- 000h @ rlad<11..0>,
     OTHERWISE -> absad <- rlad)),
  em EQ 1                               {extended control mode}
   (absad<25..0>,                       {absolute (physical) address}
    rlad<25..0>,                        {real address}
    prfx := 00 @ PR<8..19>,             {address prefix}
    DECODE rlad<13..0>
    ((00b @ 000h) -> absad <- prfx @ rlad<11..0>,
     (prfx) -> absad <- 00b @ 000h @ rlad<11..0>,
     OTHERWISE -> absad <- rlad)),

{Assigned Storage Locations (most are real addresses):}
  asl[0..796] := Mp[0..796]<0..7>,      {reserved memory locations}
  {example assignments:}
    initial_PSW := asl[0..7],           {absolute address}
    restart_new_PSW := asl[0..7],       {after initial loading}
    initial_CCW - 1 := asl[8..15],      {absolute address}
    restart_old_PSW := asl[8..15],      {after initial loading}
    initial_CCW - 2 := asl[16..23],     {absolute address}
    external_old_PSW := asl[24..31],    {during external interruption}
    supervisor-call_PSW := asl[32..39], {during supervisor call}
    program_old_PSW := asl[40..47],     {during a program interruption}
    machine-check_PSW := asl[48..55],   {during a machine check}
    input-output_PSW := asl[56..63],    {during an I/O interruption}
    CPU_identity := asl[795],           {for dual address-space tracing}
```

Figure B-1   IBM System/370 ISP (Continued).

```
{Data Formats:}
  {binary integers}
  uby<7..0> := by<0..7>,                    {unsigned byte, uby<7> is msb}
  uih<15..0> := hw<0..15>,                  {unsigned integer halfword}
  uiw<31..0> := wr<0..31>,                  {unsigned integer word}
  sih<15..0> := hw<0..15>,                  {signed integer halfword}
    sgn := sih<15>,                         {sign bit}
    int<14..0> := sih<14..0>,               {integer magnitude}
  siw<31..0> := wr<o..31>,                  {signed integer word}
    sgn := siw<31>,                         {sign bit}
    int<30..0> := siw <30..0>,              {integer magnitude}
  {Note-negative values are expressed in 2's complement notation.}
  {decimal integers}
  ((zdnum[1..m] := by[k] @ by[k+n] &(k =: 0, 1..))
      &(n =: 0..m - 1),                     {zoned decimal number}
    zdig[n]<0..7> := zdnum[n]<0..7>
      &(n =: m),                            {a single zoned digit}
    zdig<0..7> := zone<0..3> @ dec<3..0>,{zone field and decimal field}
    szd := zone(zdig[m]),                   {zoned decimal sign in ms digit}
    zone(zdig[p]) := Fh &(p =: 1..m - 1)){other zone values set to 1111b}
      &(m =: 1..16),                        {up to 16 digits allowed}
  {Note-Zoned decimal numbers are packed for decimal number processing.}
  ((pdnum[1..m]<0..3> := by[k] @ k+[n] &(k =: 0, 1..))
        &(n =: 0..m DIV 2 - 1),             {packed decimal number}
    pdig[n]<0..3> := pdnum[n]<0..3>
      &(n =: 1.. m - 1),                    {a single packed digit}
    dec<3..0> := pdig<0..3>,                {decimal-digit values}
    spd<0..3) := pdig[m])                   {optional sign digit}
    m REM 2 EQ 1 -> pdig[1] <- 0h,)         {most-significant digit}
      &(m =: 1..32),                        {up to 31 digits allowed}
  {Note-For sign fields, 1100, 1010, 1110, or 1111 represent plus, whereas
    1101 or 1011 represent minus.}
  {floating-point numbers}
  sfp<0..31> := wr<0..31>,                  {short floating-point number}
    sgfr := sfp<0>,                         {sign of the fraction}
    mgfr(23..0> := sfp<8..31>,              {fraction, msb = bit 23}
    chfp<6..0> := sfp<1..7>,                {characteristic, excess-64 format}
  lfp<0..63> := dw<0..63>,                  {long floating-point number}
    sgfr := lfp<0>,                         {sign of the fraction}
    mgfr(55..0> := lfp<8..63>,              {fraction, msb = bit 55}
    chfp<6..0> := lfp<1..7>,                {characteristic, excess-64 format}
  xfp<0..127> := dw[k]<0..63> @ dw[k + 8]<0..63>
      &(k =: 0, 8..),                       {extended floating-point number}
    sgfr := xfp<0>,                         {sign of the fraction}
    mgfr<111..0> := xfp<8..63>,             {fraction, msb = bit 111}
    chfp<6..0> := xfp<1..7>,                {characteristic, excess-64 format}
    xfp<63> := sgfr,                        {sign value is copied}
    xfp<65..71> := chfp,                    {characteristic is copied}
  {Note-Floating-point magnitude is expressed as a binary fraction.}

{Instruction Formats:}
  instr\instruction<0..47>,
  SELECT instr<0,1>                         {instruction bits 1 and 2}
  {RR (register and register) format:}
  ((00)(instr<0..15>,                       {halfword instruction}
      op<0..7> := instr<0..7>,              {one-byte operation code}
      r1<3..0> := instr<8..11>,             {argument 1 is in register r1}
      r2<3..0> := instr<12..15>),           {argument 1 is in register r2}
  {RX (register and indexed) format:}
    (01)(instr<0..31>,                      {fullword instruction}
      op<0..7> := instr<0..7>,              {one-byte operation code}
```

Figure B-1 IBM System/370 ISP (Continued).

```
                r1<3..0> := instr<8..11>,       {argument 1 is in register r1}
                x2<3..0> := instr<12..15>,      {argument 2 index in register x2}
                b2<3..0> := instr<16..19>,      {argument 2 base in register b2}
                d2<11..0> := instr<20..31>,     {argument 2 displacement}
          {RRE (register-register-extended), RS (register and storage), S (implied
          and storage), SI (storage and immediate) formats:}
          (10)(instr<0..31>,                    {fullword instruction}
                instr<2,3> EQ 11                 {op = Bxxxh (RRE or S format)}
                (op<0..15> := instr<0..15>,      {halfword operation code}
                 op<8..11> EQ 2h                 {RRE format}
                 (instr<16..23> := xxxxxxxx,     {undefined}
                  r1<3..0> := instr<24..27>,     {argument 1 is in register r1}
                  r2<3..0> := instr<28..31>),    {argument 1 is in register r2}
                 op<8..11> NE 2h                 {S format}
                 (b2<3..0> := instr<16..19>,     {argument-2 base in register b2}
                  d2<11..0> := instr<20..31>)),  {argument-2 displacement}
                instr<2,3> NE 11                 {op = 8xh, 9xh, or Axh}
                (op<0..7> := instr<0..7>,        {one-byte operation code}
                 r1<3..0> := instr<8..11>,       {argument 1 is in register r1}
                 r3<3..0> := instr<12..15>),     {argument 3 is in register r3}
                 b2<3..0> := instr<16..19,       {argument-2 base in b2}
                 d2<11..0> := instr<20..31>)),   {argument-2 displacement}
                 i2<0..7> := instr<8..15>,       {immediate argument}
                 b1<3..0> := instr<16..19,       {argument-1 base in b1}
                 d1<11..0> := instr<20..31>))),  {argument-1 displacement}
          {SS (storage and storage), SSE (storage and storage extended)}
          (11)(instr<0..47>,                     {3-halfword instruction}
                instr<3> EQ 1                     {op = Dxh or Fxh (SS format)}
                (op<0..7> := instr<0..7>,        {one-byte operation code}
                 l1<7..0> := instr<8..11>,       {length of first operand}
                 l2<7..0> := instr<12..15>,      {length of second operand}
                 ll<15..0> := l1 @ l2,           {long operand length (both)}
                 b1<3..0> := instr<16..19>,      {argument-1 base in register b1}
                 d1<11..0> := instr<20..31>,     {argument-1 displacement}
                 b2<3..0> := instr<32..35>,      {argument-2 base in register b2}
                 d2<11..0> := instr<36..47>),    {argument-2 displacement}
                instr<3> EQ 0                     {op = Exxh (SSE format)}
                (op<0..15> := instr<0..15>,      {halfword operation code}
                 b1<3..0> := instr<16..19>,      {argument-1 base in register b1}
                 d1<11..0> := instr<20..31>,     {argument-1 displacement}
                 b2<3..0> := instr<32..35>,      {argument-2 base in register b2}
                 d2<11..0> := instr<36..47>))),  {argument-2 displacement}

  {Instruction Interpretation:}
    WHILE machine_state EQ 01 ->               {operating state}
     ("interrupt"(conditions);                 {see Interrupt Processing}
       (instr<0..15> <- Mv[insad] @ Mv[insad + 1], insadd <- insad + 2);
      instr<0,1> NE 00 -> (instr<16..31> <- Mv[insad] @ Mv[insad + 1],
        insadd <- insad + 2);
      instr<0,1> EQ 11 -> (instr<32..47> <- Mv[insad] @ Mv[insad + 1],
        insadd <- insad + 2);
      "execute"(instr)),                        {see Instruction Execution}

  PROC "interrupt"(conditions): ({definition not included here}),

  PROC "except"(conditions): ({definition not included here}),

  {Operand Address Generation (logical addresses):}
    {based addressing without indexing}
     (logaddr_1 <- GR[b1]<8..31> + d1<0..11>, {logical address 1}
      logaddr_2 <- GR[b2]<8..31> + d2<0..11>, {logical address 2}
```

Figure B-1   IBM System/370 ISP (Continued).

```
{based addressing with indexing}
   logaddr <- GR[b2]<8..31> + GR[i2]<8..31> + d2<0..11>),

{Instruction Execution:}
  PROC "execute"(instr):
  (aricond<0,1>,                          {arithmetic result conditions}
  {Note- 00 = zero, 01 = negative, 10 = positive, 11 = overflow.}
   logicond<0,1>,                         {logic-unit result conditions}
  {Note- x0 = zero, x1 = not zero, 0x = no carry, 1x = carry}
   DECODE instr<0,1>
   ((00) ->                              {RR-format instructions}
    (DECODE instr<0..7>
     ((1Ah) -> (GR[r1] <- GR[r1] + GR[r2],
              cc <- aricond),            {AR, add register}
      (07h) -> (r1<cc> EQ 1 AND r2 NE 000 -> insadd <- GR[r2]<8..31>,
              r1 EQ 111 AND r2 EQ 000 -> "sync"(condits)),
          {BCR, branch on condition. Sync is a machine-check procedure}
      (26h) -> (FR[r1] @ FR[r1 + 2] <- (FR[r1] @ FR[r1 + 2]) * (FR[r2] @
          FR[r2 + 2]), cc <- aricond),  {MXR, multiply extended operands}
      {......other instructions..........} )),
   (01) ->                              {RX-format instructions}
    (DECODE instr<0..7>
     ((5Eh) -> (GR[r1] <- GR[r1] + Mv[GR[b2] + GR[x2] + d2],
              cc <- logicond),          {AL, add logical}
      (05h) -> (GR[r1] <- inslen @ cc @ prmsk @ insad; r2 NE 000 ->
          (insad <- GR[r2]<8..31>))),   {BALR, branch and link, register}
      {......other instructions..........} )),
   (10) ->                              {RRE, RS, S, SI instructions}
    (instr<2,3> EQ 11 ->                 {halfword operator field}
    (DECODE instr<0..15>
     ((B218h) -> (event_flag <- CR[1]<31> EQ 1;
          (PSW<5,12,16> EQ 110 AND CR[5]<0> EQ 1 ->
              (arg<0..23> <- [GR[b2]<8..31> + d2<0..11>];
  {Program Call Number, pcno, is used for indirect addressing to
  another program or program segment.}
          pcno<0..19> <- wr[absad(rlad(arg))]<12..31>;
          link<0..31> <- wr[absad(CR[5]<8..24> @ 0000000
                                  + pcno<0..11> @ 00)];
  {Entry, a quadword in a table, is the second level of indirection in
  a program or a subprogram.}
          (pcno<12..17> LE link<26..31> AND link<0> EQ 0 ->
              entry<0..127> <- qw[absad(link<8..25> @ 00c
                              + pcno<12..19> @ 0h)],
          pcno<12..17> GT link<26..31> OR link<0> EQ 1 -> "except(cond));
          link<1..7> NE 0000000 OR entry<32..39> NE 00h -> "except(cond);
          PSW<15> EQ 1 ->
          (CR[3]<0..15> AND entry<0..15>) EQ 0000h -> "except"(cond);
           (GR[3]<0..15> <- CR[3]<0..15>, GR[3]<16..31> <- CR[4]<16..31>,
           CR[3]<16..31> <- CR[4]<16..31>, GR[4] <- entry<64..95>,
           GR[14] <- 00h @ PSW<40..62> @ PSW<15>, PSW<15> <- entry<63>,
           PSW<40..63> <- entry<40..62> @ 0, CR[7] <- CR[1],
           CR[3]<0..15> <- entry<96..111> OR CR[3]<0..15>);
          entry<16..31> NE 0000h ->     {PC with space switching}
          (CR[14]<12> EQ 0 -> "except"(cond);
  {Address-Space Number (ASN) Link is a reference to the quadword,
  ASN_Value that contains the new program-reference information.}
          asn_link<0..31> <- wr[absad(entry<16..25> @ 0c
                              + CR[14]<20..31> @ 000h)];
          asn_link<0..7> @ asn_link<28..31> NE 000h -> "except"(cond);
          asn_value<0..127> <- qw[absad(asn_link<8..27> @ 0h
                                      + entry <26..31> @ 0h)];
          asn_value<0> EQ 1 -> "except"(cond);
```

Figure B-1   IBM System/370 ISP (Continued).

```
            CR[4]<0..11> GT asn_value<48..59> -> "except"(cond);
{Auth identifiers if the current program is authorized to reset
 Control Registers 1, 4, and 5.}
         auth<0..7> <- by(absad(asn_value<8..29> @ 00 + CR[4]<0..13>));
         SELECT CR[4]<14,15>
         ((00)(authbit := auth<0>),
          (01)(authbit := auth<2>),
          (10)(authbit := auth<4>),
          (11)(authbit := auth<6>));
         authbit EQ 1 -> (CR[4]<0..15> <- asn_value<32..47>,
                          CR[4]<16..31> <- entry<16..31>,
                          CR[1] <- asn_value<64..95>,
                          CR[5] <- asn_value96..127>))),
      PSW<5,12,16> NE 110 OR CR[5]<0> EQ 1 -> "except"(cond));
    event_flag OR CR[1]<31> EQ 1 -> "interrupt"(conditions)),
                                      {PC, program call}
  {.......other instructions..........} )),
 instr<2,3> NE 11 ->                    {byte operator field}
 (DECODE instr<0..7>
{Temp is a value temporarily held in a working register.}
  ((8Bh) -> (temp<5..0> <- d2<11..6>,
           while temp<5..0> GT 00c ->
             (GR[r1]<0> NE GR[r1]<1> ->
              (cc<01> <- 11, fm EQ 1 -> "except"(cond));
             (GR[r1]<1..30> <- GR[r1]<2..31>,
              GR[r1]<31> <- 0); temp<5..0> <- temp<5..0> - 1)),
                               {SLA, shift left single}
    (92h) -> (by[absad(rlad(GR[b1] + d1)] <- i2),
                               {MVI, move immediate}
   {.......other instructions..........} )),
 (11) ->                               {SS-, SSE-format instructions}
 (instr<3> EQ 1 ->
 (DECODE instr<0..7>                   {byte operator field}
{Pdig is a packed-decimal byte. Zdig is a zoned-decimal byte. Both
 are defined in Data Formats above.}
  ((F2h) -> ((pdig[1]<<0..3> @ pdig[2]<0..3> :=
                         by[absad(rlad(GR[b1] + d1))],
             zdig[1]<0..7> := by[absad(rlad(GR[b2] + d2))],
             k := (l1 + 1) * 2, m := l2 + 1);
            (pdig[k]<0..2> <- 110, pdig[k]<3> <- zdig{m}<3>,
             m GE k -> (n <- 1;
                while n LT m -> (pdig[n]<0..3> <- zdig[n]<4..7>;
                n <- n + 1)),
             m LT k -> (n <- 1;
                while n LT m -> (pdig[n]<0..3> <- zdig[n]<4..7>;
                n <- n + 1),
                while n GE m  AND n LT k -> (pdig[n]<0..3> <- 0h;
                n <- n + 1)))), {PACK, pack digits}
    {.......other instructions..........} )),
   instr<3> EQ 0 ->
    (DECODE instr<0..15>              {halfword operator field}
    ({.......other instructions..........} )),  )),
```

{Note-Details of interrupt processing, exception processing, program-event
 recording, dual-address-space tracing, translation-lookaside-buffer
 operation, storage-key control, address-space number-table processing,
 program-counter number-table processing, storage-consistence checking,
 multiple-processor synchronization, externally initiated functions, and
 initial program loading are not described here.}

{Ref. IBM System/370 Principles of Operation, 10th ed., IBM Corp.,
 Poughkeepsie, NY, May, 1983.}

Figure B-1   IBM System/370 ISP (Continued).

{DEC VAX ISP}

```
{Pc State:}
  GR[0..15]<31..0>,                         {General Registers}
  AP<31..0> := GR[12],                       {Argument Pointer}
  FP<31..0> := GR[13],                       {Frame Pointer}
  SP<31..0> := GR[14],                       {Stack Pointer}
  PC<31..0> := GR[15],                       {Program Counter}
  PSL<31..0>,                                {Processor-Status Longword

{Selected Privileged Registers:}
  ARPR(#00h..3Fh)<31..0>,                    {Architectural-Processor Registers}
  KSP := ARPR(#00),                          {Kernel Stack Pointer}
  ESP := ARPR(#01),                          {Executive Stack Pointer}
  SSP := ARPR(#02),                          {Supervisor Stack Pointer}
  USP := ARPR(#03),                          {User Stack Pointer}
  ISP := ARPR(#04),                          {Interrupt Stack Pointer}
  P0BR := ARPR(#08),                         {Program-Region Base Register}
  P0LR := ARPR(#19),                         {Program-Region Length Register}
  P1BR := ARPR(#0A),                         {Control-Region Base Register}
  P1LR := ARPR(#0B),                         {Control-Region Length Register}
  NICR := ARPR(#19),                         {Next-Interval-Count Register}
  ICR := ARPR(#1A),                          {Interval-Count Register}
  ICCS := ARPR(#18),                         {Interval-Clock-Control/Status R.}
  PCBB := ARPR(#10),                         {Process-Control-Block Base}
  TODR := ARPR(#1B),                         {Time-Of-Day Register}
  RXCS := ARPR(#20),                         {Receive Control/Status Register}
  RXDB := ARPR(#21),                         {Receive Data Buffer}
  TXCS := ARPR(#22),                         {Transmit Control/Status Register}
  TXDB := ARPR(#23),                         {Transmit Data Buffer}
  SID := ARPR(#3E),                          {System Identification}
  ASTR := ARPR(#13),                         {Asynchronous System-Trap Register}
  PME := ARPR(#3D),                          {Performance-Monitor-Enable Register}

{Processor-Status-Longword Assignments:}
  PSL<15..8> := 00h,
  PSL<29,28,21> := 0c,
  IPL<4..0> := PSL<20..16>,                  {Interrupt-Processor Level}
  PM<1,0> := PSL<23,22>,                     {Previous Mode}
  CM<1,0> := PSL<25,24>,                     {Current Mode}
  IS := PSL<26>,                             {Interrupt Stack}
  FPD := PSL<27>,                            {First-Part Done}
  TP := PSL<30>,                             {Trace Pending}
  CM := PSL<31>,                             {Compatibility Mode}
  PSW<15..0> := PSL<15..0>,                  {Processor-Status Word}
  C := PSW<0>,                               {Carry Bit}
  V := PSW<1>,                               {Overflow}
  Z := PSW<2>,                               {Zero}
  N := PSW<3>,                               {Negative}
  T := PSW<4>,                               {Trace Enable}
  IV := PSW<5>,                              {Integer-Overflow Trap}
  FU := PSW<6>,                              {Floating-Underflow Trap}
  DV := PSW<7>,                              {Digital-Overflow Trap}

{ICCS Register Assignments:}
  RUN := ICCS<0>,                            {Run Bit}
  XFR := ICCS<1>,                            {Transfer NICR}
  SGL := ICCS<2>,                            {Signal ICR}
  IE := ICCS<3>,                             {ICR-Interrupt Enable}
  INT := ICCS<4>,                            {ICR-Interrupt Request}
  ERR := ICCS<5>,                            {Error Bit}
```

Figure B-2 Digital Equipment VAX ISP.

```
{Mp State:}
  Mp[0..size * 2²⁰ - 1]<7..0>                {physical memory}
       &(size =: 2, 4..max),                 {max is model-dependent, 8 to 64}
  Mv[0..2³²-1]<7..0>,                         {virtual memory}
  (by[k] := Mv[k],                           {byte-addressible virtual memory}
   wd<15..0> := by[k + 1]<7..0> @ by[k]<7..0>,    {word}
   lw<31..0> := wd[k + 2]<15..0> @ wd[k]<15..0>,  {longword}
   qw<63..0) := lw[k + 4]<31..0> @ lw[k]<31..0>,  {quadword}
   ow<127..0> := qw[k + 8]<63..0) @ qw[k]<63..0)) {octaword}
       &(k =: 0..2³²-1),                      {arbitrary byte boundaries}

{Process Control Block (PCB), in Mp:}
  PCB[0..24][3..0]<7..0>,                     {Process Control Block}
  PCB[0] := Mp[PCBB],                         {physical memory location}

{Data Formats:}
  (bi<r..0> := by[m + r DIV 8..m]<7..0>,{binary integer}
   ui<r..0> := bi<r..0>,                      {unsigned integer}
   si<r..0> := bi<r..0>,                      {signed integer}
    in<r-1..0> := si<r-1..0>,                 {integer value}
    sg := si<r>)                              {sign}
       &(r =: 7, 15, 31, 63, 127)            {byte, word, longword, etc}
  ((bf<s..0>,                                 {1- to 32-bit field}
    bf<s> := by[k + s DIV 8]<x>, x := (s - 1) MOD 8)
       &(s =: 0..31),
   cs[u..t]<7..0> := by[k + u] @ cs[u + 1..t]
       &(u =: 0..t) &(t =: 0..2¹⁶-1),         {variable-length character string}
   ns[v - u..0]<3..0> := by[k + u]<3..0> @ ns[v - (u + 1)..0]
       &(u =: 0..v) & (v =: 0..31),           {variable-length numeric string}
   pd[2*u + 1]<3..0> @ pd[2*u]<3..0> := dd[u]<7..0>,
   dd[(w - u)..0] := by[k + u] @ dd[w - (u + 1)..0]
       &(u =: 0..w) &(w =: 0..15),            {variable-length packed decimal}
   Df<63..0> := qw[k],                        {floating-point type D}
   Ds := Df<15>,                              {sign of fraction}
   De<7..0> := Df<14..7>,                     {exponent (base2)}
   Dm<54..0> := Df<6..0> @ Df<31..16> @ Df<47..32>
                       @ Df<63..48>,          {fractional mantissa}
   Ff<31..0> := lw[k],                        {floating-point type F}
   Fs := Ff<15>,                              {sign of fraction}
   Fe<7..0> := Ff<14..7>,                     {exponent (base2)}
   Fm<22..0> := Ff<6..0> @ Ff<31..16>,        {fractional mantissa}
   Gf<63..0> := qw[k],                        {floating-point type G}
   Gs := Gf<15>,                              {sign of fraction}
   Ge<10..0> := Gf<14..4>,                    {exponent (base2)}
   Gm<51..0> := Gf<3..0> @ Gf<31..16> @ Gf<47..32>
                       @ Gf<63..48>,          {fractional mantissa}
   Hf<127..0> := ow[k],                       {floating-point type H}
   Hs := Hf<15>,                              {sign of fraction}
   He<14..0> := Hf<14..0>,                    {exponent (base2)}
   Hm<111..0> := Hf<31..16> @ Hf<47..32> @ Hf<63..48> @ Hf<79..64>
    @ Hf<95..80> @ Hf<111..96> @ Hf<127..112>)   {fractional mantissa}
       &(k =: 0..2³²-1),                      {any addressable byte}

{Instruction Formats:}
  (ins\inst[0..p]<7..0> := by[k..k + p]
           &(p =: 0..103),                    {1- to 104-byte instructions}
   ins := shop OR opargs,                     {general instruction format}
  (opargs := shop<7..0> @ rand[1..m]<8*n - 1..0> OR
       lnop<15..0> @ rand[1..m]<8*n - 1..0>,
   rand[m] := argspec<7..0> OR argspec<7..0> @ arg<(8*(n - 1) - 1)..0>)
           &(m =: 1..6) &(n =: 1..17),        {operator and operands}
```

Figure B-2   Digital Equipment VAX ISP (Continued).

```
     shop<7..0> := by[k]<7..0>,              {short operator}
     lnop<15..0> := by[k + 1]<7..0> @ by[k]<7..0>) {long operator}
          &(k =: 0..2^32-1),                 {any addressable byte}
  mode<3..0> := argspec<7..4>,               {mode specifier}
  reg<3..0> := argspec<3..0>,                {register selector}
  slit<7..0> := argspec<7..0>,               {short literal operand}
  slit<7,6> := 00,                           {modes 0h, 1h, 2h, 3h}
  lit<5..0> := slit<5..0>,                   {literal integer value}

{Operand Addressing Mechanisms:}
  PROC "getarg"(argspec, arg): {Get argspec; from mode define argument.}
  ((DECODE mode<3..0>
    ((0h,1h,2h,3h) -> ((arg<5..0> := by[PC]<5..0>, PC <- PC + 1)), {slit}
     (4h) -> ((temp <- r * GR[PC], PC <- PC + 1); "getarg"(by[PC],arg1);
              arg<s..0> := temp + arg1),        {indexed}
     (5h) -> ((arg<s..0> := GR[reg], PC <- PC + 1)),   {register}
     (6h) -> ((arg<s..0> := M[GR[reg]], PC <- PC + 1), {register-deferred}
     (7h) -> (GR[reg] <- GR[reg] - r; (arg<s..0> := M[GR[reg]],
                                  PC <- PC + 1)),   {autodecrement}
     (8h) -> ((arg<s..0> := M[GR[reg]], PC <- PC + 1);
                                  GR[reg] <- GR[reg] + r), {autoincrement}
     (9h) -> ((arg<s..0> := M[wd[GR[reg]]], PC <- PC + 1);
                                  GR[reg] <- GR[reg] + 4), {autoinc.-deferred}
     (Ah) -> (PC <- PC + 1; (arg<s..0> := M[GR[reg] + by[PC]],
                                  PC <- PC + 1)),       {byte displacement}
     (Bh) -> (PC <- PC + 1; (arg<s..0> := M[wd[GR[reg] + by[PC]]],
                                  PC <- PC + 1))),      {byte displ.-def.}
   {Ch, Dh, Eh, Fh are similar to Ah and Bh, but with word
       and longword, rather than byte displacements}
   s := 8 * r - 1, r EQ 1 (M := by), r EQ 2 (M := wd), r EQ 4 (M := lw)),
       &(r =: 1, 2, 4)) {8 and 16 also allowed for mode 8h}

{Instruction Execution Cycle:}
  ir<7..0>,                            {1-byte Instruction Register}
  WHILE Run EQ 1 ->
  ("process_interrupt"(conditions); "process_exception"(conditions);
  (ir <- by[PC], PC <- PC + 1);         {Fetch Instruction Byte}
  DECODE ir<7..0>
    ((00h) -> (Run <- 0),                        {Halt}
     (01h) -> (),                                {Noop}
     (04h) -> (SP <- FP + 4; "pop"(4, SP, temp); "pop"(4, SP, PC);
               "pop"(4, SP, FP); "pop"(4, SP, AP);
               (rstr<11..0> <- temp<27..16>, n <- 0); {build restore mask}
               WHILE n LT 12 -> (rstr<n> EQ 1 -> "pop"(4, SP, GR[n]);
                           n <- n + 1); (SP <- SP + temp<31,30>,
               PSW <- temp<15..0>); temp<29> EQ 1 -> ("pop"(4, SP, temp2);
               SP <- SP + 4 * temp2)),          {Return From Procedure}
     (05h) -> ("pop"(4, SP, PC)),                {Return from Subroutine}
     (30h) -> ("push"(4, SP, PC - 1); PC <- PC + wd[PC]),{Br. to S/R (wd)}
     (12h) -> (Z EQ 0 -> PC <- PC + by[PC]),     {Branch Not Equal}
     (16h) -> ("push"(4,SP, PC - 1); "getarg"(by[PC], arg);
               PC <- arg)),                      {Jump to Subroutine}
     (40h) -> (("getarg"(by[PC], arg1), PC <- PC + 1);
               "getarg"(by[PC], arg2), PC <- PC + 1);
               arg2 <- arg1 + arg2),             {Add F_float. 2 Operand}
               {. . . other 1-byte instructions}
     (FDh) -> ((ir <- by[PC], PC <- PC + 1); DECODE ir<7..0>
               ((40h) -> ({Add G_float. 2 operand, similar to F_float.}),
               ({other 2-byte instructions}))))),
```

{Ref. VAX Architecture Handbook, Digital Equipment Corp., Maynard, MA, 1986.}

Figure B-2   Digital Equipment VAX ISP (Continued).

{Motorola MC68000/MC68010/MC68020 ISP}

```
{Pc State:}
  GR[0..15]<31..0>,                   {General Registers}
  DA[0..7] := GR[0..7],               {Data Registers}
  AD[0..7] := GR[8..15],              {Address Registers}
  SP := AD[7],                        {Stack Pointer (User/Supervisor)}
  PC<31..0>,                          {Program Counter}
  SR<15..0>,                          {Status Register}
  CCR<7..0> := SR<7..0>,              {Condition-Code Register}
  VBR<31..0>,                         {Vector-Base Register*}
  SFC<3..0>,                          {Supervisor Function Code*}
  DFC<3..0>,                          {Data Function Code*}
  SCR<15..0>,                         {System-Control Register**}
     {* Not available in MC68000 processor.}{** M68020 only.}
  {Note-MC68000 and MC68010 have 16-bit data bus and 24-bit address bus.
     MC68020 has 32-bit data and address buses.}

{Status and Condition Code Register Assignments:}
  T  := SR<15>,      {Trace mode}         X := CCR<4>,    {Extend}
  S  := SR<13>,      {Supervisor state}   N := CCR<3>,    {Negative}
  I1 := SR<10>,      {Interrupt mask 1}   Z := CCR<2>,    {Zero}
  I2 := SR<9>,       {Interrupt mask 2}   V := CCR<1>,    {Overflow}
  I3 := SR<8>,       {Interrupt mask 3}   C := CCR<0>,    {Carry}
  SR<14,12,11> := xxx,   {Reserved}       CCR<7..5> := xxx,    {Reserved}

{Memory State:}
  Mv[0..maxmem - 1]<7..0>,              {Virtual memory space, bytes}
  maxmem := 2^24,                       {Maximum virtual-memory size***}
  {*** MC68020 can address 2^32 bytes of virtual memory (maxmem = 2^32).}
  {Note-Paging and segmentation are supported by MC68010 and MC68020.}

{Data Formats:}
  (by[k]<7..0> := Mv[k]<7..0>,          {Byte}
   wo[m]<15..0> := by[m] @ by[m + 1],   {Word (even byte boundaries)}
   lw[m]<31..0> := wo[m] @ wo[m + 3])   {Longword}
     &(k =: 0..maxmem), &(m =: 0, 2..k - 1),
  {Bytes, words, or longwords hold unsigned or 2's complement integers.}
  bcd<3..0>,                            {Binary-coded decimal digit}
  bcd[0,1] := by<7..0>,                 {Byte-packed BCD digit}
  bcd[0..3] := wo<15..0>,               {Word-packed BCD digit}
  bcd[0..7] := lw<31..0>,               {Longword-packed BCD digit}

{Instruction Formats:}
  (ins := wo[p..p + q] &(q =: 0, 2..8), {1- to 5-word instruction}
   op<15..0> := wo[p]<15..0>,           {Operation word}
   sx[0]<15..0> := wo[p + 2],           {Source first word}
   sx[1]<15..0> := wo[p + 4],           {Source second word}
   (dx[0]<15..0> := wo[p + r],          {Destination argument}
   dx[1]<15..0> := wo[p + r + 2]) &(r =: 2, 4, 6),
   iw<15..0> := wo[p + 2],              {Immediate source argument}
   il<31..0> := wo[p + 2] @ wo[p + 4]) &(p =: 0, 2..k - 1),

{Instruction Interpretation:}
  WHILE NOT exception -> {execution loop} (op <- wo[PC], PC <- PC + 2;
  (op<15> EQ 1 OR {others} -> "execute"(op), {Single-word instructions}
  op<15..0> = {1-ex. code} -> ("get-argument"(mode, reg); "execute"(op)),
  op<15..0> = {2-ex. code} -> ("get-argument"(mode, reg);
     "get-argument"(mode, reg); "execute"(op)))), {end of loop}
     {Operator specifies zero to four extension words of instruction.}
  "exception"(exception_condition);
```

Figure B-3   Motorola M68000 ISP.

```
{Argument Fetch:}
  PROC "get-argument"(mode, reg):
  (mode<2..0> @ reg<2..0> := op<5..0>,   {Mode and register fields}
   sz<1,0>\size_field ,                   {Argument-size designator}
  {Note-Not all instructions contain size_field or mode and reg fields.}
   DECODE sz<1,0>
   ((00) -> (ar[ex] := by[ex]<7..0>, size <- 1),   {Byte argument}
    (01) -> (ar[ex] := wo[ex]<15..0>, size <- 2),   {Word argument}
    (10) -> (ar[ex] := lw[ex]<31..0>, size <- 4),   {Longword argument}
    (11) -> "exception"(size-error)),
   DECODE mode<2..0>
   ((000) -> arg <- DA[reg],
    (001) -> arg <- AD[reg],
    (010) -> arg <- ar[AD[reg]],
    (011) -> (arg <- ar[AD[reg]]; AD[reg] <- AD[reg] + size),
    (100) -> (AD[reg] <- AD[reg] - size; arg <- ar[AD[reg]]),
    (101) -> (arg <- ar[AD[reg] + wo[PC]], PC <- PC + 2),
    (110) -> (arg <- ar[AD[reg] + wo[PC<7..0>] + GR[wo[PC<15..12>]]],
              PC <- PC + 2),
    (111) -> DECODE reg<2..0>
             ((000) -> (arg <- ar[wo[PC]], PC <- PC + 2),
              (001) -> (arg <- ar[wo[PC] @ wo[PC + 2]], PC <- PC + 4),
              (010) -> (arg <- ar[PC + wo[PC]], PC <- PC + 2),
              (011) -> (arg <- ar[PC + wo[PC<7..0>] + GR[wo[PC<15..12>]]],
                        PC <- PC + 2),
              (100) -> (optype EQ byte_op -> (arg <- ar[PC], PC <- PC + 2),
                        optype EQ word_op -> (arg <- ar[PC], PC <- PC + 2),
                        optype EQ long_op -> (arg <- ar[PC], PC <- PC + 4))))),
  {Note-Optype (byte, word, longword) is instruction-dependent.}

{Instruction Execution:}
  PROC "execute"(op):
  (DECODE op<15..0>
   ((1101xxxxxxxxxxxx) -> (sz<1,0> <- op<7,6>; "get_argument"(mode, reg);
    (op<8> EQ 0 -> DA[op<11..9>] <- DA[op<11..9>] + arg,
     op<8> EQ 1 -> (mode<2..0> EQ 111 AND reg<2,1> NE 00 ->
                    "exception"(argtype); (arg <- DA[op<11..9>] + arg)),
            "set_conditions"(1,1,1,1,1))){set all}, {Add}
    (00000110xxxxxxxx) -> ((sz<1,0> <- op<7,6>; "get_argument"(mode, reg),
           mode<2..0> EQ 111 AND reg<2,1> NE 00 OR mode<2..0> EQ 001 ->
                    "exception"(argtype));
     ((size EQ 1 -> arg <- arg + by[PC], PC <- PC + 2),
      (size EQ 2 -> arg <- arg + wo[PC], PC <- PC + 2),
      (size EQ 4 -> arg <- arg + lw[PC]; PC <- PC + 4));
      CCR<4..0> <- 00000; "set_conditions"(1,1,1,1,1)), {Add Immediate}
    (0100100001xxxxxx) -> ((sz<1,0> <- 10; "get_argument"(mode, reg),
           mode<2..0> EQ 111 AND reg<2..0> EQ 100 -> "exception"(argtype));
     SP <- SP - 2; lw[SP] <- arg), {Push Effective Address}
    (0100111010xxxxxx) -> ((sz<1,0> <- 10; "get_argument"(mode, reg),
           mode<2..0> EQ 111 AND reg<2> EQ 1 OR mode<2,1> EQ 00 OR
           mode<2..0> EQ 011 OR mode<2..0> EQ 100 -> "exception"(argtype));
     SP <- SP- 4; lw[SP] <- PC; PC <- arg), {Jump to Subroutine}
    (0100111001110101) -> (PC <- lw[SP]; SP <- SP + 4), {Return from S/R}
    (0100111001110010) -> (S EQ 0 -> "exception"(argtype) {Privileged};
     SR <- wo[PC]; PC <- PC + 2; "execute"(0100111001110010)), {Stop}
    { other instructions} )),
  PROC "set_conditions"(xc,nc,zc,vc,cc): {Definition not included here.},
  PROC "exception"(exception_condition): {Definition not included here.},
```

{Ref. Motorola, M68000 16/32-Bit Microprocessor Programmer's Reference
Manual, 4th Ed., Prentice-Hall, Englewood Cliffs, NJ, 1984.}

Figure B-3   Motorola M68000 ISP (Continued).

{NSC NS32000 CPU ISP}

{Pc State:}
  GR[0..7]<31..0>,{General Registers} PC<31..0>,   {Program Counter}
  SB<31..0>,   {Static Base}   FP<31..0>,   {Frame Pointer}
  SP[0]<31..0>,   {Interrupt Stack} SP[1]<31..0>,   {User Stack}
  INB<31..0>,   {Interrupt Base}   PSR<15..0>,   {Processor Status}
  MOD<15..0>,   {Module Register} CFG<7..0>,   {Configuration}
  {Note-Configuration register is accessible only in privileged mode.}

{Processor Status Register:}
  C := PSR<0>,   {Carry Flag}   N := PSR<7>,   {Negative Flag}
  T := PSR<1>,   {Trace Flag}   U := PSR<8>,   {User Mode Flag}
  L := PSR<2>,   {Low Flag}   S := PSR<9>,   {Stack Flag}
  F := PSR<5>,   {General Flag}   P := PSR<10>,   {Trap Pending Flg}
  Z := PSR<6>,   {Zero Flag}   I := PSR<11>,   {Interrupt Enable}
          PSR<15..12,4,3> := xxxxxx,   {Reserved Bits}

{Memory State:}
  Mp := [0..2^20 - 1][0..2^12 - 1]<7..0>, {Physical memory, byte-addressed}
  Mv := [0..2^10 - 1][0..2^10 - 1][0..2^12 - 1]<7..0>, maxmem := 2^32, {With
  NS32382 MMU; NS32082 MMU allows 2^24 bytes of memory. Virtual memory is
  addressed as: [page index][pointer index][offset]}

{Data Formats:}
  (by[k]<7..0> := Mv[k]<7..0>,   {Byte}
   wo[m]<15..0> := by[m + 1]<7..0> @ by[m]<7..0>,   {Word}
   dw[m]<31..0> := wo[m + 2]<15..0> @ wo[m]<15..0>) {Doubleword}
     &(k =: 0..maxmem - 1) &(m =: 0, 2..k - 1),   {even byte boundaries}
  {Bytes, words, or doublewords hold unsigned or 2's-complement integers.}
  bcd<3..0>,   {Binary-coded decimal digit}
  bcd[0,1] := by<7..0>,   {Byte-packed BCD digit}
  bcd[0..3] := wo<15..0>,   {Word-packed BCD digit}
  bcd[0..7] := dw<31..0>,   {Doubleword-packed BCD digit}

{Instruction Formats:}
  (ins<m..0>,   {1-, 2-, or 3-byte instructions}
   gna<4..0> := ins<m - 5..m - 9>,   {optional general-register field}
   gnb<4..0> := ins<m..m - 4>,   {optional general-register field}
   ext[1..n]<7..0>,   {optional extension bytes}
   ix[1]<7..0> := ext[1]<7..0>,   {optional first index byte}
   ix[2]<7..0> := ext[2]<7..0>,   {optional second index byte}
   ix[p]<7..0> := mode<4..0> @ reg<2..0>,{mode and register designators}
   dsim[1][1..r]<7..0> := ext[q..q + r],{displacement or immediate fields}
   dsim[2][1..t]<7..0> := ext[s..s + t],{1 to 4 bytes each}
   impl[1..v]<7..0> := ext[u..u + v],   {implicit displ. or immediate}
   q := p + 1, s := q + r + 1, u := s + t + 1, n := p + r + t + v)
   &(m =: 7, 15, 23) &(p =: 0..2) &(r =: 0..4) &(t =: 0..4) &(v =: 0..4),
          {Instructions can be from 1 to 17 bytes long.}

{Instruction Interpretation:}
  WHILE NOT exception ->   {execution loop}
  (ins<23..0> <- 000000h;   {clear instruction register}
  (ins<7..0> <- by[PC], PC <- PC + 1); {first instruction byte}
  DECODE ins<2..0>
  ((010) -> "execute"(1, ins),   {1-byte instruction}
   (110) -> ((ins<15..8> <- by[PC], ins<23..16> <- by[PC + 1],
     PC <- PC + 2); "execute"(3, ins)), {3-byte instruction}
   (OTHERWISE) -> ((ins<15..8> <- by[PC], PC <- PC + 1);
              "execute"(2, ins)));   {2-byte instruction}
  "process_exception"(condition),
  PROC "process_exception"(condition): {Procedure not defined here.},

Figure B-4   National Semiconductor NS32000 ISP.

```
{Instruction Execution:}
  PROC "execute"(ins_size, ins)
  (ins_size EQ 1 -> DECODE ins<7..0>      {1-byte instructions}
          ((02h) -> ("get_ext"(disp, 1); )("push"(PC, SP[S]),
              PC <- PC + disp),             {Branch to subroutine}
              (62h) -> ("get_ext"(disp, 1); temp <- 1; WHILE temp LT 8 ->
                  ("push"(GR[disp[temp]], SP[S]), temp <- temp + 1)),
                  {Save on stack those general registers designated in disp}
              (E2h) -> "process_exception"(SVC), {Supervisor call trap}
                  {other single-byte instructions}         ),
      ins_size EQ 2 -> DECODE ins<15..0>    {2-byte instructions}
          ((xxxxxxxxxx0000xx) -> ("arg_size"(ins<1,0>);
              "get_arg"(ins<15..11>, src); "get_arg"(ins<10..6>, dest);
              dest <- src + dest; "set_flags"(1,0,0,1,0,0)),    {Add}
              {other two-byte instructions} ),
      ins_size EQ 3 -> DECODE ins<23..0>    {3-byte instructions}
          ((xxxxxxxxxx0000xx11001110) -> ("arg_size"(ins<9,8>);
              "get_arg"(ins<23..19>, block1); "get_arg"(ins<18..14>, block2);
              "get_ext"(disp, 1); temp <- 0; WHILE temp LT disp * size ->
              (by[block2 + temp] <- by[block2 + temp]; temp <- temp + 1),
              {Move block of integers from block1 to block2}
              {other three-byte instructions}      )),

{Argument Fetch:}
  PROC "get_arg"(gen, arg):
  (DECODE gen<4,3>
    ((00) -> arg <- GR[gen<2..0>],          {register mode}
     (01) -> ("get_ext"(disp1, size); arg <- ar[GR[gen<2..0>] + disp1]),
     (11) -> gen<2> EQ 0 -> ("get_ext"(disp1, size); DECODE gen<1,0>
                  ((00) -> arg <- ar[FP + disp1],
                   (01) -> arg <- ar[SP[S] + disp1],
                   (10) -> arg <- ar[SB + disp1],
                   (11) -> arg <- ar[PC + disp1]),
              gen<2> EQ 1 -> (DECODE gen<1,0> ((00) -> scale <- 1, (01) ->
                      scale <- 2, (10) -> scale <- 4, (11) -> scale <- 8);
                      index <- by[PC]; "get_arg"(index<7..3>, arg1);
                      arg <- arg1 + ar[GR[index<2..0>] * scale]),
     (10) -> (gen<2> EQ 0 -> ("get_ext"(disp1, size);
                  "get_ext"(disp2, size); DECODE gen<1..0>
                      ((00) -> arg <- ar[disp2 + dw[FP + disp1]],
                       (01) -> arg <- ar[disp2 + dw[SP[S] + disp1]],
                       (10) -> arg <- ar[disp2 + dw[SB + disp1]],
                       (11) -> "process_exception"(code-error))),
              gen<2> EQ 1 -> DECODE gen<1,0>
                      ((00) -> ("get_ext"(immed, size); arg <- immed),
                       (01) -> ("get_ext"(disp, size); arg <- ar[disp]),
                       (10) -> {access via link table; not defined here},
                       (11) -> {stack mode; not defined here}),
  PROC "arg_size"(code<1,0>)
  (DECODE code<1,0>
    ((00) -> (ar[ex] := by[ex]<7..0>, size <- 1),    {Byte argument}
     (01) -> (ar[ex] := wo[ex]<15..0>, size <- 2),   {Word argument}
     (11) -> (ar[ex] := dw[ex]<31..0>, size <- 4),   {Doubleword argument}
     (10) -> "process_exception"(size-error))),
  PROC "set_conditions"(cx,tx,lx,fx,zx,nx): {Sets values of C, T, L, F, Z,
      N flags. Definition not included here.},
  PROC "get_ext"(field, quan): {Gets instruction extension of "quan" bytes
      from memory and assigns it to "field". Not defined here.}
```

{Ref. Hunter, C., Series 32000 Programmer's Reference Manual, (National
Semiconductor Corp.), Prentice-Hall, Englewood Cliffs, NJ, 1987.}

Figure B-4   National Semiconductor NS32000 ISP (Continued).

{Intel 80386 ISP}

```
{Pc State:}
  GR[0..7]<31..0>,         {General Registers}
  EAX := GR[0],    {Accumulator}      ECX := GR[1],     {Count Register}
  EDX := GR[2],    {Data Register}    EBX := GR[3],     {Base Register}
  ESP := GR[4],    {Stack Pointer}    EBP := GR[5],     {Base Pointer}
  ESI := GR[6],    {Source Index}     EDI := GR[7],     {Data Index}
  SSR[0..5]<15..0>,        {Segment Registers, pointers to SDR[0..5] in Mp}
  CS := SSR[0],    {Current Code}     SS := SSR[1],     {Current Stack}
  DS := SSR[2],    {Data Segment D}   ES := SSR[3],     {Data Segment E}
  FS := SSR[4],    {Data Segment F}   GS := SSR[5],     {Data Segment G}
  EIP<31..0>,   {Instruction Pointer}   IP<15..0> := EIP<15..0>, {16-bit}
  EFLAGS<31..0>,    {Flags Register}  FLAGS<15..0> := EFLAGS<15..0>,
  GDTR<47..0>,               {Global Descriptor Table pointer}
  IDTR<47..0>,               {Interrupt Descriptor Table pointer}
  TSR<15..0>,                {Task-State Register, points to SDR[6]}
  LDTR<15..0>,               {Local Descriptor Table Reg., points to SDR[7]}
  SDR[0..7]<63..0>,     {active Segment Descriptor Registers (transparent)}
  CR0<31..0>, CR1<31..0>, CR2<31..0>,        {Control Registers}
  DR[0..7]<31..0>,         {Debug Registers (breakpoints, control, status)}
  TR[6,7]<31..0>,            {Test control and status Registers}

{General Register 8/16-bit Register Aliases:}
  AX<15..0> := EAX<15..0>,           BX<15..0> := EBX<15..0>,
  CX<15..0> := ECX<15..0>,           DX<15..0> := EDX<15..0>,
  SI<15..0> := ESI<15..0>,           DI<15..0> := EDI<15..0>,
  BP<15..0> := EBP<15..0>,           SP<15..0> := ESP<15..0>,
  AH<7..0> := AX<15..8>,             AL<7..0> := AX<7..0>,
  BH<7..0> := BX<15..8>,             BL<7..0> := BX<7..0>,
  CH<7..0> := CX<15..8>,             CL<7..0> := CX<7..0>,
  DH<7..0> := DX<15..8>,             DL<7..0> := DX<7..0>,

{Flag and selected Segment Descriptor Assignments:}
  CF := FLAGS<0>,    {Carry Flag}       PF := FLAGS<2>,    {Parity Flag}
  AF := FLAGS<4>,    {Auxiliary Carry}  ZF := FLAGS<6>,    {Zero Flag}
  SF := FLAGS<7>,    {Sign Flag}        TF := FLAGS<8>,    {Trap Flag}
  IF := FLAGS<9>,    {Interrupt Enable} DF := FLAGS<10>,   {Direction Flag}
  OF := FLAGS<11>,   {Overflow Flag}    NT := FLAGS<14>,   {Nested-Test bit}
  IOP<1,0> := FLAGS<13,12>      {Input/Output Privilege Level}
  VM := EFLAGS<17>, {Virtual Mode}      RF := EFLAGS<16>, {Resume Flag}
  (sg_bs[j]<31..0> := SDR[j]<63..56,39..32,31..0>,   {segment base address}
   sg_lm[j]<19..0> := SDR[j]<35..32,15..0>,   {segment limit (bytes/pages)}
   G := SDR[j]<55>, {bytes or pages}  D := SDR[j]<54>, {Default arg. size}
   acc_rts<7..0> := SDR[j]<15..8> &(j =: 0..7),    {segment access rights}

{Mp State:}
  Mp[0..maxmem - 1]<7..0> &(maxmem =: 0..2³²), {byte-addressable memory}
  Mpp[0..maxmem DIV 4096][0..2¹²]<7..0>,       {paged memory (optional)}
  Mv[0..2³² - 1]<7..0>,        {segmented virtual memory}

{Data Formats:}
  (by[k]<7..0> := Mv[k]<7..0>,                          {byte}
   wd[k]<15..0> := by[k + 1]<7..0> @ by[k]<7..0>,       {word}
   dw[k]<31..0> := wd[k + 2]<15..0> @ wd[k]<15..0>,   {double word}
   qw[k]<63..0> := wd[k + 4]<31..0> @ wd[k]<31..0>,   {quadword}
   0h @ bcd[k]<3..0> := by[k]<7..0>,          {binary-coded decimal}
   pd[m + 1]<3..0> @ pd[m]<3..0> := by[m]<7..0> &(m =: k)) {packed bcd}
       &( k =: 0..2³² - 1)
  {Note-Bytes, words, double words, quadwords can hold signed or unsigned
   integer values. Bit, byte, and word strings can be of arbitrary length.}
```

Figure B-5   Intel 80386 ISP.

```
{Instruction Formats:}
  ins[0..11]<7..0>,                        {one- to twelve-byte instructions}
  op<7..0> := ins[0]<7..0>,                {first primary operation-code byte}
  op2<7..0> := ins[1]<7..0>,               {second primary operation-code byte}
  mrm<7..0> := ins[q]<7..0> &(q =: 1,2),   {mode/register byte}
  sib<7..0> := ins[r]<7..0> &(r =: 2,3),   {scaled-index byte}
  (disp[0..3]<7..0> := ins[s..s + u] &(s =: 1..4),      {displacement}
   imm[0..3]<7..0> := ins[t..t + u] &(t =: 1..8))       {immediate data}
        &(u =: 0,1,3),
  mode<1,0> := mrm<7,6>, {mode}        r/m<2..0> := mrm<2..0>,   {reg./mem.}
  opx<2..0> := mrm <5..3>, {op. ext.} grg<2..0> := mrm<5..3>,    {register}
  ss<1,0> := sib<7,6>, index<2..0> := sib<5..3>, base<2..0> := sib<2..0>,

{Instruction Interpretation and Execution:}
  WHILE interrupt EQ 0 -> ((op <- by[sg_bs[CS] + PC], PC <- PC + 1,
    ad_sz <- D, rn_sz <- D); "execute"(op)); "proc_inter"(int_cond),

PROC "execute"(op):
  (continue EQ 0 -> DECODE op<7..0>     {prefix or 1-byte operators}
  ((67h) -> ((ad_sz <- NOT D, op <- by[sg_bs[0] {CS} + PC],
      PC <- PC + 1); "execute"(op); ad_sz <- D),   {address-size prefix}
   (66h) -> ((rn_sz <- NOT D, op <- by[sg_bs[0] {CS} + PC],
      PC <- PC + 1); "execute"(op); rn_sz <- D),   {operand-size prefix}
      {Bus lock and segment override prefix bytes are similar.}
   (0Fh) -> ((continue <- 1, op <- by[sg_bs[0] {CS} + PC], PC <- PC + 1);
      "execute"(op); continue <- 0),               {two-byte-op prefix}
   (C6h,C7h) -> ((w <- op<0>, mrm <- by[sg_bs[0] {CS} + PC],
      PC <- PC + 1); (w EQ 0 -> dt <- (by[sg_bs[0] + PC], PC <- PC + 1),
      w EQ 1 -> (rn_sz EQ 0 -> (dt <- wd[sg_bs[0] + PC], PC <- PC + 2),
             rn_sz EQ 1 -> (dt <- dw[sg_bs[0] + PC], PC <- PC + 4)));
      (mode NE 11 -> ("get_addr"(w, rn_sz, mode, reg, sib, addr);
         rand[seg_base + offset] <- dt),
       mode EQ 11 ->
         (w EQ 0 -> (r/m<2> EQ 0 -> GR[r/m<1,0>]<7..0> <- dt,
                     r/m<2> EQ 1 -> GR[r/m<1,0>]<15..8> <- dt),
          w EQ 1 -> (rn_sz EQ 0 -> GR[r/m]<15..0> <- dt,
                     rn_sz EQ 1 -> GR[r/m]<31..0> <- dt)))),
      {Move immediate to register/memory (note operand size variations)}
   (00h,01h) -> ((w <- op<0>, mrm <- by[sg_bs[0] {CS} + PC],
      PC <- PC + 1); (w EQ 0 -> (r/m<2> EQ 0 -> dt <- GR[r/m<1,0>]<7..0>,
                     r/m<2> EQ 1 -> dt <- GR[r/m<1,0>]<15..8>),
             w EQ 1 -> (rn_sz EQ 0 -> dt <- GR[r/m]<15..0> ,
                     rn_sz EQ 1 -> dt <- GR[r/m]<31..0>)));
      (mode NE 11 -> ("get_addr"(w, rn_sz, mode, reg, sib, addr);
         rand[seg_base + offset] <- rand[seg_base + offset] + dt),
       mode EQ 11 ->
         (w EQ 0 ->
      (r/m<2> EQ 0 -> GR[r/m<1,0>]<7..0> <- GR[r/m<1,0>]<7..0> + dt,
       r/m<2> EQ 1 -> GR[r/m<1,0>]<15..8> <- GR[r/m<1,0>]<15..8> + dt),
          w EQ 1 ->
      (rn_sz EQ 0 -> GR[r/m]<15..0> <- GR[r/m]<15..0> + dt,
       rn_sz EQ 1 -> GR[r/m]<31..0> <- GR[r/m]<31..0> + dt)))),
      {Add register to register/memory (note operand size variations)}
             {other 1-byte instructions} ),
  continue EQ 1 -> DECODE op<7..0>     {two-byte operators}
  ((84h) ->
   ((ad_sz EQ 0 -> (dspl <- wd[sg_bs[0] {CS} + PC], PC <- PC + 2),
     ad_sz EQ 1 -> (dspl <- dw[sg_bs[0] {CS} + PC], PC <- PC + 4));
    ZF EQ 1 -> PC <- PC + dspl),     {Jump on equal (full displacement)}
             {other 2-byte instructions} )),
```

Figure B-5   Intel 80386 ISP (Continued).

```
PROC "get_addr"(w, sz, mode, reg, sib, addr):
  ((w EQ 0 (rand[x] := by[x]),                          {byte argument}
    w EQ 1 (sz EQ 0 (rand[x] := wd[x])                  {word argument}
            sz EQ 1 (rand[x] := dw[x]))),               {doubleword argument}
   mode NE 11 ->
   (ad_sz EQ 0 ->              {16-bit operation}
   (SELECT mode<1,0>
   ((01) (dspl := disp[0]<7..0>),                               {byte displacement}
    (10) (dspl := disp[1]<7..0> @ disp[0]<7..0>),       {word displacement}
    (00) (reg NE 110 (dspl := ),                        {null displacement}
          reg EQ 110 (dspl := disp[0]<<7..0> @ disp[1]<7..0>))),   {word}
    DECODE reg<2..0>
    ((000) -> (seg_base <- sg_bs[2] {DS},
                offset <- BX + SI + dspl),       {source-indexed based address}
      (001) -> (seg_base <- sg_bs[2] {DS},
                offset <- BX + DI + dspl),       {data-indexed based address}
      (010) -> (seg_base <- sg_bs[1] {SS},
                offset <- BP + SI + dspl),       {source-indexed stack address}
      (011) -> (seg_base <- sg_bs[1] {SS},
                offset <- BP + DI + dspl),       {data-indexed stack address}
      (100) -> (seg_base <- sg_bs[2] {DS},
                offset <- SI + dspl),            {source-indexed direct address}
      (101) -> (seg_base <- sg_bs[2] {DS},
                offset <- DI + dspl),            {data-indexed direct address}
      (110) -> (mode NE 00 -> (seg_base <- sg_bs[1] {SS},
                                offset <- BP + dspl),          {stack address}
                mode EQ 00 -> (seg_base <- sg_bs[2] {DS},
                                offset <- dspl)),              {direct address}
      (111) -> (seg_base <- sg_bs[2] {DS}, offset <- BX + dspl));  {based}
    addr <- seg_base + offset)),              {virtual address of operand}
   ad_sz EQ 1 ->              {32-bit operation}
   (SELECT mode<1,0>
    ((01) (dspl := disp[0]<7..0>),                          {byte displacement}
     (10) (dspl := disp[3..0]<7..0>),                       {doubleword displacement}
     (00) (reg NE 101 (dspl := ),                           {null displacement}
           reg EQ 110 (dspl := disp[3..0]<7..0>))),         {doubleword}
     (reg EQ 100 -> ((sib <- by[sg_bs[0] {CS} + PC], PC <- PC + 1);
                 (DECODE ss<1,0> ((00) -> sf <- 1, (01) -> sf <- 2,
                    (10) -> sf <- 4, (11) -> sf <- 8),    {set scale factor}
                 index EQ 100 -> ss EQ 00 -> ix_val <- ,       {null index}
                 index NE 100 -> ix_val <- GR[index]);  {general register}
                 sc_ix <- sf * ix_val;                  {scaled index value}
                 DECODE base<2..0>
                 ((101) -> (mode EQ 00 -> seg_base <- sg_bs[2] {DS},
                    mode EQ 01 OR mode EQ 10 -> seg_base <- sg_bs[1]) {SS},
                  (100) -> seg_base <- sg_bs[1] {SS},
                  (OTHERWISE) -> seg_base <- sg_bs[2] {DS});
                 base_val <- GR[base];
                 mode EQ 00 AND base EQ 101 -> base_val <- ;       {null}
                 offset <- base_val + sc_ix + dspl),        {indexed address}
     reg EQ 101 ->
     (mode EQ 00 -> (seg_base <- sg_bs[2] {DS}, offset <- displ),  {direct}
      mode NE 00 -> (seg_base <- sg_bs[1] {SS}, offset <- GR[reg] + dspl)),
                                                        {stack operation}
     reg NE 100 AND reg NE 101 -> (seg_base <- sg_bs[2] {DS},
                    offset <- GR[reg] + dspl));             {based address}
    addr <- seg_base + offset)),              {virtual address of operand}
   mode EQ 11 -> {argument addressing error} ),
```

{Ref. 80386 High Performance 32-bit Microprocessor with Integrated Memory
Management (Version-002), Intel Corp., Santa Clara, CA, 1986.}

Figure B-5   Intel 80386 ISP   (Continued).

{MIPS 2000/3000 ISP}

```
{Pc State:}
  GR[0..31]<31..0>,                    {General Registers}
  GR[0]<31..0> := 00000000h,           {constant zero}
  LR<31..0> := GR[31]<31..0>,          {Link Register}
  HM<31..0>,                           {High Multiply-divide register}
  LM<31..0>,                           {Low Multiply-divide register}
  PC<31..0>,                           {Program Counter}

{System Control Processor State:}
  TLB[0..63]<63..0>,                   {Translation Lookaside Buffer}
  TR<63..0>,   {TLB interface Reg.} HI<63..32> := TR<63..32>, {High}
  LO<31..0> := TR<31..0>,   {Low}  PID<5..0> := HI<43..38>, {Process ID}
  VPN<19..0> := HI<63..44>, {Page} PFN<19..0> := LO<31..12>, {Page Frame}
  N := LO<11>, {Non cachable}         D := LO<10>, {Dirty page}
  V := LO<9>,  {Valid entry}          G := LO<8>,  {Global entry}
  IX<31..0>,   {TLB Index Register} RN<31..0>,    {TLB Random Register}
  SR<31..0>,   {Status Register}     CR<31..0>,    {Cause Register}
  CX<31..0>,   {Context Register}    PR<31..0>,    {Processor Revision No.}
  BVA<31..0>,  {Bad Virtual Addr.}   EPC<31..0>,   {Exception Program Ctr.}

{Status Register and Cause Register Bit Assignments:}
  CU<3..0> := SR<31..28>,          {coprocessor usability}
  IM<7..0> := SR<15..8>,           {(hardware or software) interrupt mask}
  SR<27..23> @ SR<7,6> := 0000000, BEV := SR<22>, {bootstrap exc. vector}
  TS := SR<21>,  {TLB shutdown}     PE := SR<20>,  {parity error}
  CM := SR<19>,  {cache miss}       PZ := SR<18>,  {parity zero}
  SC := SR<17>,  {swap caches}      IC := SR<16>,  {isolate D cache}
  Uo := SR<5>,   {old mode = user}  Eo := SR<4>,   {old interrupt enable}
  Up := SR<3>,   {prev.mode = user} Ep := SR<2>,   {prev.interrupt enable}
  Uc := SR<1>,   {curr.mode = user} Ec := SR<0>,   {curr.interrupt enable}
  IP<7..0> := CR<15..8>,   {(hardware or software) interrupt pending}
  Exc<3..0> := CR<5..2>,   {exception code, as follows: 0h-Ext interrupt,
    1h-TLB modified, 2h-TLB miss,rd,    3h-TLB miss,wr,  4h-Addr err,rd,
    5h-Addr err,wr,  6h-Bus err,ins,  7h-Bus err,data, 8h-System call,
    9h-Breakpoint,   10h-Reserved ins.,11h-Coproc flt,  12h-Arith ovflow.}
  BD := CR<31>,   {branch delay}    CE<1,0> := CR<29,28>, {coprocessor}

{Floating-point Coprocessor State:}
  FGR[0..31]<31..0>,      {Floating-point General Registers, used in pairs}
  FCR<31..0>,  {Fl-pt Control Reg.} FPI<31..0>, {Fl-pt Processor Ident}

{Mp State:}
  Mp[0..maxframes][0..2¹² - 1]<7..0> &(maxframes =: 0..2²⁰ - 1),
  Mv[0..2³² - 1]<7..0>,               {Virtual Memory}
  Mu[0..2³¹ - 1]<7..0> := Mv[0..2³¹ - 1]<7..0>,   {user space}
  Mk[0..2³² - 1]<7..0> := Mv[0..2³² - 1]<7..0>,   {kernel (system) space}
  Mk[0..2³¹ - 1]<7..0> := Mu[0..2³¹ - 1]<7..0>,   {shared space}
  Mk[2³¹..5*2²⁹ - 1] := Mp[0..2²⁹ - 1],      {cached direct mapped}
  Mk[5*2²⁹..3*2³⁰ - 1] := Mp[0..2²⁹ - 1],    {non-cached d-m space}

{Data Formats:}
  (by[k]<7..0> := Mp[k]<7..0>,
  mem_config EQ big_endian          {set at hardware reconfiguration}
    (hw[m]<15..0> := by[m]<7..0> @ by[m + 1]<7..0>,
     wd[n]<31..0> := hw[n]<15..0> @ hw[n + 2]<15..0>),
  mem_config EQ little_endian       {set at hardware reconfiguration}
    (hw[m]<15..0> := by[m + 1]<7..0> @ by[m]<7..0>,
     wd[n]<31..0> := hw[n + 2]<15..0> @ hw[n]<15..0>))
       &(m =: 0, 2..k - 1) &( n =: 0, 4..k - 3) &(k =: 0..2³² - 1),
```

Figure B-6   MIPS, Inc., 2000/3000 ISP.

```
{Instruction Formats:}
  ins<31..0>,                          {fixed instruction size, I-,J-,R-type}
  op<5..0> := ins<31..26>,             {operator field}
  jtarg<25..0> := ins<25..0>,          {jump target (J-type instruction)}
  sreg<4..0> := ins<25..21>,           {source register (I-type and R-type)}
  treg<4..0> := ins<20..16>,           {target register (I-type and R-type)}
  immed<15..0> := ins<15..0>,          {immediate or displacement (I-type)}
  dreg<4..0> := ins<15..11>,           {destination register (R-type)}
  shamnt<5..0> := ins<10..6>,          {shift amount (R-type)}
  funct<5..0> := ins<5..0>,            {function selection (R-type)}

{Instruction Interpretation and Execution:}
  {"get" & "access_TLB" parameters. cache: I_cache := 0, D_cache := 1;
  r/w: read := 0, write := 1; size: byte := 00, hlfwd := 01, word := 11}
  WHILE NOT ex_cond -> (("access_TLB"(11, 1, wd[PC], arg), PC <- PC + 4));
    "get"(arg, 0, ins); "execute"(ins)); "excep"(ex_cond),
  {Note-Execution takes place in a 5-stage pipeline as follows (in RTL):
  t0: fetch instruction (via I_cache); t1: decode and get arguments;
  t2: ALU operation; t3: memory operation (via D_cache); t4: writeback.
  The compiler must allow for delays with branch and load operations.
  Ex_cond causes a halt of execution at the end of any clock time. The
  operating system places a process identifier value in PID<5..0>.}

PROC "access_TLB"(r/w, size, addr, arg): {address translation}
  ((index := IX<13..8>, BVA <- addr, VPN <- BVA<31..12>, CX<20..2> <-
  VPN<18..0>); (size AND addr<1,0>) NE 00 OR VPN<63> EQ 1 AND Uc EQ 1 ->
  {addr error} (r/w EQ 0 -> "excep"(4h), r/w EQ 1 -> "excep"(5h));
  index <- 00c; WHILE index LE 77c AND VPN NE TLB[i]<63..44> ->
  (index <- index + 1); (index GT 77c -> TLB_miss <- 1, (index LE 77c ->
  TLB_miss <- 0; LO <- TLB[i]<31..0>; TLB[i]<43..38> NE PID AND G EQ 0 OR
  V EQ 0 -> TLB_miss <- 1)); TLB_miss EQ 1 -> (r/w EQ 0 -> "excep"(2h),
  r/w EQ 1 -> "excep"(3h)); TLB_miss EQ 0 AND D EQ 0 AND r/w EQ 1 ->
  {TLB modified} "excep"(1h); arg <- PFN<19..0> @ addr<11..0>),

PROC "get"(arg, cache, result): {Use arg to access memory via cache to get
  result. Procedure not defined here.}

PROC "excep"(Exc<3..0>): {Branch to exception handler with condition.}
  ((ex_cond <- 1, br_ins EQ 1 {branch} -> (BD <- 1, PC <- PC - 4));
  (EPC <- PC, SR<5..0> <- SR<3..0> @ 00, PC <- 80000080h)),

PROC "execute"(ins):              {instruction execution}
  (br_ins <- 0; DECODE ins<31..26>
  ((00c) -> DECODE funct<5..0>      {special-function operations}
    ((00c) -> GR[dreg] <- GR[treg] * shamnt, {Shift Left Logical}
    (10c) -> (br_ins <- 1, PC <- GR[sreg]),      {Jump Register}
    (14c) -> "excep"(8h),            {System call exception}
    (21c) -> HI <- GR[sreg],         {Move To HI}
    (40c) -> (GR[treg] <- GR[sreg] + immed, "ALU_test"(cond)), {ADD}
    (52c) -> (GR[sreg] LT GR[treg] GR[treg] <- 1,
             GR[sreg] GE GR[treg] GR[treg] <- 0)), {Set on Less Than}
  (03c) -> ((br_ins <- 1, temp <- PC<31..28> @ jtarg<25..0> @ 00,
             GR[31 <- PC + 8); {delay} PC <- temp),   {Jump and Link}
  (10c) -> (GR[treg] <- GR[sreg] + immed, "ALU_test"(cond)), {ADDImmed}
  (20c) -> SR<3..0> <- SR<5..2>,         {Return from Exception}
  (43c) -> (temp <- GR[sreg] + immed; "access_TLB"(0, 11, temp, arg);
             "get"(arg, 1, res); {delay} Gr[treg] <- res),   {Load Word}
                {other operations} )),
```

{Ref. Kane, G., MIPS R2000 RISC Architecture, (MIPS, Inc.), Prentice Hall,
Englewood Cliffs, NJ, 1987.}

Figure B-6   MIPS, Inc., 2000/3000 ISP   (Continued).

{Sun SPARC ISP}

```
{Pc State:}
  WR[0..16*windows - 1]<31..0> &(windows =: 2..32),  {Windowed Registers}
  G[0..7]<31..0>, G[0] := 00000000h,          {Global registers}
  FR[0..31]<31..0>,                  {Floating-point (FPU) Registers}
  PSR<31..0>,                        {Processor State Register}
  CSR<31..0>,                        {Coprocessor State Register}
  FSR<31..0>,                        {Floating-point State Register}
  TBR<31..0>,                        {Trap Base Register}
  WIM<31..0>,   {Window Invalid Mask}  Y<31..0>,   {Y register}
  PC<31..0>,   {Program Counter}      nPC<31..0>, {next Program Counter}
  CQ<63..0>,   {Coprocessor Queue}    FQ<63..0>,  {Floating-point Queue}
  (n GT 7 (r[n] := WR[(n-8) + 16*WP]),     {r[n] are working registers}
   n LE 7 (r[n] := G[n])) &(n =: 0..31),   {WP is current Window Pointer}
  {rlocals: n := 16..23; overlapped rins: n := 8..15, routs: n := 24..31}

{PSR and TBR Bit Assignments:}
  impl<3..0> := PSR<31..28>,             {processor implementation number}
  ver<3..0> := PSR<27..24>,              {constant, depends on impl}
  N := PSR<23>, {ALU Negative}           Z := PSR<22>, {ALU Zero}
  V := PSR<21>, {ALU Overflow}           C := PSR<20>, {ALU Carry}
  PSR<19..14> := xxc,                    {reserved for system}
  EC := PSR<13>, {Enable Coprocessor} EF := PSR<12>, {Enable FPU}
  PIL<3..0> := PSR<11..8>,               {Processor Interrupt Level}
  S := PSR<7>, {Supervisor mode}         PS := PSR<6>, {Previous S value}
  ET := PSR<5>, {Trap Enable}            WP<4..0> := PSR<4..0>, {Window Ptr.}
  TBA<19..0> := TBR<31..12>,             {Trap Base Address}
  tt<7..0> := TBR<11..4>, {trap type} TBR<3..0> := 0h,

{Mp State:}
  Mp[0..maxmem - 1]<7..0> &(maxmem =: 0..2^32),
  Mv[0..2^32 - 1]<7..0>,   {MMU and cache are defined by system designer.}

{Data Formats:}
  (by[k]<7..0> := Mv[k]<7..0>,
   hw[m]<15..0> := by[m]<7..0> @ by[m + 1]<7..0> &(m =: 0,2..k - 1),
   wd[n]<31..0> := hw[n]<15..0> @ hw[n + 2]<15..0> &(n =: 0,4..k - 3),
   dw[p]<63..0> := wd[p]<31..0> @ wd[p + 4]<31..0> &(p =: 0,8..k - 7))
        &(k =: 0..2^32 - 1),
  {Signed and unsigned byte, halfword, word, and doubleword integer; IEEE
  format single, double, and extended floating-point values are included.}

{Instruction Formats:}
  ins<31.0>,                         {uniform-size instruction, 3 formats}
  op<1,0> := ins<31,10>,             {format-selector operator}
  disp30<29..0> := ins<29..0>,       {sign-ext. displacement (format 1)}
  a := ins<29>,                      {annul (next instr.) bit (format 2)}
  cond<3..0> := ins<28..25>,         {condition code (format 2)}
  op2<2..0> := ins<24..22>,          {format-2 operator}
  disp22<21..0> := ins<21..0>,       {sign-ext. displacement (format 2)}
  rd<4..0> := ins<29..25>,           {source/dest. register (format 2 or 3)}
  imm22<21..0> := ins<21..0>,        {immediate value (format 2)}
  op3<5..0> := ins<24..19>,          {format-3 operator}
  rs1<4..0> := ins<18..14>,          {first source register (format3)}
  i := ins<13>,                      {second-operand selector (format 3)}
  asi<7..0> := ins<12..5>,           {address-space identifier (format 3)}
  rs2<4..0> := ins<4..0>,            {second source register (format3)}
  simm13<12..0> := ins<12..0>,       {sign-ext. immediate value (format 3)}
  shcnt<4..0> := ins<4..0>,          {shift count (field of simm13)}
  op4<8..0> := ins<13..5>,           {FPop or CPop operator (format 3)}
```

Figure B-7 Sun SPARC ISP.

```
{Instruction Interpretation and Execution:}    {clock times T0, T1, T2, T3}
   WHILE mode EQ execute ->                  {other modes are reset and error}
   ({T0 } interrupt EQ 1 -> "proc_inter"(int_cond);
          trap EQ 1 -> "proc_trap"(tr_cond);
          ins <- wd[PC];
   {T1 } (mem_excep EQ 1 -> (trap <- 1, tr_cond <- ins_access),
          mem_excep EQ 0 -> (PC <- nPC, nPC <- nPC + 4, (annul EQ 0 ->
                           "exec_ins"(ins<31,30>), annul EQ 1 -> annul <- 0)));
   {T2, T3: times for instruction execution and writeback} ),
   {Note-Reset and error modes not defined here. Interrupt, int_cond, trap,
   tr_cond, mem_excep are not defined here. Annul can be set by a of prior
   instruction. An 4-stage pipeline is used for instruction overlap.}

PROC exec_ins(op):  {executed in times T2, T3, unless delay (T4) is noted}
   (DECODE op<1,0>
    ((00) -> DECODE op2<2..0>                       {format-2 instructions}
        ((000) -> (trap <- 1, tr_cond <- illeg_ins)),     {Unimplemented}
         (010) -> (PC <- nPC, DECODE cond<3..0>       {Branch on condition}
            ((1001) -> ((Z EQ 0 -> (nPC <- NPC + 4, annul <- a),
                         Z EQ 1 -> nPC <- 4 * displ22;{T4})),   {equal}
                   {other conditions} ),
          (100) -> rd NE 0 -> r[rd] <- imm22<21..0> @ 0000000000, {Set Hi}
         {other format-2 instructions} ),
     (01) -> ((r[15] <-PC, PC <- nPC, nPC <- PC + 4 * disp30);{T4}), {Call}
     (10) -> DECODE op3<5..0>                         {format-3 instructions}
        ((20c) -> ((i EQ 0 -> result <- r[rs1] + r[rs2],
                    i EQ 1 -> result <- r[rs1] + simm13];
              ("ALU_test"(N,Z,V,C), rd NE 0 -> r[rd] <- result)),{Addcc}
         (51c) -> (S EQ 0 -> (trap <- 1, tr_cond <- priv_ins),
                   S EQ 1 -> rd NE 0 -> r[rd] <- PSR),         {Read PSR}
         (66c) -> DECODE op4<8..0> ({defin.}),   {Coprocessor operations}
         (70c) -> ((i EQ 0 -> jmp_addr <-r[rs1] + r[rs2],
                    i EQ 1 -> jmp_add <-r[rs1] + simm13);
              (jmp_add<1,0> NE 00 -> (trap <- 1, tr_cond <- mem_align),
               jmp_add<1,0> EQ 00 -> (rd NE 0 -> r[rd] <- PC,
                   PC <- nPC, nPC <- jmp_add); {T4})), {Jump & Link}
         (74c) -> (temp <- (CWP - 1) MOD windows; "masked"(temp, WIM, q);
                   (q EQ 1 -> (trap <- 1, tr_cond <- window_msk)),
                   q EQ 0 -> ((i EQ 0 -> result <- r[rs1] + r[rs2],
                               i EQ 1 -> result <- r[rs1] + simm13);
                    (CWP <- temp, rd NE 0 -> r[rd] <- result)))), {Save}
             {other format-3 instructions}),
     (11) -> DECODE op3<5..0>             {Load/Store format-3 instructions}
        ((00c) -> ((i EQ 0 -> addr <- r[rs1] + r[rs2],
                    i EQ 1 -> addr <- r[rs1] + simm13);
             (S EQ 0 -> addr_space <- 10, S EQ 1 -> addr_space <- 11);
             (addr<1,0> NE 00 -> (trap <- 1, tr_cond <- mem_align),
              addr<1,0> EQ 00 -> rd NE 0 -> wd[addr]; {T4})), {Load}
             {other Load/Store format-3 instructions}),

PROC "proc_inter"(int_cond): {Interrupt processor not defined here.}

PROC "proc_trap"(tr_cond): {Trap processing procerdure not defined here.}

PROC "masked"(value, mask, result): {Test of binary value against bit mask
   to yield true or false not defined here.}

PROC "ALU_test"(N,Z,V,C): {Test to set condition codes not defined here.}

{Ref. The SPARC™ Architecture Manual, Version 7, Sun Microsystems, Inc.,
   Mountain View, CA, 1987.}
```

Figure B-7   Sun SPARC ISP (Continued).

References

[AdamG85] Adams, G. B., III, R. L. Brown, and P. J. Denning. *An Evaluation Study of Dataflow Computation,* Research Institute on Advanced Computer Science Report TR-85.2. Moffett Field, CA: NASA Ames Research Center, 1985.

[AgraA83] Agrawala, A. K., and V. Herzog (eds.). Special issue on performance evaluation of multiple processor systems. *IEEE Trans. Computers,* C-32/1 (January 1983).

[AgraD86] Agrawal, D. P., V. K. Janakiram, and G. G. Pathak. Evaluating the performance of multicomputer configurations. *IEEE Computer,* 19/5 (May 1986).

[AllaS80] Allan, S. J., and A. E. Oldehoeft. A flow analysis procedure for the translation of high-level languages to a data flow language. *IEEE Trans. Computers,* C-29/9 (September 1980).

[AlleA80] Allen, A. O. Queuing models of computer systems. *IEEE Computer,* 13/4 (April 1980).

[AlleC86] Alley, C. L., and K. Atwood. *Microelectronics.* Englewood Cliffs, NJ: Prentice-Hall, 1986.

[AlleF76] Allen, F. E., and J. Cocke. A program data flow analysis procedure. *Commun. ACM,* 19/3 (March 1976).

[AmdaG64] Amdahl, G. M., G. A. Blaauw, and F. P. Brooks. Architecture of the IBM System 360. *IBM J. Res. & Dev.,* 8/2 (April 1964).

[AndeJ61] Anderson, J. P. A computer for direct execution of algorithmic languages. In *Proceedings of the Eastern Joint Computer Conference.* Montvale, NJ: AFIPS, 1961.

[AndeJ62] Anderson, J. P., S. A. Hoffman, J. Shifman, and R. J. Williams. D825- A multiple computer system for command and control. In *Proceedings of the Fall Joint Computer Conference.* Montvale, NJ: AFIPS, 1962.

[Arvin77] Arvind and K. P. Gostelow. A computer capable of exchanging processors for time. In *Proceedings of the 1977 IFIP Congress*. Amsterdam: North Holland, 1977.

[Arvin81] Arvind and J. B. Dennis. *Proceedings of the 1981 Conference on Functional Programming Languages and Computer Architecture*. New York: ACM, 1981.

[AstrM52] Astrahan, M. M., and N. Rochester. The logical organization of the new IBM scientific calculator. In *Proceedings of the ACM Pittsburgh Conference*. New York: ACM, 1952.

[BackJ78] Backus, J. Can programming be liberated from the von Neumann style? A functional style and its algebra of programs. *Commun. ACM,* 21/8 (August 1978).

[BaerJ80] Baer, J. L. *Computer Systems Architecture*. Potomac, MD: Computer Science Press, 1980.

[BarbM75] Barbacci, M. R. A comparison of register transfer languages for describing computers and digital systems. *IEEE Trans. Computers*, C-24/2 (February 1975).

[BarbM81] Barbacci, M. R. Instruction set processor specifications (ISPS). *IEEE Trans. Computers,* C30/1 (January 1981).

[BarnG68] Barnes, G. H., R. M. Brown, M. Kato, D. J. Kuch, D. L. Slotnick, and R. A. Stokes. The ILLIAC IV computer. *IEEE Trans. Computers*, C-17/8 (August 1968). (Reprinted in [BellC71].)

[BartR61] Barton, R. S. A new approach to the functional design of a digital computer. In *Proceedings of the Western Joint Computer Conference*. Montvale, NJ: AFIPS, 1961.

[BatcK77] Batcher, K.E. STARAN series E. In *Proceedings of the 1977 International Conference on Parallel Processing*. New York: IEEE, 1977.

[BatcK80] Batcher, K. E. Architecture of a Massively Parallel Processor. *IEEE Trans. Computers,* C-29/9 (September 1980).

[BatcT87] Batchman, T. E., and E. A. Parrish, Jr. (eds.). Integrated optical computers. *IEEE Computer*, 20/12 (December 1987).

[BeicF84] Beichter, F. W., O. Herzog, and H. Petzsch. SLAN-4: A software specification and design language. *IEEE Trans. Software Eng.*, SE-10/2 (March 1984).

[BellC70] Bell, C. G., and A. Newell, The PMS and ISP descriptive systems for computer structures. In *Proceedings of the 1970 Spring Joint Computer Conference*. Montvale, NJ: AFIPS, 1970.

[BellC71] Bell, C. G., and A. Newell. *Computer Structures: Readings and Examples*. New York: McGraw-Hill, 1971.

[BellC78a] Bell, C. G., S. H. Fuller, and D. Siewiorek (eds.). *Commun. ACM*, 21/1 (January 1978).

[BellC78b] Bell, C. G., J. C. Mudge, and J. E. McNamara. *Computer Engineering: A DEC View of Hardware System Design*. Marlboro, MA: Digital Press, 1978.

[BellJ74] Bell, J., D. Casasent, and C. G. Bell, An investigation of alternative cache organizations. *IEEE Trans. Computers*, C-23/4 (April 1974).

[BergG86] Bergland, G. D., and P. Zave (eds.). *IEEE Trans. Software Eng.*, SE-12/2 (February 1986).

[BerkK78] Berkling, K. J. Reduction languages for reduction machines. In *Proceedings of the 2nd International Symposium on Computer Architecture*. New York: IEEE, 1975.

[BhuyL87] Bhuyan, L. H. (ed.). Interconnection networks. *IEEE Computer,* 20/6 (June 1987).

[BicLu87] Bic, L., and A. C. Shaw. *The Logical Design of Operating Systems,* 2nd Ed. Englewood Cliffs, NJ: Prentice-Hall, 1987.

[BlanB81] Blanchard, B. S., and W. J. Fabrycky. *Systems Engineering and Analysis*. Englewood Cliffs, NJ: Prentice-Hall, 1981.

[BlocE59] Block, E. The engineering design of the Stretch computer. In *Proceedings of the Eastern Joint Computer Conference*. Montvale, NJ: AFIPS, 1959. (Reprinted in [BellC71].)

[BokhS87] Bokhari, S. H. Multiprocessing the sieve of Eratosthenes. *IEEE Computer*, 20/4 (April 1987).

[BorgB78] Borgeson, B. R., M. L. Hanson, and P. A. Hartley. The evolution of the Sperry Univac 1100 series: A history, analysis, and projection. *Commun. ACM*, 21/1 (January 1978).

[BoukW72] Bouknight, W. J., S. A. Denenberg, D. A. McIntyre, J. M. Randall, A. M. Sameh, and D. L. Slotnick. The ILLIAC IV system. *Proc. IEEE*, 60/4 (April 1972). (Reprinted in [SiewD82].)

[BuchW53] Buchholz, W. The system design of the IBM type 701 computer. *Proc. IRE*, 41/10 (October 1953).

[BuchW86] Buchholz, W. The IBM System/370 vector architecture. *IBM Syst. J.*, 25/1 (1986).

[BullD77] Bullman, D. M. (ed.). Stack-based computers, special issue. *IEEE Computer*, 10/5 (May 1977).

[BurkA46] Burks, A. W., H. H. Goldstine, and J. von Neumann. *Preliminary Discussion of the Logical Design of an Electronic Computing Instrument*, Report to U.S. Army Ordnance Department. Princeton, NJ: Institute for Advanced Study, Princeton University, 1946. (Published in [TaubA63]. Parts I and II are reprinted in *Datamation*, 8/9 (September 1962) and 8/10 (October 1962). Part I is reprinted in [BellC71].)

[CandC85] Candrell, C., Jr. *System Development Standards*. New York: McGraw-Hill, 1985.

[CascR78] Case, R. P., and A. Padegs. Architecture of the IBM System/370. *Commun. ACM*, 21/1 (January 1978).

[CharA81] Charlesworth, A. E. An approach to scientific array processing. *IEEE Computer*, 14/9 (September 1981).

[ChuYa75] Chu, Y. *High Level Language Computer Architecture*. New York: Academic Press, 1975.

[ChuYa81] Chu, Y. (ed.). High level computer architecture, special issue. *IEEE Computer*, 14/7 (July 1981).

[ClarK82] Clark, K. L., and S. A. Tarlund (eds.). *Logic Programming*. London: Academic Press, 1982.

[CoffE73] Coffman, E. G., Jr., and P. J. Denning. *Operating Systems Theory*, Englewood Cliffs, NJ: Prentice-Hall, 1973.

[CorbF62] Corbato, F. J., M. M. Daggett, and R. C. Daley. An experimental time sharing system. In *Proceedings of the Spring Joint Computer Conference*. Montvale, NJ: AFIPS, 1962.

[CorbF65] Corbato, F. J., and V. A. Vyssotsky. Introduction and overview of the Multics system. In *Proceedings of the Fall Joint Computer Conference*. Montvale, NJ: AFIPS, 1965.

[CormR83] Cormier, R. L., R. J. Dugan, and R. R. Guyette. System/370 extended architecture: The channel subsystem. *IBM J. Res. & Dev.*, 27/3 (May 1983).

[CrayR82] Cray Research, Inc. *CRAY X-MP Series of Computers*, Publication MP-0001. Chippewa Falls, MN, 1982.

[CvetZ87] Cvetanovic, Z. The effects of problem partitioning, allocation, and granularity on the performance of multiple-processor systems. *IEEE Trans. Computers*, C36/4 (April 1987).

[DahlS78] Dahlby, S. H., G. G. Henry, D. N. Reynolds, and P. T. Taylor. The IBM System/38: A high level machine. In *IBM System/38: Technical Developments*. White Plains, NY: IBM Corp., 1978. (Reprinted in [SiewD82].)

[DaleR68] Daley, R. C., and J. B. Dennis. Virtual memory, processes, and sharing in MULTICS. *Commun. ACM*, 11/5 (May 1968).

[DarlJ81] Darlington, J., and M. Reeve. ALICE: A multiprocessor reduction machine for parallel evaluation of applicative languages. In *Proceedings of the International Symposium on Functional Programming Languages and Computer Architecture.* New York: ACM, 1981.

[DaviA82] Davis, A. M. The design of a family of application oriented requirements languages. *IEEE Computer,* 15/5 (May 1982).

[DaviG60] Davis, G. M. The English Electric KDF9 computer system. *Computer Bull.,* 4/3 (December 1960).

[DennJ80] Dennis, J. B. Data flow supercomputers. *IEEE Computer,* 13/11 (November 1980).

[DennP87] Denning, P. S. Evaluating supercomputers. *American Scientist,* 75/2 (March-April 1987).

[Digi86a] Digital Equipment Corp. *VAX Architecture Handbook.* Maynard, MA, 1986.

[Digi86b] Digital Equipment Corp. *VAX Hardware Handbook, Vol. 1 and Vol. 2.* Maynard. MA, 1986.

[DongJ85] Dongarra, J. J., and I. S. Duff. *Advanced Computer Architectures,* Technical Memorandum No. 57. Argonne, IL: Argonne National Laboratory, 1985.

[EckeJ51] Eckert, J. P., J. R. Weiner, H. F. Welsh, and H. F. Mitchell. The UNIVAC system. In *Proceedings of the AIEE-IRE Conference.* New York: IEEE. December 1951. (Reprinted in [BellC71].)

[EinDP85] Ein-Dor, P. Grosch's law revisited: CPU power and the cost of computation. *Commun. ACM,* 28/2 (February 1985).

[EnslP77] Enslow, P. H., Jr. Multiprocessor organization-A survey. *Computer Surveys,* 9/1 (March 1977).

[EverR57] Everett, R. R., C. A. Zracket, and H. D. Benington. SAGE- A data processing system for air defense. In *Proceedings of the Fall Joint Computer Conference.* Montvale, NJ: AFIPS, 1957.

[FengT81] Feng, T. Y. A survey of interconnection networks. *IEEE Computer,* 14/12 (December 1981).

[FerrD78] Ferrari, D. *Computer Systems Performance Evaluation.* Englewood Cliffs, NJ: Prentice-Hall, 1978.

[FeusE73] Feustel, E. A. On the advantages of tagged architecture. *IEEE Trans. Computers,* C-22/7 (July 1973).

[FishA85] Fisher, A. L., and H. T. Kung. Special purpose VLSI architectures: General discussion and a case study. In [KungS85].

[FlynM66] Flynn, M. J. Very high speed computing systems. *Proc. IEEE,* 54/12 (December 1966).

[FlynM76] Flynn, M. J. Some computer organizations and their effectiveness. *IEEE Trans. Computers,* C-21/9 (September 1976).

[FlynM79] Flynn, M. J., and L. W. Hoevel. *A Theory of Interpretive Architectures: Ideal Language Machines,* Computer Syst Laboratory Technical Report No. 170. Stanford, CA: Stanford University, 1979.

[FlynM80] Flynn, M. J. Directions and issues in architecture and language. *IEEE Computer,* 13/10 (October 1980).

[FortJ87] Fortes, J. A. B., and B. W. Wahl (eds.). Systolic arrays, special issue. *IEEE Computer,* 20/7 (July 1987).

[FreeH83] Freeman, H. A. (ed.). Network Interconnection. *IEEE Computer,* 16/9 (September 1983).

[FullS77a] Fuller, S. H., H. S. Stone, and W. E. Burr. Initial selection and screening of the CFA candidate computer architectures. In *Proceedings of the National Computer Conference.* Montvale, NJ: AFIPS, 1977.

[FullS77b] Fuller, S. H., P. Shaman, D. Lamb, and W. E. Burr. Evaluation of computer architectures via test programs. In *Proceedings of the National Computer Conference.* Montvale, NJ: AFIPS, 1977.

[GajsD82] Gajski, D. D., D. A. Padua, D. J. Kuck, and R. H. Kuhn. A second opinion on data flow machines and languages. *IEEE Computer*, 15/2, (February 1982).

[GajsD85] Gajski, D. D., and J.-K. Pier. Essential issues in multiprocessor systems. *IEEE Computer*, 18/6 (June 1985).

[GehrE82] Gehringer, E. F., A. K. Jones, and Z. Z. Segall. The Cm* testbed. *IEEE Computer*, 15/10 (October 1982).

[GibsJ70] Gibson, J. C. *The Gibson Mix*, Technical Report TR00.2043. Poughkeepsie, NY: IBM Systems Development Division, 1970.

[GimaC87] Gimarc, C. E., and V. M. Milutinovic. A survey of RISC processors and computers of the mid-1980's. *IEEE Computer*, 20/9 (September 1987).

[GlazD86] Glazier, D. Moving pictures at 40 million instructions per second. *Intelligent Instruments and Computers.* (September/October 1986).

[GokeR73] Goke, R., and G. J. Lipovski. Banyan networks for partitioning on multiprocessor systems. In *Proceedings of the First Annual Symposium on Computer Architecture.* New York: IEEE and ACM, 1973.

[GoodH57] Goode, H. H., and R. E. Machol. *System Engineering.* New York: McGraw-Hill, 1957.

[GorsG86] Gorsline, G. W. *Computer Organization,* 2nd Ed. Englewood Cliffs, NJ: Prentice-Hall, 1986.

[GrabE59] Grabbe, E. M., S. Ramo, and D. E. Wooldridge. *Handbook of Automation, Computation, and Control, Vol. 2.* New York: Wiley, 1959.

[GrosH53] Grosch, H. R. J. High speed arithmetic: The digital computer as a research tool. *J. Opt. Soc. Am.*, 4/4 (April 1953).

[GrosT88] Gross, T. R., J. L. Hennessy, S. A. Przybylski, and C. Rowen. Measurement and evaluation of the MIPS architecture and processor. *ACM Trans. Computer Syst.*, 6/3 (August 1988).

[GurdJ86] Gurd, J. P., C. C. Kirkham, and I. Watson. The Manchester prototype dataflow computer. *Commun. ACM,* 28/1 (January 1986).

[HackJ86] Hack, J. J. Peak vs sustained performance in highly concurrent vector machines. *IEEE Computer,* 19/9 (September 1986).

[HamaV84] Hamacher, V. C., Z. G. Vranesic, and S. G. Zaky. *Computer Organization*, 2nd Edition. New York: McGraw-Hill, 1984.

[HammR50] Hamming, R. W. Error detection and error correction. *Bell Syst. Tech. J.,* 29/4 (April 1950).

[HammR86] Hamming, R. W. *Coding and Information Theory*, 2nd Ed. Englewood Cliffs, NJ: Prentice-Hall, 1986.

[HendP80] Henderson, P. *Functional Programming, Application and Implementation.* London: Prentice-Hall International, 1980.

[HennJ84] Hennessy, J. VLSI processor architecture. *IEEE Trans. Computers,* C-33/12 (December 1984).

[HeurV88] Heuring, V. P., H. F. Jordan, and J. P. Pratt. *A bit serial architecture for optical computing,* TR 88-01. Boulder, CO: Center for Optoelectronic Computing Systems, University of Colorado, 1988.

[HigbL73] Higbie, L. C. Supercomputer architecture. *IEEE Computer,* 6/12 (December 1973).

[HillW86] Hillis, W. D. *The Connection Machine.* Cambridge, MA: The MIT Press, 1986.

[HoevL79] Hoevel, L. W., and M. J. Flynn. *A Theory of Interpretive Architectures: Some Notes on DEL Design and a Fortran Case Study*, Computer Systems Laboratory Technical Report No. 171. Stanford, CA: Stanford University, 1979.

[HollM87] Holliday, M. A., and M. K. Vernon. Exact performance estimates for multiprocessor memory and bus interface. *IEEE Trans. Computers*, C-36/1 (January 1987).

[HopkM84] Hopkins, M. E. A definition of RISC. In *Proceedings of the International Workshop on High Level Computer Archi*tecture. College Park, MD: University of Maryland, 1984.

[HowaD61] Howarth, D. J., R. B. Payne, and F. H. Sumner. The Manchester University Atlas operating system, Part II: User's description. *Computer J.*, 4/3 (October 1961).

[HuntC87] Hunter, C. *Series 32000 Programmers Reference Manual*. Englewood Cliffs, NJ: Prentice-Hall, 1987.

[HuskH76] Huskey, H. D. (ed.). *IEEE Trans. Computers*, C-25/12 (December 1976).

[HsaiD83] Hsaio, D. K. (ed.). *Advanced Database Machine Architecture*. Englewood Cliffs, NJ: Prentice-Hall, 1983.

[HwanA84] Hwang, A. Architectural considerations involved in the design of an optical digital computer. *Proc. IEEE*, 72/7 (July 1984).

[HwanK84] Hwang, K., and F. A. Briggs. *Computer Architecture and Parallel Processing*. New York: McGraw-Hill, 1984.

[IEEE 83] *ANSI/IEEE Standard 796-1983, Standard Microcomputer Bus System*. New York: IEEE, 1983.

[IEEE 85] *ANSI/IEEE Standard 754-1985, Binary Floating-Point Arithmetic*. New York: IEEE, 1985.

[Intel79] Intel Corp. *The 8086 Family User's Manual*. Santa Clara, CA, 1979.

[Intel83] Intel Corp. *Microprocessor and Peripherals Handbook*. Santa Clara, CA, 1983.

[Intel85] Intel Corp. *Solutions*. Santa Clara, CA, November/December 1985.

[JackM83] Jackson, M. A. *System Development*. London: Prentice-Hall International, 1983.

[JoneA80] Jones, A. K., and P. Schwarz. Experience using multiprocessor systems-A status report. *Computer Sur*veys, 12/2 (February 1980).

[JordH84] Jordan, H. F. Experience with pipelined multiple instruction streams. *Proc. IEEE*, 72/1 (January 1984).

[JordH85] Jordan, H. F. HEP architecture programming and performance. In [KowaJ85].

[JordH86] Jordan, H. F. Structuring parallel algorithms in an MIMD, shared memory environment. *Parallel Processing*, 3 (May 1986).

[JordK87] Jordan, K. E. Performance comparisons of very large scale scientific computers. *IEEE Computer*, 20/3 (March 1987).

[KaneG87] Kane, G. *MIPS R2000 RISC Architecture*. Englewood Cliffs, NJ: Prentice-Hall, 1987.

[KatzJ77] Katzman, J. A. *System Architecture for NonStop Computing*. Cupertino, CA: Tandem Computers, 1977. (Also in *Proceedings of Compcon 77*. New York: IEEE, 1977. Also reprinted in [SiewD82].)

[KilbT56] Kilburn, T., D. B. G. Edwards, and C. E. Thomas. The Manchester University Mark II digital computing machine. *Proc. IEE (U.K.), Part B*, 103 (supp 2) (1956).

[KilbT61] Kilburn, T., D. J. Howarth, R. B. Payne, and F. H. Sumner. The Manchester University Atlas operating system, Part I: Internal organization. *Computer J.*, 4/3 (October 1961).

[KingD84] King, D. *Current Practice in Software Development*. New York: Yourdon Press, 1984.

[KleiL75] Kleinrock, L. *Queuing Systems, Vol. I: Theory*. New York: Wiley, 1975.

[KleiL76] Kleinrock, L. *Queuing Systems, Vol. II: Computer Applications.* New York: Wiley, 1976.

[KnigK66] Knight, K. E. Changes in computer performance. *Datamation*, 12/9 (September 1966).

[KoggP81] Kogg, P. M. *The Architecture of Pipelined Computers.* New York: McGraw-Hill, 1981.

[KowaJ85] Kowalik, J. S. (ed.). *Parallel MIMD Computation: HEP Supercomputer and its Applications.* Cambridge, MA: The MIT Press, 1985.

[KowaR79] Kowalski, R. A. *Logic for Problem Solving.* Amsterdam: Elsevier-North Holland, 1979.

[KozdE80] Kozdrowicki, E. W., and D. J. Theis. Second generation of vector supercomputers. *IEEE Computer*, 13/11 (November 1980).

[KranF60] Krantz, F. H., and W. D. Murray. A survey of digital methods for radar data processing. In *Proceedings of the Eastern Joint Computer Conference.* Montvale, NJ: AFIPS, 1960.

[KuckD72] Kuck, D. J., Y. Maraoka, and S.-C. Chen. On the number of operations simultaneously executable in FORTRAN-like programs and their resulting speed. *IEEE Trans. Computers*, C-21/12 (December 1972).

[KuckD76] Kuck, D. J. Parallel processing of ordinary programs. In Rubinoff, M., and M. C. Yovitts (eds.). *Advances in Computers, Vol. 15.* New York: Academic Press, 1976.

[KuckD77] Kuck, D. J., D. H. Lawrie, and A. H. Sameh (eds.). *High Speed Computer and Algorithm Organization.* New York: Academic Press, 1977.

[KuckD78] Kuck, D. J. *The Structure of Computers and Computations, Vol. 1.* New York: Wiley, 1978.

[KuckD82] Kuck, D. J., and R. A. Stokes. The Burroughs Scientific Processor (BSP). *IEEE Trans. Computers*, C-31/5 (May 1982).

[KungH82] Kung, H. T. Why systolic architectures. *IEEE Computer*, 15/1 (January 1982).

[KungS85] Kung, S. Y., H. J. Whitehorse, and T. Kailath (eds.). *VLSI and Modern Signal Processing.* Englewood Cliffs, NJ: Prentice-Hall, 1985.

[KungS87] Kung, S. Y. *VLSI Array Processors.* Englewood Cliffs, NJ: Prentice-Hall, 1987.

[LaveS83] Lavenberg, S. *Computer Performance Modeling Handbook.* London: Academic Press, 1983.

[LawrD75] Lawrie, D. H. Access and alignment of data in an array processor. *IEEE Trans. Computers*, C-24/12 (December 1975).

[LawrD82] Lawrie, D. H., and C. R. Vora. The prime memory system for array access. *IEEE Trans. Computers*, C-31/5 (May 1982).

[LeviA84] Levinthal, A., and T. Porter. CHAP, a SIMD graphics processor. *Computer Graphics*, 18/3 (July 1984).

[LinKS87] Lin, K.-S. (ed.). *Digital Signal Processing Applications with the TMS 320 Family.* Englewood Cliffs, NJ: Prentice-Hall, 1987.

[LippR87] Lippmann, R. P. An introduction to computing with neural nets. *IEEE ASSP*, 3/4 (April 1987). (Reprinted in *Computer Architecture News (ACM)*. 16/1 [Mar 1988].)

[LiuMT82] Liu, M. T., and J. Rothstein (eds.). Special issue on parallel and distributed processing. *IEEE Trans. Computers*, C-31/11 (November 1982).

[LouiT81] Louie, T. Array processors: A selected bibliography. *IEEE Computer*, 14/9 (Sepember 1981).

[LundS87] Lundstrom, S. F. Applications considerations in the design of highly concurrent multiprocessors. *IEEE Trans. Computers*, C-36/11 (November 1987).

[MacLB83] MacLennan, B. J. *Principles of Programming Languages: Design, Evaluation, and Implementation.* New York: Holt, Rinehart and Winston, 1983.

[MaekM87] Maekawa, M., A. E. Oldehoeft, and R. R. Oldehoeft. *Operating Systems, Advanced Concepts.* Menlo Park, CA: BenjaminCummings, 1987.

[MagoG80] Mago, G. A. A cellular computer architecture for functional programming. In *Digest of COMPCOM Spring 80.* New York: IEEE, 1980.

[ManoM79] Mano, M. M. *Digital Logic and Computer Design.* Englewood Cliffs, NJ: Prentice-Hall, 1979.

[ManoM82] Mano, M. M. *Computer System Architecture,* 2nd Ed. Englewood Cliffs, NJ: Prentice-Hall, 1982.

[McCaJ60] McCarthy, J. Recursive functions of symbolic expressions and their computation by machine. *Commun. ACM,* 3/4 (April 1960).

[McKeR76] McKeag, R. M., and R. Wilson. *Studies in Operating Systems.* London: Academic Press, 1976.

[MeyeR70] Meyer, R. A., and L. H. Seawright. A virtual machine time-sharing system. *IBM Syst. J.,* 9/3 (1970).

[MillJ85] Mills, J. A. A pragmatic view of the system architect. *Commun. ACM,* 28/7 (July 1985).

[MillR73] Miller, R. E. A comparison of some theoretical models of parallel computation. *IEEE Trans. Computers,* C-22/8 (August 1973).

[MiluV86] Milutinovic, V. (ed.). Artificial neural systems. *IEEE Computer,* 19/10 (October 1986).

[MoonD87] Moon, D. A. Symbolics architecture. *IEEE Computer,* 20/1 (January 1987).

[Motor84] Motorola Inc. *M68000 16-/32-Bit Microprocessor, Programmer's Reference Manual,* 4th Ed. Englewood Cliffs, NJ: Prentice-Hall, 1984.

[NashJ79] Nash, J., and M. Spak. Hardware and software tools for the development of a microprogrammed microprocessor. In *Proceedings of the 12th Annual Microprogramming Workshop.* New York: IEEE, 1979. (Also published as *ACM SIGMICRO Newsletter,* 10/4 [December 1979]).

[Natio85] National Semiconductor Corp. *Series 32000 Databook.* Santa Clara, CA. 1985.

[NoycR77] Noyce, R. N. Large scale integration: What is yet to come? *Science,* 195/4283 (Mar 1977).

[OrgaE72] Organick, E. I. *The Multics System: An Examination of its Structure.* Cambridge, MA: The MIT Press, 1972.

[OrgaE73] Organick, E. I. *Computer Systems Organization- The B5700/B6700 Series.* New York: Academic Press, 1973.

[OrgaE78] Organick, E. I., and J. A. Hinds. *Interpreting Machines: Architecture and Programming of the B1700/B1800 Series.* New York: Elsevier North-Holland, 1978.

[PadeA83] Padegs, A. System/370 extended architecture: Design considerations. *IBM J. Res. & Dev.,* 27/3 (May 1983).

[PadeA88] Padegs, A., B. B. Moore, R. M. Smith, and W. Buchholz. The IBM System/370 vector architecture: Design considerations. *IEEE Trans. Computers,* 37/5 (May 1988).

[PaduD80] Padua, D. A., D. J. Kuck, and D. L. Lawrie. High speed multiprocessor and compiler techniques. *IEEE Trans. Computers,* C-29/9 (September 1980).

[ParkD83] Parkinson, D., and H. M. Liddell. The measurement of performance on a highly parallel system. *IEEE Trans. Computers,* C-32/1 (January 1983).

[PateJ81] Patel, J. H. Performance of processor-memory interconnections for multiprocessors. *IEEE Trans. Computers,* C-30/10 (October 1981).

[PattD82] Patterson, D. A., and C. H. Sequin. A VLSI RISC. *IEEE Computer*, 15/9 (September 1982).

[PattD85] Patterson, D. A. Reduced instruction set Computers. *Commun. ACM*, 28/1 (January 1985).

[PattP85] Patton, P. P. Multiprocessors, architecture and applications. *IEEE Computer*, 18/6 (June 1985).

[PeasM77] Pease, M. C. The indirect binary n-cube microprocessor array. *IEEE Trans. Computers*, C25/5 (May 1977).

[PeleA76] Peled, A., and B. Liu. *Digital Signal Processing*. New York: Wiley, 1976.

[PeteJ83] Peterson, J. L. *Petri-Net Theory and the Modeling of Systems*. Englewood Cliffs, NJ: Prentice-Hall, 1983.

[PeteJ85] Peterson, J. L., and A. Silberschatz. *Operating System Concepts*, 2nd Ed. Reading, MA: Addison Wesley, 1985.

[PortR60] Porter, R. E. The RW400-A new polymorphic data system. *Datamation*, 6/1 (January 1960).

[PresR87] Pressman, R. S. *Software Engineering: a Practitioner's Approach*, 2nd ed. New York: McGraw-Hill, 1987.

[RadiG82] Radin, G. The 801 minicomputer. In *Proceedings of the Symposium on Architectural Support for Programming Languages and Operating Systems*. New York: ACM, 1982.

[RadiG83] Radin, G. The 801 Minicomputer. *IBM J. Res. & Dev.*, 27/3 (May 1983).

[RamaC77] Ramamoorthy, C. V., and H. F. Li. Pipeline architecture. *Computing Surveys*, 9/1 (March 1977).

[RandB73] Randell, B. *The Origins of Digital Computers: Selected Papers*. Berlin: Springer-Verlag, 1973.

[RausT80] Rauscher, T. G., and P. M. Adams. Microprogramming: A tutorial and survey of recent developments. *IEEE Trans. Computers*, C-29/1 (January 1980).

[ReilJ82] Reilly, J., A. Sutton, R. Nasser, and R. Griaconi. Process controller for the IBM 3081. *IBM J. Res. & Dev.*, 26/1 (January 1982).

[RitcD78] Ritchie, D. M., and K. Thompson. The UNIX time-sharing system. *Bell Syst. Tech. J.*, 57/6 (June 1978).

[RoseS69] Rosen, S. Electronic computers: A historical survey. *Computing Surveys*, 1/1 (March 1969).

[RussR78] Russell, R. M. The CRAY-1 supercomputer. *Commun. ACM*, 21/1 (January 1978).

[RzepW85] Rzepka, W., and Y. Ohno (eds.). Requirements engineering environments. *IEEE Computer*, 18/4 (April 1985).

[SammJ69] Sammet, J. *Programming Languages, History and Fundamentals*. Englewood Cliffs, NJ: Prentice-Hall, 1969.

[SangJ86] Sanguinetti, J. Performance of a message-based multiprocessor. *IEEE Computer*, 19/9 (September 1986).

[SatyM80] Satyanarayanan, M. *Multiprocessors: A Comparative Study*. Englewood Cliffs, NJ: Prentice-Hall, 1980.

[SaueC81] Sauer, C. H., and K. M. Chandry. *Computer System Performance Modeling*. Englewood Cliffs, NJ: Prentice-Hall, 1981.

[SeitC86] Seitz, C. L. The Cosmic Cube. *Commun. ACM*, 28/1 (January 1986).

[ShawA74] Shaw, A. C. *The Logical Design of Operating Systems*. Englewood Cliffs, NJ: Prentice-Hall, 1974.

[ShawA88] Shaw, A. C. (ed.). Special section on operating systems. *Commun. ACM*, 31/3 (March 1988).

[ShriB88] Shriver, B. D. (ed.). Artificial neural systems. *IEEE Computer*, 21/3 (March 1988).

[SiegH84] Siegel, H. J. *Interconnection Networks for Large-Scale Parallel Processing*. Lexington, MA: Lexington Books, 1984.

[SiewD82] Siewiorek, D. P., C. G. Bell, and A. Newell. *Computer Structures: Principles and Examples*. New York: McGraw-Hill, 1982.

[SlotD62] Slotnick, D. L., W. C. Borek, and R. C. McReynolds. The Solomon Computer. In *Proceedings of the Fall Joint Computer Conference*. Montvale, NJ: AFIPS, 1962.

[SmitB78] Smith, B. J. A pipelined, shared resource MIMD computer. In *Proceedings of the 1978 International Conference on Parallel Processing*. New York: IEEE and ACM, 1978.

[SpraJ80] Spragins, J. (ed.). Analytical queuing models. *IEEE Computer*, 13/4 (April 1980).

[StalW86] Stallings, W. *Reduced Instruction Set Computers*. Washington, DC: IEEE Computer Society Press, 1986.

[StalW87] Stallings, W. *Computer Organization and Architecture*. New York: MacMillan, 1987.

[StokR77] Stokes, R. A. Burroughs Scientific Processor. In [KuckD77].

[StonH71] Stone, H. S. Parallel processing with a perfect shuffle. *IEEE Trans. Computers*, C-20/2 (February 1971).

[StonH87] Stone, H. S. *High Performance Computer Architecture*. Reading, MA: Addison-Wesley, 1987.

[StoyJ77] Stoy, J. E. *Denotational Semantics: The Scott-Strachey Approach to Programming Language Theory*. Cambridge, MA: The MIT Press, 1977.

[StreW78] Strecker, W. D. VAX-11/780: A virtual address extension to the DEC PDP-11 family. In *Proceedings of the 1978 National Computer Conference*. Montvale, NJ: AFIPS, 1978. (Reprinted in [BellC78b]).

[SussG81] Sussman, G. J., J. Holloway, G. L. Steel, Jr., and A. Bell. Scheme-79--Lisp on a chip. *IEEE Computer*, 14/7 (July 1981).

[TaneA78] Tanenbaum, A. S. Implications of structured programming for machine architecture. *IEEE Trans. Computers*, C-27/3 (March 1978).

[TaneA81] Tanenbaum, A. S. *Computer Networks*. Englewood Cliffs, NJ: Prentice-Hall, 1981.

[TaneA84] Tanenbaum, A. S. *Structured Computer Organization*, 2nd Ed. Englewood Cliffs, NJ: Prentice-Hall, 1984.

[TaubA63] Taub, A. H. (ed.). *The Collected Works of John von Neumann, Vol. 5*. New York: Macmillan, 1963.

[TennR81] Tennent, R. D. *Principles of Programming Languages*. London: Prentice-Hall International, 1981.

[Texas85] Texas Instruments. *TMS32020 User's Guide, Digital Signal Processors Products*. Dallas, TX, 1985.

[ThomR63] Thompson, R. N., and J. A. Wilkinson. The D825 automatic operating and scheduling program. In *Proceedings of the Spring Joint Computer Conference*. Montvale, NJ: AFIPS, 1963.

[ThorJ64] Thornton, J. E. Parallel operation of the Control Data 6600. In *Proceedings of the Fall Joint Computer Conference, Part II*. Montvale, NJ: AFIPS, 1964. (Reprinted in [BellC71].)

[ThurK83] Thurber, K. J., and P. C. Patton. *Computer System Requirements*. Lexington, MA: Lexington Books, 1983.

[TrelP82] Treleaven, P. C., D. R. Brownbridge, and R. P. Hopkins. Data-driven and demand-driven computer architecture. *Computer Surveys*, 14/1 (January 1982).

[TrelP83] Treleaven, P. C. The new generation of computer architecture. In *Proceedings of the 10th Annual Symposium on Computer Archit*ecture. New York: ACM, 1983.

[TrivK82] Trivedi, K. S. *Probability and Statistics with Reliability, Queuing, and Computer Science Applications*. Englewood Cliffs, NJ: Prentice-Hall, 1982.

[TroyJ77] Troy, J. L. *PEPE Hardware Reference Manual*, System Development Corp. TM-NU-051/001/00. Detroit, MI: Unisys Corp, 1977.

[TsaoC84] Tsao, C. D., and F. Ricci (eds.). Architectures of Local Area Networks (LANs). *IEEE Communications*, 22/8 (August 1984).

[TuckS86] Tucker, S. G. The IBM 3090 system: An overview. *IBM Syst. J.*, 25/1, 1986.

[TurnD79] Turner, D. A. A new implementetion technique for applicative languages. *Software-Practice and Experience*, 9/1 (January 1979).

[USAF-74] *MIL-STD-499A(USAF), Engineering Management*. Washington, DC: U.S. Government Printing Office, 1974.

[WakeJ78] Wakerly, J. *Error Detecting Codes, Self Checking Circuits and Applications*. New York: Elsevier NorthHolland, 1978.

[WatsI82] Watson, I., and J. Gurd. A practical data flow computer. *IEEE Computer*, 15/2 (February 1982).

[WatsW72] Watson, W. J. The TI ASC-A highly modular and flexible super computer architecture. In *Proceedings of the Fall Joint Computer Conference*. Montvale, NJ: AFIPS, 1972.

[WebeH67] Weber, H. A microprogrammed implementation of Euler on IBM System/360 model 30. *Commun. ACM*, 10/9 (September 1967).

[WeidN71] Weiderman, N. *Synchronization and Simulation in Operating System Construction*, Tech. Rep. 71102. PhD thesis, Computer Science Department. Ithaca, NY: Cornell University, 1971.

[WestL87] West, L. C. Picosecond integrated optical logic. *IEEE Computer*, 20/12 (December 1987).

[WiecC82] Wiecek, C. A. A case study of VAX-11 instruction set usage for compiler execution. In *Proceedings of the Symposium on Architectural Support for Programming Languages and Operating Syst*ems. New York: ACM, 1982.

[WienR83] Wiener, R., and R. Sincovec. *Programming in ADA*. New York: Wiley, 1983.

[WilkM51] Wilkes, M. V. The best way to design an automatic calculating machine. In *Proceedings of the Manchester University Inaugural Computer Conference*. London: Ferranti, 1951.

[WillC86] Williams, C. S. *Designing Digital Filters*, Englewood Cliffs, NJ: Prentice-Hall, 1986.

[WindR73] Winder, R. O., and K. R. Kaplan. Cache-based comupter systems. *IEEE Computer*, 6/3 (March 1973).

[WirtN75] Wirth, N. An assessment of the programming language PASCAL. *IEEE Trans. Software Eng.*, 1/2 (June 1975).

[WirtN77] Wirth, N. Modula, a language for modular multiprogramming. *Software-Practice and Experience*. 7/1 (January 1977).

[WirtN86] Wirth, N. Microprocessor architectures: A comparison based on code generation by compiler. *Commun. ACM*, 29/10 (October 1986).

[WuChu81] Wu, C.l. (ed.). Interconnection Networks. *IEEE Computer*, 14/12 (December 1981).

[WuChu85] Wu, C.l. (ed.). Multiprocessing technology. *IEEE Computer*, 18/6 (June 1985).

[WuC&F80] Wu, C.l., and T. Y. Feng. On a class of multistage interconnection networks. *IEEE Trans. Computers,* C29/8 (August 1980).

[WuC&F81] Wu, C.l., and T. Y. Feng. Universality of a shuffle exchange network. *IEEE Trans. Computers,* C30/5 (May 1981).

[WulfW81] Wulf, W. A. Compilers and computer architecture. *IEEE Computer,* 14/7 (July 1981).

[YauSS77] Yau, S. S., and H. S. Fung. Associative processor architecture-A survey. *Computer Surveys,* 9/1 (March 1977).

Index

Access time, memory, 104–6, 120–21
Accumulator, 7, 303–4
Adder, full, 227
Address, memory:
  effective, 179 (*see also* ISP)
  logical, 111–12, 124–25
  physical, 111–12, 124
Address translation (*see* ISP)
Addressing (modes), 178, 202
  direct, 179
  displacement, 179
  example (*see* ISP, example)
  immediate, 179, 202
  indexed, 179
  indirect, 179–81, 213–14
  literal, 179
  memory block, 121
  register, 179, 181, 202
  register-based, 202
  register indirect, 179, 202
  relative, 179–80
Advanced Micro Devices (AMD):
  AM2901, 211–12
  AM2910, 209–12
Aiken, H., 3
Air Force, U.S., 52
ALGOL (*see* Languages, programming)
ALU (arithmetic and logic unit), 2, 196–97, 201–4, 226–34, 245, 304–6, 374, 390–91, 395

Ametek System 14, 333
Analytic engine (Babbage), 19
Antenna steering, 379–82
Argonne National Laboratory, 4
Arithmetic, 7
Arithmetic and logic unit (*see* ALU)
Army, U.S., 373
Array (*see* Data type)
Array processing, 301, 309, 311–12, 317–20, 328, 334–37
Array processor (*see* ILLIAC IV; MPP; PEPE; STARAN)
Arvind, 364
ASCII (American Standard Code for Information Interchange), 131, 257–58, 280
Assembly language (*see* Language, programming)
Associative processor, 375–77
Asynchronous communication, 280
Atanasoff, J., 3, 101
ATLAS computer (Manchester U.), 153, 187
Availability, 82

B-tubes, 19
Babbage, C., 3, 19
Back-end processor, 288–89
Backus, J., 364

Backus-Naur form (BNF), 402
Ballistic Missile Defense Agency (U.S. Army), 373
Banyan network, 325
Barbacci, M. R., 14, 401
Barrel shifter, 323–24
Bell, C. G., 13, 33, 38, 401
Bell (Telephone) Laboratories, 3, 101, 154, 391
Bendix Corp., 4
Benes network, 325–26
Berlin, Tech. Hoschule, 3
Bit-slice processor, 211–12
Block-oriented RAM, 105, 123
Bokhari, S. H., 337–38
Boole, G., 3
Breadboard, 33
Breakpoint, 217, 219
Briggs, F. A., 92–93, 337
Bubble memory, 124
Buffer:
  input/output, 256–57
  translation, 287
Bull, Cie. Machines, 4
Burks, A. W., 36
Burroughs, 4, 161, 234, 301, 369, 373 (*see also* Unisys)
  B160/B260/B300, 55
  B1700/B1800/B1900, 209, 247
  B2500/B3500/B4500, 56
  B5000, 19, 88, 153, 161–62

446

B5500/B6500, 56, 64, 101, 128, 152, 188, 213, 247, 318
B6700, 97, 162–63, 239
B7800, 330
D825, 19, 56–57, 72, 81, 92, 97, 303, 327, 344
Burroughs Scientific Processor (BSP), 328–31, 336, 344–45, 375
Bus (*see* Switch)

Cache conflict, 114–15
Cache memory, 10, 59–60, 66, 113–19, 130, 135, 157, 219, 221–23, 285–88, 301
   associative, 115–16, 119
   direct-mapped, 114–16, 119
   locations in system, 83–85, 119
   set-associative, 115–17
Cache performance, 116–17
Cache replacement strategy, 119
Cambridge University, 4, 369
California, U. of (Berkeley), 159, 220, 247 (*see also* RISC)
California Inst. of Technology, 332
Capacity, memory, 101–4, 106, 111, 128–31, 388
Carnegie-Mellon University, 331
   C.mmp, 72, 97, 331, 344
   Cm*, 64–65, 97, 331, 344
Carr, J. W., 19
Carry, 227–28
Carry lookahead, 228
Cathode-ray tube, 76
CCD (charge-coupled device), 124
CCITT, 280
CHAP computer, 383
Chicago, U. of, 4
Chip, 5 (*see also* Technology)
Circuit switching, 67, 323
Clock, computer, 14, 15, 203, 232–34, 316, 328, 330
CMOS (complementary MOS), 108, 303
Coche, J., 220
Code, character, 258
Collision vector, pipeline, 234
Colorado, U. of (Boulder), 391
Combinator, 367–69
Communication processing, 280
Compatibility, 58, 128, 391–92
Compiler, 141, 220, 237, 240–41
   optimizing, 221, 223–25
   vectorizing, 393
Compiler requirements, 152
Complexity, 50, 52, 219
   switch, 72–74, 77–78, 81, 98, 321–23
Component (*see* Technology)
Computer, definition, 2, 35, 410
Computer-aided tomography, 347–49
Computer architecture, definition, 1
Computer Controls Corp., 4
Computer family architecture (Dept. of Defense), 20
Concurrency (*see* Parallel processing)

Condition codes, 198–99, 202–5
Configuration control, 30
Connection Machine (Thinking Machines, Inc.), 333–34, 344
Connectivity, switch, 321–23
Consolidated Engineering Corp., 4
Content-addressable memory, 114
Context switching, 157–58, 167–72, 239
Control, aircraft, 357–58
Control:
   computer, 6–8, 33, 35, 194–95, 200–215, 219, 245, 247, 309, 362–70, 409
   disk drive, 288–89
   input/output, 61–62, 74, 76, 201, 259, 391
   memory, 266–70
   microprogrammed, 205–6, 208, 245
   peripherals (*see* Input/output)
   PMS-level, 34–35, 409
   processor, 226
   system, 360
Control Data Corp. (CDC), 4, 248, 311
   Cyber, 135, 158, 164, 188, 230, 303, 386
   Cyber 170, 19, 109, 110
   Cyber 203/205, 316–17, 320, 344, 362
   Star-100, 301, 311–14, 316–17, 320, 344, 350, 362
   160/1604/924, 55
   6600, 19, 135, 164, 230, 301, 314, 344, 386
   7600, 230, 301, 314
Control flow, 213
Control store, 14, 205–6, 208–9
Convex C-1, 279–80, 293, 298
Convolution, 361–62
Coprocessor, numeric, 57–59, 87–89
Correlation, 361–62, 384
Cosmic Cube (Calif. Inst. Technology), 332–33, 344
Cost:
   component, 194–95
   memory, 78, 82, 103, 105–7, 111
   and performance, 50, 90–95
   software, 55, 195
   switch, 72–74, 321–23
Cray, S., 314
Cray Research, Inc., 311
   Cray-1, 314–16, 328, 344, 362, 387
   Cray-2/Cray-3/Cray Y-MP, 328, 388
   Cray X-MP, 328–29
Crossbar (*see* Switch)
CTSS (computer timesharing system) (MIT), 153, 187
Curry, H. B., 367
Cvetanovic, Z., 339
Cycle time, memory, 14, 107, 387–89

Database management, 288–89
Data-driven computer, 213, 363

Data-flow analysis, 223
Data-flow computer, 213, 363–64, 383–84, 391, 398
Data operator, 33–35, 309
Data type, 172–78
   array, 144, 309–12
   character, 173
   compound, 144
   example: (*see also* ISP)
      DEC VAX, 178
      IBM System/370, 176–77
      Unisys A Series, 176–77
      Unisys 1100/2200, 176–78
   fixed-point, 173–75, 232–33, 313–14, 316
   floating-point, 173–76, 228, 230–34, 309–11, 313–15
      exponent, 173–76, 228, 232–33
      mantissa, 173–74, 228, 231–33
      range, 173–75
   integer (*see* Fixed point)
   multiple precision, 176–78
   negative values, 175
   number, 173–74
   number base, 173–74
   packed, 176
   real (*see* Floating point)
   record, 144
   structure, 144
   vector, 144
Decision tree, 30–31
Decoder, 204
Defense, Dept. of (U.S.), 20
Delay, circuit, 387–89, 394–95
Delay line, 124
Demand-driven computer, 213, 363–64
DeMorgan, A., 3
Denelcor HEP, 36–38, 53, 307–9, 344
Density, semiconductor component, 194–95, 387–88, 394
Descriptor:
   Burroughs (Unisys), 184, 213–15
   Process, 154–55
   Resource, 154
Design:
   computer, 32–33
   memory, 128–31
      examples, 130–31
   system, 356–59
Design objectives, 27–30
Diagnostics (*see* Maintenance)
Digital Equipment Corp. (DEC), 4
   LSI-11, 207
   PDP-4/PDP-7/PDP-9, 55–56
   PDP-8, 45–46, 53
   PDP-10, 191
   PDP-11, 56, 64, 207, 242, 318, 386
   VAX, 97, 130–31, 158, 167, 169–71, 178, 182–83, 198–200, 209, 217, 240–42, 248, 333–34, 386, 420–22
      attached processor (11/782), 88
      context switching, 169–71
      general registers, 158, 198, 420
      instruction formats, 183, 420

Digital Equipment Corp.
VAX (*Continued*)
internal data-bus registers, 198–200
ISP, 420–22
operating modes, 198
processor registers, 198–99
processor status longword, 199, 420
SBI (system backplane interconnect), 272
VAXbus, 272
11/780, 59–60, 70, 76, 98, 242, 248, 272
8600/8650, 272
8800, 209
Digital system, definition, 2, 54
Direct-execution architecture, 141, 211, 213, 247
Disk drives:
access time, 104, 120
block transfer time, 104, 120
characteristics, 104–6, 120, 255–56, 387
head-per-track, 288
optical, 123
DMA (direct memory access), 58, 61, 69, 259, 266–70, 283–84, 288, 298
DRAM (dynamic RAM), 110–11, 117–18, 129–30, 136, 194, 387–88, 394–95
Duplex organizations, 80, 327

EBCDIC (extended binary-coded decimal interchange code), 258
Eckert, J. P., 4, 8, 18–19, 101
Eckert-Mauchly Computer Corp., 4
ECL (emitter-coupled logic), 108, 110, 302
Economic issues, 25, 50
EDVAC, 8, 303
EEPROM (electronically erasable PROM), 104
Effective address (*see* Address, memory)
Electrodata, 4
Elxsi 6400, 93
Engineering Research Associates, 4
English Electric, 4
KDF-9, 19
ENIAC, 4
Environments, execution:
and contexts, 167–72, 220
control examples,
DEC VAX, 167, 168–71
IBM System/370, 171–72
Unisys A Series, 172
and stacks, 160–61, 167
EPROM (erasable PROM), 104, 108, 208
Error detection and correction, 131–33, 135, 215–17, 245, 257, 285, 303–4

Exponent (*see* Data type)
Extent, programming language, 143
Exxon Research and Engineering, 20

Failure rate, 79
Failure probability, 80
Fairchild Semiconductor, 247
Fast Fourier transform, 360–61
Fault diagnosis, 215–19, 245
Ferranti Corp., 4
Fetch-execute cycle, 202, 204, 240, 300, 391 (*see also* ISP, example)
FIFO (first-in first-out) (*see* Queue)
Fixed point (*see* Data type)
FLEX/32, 337–39
Floating point (*see* Data type)
Floating Point Systems:
FPS 164, 289–91
FPS 5000, 89
Flow tracing, 217, 219
Flynn, M. J., 247, 303
FORTRAN (*see* Language, programming)
Fragmentation, memory, 126–28
Front-end computer, 289
Fujitsu Corp., 4
Function, computer, 2, 24
Functional programming, 19, 152, 196, 363, 383, 394

Gajski, D. D., 392–93
Gallium arsenide, (GaAs), 108, 386, 389–90
General Electric Co., 4
computers, 55
programmable controller, 372–73
General Precision Equipment Co., 4
Gibson, J. C., 15
Gibson mix, 15, 20
Goldstine, H. H., 36
Goode, H. H., 52
Goodyear Aerospace, 375, 377
MPP, 377–79, 383
STARAN, 288, 375–79, 383
Graph reduction, 365–69
Grosch, H. R. J., 93
Grosch's law, 93, 95, 98
Gross, T. R., 225

Hamming, R. W., 132
Hamming code, 132–33
Hardware engine, 289–96
Hardwired control logic, 204, 206–7
Harvard University, 3, 101
HCMOS (high-speed CMOS), 108
HDLC (high-level data-link control), 281–82
Hennessy, J., 220
HEP (Heterogeneous Element Processor) (*see* Denelcor)
Heuring, V. P., 391

Hewlett-Packard Corp.:
HP3000, 161–62
RISC, 225
Higher-level language (*see* Language, programming)
History, computer, 3–6
Hit rate, cache, 117–19
HMOS (high-speed MOS), 108
Hoelvel, L. W., 247
Holliday, M. A., 340
Honeywell, Inc., 4, 55
Hopkins, M. E., 243
Husky, H. D., 18
Husky, V. R., 18
Hwang, K., 92–93, 337

IBM (International Business Machines Corp.), 4, 327
attached processor (370/AP, 3033AP), 88
disk drives (2302, 3330, 3380), 120
PC, 41, 57–58
Research Laboratory, 220
System/38, 151–52, 188, 386
System/360, 19, 56, 89, 102, 158, 196, 200, 247, 278, 386
System/370, 56, 59, 89, 102, 171–72, 176–77, 182–83, 196–98, 230, 248, 278, 413–19
external-data controller, 278–79
program-status word, 198
vector facility, 293–94, 298–99
701/704/709, 4, 9, 14, 19, 55–56, 102
801, 220–26, 239, 243
3033, 88, 102
3080/3081/3084, 59–60, 99, 102, 217–18, 278, 303
3090, 101–2, 130–31, 163–64, 217–18, 278, 298
7030 (Stretch), 301, 303–4, 344
7080/7090/7094, 19, 55–56, 102, 153, 303
9370, 130–31
ICL (International Computer, Ltd.), 4
ICT (International Computers and Tabulators), 4
Ideal computing engine, 238
IEEE (Institute of Electrical and Electronics Engineers) (*see* Standards)
ILLIAC IV, 234–35, 248, 301, 306, 309, 317–20, 322, 327–28, 331, 336, 344, 346, 350, 362, 373, 375, 379, 384, 387
Illinois, U. of, 4, 234, 301, 393
Image processing, 371–72, 378
medical, 347–49
MPP, 377–79, 383
PIXAR, 371–72, 383
Index register, 10, 19, 179, 303–4, 318
Input/output, 6–9, 62–63, 74–78
Input/output addressing:
device-addressed, 263–64

memory-mapped, 202, 245, 263–65
Input/output bus, 258–60
DEC VAX SBI, 272
IEEE standards (see Standards)
MASSBUS (DEC), 76, 272–73
Multibus (IEEE, Intel), 274, 279
RS-232 standard, 273, 280–81
S-100, 274
UNIBUS (DEC), 76, 272–73
Input/output control, 74, 76, 201, 256–57, 303–4
Input/output device controllers, 258–63
communication, 282–84
display, 255
disk drive, 255–56, 260–62
floppy disk, 255, 260–62
keyboard, 255
magnetic-tape drive, 255–56
multi-purpose, 262–64
printer, 255, 260–62
UART, USRT, USART, 282–83
Input/output peripheral device, 75–76, 254–56 (see also specific devices)
Input/output requirements, 75–76, 254–58
Institute for Advanced Study (Princeton U.), 3, 18
Instruction decoder, 204
Instruction format, 201–2
example (see also ISP, example)
DEC VAX, 183
IBM System/370, 183
Unisys A Series, 183–84
Instruction queue, 119, 163–64, 167
Instruction representation, 178
Instruction set, 7, 178, 181, 219
example:
DEC VAX, 183
IBM System/370, 183
Unisys A Series, 183–84
Intel Corp., 118, 247
Hypercube, 333
multibus, 274, 279
peripheral controllers:
8237 (DMA), 276–70
8251 (communication), 282–83
8255A (programmable interface), 262–63
8259 (interrupt), 270–71
8271 (floppy disk), 260–62
8288 (bus), 275, 298
8289 (bus arbiter), 275, 298
8295 (printer), 260–61
4040/8080 processors, 194
8086/8088 processors, 41–43, 53, 57, 158, 161, 276–78, 293, 332–33
8087 coprocessor, 57, 293, 332–33
8089 I/O processor, 43–44, 53, 276–78
80286 processor, 194, 333
80386 processor, 194, 387, 427–29
Interrupt handling, 156, 168–71, 190, 201, 303–4

Interrupt processor, 270–71
Interrupt system examples:
DEC VAX, 169–71
IBM System/370, 171–72
Unisys A Series, 172
Iowa State University, 3
ISO (International Standards Organization), 131, 257–58, 280
ISP (instruction-set processor), 7, 8, 13, 18–19, 33, 38–44, 52, 196, 213, 245–46, 389–92, 401–33
definition:
formal, 40–28
informal, 38–44, 411
example:
DEC PDP-8, 45
DEC VAX, 420–22
IBM System/370, 413–19
IBM System/370 vector facility, 294
Intel 8086, 41
Intel 8089, 43
Intel 80386, 427–29
MIPS 2000/3000, 430–31
Motorola M68000, 423–24
National NS32000 processor, 425–26
National NS32082 MMU, 287
Sun SPARC, 432–33
Texas Instruments TMS 32020, 295
von Neumann architecture, 40

Jacquard, J., 3
Jordan, H. F., 391, 393

Kent at Canterbury, U. of, 369
Knight, K. E., 15, 20
Knight's mix, 15, 20

LAN (local-area network), 68, 97
Language:
hardware description, 13, 19, 23
machine, 237
programming, 5, 19, 141–52, 196, 237, 327
ADA, 147, 394
ALGOL-60, 49, 145, 247
ALGOL-68, 147
APL, 148, 213
and architecture, 141, 152, 187, 392–95
assembly, 142–43, 196, 224, 250–51
block-structured, 19, 143, 145–48
C, 213
COBOL, 184
dynamic, 148
EUCLID, 147
Euler, 247
FORTRAN, 49, 144–45, 147, 188, 308, 316, 393

higher-level, 5, 143–52, 196, 211, 213, 220, 223–24, 236–40, 242, 248
HOPE, 152, 394
LISP, 148, 165–66, 213, 363
MIRANDA, 152, 394
MODULA 2, 147, 394
object-oriented, 150–52
parallel, 374
PASCAL, 145–47, 188–89, 213, 250–51, 354–56, 383–84, 394
PL/1, 147, 213
procedural, 14, 19, 394
PROLOG, 148, 150, 213
SIMULA, 49
SIMSCRIPT, 49
SISAL, 394
SMALLTALK, 150
simulation, 13, 19, 49–50
specification, 13, 22, 32
Language-based computers, 195, 211, 213
Language space, 211, 213
LARC (Univac), 301
Leibniz, G., 3
Librascope, 4
LIFO (last-in first-out) (see Stack)
LILITH (ETH Zurich), 243–44, 248
Link, 33–34, 410
LISP (see Language, programming)
Locality, principle of, 113
Logic programming, 19, 196, 394
Lookahead, instruction, 165, 300, 303–4
Lookaside memory, 66, 165, 167, 301
Los Alamos National Laboratory, 4
LRC (longitudinal redundancy check), 131
LRU replacement strategy, 119
LSI (large-scale integration), 194
Lundstrom, S. F., 394

Magnetic memory:
bubble, 124
core, 102, 123
disk, 103–4, 120–22, 255–56, 387
tape, 104, 106, 120, 122, 255–56
thin film, 124
Maintenance and diagnostics, 215–19, 245
Manchester University, 4, 19 (see also ATLAS)
Mantissa (see Data type, floating-point)
Manufacturing, 94–95, 98
semiconductor, 388–89
Manufacturing learning curve, 94–95
Markov process, 340, 396–97
Maryland, U. of, 247
Massachusetts Institute of Technology (MIT), 4, 153
MASSBUS (DEC), 76, 272–73
Master Control Program (Burroughs), 155, 188, 330
Matrix, 10

Matrix operations, 309–12, 334–37
Mauchly, J., 4, 8, 101
Memory, computer, 2–3, 6–7, 9, 33–34, 101–3, 409 (*see also* PMS, example)
   archival, 106, 120, 122–23
   associative, 318
   bubble, 124
   buffer, 3, 7, 124, 130
   cache (*see* Cache memory)
   disk, 288
   intermediate, 85–87, 123–24
   lookaside, 66, 165, 167, 301
   modular, 63, 285
   multiport, 59, 70, 72, 285
   nonvolatile, 102
   optical, 102, 106, 123
   physical, 125, 136, 285–86
   primary, 3, 83–86, 107, 110–13, 120–24, 129–31, 157, 263, 387
   secondary, 3, 85–86, 120–24, 129–31, 288
   tagged, 213–15, 245, 247
   tertiary, 86
   virtual, 124–28, 136, 153, 285–86, 316 (*see also* ISP, example)
Memory capacity, 101–4, 106, 111, 128–31
Memory hierarchy, 82–87, 101, 103, 137
Memory management:
   paging, 125–26, 128
   segmentation:
      continuously variable, 127–28
      paged, 126, 128
Memory protection, 156
Message switching, 67–68, 98, 323
Methodology, design, 6, 348–59, 385–86
   bottom-up, 22
   top-down, 21–23
Methodology, research, 386
MFLOPS (million floating-point operations per second), 17, 20, 234, 307–8, 314, 316–17, 320, 328, 331, 380, 382
Michigan, U. of, 19, 52
Microinstruction, 205–6
   horizontal, 206–9, 245
   LSI-11, 207
   vertical, 206–7, 245
Microprocessor, 5, 423–33
   example:
      Intel 8086, 41
      Intel 80386, 427–29
      Lilith (ETH Zurich), 243–44
      Motorola M68000, 423–24
      MIPS 2000/3000, 430–31
      National NS32000, 425–26
      Sun SPARC, 432–33
   performance comparisons, 243–44
Microprogrammable computer, 209, 247
Microprogramming, 2, 14, 194, 205–10, 213, 217, 219, 245, 247

MIDAC (U. Michigan), 19
MIMD (multiple instruction multiple data), 304–10, 326–28, 337–42, 344–45, 393
Minsky, M., 92–93
Minsky's conjecture, 92
MIPS (million instructions per second), 17, 20, 234, 334, 372
MIPS Computer Systems, Inc., 220, 430–31 (*see also* RISC)
MMU (memory-management unit), 113, 217, 219, 286–88
Mode, addressing (*see* Addressing)
Moore, G. E., 247
Morland, S., 3
MOS (metal-oxide semiconductor), 108, 388
Motorola, Inc.:
   M68000 microprocessor, 87–88, 161, 180, 208, 242–44, 248, 279–80, 290, 293, 423–24
   MC68020 processor, 87–88, 290
   MC68120 peripheral controller, 262, 264
   MC68881 coprocessor, 87–88, 290, 292, 331
   80010 RISC microprocessor, 225
MPP (Massively Parallel Processor), 377–79, 383
MSI (medium-scale integration), 194
MSYPS (million synchronizations per second), 393
MTBF (mean time between failures), 79, 82
MTR (mean time to repair), 82
Multibus (IEEE, Intel), 274, 279
Multicomputers, 303, 326–27, 332–34, 393
Multics (MIT), 153–54, 187
Multiplication, 228–29, 231–33
Multiport memory, 59, 70, 72, 285
Multiprocessing, 156, 301, 303, 326–34
   loosely-coupled, 301, 307, 327
   tightly-coupled, 301, 307, 327
Multiprocessor, 64, 91–94, 97, 100, 327–28, 393
   example (*see* Burroughs D825; Carnegie-Mellon U. C.mmp; Carnegie-Mellon U. Cm*; IBM 3084; Unisys A Series)
Multiprogramming, 91, 301

Nanodata Computer Corp. QM1, 209, 211
Nanoprogram, 207, 209, 245
NASA (National Aeronautics and Space Agency), 379
National Bureau of Standards (U.S.), 4
National Physical Laboratory (U.K.), 4
National Semiconductor, Inc.:
   NS32000, 180, 217, 219, 243–44, 248, 425–26

NS32016 microprocessor, 333
NS32032 microprocessor, 331–32, 337
NS32081 floating-point coprocessor, 331–32
NS32082 MMU, 286–88, 299, 331–32
NS32490 network interface, 283–84
NCR Tower, 153
NCUBE computer, 333
Network:
   baseline, 325–26
   Benes, 325–26
   binary N–cube, 322–26, 332, 334
   computer, 65, 68
   delta, 325
   nearest-neighbor, 322–24
   nonblocking, 325–26
   omega, 326
   shuffle exchange, 325
Newell, A., 13, 33, 38
NMOS (negative MOS), 108
North Carolina, U. of, 365
Noyce, R. N., 247
Number (*see* Data type)

One-address computer, 19
Opcode (*see* Instruction format)
Operating system, 5, 20, 90–91, 97, 128, 153–56, 171–72, 196, 213–14, 301, 327, 392–95
   requirements for, 153, 155–56
Optical computing, 390–91
Order code (*see* Instruction set)
Orthogonality, 152, 182
Overhead, processing, 236

Paged memory, 125–26, 128
   segmented, 126, 128
Parafrase compiler, 393
Parallel processing, 5, 79, 155, 195, 301, 303–11, 320, 327–34, 362–70, 392
Parity, 131–33, 215
PASCAL (*see* Language, programming)
Pascal, B., 3
Patterson, D. A., 220, 242, 247
Patton, P. C., 392
PDP- (*see* Digital Equipment Corp.)
Pennsylvania, U. of, 4, 8, 303
Pennsylvania State University, 344
PEPE (parallel-element processing ensemble), 372–75, 378, 383–84
Performance:
   computer, 13–17, 20, 25, 66, 211, 219–21, 234, 236–44, 246, 300–309, 314, 316–18, 320, 334–42, 344, 395–98
   and cost, 50, 90–95
   memory, 104–5, 107, 111
   parallel systems, 92–94, 314, 316–18, 320, 334–42, 344

system:
benchmarks, 16–17, 236, 240–41, 398
queuing models, 395–98
simple measures, 13–16
thermodynamic analogy, 17, 238–40, 246
Performance comparison, 20, 240–46
array and vector processors, 334–37
microprocessors, 243–44
multiprocessors, 337–42
Performance measures, 14–17, 395–98
Peripheral (*see* Input/output)
Petri net, 13–14, 19, 48–49, 52, 340, 396–97
Philco Corp., 4
Pier, J.-K., 392
Pipeline, arithmetic, 228, 230–34, 247, 293, 311, 313, 317, 389
Pipeline, instruction, 222–24, 247, 249, 316
Pipeline bubble, 223–24
Pipeline processor, 301, 306, 309–17, 328, 334–38, 345
PIXAR image processor, 371–72, 383
PLA (programmable logic array), 195, 204–5, 221, 290
PMOS (positive MOS), 108
PMS (processor-memory-switch), 8, 13–14, 18–19, 33–38, 401–11
definition:
formal, 402–8
informal, 33–38, 408–11
example:
Burroughs D825, 57
Caltech Cosmic Cube, 333
Carnegie-Mellon U. Cm*, 65
Connection Machine, 334
Convex C-1, 279
DEC PDP-8, 45
DEC VAX-11/780, 59
Denelcor HEP, 37
GE programmable controller, 373
IBM PC, 58
IBM 3033AP, 88
IBM 3084, 60
IBM 3090 channel subsystem, 278
FPS 5000, 89
Motorola M68000, 88
PIXAR image-processing system, 371
Sequent Balance, 322
von Neumann architecture, 36, 411
organizations:
cache locations, 84
computer network, 65
intermediate memory, 84
modular memory, 63
multiple computer, 65
multiple I/O, 63

multiprocessor, 64
uniprocessor, 62–63
Pratt, J. P., 391
Primary memory (*see* Memory, computer)
Princeton University, 3
Probabilistic model, 396–98
Processor, 6, 33–34, 87, 408–9
array, 301, 309, 311–12, 317–20, 328, 334–37
attached:
DEC VAX-11/782, 88
IBM 3033AP, 88
central, 6 (*see also* ISP, example)
input/output, 60, 74, 76, 259, 275–86
memory, 285–89
parallel (*see* Parallel processing)
pipeline, 301, 306, 309–17, 328, 334–38, 345
scalar, 314–17, 328–30
special-purpose, 288
vector, 301, 309–20, 328, 334–38
Producer-consumer example, 98
Product development, 23–24, 28
Program counter, 7, 200–201
PROLOG (*see* Language, programming)
PROM (programmable ROM), 90, 104, 108–9, 208–9, 356
Pseudoinstruction, 142–43

Queue (FIFO), 163–64, 300, 308, 310, 316
Queuing theory, 395–98

Radar signal processing:
phased-array, 358–59
search, 351–56, 383
Radar track processing, 359
Radin, G., 243, 248–49
RAM (random-access memory), 90, 208, 262, 378
Ramo-Wooldridge (TRW) RW400, 80, 97, 99, 327, 344
Rand Corp., 4
Raytheon Corp., 4
RCA (Radio Corp. of America), 4, 56
Real (*see* Data type)
Record (*see* Data type)
Reduction machine, 213, 364–69, 383, 391
Register, 2
accumulator, 7, 39–41, 45, 303–4
buffer, 258–59
display (Unisys A Series and B6700), 162–63, 200
example: (*see also* ISP, example)
CDC Cyber, 109
Cray-1, 314–16
DEC VAX, 158, 169–70, 199
FPS 164, 291
IBM 7030 (Stretch), 303–4
Scheme-79, 166

Unisys A Series, 162
Unisys 1100/2200, 109
floating-point, 292, 413, 430, 432
general, 10, 41, 109, 158, 190, 198, 200–201, 220–21, 390
index, 10, 19
instruction, 200–203, 205, 209
memory-address, 110, 201, 318–19
memory buffer, 110
memory data, 201–2
processor, VAX, 198–99
top-of-stack, 10, 161–63
Register-to-register mode, 189–90, 221, 250
Register-transfer language (RTL), 13, 19, 44–46, 48, 52
Regularity, instruction sets, 152, 182
Reliability, 74, 78–82, 327
and cost, 81
models, 80, 97
Remington Rand (Univac), 4
Requirements, system, 13
Requirements analysis, 23–26, 350
Reservation table, pipeline, 232–34, 250
Resource management, 154–55
RISC (reduced-instruction-set computer):
example:
Berkeley, 159, 220–26, 242
IBM 801, 220–26, 239, 243
MIPS 2000/3000, 225, 430–31
Motorola 80010, 225
Stanford MIPS, 220–26, 239, 247
Sun SPARC, 225, 432–33
organization, 195, 207, 211, 213, 219–26, 239–40, 245–46, 389–90
principles, 225
ROM (read-only memory), 57, 90, 104, 108–9, 208, 356
Rosenblatt, C., 400
Royal Signals and Radar Establishment (U.K.), 379
RS-232, (*see* Standards)

SAGE (air-defense system), 80, 97, 327, 344, 354, 383
Sanguinetti, J., 93
Scheduler, process, 154–55
Scheme-79, 165–66, 188
Schottky diode, 108
Scope, programming language, 143
Scoreboard (CDC), 230
Scott, D. S., 383
SDS (Scientific Data Systems), 4, 56
Segmented memory, 127–28
with paging, 126, 128
Selectron tube, 7
Semantic gap, 141, 236
Semiconductor, 5
Sequencer, microprogram, 209
Sequent Balance 8000, 331–32
Sequin, C. H., 242

Shaw, A., 392
Shifter, 201–4, 226–28
Sieve of Eratosthenes, 337–39
Signal processor, 294–96
Silicon, 5, 302, 388
SIMD (single instruction multiple data), 304–6, 311–12, 371, 376
Single-address computer, 11, 19
Single-address instruction, 10
SISD (single instruction single data), 304–6, 320, 326–28, 331, 334–37, 344–45
Software, 5, 87, 90
Software engineering, 5
SOLOMON computer, 344
Special vs. general purpose, 30–31, 347, 350, 356
Specification, 32
Sperry Corp., Sperry-Rand Corp., 4
SRAM (Static RAM), 110, 117–18, 129–30, 136, 387–88, 390, 394–95
Stack (LIFO), 10–12, 159–63, 167, 188–90, 213–14, 239, 243–44
   in arithmetic operations, 159–60
   Burroughs B6700, 162–63
   for environment switching, 160–61, 167
   Hewlett-Packard 3000, 161–62
   Lilith (ETH Zurich), 243–44
   programmed, 161
Stack pointer:
   DEC VAX, 158, 198, 420
   Intel 8086, 161
   Intel 80386, 427
   Motorola M68000, 161, 423
   National NS32000, 425
Stack registers, 161–63
Standards:
   IEEE floating point, 176, 188, 290
   IEEE instrument bus, 274
   IEEE (Intel) Multibus, 274, 279
   IEEE packet communication, 283
   IEEE S-100 bus, 274
   ISO high-level data-link control (HDLC), 281–82
   RS-232C (EIA), 273, 280–81
   USAF engineering management, 52
   USASCII/ISO character set, 258
Stanford University, 220, 225, 247 (see also RISC)
Star-100 (see CCD)
STARAN, 288, 375–79, 383
State:
   control, 200, 203
   hidden, 200, 219
   processor, 108–10, 130, 156–66
State (transition) diagram, 13, 47–48
State machine, 205
Status flag, 198–99, 202–5
Stepwise refinement, 22, 27, 29

Stibitz, G., 3
Stone, H. S., 340–41, 346, 393
Strachey, C., 383
Strela, 19
Stretch (IBM 7030), 301, 303–4, 344
String reduction, 364–65
Sun, Inc.:
   SPARC, 225, 432–33
   workstation, 153
Supervisor mode (state), 197–98, 288
Switch (see also Network), 33–34, 67–74, 320–26, 409
   bus, 57, 70–71, 201, 333–34, 340–41
   crossbar, 71–72, 76–77, 285, 321–24, 333–34, 340–41
   duplex, 74
   inverted tree, 70, 285
   input/output, 76–77
   router, 323–24, 326, 333–34
   tree, 69, 76–77
Symbolic assembler, 142
Symbolics 3600, 166, 188, 333–34
Synchronous communication, 280–82
Syntax, ISP and PMS, 402–8
System software, 90, 196
System test, 28–30
Systolic array, 213, 369-70, 379-83, 391, 398

Tagged memory, 213–15, 245, 247
Technology:
   and architecture, 193–95, 362, 369, 386–89, 399
   memory, 302–3, 387–89
   semiconductor, 5, 193, 302–3, 386–89
Testing, 28–30
Texas Instruments, Inc.:
   ASC (Advanced Scientific Computer), 248, 306–7, 309, 314, 349
   TMS32020 signal processor, 294–96, 298
Thinking Machines, Inc., 333
Three-address computer, 11, 19
Three-address instruction, 10
Tools, design, 32–33, 204
Transducer, 33–34, 409
Transfer, block, 69, 104–5, 120–21, 255–56
Triplex, 80
TTL (transistor-transistor logic), 108, 110, 303
Turing, A., 3
Two-address computer, 11, 19
Two-address instruction, 10

UART (universal asynchronous receiver-transmitter), 282–83
UNIBUS (DEC), 76, 272–73

Unisys, 4, 369, 373
   A Series, 72, 128, 152, 162–63, 172, 176–77, 183–84, 200, 211, 213, 386
   workstations, 153
   1100/2200, 9, 19, 64, 72, 109–10, 130–31, 135, 176–78, 197–200, 386
UNIVAC, 4, 89, 14, 19, 102 (see also Unisys)
   LARC, 301
   II, 55, 62
   1101/1102/1105, 55
   1103, 19, 55
   1106/1107/1108, 56, 157
   1110, 97
Unix (Bell Laboratories, ATT), 153–54, 188, 372
USART (universal synchronous-asynchronous receiver-transmitter), 282–83
User mode (space), 288
USRT (universal synchronous receiver-transmitter), 282

VAX (see Digital Equipment Corp.)
Vector operation, 293–94
Vector processor, 228, 301, 309–20, 328, 334–38
Verification, 27, 30, 33
Vernon, M. K., 340
Virtual machine, 5, 14, 19, 195–200, 209, 216, 226, 245
Virtual memory (see Memory)
VLSI (very-large-scale integration), 220, 226, 244, 369, 379
von Neumann, J., 2–3, 18–19, 22
von Neumannn architecture, 6–12, 36, 39–41, 52, 189–92, 213, 225–26, 303, 390, 398–99, 411
Voting logic, 216

Wavefront computation, 370
Weiderman, N., 20
West, L. C., 391
Wiecek, C. A., 240–41
Wilkes, M. V., 6, 194–95, 247
Williams tube, 7, 12
Windows, register, 221
Wirth, N., 243–44, 389
Writeback policy, cache, 119
Writethrough policy, cache, 119
Wulf, W. A., 152, 175, 182, 219

Xerox Data Systems, 4, 56

Zero-address computer, 11, 14, 19
Zuse, K., 3